DIRITTO INTERNAZIONALE
DEI DIRITTI UMANI

Teoria e prassi

RICCARDO PISILLO MAZZESCHI

DIRITTO INTERNAZIONALE DEI DIRITTI UMANI

Teoria e prassi

Ristampa emendata

G. Giappichelli Editore

VIA PO, 21 - TEL. 011-81.53.111 - FAX 011-81.25.100
http://www.giappichelli.it

ISBN/EAN 978-88-921-3633-5

Stampa: LegoDigit s.r.l. - Lavis (TN)

Ai miei piccoli nipoti Marco e Alessandro,
con l'augurio che crescano in una società più aperta
ai valori universali di eguaglianza e di fraternità

INDICE-SOMMARIO

pag.

Capitolo III

GLI OBBLIGHI INTERNAZIONALI

PREMESSA

Questo libro ha uno scopo didattico, per gli studenti dei corsi specialistici di tutela internazionale dei diritti umani; ma anche di consultazione per studiosi ed operatori nel campo del diritto internazionale e dei diritti umani. Ho cercato di fornire un quadro sufficientemente completo e sistematico della materia, come mi sembra necessario per un manuale, anche se il settore del diritto internazionale dei diritti umani ha ormai assunto una dimensione così ampia, da rendere difficile una sua trattazione in un volume di dimensioni contenute. Il libro cerca di dar conto della prassi e della giurisprudenza più rilevanti, ma anche di trattare questioni teoriche. Da qui deriva il suo titolo, che richiama volutamente lo scritto di un autorevole studioso del diritto internazionale [1].

Ci si potrebbe chiedere quali siano i motivi che mi hanno indotto a scrivere un nuovo libro sui diritti umani, visto il gran numero di manuali già pubblicati, negli ultimi decenni, specie in lingua inglese e francese. Un primo motivo consiste nel mio desiderio di tentare di dare un'impostazione diversa a questo volume. Infatti, molti dei manuali esistenti, ed in particolare quelli della dottrina anglo-americana, si concentrano sulla descrizione della parte istituzionale della tutela internazionale dei diritti umani (sistemi convenzionali, organi e procedure) oppure si occupano solo di alcuni diritti umani [2]. A mio avviso, anche in un'ottica didattica, gli studenti non hanno bisogno di ricevere molte informazioni e descrizioni dettagliate, che trovano facilmente su Internet e che comunque tendono presto a dimenticare; ma piuttosto di riflettere su concetti, tesi ed inquadramenti sistematici. Solo queste riflessioni sono formative per i giovani giuristi ed aiutano a comprendere come funziona il diritto, compreso il diritto internazionale dei diritti umani. In altri termini, per me non esiste alcun conflitto, ma anzi necessaria sinergia, fra scopo didattico e scientifico di un libro. Naturalmente, ciò non significa che il mio proposito di combinare nel volume teoria, prassi ed una certa completezza della materia, sia davvero riuscito.

Comunque, seguendo questa impostazione, ho scelto di dedicare poco spazio alla parte istituzionale (Cap. IV) e di approfondire invece i temi dell'impatto dei diritti umani sull'intero ordinamento internazionale (Cap. I), sulle fonti (Cap. II), sugli obblighi (Cap. III), nonché la parte del libro che tratta il contenuto dei diritti umani "fondamentali" (Cap. V), senza però trascurare gli altri diritti (Cap. VI). Sono consapevole che questa scelta può aver prodotto alcuni effetti negativi sull'omogeneità del volume, poiché ha indotto ad approfondire maggiormente alcuni argomenti ed a trattarne altri in maniera più sintetica.

---

[1] Oscar Schachter, *International Law in Theory and Practice* (1991).

[2] Fra i manuali in lingua inglese, fanno eccezione gli eccellenti libri di Tomuschat (*Human Rights. Between Idealism and Realism*) e di Kälin e Künzli (*The Law of International Human Rights Protection*), che mi hanno offerto numerosi spunti, per i quali sono grato.

D'altra parte, questa opzione di struttura dipende anche da un secondo motivo. Il libro è il frutto di riflessioni che ho svolto da un paio di decenni sui diritti umani; ma che si riallacciano a studi su temi più generali del diritto internazionale, che mi hanno indotto a seguire un *fil rouge*, che si è sviluppato nel tempo e che si è venuto collegando ad una determinata concezione sul fondamento deontologico del diritto. Questo filo conduttore, influenzato dalla mia crescente attenzione verso i diritti umani, mi ha portato ad un atteggiamento critico nei confronti della teoria del positivismo formale (pur riconoscendone il rigore di metodo) ed a coltivare un interesse per le teorie "antiformalistiche" (specie l'istituzionalismo ed il neo-costituzionalismo), che recuperano un'apertura ai valori etico-politici del diritto. Da questo approccio generale, è derivata anche l'idea che sia intellettualmente stimolante studiare non solo il diritto delle regole e ciò che il diritto è (*what the law is*), ma anche il diritto dei principi/valori e la direzione verso la quale il diritto si muove[3]; e ciò specie in un settore, quale il diritto internazionale, che ha subito di recente forti processi di cambiamento. Ed infatti, nel mio percorso di studi, ho proposto tentativi di ricollocazione sistematica di alcuni istituti classici (inadempimento dei trattati, colpa e diligenza, esaurimento dei ricorsi interni) e tentativi di rivisitazione, in chiave che ritengo più moderna, di altri temi generali (teoria degli obblighi internazionali, responsabilità degli Stati per violazione dei diritti umani, soggettività internazionale, nuovo ruolo dell'individuo, principi generali, immunità internazionali, accesso alla giustizia). I lettori noteranno che molti di questi argomenti hanno finito, inevitabilmente, per confluire, sia pure in via incidentale, anche in questo libro[4].

Desidero ringraziare Alessandra Viviani e Federico Lenzerini per la lettura del volume ed Eugenio Carli per la sua collaborazione relativa alla parte bibliografica e documentaria. Naturalmente, è soltanto mia la responsabilità per eventuali errori ed omissioni.

R.P.M.

Siena, dicembre 2019

AVVERTENZE

A. *Reperimento di atti e documenti*

Quasi tutti i materiali normativi internazionali (sentenze, decisioni, trattati ed altri atti) sono ufficialmente pubblicati sui loro siti. Pertanto, per il loro reperimento, rinviamo all'indice dei siti online.

B. *Uso delle lingue*

Per la citazione, nel testo, di brani di sentenze, trattati o altri atti normativi, ho usato di solito la lingua inglese, che è la più diffusa fra le versioni ufficiali di tali documenti. Anche nelle note, la giurisprudenza, i trattati e gli altri atti, vengono quasi sempre citati in inglese.

C. *Citazioni nelle note*

Nelle note, la dottrina è citata in forma abbreviata (cognome dell'autore ed anno di pubblicazione), rinviando alla bibliografia per un'indicazione più completa. Anche i casi vengono citati in forma sintetica, con rinvio al relativo indice per maggiori informazioni.

---

[3] Cfr. Antonio Cassese, *Self-Determination of Peoples. A Legal Reappraisal* (1995), p. 3.

[4] E spero che essi mi scuseranno se, nel tentativo di fornire ulteriori riferimenti su questi argomenti, ho spesso citato miei scritti precedenti.

ABBREVIAZIONI

A. *Acronimi*

ACHPR	African Charter on Human and Peoples' Rights of 27 June 1981
ACHR	American Convention of Human Rights of 22 November 1969
ACmHPR	African Commission on Human and Peoples' Rights
ACtHPR	African Court on Human and Peoples' Rights
ACtJHR	African Court of Justice and Human Rights
AP	Additional Protocol
AP I	Protocol Additional to the Geneva Convention of 12 August 1949 (Protection of Victims of International Armed Conflicts) of 8 June 1977
AP II	Protocol Additional to the Geneva Convention of 12 August 1949 (Protection of Victims of Non-International Armed Conflicts) of 8 June 1977
ArCHR	Arab Charter on Human Rights of 22 May 2004
ASEAN	Association of South-East Asian Nations
AU	African Union
CAT	Convention against Torture and Other Cruel, Inhuman or Degrading Treatment or Punishment of 10 December 1984
CCPR	International Covenant on Civil and Political Rights of 16 December 1966
CEDAW	Convention on the Elimination of All Forms of Discrimination against Women of 18 December 1979
CERD	International Convention on the Elimination of All Forms of Racial Discrimination of 21 December 1965
CESCR	International Covenant on Economic, Social and Cultural Rights of 16 December 1966
CFI	Court of First Instance of the European Communities
CJAU	Court of Justice of the African Union
CmHR	Commission on Human Rights
CoE	Council of Europe
CMW	International Convention on the Protection of the Rights of All Migrant Workers and Members of Their Families of 18 December 1990
CPPED	International Convention for the Protection of All Persons from Enforced Disappearance of 20 December 2006
CPPCG	Convention on the Prevention and Punishment of the Crime of Genocide of 9 December 1948
CRC	Convention on the Rights of the Child of 20 November 1989
CRPD	Convention on the Rights of Persons with Disabilities of 13 December 2006
CSCE	Conference on Security and Co-operation in Europe

CSPCA	International Convention on the Suppression and Punishment of the Crime of Apartheid of 30 November 1973
CSR	Convention relating to the Status of Refugees of 28 July 1951
CteeAT	Committee Against Torture
CteeED	Committee on Enforced Disappearances
CteeEDAW	Committee on the Elimination of Discrimination against Women
CteeERD	Committee on the Elimination of Racial Discrimination
CteeESCR	Committee on Economic, Social and Cultural Rights
CteeMW	Committee on Migrant Workers
CteeRC	Committee on the Rights of the Child
CteeRPD	Committee of the Rights of Persons with Disabilities
EC	European Community
ECCC	Extraordinary Chambers in the Courts of Cambodia
ECJ	European Court of Justice
EC Treaty	Treaty establishing the European Community (former Treaty establishing the European Economic Community of 25 March 1957)
ECHR	European Convention for the Protection of Human Rights and Fundamental Freedoms of 4 November 1950
ECHRB	European Convention for the Protection of Human Rights and Dignity of the Human Being with regard to the Application of Biology and Medicine of 4 April 1997
ECmHR	European Commission of Human Rights
ECML	European Charter for Regional or Minority Languages of 5 November 1992
ECOSOC	Economic and Social Council
ECOWAS	Economic Community of West African States
ECOWAS-CCJ	ECOWAS Community Court of Justice
ECPT	European Convention for the Prevention of Torture and Inhuman or Degrading Treatment or Punishment of 26 November 1987
ECteeSR	European Committee of Social Rights
ECtHR	European Court of Human Rights
EEC	European Economic Community
ESC	European Social Charter of 18 October 1961
ESCrev	European Social Charter revised of 3 May 1996
EU	European Union
EUCh	Charter of Fundamental Rights of the European Union
FAO	Food and Agriculture Organization
FCPNM	Framework Convention for the Protection of National Minorities of 1 February 1995
GA	General Assembly of the United Nations
GC	Geneva Conventions of 12 August 1949
GC I	Geneva Convention for the Amelioration of the Condition of the Wounded and Sick in Armed Forces in the Field of 12 August 1949
GC II	Geneva Convention for the Amelioration of the Condition of the Wounded, Sick and Shipwrecked Members of Armed Forces at Sea of 12 August 1949
GC III	Geneva Convention relative to the Treatment of Prisoners of War of 12 August 1949

GC IV	Geneva Convention relative to the Protection of Civilian Persons in Time of War of 12 August 1949
HCHR	United Nations High Commissioner for Human Rights
HRC	Human Rights Council
HRCtee	Human Rights Committee
IACAT	Inter-American Convention to Prevent and Punish Torture of 9 December 1985
IACmHR	Inter-American Commission on Human Rights
IACtHR	Inter-American Court of Human Rights
ICAO	International Civil Aviation Organization
ICC	International Criminal Court
ICJ	International Court of Justice
ICRC	International Committee of the Red Cross
ICSID	Convention on the Settlement of Investments Disputes between States and Nationals of Other States of 18 March 1965
ICTR	International Criminal Tribunal for Rwanda
ICTY	International Criminal Tribunal for the Former Yugoslavia
ILC	International Law Commission
ILO	International Labour Organization
IMT	International Military Tribunal of Nuremberg
IMTFE	International Military Tribunal for the Far East (of Tokyo)
ITLOS	International Tribunal for the Law of the Sea
ITU	International Telecommunication Union
IUSCT	Iran-United States Claims Tribunal
NATO	North Atlantic Treaty Organization
NGO	Non-Governmental Organization
OAS	Organization of American States
OAU	Organization of African Unity
OECD	Organization of Economic Co-operation and Development
OHCHR	Office of the High Commissioner for Human Rights
OSCE	Organization for Security and Co-operation in Europe
PCIJ	Permanent Court of International Justice
PSR	Protocol Relating to the Status of Refugees
Rome Statute	Rome Statute of the International Criminal Court of 17 July 1998
RSCSL	Residual Special Court for Sierra Leone
SADC	Southern African Development Community
SCSL	Special Court for Sierra Leone
SICTR	Statute of the International Criminal Tribunal for Rwanda of 8 November 1994
SICTY	Statute of the International Criminal Tribunal for the Former Yugoslavia of 25 May 1993
STL	Special Tribunal for Lebanon
TEU	Treaty on European Union
TFEU	Treaty on the Functioning of the European Union
UDHR	Universal Declaration of Human Rights of 10 December 1948
UN	United Nations
UN Charter	Charter of the United Nations
UNCC	United Nations Compensation Commission

UNHCR	Office of the United Nations High Commissioner for Refugees
UNDP	United Nations Development Programme
UNESCO	United Nations Educational, Scientific and Cultural Organization
UPR	Universal Periodic Review
VCLT	Vienna Convention on the Law of Treaties of 23 May 1969
WHO	World Health Organization
WTO	World Trade Organization

B. *Riviste, periodici e altre fonti*

ACDI	Annuaire de la Commission du droit international
AFDI	Annuaire français de droit international
AIDI	Annuaire de l'Institut de droit international
AJIL	American Journal of International Law
ASDI	Annuaire Suisse de Droit International
ASIL Proc.	American Society of International Law Proceedings
AV	Archiv des Völkerrechts
Aus.YIL	Australian Yearbook of International Law
BYBIL	British Year Book of International Law
CD	Collection of Decisions of the European Commission on Human Rights
Col.JTL	Columbia Journal of Transnational Law
Com. int.	La Comunità internazionale
CS	Comunicazioni e Studi dell'Istituto di diritto internazionale e straniero dell'Università di Milano
DUDI	Diritti umani e diritto internazionale
ECR	European Court Reports
EJIL	European Journal of International Law
ED	Enciclopedia del Diritto
EPIL	Encyclopedia of Public International Law
ESIL Proc.	European Society of International Law, Select Proceedings of the ESIL
GYIL	German Yearbook of International Law
Georg.JIL	Georgia Journal of International Law
HRQ	Human Rights Quarterly
ICJ Rep.	Reports of Judgments, Advisory Opinions and Orders of the International Court of Justice
ILM	International Legal Materials
ILR	International Law Reports
ICLQ	International and Comparative Law Quarterly
It.YIL	Italian Yearbook of International Law
JICJ	Journal of International Criminal Justice
Journ. Int. Disp. Settl.	Journal of International Dispute Settlement
Mich. JIL	Michigan Journal of International Law
Neth.ILR	Netherlands International Law Review
Neth.YIL	Netherlands Yearbook of International Law
ÖZöR	Österreichische Zeitschrift für öffentliches Recht und Völkerrecht (Austrian Journal of Public and International Law)

PCIJ Publ.	Permanent Court of International Justice Publications
Pol.YIL	Polish Yearbook of International Law
RIAA	Reports of International Arbitral Awards
Riv. int. dir. uomo	Rivista internazionale dei diritti dell'uomo
RBDI	Revue belge de droit international
RC	Recueil des Cours, The Hague Academy of International Law
RDI	Rivista di diritto internazionale
REDI	Revista española de derecho internacional
RGDIP	Revue générale de droit international public
Studi integr. eur.	Studi sull'integrazione europea
UNTS	United Nations Treaty Series
Virg.JIL	Virginia Journal of International Law
YILC	Yearbook of the International Law Commission
ZaöRV	Zeitschrift für ausländisches öffentliches Recht und Völkerrecht (Heidelberg Journal of International Law)

SITI ONLINE

African Commission on Human and Peoples' Rights
https://www.achpr.org/communications

African Court on Human and Peoples' Rights
http://en.african-court.org/index.php/cases

Committee Against Torture
https://www.ohchr.org/en/hrbodies/cat/pages/catindex.aspx

Committee on Economic, Social and Cultural Rights
https://www.ohchr.org/en/hrbodies/cescr/pages/cescrindex.aspx

Committee on Enforced Disappearances
https://www.ohchr.org/en/hrbodies/ced/pages/cedindex.aspx

Committee on Migrant Workers
https://www.ohchr.org/EN/HRBodies/CMW/Pages/CMWIndex.aspx

Committee on the Elimination of Discrimination against Women
https://www.ohchr.org/en/hrbodies/cedaw/pages/cedawindex.aspx

Committee on the Elimination of Racial Discrimination
https://www.ohchr.org/en/hrbodies/cerd/pages/cerdindex.aspx

Committee on the Rights of Persons with Disabilities
https://www.ohchr.org/en/hrbodies/crpd/pages/crpdindex.aspx

Committee on the Rights of the Child
https://www.ohchr.org/en/hrbodies/crc/pages/crcindex.aspx

Court of First Instance of the European Communities
https://curia.europa.eu/jcms/jcms/Jo2_14304/en/

Economic and Social Council
https://www.un.org/ecosoc/en/home

ECOWAS Community Court of Justice
http://prod.courtecowas.org/cases-and-decisions-2/

European Commission of Human Rights
https://www.refworld.org/publisher/COECOMMHR.html

European Committee of Social Rights
https://www.coe.int/en/web/european-social-charter/european-committee-of-social-rights

European Court of Human Rights
https://echr.coe.int/Pages/home.aspx?p=home

European Court of Justice
https://curia.europa.eu/jcms/jcms/j_6/en/

European General Court
https://curia.europa.eu/jcms/jcms/p1_217427/en/

General Assembly
https://www.un.org/en/ga/documents/index.shtml

Human Rights Committee
https://www.ohchr.org/EN/HRBodies/CCPR/Pages/CCPRIndex.aspx

Human Rights Council
https://www.ohchr.org/en/hrbodies/hrc/pages/home.aspx

Inter-American Commission on Human Rights
https://www.oas.org/en/iachr/

Inter-American Court of Human Rights
http://www.corteidh.or.cr/index-en.cfm

International Arbitral Tribunals (*RIAA*)
https://legal.un.org/riaa/

International Court of Justice
https://www.icj-cij.org/en/cases

International Criminal Court
https://www.icc-cpi.int/Pages/cases.aspx

International Criminal Tribunal for Rwanda
https://unictr.irmct.org/en/cases

International Criminal Tribunal for the Former Yugoslavia
https://www.icty.org/en/cases

International Law Commission
https://legal.un.org/ilc/

International Military Tribunal of Nuremberg
https://avalon.law.yale.edu/subject_menus/imt.asp

Permanent Court of International Justice
https://www.icj-cij.org/en/pcij

Security Council
https://www.un.org/securitycouncil/

Special Tribunal for Lebanon
https://www.stl-tsl.org/en/the-cases

INDICE DEI CASI

Corte permanente di giustizia internazionale/Permanent Court of International Justice (PCIJ)

Mavrommatis Palestine Concessions Case (Jurisdiction) (Greece v. United Kingdom), Judgment of 30 August 1924

Corte internazionale di giustizia/International Court of Justice (ICJ)

Accordance with International Law of the Unilateral Declaration of Independence in respect of Kosovo, Advisory Opinion of 22 July 2010

Application of the Convention on the Prevention and Punishment of the Crime of Genocide (Bosnia and Herzegovina v. Yugoslavia), Preliminary Objections, Judgment of 11 July 1996

Application of the Convention on the Prevention and Punishment of the Crime of Genocide (Bosnia and Herzegovina v. Serbia and Montenegro), Judgment of 26 February 2007

Application of the Convention on the Prevention and Punishment of the Crime of Genocide (Croatia v. Serbia), Judgment of 3 February 2015

Application of the Convention on the Prevention and Punishment of the Crime of Genocide (The Gambia v. Myanmar), Order of 23 January 2020

Application of the International Convention on the Elimination of All Forms of Racial Discrimination (Georgia v. Russian Federation), Request for the Indication of Provisional Measures, Order of 15 October 2008

Application of the International Convention on the Elimination of All Forms of Racial Discrimination (Georgia v. Russian Federation), Judgment of 1 April 2011

Armed Activities on the Territory of the Congo (Democratic Republic of the Congo v. Uganda), Judgment of 19 December 2005

Armed Activities on the Territory of the Congo (New Application: 2002) (Democratic Republic of the Congo v. Rwanda), Judgment of 3 February 2006

Arrest Warrant of 11 April 2000 (Democratic Republic of the Congo v. Belgium), Judgment of 14 February 2002

Avena and Other Mexican Nationals (Mexico v. United States of America), Judgment of 31 March 2004

Barcelona Traction, Light and Power Company, Limited (New Application: 1962) (Belgium v. Spain), Second Phase, Judgment of 5 February 1970

Corfu Channel Case (The United Kingdom v. Albania), Merits, Judgment of 9 April 1949

East Timor (Portugal v. Australia), Judgment of 30 June 1995

Gabčikovo-Nagymaros Project (Hungary v. Slovakia), Judgment of 25 September 1997

Jurisdictional Immunities of the State (Germany v. Italy: Greece Intervening), Judgment of 3 February 2012

LaGrand (Germany v. United States of America), Merits, Judgment of 27 June 2001
Legal Consequences for States of the Continued Presence of South Africa in Namibia (South West Africa) notwithstanding Security Council Resolution 276 (1970), Advisory Opinion of 21 June 1971
Legal Consequences of the Construction of a Wall in the Occupied Palestinian Territory, Advisory Opinion of 9 July 2004
Legal Consequences of the Separation of the Chagos Archipelago from Mauritius in 1965, Advisory Opinion of 25 February 2019
Legality of the Threat or Use of Nuclear Weapons, Advisory Opinion of 8 July 1996
Legality of Use of Force (Serbia and Montenegro v. Belgium, Canada, France, Germany, Italy, The Netherlands, Portugal and The United Kingdom), Judgments of 15 December 2004
Military and Paramilitary Activities in and against Nicaragua (Nicaragua v. United States), Jurisdiction and Admissibility, Judgment of 26 November 1984
Military and Paramilitary Activities in and against Nicaragua (Nicaragua v. United States), Merits, Judgment of 27 June 1986
Questions relating to the Obligation to Prosecute or Extradite (Belgium v. Senegal), Judgment of 20 July 2012
Pulp Mills on the River Uruguay (Argentina v. Uruguay), Judgment of 20 April 2010
Reservations to the Convention on the Prevention and Punishment of the Crime of Genocide, Advisory Opinion of 28 May 1951
United States Diplomatic and Consular Staff in Tehran (United States v. Iran), Merits, Judgment of 24 May 1980
Western Sahara, Advisory Opinion of 16 October 1975

Tribunale dei reclami Iran-Stati Uniti/Iran-United States Claims Tribunal (IUSCT)

Yeager v. Islamic Republic of Iran, Decision of 2 November 1987, 17 *Reports* 92

Altri tribunali arbitrali /Other Arbitration Tribunals

Alabama claims of the United States of America v. Great Britain, Award of 14 September 1872, in De Martens (1975), pp. 698-775; Moore (1898), pp. 495-682

Comitato dei diritti umani/Human Rights Committee (HRCtee)

A v. Australia. Communication No. 560/1993, Views of 3 April 1997
C. v. Australia, Communication No. 900/1999, Views of 28 October 2002
Ackla v. Togo, Communication No. 505/1992, Views of 25 March 1996
Alzery v. Sweden, Communication No. 1416/2005, Views of 25 October 2006
Baban et al. v. Australia, Communication No. 1014/2001, Views of 6 August 2003
Basongo Bondonga v. Democratic Republic of the Congo, Communication No. 1483/2006, Views of 30 July 2009
Baumgarten v. Germany, Communication No. 960/2000, Views of 19 September 2003
Bautista de Arellana v. Colombia, Communication No. 563/1993, Views of 27 October 1995
Bwalya v. Zambia, Communication No. 314/1988, Views of 14 July 1993
Celiberti de Casariego v. Uruguay, Communication No. 56/1979, Views of 29 July 1981
Chongwe v. Zambia, Communication No. 821/1998, Views of 25 October 2000
Coeriel and Aurik v. The Netherlands, Communication No. 453/1991, Views of 31 October 1994

Kaba v. Canada, Communication No. 1465/2006, Views of 25 March 2010
El Ghar v. Lybian Arab Jamahiriya, Communication No. 1107/2002, Views of 2 November 2004
Faure v. Australia, Communication No. 1036/2001, Views of 31 October 2005
González del Rio v. Peru, Communication No. 263/1987, Views of 28 October 1992
Gordon C. Van Duzen v. Canada, Communication No. R.12/50, Views of 7 April 1982
Gueye et al. v. France, Communication No. 196/1985, Views of 3 April 1989
Hinostroza Solís v. Peru, Communication No. 1016/2001, Views of 27 March 2006
Huamán v. Peru, Communication No. 1153/2003, Views of 24 October 2005
Hudoyberganova v. Uzbekistan, Communication No. 931/2000, Views of 5 November 2004
Judge v. Canada, Communication No. 829/1998, Views of 5 August 2003
Kall v. Poland, Communication No. 552/1993, Views of 14 July 1997
Kennedy v. Trinidad and Tobago, Communication No. 845/1999, Views of 26 March 2002
Kitok v. Sweden, Communication No. 197/1985, Views of 27 July 1988
Kivenmaa v. Finland, Communication No. 412/1990, Views of 31 March 1994
Korneenko et al. v. Belarus, Communication No. 1274/2004, Views of 31 October 2006
Lansman (Ilmari) et al. v. Finland, Communication No. 511/1992, Views of 26 October1994
Länsman (Jouni) et al. v. Finland, Communication No. 671/1995, Views of 30 October 1996
Laureano Atachahua v. Peru, Communication No. 540/1993, Views of 25 March 1996
L.T.K. v. Finland, Communication No. 185/1984, Inadmissibility decision of 9 July 1985
Leirvåg et al. v. Norway, Communication No. 1155/2003, Views of 3 November 2004
Lopez Burgos v. Uruguay, Communication No. 52/1979, Views of 29 July 1981
Love et al. v. Australia, Communication No. 983/2001, Views of 25 March 2003
Lovelace v. Canada, Communication No. 024/1977, Views of 30 July 1981
Maksudov and Others v. Kyrgyzstan and Uzbekistan, Communications Nos. 1461/2006, 1462/2006, 1476/2006, 1477/2006, Views of 16 July 2008
Marshall et al. and the Mikmaq tribal society v. Canada, Communication No. 205/1986, Views of 4 November 1991
Matkarim Aminov v. Turkmenistan, Communication No. 2220/2012, Views of 14 July 2016
Mahuika et al. v. New Zealand, Communication No. 547/1993, Views of 27 October 2000
Mojica v. Dominican Republic, Communication No. 449/1991, Views of 15 July 1994
Ng v. Canada, Communication No. 469/1991, Views of 5 November 1993
Peltonen v. Finland, Communication No. 492/1992, Views of 21 July 1994
Pereira Montero v. Uruguay, Communication No. 106/1981, Views of 31 March 1983
Poma Poma v. Peru, Communication No. 1457/2006, Views of 27 March 2009
Queenan v. Canada, Communication No. 1379/2005, Decision on admissibility of 26 July 2005
Radosevic v. Germany, Communication No. 1292/2004, Decision on admissibility of 22 July 2005
Rodríguez v. Uruguay, Communication No. 322/1988, Views of 19 July 1994
Rouse v. The Philippines, Communication No. 1089/2002, Views of 25 July 2005
Sarma v. Sri Lanka, Communication No. 950/2000, Views of 16 July 2003
Sayadi and Vinck v. Belgium, Communication No. 1472/2006, Views of 22 October 2008
Singh Bhinder v. Canada, Communication No. 208/1986, Views of 9 November 1989
Suarez de Guerrero v. Colombia, Communication No. 45/1979, Views of 31 March 1982
Teran Jijon v. Ecuador, Communication No. 277/1988, Views of 26 March 1992
V.D.A. v. Argentina, Communication No. 1608/2007, Views of 29 March 2011
Wallmann and Others v. Austria, Communication No. 1002/2001, Views of 1 April 2004
Warsame v. Canada, Communication 1959/2010, Views of 21 July 2011

Yevdokimov and Rezanov v. Russia, Communication No. 1410/2005, Views of 21 March 2011
Zalesskaya v. Belarus, Communication No. 1604/2007, Views of 28 March 2011

Comitato contro la tortura/Committee Against Torture (CteeAT)

M. Qani Halimi-Nedzibi v. Austria, Communication 8/1991, Views of 18 November 1993

Comitato sulla eliminazione della discriminazione razziale/Committee on the Elimination of Racial Discrimination (CteeERD)

Hagan v. Australia, Communication No. 26/2002, Opinion of 20 March 2003

Commissione europea dei diritti umani/European Commission of Human Righs (ECmHR)

Arrowsmith v. The United Kingdom, Decision of 16 May 1977.
Austria v. Italy, Decision of 11 January 1961
France, Norway, Denmark, Sweden and The Netherlands v. Turkey, Report of 7 December 1985
H. v. Norway, Decision of 19 May 1992
Iversen v. Norway, Decision of 17 December 1963
Lawless v. Ireland, Report of 12 April 1960
Smith Kline and French Laboratories Ltd v. The Netherlands, Decision of 4 October 1990
W.P. v. The United Kingdom, Decision of 13 May 1980
X v. Federal Republic of Germany, Decision of 5 July 1977
X v. Federal Republic of Germany, Decision of 10 March 1981

Corte europea dei diritti umani/European Court of Human Rights (ECtHR)

A. v. The United Kingdom, Judgment of 23 September 1998
A. and Others v. The United Kingdom, Grand Chamber, Judgment of 19 February 2009
Adolf v. Austria, Judgment of 26 March 1982
Ahmed and Others v. The United Kingdom, Judgment of 2 September 1998
Airey v. Ireland, Judgment of 9 October 1979
Akdivar and Others v. Turkey, Grand Chamber, Judgment of 16 September 1996
Akkoç v. Turkey, Judgment of 10 October 2000
Aksoy v. Turkey, Judgment of 18 December 1996
Aktaş v. Turkey, Judgment of 24 April 2003
Al-Adsani v. The United Kingdom, Grand Chamber, Judgment of 21 November 2001
Al-Dulimi and Montana Management Inc. v. Switzerland, Judgment of 21 June 2016
Alexandridis v. Greece, Judgment of 21 February 2008
Alikaj and Others v. Italy, Judgment of 29 March 2011
Al-Jedda v. The United Kingdom, Grand Chamber, Judgment of 7 July 2011
Al-Saadoon and Mufdhi v. The United Kingdom, Decision of 30 June 2009
Al-Saadoon and Mufdhi v. The United Kingdom, Judgment of 2 March 2010
Al-Skeini and Others v. The United Kingdom, Judgment of 7 July 2011
Andronicou and Constantinou v. Cyprus, Judgment of 9 October 1997
Anguelova v. Bulgaria, Judgment of 13 June 2002
Anheuser-Busch Inc. v. Portugal, Judgment of 11 January 2007

Assenov and Others v. Bulgaria, Judgment of 28 October 1998
Avsar v. Turkey, Judgment of 10 July 2001
Aydin v. Turkey, Judgment of 25 September 1997
Babar Ahmad and Others v. The United Kingdom, Decision of 8 July 2010
B. v. The United Kingdom, Judgment of 8 July 1987
Banković and Others v. Belgium and 16 Other States, Grand Chamber, Admissibility Decision of 12 December 2001
Bayatyan v. Armenia, Judgment of 7 July 2011
Beer and Regan v. Federal Republic of Germany, Grand Chamber, Judgment of 18 February 1999
Belgian Linguistic Case (Case relating to certain aspects of the laws on the use of languages in education in Belgium v. Belgium), Merits, Judgment of 23 July 1968
Belilos v. Switzerland, Judgment of 29 April 1988
Beyeler v. Italy, Grand Chamber, Judgment of 5 January 2000
Bosphorus Hava Yolları Turizm ve Ticaret Anonim Şirketi v. Ireland, Grand Chamber, Judgment of 30 June 2005
Bozcaada Kimisis Teodoku Rum Ortodoks Kilisesi Vakfı v. Turkey, Judgment of 3 March 2009
Brannigan and McBride v. The United Kingdom, Judgment of 26 May 1993
Buckley v. The United Kingdom, Judgment of 25 September 1996
Burghartz v. Switzerland, Judgment of 22 February 1994
Buscarini and Others v. San Marino, Grand Chamber, Judgment of 18 February 1999
C.N. v. The United Kingdom, Judgment of 19 October 2012
Çakici v. Turkey, Judgment of 8 July 1999
Calvelli and Ciglio v. Italy, Grand Chamber, Judgment of 17 January 2002
Campbell and Cosans v. The United Kingdom, Judgment of 25 February 1982
Cara-Damiani v. Italy, Judgment of 7 February 2012
Casa di Cura Valle Fiorita S.r.l. v. Italy, Judgment of 13 December 2018
Casado Coca v. Spain, Judgment of 24 February 1994
Case of United Communist Party of Turkey and Others v. Turkey, Judgment of 30 January 1998
Catan and Others v. Moldova and Russia, Grand Chamber, Judgment of 19 October 2012
Cengiz and Others v. Turkey, Judgment of 1 December 2015,
Centro Europa 7 s.r.l. and Di Stefano v. Italy, Judgment of 7 June 2012
Cestaro v. Italy, Judgment of 7 April 2015
Chahal v. UK, Judgment of 15 November 1996
Chinnici v. Italy (No. 2), Judgment of 14 April 2015
Chiragov and Others v. Armenia, Grand Chamber, Judgment of 16 June 2015
Chitos v. Greece, Judgment of 4 June 2015
Chovancik v. Slovakia, Judgment of 17 June 2003
Connors v. The United Kingdom, Judgment of 27 May 2004
Contrada v. Italy (No. 3), Judgment of 14 April 2015
Cyprus v. Turkey, Grand Chamber, Judgment of 10 May 2001
De Haes and Gijsels v. Belgium, Judgment of 24 February 1997
Depalle v. France, Grand Chamber, Judgment of 29 March 2010
Dink v. Turkey, Judgment of 14 September 2010
D.H. and Others v. Czech Republic, Grand Chamber, Judgment of 13 November 2007
D.J. v. Croatia, Judgment of 24 July 2012
Djavit An v. Turkey, Judgment of 20 February 2003
Dubowska and Skup v. Poland, Decision of 18 April 1997

Dudgeon v. The United Kingdom, Judgment of 22 October 1991
Ebrahimian v. France, Judgment of 26 November 2015
Edwards v. The United Kingdom, Judgment of 16 December 1992
Edwards Paul and Audrey v. The United Kingdom, Judgment of 14 March 2002
El-Masri v. The Former Yugoslav Republic of Macedonia, Grand Chamber, Judgment of 13 December 2012
Engel and Others v. The Netherlands, Judgment of 8 June 1976
Ergi v. Turkey, Judgment of 28 July 1998
Fabris v. France, Grand Chamber, Judgment of 7 February 2013
Fadeyeva v. Russia, Judgment of 9 June 2005
Filip v. Rumenia, Judgment of 14 December 2006
France, Norway, Denmark, Sweden, Netherlands v. Turkey, Decision of 6 December 1983
Fretté v. France, Judgment of 26 February 2002
Fuklev v. Ukraine, Judgment of 7 June 2002
Gaskin v. The United Kingdom, Judgment of 7 July 1989
Gentilhomme, Schaff-Benhadji and Zerouki v. France, Judgment of 14 May 2002
Gitonas and Others v. Greece, Judgment of 1 July 1997
Giuliani and Gaggio v. Italy, Grand Chamber, Judgment of 24 March 2011
Golder v. The United Kingdom, Judgment of 21 February 1975
Gongadze v. Ukraine, Judgment of 8 November 2005
Goodwin v. The United Kingdom, Grand Chamber, Judgment of 27 March 1996
Goodwin Christine v. The United Kingdom, Grand Chamber, Judgment of 11 July 2002
Grande Stevens and Others v. Italy, Judgment of 4 March 2014
Graziani-Weiss v. Austria, Judgment of 18 October 2011
Greek Case – Denmark v. Greece, Norway v. Greece, Sweden v. Greece, Netherlands v. Greece, Report of 5 November 1969
Grzelak v. Poland, Judgment of 15 June 2010
Guillot v. France, Judgment of 24 October 1996
Güleç v. Turkey, Judgment of 27 July 1998
Gustafsson v. Sweden, Grand Chamber, Judgment of 25 April 1996
Haas v. Switzerland, Judgment of 20 January 2011
Hadjianastassiou v. Greece, Judgment of 16 December 1992
Handyside v. The United Kingdom, Judgment of 7 December 1976
Hardy and Maile v. The United Kingdom, Judgment of 14 February 2012
Harkins and Edwards v. The United Kingdom, Judgment of 17 January 2012
Hasan and Eylem Zengin v. Turkey, Judgment of 9 October 2007
Hassan v. The United Kingdom, Grand Chamber, Judgment of 16 September 2014
Hatton and Others v. The United Kingdom, Judgment of 8 July 2003
Herczegfalvy v. Austria, Judgment of 24 September 1992
Hirsi Jamaa and Others v. Italy, Grand Chamber, Judgment of 23 February 2012
Hirst v. The United Kingdom (No. 2), Judgment of 6 October 2005
Iatridis v. Greece, Grand Chamber, Judgment of 25 March 1999
Ilaşcu and Others v. Moldova and Russia, Grand Chamber, Judgment of 8 July 2004
Ilhan v. Turkey, Grand Chamber, Judgment of 27 June 2000
Informationsverein Lentia and Others v. Austria, Judgment of 24 November 1993
Ireland v. The United Kingdom, Judgment of 18 January 1978
Isayeva v. Russia, Judgment of 24 February 2005
Isayeva, Yusupova and Bazayeva v. Russia, Judgment of 24 February 2005

Issa and Others v. Turkey, Judgment of 16 November 2004
Jahn and Others v. Germany, Grand Chamber, Judgment of 30 June 2005
Jaloud v. The Netherlands, Grand Chamber, Judgment of 20 November 2014
James and Others v. The United Kingdom, Judgment of 21 February 1986
Janowski v. Poland, Grand Chamber, Judgment of 21 January 1999
Jersild v. Denmark, Grand Chamber, Judgment of 23 September 1994
Jones and Others v. The United Kingdom, Judgment of 14 January 2014
Kafkaris v. Cyprus, Grand Chamber, Judgment of 12 February 2008
Kasymakhunov and Saybatalov v. Russia, Judgment of 14 March 2013
Kaya v. Turkey, Judgment of 19 February 1998
Khatsiyeva and Others v. Russia, Judgment of 17 January 2008
Keenan v. The United Kingdom, Judgment of 3 April 2001
Kelly and Others v. The United Kingdom, Judgment of 4 May 2001
Kılıç v. Turkey, Judgment of 28 March 2000
Kjeldsen, Busk Madsen and Pedersen v. Denmark, Judgment of 7 December 1976
Klass and Others v. Germany, Judgment of 6 September 1978
Koch v. Germany, Judgment of 19 July 2012
Kokkinakis v. Greece, Judgment of 25 May 1993
König v. Germany, Judgment of 28 June 1978
Kononov v. Latvia, Judgment of 17 May 2010
Kopecký v. Slovakia, Grand Chamber, Judgment of 28 September 2004
Konečný v. Czech Republic, Judgment of 26 October 2004
Köse and 93 Others v. Turkey, Decision of 24 January 2006
Kruslin v. France, Judgment of 24 April 1990
Kurt v. Turkey, Judgment of 25 May 1998
L.C.B. v. The United Kingdom, Judgment of 9 June 1998
Labita v. Italy, Grand Chamber, Judgment of 6 April 2000
Lautsi v. Italy, Judgment of 3 November 2009
Lautsi and Others v. Italy, Grand Chamber, Judgment of 18 March 2011
Lawless v. Ireland (No. 3), Judgment of 1 July 1961
Leela Forderkreis E.V. and Others v. Germany, Judgment of 6 November 2008
Leyla Şahin v. Turkey, Grand Chamber, Judgment of 10 November 2005
Lingens v. Austria, Judgment of 8 July 1986
Lithgow and Others v. The United Kingdom, Judgment of 8 July 1986
Loizidou v. Turkey (preliminary objections), Grand Chamber, Judgment of 23 March 1995
Loizidou v. Turkey (merits), Grand Chamber, Judgment of 18 December 1996
Loizidou v. Turkey (Article 50), Grand Chamber, Judgment of 28 July 1998
López Ostra v. Spain, Judgment of 9 December 1994
M.C. v. Bulgaria, Judgment of 4 December 2003
M.S.S. v. Belgium and Greece, Grand Chamber, Judgment of 21 January 2011
Mahmut Kaya v. Turkey, Judgment of 28 March 2000
Makaratzis v. Greece, Grand Chamber, Judgment of 20 December 2004
Maktouf and Damjanović v. Bosnia and Herzegovina, Grand Chamber, Judgment of 18 July 2013
Marckx v. Belgium, Judgment of 13 June 1979
Markt Intern Verlag GmbH and Klaus Beermann v. Germany, Judgment of 20 November 1989
Maslova and Nalbandov v. Russia, Judgment of 24 January 2008
Mastromatteo v. Italy, Grand Chamber, Judgment of 24 October 2002
Mathieu-Molin and Clerfayt v. Belgium, Judgment of 2 March 1987

Matter v. Slovakia, Judgment of 5 July 1999
Matthews v. The United Kingdom, Grand Chamber, Judgment of 18 February 1999
McCann and Others v. The United Kingdom, Grand Chamber, Judgment of 27 September 1995
Medvedyev and Others v. France, Grand Chamber, Judgment of 29 March 2010
Members of the Gldani Congregation of the Jehovah's Witnesses v. Georgia, Judgment of 3 May 2007
Mikayil Mammadov v. Azerbaijan, Judgment of 22 May 2014
Moldovan and Others v. Romania (No. 2), Judgment of 12 July 2005
Moustaquim v. Belgium, Judgment of 18 February 1991
Müller and Others v. Switzerland, Judgment of 24 May 1988
Nachova and Others v. Bulgaria, Judgment of 26 February 2004
Nachova and Others v. Bulgaria, Grand Chamber, Judgment of 6 July 2005
Nada v. Switzerland, Grand Chamber, Judgment of 12 September 2012
Naletilić v. Croatia, Decision of 4 May 2000
NA. v. The United Kingdom, Judgment of 17 July 2008
Nasr and Ghali v. Italy, Judgment of 23 February 2016
N.B. v. Slovakia, Judgment of 12 June 2012
Nikolova and Velichkova v. Bulgaria, Judgment of 20 December 2007
Norris v. Ireland, Judgment of 26 October 1988
Oberschlick v. Austria, Judgment of 23 May 1991
Öcalan v. Turkey, Judgment of 12 March 2003
Öcalan v. Turkey, Grand Chamber, Judgment of 12 May 2005
Öcalan v. Turkey (No. 2), Judgment of 18 March 2014
Oğur v. Turkey, Grand Chamber, Judgment of 20 May 1999
Open Door and Dublin Well Woman v. Ireland, Judgment of 29 October 1992
Osman v. The United Kingdom, Grand Chamber, Judgment of 28 October 1998
Otto-Preminger-Institut v. Austria, Judgment 20 September 1994
Ouranio Toxo v. Greece, Judgment of 20 October 2005
Öztürk v. Germany, Judgment of 21 February 1984
P. and S. v. Poland, Judgment of 30 October 2012
Perinçek v. Switzerland, Grand Chamber, Judgment of 15 October 2015
Perk and Others v. Turkey, Judgment of 28 March 2006
Perna v. Italy, Grand Chamber, Judgment of 6 May 2003
Pierre-Bloch v. France, Judgment of 21 October 1997
Pine Valley Developments Ltd and Others v. Ireland, Judgment of 29 November 1991
Pla and Puncernau v. Andorra, Judgment of 13 July 2004
Pressos Compania Naviera S.A. and Others v. Belgium, Judgment of 20 November 1995
Pretty v. The United Kingdom, Judgment of 29 April 2002
Rackete and Others v. Italy, Decision (on interim measures) of 25 June 2019
R.R. v. Poland, Judgment of 26 May 2011
Ramsahai and Others v. The Netherlands, Grand Chamber, Judgment of 15 May 2007
Rantsev v. Cyprus and Russia, Judgment of 7 January 2010
Refah Partisi (the Welfare Party) and others v. Turkey, Grand Chamber, Judgment of 13 February 2003
Renolde v. France, Judgment of 16 October 2008
Rivière v. France, Judgment of 11 July 2006
Saadi v. Italy, Grand Chamber, Judgment of 28 February 2008
Sadak and others v. Turkey (No. 2), Judgment of 11 June 2002

Şahin v. Turkey, Grand Chamber, Judgment of 10 November 2005
Sakik and Others v. Turkey, Judgment of 26 November 1997
Saoud v. France, Judgment of 9 October 2007
Sciacca v. Italy, Judgment of 11 January 2005
Scollo v. Italy, Judgment of 28 September 1995
Scoppola v. Italy (No. 3), Grand Chamber, Judgment of 22 May 2012
Scordino and Others v. Italy (No. 1), Decision of 27 March 2003
Scordino and Others v. Italy (No. 1), Grand Chamber, Judgment of 29 March 2006
Seguin v. France, Decision of 7 March 2000
Selmouni v. France, Grand Chamber, Judgment of 28 July 1999
Sigurjónsson v. Iceland, Judgment of 30 June 1993
Siliadin v. France, Judgment of 26 July 2005
Sinan Işik v. Turkey, Judgment of 2 February 2010
Soering v. The United Kingdom, Judgment of 7 July 1989
Sørensen and Rasmussen v. Denmark, Grand Chamber, Judgment of 11 January 2006
Sporrong and Lönnroth v. Sweden, Judgment of 23 September 1982
Stafford v. The United Kingdom, Grand Chamber, Judgment of 28 May 2002
Stichting Mothers of Srebrenica and Others v. The Netherlands, Decision of 11 June 2013
Streletz, Kessler and Krenk v. Germany, Grand Chamber, Judgment 22 March 2001
Sulejmanovic v. Italy, Judgment of 16 July 2009
Sunday Times v. The United Kingdom (No. 1), Judgment of 26 April 1979
Taranenko v. Russia, Judgment of 15 May 2014
T.I. v. The United Kingdom, Judgment of 7 March 2000
Thlimmenos v. Greece, Grand Chamber, Judgment of 6 April 2000
Thorgeir Thorgeirson v. Island, Judgment of 25 June 1992
Torreggiani and Others v. Italy, Judgment of 8 January 2013
Trijonis v. Lithuania, Decision of 17 March 2005
Trijonis v. Lithuania, Judgment of 15 December 2005
Tyrer v. The United Kingdom, Judgment of 25 April 1978
Tysiąc v. Poland, Judgment of 27 March 2007
V.C. v. Slovakia, Judgment of 8 November 2011
Velikova v. Bulgaria, Judgment of 18 May 2000
VgT Verein gegen Tierfrabriken v. Switzerland, Judgment of 28 June 2001
Vilvarajah and Others v. The United Kingdom, Judgment of 30 October 1991
Vinter and Others v. The United Kingdom, Grand Chamber, Judgment of 9 July 2013
Vo v. France, Grand Chamber, Judgment of 8 July 2004
Waite and Kennedy v. Germany, Grand Chamber, Judgment of 18 February 1999
Weber v. Switzerland, Judgment of 22 May 1990
Wemhoff v. Germany, Judgment of 27 June 1968
Wingrove v. The United Kingdom, Judgment of 25 November 1996
X and Y v. The Netherlands, Judgment of 26 March 1985
X, Y and Z v. The United Kingdom, Grand Chamber, Judgment of 22 April 1997
Yaşa v. Turkey, Judgment of 2 September 1998
Young, James and Webster v. The United Kingdom, Judgment of 13 August 1981
Z and Others v. The United Kingdom, Grand Chamber, Judgment of 10 May 2001
Zana v. Turkey, Grand Chamber, Judgment of 25 November 1997
Zdanoka v. Latvia, Judgment of 17 June 2004
Zdanoka v. Latvia, Grand Chamber, Judgment of 16 March 2006

Comitato europeo dei diritti sociali/ European Committee of Social Rights (ECteeSR)

Confederazione Generale Italiana del Lavoro (CGIL) v. Italy, Complaint No. 91/2013, Decision of 12 October 2015
Finnish Society of Social Rights v. Finland, Complaint No. 88/2012, Decision of 9 September 2014
Finnish Society of Social Rights v. Finland, Complaint No. 106/2014, Decision on admissibility and the merits of 8 September 2016
International Federation of Human Rights Leagues (FIDH) v. France, Complaint No 14/2003, Decision of 8 September 2004

Corte di giustizia delle Comunità Europee (ora dell'Unione Europea) /European Court of Justice (ECJ)

Accession by the Community to the European Convention for the Protection of Human Rights and Fundamental Freedoms, Opinion 2/94 of 28 March 1996
Brüstle v. Greenpeace eV, Case C-34/1018, Judgment of 18 October 2011
European Commission and Others v. Kadi, Joined Cases C-584/10 P, C-593/10 P and C-595/10 P, Judgment of 18 July 2013
Hauer v. Land Rheinland-Pfalz, Case C-44/79, Judgment of 13 December 1979
Internationale Handelsgesellschaft mbH v. Einfuhr– und Vorratsstelle für Getreide und –Futtermittel, Case 11/70, Judgment of 17 December 1970
Kadi and Al Barakaat International Foundation v. Council and Commission, Joined Cases C-402/05 P and C-415/05 P, Judgment of 3 September 2008
Meryem Demirel v. Stadt Schwäbisch Gmünd, Case C-12/86, Judgment of 30 September 1987
Nold, Kohlen– und Baustoffgroßhandlung v. Commission, Case 4-73, Judgment of 14 May 1974
Stauder v. City of Ulm – Sozialamt, Case 29/69, Judgment of 12 November 1969
Stork & Cie v. High Authority of the European Coal and Steel Community, Case 1/58, Judgment of 4 February 1959
The Society for the Protection of Unborn Children Ireland Ltd v. Stephen Grogan and Others, Case C-159/90, Judgment of 4 October 1991
Wachauf v. Bundesamt für Ernährung und Forstwirtschaft, Case C-5/88, Judgment of 13 July 1989

Tribunale di primo grado delle Comunità Europee/Court of First Instance(CFI) (ora Tribunale dell'UE/European General Court (EGC))

Kadi v. Council and Commission, Case T-315/01, CFI Judgment of 21 September 2005
Kadi v. European Commission, Case T-85/09, EGC Judgment of 30 September 2010
Yusuf and Al Barakaat International Foundation v. Council and Commission, Case T-306/01, CFI Judgment of 21 September 2005

Commissione interamericana dei diritti umani/ Inter-American Commission on Human Rights (IACmHR)

Baby Boy Case (Christian S. White and Gary K. Potter v. United States), Case 2141, Report No. 23/81 of 6 March 1981
Coard et al. v. United States, Case 10.951, Report No. 109/99 of 29 September 1999
Ecuador v. Colombia (Inter-state Petition IP-02 Admissibility Franklin Guillermo Aisalla Molina), Report No. 112/10, Decision on admissibility of 21 October 2010

Garay Hermosilla et al. v. Chile, Case 10.843, Report No. 36/96 of 15 October 1996
"Haitian Interdiction" (Haitian Center for Human Rights et al. v. United States), Case 10.675, Report No. 28/93, Decision on admissibility of 13 October 1993
"Haitian Interdiction" (Haitian Center for Human Rights et al. v. United States), Case 10.675, Report No. 51/96, Decision on the merits of 13 March 1997
Raquel Martín de Mejía v. Peru, Case 10.970, Report No. 5/96 of 1 March 1996
Romer Morales Zegarra et al. v. Peru, Cases 10.827 and 11.984, Report No. 57/99 of 13 April 1999
Salas and Others v. United States, Case 10.573, Report No. 31/93, Decision on admissibility of 14 October 1993

Corte interamericana dei diritti umani/Inter-American Court of Human Rights (IACtHR)

Aloeboetoe et al. v. Suriname (Merits), Judgment of 4 December 1991
Aloeboetoe et al. v. Suriname (Reparations), Judgment of 10 September 1993
Bámaca-Velásquez v. Guatemala (Reparations), Judgment of 22 February 2002
Barrios Altos v. Peru (Merits), Judgment of 14 March 2001
Barrios Altos v. Peru (Reparations), Judgment of 30 November 2001
Bueno Alves v. Argentina, Judgment of 11 May 2007
Caballero Delgado and Santana v. Colombia, Judgment of 8 December 1995
Caesar v. Trinidad and Tobago, Judgment of 11 March 2005
Cantoral Benavides v. Peru (Merits), Judgment of 18 August 2000
Cantoral Benavides v. Peru (Reparations), Judgment of 3 December 2001
Case of the Girls Yean and Bosico v. Dominican Republic, Judgment of 8 September 2005
Castillo Petruzzi et al. v. Peru, Judgment of 30 May 1999
Claude-Reyes et al. v. Chile, Judgment of 19 September 2006
Godínez Cruz v. Honduras (Merits), Judgment of 20 January 1989
Goiburù et al. v. Paraguay (Merits), Judgment of 22 September 2006
González et al. ("Cotton Field") v. Mexico, Judgment of 16 November 2009
Habeas Corpus in Emergency Situations (Arts. 27(2), 25(1) and 7(6) American Convention on Human Rights), Advisory Opinion of 30 January 1987
Heliodoro Portugal v. Panama, Judgment of 12 August 2008
Hilaire v. Trinidad and Tobago (Preliminary Exceptions), Judgment of 1° September 2001
Hilaire, Constantine and Benjamin et al. v. Trinidad and Tobago, Judgment of 21 June 2002
Ituango Massacres v. Colombia, Judgment of 1 July 2006
Ivcher Bronstein v. Peru, Judgment of 24 September 1999
Juan Humberto Sánchez v. Honduras, Judgment of 7 June 2003
Judicial Guarantees in States of Emergency (Arts. 27(2), 25 and (8) American Convention on Human Rights), Advisory Opinion of 6 October 1987
"Juvenile Reeducation Institute" v. Paraguay, Judgment of 2 September 2004
Kuna Indigenous People of Maduganbí and the Emberá Indigenous People of Bayano and their members v. Panama, Judgment of 14 October 2014
Maritza Urrutia v. Guatemala, Judgment of 27 November 2003
Masacre de las Dos Erres v. Guatemala, Judgment of 24 November 2009
Mayagna (Sumo) Awas Tingni Community v. Nicaragua (Merits), Judgment of 31 August 2001
Miguel Castro Castro Prison v. Peru, Judgment of 25 November 2006
Moiwana Community v. Suriname (Merits), Judgment of 15 June 2005
Montero Aranguren et al. (Detention Center of Catia) v. Venezuela, Judgment of 5 July 2006

Neira Alegría et al. v. Peru (Merits), Judgment of 19 January 1995
Olmedo Bustos et al. ("The Last Temptation of Christ") v. Chile, Judgment of 5 February 2001
Paniagua Morales and Others ("White Van") v. Guatemala, Judgment of 8 March 1998
Proposed Amendments of the Naturalization Provisions of the Constitution of Costa Rica, Advisory Opinion of 19 January 1984
Saramaka People v. Suriname, Judgment of 28 November 2007
Sawhoyamaxa Indigenous Community v. Paraguay, Judgment of 29 March 2006
States of Emergency, Advisory Opinion of 30 January 1987
The Environment and Human Rights (State obligations in relation to the environment in the context of the protection and guarantee of the rights to life and to personal integrity – interpretation and scope of Articles 4(1) and 5(1) of the American Convention on Human Rights), Advisory Opinion of 15 November 2017
The Right to Information on Consular Assistance in the Framework of the Guarantees of the Due Process of Law, Advisory Opinion of 1 October 1999
The "Street Children" (Villagrán Morales et al.) v. Guatemala (Merits), Judgment of 19 November 1999
The "Street Children" (Villagrán Morales et al.) v. Guatemala (Reparations), Judgment of 26 May 2001
Tibi v. Ecuador, Judgment of 7 September 2004
Trujillo-Oroza v. Bolivia (Reparations), Judgment of 27 February 2002
Vargas Areco v. Paraguay, Judgment of 26 September 2006
Velásquez Rodríguez v. Honduras (Merits), Judgment of 29 July 1988
Ximenes Lopes v. Brasil, Judgment of 4 July 2006
Yakye Axa Indigenous Community v. Paraguay (Merits), Judgment of 17 June 2005

Commissione africana dei diritti dell'uomo e dei popoli/African Commission on Human and Peoples' Rights (ACmHPR)

Amnesty International, Comité Loosli Bachelard, Lawyers' Committee for Human Rights, Association of Members of the Episcopal Conference of East Africa v. Sudan, Communications Nos. 48/1990-50/1991-52/1991-89/1993, Decision of 15 November 1999
Curtis Francis Doebbler v. Sudan, Communication No. 236/00, Decision of 4 May 2003
Free Legal Assistance Group, Lawyers' Committee for Human Rights, Union Interafricaine des Droits de l'Homme, Les Témoins de Jehovah v. The Democratic Republic of Congo, Communications Nos. 25/89-47/90-56/91-100/93, Decision of 4 April 1996
Garreth Anver Prince v. South Africa, Communication No. 255/02, Decision of 7 December 2004
Institute for Human Rights and Development in Africa (on behalf of Sierra Leonean refugees in Guinea) v. Guinea, Communication No. 249/02, Decision of 7 December 2004
Malawi African Association, Amnesty International and Others v. Mauritania, Communications Nos. 54/91-61/91-96/93-98/93-164/97-196/97-210/98, Decision of 11 May 2000
Purohit and Moore v. Gambia, Communication No. 241/01, Decision of 29 May 2003
Social and Economic Rights Action Center (SERAC) and Center for Economic and Social Rights (CESR) v. Nigeria ("Ogoniland"), Communication No. 155/96, Decision of 27 October 2001
Zimbabwe Human Rights NGO Forum v. Zimbabwe, Communication No. 245/02, Decision of 15 May 2006

Corte africana dei diritti dell'uomo e dei popoli/African Court on Human and Peoples' Rights (ACtHPR)

African Commission on Human and Peoples' Rights v. Republic of Kenya, Judgment of 26 May 2017

APDF & IHRDA (Association pour le progrès et la défense des droits des femmes maliennes and the Institute for Human Rights and Developments in Africa) v. Republic of Mali, Judgment of 11 May 2018

Corte di giustizia dell'ECOWAS/ ECOWAS Community Court of Justice (CCJ)

Hadijatou Mani Koraou v. Niger, Judgment of 27 October 2008

The Registered Trustees of the Socio-Economic Rights and Accountability Project (SERAP) v. Nigeria & UBEC, Judgment of 30 November 2010

Tribunale militare internazionale di Norimberga/International Military Tribunal of Nuremberg (IMT)

The United States et al. v. Göring et al., Judgment of 1 October 1946, in *Trial of the Major War Criminals before the International Military Tribunal, Nuremberg, 14 November 1945-1 October 1946*, vol. I, Nuremberg, 1947, pp. 1-367; rep. in *AJIL*, vol. 41, 1947, pp. 172-333.

The United States v. Wilhelm von Leeb et al. (High Command Case), Judgment of 27 October 1948, in *Trials of the War Criminals Before the Nuremberg Military Tribunals under Control Law No. 1, Nuremberg, October 1946-April 1949*, vol. IX, Washington, 1950, pp. 462-697

Tribunale penale internazionale per la ex Jugoslavia/International Criminal Tribunal for the Former Yugoslavia (ICTY)

Delalić (*Prosecutor v. Delacić et al.*), Trial Chamber, Case No. IT-96-21-T, Judgment of 16 November 1998

Delalić (*Prosecutor v. Delacić et al.*), Appeals Chamber, Case No. IT-96-21-A, Judgment of 20 February 2001

Furundžija (*Prosecutor v. Anto Furundžija*), Trial Chamber, Case No. T-95-17/1-T, Judgment of 10 December 1998

Jelisić (*Prosecutor v. Jelisić*), Trial Chamber, Case No. IT-95-10-T, Judgment of 14 December 1999.

Jelisić (*Prosecutor v. Jelisić*), Appeals Chamber, Case No. IT-95-10-A, Judgment of 5 July 2001.

Kunarac (*Prosecutor v. Kunarac et al.*), Trial Chamber, Case No. IT-96-23&23/1-T, Judgment of 22 February 2001

Kunarac (*Prosecutor v. Kunarac et al.*), Appeals Chamber, Case No. IT-96-23&23/1-A, Judgment of 12 June 2002

Kvočka (*Prosecutor v. Kvočka et al.*), Trial Chamber, Case No. IT-98-30/1-T, Judgment of 2 November 2001

Kvočka (*Prosecutor v. Kvočka et al.*), Appeals Chamber, Case No. IT-98-30/1-A, Judgment of 28 February 2005

Mladić (*Prosecutor v. Ratko Mladić*), Trial Chamber I, Case No. IT-09-92-T, Judgment of 22 November 2017

Tadić (*Prosecutor v. Dusko Tadić*), Appeals Chamber, Case No. IT-94-1-AR72, Decision on the Defence Motion for Interlocutory Appeal on Jurisdiction, Decision of 2 October 1995
Tadić (*Prosecutor v. Dusko Tadić*), Appeals Chamber, Case No. IT-94-1-A, Judgment of 15 July 1999

Tribunale penale internazionale per il Ruanda/International Criminal Tribunal for Rwanda (ICTR)

Akayesu (The Prosecutor v. Jean-Paul Akayesu), Chamber I, Case No. ICTR-96-4-T, Judgment of 2 September 1998
Akayesu (The Prosecutor v. Jean-Paul Akayesu), Case No. ICTR-96-4, Judgment of 1 June 2001
Kayishema et al. (The Prosecutor v. Clément Kayishema et al.), Appeals Chamber, Case No. ICTR-95-1-A, Judgment of 1 June 2001

Tribunale speciale per il Libano/Special Tribunal for Lebanon (STL)

El Sayed (In the matter of El Sayed), Case No. CH/PRES/2010/01, Order of 15 April 2010

Tribunali nazionali/National Courts

Canada

Supreme Court

Kazemi Estate v. Islamic Republic of Iran, Judgment of 10 October 2014, [2014] 3 SCR 176
Re Secession of Quebec (Reference by the Governor in Council concerning Certain Questions relating to the Secession of Quebec from Canada), Advisory Opinion of 20 August 1998, [1998] 2 SCR 217
Suresh v. Canada (Minister of Citizenship and Immigration), Judgment of 1 November 2002, [2002] 1 S.C.R. 3

Francia

French Court of Cassation (Cour de Cassation, Chambre Criminelle)

Khadafi, Judgment of 13 March 2001, *RGDIP*, vol. 105, 2001, p. 473.

Germania

Federal Constitutional Court (Bundesverfassungsgericht)

"*Solange I*", Order of 29 May 1974, BVerfGE 37, 271

Grecia

Supreme Court

Margellos and Others v. Federal Republic of Germany, Judgment of 17 September 2002, *ILR*, vol. 129, 2007, p. 533

Italia

Corte Costituzionale

Frontini, sentenza 18 dicembre 1973, n. 183, *www.cortecostituzionale.it*

Ordinanza 8 aprile 2013, n. 69, *www.cortecostituzionale.it*
Sentenza 22 ottobre 2014, n. 238, *www.cortecostituzionale.it*
Sentenza 20 giugno 2019, n.194, *www.cortecostituzionale.it*

Corte di Cassazione
Allen c. Min. Int., sentenza 26 maggio 1997, n. 4674, *RDI*, vol. 80, 1997, p. 844
Boyisele Kumayo c. Min. Int., sentenza 17 dicembre 1999, n. 907, *http://pluris-cedam.utetgiuridica.it*
Ferrini c. Repubblica Federale di Germania, sentenza 11 marzo 2004, n. 5044, *RDI*, vol. 87, 2004, p. 539
Medero et al. (caso *Abu Omar*), sentenza 25 settembre 2014, n. 39788, *www.cortedicassazione.it*
Milde, sentenza 13 gennaio 2009, n. 1072, *RDI*, vol. 92, 2009, p. 618
Min. Int. c. Yarbo Musa, sentenza 23 febbraio 2018, n.4455, *www.cortedicassazione.it*
Nasr et al. (caso *Abu Omar*), sentenza 19 settembre 2012, n. 46340, *www.penalecontemporaneo.it*

Corte d'appello di Milano
Abu Omar et al., sentenza 12 febbraio 2013 n. 6709, *www.penalecontemporaneo.it*
Courtney et al. (caso *Abu Omar*), sentenza 15 dicembre 2010, n. 3688, *www.penalecontemporaneo.it*

Tribunale di Agrigento (Ufficio GIP)
Rackete (caso *Sea Watch 3*), ordinanza 2 luglio 2019, *Giur. pen.*, 4 luglio 2019

Tribunale di Catania (sez. Reati Ministeriali)
Caso *Diciotti*, relazione 7 dicembre 2018 (depositata il 22 gennaio 2019), *www.penalecontemporaneo.it*

Paesi Bassi

Supreme Court (Hoge Raad)
State of the Netherlands v. Mustafić et al., Judgment of 6 September 2013, *www.rechtspraak.nl/Organisatie/Hoge-Raad/Supreme-court/*

The Hague Court of Appeal
Mehida Mustafić-Mujić et al. v. The Netherlands, Judgment of 5 July 2011, *http://uitspraken-rechtspraak.nl/inziendocument?id=ECLI:NL:GHSGR:2011:BR53886*

Polonia

Supreme Court
Natoniewski v. The Federal Republic of Germany and The Federal Chancellery for Payment, Judgment of 29 October 2010, *Pol.YBIL*, vol. 30, 2010, p. 299

Regno Unito

House of Lords
Al-Skeini and Others v. Secretary of State for Defence, Judgment of 13 June 2007, [2007] UKHL 26
Jones and Mitchell v. Ministry of Interior Al-Mamlaka Al-Arabiya AS Saudiya (the Kingdom of Saudi Arabia) and Others, Judgment of 14 June 2006, [2006] UKHL 26

"*Pinochet I*" *(Regina v. Bartle and the Commissioner of Police for the Metropolis and Other, Ex Parte Pinochet* and *Regina v. Evans and Another and the Commissioner of Police for the Metropolis and Others, Ex Parte Pinochet)*, Judgment of 25 November 1998, *ILR*, vol. 119, 2002, p. 51

"*Pinochet II*" *(Regina v. Bow Street Metropolitan Stipendiary Magistrate, Ex Parte Pinochet Ugarte (No. 2))*, Judgment of 15 January 1999, [1999] UKHL 1

"*Pinochet III*" *(Regina v. Bartle and the Commissioner of Police for the Metropolis and Others, Ex Parte Pinochet; Regina v. Evans and Another and the Commissioner of Police for the Metropolis and Others, Ex Parte Pinochet)*, Judgment of 24 March 1999, *ILR*, vol. 119, 2002, p. 135

High Court of Justice

Al-Skeini and Others v. Secretary of State for Defence, Judgment of 14 December 2004, [2004] EWHC 2911 Admin

Serdar Mohammed v. Ministry of Defence, Judgment of 2 May 2014, [2014] EWHC 1369 (QB)

Court of Appeal (Civil Division)

Al-Skeini and Others v. Secretary of State for Defence, Judgment of 21 December 2005, [2005] EWCA Civ 1609

Stati Uniti

Supreme Court

In re Yamashita, Judgment of 4 February 1946, 327 U.S. 1 (1946)

INDICE DI COMMENTI E RACCOMANDAZIONI DEI *TREATY-BODIES*

Comitato dei diritti umani/Human Rights Committee (HRCtee)

a) Concluding Observations

Concluding Observations: *Chile*, 30 March 1999
Concluding Observations: *Guatemala*, 27 August 2001
Concluding Observations: *Iraq*, 30-31 October 1991
Concluding Observations: *Israel*, 18 August 1998
Concluding Observations: *Israel*, 21 August 2003
Concluding Observations: *Netherlands*, 27 August 2001
Concluding Observations: *Poland*, 23 November 2016
Concluding Observations: *Suriname*, 4 May 2004
Concluding Observations: *Yemen*, 12 August 2002

b) General Comments

General Comment No. 6: *Article 6 (The right to life)*, 30 April 1982
General Comment No. 8: *Article 9 (Right to liberty and security of persons)*, 30 June 1982
General Comment No. 18: *Non-discrimination*, 10 November 1989
General Comment No. 20: *Prohibition of torture, or other cruel, inhuman or degrading treatment or punishment, Article 7*, 10 March 1992
General Comment No. 22: *The right to freedom of thought, conscience and religion (Article 18)*, 30 July 1993
General Comment No. 23: *The right of minorities (Article 27)*, 8 April 1994
General Comment No. 24: *Issues relating to reservations made upon ratification or accession to the Covenant or the Optional Protocols thereto, or in relation to declarations under article 41 of the Covenant*, 4 November 1994
General Comment No. 25: *The right to participate in public affairs, voting rights and the right to equal access to public service (Article 25)*, 12 July 1996
General Comment No. 26: *Continuity of obligations*, 8 December 1997
General Comment No. 27: *Freedom of movement (Article 12)*, 2 November 1999
General Comment No. 28: *Article 3 (The equality of rights between men and women)*, 29 March 2000
General Comment No. 29: S*tates of emergency (Article 4)*, 31 August 2001
General Comment No. 31: *Nature of the general legal obligation imposed on States parties to the Covenant*, 26 May 2004
General Comment No. 32: *Article 14: Right to equality before courts and tribunals and to a fair trial*, 23 August 2007
General Comment No. 35: *Article 9 (Liberty and security of person)*, 23 October 2014

General Comment No. 34: *Article 19: Freedoms of opinion and expression*, 12 September 2011
General Comment No. 36: *Article 6 (the right to life)*, 3 September 2019

Comitato sui diritti economici, sociali e culturali/Committee on Economic, Social and Cultural Rights (CteeESCR)

a) Concluding Observations

Concluding Observations: *Israel*, 23 May 2003

b) General Comments

General Comment No. 3: *The nature of States parties' obligations (art. 2, para. 1, of the Covenant)*, 14 December 1990
General Comment No. 4: *The right to adequate housing (art. 11 (1) of the Covenant)*, 13 December 1991
General Comment No. 7: *The right to adequate housing (art. 11 (1) of the Covenant): Forced evictions*, 16 May 1997
General Comment No. 11: *Plans of action for primary education (article 14 of the International Covenant on Economic, Social and Cultural Rights)*, 10 May 1999
General Comment No. 12: *The right to adequate food (art. 11)*, 12 May 1999
General Comment No. 13: *The right to education (article 13 of the Covenant)*, 8 December 1999
General Comment No. 14: *The right to the highest attainable standard of health (article 12 of the International Covenant on Economic, Social and Cultural Rights)*, 11 August 2000
General Comment No. 15: *The right to water (arts. 11 and 12 of the International Covenant on Economic, Social and Cultural Rights)*, 20 January 2003
General Comment No. 17: *The right of everyone to benefit from the protection of the moral and material interests resulting from any scientific, literary or artistic production of which he or she is the author (article 15, paragraph 1(c), of the Covenant)*, 12 January 2006
General Comment No. 18: *The right to work (art. 6 of the International Covenant on Economic, Social and Cultural Rights)*, 6 February 2006
General Comment No. 23: *The right to just and favorable conditions of work (article 7 of the International Covenant on Economic, Social and Cultural Rights)*, 27 April 2016

Comitato sulla eliminazione della discriminazione razziale/ Committee on the Elimination of Racial Discrimination (CteeERD)

a) Recommendations

General Recommendation No. VIII *concerning the interpretation and application of article 1, paragraphs 1 and 4 of the Convention*, 38th Session (1990)

Capitolo I

I DIRITTI UMANI NELL'ORDINAMENTO INTERNAZIONALE

Sezione I

FONDAMENTO E SVILUPPO STORICO DEI DIRITTI UMANI INTERNAZIONALI

1. *Nozione e fondamento dei diritti umani*

La nozione di "diritti umani" è apparentemente semplice; ma in realtà piuttosto complessa. Infatti, essi sono stati, nella storia della filosofia giuridica, via via definiti con termini diversi (diritti naturali, innati, originari, morali, fondamentali); la loro origine storica viene situata in tempi diversi; il loro fondamento giuridico è stato spiegato in maniera diversa dal giusnaturalismo, dal positivismo, dal realismo giuridico; e la nozione medesima di "diritti umani" si è progressivamente molto ampliata.

Secondo alcuni autori, i diritti umani sono quelle libertà, immunità e benefici che, secondo i valori contemporanei accettati, tutti gli esseri umani dovrebbero essere capaci di pretendere, come diritti veri e propri, dalla società in cui essi vivono [1]. Secondo altri, sono diritti umani quelli che hanno la natura di diritti fondamentali ed essenziali della persona e quindi sono imprescrittibili, inalienabili, irrinunciabili ed universali [2]. Secondo altri ancora, i diritti umani costituiscono un minimo invalicabile per ogni essere umano che il diritto deve proteggere a qualsiasi costo [3].

Queste definizioni sono piuttosto simili; tuttavia esse non sembrano sufficientemente precise da distinguere chiaramente i diritti umani da altri diritti "ordinari". Pertanto, si apre il problema del fondamento giuridico dei diritti umani, specie nell'ottica dell'ordinamento internazionale.

Secondo una prima opinione, si può ritenere che un certo diritto costituisca un "diritto umano" quando corrisponde alla natura umana, cioè alla ragione ed alla volontà tipiche della specie umana. Questa tesi ha un'impostazione di fondo giusnaturalistica e presenta lo

---

[1] Henkin (1995), p. 886.

[2] Zanghì (2013), p. 4.

[3] Focarelli (2008), p. 342.

svantaggio di lasciare un margine di soggettività nel trovare una definizione di "natura umana" che sia universalmente accettata nel mondo multiculturale contemporaneo.

Altri autori hanno sostenuto la tesi dell'"auto-evidenza" dei diritti umani. Essi sarebbero così evidenti e così immediati, che non richiederebbero di cercarne una giustificazione razionale ed un fondamento giuridico. Ma anche questa tesi si presta ad interpretazioni soggettive diverse da parte dei vari gruppi di Stati aventi tradizioni, religioni e culture diverse.

La terza tesi, a nostro avviso la più convincente, ritiene che i diritti umani si fondino semplicemente sul consenso. In altri termini sono diritti umani quei diritti che vengono riconosciuti come tali in un certo ordinamento giuridico sulla base di un consenso generalizzato dei soggetti di tale ordinamento. Nell'ordinamento giuridico internazionale sarà il consenso della comunità internazionale a stabilire quali diritti possano essere definiti come "diritti umani internazionali". Un problema diverso (la cui risposta è più restrittiva) è quello di accertare quali diritti umani siano davvero universali, perché affermatisi nel diritto internazionale generale [4].

2. *Precedenti storici*

2.1. *Cenni sullo sviluppo storico dei diritti umani nei diritti nazionali*

Se si vuole risalire ai tempi antichi, si può sostenere che l'idea di alcuni diritti umani può essere rintracciata nella Bibbia, nel Codice di Hammurabi, nelle leggi di città greche come Atene, nonché in alcuni precetti di varie religioni o filosofie, come il Buddismo, il Confucianesimo, l'Hinduismo.

Tuttavia, uno sviluppo più interessante si ha molti secoli più tardi con alcuni documenti nazionali inglesi, come la celebre *Magna Charta Libertatum* del 1215, l'*Habeas Corpus Act* del 1679 ed il *Bill of Rights* del 1689. Nei tempi più moderni, presentano grande importanza alcune dichiarazioni statunitensi, quali la *Virginia Declaration of Rights* del 12 giugno 1776 [5], l'*American Declaration of Independence* del 4 luglio 1776 [6], ed il *Bill of Rights* adottato nel 1789 e ratificato nel 1791 [7]. Infine, si deve ricordare, fra i documenti francesi, la Dichiarazione dei diritti dell'uomo e del cittadino del 1789 [8]. In seguito, molti Stati seguirono, nelle loro carte costituzionali, gli esempi degli USA e della Francia [9].

Peraltro, si deve notare che, in questi strumenti, al di là del linguaggio di stampo universalistico, i diritti umani sono essenzialmente intesi come diritti dei cittadini; e che essi rilevano sul piano del diritto costituzionale interno e non su quello del diritto internaziona-

[4] Vedi *infra*, par. 4 e Cap. V, Sez. I.

[5] Art. 1: [...] all men are by nature equally free and independent, and have certain inherent rights [...]".

[6] "We hold these truths to be self-evident, that all men are created equal, that they are endowed by their Creator with certain inalienable Rights, that among these are Life, Liberty and the pursuit of Happiness ...".

[7] Si tratta di dieci emendamenti alla Costituzione degli USA del 1787.

[8] Art. 1: "Gli uomini nascono e rimangono liberi e uguali nei diritti. Le distinzioni sociali non possono essere fondate che sull'utilità comune"; Art. 2: "Il fine di ogni associazione politica è la conservazione dei diritti naturali ed imprescrittibili dell'uomo. Questi diritti sono la libertà, la proprietà, la sicurezza e la resistenza all'oppressione".

[9] Vedi, ad es., i Paesi Bassi (1798), la Svezia (1809), la Spagna (1812), la Norvegia (1814), il Belgio (1831), il Regno di Sardegna (1848), la Danimarca (1849), la Prussia (1850).

le. È infatti estranea l'idea che uno Stato possa far valere i diritti umani delle persone contro un altro Stato, e specie contro lo Stato di nazionalità della persona. In altri termini, i diritti umani non ebbero alcun impatto sui rapporti internazionali fra Stati nei secoli XVIII e XIX ed un impatto minimo durante la prima metà del XX secolo.

2.2. *Il ruolo dell'individuo nel diritto internazionale classico*

Secondo la concezione del diritto internazionale classico, predominante fino alla metà del XX secolo, gli individui non erano soggetti del diritto internazionale, il loro ruolo era in sostanza irrilevante ed essi erano sottoposti al potere di governo esclusivo dello Stato del quale erano "sudditi". Il diritto internazionale regolava formalmente solo rapporti fra Stati. Anche dal punto di vista sostanziale, il diritto internazionale si occupava quasi esclusivamente di disciplinare rapporti interstatali e pertanto il modo con cui lo Stato trattava i propri sudditi era una questione c.d. di "dominio riservato" (*domestic jurisdiction*) di tale Stato. In realtà alcuni limiti alla sovranità territoriale degli Stati esistevano già nel diritto internazionale classico; ma gli individui traevano solo un beneficio indiretto da tali limiti e non veri e propri diritti sul piano del diritto internazionale. Vediamo sinteticamente questi limiti.

2.3. *Obbligo di protezione degli stranieri e dei loro beni*

Il diritto internazionale tradizionale ha riconosciuto fin dai primi secoli del suo sviluppo che gli Stati hanno un obbligo di proteggere gli stranieri che si trovano nel proprio territorio o sotto la propria giurisdizione da offese relative alla loro persona o ai loro beni, mediante misure di prevenzione e di repressione che si conformino a certi standard minimi di civiltà e di giustizia. Ma tale obbligo, di natura consuetudinaria, era concepito solo come operante fra lo Stato territoriale e lo Stato di nazionalità dello straniero; l'individuo vittima era considerato solo come possibile "beneficiario di fatto" di tale obbligo. Pertanto, quando l'individuo straniero subiva dallo Stato territoriale una violazione di tale obbligo di protezione, soltanto lo Stato nazionale dello straniero aveva il diritto di agire, sul piano internazionale, contro lo Stato offensore, in base alle regole sulla protezione diplomatica e sulla responsabilità internazionale degli Stati.

In sostanza, l'individuo era un "oggetto" e non un "soggetto" del diritto internazionale; ed egli non aveva un vero e proprio diritto neppure a ricevere dal proprio Stato nazionale la riparazione che questo fosse eventualmente riuscito ad ottenere dallo Stato offensore.

2.4. *Intervento umanitario*

La dottrina dell'intervento umanitario, già sostenuta da alcuni internazionalisti nel XVII secolo, riconosceva come legittimo l'uso della forza armata da parte di uno o più Stati quando era necessaria per far cessare il maltrattamento di individui in uno Stato estero, e quando tale maltrattamento era così brutale e sistematico da offendere la coscienza della comunità degli Stati [10]. Di fatto, l'intervento umanitario fu usato soprattutto nel XIX

---

[10] Buergenthal *et al.* (2004), p. 3.

secolo dalle Potenze europee per tutelare i cristiani perseguitati nei territori dell'Impero Ottomano. La dottrina fu talora utilizzata in maniera abusiva e come pretesto degli Stati più forti per occupare o invadere il territorio di Stati più deboli.

Tuttavia, la dottrina dell'intervento umanitario mise in evidenza il fatto che esistevano alcuni limiti alla libertà degli Stati nel trattamento dei propri sudditi, quando si trattava di gravissime violazioni dei diritti umani di questi ultimi.

2.5. *Trattati contro la schiavitù e sulla protezione di gruppi religiosi*

Nel XIX secolo, la concezione strettamente interstatale del diritto internazionale era largamente dominante; ma vi era la possibilità, sia pure in casi rari e isolati, che uno Stato, tramite un trattato bilaterale o multilaterale, stabilisse degli obblighi volti ad accordare certi diritti agli individui. In questo modo il trattamento degli individui diveniva oggetto di un obbligo internazionale fra gli Stati parti e usciva dalla sfera del dominio riservato di tali Stati [11]. Questo processo di "internazionalizzazione" di interessi individuali già ebbe inizio dopo il Congresso di Vienna del 1815.

Il Congresso adottò una Dichiarazione sul commercio degli schiavi, che raccomandava agli Stati la sua abolizione, affermando che la schiavitù era incompatibile con i principi di umanità e di moralità internazionale [12]. In seguito, questo obiettivo fu incluso in una serie di trattati bilaterali, in un trattato multilaterale del 1842 fra Stati europei e latino-americani, nel *Berlin Congo Act* del 1885 e nel *General Act* della Conferenza di Bruxelles del 1890 sulla soppressione della schiavitù. Nel 1900, come vedremo [13], il tema fu ripreso nell'importante Convenzione sulla schiavitù del 1926 della Società delle Nazioni e in altri trattati successivi.

Sviluppi simili si verificarono in tema di protezione delle minoranze religiose. Già nel XVII secolo alcuni trattati contenevano norme a tutela delle minoranze religiose. Quindi il Congresso di Vienna impose ad alcuni Stati l'obbligo di garantire non discriminazione fra le varie minoranze religiose e la libertà di praticare la religione cattolica in certi territori. In seguito, nel Trattato di Berlino del 1878 uno status giuridico speciale fu garantito ad alcuni gruppi religiosi [14].

2.6. *La nascita del diritto internazionale umanitario*

Il diritto internazionale umanitario (originariamente denominato *ius in bello*) si occupa della protezione delle vittime dei conflitti armati e di proibire certi mezzi e metodi di guerra considerati inumani, allo scopo di "umanizzare" per quanto possibile tramite regole giuridiche i conflitti armati. La sua origine è assai più antica rispetto al diritto internazionale dei diritti umani, anche se attualmente questi due settori giuridici tendono ad avvicinarsi e ad essere complementari.

La nascita del diritto internazionale umanitario moderno si fa risalire alla metà del XIX

---

[11] Buergenthal *et al.* (2004), p. 6.

[12] Kälin, Künzli (2009), p. 8.

[13] Vedi *infra*, Cap. V, par. 15.

[14] Buergenthal *et al.* (2004), p. 7.

secolo, quando lo svizzero Henry Dunant propose delle misure per la protezione delle vittime di guerra, che portarono alla creazione del Comitato Internazionale della Croce Rossa e quindi alla redazione della Convenzione di Ginevra del 1864 per il miglioramento delle condizioni dei feriti e dei malati nelle forze armate [15]. Nel frattempo, il Presidente degli USA Lincoln aveva emanato nel 1863 il c.d. Codice *Lieber*, che stabiliva una serie di regole e di istruzioni per lo svolgimento delle operazioni militari nel corso della guerra civile americana. La tappa successiva di questo processo di sviluppo fu la Dichiarazione di San Pietroburgo del 1868, nella quale si proibiva l'uso di certe armi e nel cui Preambolo si dichiarava solennemente che "il solo scopo legittimo che gli Stati dovrebbero perseguire durante la guerra è quello di indebolire le forze militari del nemico".

Gli sviluppi successivi, di grande importanza, furono le Convenzioni dell'Aja del 1899 e quelle del 1907. Particolarmente significativa è la IV Convenzione dell'Aja del 1907, sulle leggi e gli usi della guerra terrestre, il cui Preambolo contiene la celebre "Clausola Martens", secondo la quale, in assenza di una regola giuridica specifica applicabile al caso, gli abitanti ed i belligeranti

> "remain under the protection and the rule of the principles of the law of nations, as they result from the usages established among civilized peoples, from the laws of humanity, and the dictates of the public conscience".

Si deve notare che queste prime regole del diritto internazionale umanitario si fondavano sul principio di reciprocità ed erano concepite strutturalmente nel quadro del diritto internazionale tradizionale di natura interstatale; e quindi non attribuivano veri e propri diritti agli individui sul piano del diritto internazionale. Tuttavia, gran parte di tali regole era, di fatto, destinata a tutelare anche interessi individuali e quindi rappresentava un segnale di crescita del ruolo dell'individuo nel diritto internazionale.

Il diritto internazionale umanitario fu riveduto, aggiornato ed ulteriormente sviluppato nel secolo XX, specie dopo la Seconda Guerra Mondiale. Non vi è dubbio che la posizione giuridica dell'individuo è sostanzialmente cambiata nel diritto umanitario contemporaneo.

2.7. *La Società delle Nazioni e il sistema dei mandati*

Alcuni sviluppi importanti in relazione a specifici diritti umani si verificarono dopo la Prima Guerra Mondiale. Il Presidente degli USA Woodrow Wilson aveva presentato al Congresso nel 1918 i suoi "Quattordici Punti", un programma ambizioso volto a creare una comunità internazionale più pacifica e giusta. Egli auspicava, fra l'altro, la realizzazione del principio di autodeterminazione dei popoli, sia pure limitato agli Stati occidentali, attraverso una rideterminazione delle frontiere sulla base del principio della nazionalità ed il riconoscimento della statualità a entità nazionali in cerca di autonomia. Il principio non fu accolto; ma esercitò una certa influenza sulla Società delle Nazioni (SdN).

In realtà il Patto della Società delle Nazioni, approvato il 28 aprile 1919 e inserito nel Trattato di pace di Versailles del 28 giugno 1919 [16], non conteneva delle disposizioni generali dedicate ai diritti umani. L'idea che i diritti umani, in linea generale, dovessero essere

---

[15] Kälin, Künzli (2009), p. 11.

[16] Il Trattato di Versailles fu firmato da 44 Stati ed entrò in vigore il 10 gennaio 1920.

protetti a livello internazionale non era ancora matura nella comunità internazionale. Tuttavia, il Patto conteneva due disposizioni, gli artt. 22 e 23, che erano destinati ad avere un'influenza sullo sviluppo di alcuni diritti umani.

L'art. 22 del Patto stabiliva il sistema dei mandati della Società delle Nazioni, che si applicava alle colonie ed ai territori non autonomi degli Stati che avevano perso la Prima Guerra Mondiale e che trasformava tali colonie in Mandati della SdN affidati in amministrazione alle Potenze vincitrici. Lo scopo finale dei mandati era quello di realizzare con il tempo l'autodeterminazione di tali colonie e territori. Nel frattempo, le Potenze affidatarie del mandato si impegnavano con la SdN ad amministrare i territori promovendo il benessere materiale e morale, ed il progresso sociale, degli abitanti. La Commissione dei mandati (*Mandates Commission*) della SdN gradualmente acquistò con il tempo maggiori poteri nel controllare l'amministrazione dei mandati ed il modo con cui le popolazioni native venivano trattate. Tuttavia, la dissoluzione della SdN pose termine a questo sviluppo. In sua sostituzione, le Nazioni Unite stabilirono il Sistema di amministrazione fiduciaria (*Trusteeship System*), che fu incaricato di poteri di controllo sui restanti mandati e gli altri territori non autonomi.

2.8. *La protezione dei lavoratori*

Nel Trattato di pace di Versailles si riconosceva l'esigenza di proteggere i lavoratori, poiché si affermava che la pace mondiale "può essere stabilita solo se essa si basa sulla giustizia sociale". L'art. 427 del Trattato enunciava una serie di obiettivi più specifici in materia di protezione dei lavoratori [17].

Anche l'art. 23 del Patto della Società delle Nazioni si occupava, fra l'altro, di questioni relative a "condizioni di lavoro eque ed umane per uomini, donne e fanciulli"; e contemplava la creazione di un'organizzazione internazionale per promuovere tale obiettivo. In effetti fu creata l'Organizzazione Internazionale del Lavoro (ILO), che riuscì rapidamente a predisporre e far adottare dagli Stati parti alcune convenzioni importanti, come quella sul lavoro di 8 ore (Convenzione n. 1 del 1919), sulla protezione della maternità (Convenzione n. 3 del 1919), quella sul lavoro notturno da parte di giovani lavoratori (Convenzione n. 6 del 1919), quella sul lavoro forzato (Convenzione n. 29 del 1930).

2.9. *Il sistema di protezione delle minoranze*

La Società delle Nazioni ha anche esercitato un ruolo importante nella creazione di un sistema internazionale per la protezione delle minoranze. Questa materia non era regolata dal Patto della SdN. Tuttavia, alcuni Stati dell'Europa centrale ed orientale, che erano stati creati dopo il collasso dell'Impero Ottomano e dell'Impero Austro-Ungarico, includevano nel proprio territorio gruppi di minoranze etniche, linguistiche e religiose, che avevano motivi storici per temere che i nuovi Stati non avrebbero rispettato la loro autonomia culturale. Pertanto, gli Stati vincitori della Prima Guerra Mondiale riuscirono ad imporre, ai suddetti Stati, trattati o dichiarazioni unilaterali, che contenevano garanzie di protezione di

[17] Vedi Kälin, Künzli (2009), pp. 12-13.

tali minoranze. Si possono ricordare i trattati di pace con Austria, Bulgaria, Ungheria e Turchia; gli accordi speciali con Cecoslovacchia, Grecia, Polonia, Romania e Iugoslavia; e le dichiarazioni unilaterali di Albania, Finlandia, Estonia, Lituania e Lettonia.

Questi Stati si obbligavano a non effettuare discriminazioni contro i membri delle minoranze protette ed a garantire loro protezione della vita e della persona, libertà di credo e di pratica religiosi e certi diritti linguistici. Per rafforzare l'adempimento di tali obblighi, gli Stati in questione convenivano che i propri obblighi fossero posti sotto la garanzia della SdN. Quest'ultima esercitò la propria funzione di controllo sviluppando un sistema per trattare le petizioni da parte delle minoranze, che lamentavano violazioni dei propri diritti. Le petizioni venivano esaminate da un Comitato di tre membri del Consiglio della SdN presso il quale gli Stati coinvolti potevano presentare le proprie osservazioni; e, quando fosse opportuno, si chiedeva alla Corte Permanente di Giustizia Internazionale di fornire un parere consultivo su controverse questioni giuridiche.

Questo sistema di protezione internazionale delle minoranze costituiva un esperimento interessante per quell'epoca. Tuttavia, è anche vero che i trattati sulla protezione delle minoranze si mantenevano nel solco del diritto internazionale tradizionale, poiché stabilivano soltanto obblighi degli Stati nei confronti di altri Stati e della SdN, e non creavano veri e propri diritti sostanziali, a livello internazionale, né per le minoranze come enti collettivi, né per i singoli membri delle minoranze. Questi ultimi avevano solo il diritto di sottoporre petizioni alla SdN.

2.10. *I limiti dei precedenti storici finora trattati*

Si sono visti finora alcuni precedenti storici, che indicano l'esistenza di limiti al principio generale del dominio riservato dello Stato nel trattamento dei propri sudditi e, parallelamente, una sempre maggiore attenzione del diritto internazionale per gli interessi ed il ruolo dell'individuo.

Tuttavia, si devono sottolineare tre limiti importanti che caratterizzavano i suddetti sviluppi. Il primo è che essi avevano carattere assai specifico e settoriale. Il secondo limite è che molti dei trattati sopra citati perseguivano in realtà interessi politici o economici degli Stati, più che motivazioni di carattere umanitario. Il terzo limite è che la dottrina all'epoca prevalente, di formazione positivistica, continuava ad interpretare tali trattati come formalmente regolanti solo rapporti fra Stati, dai quali non discendevano veri e propri diritti per gli individui sul piano internazionale. Questa tesi fu avallata anche dalla Corte Permanente di Giustizia Internazionale (PCIJ) nella sentenza del 1924 sul caso *Mavrommatis*, nella quale la Corte formulò in termini tradizionali l'istituto della protezione diplomatica affermando che:

> "By taking up the case of one of its subjects and by resorting to diplomatic action or international judicial proceedings on his behalf, a State is in reality asserting its own right – its rights to ensure, in the person of its subjects, respect for the rules of international law" [18].

---

[18] PCIJ, *Mavrommatis Palestine Concessions*, p. 12.

3. *La svolta dopo la Seconda Guerra Mondiale: la teoria dei diritti umani si impone a livello internazionale*

Nel periodo successivo alla Seconda Guerra Mondiale, sotto la spinta dell'opinione pubblica mondiale, gli sforzi per una tutela internazionale dei diritti umani, avente un carattere generale e non solo settoriale, si moltiplicano. Gli individui vengono considerati come persone umane da tutelare in quanto tali, e quindi anche verso il proprio Stato nazionale. Pertanto, il tema dei diritti umani, nella loro globalità, diviene un tema centrale sulla scena internazionale.

Il motivo più importante di questo radicale cambiamento è certamente la consapevolezza da parte della comunità internazionale che il sistema nazista e gli altri regimi totalitari avevano dimostrato, prima e durante la guerra, un disprezzo assoluto per i diritti umani più essenziali e che la protezione dei diritti umani tramite le costituzioni dei singoli Stati non era sufficiente. Occorreva invece creare un nuovo ordine mondiale, che fosse fondato sulla pace e sulla tutela internazionale dei diritti umani. Queste idee furono sostenute inizialmente soprattutto dagli Stati occidentali, in virtù delle loro tradizioni costituzionali; furono inserite nella Carta Atlantica del 1941; e furono riprese nella Conferenza di Dumbarton Oaks del 1944, in cui si proponeva l'istituzione delle Nazioni Unite (NU).

Infine, le potenze occidentali, alla Conferenza di San Francisco del 1945, crearono l'Organizzazione delle Nazioni Unite (NU), affidandole come parte importante del suo mandato la promozione e la protezione dei diritti umani. L'idea di fondo era quella di elaborare dei principi sui diritti umani che dovessero guidare l'azione delle NU e degli Stati membri, con lo scopo di creare gradualmente un sistema ampio di protezione dei diritti umani in tempo di pace, tramite la sua progressiva codificazione in una serie di trattati e di meccanismi internazionali di garanzia. Questo scopo si è realizzato con il tempo, dando luogo al c.d. sistema di tutela dei diritti umani delle NU [19]. Si tratta di un sistema di tutela dei diritti umani a livello (almeno tendenzialmente) universale. A questo si sono aggiunti progressivamente nel tempo alcuni sistemi di tutela dei diritti umani a livello regionale, aventi caratteristiche talora più avanzate rispetto al sistema delle NU [20].

Si può pertanto oggi parlare, in senso più generale e complessivo, di un "sistema internazionale di tutela dei diritti umani". Questo sistema internazionale si è realizzato progressivamente attraverso norme e meccanismi di garanzia (organi e procedure), il cui ampio percorso di evoluzione esamineremo in seguito. Per ora è sufficiente notare che il movimento internazionale per la tutela dei diritti umani, sviluppatosi in maniera generalizzata, e non più soltanto in maniera limitata e settoriale, a partire dall'entrata in vigore della Carta delle NU, si è tradotto, sul piano giuridico, nell'adozione di molti atti di *soft law*, nella conclusione di numerosi accordi internazionali su scala regionale e su scala universale [21], ed anche nella creazione di alcune norme di diritto internazionale generale [22]. Si può inol-

---

[19] Vedi *infra*, Cap. IV, Sez. I.

[20] Vedi *infra*, Cap. IV, Sezz. II e III.

[21] Questi accordi contengono sia un catalogo dettagliato di diritti umani che gli Stati parti sono obbligati ad accordare a tutti gli individui sottoposti alla loro giurisdizione, sia strumenti di garanzia e di controllo.

[22] Queste norme includono consuetudini, principi di diritto internazionale e principi generali di diritto riconosciuti dalle nazioni civili *in foro domestico*.

tre ricordare che, grazie all'attività degli organi internazionali di controllo istituiti da alcuni dei trattati suddetti, esiste ormai una vasta prassi internazionale giurisprudenziale e quasi-giurisprudenziale in materia di diritti umani.

In definitiva, si può affermare che la teoria dei diritti umani ha caratterizzato fortemente la fase di sviluppo della comunità internazionale che si è svolta dopo la Seconda Guerra Mondiale e che tale teoria ha condotto all'affermazione e progressivo consolidamento di un nuovo, vasto ed importante, settore normativo dell'ordinamento internazionale, il c.d. diritto internazionale dei diritti umani.

Ma in realtà occorre sottolineare il fatto che la teoria dei diritti umani ha esercitato anche un ruolo più ampio, poiché, radicandosi a fondo nella vita della comunità internazionale, ha finito per produrre una grande influenza sui principi generali che regolano tale comunità e quindi anche, come vedremo [23], un impatto sull'ordinamento internazionale complessivamente considerato. In questo senso, si può forse parlare di un processo di cambiamento strutturale del diritto internazionale.

Ciò è dovuto, a nostro parere, sostanzialmente a due motivi, fra loro collegati. Il primo è che la teoria dei diritti umani è per sua natura "sovversiva" o "rivoluzionaria" [24] rispetto alla struttura tradizionale dei rapporti fra Stati, perché si pone in contrasto con il principio di sovranità, che è il principio base del diritto internazionale tradizionale e che ha impedito a lungo agli Stati di ingerirsi nell'organizzazione interna degli altri Stati e nel modo con cui questi trattano i propri cittadini. Il secondo motivo è che tale teoria mette al centro dell'attenzione l'individuo, che non è più preso in considerazione come oggetto della sovranità statale, ma considerato in sé stesso, come persona umana, e tende ad assumere un ruolo sempre più importante e centrale nella vita della comunità internazionale. Anche in questo senso la teoria dei diritti umani è "sovversiva", perché si pone in contrasto con la concezione tradizionale per cui soltanto gli Stati e gli altri enti sovrani sono i soggetti dell'ordinamento internazionale.

Nella prossima sezione, esamineremo più a fondo l'impatto della teoria dei diritti umani sulla struttura del diritto internazionale.

4. *Scopi generali dei diritti umani*

4.1. *Dignità della persona umana e valori universali*

All'inizio di questo capitolo abbiamo visto, in estrema sintesi, le tesi principali sulla nozione e sul fondamento dei diritti umani. Conviene ora affrontare il problema degli obiettivi generali perseguiti da tali diritti nell'ordinamento internazionale. In sintesi, si può dire, a mio avviso, che le norme internazionali sui diritti umani perseguono contemporaneamente due scopi generali: *a*) quello di proteggere la dignità della persona umana e di difenderla nei confronti dello Stato; *b*) quello di realizzare un valore universale dell'ordinamento internazionale contemporaneo.

Il primo scopo è assai evidente. Sotto la spinta di vari fattori storici, che abbiamo bre-

---

[23] Vedi *infra*, Sez. II.

[24] Cfr. Cassese (1984), p. 321; Id. (2003-2004), vol. II, pp. 83-84.

vemente descritto, la comunità internazionale si è convinta che fosse necessario creare un regime giuridico *internazionale* di tutela dell'individuo nei confronti dello Stato, e specie nei confronti del proprio Stato. Ciò significa anche che il diritto internazionale dei diritti umani tende a creare un regime giuridico di tutela degli *interessi individuali* che tendono a prevalere sugli interessi statali, per il semplice fatto che i diritti umani sono, in linea di massima, diritti che l'individuo vanta *contro* lo Stato. In questo senso, a mio avviso, si può ritenere che il *principio di preminenza dell'individuo* (o della persona umana) costituisca un principio-guida del diritto internazionale dei diritti umani.

Il secondo scopo è strettamente collegato al primo. Infatti, sotto la spinta della tutela degli interessi essenziali degli individui, le norme internazionali sui diritti umani hanno oggi lo scopo di realizzare anche un interesse comunitario degli Stati, che prevale sui loro interessi individuali; e ciò perché si riconosce che la tutela dei diritti umani persegue alti obiettivi di umanità, di civiltà e di moralità, e costituisce un *valore centrale ed universale* per l'odierna comunità internazionale. Pertanto, si può ritenere che il *principio di universalità* dei diritti umani costituisca un secondo principio-guida del diritto internazionale dei diritti umani.

Tuttavia, questa seconda conclusione non è scontata, poiché il concetto stesso di universalismo dei diritti umani è controverso e deve confrontarsi con fenomeni di particolarismo e di multiculturalismo che sono presenti nella realtà della comunità internazionale. Il problema merita qualche riflessione.

4.2. *Il problema dell'universalismo dei diritti umani in un mondo multiculturale*

Conviene affrontare il problema dell'universalismo dei diritti umani solo dal punto di vista giuridico[25]. Nel linguaggio comune, si dà spesso per scontato che i diritti umani siano universali, nel duplice senso che appartengano a tutte le persone e che siano globalmente riconosciuti. Ma in realtà la questione è più complessa, e può essere riassunta e semplificata in una domanda: è possibile l'universalismo dei diritti umani in un mondo multiculturale[26]? E in una realtà contemporanea che vede il rinascere dei nazionalismi e dei particolarismi? Cosa significa esattamente, nel diritto internazionale, l'universalismo dei diritti umani?

A mio avviso, la *vocazione* universalistica dei diritti umani è indubbia e non può essere messa in discussione, se non si vuole addirittura rinunciare a credere all'esistenza dei diritti umani internazionali. Questi ultimi sono, per definizione, diritti che *dovrebbero* spettare a tutte le persone umane e che tutti gli Stati *dovrebbero* riconoscere. L'idea che tutti gli Stati devono garantire i diritti fondamentali a tutti gli esseri umani, e in uguale misura, risulta nitidamente dall'art. 1 della Dichiarazione universale dei diritti dell'uomo, secondo cui:

> "All human beings are born free and equal in dignity and rights […]"[27].

Inoltre, come si è detto sopra, anche nella comunità degli Stati si è affermata l'idea del valore centrale e universale della tutela dei diritti umani; e pertanto si può dire che il *principio dell'universalità è un principio-guida* che opera nell'intero settore.

---

[25] E quindi trascurando gli aspetti filosofici, storici, sociali, culturali, ecc.

[26] Vedi, di recente, Lenzerini (2014).

[27] UDHR, art. 1.

Tuttavia, questa *vocazione* universalistica dei diritti umani deve fare i conti con un mondo multiculturale, nel quale esistono concezioni diverse su quali diritti e quali valori siano davvero fondamentali; e con la realtà giuridica, per la quale soltanto *alcuni* diritti umani sono regolati dal diritto internazionale generale. In sintesi, si contrappongono due tendenze o, se si vuole, due principi contrastanti: universalismo e multiculturalismo/particolarismo. Ma, poiché, nella teoria dei diritti umani, anche il multiculturalismo viene riconosciuto come un valore da difendere [28], si pone l'esigenza di tentare di conciliare, in qualche modo, i due principi.

A mio avviso, questa conciliazione è possibile se si riconosce che, nel diritto internazionale, si è finora realizzato un *equilibrio* (o un compromesso) fra universalismo e multiculturalismo: la *vocazione* universalistica dei diritti umani agisce come forza trainante dell'intero settore, ma essa si è realizzata pienamente, *da un punto di vista giuridico*, soltanto in parte; cioè per quel numero limitato di diritti umani che sono regolati dal diritto internazionale generale (principi del diritto internazionale, diritto consuetudinario, principi generali di diritto riconosciuti *in foro domestico*). In altri termini, tale vocazione si è realizzata per quei diritti umani che godono del consenso generale della comunità internazionale, consenso che si esprime in modo diverso nelle diverse fonti succitate del diritto internazionale generale [29]. Inoltre, come vedremo [30], questo consenso generale della comunità internazionale è rafforzato anche dal fatto che i diritti umani regolati dal diritto internazionale generale finiscono, quasi sempre (ma non sempre), per coincidere con i diritti umani regolati dallo *ius cogens*; cioè riconosciuti come valori essenziali, fondamentali e non derogabili della comunità internazionale.

Tuttavia, l'universalismo giuridico dei diritti umani incontra ancora molti limiti, perché la maggior parte dei diritti umani, come vedremo, è regolata solo dal diritto internazionale convenzionale; cioè da norme che vincolano solo gli Stati che le hanno volontariamente accettate e ratificate. È in questo aspetto che si esprime il principio del *multiculturalismo/particolarismo*: è chiaro che quei diritti umani che sono regolati soltanto da trattati, e da trattati ratificati solo da una parte degli Stati esistenti, non possono essere considerati *concretamente* come universali, da un punto di vista giuridico. Quei diritti non spettano a tutte le persone umane e non obbligano tutti gli Stati. In altri termini, il diritto internazionale convenzionale lascia gli Stati liberi, anche sulla base della propria cultura dei diritti umani, di accettare o meno di obbligarsi al rispetto di certi diritti. Per fare un esempio (seppure non edificante), se quelle norme dei trattati sui diritti umani, che stabiliscono il principio di uguaglianza fra uomo e donna, non sono accettate dagli Stati del mondo musulmano, ciò impedisce che esse diventino norme di diritto internazionale generale. Un discorso simile si potrebbe fare per altri diritti umani che sono accettati solo da una parte degli Stati, come, ad esempio, il divieto della pena di morte.

Inoltre, si consideri un altro aspetto nel quale si esprime il rapporto fra universalismo e multiculturalismo/particolarismo; e cioè nel fatto che il contenuto della norma consuetudinaria (o comunque di diritto internazionale generale) su un determinato diritto umano non è identico a quello delle corrispondenti norme convenzionali sul medesimo diritto. Di soli-

---

[28] Cfr. Lenzerini (2014); Crawford (2013), pp. 325-341.

[29] Vedi *infra*, Cap. II.

[30] Vedi *infra*, Cap. V, parr. 4.4 e 4.5.

to, il contenuto della norma consuetudinaria è più generale, più semplice e più essenziale, come vedremo meglio in seguito. Ad esempio, il diritto alla vita nel diritto consuetudinario significa, in sostanza, il divieto di privazione arbitraria della vita[31]. Invece, nelle numerose norme convenzionali che lo regolano, il diritto alla vita ha un contenuto più complesso e dettagliato, e prevede restrizioni e deroghe, nonché criteri per definire meglio il criterio di arbitrarietà. Per fare un altro esempio, il diritto di accesso alla giustizia, nel diritto consuetudinario, ha un contenuto sintetico ed essenziale[32], mentre nelle varie norme convenzionali esso si specifica in disposizioni dettagliate sul giusto processo e sui ricorsi interni effettivi, che stabiliscono un regime giuridico complesso, con una serie di garanzie sostanziali e procedurali. E queste disposizioni convenzionali variano a seconda dei diversi trattati e dei diversi sistemi convenzionali sui diritti umani, lasciando uno spazio al particolarismo e al regionalismo.

Ma si deve notare che il diritto convenzionale sui diritti umani non esprime solo la tendenza favorevole al multiculturalismo. Esso può anche, nel difficile *equilibrio* fra le due tendenze, esprimere la *vocazione* universalistica. Infatti, in primo luogo, alcuni trattati sui diritti umani sono stati ratificati da un numero altissimo di Stati[33] e quindi essi sono "quasi-universali". In secondo luogo, come vedremo meglio in seguito[34], il diritto convenzionale può avere, a certe condizioni, un notevole impatto sullo sviluppo progressivo del diritto internazionale generale (specie quello consuetudinario). In terzo luogo (ed anche questo punto sarà approfondito in seguito[35]), il principio universalistico esercita un'influenza su certi caratteri "speciali" del diritto convenzionale dei diritti umani, poiché tende a favorire la più ampia partecipazione possibile a tali trattati da parte degli Stati ed a ampliare la loro sfera di applicazione.

In sintesi, a mio parere, il rapporto fra universalismo e multiculturalismo dei diritti umani può essere visivamente rappresentato da due cerchi concentrici: il più grande rappresenta tutti i diritti umani mentre il più piccolo, al suo interno, rappresenta i diritti umani regolati dal diritto internazionale generale, che definiamo, per ora in via provvisoria, come diritti umani "fondamentali"[36]. Via via che il diritto internazionale dei diritti umani si sviluppa e si amplia progressivamente, il cerchio piccolo tende ad allargarsi; e quindi tende a diminuire la differenza fra le dimensioni dei due cerchi. In altri termini, l'universalismo si rafforza a spese del multiculturalismo/particolarismo. Ma, ovviamente, si tratta di un processo molto lento e non sempre lineare e continuo; e probabilmente i due cerchi non finiranno mai per coincidere.

---

[31] Vedi *infra*, Cap. V, par. 7.

[32] Vedi *infra*, Cap. V, par. 18.

[33] Vedi, ad es. la Convenzione sui diritti del fanciullo (*infra*, Cap. IV, par. 5.2.7.).

[34] Vedi *infra*, Cap. II, par. 3.2.

[35] Vedi *infra*, Cap. II, parr. 9 e 10.

[36] Per un approfondimento di questa nozione vedi *infra*, Cap. V, Sez. I.

Sezione II
L'IMPATTO DEI DIRITTI UMANI SUL DIRITTO INTERNAZIONALE

5. *Diritti umani e processo di modernizzazione del diritto internazionale*

Come si è detto sopra, la teoria dei diritti umani ha via via assunto un ruolo centrale nel diritto internazionale e si è radicata a fondo nella dinamica della società internazionale contemporanea.

Ciò significa, a mio avviso, che tale teoria ha anche prodotto un fenomeno di innovazione e modernizzazione sia su alcuni aspetti generali e strutturali del diritto internazionale sia su molti settori specifici di tale diritto [37]. A questo proposito, una parte della dottrina ha parlato di un processo di "umanizzazione" del diritto internazionale, volendo significare che il diritto internazionale "classico" o "tradizionale", formato essenzialmente da norme c.d. "stato-centriche" (cioè protettive dei rapporti interstatali), pur restando in gran parte attuale anche nel mondo contemporaneo, ha via via e progressivamente lasciato uno spazio anche ad un diritto internazionale "nuovo", formato da norme c.d. "umano-centriche" (cioè tese a proteggere anche e soprattutto la persona umana) [38].

Tuttavia, si deve avvertire subito che un'altra parte della dottrina non è d'accordo sull'esistenza di tale processo di modernizzazione e di "umanizzazione" del diritto internazionale; o comunque tende a sminuirne molto l'importanza [39].

A queste due opinioni diverse corrispondono, in gran parte, due teorie generali assai diverse sulla coerenza e completezza dell'ordinamento internazionale e sul problema connesso dell'esistenza o meno dei c.d. regimi *self-contained* [40]. Queste teorie conducono a concepire in maniera assai differente anche il settore specifico costituito dal diritto internazionale dei diritti umani: si tratta di un sistema chiuso ed isolato, incapace di comunicare e di interagire con il diritto internazionale generale e con altri settori specifici di tale diritto (e quindi si tratta in sostanza di un regime *self-contained*) oppure, viceversa, si tratta di un settore che comunica e interagisce con l'ordinamento internazionale complessivamente considerato? Come è chiaro, soltanto quest'ultima concezione del diritto internazionale dei diritti umani consente di ipotizzare che esso abbia prodotto il suddetto fenomeno di modernizzazione dell'intero ordinamento internazionale. Pertanto conviene approfondire il discorso sulle due teorie generali in questione.

---

[37] Si veda, per opere classiche, Friedmann (1964); Jennings (1979); Simma (1994); Tomuschat (1993); Carrillo Salcedo (1997).

[38] Vedi, in particolare, Simma (1993); Meron (2003); Meron (2006); Pisillo Mazzeschi (2004a), pp. 16-36; Pisillo Mazzeschi (2008), pp. 198-220; Sicilianos (2012); Pisillo Mazzeschi, De Sena (eds.) (2018).

[39] Vedi, ad es., Weil (1983); Weil (1992), spec. pp. 25-39 e 66-81; Combacau (1986); Combacau, Sur (2006), pp. 17-28; Pellet (2000).

[40] Sulla teoria dei regimi *self-contained*, vedi Simma (1985); Simma, Pulkowski (2006). Vedi anche Pisillo Mazzeschi (2014a), pp. 278-287.

6. *Il diritto internazionale dei diritti umani come regime* self-contained?

Una parte della dottrina internazionalistica (composta specie dagli autori specializzati in singoli settori) aderisce alla prima delle due teorie generali sopra indicate; e cioè si fonda, già in partenza, su una concezione "particolaristica" del diritto internazionale, che considera tale diritto come un insieme di sottosistemi normativi scarsamente interconnessi fra loro, per la carenza di principi sovraordinati comuni[41]. Ciò conduce a favorire la teoria generale dei regimi *self-contained*; e quindi anche l'idea che il sistema internazionale dei diritti umani costituisca, in tutto o in parte, un regime *self-contained*; cioè un regime speciale di per sé chiuso e sufficiente, che esclude il ricorso a norme diverse da quelle proprie del regime in oggetto, e quindi esclude anche il funzionamento del diritto internazionale generale o, quantomeno, lo ammette solo in casi eccezionali e residuali.

D'altra parte, l'idea che il diritto internazionale dei diritti umani costituisca un regime *self-contained* viene accolta, su basi meno teoriche e più pragmatiche, anche da molti studiosi specializzati nel settore dei diritti umani, i quali tendono, probabilmente mossi anche da un sincero entusiasmo ed ottimismo per i rapidi sviluppi del settore, ad accentuare l'importanza di tali sviluppi e, di conseguenza, anche le differenze fra il regime giuridico dei diritti umani ed il diritto internazionale generale. In sostanza, ciò significa che, per questi autori, le caratteristiche peculiari del regime dei diritti umani non incidono sul diritto internazionale generale. Pertanto questa tendenza conduce anch'essa ad "isolare" la tutela internazionale dei diritti umani rispetto al tradizionale sistema complessivo del diritto internazionale. Lo strumento giuridico principale, che può fornire la base teorica a questo approccio "particolaristico", è, come si è detto sopra, il concetto di regime *self-contained*. Si tratta, a nostro avviso, di un risultato paradossale per i sostenitori dei diritti umani (gli *human rights lawyers*), perché significa, in un certo senso, chiudere questo settore in una sorta di "ghetto" ed ammettere che esso non riesce ad incidere sull'intero ordinamento internazionale.

Al contrario, in maniera inversa ed opposta, un'altra parte della dottrina internazionalistica (formata specie dagli studiosi c.d. "generalisti") si basa su una concezione di fondo assai diversa circa la struttura stessa del diritto internazionale e considera tale diritto come un ordinamento giuridico unico, e con forti caratteri di completezza e coerenza sistematica (concezione "universalistica" del diritto internazionale). Questa dottrina, alla quale riteniamo di aderire, tende in linea di massima a respingere il concetto di regimi *self-contained*, intesi come sistemi totalmente chiusi verso l'esterno, ed invece ad accettare solo la possibilità di regimi speciali, specie di natura convenzionale, che funzionino nel quadro dei normali rapporti fra diritto generale e diritto speciale. Inoltre, l'esistenza di un regime speciale, che deroghi al diritto internazionale generale, dovrebbe risultare da elementi certi; e cioè dal fatto che gli Stati parti di un regime speciale convenzionale abbiano chiaramente manifestato tale volontà derogatoria.

Questa concezione generale si applica anche al campo specifico dei diritti umani. La

---

[41] Sul problema della c.d. "frammentazione" del diritto internazionale vedi ILC, *Fragmentation of International Law: Difficulties Arising from the Diversification and Expansion of International Law, Report of the Study Group of the International Law Commission (Finalized by Martti Koskenniemi)*, A/CN.4/L.682 of 13 April 2006; Koskenniemi, Leino (2002). In senso critico, vedi Conforti (2007); Benvenisti (2008); Simma (2009).

dottrina in esame mostra la tendenza a non "isolare" il diritto internazionale dei diritti umani rispetto al diritto internazionale generale ed agli altri settori specialistici di tale diritto; e quindi a ritenere che la tutela internazionale dei diritti umani, pur costituendo per molti aspetti un regime speciale che può derogare al diritto internazionale generale, in base al criterio di specialità, faccia comunque parte del sistema generale ed interagisca con tale sistema e con altri regimi speciali, con la possibilità di reciproche influenze, interazioni e coordinamenti. È chiaro che questa dottrina è assai più incline ad ammettere che si sia realizzato quel processo di "umanizzazione" del diritto internazionale di cui abbiamo parlato nel paragrafo precedente. Pertanto, se ciò è vero, si deve concludere che sono gli autori generalisti, più che gli specialisti dei diritti umani, che riconoscono più facilmente l'impatto innovatore di tali diritti sull'intero sistema del diritto internazionale.

Per concludere, si deve sottolineare il fatto che, anche al di là delle premesse teoriche e dottrinali di partenza, è l'esame concreto della realtà del diritto internazionale contemporaneo che dimostra la correttezza della seconda teoria sopra descritta. Infatti, come vedremo subito, è assai difficile negare che la teoria dei diritti umani, trasportata sul piano internazionale, abbia prodotto un notevole impatto sull'ordinamento internazionale[42]. Per ragioni sistematiche, distingueremo fra due fenomeni di cambiamento: *a*) un vero e proprio processo di modifica strutturale dell'ordinamento giuridico internazionale; *b*) un impatto su una serie di settori specifici del diritto internazionale.

7. *Influenza della teoria dei diritti umani sulla struttura tradizionale dell'ordinamento internazionale*

7.1. *Ampliamento del contenuto del diritto internazionale*

Secondo la definizione classica o tradizionale, assolutamente dominante fino alla metà del XX secolo, il diritto internazionale è l'ordinamento giuridico che regola i rapporti fra Stati (o fra Stati ed altri enti sovrani). Questa affermazione intende prima di tutto mettere in rilievo che il diritto internazionale regola *materialmente* rapporti fra Stati; cioè che il suo *contenuto tipico* è quello di disciplinare materie attinenti a rapporti interstatali, a relazioni e questioni giuridiche per così dire "esterne" e di interesse tipicamente diplomatico.

La teoria dei diritti umani ha prodotto una frattura notevole rispetto a tale contenuto, poiché ha trasferito a livello giuridico internazionale i rapporti fra lo Stato e i suoi cittadini ed ha attribuito all'individuo un ruolo centrale. In tal modo essa ha prodotto un notevole *ampliamento del contenuto materiale* del diritto internazionale[43]. Infatti il diritto internazionale contemporaneo non disciplina più soltanto rapporti tipicamente interstatali, ma anche, e sempre di più, moltissimi rapporti che si svolgono all'interno delle varie comunità statali, che intercorrono fra Stati ed individui, e che interessano tutti gli operatori giuridici interni e tutti gli individui[44]. Si potrebbe dire, con espressione sintetica, che il diritto internazionale non è più soltanto un diritto per gli Stati, ma anche un diritto per gli individui. In

---

[42] Vedi Pisillo Mazzeschi (2014b).

[43] *Ibidem*, p. 90.

[44] Cfr. Conforti (2006), p. 3.

questo processo di cambiamento ha giocato un ruolo primario e fondamentale la teoria internazionale dei diritti umani, poiché essa, come si è detto, ha internazionalizzato i rapporti fra lo Stato ed i suoi cittadini, che per secoli erano questioni di competenza domestica (o dominio riservato), esclusi dalla sfera stessa di applicazione del diritto internazionale. Tale teoria ha prodotto inoltre una spinta dinamica per lo sviluppo di altri settori del diritto internazionale contemporaneo, che disciplinano anch'essi rapporti fra Stati ed individui o rapporti interindividuali: basti pensare al diritto internazionale penale ed al diritto internazionale umanitario contemporaneo.

7.2. *Allargamento dei soggetti del diritto internazionale: il nuovo ruolo dell'individuo*

Un secondo elemento della nozione tradizionale del diritto internazionale riguarda i suoi soggetti o destinatari formali. Nel diritto internazionale classico solo gli Stati sono destinatari *formali* delle norme internazionali e considerati soggetti. Gli individui sono ritenuti solo "oggetti" o, quantomeno, meri "beneficiari di fatto" delle norme internazionali. In epoca più recente, si è affermata anche la soggettività internazionale delle organizzazioni internazionali.

La teoria dei diritti umani internazionali ha, secondo l'opinione oramai dominante, dato un contributo fondamentale per cambiare radicalmente tale concezione tradizionale [45]. Oggi si ammette che il diritto internazionale contemporaneo regola *formalmente e direttamente* (cioè senza necessità di essere recepito dal diritto interno) anche *alcuni* rapporti fra Stati ed individui (ed altri enti non statali) ed *alcuni* rapporti interindividuali. In altri termini gli individui sono adesso destinatari diretti di *alcune* norme internazionali, non solo primarie, ma anche secondarie e terziarie, e quindi anche di diritti e obblighi sul piano internazionale. La stessa Corte internazionale di giustizia (CIG) ha stabilito che la Convenzione di Vienna del 1963 sulle relazioni consolari contiene norme che attribuiscono diritti agli individui [46].

Le norme internazionali sui diritti umani sono l'esempio principale, anche se non il solo, di norme che impongono obblighi ad uno Stato cui corrispondono sia diritti di altri Stati, sia *diritti di individui*. Ed anzi, conviene ribadire qui quanto già abbiamo detto [47]: cioè che il principio della *preminenza dell'individuo* domina l'intero settore del diritto internazionale dei diritti umani. Quanto agli obblighi, sono le norme del diritto internazionale penale l'esempio principale di norme internazionali che impongono direttamente obblighi agli individui.

In dottrina, poiché non vi è accordo unanime sul concetto di soggettività internazionale, si discute ancora se questo cambiamento significa che gli individui sono "soggetti" del diritto internazionale, oppure "soggetti parziali o limitati", oppure solo dotati di certe capacità [48]. A nostro avviso, si tratta oramai di una discussione solo teorica, che non incide

---

[45] Vedi Pisillo Mazzeschi (2004a), pp. 16-36; Id. (2014a), pp. 287-294.

[46] ICJ, *LaGrand*, p. 466; ICJ, *Avena*, p. 121. Vedi anche IACtHR, *The Right to Information on Consular Assistance*, par. 80.

[47] Vedi *supra*, par. 4.

[48] Vedi Pisillo Mazzeschi (2014a), pp. 287-294.

molto sulla realtà, che consiste nel determinare, in concreto e volta per volta, quali siano i *destinatari* di ogni singola norma internazionale ed i titolari di ogni singolo diritto o obbligo internazionale. Volendo, questa soluzione, di natura pragmatica, potrebbe concretizzarsi nella tesi, mutuata dai diritti interni, di ritenere che gli individui siano soggetti internazionali, ma che abbiano capacità volta per volta diverse (e talora nessuna capacità), a seconda dei singoli settori e delle singole norme del diritto internazionale.

In ogni caso, è chiaro che la teoria dei diritti umani, anche su questo aspetto della soggettività, ha modificato radicalmente un elemento fondamentale, che aveva caratterizzato per secoli la struttura tradizionale di tale diritto. Oggi si può sostenere che la comunità internazionale deve essere intesa in senso lato, come comprendente anche gli individui ed altri attori non statali.

7.3. *Modifica della natura tipica del diritto internazionale*

Un terzo elemento della nozione tradizionale del diritto internazionale riguarda la sua *funzione tipica* e la sua *natura giuridica*[49]. Il diritto internazionale classico, specie quello consuetudinario, ha la funzione tipica di regolare la coesistenza fra Stati, nel quadro di una struttura paritaria e orizzontale della società internazionale. Di conseguenza, esso si fonda essenzialmente sui principi di reciprocità e bilateralità ed ha pertanto una natura giuridica tipicamente "privatistica", cioè tesa a regolare gli interessi individuali dei singoli Stati. Questa natura privatistica concerne due aspetti principali: *a*) l'assenza degli interessi collettivi degli Stati; *b*) l'assenza di valori fondamentali appartenenti all'intera comunità internazionale. Il primo aspetto è illustrato dal fatto che le norme internazionali tradizionali, anche quando sono indirizzate a più Stati, operano in maniera bilaterale e reciproca. Il secondo aspetto è mostrato dal fatto che le norme tradizionali consuetudinarie hanno quasi tutte natura dispositiva, cioè possono essere derogate dagli Stati mediante accordo. Ciò conferma che il diritto internazionale classico non riconosce l'esistenza di valori fondamentali dell'intera comunità internazionale, che siano di natura inderogabile.

Per un processo storico naturale, l'ampliamento del contenuto materiale del diritto internazionale ha prodotto anche un'estensione della sua funzione e della sua natura: il c.d. diritto internazionale della coesistenza, tutto impostato su una concezione individualistica e "privatistica" dei rapporti fra Stati, sui principi della reciprocità e del "bilateralismo" in materia di responsabilità fra Stati, pur sopravvivendo, ha lasciato via via spazio anche al c.d. diritto internazionale della cooperazione, che si è sempre di più aperto alla tutela di interessi collettivi, solidaristici e talora addirittura comunitari degli Stati[50]. In altri termini, vi è stato non solo un fenomeno di aumento quantitativo della cooperazione fra Stati, ma anche un'apertura progressiva verso una concezione "pubblicistica" dei rapporti fra Stati, quantomeno a livello normativo, se non ancora a livello istituzionale.

Questo fenomeno di cambiamento è stato provocato da una serie complessa di fattori; ma si deve riconoscere che la teoria dei diritti umani ha esercitato un ruolo fondamentale, che è bene evidenziato dai concetti di obblighi *erga omnes* e di *ius cogens*.

---

[49] Vedi Pisillo Mazzeschi (2014b), pp. 90-92.

[50] Si veda, *supra*, la dottrina citata nel par. 5.

7.3.1. *Obblighi* erga omnes *e valori collettivi*

Il primo concetto è legato alla nascita, nel diritto internazionale contemporaneo, di alcuni interessi *collettivi e comunitari* degli Stati.

Come si è già accennato, nel diritto internazionale tradizionale, di solito le norme creano vincoli bilaterali fra Stati; cioè creano diritti ed obblighi reciproci fra di essi. In altri termini, tali norme hanno natura "sinallagmatica". Ciò si verifica non solo per le norme derivanti dai trattati bilaterali; ma anche per quelle derivanti dai trattati multilaterali o dal diritto consuetudinario. Infatti, anche quest'ultime due categorie di norme, pur indirizzandosi come destinatari ad una pluralità di Stati, sono suscettibili di essere scomposte in un fascio di rapporti bilaterali fra Stati. Questa scomposizione si vede bene in caso di violazione della norma, poiché solo lo Stato leso (cioè lo Stato il cui diritto soggettivo è stato violato e che ha subìto un danno) ha una legittimazione attiva a far valere il rapporto di responsabilità (principio del bilateralismo). Naturalmente vi erano, anche nel diritto internazionale tradizionale, alcune eccezioni al principio di reciprocità ed alla regola della natura "sinallagmatica" delle norme internazionali. Ma esse erano, appunto, solo isolate eccezioni. Il principio di reciprocità era dominante perché rispecchiava bene la struttura paritaria ed esclusivamente orizzontale della comunità internazionale, l'assenza di intensi legami giuridici fra Stati e l'assoluta prevalenza degli interessi individuali ed egoistici degli Stati su quelli di natura collettiva.

La situazione è molto cambiata nel diritto internazionale contemporaneo, poiché esistono adesso molti esempi di norme internazionali che non si basano sulla reciprocità, ma sull'opposto principio c.d. della solidarietà. Si tratta appunto delle norme che istituiscono vincoli od obblighi solidali o, come si usa dire più spesso, obblighi *erga omnes* [51]. Questo termine significa che l'obbligo esiste verso tutti i membri della comunità internazionale (obblighi *erga omnes*) oppure verso tutti i contraenti di un trattato multilaterale (obblighi *erga omnes partes*); e cioè che la sua violazione da parte di uno Stato *interessa* tutti gli altri Stati o, quantomeno, tutti gli altri Stati parti di un trattato. Cioè la solidarietà dell'obbligo può derivare sia da una norma consuetudinaria che da una norma pattizia. È evidente che questa evoluzione del diritto internazionale contemporaneo è legata al progressivo emergere in tale ordinamento di *valori collettivi* della comunità internazionale. Le norme che proteggono tali valori hanno un carattere "pubblicistico" più che "privatistico" e pertanto si pongono su un piano diverso rispetto alle altre norme dell'ordinamento e tendono a creare obblighi di natura solidale nel senso che impegnano ogni Stato nei confronti di ogni altro Stato nel quadro dell'intera comunità internazionale (o nell'ambito di un gruppo più ristretto di Stati che condividono tali valori collettivi).

Si deve sottolineare che l'impulso iniziale e la spinta decisiva per lo sviluppo del concetto di obblighi *erga omnes* sono derivati proprio dal settore dei diritti umani, come è dimostrato dal fatto che la Corte internazionale di giustizia, nel celebre brano della sentenza *Barcelona Traction* in cui enuclea il concetto di obblighi *erga omnes*, include soprattutto esempi relativi ai diritti umani [52]. Infatti, le norme consuetudinarie ed i trattati sui diritti umani sono

---

[51] Sugli obblighi *erga omnes* la bibliografia è vastissima. Ci si limita a rinviare a: Simma (1994); Ragazzi (1997); Picone (2005); Ronzitti (2007); Pisillo Mazzeschi (2008), pp. 249-256.

[52] ICJ, *Barcelona Traction*, Judgment of 5 February 1970, parr. 32-34.

esempi paradigmatici di norme che contengono obblighi *erga omnes*, nel senso che essi obbligano ogni Stato nei confronti di tutti gli altri Stati o (nel caso dei c.d. obblighi *erga omnes partes*) nei confronti di tutti gli altri Stati parti di un trattato multilaterale.

Da ciò conseguono effetti importanti specie nel settore della *responsabilità* internazionale, poiché la violazione degli obblighi *erga omnes* lede un diritto, o comunque un interesse giuridico, di tutti gli altri Stati o di ogni altro Stato parte del trattato multilaterale [53]. Pertanto, è evidente che il nuovo concetto di obblighi solidali, pur convivendo con i tradizionali concetti di obblighi bilaterali e reciproci, ha introdotto un cambiamento notevole nella funzione e natura tipica del diritto internazionale classico, poiché il riconoscimento di valori solidali, come si è detto, costituisce una spinta verso una natura "pubblicistica" (o, secondo alcuni, "verticalistica" o "costituzionalistica") del diritto internazionale.

7.3.2. Ius cogens *e valori fondamentali*

Un discorso simile si può fare per il concetto di *ius cogens* [54], che trae origine dallo sviluppo, nel diritto internazionale contemporaneo, di alcuni valori *essenziali, fondamentali e non derogabili* dell'intera comunità internazionale. Il concetto giuridico di *ius cogens*, ormai universalmente riconosciuto, non deve essere confuso con quello di obblighi *erga omnes*, perché il primo non riguarda la struttura particolare dell'obbligo, ma piuttosto il valore, la forza di resistenza e (secondo la tesi preferibile) anche il rango gerarchico della norma. Inoltre, la nozione di *ius cogens* è più restrittiva di quella di obblighi *erga omnes*. Tuttavia, vi sono anche forti affinità fra i due concetti, poiché alla loro base vi è l'idea che nel diritto internazionale contemporaneo vi sono dei valori "comunitari" o "pubblici", che devono essere tutelati.

La teoria dei diritti umani ha giocato un ruolo importante anche nel far emergere e affermare nel diritto internazionale il concetto di *ius cogens* e, in pratica, molte norme inderogabili corrispondono a norme consuetudinarie o a principi generali di diritto internazionale sui diritti umani "fondamentali", che stabiliscono anche obblighi *erga omnes*, quali, ad esempio, il divieto di genocidio, di crimini contro l'umanità, di tortura, di schiavitù, di discriminazione razziale, di *apartheid*.

Pertanto, la teoria dei diritti umani ha contribuito, tramite i concetti di obblighi *erga omnes* e di *ius cogens*, a cambiare la funzione e la natura giuridica tipiche del diritto internazionale nel senso di una loro modernizzazione: accanto alla dimensione privatistica del diritto internazionale, una sua dimensione pubblicistica si è gradualmente sviluppata e affermata. Come vedremo subito, anche il concetto di *ius cogens* (come quello di obblighi *erga omnes*) ha importanti effetti nel campo della responsabilità degli Stati.

---

[53] Vedi ILC, *Draft Articles on Responsibility of States for Internationally Wrongful Acts*, 1 August 2001, artt. 48 e 54.

[54] Anche sul concetto di *ius cogens* la bibliografia è sterminata. Ci si limita a rinviare a: Ronzitti (1978); Gaja (1981); Hannikainen (1988); Kolb (2001a); Orakhelashvili (2006); Picone (2008); ed ai lavori della Commissione del diritto internazionale, in particolare ai rapporti presentati dal Relatore Speciale: Tladi (2016); Id. (2017); Id. (2018); Id. (2019).

7.4. *Modernizzazione del regime della responsabilità internazionale degli Stati*

La teoria dei diritti umani, insieme ad altri fattori, ha prodotto notevoli cambiamenti anche nel settore tradizionale della responsabilità degli Stati, incidendo sugli elementi fondamentali di tale settore, che erano costituiti dal principio del "bilateralismo" e dal principio del carattere esclusivamente interstatale della responsabilità. Essa ha modernizzato tali aspetti, poiché i cambiamenti strutturali sopra menzionati (specie quello attinente al nuovo ruolo dell'individuo e quello attinente alla nuova natura "pubblicistica" del diritto internazionale) hanno inciso anche sulla fase "patologica" del diritto internazionale, rappresentata dalla responsabilità internazionale [55].

Più in particolare, tali cambiamenti hanno: *a*) ampliato la sfera degli Stati legittimati ad invocare la responsabilità dello Stato accusato dell'illecito; *b*) stabilito, accanto al regime ordinario di responsabilità dello Stato, anche un regime di responsabilità "aggravata"; *c*) ammesso la possibilità di una responsabilità internazionale degli Stati verso gli individui. Vediamo separatamente questi tre aspetti.

7.4.1. *Invocazione della responsabilità per violazione di obblighi* erga omnes

Per quanto riguarda il primo aspetto, si è già visto che un fattore importante del processo di cambiamento del diritto internazionale contemporaneo, tramite l'impulso decisivo dato dalla teoria dei diritti umani, concerne il ruolo via via crescente degli interessi collettivi e comunitari degli Stati. Questo sviluppo è rappresentato soprattutto dal fatto che esistono adesso molte norme internazionali che stabiliscono obblighi solidali (o *erga omnes*). Ciò vale molto nel settore dei diritti umani, poiché le ormai numerosissime norme convenzionali sui diritti umani stabiliscono in linea di principio obblighi *erga omnes partes*; e le meno numerose norme di diritto internazionale generale sui diritti umani stabiliscono obblighi *erga omnes*.

Ciò premesso, i cambiamenti ed i problemi più importanti riguardano la responsabilità degli Stati per la violazione degli obblighi *erga omnes*. In linea generale si può dire che la solidarietà dell'obbligo comporta soprattutto un'estensione degli Stati che sono legittimati ad invocare la responsabilità dello Stato autore della violazione. Ma, più in particolare, si deve stabilire in concreto quali Stati siano legittimati ad invocare la responsabilità e quali conseguenze dell'illecito essi possano far valere.

Su questo punto non fornisce molto aiuto la nota giurisprudenza della CIG che per prima ha sviluppato il concetto di obblighi *erga omnes*. Nel parere consultivo del 1951 sulle *Riserve alla Convenzione sul genocidio* [56] e nella sentenza *Barcelona Traction* del 1970 [57] la Corte sembra orientata a riconoscere che la violazione da parte di uno Stato di un obbligo *erga omnes* lede un *interesse giuridico* e non un vero e proprio diritto soggettivo degli altri Stati. Ma essa non entra nel merito delle forme e dei modi con cui tali Stati possano reagire alla violazione.

Questi ultimi aspetti sono stati invece dibattuti a lungo, come è noto, durante i lavori

---

[55] Vedi Pisillo Mazzeschi (2014b), pp. 93-98.

[56] ICJ, *Reservations to the Convention on the Prevention and Punishment of the Crime of Genocide*, p. 23.

[57] ICJ, *Barcelona Traction*, p. 32, parr. 33-34.

della CDI sulla responsabilità degli Stati; e vi è stato anche un approccio generale piuttosto diverso fra il Progetto adottato in prima lettura nel 1996 ed il Progetto finale della CDI del 2001 [58]. Quest'ultimo Progetto opera una distinzione generale fra Stati lesi (art.42) e Stati non lesi ma pur sempre legittimati ad invocare la responsabilità dello Stato offensore (art.48). Gli Stati lesi possono far valere tutte le conseguenze dell'illecito internazionale (richiesta di cessazione dell'illecito, garanzie di non ripetizione, riparazione, contromisure).

Invece, gli Stati non lesi, ma legittimati a far valere la responsabilità per violazione di obblighi *erga omnes*, possono far valere solo alcune delle conseguenze dell'illecito [59]: la cessazione dell'illecito e garanzie e assicurazioni di non ripetizione, nonché la riparazione dell'illecito, ma solo nell'interesse dello Stato leso (se vi sia uno Stato leso) e dei "beneficiari" dell'obbligo violato (ad es., gli individui vittime delle violazioni dei diritti umani). Inoltre, sembra che essi possano adottare contro lo Stato responsabile altre "misure lecite" previste dal diritto internazionale (art. 54) [60]. A noi sembra che, quando la violazione di un obbligo *erga omnes* non comporti anche una grave violazione dello *ius cogens*, il concetto di "misure lecite" dovrebbe essere interpretato in maniera restrittiva; cioè dovrebbe essere limitato a ritorsioni pacifiche. Infatti, è logico che le conseguenze giuridiche di una semplice violazione di un obbligo solidale debbano essere più lievi di quelle derivanti da una grave violazione dello *ius cogens*.

In conclusione, l'ampliamento della sfera degli Stati che possono invocare la responsabilità per violazione di obblighi *erga omnes* costituisce un cambiamento significativo del regime della responsabilità degli Stati.

7.4.2. *Responsabilità aggravata per violazioni di obblighi derivanti da norme di* ius cogens

Venendo al secondo cambiamento sopra accennato del regime della responsabilità internazionale, esso è stato prodotto dal concetto di *ius cogens*. Si era già visto che un fattore importante del processo di cambiamento strutturale del diritto internazionale è costituito dalla nascita e consolidamento delle norme di *ius cogens*. Nell'ottica della responsabilità degli Stati, la nozione di *ius cogens* ha contribuito a creare, nel quadro del relativo Progetto della Commissione del diritto internazionale (CDI/ILC), il concetto di "crimini internazionali degli Stati", che è stato in seguito sostituito dalla nozione di "gravi violazioni di obblighi derivanti da norme imperative del diritto internazionale generale" (art. 40 del Progetto) [61].

Queste particolari violazioni producono una responsabilità "aggravata" dello Stato offensore, poiché producono alcune conseguenze particolari (art. 41), che si aggiungono alle

---

[58] ILC, *Draft Articles on Responsibility of States for Internationally Wrongful Acts*, 1 August 2001.

[59] *Ibidem*, vedi l'art. 48(2).

[60] Art. 54 (*Measures taken by States other than an injured State*): "This chapter does not prejudice the right of any other State, entitled under article 48, paragraph 1, to invoke the responsibility of another State, to take lawful measures against that State to ensure cessation of the breach and reparation in the interest of the injured State or of the beneficiaries of the obligation breached".

[61] Art. 40 (*Application of this chapter*): "1. This chapter applies to the international responsibility which is entailed by a serious breach by a State of an obligation arising under a peremptory norm of general international law. 2. A breach of such an obligation is serious if it involves a gross or systematic failure by the responsible State to fulfil the obligation".

normali conseguenze dell'illecito, e che comportano un coinvolgimento di tutti gli Stati diversi da quello responsabile in alcuni obblighi: quello di cooperare per porre fine, con mezzi leciti, alla violazione; quello di non riconoscere come legittima una situazione creata attraverso la violazione; ed infine quello di non prestare aiuto o assistenza nel mantenere la situazione illecita.

In realtà, queste conseguenze particolari, anche se contribuiscono ad aggravare la responsabilità dello Stato che ha violato lo *ius cogens*, non appaiono molto incisive e sono inferiori rispetto alle attese, tenendo conto che esse dovrebbero sanzionare violazioni gravi di valori fondamentali dell'intera comunità internazionale. Tuttavia, si deve considerare che gli artt. 55, 56 e 59 del Progetto lasciano impregiudicate le regole sulla responsabilità stabilite dal diritto internazionale, perché sono norme speciali o perché non sono espressamente previste dal Progetto o perché sono sancite dalla Carta delle NU.

Inoltre, per le gravi violazioni dello *ius cogens*, ci sembra applicabile anche l'art. 54 del Progetto. Esso afferma il diritto di ogni Stato diverso da quello leso e legittimato ad invocare la responsabilità di prendere "misure lecite" contro lo Stato responsabile della violazione, per assicurare la cessazione dell'illecito e la riparazione nell'interesse dello Stato leso e dei beneficiari dell'obbligo violato. Il Progetto non specifica il concetto di "misure lecite"; ma, alla luce del Commento dell'art. 54[62] e dei citati artt. 55, 56 e 59, si può ritenere che, per definire tale concetto, si possa ricorrere al diritto internazionale (anche nel suo sviluppo progressivo) ed alla Carta delle NU. Pertanto, in caso di gravi violazioni dello *ius cogens* (ad es., *gross violations* dei diritti umani) ci sembra che le "misure lecite" possano comprendere: *a*) ritorsioni pacifiche contro lo Stato autore dell'illecito, *b*) contromisure pacifiche; *c*) misure non comportanti l'uso della forza raccomandate o decise dal Consiglio di sicurezza (CdS) *ex* art. 41 della Carta delle NU quando le gravi violazioni dello *ius cogens* determinano una delle condizioni previste dall'art. 39 della Carta; *d*) misure implicanti l'uso della forza decise o autorizzate dal CdS, sempre nei casi previsti dall'art. 39 della Carta.

In conclusione, il regime di responsabilità aggravata per le violazioni dello *ius cogens* appare poco incisivo nel Progetto della CDI, ma può rafforzarsi in futuro tramite un'interpretazione dinamica del diritto internazionale. In ogni caso, tale regime ha creato una modernizzazione importante del settore della responsabilità degli Stati.

7.4.3. *Responsabilità degli Stati verso gli individui e diritto individuale alla riparazione*

La teoria dei diritti umani, contribuendo molto a far affermare il concetto che l'individuo può essere destinatario diretto di *alcune* norme internazionali, ha prodotto un altro cambiamento nel settore della responsabilità degli Stati, poiché ha messo in crisi il principio classico del carattere solo interstatale del rapporto di responsabilità. Infatti, gli individui possono, *in certe circostanze*, essere destinatari di norme internazionali *secondarie*[63]; e quindi possono invocare e far valere la responsabilità di uno Stato. In altre parole, quando l'obbligo inter-

[62] ILC, *Draft articles on Responsibility of States for Internationally Wrongful Acts, with commentaries*, *YILC*, 2001, vol. II (2), pp. 137-139.

[63] Vedi ICJ, *LaGrand* e *Avena*.

nazionale primario violato dallo Stato ha per destinatari formali non solo altri Stati ma *anche individui*, tale Stato assume una responsabilità internazionale non solo verso altri Stati ma *anche verso gli individui*, che diventano anch'essi soggetti attivi del rapporto di responsabilità [64]. Queste conclusioni sono assai importanti per il settore dei diritti umani, dove pertanto è possibile concepire oggi una vera e propria responsabilità internazionale dello Stato verso gli individui. In tale materia, gli aspetti più importanti riguardano la legittimazione degli individui ad invocare la responsabilità e il loro diritto alla riparazione.

Il Progetto della CDI sulla responsabilità degli Stati, purtroppo, si occupa solo della responsabilità internazionale dello Stato *verso altri Stati*, e quindi sotto questo profilo è assai conservatore. Tuttavia, la CDI ha implicitamente ammesso che il diritto internazionale contemporaneo può contenere norme sulla responsabilità di uno Stato verso un individuo (v. art. 33.2 Progetto) [65].

Il diritto di un individuo di *invocare*, a livello internazionale, la responsabilità di uno Stato è dimostrato dai numerosi casi in cui un individuo può iniziare un'azione dinanzi ad organi internazionali giurisdizionali o quasi-giurisdizionali di controllo sui diritti umani contro lo Stato autore della violazione.

Quanto al diritto dell'individuo di pretendere la *riparazione* [66], la sua esistenza nel diritto internazionale è dimostrata da numerose norme convenzionali sui diritti umani, che stabiliscono che lo Stato responsabile ha un obbligo di riparare l'offesa nei confronti dell'individuo vittima. Inoltre, la prassi degli organi internazionali di controllo sui diritti umani dimostra, molto chiaramente, che le decisioni di tali organi spesso stabiliscono una riparazione (restituzione, risarcimento o soddisfazione) che è direttamente a favore dell'individuo vittima, anche se l'obbligo di riparare spetta poi in pratica allo Stato responsabile della violazione. Inoltre, in sostegno a questa conclusione, quantomeno con riferimento alle gravi e sistematiche violazioni dei diritti umani, si possono citare anche il parere consultivo del 2004 della Corte internazionale di giustizia nel caso delle *Conseguenze della costruzione di un muro in Palestina* [67]; la Risoluzione dell'Assemblea Generale delle NU del 2005 sui *Principi e linee-guida sul diritto alla riparazione per le vittime di gravi violazioni dei diritti umani* [68]; il Rapporto adottato nel 2004 dalla Commissione di inchiesta sul Darfur [69]; ed una risoluzione del 2009 dell'*Institut de Droit International* [70].

Pertanto, si può concludere che l'individuo è oggi titolare di un *diritto alla riparazione per violazione dei diritti umani*, conferito direttamente dal diritto internazionale. Si tratta di un altro importante sviluppo nel settore della responsabilità degli Stati.

---

[64] Pisillo Mazzeschi (2004b).

[65] Art. 33(2): "This part is without prejudice to any right, arising from the international responsibility of a State, which may accrue directly to any person or entity other than a State".

[66] Vedi Pisillo Mazzeschi (1999b); Bartolini (2009). Sul diritto alla riparazione per violazione dei diritti umani fondamentali vedi anche *infra*, Cap. V, par. 19.

[67] ICJ, *Legal Consequences of the Construction of a Wall*, parr. 151-153.

[68] *Basic Principles and Guidelines on the Right to a Remedy and Reparation for Victims of Flagrant Violations of Human Rights and Serious Breaches of Humanitarian Law*, UN Doc. A/RES/60/147, 16 December 2005.

[69] *Report of the International Commission of Inquiry on Darfur to the United Nations Secretary General, Pursuant to Security Council Resolution 1564 of 18 September 2004*, Geneva, 25 January 2005, parr. 595-599.

[70] Institut de Droit International, *Immunity from Jurisdiction of the State and of Persons Who Act on Behalf of the State in Case of International Crimes*, Naples, 10 September 2009.

7.5. *Rapporto fra diritto internazionale e diritti statali: verso una sempre maggiore armonizzazione e integrazione fra i due diritti*

Infine, la teoria dei diritti umani ha, a nostro parere, contribuito a modificare, quantomeno in parte, anche un altro elemento distintivo della nozione tradizionale del diritto internazionale: quello relativo alla sua autonomia, derivante da una separazione netta ed assoluta fra ordinamento internazionale ed ordinamenti statali. Questa autonomia è bene rappresentata dalla tradizionale concezione dualista (o pluralista) dei rapporti fra diritto internazionale e diritto interno, secondo la quale i due ordinamenti giuridici sono separati e distinti, perché differiscono per l'origine delle fonti, per le norme, per il contenuto tipico delle norme e per i destinatari formali delle medesime.

In realtà, la dottrina contemporanea maggioritaria ha abbandonato le vecchie posizioni teoriche nette a favore del dualismo o del monismo; e si deve infatti riconoscere che la contrapposizione netta e radicale di un tempo fra le due concezioni non ha più molto senso, specie se esse restano fondate solo su rigidi presupposti teorici e astratti. Si devono invece esaminare i due diversi orientamenti come modelli metodologici di carattere generale, che esprimono delle linee generali di tendenza della realtà internazionale. In quest'ottica, si deve ammettere che tale realtà impone oggi di rivedere quantomeno certi aspetti della concezione dualista tradizionale, perché alcune delle differenze sopra indicate fra i due ordinamenti sono venute meno ed altre si stanno assai riducendo [71].

In primo luogo, è ormai venuta a cadere in gran parte la distinzione fra i due ordinamenti che si basava sulla diversità dei loro rispettivi contenuti. Come si è visto il diritto internazionale, che un tempo regolava solo la materia dei rapporti fra Stati, adesso regola anche, in larga misura, materie attinenti a rapporti individuali o fra Stati e individui: il diritto internazionale dei diritti umani ne è un esempio paradigmatico. In secondo luogo, è venuta a cadere anche la distinzione fra i due ordinamenti che si basava sulla diversità dei loro rispettivi destinatari formali. Oggi il diritto internazionale crea direttamente diritti ed obblighi anche per gli individui. In terzo luogo, anche sul piano delle norme, le differenze fra diritto internazionale e diritto interno si stanno sempre più riducendo. In quarto luogo, per quanto riguarda l'applicazione del diritto internazionale all'interno degli Stati, si può notare che convivono nella prassi degli Stati metodi di trasformazione o nazionalizzazione delle norme internazionali, ispirati ad un modello dualista, con metodi di ricezione diretta delle norme internazionali, ispirati ad un modello tendenzialmente monista. Anche i conflitti fra diritto internazionale e diritto interno vengono risolti, nella prassi degli Stati, talora con la prevalenza del diritto internazionale, in un'ottica più monista, e talora con quella del diritto interno, in una prospettiva dualista.

In conclusione, alcuni dati della realtà internazionale contemporanea si conformano più ad una visione dualista dei rapporti fra diritto internazionale e diritto interno, mentre altri dati si addicono più ad una visione monista. Altri dati, infine, hanno carattere ambivalente. Ciò conferma, come si era detto prima, che oggi non ha più molto senso voler interpretare i rapporti fra diritto internazionale e diritto interno secondo un modello rigidamente dualista oppure rigidamente monista.

D'altra parte, si possono concepire il dualismo ed il monismo non solo come due diver-

---

[71] Vedi Ferrari Bravo (2002), pp. 99-150; Pisillo Mazzeschi (1994a); Id. (2004a), pp. 33-36.

si modelli concettuali d'interpretazione dei rapporti fra diritto internazionale e diritto interno, ma anche e soprattutto come due diversi modelli politici di società internazionale, uno fondato sul *nazionalismo-pluralismo* e l'altro sull'*universalismo* [72]. In questo senso, si deve ammettere che la struttura dell'attuale società internazionale è tuttora formata essenzialmente da Stati e che il diritto internazionale è tuttora in larga misura incentrato sul principio della sovranità degli Stati; e che quindi esso non lascia per ora uno spazio ampio ad una comunità umana universale, che leghi gli individui al di là delle barriere nazionali.

Tuttavia, è anche vero che tale *comunità umana universale* è oggi presente sulla scena internazionale, sta assumendo un ruolo sempre più importante, e sta esercitando forti pressioni sulla comunità degli Stati, affinché il diritto internazionale si occupi sempre di più degli interessi dell'uomo e dell'umanità. Questa pressione della comunità umana, che si fonda in gran parte sulla *forza della teoria dei diritti umani*, ha prodotto, come si è visto, una vera e propria rivoluzione nel contenuto materiale del diritto internazionale e nei soggetti del diritto internazionale e sta producendo anche modifiche strutturali nella funzione e natura tipiche del diritto internazionale. Pertanto, in definitiva, se si guardano le linee di tendenza del diritto internazionale, si possono cogliere segni di superamento della sovranità assoluta dello Stato e della struttura della comunità internazionale fondata solo sulla uguaglianza sovrana degli Stati. Tuttavia, si deve ammettere che, recentemente, vi sono anche preoccupanti segni di natura opposta, fondati sulla rinascita del nazionalismo-pluralismo.

Infine, sul piano più giuridico dei rapporti fra diritto internazionale e diritto interno, si può constatare che il diritto internazionale invade sempre più i settori che erano riservati all'esperienza giuridica nazionale ed esercita una pressione via via crescente sulle realtà nazionali. In altri termini, si assiste oggi ad un'evoluzione verso una sempre maggiore comunicazione, armonizzazione ed integrazione fra ordinamento internazionale ed ordinamenti statali. Si tratta di un'evoluzione naturale poiché, nel mondo contemporaneo caratterizzato dalla interdipendenza e dalla globalizzazione, è "inconcepibile che il mondo giuridico possa rimanere distribuito in celle reciprocamente impermeabili" [73].

7.6. *Incidenza del diritto internazionale dei diritti umani sulle fonti e sugli obblighi internazionali (rinvio)*

Questi temi saranno trattati in seguito, nei capitoli II e III.

8. *Impatto dei diritti umani su settori specifici del diritto internazionale*

La teoria dei diritti umani, impiantata nel sistema del diritto internazionale, ha prodotto non solo dei cambiamenti di carattere generale ed anche strutturale su tale sistema, ma anche dei cambiamenti, più circoscritti, sulle fonti del diritto internazionale e su certi specifici settori di tale diritto. Rinviando per ora il discorso sulle fonti [74], vediamo adesso in sin-

[72] Qui si intende il termine "universalismo" in senso lato, riferito ad un modello politico di società internazionale. Quindi in senso diverso rispetto al principio di universalismo dei diritti umani esaminato *supra*, par. 4.

[73] Ferrari Bravo (2002), p. 149.

[74] Vedi *infra*, Cap. II.

tesi l'impatto che la teoria dei diritti umani ha esercitato sul contenuto delle norme di carattere sostanziale (o materiale) del diritto internazionale generale, non solo nei settori nei quali vengono più in evidenza gli interessi degli individui, ma anche in settori tradizionalmente riservati agli interessi interstatali [75]. Faremo solo alcuni esempi.

Il diritto internazionale umanitario ed il diritto internazionale penale sono le due aree che, essendo strettamente collegate ai diritti umani, sono state più influenzate da questi ultimi.

Le norme del diritto internazionale umanitario, sviluppatesi in un primo tempo nel quadro di una logica solo interstatale, hanno subìto cambiamenti notevoli a partire dalla seconda metà del XX secolo e vengono adesso lette non solo nella vecchia ottica interstatale, ma anche, e sempre di più, nella nuova ottica dei diritti umani e dei rapporti fra Stati ed individui. Inoltre, l'aspetto strettamente umanitario di tali norme prevale adesso su quello più strettamente bellico. In altri termini, si può dire che il diritto internazionale umanitario ha molto mitigato il suo carattere originale solo interstatale, in misura tale che oggi si tende a riconoscere che l'individuo può essere un destinatario diretto di alcune norme di tale diritto. Inoltre, si è realizzata con il tempo una confluenza fra il diritto internazionale umanitario ed il diritto internazionale dei diritti umani; e si è riconosciuto che alcuni diritti umani sono applicabili anche durante i conflitti armati. In particolare, viene in rilievo il diritto alla vita, protetto da tutti i principali trattati sui diritti umani, nei casi in cui sia arbitrariamente privato da un atto illecito secondo il diritto internazionale umanitario. Questo sviluppo consente agli individui vittime di violazioni di ricorrere agli organi internazionali di controllo sui diritti umani, che non sono invece previsti dal diritto internazionale umanitario.

Ancora più accentuata è stata l'influenza della teoria dei diritti umani sulle norme, di assai più recente formazione, del diritto internazionale penale [76]. Tali norme sono in gran parte fondate sulla logica dei diritti umani e appaiono come un vero e proprio percorso parallelo preso dal diritto internazionale contemporaneo, con lo scopo di rafforzare, tramite lo strumento della responsabilità penale individuale, la protezione dei diritti umani fondamentali in tempo di pace ed in tempo di conflitti armati [77].

Un altro settore normativo recente che ha subìto l'influenza della teoria dei diritti umani è costituito dal diritto internazionale dell'ambiente. Accanto alle norme di carattere interstatale, che si sono sviluppate per prime, si stanno adesso formando anche norme che attengono a rapporti fra Stati ed individui e che mirano a proteggere diritti individuali, che si configurano sostanzialmente come diritti umani; quali, ad es., il diritto dell'individuo ad un ambiente sano [78] ed il diritto di essere informato e di partecipare a certe decisioni statali suscettibili di avere impatto dannoso sull'ambiente. Inoltre, specie in relazione ad attività pericolose o ultra-pericolose, vi sono trattati internazionali che tendono a stabilire norme uniformi di diritto interno indirizzate soprattutto agli individui, come, ad es., le norme sulla responsabilità civile interna nel campo dell'energia nucleare, del trasporto marittimo di

---

[75] Vedi Kamminga, Scheinin (2009); Pisillo Mazzeschi (2008), pp. 208-212; Id. (2104b), pp. 99-100.

[76] Vedi *infra*, Cap. V, par. 9.

[77] Si pensi, ad es., al sistema di riparazione per le vittime dei crimini internazionali previsto dall'art. 75 dello Statuto di Roma istitutivo della Corte penale internazionale.

[78] Vedi *infra*, Cap. VI, par. 20.2.

materiale nucleare, dell'inquinamento da idrocarburi, del trasporto marittimo di sostanze pericolose e tossiche.

La teoria dei diritti umani ha esercitato un impatto anche su alcuni settori normativi assai più antichi del diritto internazionale. Ad esempio, le norme consuetudinarie sul trattamento degli stranieri sono state molto influenzate dalla teoria dei diritti umani, tanto che alcuni autori addirittura ritengono che le norme sul trattamento degli stranieri siano state assorbite da quelle sui diritti umani. Per parte nostra non condividiamo tale posizione estrema; ma dobbiamo riconoscere che varie norme consuetudinarie sul trattamento degli stranieri si sono molto modificate [79]. Ad esempio, le norme sull'ammissione e allontanamento degli stranieri [80] hanno subìto cambiamenti per effetto dei diritti dei rifugiati, del divieto di *refoulement* verso certi Stati, del divieto di estradizione per reati politici. Parimenti le norme sulla protezione degli stranieri e dei loro beni hanno subìto cambiamenti per effetto del divieto di discriminazione e del diritto ad un rimedio interno effettivo, che ha sostanzialmente assorbito il vecchio divieto di diniego di giustizia.

Anche le norme secondarie in tema di trattamento degli stranieri, in particolare quelle sulla protezione diplomatica, hanno subìto un processo di ammodernamento ispirato dall'idea della protezione di interessi individuali, se non dei diritti umani [81]. I segnali di cambiamento più significativi sono rappresentati da alcune recenti decisioni della Corte internazionale di giustizia e della Corte interamericana dei diritti umani [82], che riconoscono espressamente che le norme internazionali sul trattamento degli stranieri impongono allo Stato territoriale obblighi *internazionali* non solo verso lo Stato nazionale dello straniero ma *anche verso lo stesso individuo straniero*. Da ciò deriva logicamente la conseguenza che, nel caso di un individuo che abbia sofferto una lesione da parte di uno Stato estero per la violazione di una norma sul trattamento degli stranieri, sorge un rapporto di responsabilità internazionale non solo fra Stato autore dell'illecito e Stato nazionale dell'individuo, ma *anche fra Stato autore ed individuo*. È chiaro che questa conclusione è destinata ad influire anche sulle norme secondarie tradizionali in tema di protezione diplomatica, poiché essa conduce verso il nuovo concetto per cui lo Stato nazionale, nel ricorrere all'azione in protezione diplomatica, asserisce non solo il proprio diritto, ma *anche il diritto del proprio cittadino*. E pertanto anche il diritto alla riparazione appartiene sia allo Stato leso che all'individuo leso. Ciò può condurre a cambiare anche il regime giuridico che regola il rapporto fra l'individuo leso ed il proprio Stato nazionale, ed a sostenere che l'individuo ha, quantomeno in certe circostanze, nei confronti del proprio Stato nazionale, un diritto alla protezione diplomatica, o quantomeno un diritto ad un controllo giurisdizionale sulla ragionevolezza della decisione dello Stato circa l'esercizio o meno della protezione diplomatica; ed anche un diritto ad ottenere la riparazione, se il proprio Stato nazionale esercita con successo la protezione diplomatica. Alcuni di questi cambiamenti sono stati riconosciuti, sia pure a titolo di sviluppo progressivo del diritto internazionale, nel noto art. 19 del Progetto della CDI sulla protezione diplomatica approvato nel 2006 [83].

---

[79] Vedi Pisillo Mazzeschi (2011).

[80] Vedi *infra*, Cap.VI, parr. 13, 14 e 15.

[81] Cfr. Pisillo Mazzeschi (2009).

[82] ICJ, *LaGrand*; ICJ, *Avena*.

[83] ILC, *Draft Articles on Diplomatic Protection*, 8 August 2006, Art. 19 (*Recommended practice*): A State

Infine, come si era detto, l'impatto della teoria dei diritti umani si è avuto non solo nei settori del diritto internazionale di maggior interesse per gli individui, ma anche in quelli tradizionalmente dominati dagli interessi statali. Si pensi, ad esempio, al gruppo di norme consuetudinarie relativo alle immunità degli Stati ed alle immunità funzionali degli organi statali. Come è noto, vi è la tendenza del diritto contemporaneo a prevedere eccezioni a tali immunità nel caso di *gross violations* dei diritti umani [84]. Inoltre, a tutela dei diritti dei lavoratori, si può ricordare la tendenza, nella prassi internazionale più recente, ad escludere l'immunità giurisdizionale degli Stati esteri nelle controversie relative a rapporti di lavoro svoltisi nello Stato del foro. Anche varie norme del diritto internazionale dell'economia e dello sviluppo appaiono adesso influenzate dalla teoria dei diritti umani: si pensi, ad es., a come il diritto di autodeterminazione dei popoli, la Dichiarazione sul nuovo ordine economico internazionale con la sua Carta dei diritti e doveri economici degli Stati e la Dichiarazione sul diritto allo sviluppo abbiano inciso sulla disciplina tradizionale del diritto internazionale in materia di protezione di beni stranieri, di nazionalizzazioni e di investimenti all'estero e sul ruolo e la funzione delle istituzioni economiche internazionali. Infine, anche le norme sul diritto del mare e quelle sugli spazi comuni hanno sentito l'impatto dell'ideologia dei diritti umani, nonostante si tratti di aree normative piuttosto lontane dal campo degli interessi individuali: si pensi solo all'idea dei fondi marini e di certi spazi comuni come "patrimonio comune dell'umanità".

In conclusione, per quanto riguarda il contenuto delle norme internazionali materiali, non vi è forse alcun settore dell'ordinamento internazionale che sia sfuggito all'impatto della teoria dei diritti umani.

---

entitled to exercise diplomatic protection according to the present draft articles, should: a) Give due consideration to the possibility of exercising diplomatic protection, especially when a significant injury has occurred; b) Take into account, wherever feasible, the views of the injured person with regard to resort to diplomatic protection and the reparation to be sought; and c) Transfer to the injured person any compensation obtained for the injury from the responsible State subject to any reasonable deductions".

[84] Vedi *infra*, Cap. V, parr. 18.3.2 e 19.2.1.

Capitolo II
LE FONTI INTERNAZIONALI

1. *Il sistema delle fonti del diritto internazionale dei diritti umani*

Si è visto che il sistema internazionale di tutela dei diritti umani è composto da norme primarie e secondarie e che il diritto internazionale dei diritti umani è parte integrante e non autonoma dell'intero e unitario ordinamento internazionale. Pertanto è evidente che le fonti del diritto internazionale dei diritti umani sono le medesime fonti del diritto internazionale; e cioè la consuetudine, i principi generali del diritto internazionale [1], i principi generali di diritto riconosciuti dalle nazioni civili *in foro domestico*, i trattati e le fonti derivanti da trattati. Non è invece una fonte in senso proprio la *soft law*, che peraltro, come vedremo, ha un ruolo importante in materia di diritti umani.

Si deve subito premettere che, in materia di diritti umani internazionali, la fonte più importante è costituita dai trattati, specie da molti trattati multilaterali sia a carattere universale che regionale. Ma, in questo capitolo, seguiremo l'ordine tradizionale di gerarchia delle fonti, partendo dal diritto internazionale generale e proseguendo con il diritto internazionale convenzionale e quindi con le fonti previste da accordi.

2. *Elementi di "specialità" in tale sistema? Il ruolo di due principi-guida: universalità dei diritti umani e preminenza dell'individuo*

Il problema più interessante, a mio avviso, è se le fonti del diritto internazionale dei diritti umani presentino elementi di specialità o di peculiarità rispetto al normale funzionamento delle fonti del diritto internazionale. Ribadiamo che qui per "specialità" non si intende indicare un regime separato e autonomo, un regime "*self-contained*", di fonti; ma soltanto l'eventuale esistenza di alcune regole specifiche o particolari, che deroghino o integrino parzialmente le regole tradizionali sul funzionamento delle fonti del diritto internazionale, secondo la normale regola della *lex specialis*. In effetti, è il problema circa l'eventuale specialità delle fonti che giustifica un'indagine *ad hoc* nel presente libro, che altrimenti potrebbe limitarsi a rinviare alla parte sulle fonti contenuta in un manuale generale di diritto internazionale.

---

[1] Questa fonte è adesso ammessa dalla dottrina prevalente. Ma una parte di essa nega ancora l'esistenza di tali principi come fonte autonoma del diritto internazionale. Sul tema vedi, di recente, Pisillo Mazzeschi, Viviani (2018), pp. 113-161.

Esamineremo le fonti sopraindicate in quest'ottica. La nostra tesi, che cercheremo di dimostrare e che qui anticipiamo, è che in effetti le fonti del diritto internazionale dei diritti umani presentino alcuni caratteri speciali; e che ciò si possa spiegare per l'operare di *due principi-guida* generali che regolano tale settore normativo, e dei quali abbiamo già parlato: *a*) il principio di *preminenza dell'individuo* (o della persona umana); *b*) il principio di *universalità* dei diritti umani [2].

Come si è già detto, questi due principi sono espressione del fatto che le norme internazionali sui diritti umani hanno un *duplice scopo*: *a*) quello di proteggere gli *individui*, come principali destinatari delle norme medesime; *b*) quello di perseguire anche un interesse comunitario degli Stati, i quali hanno preso coscienza che la tutela dei diritti umani costituisce un valore centrale ed universale [3] nell'ordinamento internazionale contemporaneo.

Questo *duplice scopo* delle norme sui diritti umani (e quindi implicitamente l'esistenza dei due principi suddetti) viene evidenziato, in maniera esemplare, nel celebre parere del 1951 della Corte internazionale di giustizia sulle *Riserve alla Convenzione sul genocidio,* laddove la Corte afferma, a proposito di tale Convenzione:

> "The objects of such a convention must also be considered. The Convention was manifestly adopted for a purely humanitarian and civilizing purpose. It is indeed difficult to imagine a convention that might have this *dual character* to a greater degree, since its object on the one hand is to *safeguard the very existence of certain human groups* and on the other to confirm and endorse the most elementary principles of morality. In such a convention the contracting States do not have any interests of their own; they merely have, one and all, a *common interest*, namely the accomplishment of those high purposes which are the *raison d'être* of the convention" [4].

A mio avviso, le parole della Corte sul "duplice carattere" della Convenzione sul genocidio possono essere riferite, *mutatis mutandis*, a tutte le norme internazionali sui diritti umani [5], nelle quali convive la vocazione comunitaria/universalistica con quella di difesa della persona umana [6].

Ciò premesso, si tratta adesso di verificare se i due principi-guida suddetti abbiano prodotto anche un impatto sul sistema delle fonti del diritto internazionale dei diritti umani, tale da conferire alcuni caratteri di "specialità" a tale sistema rispetto a quello tradizionale dell'ordinamento internazionale.

---

[2] Vedi *supra*, Cap. I, par. 4.

[3] Ma vedi anche i limiti dell'universalismo: *supra*, Cap. I, par. 4.2.

[4] ICJ, *Reservations to the Convention on the Prevention and Punishment of the Crime of Genocide*, p. 23 (corsivi aggiunti).

[5] Sul punto vedi anche Russo (2012), p. 11.

[6] Vedi *supra*, Cap. I, par. 4.

Sezione I

DIRITTO INTERNAZIONALE GENERALE

Una parte della dottrina sostiene che nel settore della tutela internazionale dei diritti umani (ed anche in settori ad esso strettamente collegati quali il diritto internazionale penale ed il diritto internazionale umanitario) i processi di formazione (o quantomeno di rilevazione)[7] del diritto internazionale generale abbiano caratteri diversi e innovativi rispetto a quelli tradizionali. Peraltro, nel quadro di questo generale orientamento dottrinale, si possono distinguere varie tesi più specifiche, che riguardano: *a*) il diritto consuetudinario; *b*) i principi generali di diritto riconosciuti dalle nazioni civili *in foro domestico*; *c*) i principi generali del diritto internazionale; *d*) lo *ius cogens*. Esaminiamo separatamente queste quattro fonti.

3. *Diritto consuetudinario*

3.1. *Un concetto moderno di consuetudine in materia di diritti umani*

Come è noto, vi sono diverse concezioni in dottrina sul modo di formazione e rilevazione delle norme di diritto internazionale consuetudinario. Semplificando, si può distinguere fra una concezione "tradizionale" ed una "moderna"[8].

In sintesi, l'approccio tradizionale richiede due elementi costitutivi per la formazione di una norma consuetudinaria: la prassi degli Stati (c.d. *diuturnitas*) e il convincimento degli Stati che tale prassi sia giuridicamente obbligatoria (c.d. *opinio iuris*). Inoltre, un'ampia parte della dottrina che condivide questa concezione ritiene che, sia pure nel quadro del concetto dualista di consuetudine, si debba attribuire più importanza all'elemento *diuturnitas*, perché esso è più certo e stabile rispetto all'elemento *opinio iuris*[9]; e che la *diuturnitas* debba essere intesa in senso restrittivo come prassi "reale" (cioè comportamenti concreti degli Stati) e non come prassi "scritta o orale"[10].

Al contrario, l'approccio moderno tende a mettere in discussione il concetto dualista classico di consuetudine e/o il modo di interpretare la *diuturnitas*. Più in particolare, una buona parte della dottrina contemporanea, e specie quella specializzata nei diritti umani, sostiene che il metodo di formazione (o rilevazione) delle norme consuetudinarie, nei settori dei diritti umani, del diritto internazionale umanitario e del diritto internazionale pena-

---

[7] In realtà a noi sembra che, nel diritto internazionale generale, la linea di confine fra i procedimenti di rilevazione e quelli di formazione del diritto sia assai sottile. Conviene pertanto in questa sede parlare solo di metodi di formazione del diritto generale.

[8] Queste due concezioni sono state recentemente descritte dal Relatore Speciale Michael Wood nei lavori della CDI su "*Identification of Customary International Law*". Vedi Wood (2013), parr. 95-101 (con ampi riferimenti alla dottrina).

[9] Vedi Wood (2013), par. 96.

[10] Vedi, fra gli altri, Thirlway (1972), p. 58. Sul contrasto fra prassi "reale" ed "orale" vedi Simma (1993), pp. 213-223; Simma, Alston (1992), pp. 88-100; Simma, Paulus (1999), pp. 307-308 e 316.

le, sarebbe innovativo rispetto a quello tradizionale. La novità riguarderebbe due aspetti diversi, ma strettamente collegati.

In primo luogo, alcuni autori sostengono che vi è una tendenza ad estendere il concetto di *diuturnitas*, al fine di comprendere non solo la c.d. "prassi reale" degli Stati, costituita dai loro comportamenti concreti, ma anche la c.d. "prassi scritta e orale", composta da una serie di atti giuridici, nonché di affermazioni e dichiarazioni degli Stati, quali, ad esempio, dichiarazioni ufficiali da parte di organi statali, atti legislativi, decisioni di giudici interni e di organi esecutivi, istruzioni alle forze armate, commenti su progetti di trattati, memorie dinanzi a tribunali internazionali, risoluzioni e dichiarazioni nel quadro di organizzazioni internazionali [11]. Secondo alcuni, la prassi scritta e orale sarebbe addirittura divenuta più rilevante della prassi reale [12].

In secondo luogo, altri autori ritengono che, nel diritto internazionale contemporaneo, vi sia anche la tendenza ad attribuire un ruolo più importante all'elemento dell'*opinio iuris* e addirittura ad invertire la logica tradizionale nella rilevazione della consuetudine, secondo la quale l'accertamento della *diuturnitas* è preliminare e fondamentale, mentre l'accertamento dell'*opinio iuris* serve solo a confermare l'esistenza della consuetudine. Invece, secondo la dottrina in esame, l'accertamento dell'*opinio iuris* costituirebbe la fase più importante nel processo di rilevazione della consuetudine [13].

In realtà, i due aspetti sopraindicati possono essere considerati come complementari. Infatti la prassi scritta e orale degli Stati può avere una doppia funzione: quella di costituire una prova sia della *diuturnitas* che dell'*opinio iuris*. Pertanto, il risultato complessivo del nuovo metodo di formazione/rilevazione della consuetudine è quello di privilegiare l'*opinio iuris* rispetto alla *diuturnitas*.

A mio avviso, questo metodo moderno che, sia pure nel quadro della concezione dualista della consuetudine, favorisce la prassi "scritta e orale" e privilegia l'elemento dell'*opinio iuris*, deve essere approvato in linea generale. Ma soprattutto questo metodo è convincente nel settore dei diritti umani, inteso in senso ampio, come comprendente il diritto internazionale penale e il diritto internazionale umanitario [14].

Ciò è confermato dalla prassi internazionale. Infatti, a sostegno del nuovo metodo di formazione/rilevazione della consuetudine, si possono citare alcune importanti sentenze

---

[11] Vedi, ad es., Schachter (1991), pp. 335-342; Meron (2006), pp. 360-366; Pisillo Mazzeschi (2008), p. 205.

[12] Wouters, Ryngaert (2009), pp. 115-118 e 123.

[13] Vedi Abi-Saab (1985), pp. 3-4 e 13; Id. (1987), pp. 169-178; Id. (1988), pp. 729-738; Schachter (1991), pp. 338-342; Tomuschat (1999), pp. 333-334; Cassese (2000), pp. 213-215; Wouters, Ryngaert (2009), pp. 127-131.

[14] Tuttavia, si deve notare che la dottrina favorevole al nuovo metodo di rilevazione e/o formazione della consuetudine internazionale ha trovato una forte opposizione in un'altra parte della dottrina. Alcuni autori (v. ad es. Simma, Alston (1992) p. 104) hanno sostenuto che tale metodo, privilegiando la c.d. *paper practice* (cioè la prassi scritta e orale), rispetto alla prassi reale e concreta degli Stati, si concretizza in una "*strained, or even denaturated, 'new' theory of custom*" e finisce per trasformare il processo di formazione del diritto consuetudinario in un esercizio di retorica. Secondo questi studiosi, l'argomento più forte, che si oppone ad un uso assai ampio del diritto consuetudinario nel settore dei diritti umani, sarebbe costituito dalla chiara contraddizione tra la prassi reale e l'*opinio iuris* degli Stati. In realtà, ci sembra che questo argomento sia un po' circolare: poiché esso parte dalla premessa che l'unico elemento fondamentale della consuetudine sia la prassi reale e concreta, esso è indotto a concludere che, laddove tale elemento manchi, non vi può essere consuetudine.

internazionali. I precedenti più antichi sono costituiti da due sentenze dei tribunali militari di Norimberga [15]. In seguito, il nuovo metodo trova una conferma importante da parte della Corte internazionale di giustizia in un settore diverso del diritto internazionale. Infatti, nella sentenza del 1986 sul caso *Nicaragua*, in relazione alla norma consuetudinaria sul divieto dell'uso della forza armata, la Corte ha affermato che essa "must satisfy itself that the existence of the rule in the *opinio juris* of States is confirmed by practice" [16]; e quindi ha applicato un metodo di rilevazione del diritto consuetudinario nel quale l'accertamento dell'*opinio iuris* logicamente precede l'esame della *diuturnitas*. Ma l'esempio più significativo del nuovo metodo di rilevazione della consuetudine è rappresentato dalla notissima decisione della Camera d'Appello del Tribunale Penale Internazionale per la ex Iugoslavia nel caso *Tadić* [17]. Come è noto, il c.d. metodo *Tadić* è stato poi ripreso nello studio del Comitato Internazionale della Croce Rossa del 2005 sul diritto internazionale umanitario consuetudinario [18].

Conviene adesso chiederci perché la prassi internazionale favorevole al nuovo metodo di formazione della consuetudine si concentri specie su alcuni settori del diritto internazionale. A mio avviso, vi sono due motivi, che spiegano la preminenza dell'elemento *opinio iuris*. In primo luogo, nei settori della tutela dei diritti umani e del diritto internazionale penale, le norme di diritto consuetudinario sono caratterizzate da una forte *opinio iuris* della comunità internazionale (che emerge da dichiarazioni di Stati, da trattati multilaterali, da risoluzioni di organizzazioni internazionali, da altri atti di *soft law*, ecc.) e, al contrario, da una prassi "reale" e interstatale piuttosto scarsa o talora addirittura contraddittoria. L'esiguità di tale prassi dipende, in larga misura, dal fatto che in tali settori, che regolano soprattutto rapporti fra Stati e individui, le violazioni delle norme tendono a verificarsi all'interno di uno Stato; e pertanto gli altri Stati sono restii a reagire sul piano internazionale.

In secondo luogo, in questi settori del diritto internazionale vengono in rilievo anche gli *interessi comunitari* degli Stati ed i valori fondamentali della comunità internazionale; e l'*opinio iuris* ha il pregio di indicare con più evidenza e immediatezza, rispetto alla *diuturnitas*, la coscienza o il consenso collettivi della comunità internazionale nel suo insieme. E in questo aspetto si può notare l'incidenza del principio di *universalità* dei diritti umani sulla formazione del diritto consuetudinario.

Tuttavia, si deve ammettere che il nuovo metodo di formazione/rilevazione della consuetudine non è neutrale dal punto di vista dei valori e degli interessi, poiché, privilegiando l'*opinio iuris* rispetto alla *diuturnitas*, finisce per favorire l'accertamento del diritto consuetudinario e quindi per favorire la protezione dei diritti umani rispetto alla sovranità degli Stati. Si potrebbe aggiungere che, se l'interprete intende privilegiare lo sviluppo progressivo dei suddetti settori normativi, egli potrebbe e forse dovrebbe rivalutare, nel quadro dell'*opinio iuris seu necessitatis*, l'elemento più dinamico del senso di doverosità so-

---

[15] ITM, *The United States et al. v. Göring et al*, spec. pp. 218-224; US Military Tribunal Nuremberg, *The United States v. von Leeb et al.*, spec. pp. 485-491.

[16] ICJ, *Military and Paramilitary Activities*, parr. 184-188.

[17] ICTY, *Tadić*, 2 October 1995, par. 99.

[18] Henckaerts, Doswald-Beck (2005), vol. 1, pp. xxxii-xxxviii. Vedi anche Wouters, Ryngaert (2009), pp. 116-117.

ciale e di aspettativa di legittimità (*opinio necessitatis*), rispetto all'altro elemento più statico della convinzione di legalità (*opinio iuris* in senso stretto).

3.2. *Il ruolo dei trattati sui diritti umani nella formazione della consuetudine*

Nel discorso generale svolto nel precedente paragrafo, si inserisce il tema più particolare del ruolo che i trattati sui diritti umani (*rectius*, le singole norme di tali trattati) possono giocare nella formazione di norme consuetudinarie. Più precisamente, il problema è se la presenza costante ed uniforme, nei trattati sui diritti umani, di una norma di contenuto identico o simile su un determinato diritto (ad esempio, sul divieto di tortura) possa avere un impatto, e quale impatto, nella formazione di una norma consuetudinaria avente un analogo contenuto.

In realtà il tema dei rapporti fra trattati e consuetudine è molto complesso, ha dato vita ad un ampio dibattito dottrinale, e non può qui essere affrontato [19]. In estrema sintesi, si può solo dire che, di solito, esso si concentra sul problema del rapporto fra trattati di codificazione del diritto internazionale, predisposti sulla base dell'art. 13 della Carta delle NU, e consuetudine. L'opinione dominante, confortata dalla giurisprudenza internazionale, è che i trattati di codificazione del diritto internazionale possono dare un contributo al processo di formazione del diritto consuetudinario, poiché essi possono esprimere, sia pure in varia misura, l'*opinio iuris* e la *diuturnitas* degli Stati. Più in particolare, essi possono produrre tre effetti diversi sulla consuetudine: *a*) un effetto dichiarativo di una norma preesistente di diritto consuetudinario; *b*) un effetto "costitutivo" di una nuova regola consuetudinaria, e cioè il punto di partenza o una tappa intermedia del processo di formazione di tale regola; *c*) un effetto "cristallizzatore" di una regola consuetudinaria che era già in via di formazione [20]. Inoltre, all'interno del medesimo trattato di codificazione possono coesistere regole "dichiarative", "costitutive" e "cristallizzatrici".

In realtà, i trattati sui diritti umani non sono classificabili, a stretto rigore, fra i trattati di codificazione del diritto internazionale *ex* art. 13 della Carta delle NU. Tuttavia, essi, specie quando sono promossi dalle NU ed hanno carattere universale, condividono molti aspetti di tali trattati di codificazione. Infatti, il loro scopo è anche quello di contribuire a chiarire ed a sviluppare progressivamente il diritto internazionale dei diritti umani. Pertanto, si può ritenere che i trattati sui diritti umani, e le singole norme in essi contenute, possono produrre i suddetti tre effetti. Ma anche i trattati sui diritti umani esistenti nel quadro di sistemi regionali possono incidere sul diritto consuetudinario, sia perché anch'essi possono esprimere l'*opinio iuris* e la *diuturnitas* di un consistente gruppo regionale di Stati, sia perché essi esercitano influenza sui trattati universali, dal punto di vista applicativo ed interpretativo.

Questo processo di reciproca influenza fra trattati universali e regionali sui diritti umani viene molto accresciuto nei trattati che dispongono di organi internazionali di controllo, quali, ad esempio, i *Treaty Bodies* delle NU, la Corte europea, la Corte e Commissione in-

---

[19] Fra i contributi classici, vedi Baxter (1965-66): Id. (1970); D'Amato (1971), pp. 103-166; Thirlway (1972). Più di recente, cfr. Dinstein (2006); Crawford (2013), pp. 115-146.

[20] Vedi anche Pisillo Mazzeschi (1994b), spec. pp. 202-204.

teramericane, la Corte e la Commissione africane [21]. Infatti, la giurisprudenza e prassi applicativa dei trattati ad opera di tali organi di controllo dimostra chiaramente l'esistenza di questa reciproca influenza. Comunque tale prassi, pur non essendo configurabile come *diuturnitas* e *opinio iuris* degli Stati, è assai utile come indicazione autorevole per comprendere come norme convenzionali si riflettano in norme consuetudinarie.

Si consideri, inoltre, quanto abbiamo già detto, nel paragrafo precedente, circa il fatto che, nel settore dei diritti umani, la prassi "reale" e interstatale è esigua, perché gli Stati sono molto restii a reagire sul piano internazionale alle violazioni delle norme sui diritti umani, che tendono a verificarsi all'interno di un singolo Stato e solo raramente a colpire interessi diretti e materiali di altri Stati. La scarsità di prassi interstatale finisce inevitabilmente per far privilegiare, nella ricostruzione delle consuetudini, l'elemento dell'*opinio iuris* rispetto all'elemento della *diuturnitas*. E tale scarsità, al contempo, finisce per aumentare il ruolo della prassi applicativa dei trattati sui diritti umani da parte degli organi internazionali di controllo. Infine, si aggiunga il peso interpretativo dei *General Comments* dei *Treaty Bodies*.

In definitiva, non ci sembra azzardato sostenere che i trattati sui diritti umani (e le norme aventi contenuto costante ed uniforme in essi contenute), per le ragioni sopra indicate, producono un contributo importante alla formazione di regole consuetudinarie, contributo equiparabile a quello prodotto dai trattati di codificazione e sviluppo progressivo del diritto internazionale.

4. *Principi generali di diritto riconosciuti dalle nazioni civili* in foro domestico

Anche i principi generali di diritto riconosciuti dalle nazioni civili [22], intesi come principi che hanno origine e trovano applicazione uniforme nei diritti statali, possono avere un ruolo innovativo ed originale in materia di diritti umani.

Questa tesi è stata sostenuta da alcuni illustri studiosi. Conforti [23] ha sostenuto, fin dal 1976, che questa categoria di fonti del diritto internazionale può comprendere quei principi, universalmente presenti nei diritti interni, che mirano a salvaguardare la dignità umana, quali, ad esempio, i principi che vietano l'*apartheid*, la discriminazione razziale, la tortura, il massacro, il genocidio, la schiavitù ed altri metodi di governo disumani. Con questa tesi, l'illustre autore ha aperto un nuovo metodo per la rilevazione di alcuni diritti umani fondamentali dal diritto internazionale generale, senza bisogno di ricorrere al diritto consuetudinario classico e quindi anche all'elemento costituito da una consolidata *diuturnitas* a livello interstatale (la *diuturnitas* sarebbe invece costituita dalla loro uniforme applicazione nei diritti statali). In effetti, l'origine "interna" di *alcuni* diritti umani fondamentali appare più convincente rispetto ad una loro origine "internazionale": si pensi, ad esempio, al divieto di tortura che probabilmente si è affermato negli ordinamenti interni della grande maggioranza degli Stati prima ancora che a livello internazionale.

---

[21] Vedi *infra*, Cap. IV.

[22] Vedi l'art. 38, n. 1, lett. *c*, dello Statuto della Corte internazionale di giustizia.

[23] Conforti (1976), pp. 27-28: Id. (2018), pp. 49-52.

Una tesi simile, ma non identica, è stata sostenuta da Henkin[24]. Secondo questo autore, esistono norme di diritto internazionale generale sui diritti umani che non sono fondate sulla consuetudine o sulla prassi interstatale, né sul consenso degli Stati, ma che sono "costituzionali" nel senso che esse derivano dai diritti contenuti nelle costituzioni nazionali contemporanee. Anche Cassese[25], pur ritenendo che i principi generali di diritto di origine interna siano soltanto una fonte sussidiaria del diritto internazionale, sostiene che tale categoria è utile per disciplinare settori nuovi; e fa notare come i tribunali penali internazionali abbiano utilizzato frequentemente i principi generali di diritto penale riconosciuti dai principali sistemi giuridici interni.

Si deve rilevare che anche la tesi che utilizza i principi generali di diritto applicati *in foro domestico*, come metodo di rilevazione e/o formazione delle norme di diritto internazionale generale sui diritti umani, ha incontrato opposizione da parte di vari studiosi. Costoro ritengono che l'identificazione di tali principi si presti ad incertezze e ad interpretazioni soggettive, quando manchi una loro conferma nella prassi interstatale. A nostro avviso, tale critica investe, più che il metodo sopradescritto di utilizzo dei principi generali, la stessa validità di tale fonte del diritto internazionale. Infatti, se si richiede che i principi generali riconosciuti in *foro domestico* debbano trovare conferma in una prassi *interstatale* costante e consolidata, viene a cadere ogni differenza fra tali principi e le consuetudini: in sostanza, tali principi vengono concepiti solo come mezzi di prova del processo di formazione di *diuturnitas* e di *opinio iuris*. Quindi, si dovrebbe logicamente escludere che tali principi costituiscano una fonte autonoma del diritto internazionale. Ma la prassi e la giurisprudenza internazionale smentiscono questa tesi. Basti pensare, oltre alla già citata giurisprudenza dei tribunali penali internazionali, alla giurisprudenza dei tribunali amministrativi interni delle organizzazioni internazionali ed a quella della Corte di giustizia dell'UE in materia di diritti umani.

In conclusione, a noi sembra che, una volta cadute in gran parte le vecchie differenze di contenuto materiale fra diritto internazionale e diritti statali, i principi generali di diritto applicati *in foro domestico* si prestino ad essere utilizzati soprattutto nei settori del diritto internazionale che sono nuovi, che regolano materie interne e che contengono norme che creano direttamente *diritti ed obblighi per gli individui* ed altri *non-state actors*. In questi settori, tali principi, che non tengono conto della tradizionale *diuturnitas* interstatale, hanno notevoli potenzialità dinamiche nell'ordinamento internazionale. Ciò vale in modo particolare per il diritto internazionale dei diritti umani dove il *principio di preminenza dell'individuo* suggerisce all'interprete un uso ampio dei principi generali di diritto riconosciuti *in foro domestico*.

5. *Principi generali del diritto internazionale*

I principi generali del diritto internazionale, cioè i principi che non derivano dai sistemi giuridici statali ma che hanno origine direttamente nell'ordinamento internazionale, costi-

[24] Henkin (1995-96), pp. 31-45.

[25] Cassese (2013), pp. 293-295.

tuiscono da sempre un tema assai controverso nella dottrina internazionalistica. Gli autori più tradizionalisti negano l'esistenza di tali principi come fonti autonome [26]. Altri propongono una serie di tesi conservatrici che tendono a limitare gravemente il ruolo di tali principi. Fra queste ultime tesi [27], quella oggi prevalente è che tali principi derivino da norme consuetudinarie già esistenti, tramite un processo di induzione o astrazione o generalizzazione.

Tuttavia, la tesi oggi dominante è che la categoria dei principi generali del diritto internazionale debba essere ammessa fra le fonti autonome del diritto internazionale contemporaneo [28]. Ma restano da chiarire il fondamento, il metodo di rilevazione e le funzioni di tali principi [29].

A nostro parere, la tesi che i principi derivino per astrazione da norme consuetudinarie già esistenti può essere accolta; ma *soltanto riguardo ad alcuni* principi generali del diritto internazionale, che sono di solito i più antichi e quelli che operano nei settori più tradizionali del diritto internazionale. Si possono citare, ad esempio, i principi della sovranità territoriale, dell'uguaglianza formale fra Stati, dell'effettività, della libertà dei mari, della responsabilità degli Stati per illecito e della legittima difesa. Per rilevare questi principi, l'interprete ricava un principio vago e generale da norme consuetudinarie specifiche o da gruppi di tali norme. In sostanza, questi principi hanno la stessa natura delle norme consuetudinarie, ma un contenuto più generale ed indeterminato. Pertanto, la differenza fra questi principi e le norme consuetudinarie dalle quali essi sono "astratti" è relativa, perché i criteri della generalità e vaghezza sono anch'essi relativi.

Tuttavia, *in aggiunta* a tali principi, vi sono anche *altri principi*, che sono di solito i più recenti e che operano nei settori più nuovi del diritto internazionale [30]. Essi sono più interessanti perché hanno un *fondamento ed un metodo di rilevazione diverso*, che è stato messo in evidenza da alcuni studiosi autorevoli [31]. Ciò consiste nel fatto che questi principi non sono basati su norme consuetudinarie già esistenti, ma sulla circostanza che su di essi vi è un *riconoscimento e consenso generale* da parte della comunità internazionale. Inoltre, a nostro avviso, la comunità internazionale va qui intesa in senso lato; cioè non limitata agli Stati ed alle organizzazioni internazionali, ma comprendente anche altri "attori", quali organizzazioni non governative, individui, gruppi di individui, enti giuridici, associazioni e movimenti politici che rappresentano in vari modi la società civile. Si noti che tale *riconoscimento e consenso generale* non dipende dagli elementi classici della *diuturnitas* e del-

---

[26] Vedi, ad es., Scelle (1934), pp. 312-315; Kelsen (1966), pp. 440, 539-540; Tunkin (1974), pp. 190-203.

[27] Sulle varie tesi vedi, da ultimo, Pisillo Mazzeschi, Viviani (2018), pp. 123-137.

[28] Vedi, fra gli altri, Simma, Alston (1992), p. 102 ss.; Simma (1993), pp. 221-223 e 224-229; Charney (1993), pp. 537-538 e 543-550; Simma, Paulus (1999), pp. 306-308; Tomuschat (1999), pp. 335-340; Id. (2018), pp. 192-194; Dupuy (2002), pp. 186-187; Cannizzaro (2012), pp. 125-131; Cassese (2013), pp. 289-290. Vedi anche, sia pure con un'impostazione più prudente, Gaja (1986), p. 533 ss.; Id. (2012), parr. 18-20.

[29] Cfr. Pisillo Mazzeschi, Viviani (2018), pp. 134-137.

[30] *Ibidem*, pp. 142-155.

[31] Per la dottrina meno recente vedi Verdross (1968). Fra gli autori più recenti vedi, fra gli altri, Simma (1993), pp. 224-229; Simma, Alston (1992), pp. 102-106; Bassiouni (1990), pp. 768-769; Dupuy (2002), pp. 186-187; Tomuschat (1999), p. 356; Gaja (2012), parr. 18-20; Cançado Trindade, Separate Opinion, in ICJ, *Pulp Mills on the River Uruguay*, par. 39. Vedi anche, per una tesi simile, Charney (1993), pp. 543-551; Henkin (1995-96), pp. 37-39.

l'*opinio iuris* che caratterizzano le norme consuetudinarie; ma dal fatto che la comunità internazionale crede che questi principi esprimano valori giuridici internazionali condivisi, e talora perfino valori fondamentali e quindi inderogabili. Questa convinzione deriva in gran parte dal valore etico-giuridico di tali principi e si può desumere da molti elementi della prassi, anche orale, dei suddetti "attori" della comunità internazionale. Fra tali elementi, ha particolare importanza la formulazione espressa di tali principi in fori, organizzazioni o istituzioni internazionali, quali l'Assemblea Generale delle NU, il Consiglio dei diritti umani o gli organi assembleari di altre organizzazioni internazionali.

Alcuni di questi principi hanno carattere dispositivo, ad esempio il principio di risoluzione pacifica delle controversie, quello che vieta l'uso dannoso del territorio statale, quello che dichiara le risorse dei fondi oceanici come patrimonio comune dell'umanità. Altri principi (ai nostri fini più importanti) hanno carattere inderogabile (di *ius cogens*), ad esempio il principio che vieta la minaccia o l'uso della forza, quello di autodeterminazione dei popoli, i principi che vietano il genocidio, le violazioni gravi e sistematiche di diritti umani fondamentali (c.d. *gross violations*), e le *grave breaches* del diritto internazionale umanitario.

Come si vede, molti di questi principi aventi carattere inderogabile appartengono al settore dei diritti umani. E infatti, in dottrina, i principali fautori di questi principi ritengono che proprio su di essi si fondi gran parte del diritto internazionale generale in materia di diritti umani [32]. In effetti, ciò trova conferma in alcune importanti sentenze ed alcuni pareri consultivi della CIG, in materia di diritti umani e di diritto umanitario, che stabiliscono, in maniera più o meno esplicita, l'esistenza di questi principi. Si possono ricordare: il parere del 1975 sul caso *Western Sahara* (sul principio di autodeterminazione dei popoli) [33]; il parere del 1951 sulle *Riserve alla Convenzione sul genocidio* (sul principio che vieta il genocidio) [34]; le sentenze nei casi *Corfu Channel* [35], *Barcelona Traction* [36] e *US Diplomatic and Consular Staff in Tehran* [37] (sul principio che vieta le gravi violazioni di diritti umani fondamentali); la sentenza del 1986 nel caso *Nicaragua* [38] (sul principio che vieta le *grave breaches* del diritto umanitario) [39].

Si può notare che questi principi in materia di diritti umani hanno un contenuto assai ampio. Ma questo è un carattere distintivo di tutti i principi. Infatti conviene ribadire che i

[32] Cfr. Simma (1993), pp. 224-229; Simma, Alston (1992), pp. 102-106.

[33] ICJ, *Western Sahara*, p. 12.

[34] ICJ, *Reservations to the Convention on the Prevention and Punishment of the Crime of Genocide*, p. 15.

[35] ICJ, *Corfu Channel*, p. 22.

[36] ICJ, *Barcelona Traction*, p. 3.

[37] ICJ, *United States Diplomatic and Consular Staff*, p. 3.

[38] ICJ, *Military and Paramilitary Activities*, Judgment of 27 June 1986, parr. 219-221.

[39] Secondo alcuni autori (Simma (1993), pp. 225-226; Simma, Alston (1992), pp. 103-108), un ulteriore argomento in favore dei principi generali nel campo dei diritti umani deriverebbe dal concetto di *ius cogens*. Lo *ius cogens* non sarebbe costituito da norme consuetudinarie, bensì proprio da principi generali del diritto internazionale. E poiché i diritti umani fondamentali apparterrebbero quasi tutti allo *ius cogens*, per la loro rilevazione avrebbe importanza decisiva una "forte" *opinio iuris*, in presenza della quale la *diuturnitas* non sarebbe più necessaria, come elemento costitutivo del diritto internazionale generale. A mio avviso questa tesi non è totalmente condivisibile, poiché lo *ius cogens* comprende sia alcune norme consuetudinarie sia alcuni principi generali del diritto internazionale.

principi generali del diritto internazionale devono essere tenuti distinti dalle norme consuetudinarie, perché i primi caratterizzano l'intero ordinamento giuridico internazionale o, più spesso, un suo settore specifico, come nel caso dei diritti umani. Inoltre i principi, di solito ma non sempre, stanno al fondamento di un gruppo di altre norme più specifiche, hanno un grado più alto di generalità rispetto alle norme consuetudinarie, esprimono scopi e valori generali ed hanno un contenuto teleologico e flessibile invece di stabilire una condotta precisa e ben determinata [40].

Peraltro, i principi in questione (quelli fondati sul *riconoscimento generale*) esprimono spesso le tendenze evolutive del diritto internazionale o di certi suoi settori; e quindi possono influenzare la formazione di norme consuetudinarie, che abbiano carattere più preciso e specifico. In materia di diritti umani, ad esempio, il principio del divieto di *gross violations* dei diritti umani ha favorito la formazione di norme consuetudinarie più specifiche quali, ad esempio, i divieti di tortura, di schiavitù e di privazione arbitraria della vita. Parimenti, il principio generale di non discriminazione, alla base della Dichiarazione universale dei diritti dell'uomo, ha influenzato la formazione di norme più specifiche sui divieti di discriminazione razziale e di *apartheid*. Anche il principio di autodeterminazione dei popoli, sorto in origine, con la Carta delle NU, come principio generale, si è poi concretizzato in norme consuetudinarie, che lo hanno specificato in alcune aree [41].

In conclusione, si può ritenere che vi siano *due categorie di principi* generali del diritto internazionale, che, in linea di massima, si sono sviluppati in periodi storici diversi ed in modi diversi. Quando la comunità internazionale era poco numerosa e consisteva solo di Stati, i valori ed i principi generali che regolavano tale comunità dovevano affermarsi tramite le fonti formali, e sostanzialmente tramite il diritto consuetudinario tradizionale che era una garanzia di stabilità e certezza, specie in virtù del suo elemento della *diuturnitas* interstatale. Quindi tali principi derivavano da norme consuetudinarie già esistenti. Quando, invece, in tempi più recenti la comunità internazionale si è estesa anche ad altri "attori", i valori ed i principi generali di questa comunità si sono potuti esprimere anche al di fuori delle fonti formali e del diritto consuetudinario tradizionale, fondandosi invece sul *riconoscimento e consenso generale e diretto* da parte della base sociale del sistema giuridico, cioè da parte della comunità internazionale nel suo insieme. Si tratta di una categoria più moderna di principi.

In conclusione, si può dire che la teoria dei diritti umani internazionali ha avuto un ruolo importante nella creazione e sviluppo dei "nuovi" principi del diritto internazionale; e quindi, più in generale, nel modernizzare la fonte costituita dai principi generali del diritto internazionale e nel far crescere la sua importanza nell'ordinamento internazionale contemporaneo. In sintesi, tale teoria ha contribuito ad ampliare il sistema delle fonti del diritto internazionale generale. In questo senso, si può sostenere che vi è stato anche qui un impatto del principio-guida dell'*universalità* dei diritti umani e, sia pure in maniera minore, dell'altro principio-guida della *preminenza dell'individuo*.

---

[40] Sulla distinzione fra principi e norme, nella teoria generale del diritto, vedi Guastini (1993), pp. 76-79 e 447-461.

[41] Vedi *infra*, Cap. V, par. 24.

6. Ius cogens

Il tema dello *ius cogens* è già stato affrontato, nel Capitolo I, ma solo in relazione all'impatto che il concetto ha avuto sulla funzione e natura giuridica del diritto internazionale e sul regime della responsabilità degli Stati [42]. Si tratta ora, invece, di affrontare in maniera sintetica l'argomento dal punto di vista della sua incidenza sul sistema delle fonti, con particolare riguardo alle norme sui diritti umani.

Si deve preliminarmente chiarire che lo *ius cogens* non è, in senso stretto, una fonte autonoma del diritto internazionale; ma piuttosto un carattere speciale che assumono certe norme del diritto internazionale generale. Come si è già detto [43], le norme di *ius cogens* (o cogenti o imperative o perentorie) esprimono valori *fondamentali ed essenziali* dell'intera comunità internazionale. Esse sono una categoria piuttosto ristretta di norme consuetudinarie e (a mio avviso) anche di principi generali di diritto internazionale [44], che sono sorretti da una particolare *opinio iuris* (per le norme consuetudinarie) o da una particolare convinzione (per i principi) da parte della comunità internazionale. Quest'ultima deve essere convinta che certe condotte sono non solo giuridicamente vincolanti ma anche *inderogabili*. La *convinzione di inderogabilità* è il punto cruciale per poter affermare il carattere imperativo di una norma. Inoltre, conviene ricordare che le norme imperative contengono obblighi *erga omnes*; ma che la nozione di *ius cogens* è più restrittiva di quella di obblighi *erga omnes*.

Gli effetti delle norme cogenti sono molteplici [45]. In primo luogo, in base al loro significato originario stabilito dalla Convenzione di Vienna sul diritto dei trattati del 1969, le norme cogenti invalidano o estinguono i trattati che siano ad esse contrari [46]. In secondo luogo, le norme cogenti prevalgono, in caso di conflitto, sulle norme consuetudinarie dispositive e sui principi di diritto internazionale dispositivi. Ciò dipende dal fatto che le norme cogenti hanno una forza di resistenza speciale o (secondo la tesi preferibile) addirittura un rango superiore, che le pone al vertice delle fonti internazionali. Questo effetto delle norme cogenti è, ai nostri fini, particolarmente importante [47]. Inoltre, le norme cogenti hanno altri effetti interessanti, quali quello di invalidare fonti derivate da trattati, se sono ad esse contrarie; quello di impedire ad uno Stato di invocare una causa di giustificazione dell'illecito in relazione ad una condotta contraria ad una norma cogente; quello di impedire la validità di una situazione (ad esempio un regime di *apartheid*) frutto della violazione di una norma cogente. Infine, come si è già visto [48], la violazione di una norma cogente crea una responsabilità aggravata, che comporta particolari conseguenze sul piano delle reazioni degli altri Stati.

Tutti questi aspetti sono assai rilevanti in materia di diritti umani. Infatti, come si è in parte già detto, vi è un certo numero di principi e di norme consuetudinarie sui diritti uma-

---

[42] Vedi *supra*, Cap. I, parr. 7.3.2 e 7.4.2.

[43] Cfr. *supra*, Cap. I, par. 7.3.2.

[44] Cfr. Pisillo Mazzeschi, Viviani (2018), pp. 142-150.

[45] Sul punto vedi la sintetica, ma eccellente, descrizione di Ronzitti (2007).

[46] Vedi gli artt. 53 e 64 della Convenzione di Vienna.

[47] Vedi *infra*, Cap. V, parr. 18.3.2 e 19.2.1.

[48] Vedi *supra*, Cap. I, par. 7.4.2.

ni che ha il carattere di *ius cogens* [49]. Fra i principi generali di diritto internazionale, si possono citare l'autodeterminazione dei popoli [50], il divieto di *gross violations* dei diritti umani, il divieto di genocidio e di altri crimini internazionali [51]. Fra le norme consuetudinarie, si possono ricordare: i divieti di pratiche di tortura e di trattamenti o punizioni inumani [52]; di schiavitù e tratta degli schiavi [53]; di sistematica discriminazione razziale e di *apartheid* [54].

Pertanto, si può concludere che la teoria dei diritti umani internazionali ha contribuito in maniera assai importante anche all'affermazione e consolidamento del concetto di *ius cogens* nell'ordinamento internazionale. E su questo contributo hanno giocato un ruolo i principi-guida dell'*universalità dei diritti umani* e della *preminenza dell'individuo*.

7. *Conclusioni*

Dall'analisi fin qui svolta, sui metodi di formazione/rilevazione del diritto internazionale generale in materia di diritti umani, ci sembra si possano trarre alcune conclusioni, che avevamo in sintesi anticipato.

Una prima conclusione è che l'elemento della *diuturnitas* internazionale, specie intesa in senso classico come "prassi reale" interstatale, tende a indebolirsi a favore dell'elemento dell'*opinio iuris* (nel diritto consuetudinario) o del riconoscimento/consenso generalizzato e "immediato" della comunità internazionale (nei principi generali del diritto internazionale) o della prassi nazionale (nei principi generali di diritto riconosciuti *in foro domestico*). Questa tendenza, che cerca in vari modi di porre rimedio alla scarsità di *diuturnitas* interstatale in materia di diritti umani, favorisce la formazione e la rilevazione del diritto internazionale generale in tale settore. E pertanto essa è un effetto del principio-guida di *universalità dei diritti umani*. Il principio generale del rispetto della dignità umana e la sua valenza universale, sorretta dal riconoscimento generalizzato da parte della comunità internazionale nel suo insieme, hanno dato e danno una spinta propulsiva verso l'ampliamento della sfera di applicazione del diritto internazionale generale in materia di diritti umani. Come avevamo detto nel Capitolo I, l'universalismo si rafforza a spese del multiculturalismo.

Una seconda conclusione è che il ricorso più ampio all'*opinio iuris* ed al consenso "immediato" della comunità internazionale sono due fattori che si prestano non solo ad ampliare la sfera di applicazione del diritto internazionale generale in materia di diritti umani, ma anche a colmare le lacune delle norme più specifiche, ad interpretarle in senso dinamico, a adattarle ai singoli casi concreti ed a fornire maggiore completezza e coerenza sistematica all'intero settore normativo dei diritti umani. Anche queste tendenze rispondono al principio-guida di *universalità dei diritti umani*. In altri termini, il riconoscimento da parte della comunità internazionale nel suo insieme che la tutela dei diritti umani costitui-

---

[49] Vedi anche *infra*, Cap. V, par. 4.5.

[50] Vedi *infra*, Cap. V, par. 24.

[51] Vedi *infra*, Cap. V, par. 9.

[52] Vedi *infra*, Cap. V, par. 8.

[53] Vedi *infra*, Cap. V, par. 15.

[54] Vedi *infra*, Cap. V, par. 22.

sce un valore universale nell'ordinamento internazionale contemporaneo motiva l'interesse forte di tale comunità a favorire lo sviluppo progressivo di tale settore normativo, anche con strumenti diversi e complementari rispetto a quello dell'ampliamento del diritto internazionale generale.

Una terza conclusione è che le tendenze suddette finiscono per rafforzare anche il principio-guida di *preminenza dell'individuo*, e quindi dei diritti individuali su quelli statali. Infatti l'estensione del diritto internazionale generale in materia di diritti umani significa una parallela restrizione della sovranità degli Stati. Inoltre la preminenza dell'individuo è particolarmente evidente per quel nucleo di diritti umani che sono tutelati da norme di *ius cogens*, che sono sottratte al potere della "volontà contrattuale" degli Stati.

In conclusione, come si era già detto [55], le vecchie norme "stato-centriche" lasciano via via uno spazio anche alle nuove norme "umano-centriche", ed il diritto internazionale, tramite un processo di "umanizzazione", diventa un diritto non solo per gli Stati, ma anche per gli individui. Questo processo ha investito, in una certa misura, anche le fonti del diritto internazionale generale.

Sezione II
TRATTATI

8. *Possibili motivi per la "specialità" dei trattati sui diritti umani*

Anche in relazione ai trattati sui diritti umani, una buona parte della dottrina sostiene che si applichino regole *diverse e innovative* rispetto a quelle tradizionali del diritto dei trattati. In questo senso si dice che i trattati sui diritti umani sono "speciali" rispetto agli altri trattati [56]. Tale carattere "speciale" viene giustificato con opinioni o motivazioni diverse [57], talora alternative e talora cumulative: *a*) il carattere *erga omnes* (o non reciproco) degli obblighi assunti dagli Stati parti; *b*) il carattere "oggettivo" dei medesimi obblighi e la loro garanzia collettiva [58]; *c*) il carattere cogente delle norme convenzionali sui diritti umani; *d*) la tesi per cui i trattati sui diritti umani avrebbero una natura "costituzionale"; *e*) la tesi per cui i trattati sui diritti umani avrebbero come destinatari formali gli individui accanto agli Stati.

A nostro parere, come cercheremo di dimostrare, non è corretto parlare di "specialità" dei trattati sui diritti umani, nel senso che essi siano regolati da un regime speciale, diverso, separato ed autonomo, di diritto dei trattati; cioè da un regime *self-contained* [59]. Piuttosto si deve riconoscere che vi sono alcuni principi generali [60], che caratterizzano i trattati

---

[55] Vedi *supra*, Cap. I, par. 5.

[56] Vedi, ad es., Focarelli (2013), p. 101.

[57] Su queste varie opinioni vedi l'ottima analisi di Russo (2012), pp. 280-304.

[58] Per questa tesi cfr. Sudre (2006), pp. 58-60.

[59] Vedi *supra*, Cap. I, par. 6.

[60] Cfr. Sudre (2006), pp. 57 ss. e 189 ss.

sui diritti umani (ma non solo questi) rispetto ad altri trattati internazionali; e che essi possono dar luogo ad alcune regole speciali, che, sulla base del criterio della *lex specialis*, si limitano a integrare, e talora a derogare, le regole internazionali tradizionali sul diritto dei trattati. In sostanza, i trattati sui diritti umani possiedono alcuni *caratteri peculiari*.

La nostra tesi, che qui anticipiamo, è che tali caratteri peculiari derivino, anche in questo caso, dal principio di *preminenza dell'individuo* e, in misura minore, dal principio della *universalità dei diritti umani*. Si tratta adesso di approfondire il tema della "specialità" dei trattati sui diritti umani, esaminando, separatamente ed in maniera critica, le varie tesi che cercano di spiegare tale "specialità".

8.1. *Non reciprocità e obblighi* erga omnes partes

Secondo una prima opinione, la differenza fra i trattati sui diritti umani e gli altri trattati sarebbe costituita dalla *mancanza di reciprocità* degli obblighi assunti dagli Stati nei primi trattati. La tesi della assenza di reciprocità degli obblighi convenzionali sui diritti umani, che sembra evocare per alcuni aspetti la vecchia ed oramai obsoleta distinzione fra trattati-legge e trattati-contratto, è stata affermata varie volte nella giurisprudenza internazionale. Già la Corte internazionale di giustizia, nel suo parere del 1951 sulle *Riserve alla Convenzione sul genocidio*, aveva sostenuto una tesi simile, affermando che:

> "In such a convention the contracting States do not have any interests of their own; they merely have, one and all, a common interest, namely the accomplishment of those high purposes which are the *raison d'être* of the convention. Consequently, in a convention of this type, one cannot speak of individual advantages or disadvantages to States, or of the maintenance of a perfect contractual balance between rights and duties" [61].

In maniera ancora più netta si è espresso, dopo alcuni anni, il Comitato dei diritti umani, il quale, in relazione ai trattati sui diritti umani, ha affermato:

> "[...] such treaties, and the Covenant specifically, are not a web of inter-State exchanges of mutual obligations. [...] The principle of inter-State reciprocity has no place" [62].

L'idea della non-reciprocità degli obblighi convenzionali sui diritti umani è stata sostenuta anche dalla Corte interamericana dei diritti umani, laddove ha affermato:

> "The American Convention and the other human rights treaties [....] have a special character that sets them apart from other treaties. The latter govern mutual interests between and among the States parties [...]" [63].

Infine, anche la Commissione e la Corte europea dei diritti umani hanno affermato numerose volte l'idea della non-reciprocità degli obblighi convenzionali sui diritti umani, anche se esse (come vedremo) preferiscono usare il concetto, analogo ma non identico, del carattere "oggettivo" di tali obblighi.

Quanto alla dottrina, essa di solito concorda sul fatto che gli obblighi convenzionali sui

---

[61] ICJ, *Reservations to the Convention on the Prevention and Punishment of the Crime of Genocide*, p. 23.

[62] HRCtee, General Comment No. 24, 4 November 1994, par. 19.

[63] Vedi, ad es., IACtHR, *Ivcher Bronstein*, par. 42.

diritti umani siano, in linea di massima, caratterizzati da mancanza di reciprocità; ma alcuni autori rilevano giustamente che tali trattati, se escludono la reciprocità intesa come scambio di interessi e benefici tangibili fra gli Stati, non escludono invece la reciprocità intesa come impegno giuridico di diritti ed obblighi reciproci fra gli Stati parti [64]. In altri termini, si potrebbe dire che gli impegni convenzionali sui diritti umani superano e oltrepassano, ma non escludono, l'elemento della reciprocità. In questo senso è esemplare l'affermazione della Corte europea dei diritti umani, che, nel caso *Irlanda c. Regno Unito*, ha affermato:

> "unlike international treaties of the classic kind, the Convention comprises more than reciprocal engagements between contracting States. It creates, over and above a network of mutual, bilateral undertakings, objective obligations" [65].

In realtà, a nostro parere, la tesi della mancanza di reciprocità nei trattati sui diritti umani, pur con le sue imprecisioni terminologiche, equivale, nella sostanza, alla tesi, più utilizzata in dottrina che in giurisprudenza ma terminologicamente più precisa, secondo la quale tali trattati contengono obblighi *erga omnes partes*. Questa seconda tesi è più corretta, perché esprime meglio il fatto che, nei trattati sui diritti umani, in forza della solidarietà degli obblighi assunti, ogni Stato parte si obbliga nei confronti di tutti gli altri Stati parti ad eseguire i suoi obblighi e che, parallelamente, ogni Stato contraente ha un diritto all'esecuzione degli obblighi ad opera di tutti gli altri Stati contraenti [66]. Infine, il concetto di solidarietà degli obblighi esprime meglio anche l'idea che questi hanno la funzione di tutelare valori collettivi e di carattere pubblicistico [67].

Si può aggiungere che il concetto di obblighi *erga omnes partes* contiene due elementi, che, a prima vista, non appaiono evidenti nel concetto di obblighi non reciproci: *a*) lo scopo collettivo e solidale degli Stati parti che si obbligano a rispettare i *diritti degli individui* a prescindere dalla loro nazionalità; *b*) il fatto che la violazione di uno Stato parte *legittima* tutti gli altri Stati parti ad invocare la responsabilità del primo Stato; cioè il superamento del principio tradizionale del bilateralismo nella responsabilità interstatale. In realtà, come abbiamo già visto, l'elemento più importante degli obblighi *erga omnes partes* consiste proprio nell'estensione della legittimazione ad invocare la responsabilità dello Stato autore dell'illecito [68]. Tuttavia, questi due elementi, sebbene a prima vista non evidenti, sono impliciti anche nella tesi della non reciprocità degli obblighi convenzionali sui diritti umani.

In conclusione, il concetto di obblighi *erga omnes partes* è adatto, più che quello un po' ambiguo di non-reciprocità, a definire la natura particolare degli obblighi convenzionali sui diritti umani. Ma tale concetto non è sufficiente *da solo* per spiegare la differenza fra i trattati sui diritti umani e gli altri trattati. Infatti i trattati sui diritti umani non sono certamente i soli trattati che contengono obblighi *erga omnes partes*.

---

[64] Vedi Simma (1994), p. 369.

[65] ECtHR, *Ireland v. UK*, p. 90, par. 239.

[66] Simma (1994), p. 369.

[67] Vedi *supra*, Cap. I, par. 7.3.1.

[68] Vedi *supra*, Cap. I, par. 7.4.1.

8.2. *Tesi sul carattere "oggettivo" degli obblighi convenzionali sui diritti umani. Critica*

In base ad una seconda opinione, gli obblighi convenzionali sui diritti umani si caratterizzerebbero, rispetto ad altri obblighi convenzionali, per il fatto di avere un carattere "oggettivo" o, con una espressione analoga, per il fatto di stabilire un regime giuridico "oggettivo". Come si è detto sopra, questa terminologia viene usata soprattutto dagli organi di controllo della Convenzione europea dei diritti umani.

La Commissione e la Corte europea dei diritti umani hanno usato il concetto di "obblighi oggettivi" fin dalla celebre decisione del 1961 nel caso *Austria c. Italia*[69]. In alcuni passaggi importanti della decisione si legge:

> "[...] les Etats contractants n'ont pas voulu se concéder des droits et obligations réciproques utiles à la poursuite de leurs intérêts nationaux respectifs, mais réaliser les objectifs et idéaux du Conseil de l'Europe [...] et instaurer un ordre public communautaire [...]".
> "[...] les obligations souscrites par les Etats contractants [...] ont essentiellement un caractère objectif [...]".
> "[...] le caractère objectif desdites engagements apparaît également dans le mécanisme érigé dans la Convention pour en garantir le respect; [...] qu'un Etat contractant, lorsqu'il saisit la commission [...] ne doit donc pas être considéré comme agissant pour faire respecter ses droits propres, mais plutôt comme soumettant à la commission une question qui touche à l'ordre public de l'Europe".

In seguito, gli organi di Strasburgo hanno ribadito molte volte i medesimi concetti, affermando: *a*) che la Convenzione europea va oltre la tradizionale reciprocità degli obblighi convenzionali, poiché crea, oltre e sopra ad un fascio di impegni reciproci, obblighi oggettivi; *b*) che tali obblighi oggettivi beneficiano di un meccanismo di "garanzia collettiva", perché permette ad ogni Stato contraente di adire gli organi di controllo anche se la violazione ad opera di un altro Stato non crea un pregiudizio ad un proprio cittadino; *c*) che la Convenzione stabilisce "uno strumento costituzionale dell'ordine pubblico europeo"[70].

Anche la Corte interamericana dei diritti umani ha talora fatto ricorso alla nozione di "obblighi oggettivi":

> "The American Convention and the other human rights treaties are inspired by a set of higher common values [...] are endowed with specific supervisory mechanisms, are applied as a collective guarantee, embody essentially objective obligations, and have a special character that sets them apart from other treaties"[71].

In realtà, il concetto di "obblighi oggettivi" non è del tutto chiaro e spesso viene confuso con quelli, sopra esaminati, di "obblighi non-reciproci" o di "obblighi *erga omnes partes*". Ma, a nostro avviso, il concetto di "obblighi oggettivi" contiene, rispetto agli altri due concetti, un *quid pluris*, costituito da due elementi, che risultano piuttosto chiari specie dalla giurisprudenza degli organi della CEDU: *a*) lo scopo comune degli Stati parti di rea-

---

[69] ECmHR, *Austria v. Italy*, pp. 18-19.

[70] ECtHR, *Loizidou v. Turkey* (*preliminary objections*), Judgment of 23 March 1995, parr. 70 e 75; *Ireland v. UK*, par. 239.

[71] IACtHR, *Ivcher Bronstein*, par. 42.

lizzare, anziché i propri interessi nazionali, gli obiettivi e ideali del Consiglio d'Europa, e quindi un "ordine pubblico europeo"; *b*) l'esistenza di un meccanismo di garanzia collettiva, che è idoneo a realizzare tale scopo.

Questi due elementi sono presenti, *mutatis mutandis*, anche in altri sistemi convenzionali sui diritti umani, come, ad esempio, nel sistema interamericano, in quello africano, nel sistema dei *Treaty Bodies* delle NU; ma non in tutti i trattati sui diritti umani. Pertanto si può concludere che, mentre il carattere "*erga omnes partes*" degli obblighi convenzionali è presente, in linea di massima, in tutti i trattati sui diritti umani, il carattere "oggettivo" di tali obblighi è presente solo in alcuni sistemi convenzionali più progrediti; cioè in quei sistemi dove: *a*) lo scopo collettivo e solidaristico degli Stati parti del trattato di proteggere i diritti umani di tutti gli individui si accompagna anche allo scopo più ampio di realizzare gli obiettivi dell'organizzazione internazionale che unisce gli Stati; *b*) il meccanismo di garanzia collettiva non si limita alla possibilità di tutti gli Stati di reagire alla violazione ad opera di uno Stato con i mezzi tradizionali del diritto internazionale generale; ma si estende fino alla legittimazione di ogni Stato parte (e talora anche dell'individuo vittima) a far valere la violazione, dinanzi ad organi giurisdizionali o quasi-giurisdizionali di controllo, contro un altro Stato parte anche quando la violazione non colpisce un suo cittadino o un suo interesse specifico. In altri termini, negli "obblighi oggettivi" la garanzia collettiva stabilita per la loro osservanza è più "progredita" ed efficace, perché è istituzionalizzata.

Pertanto, si può concludere che il carattere "oggettivo" degli obblighi convenzionali sui diritti umani è adatto a definire la natura particolare di *alcuni* obblighi convenzionali sui diritti umani; ma *non* è idoneo a spiegare la "specialità" di *tutti* i trattati sui diritti umani.

8.3. *Tesi sul carattere cogente delle norme sui diritti umani. Critica*

Secondo una terza opinione, sostenuta in dottrina da qualche autore, i trattati sui diritti umani si caratterizzerebbero dagli altri trattati perché le norme sui diritti umani rappresenterebbero valori universali ed avrebbero per tale motivo carattere di *ius cogens* [72]. Ciò sarebbe confermato dal fatto che i trattati di natura più generale sui diritti umani prevedono espressamente che certi diritti siano inderogabili.

Tuttavia, a questa opinione si possono muovere varie obiezioni. In primo luogo, i trattati sopra indicati definiscono alcuni diritti umani come "inderogabili in stati di emergenza", ma questo concetto, come vedremo [73], non corrisponde a quello del carattere cogente (di *ius cogens*) dei diritti umani. In secondo luogo, tali trattati stabiliscono espressamente che *solo alcuni* dei diritti protetti sono "inderogabili in stati di emergenza".

In terzo luogo, come vedremo [74], si deve osservare, sulla base della prassi e della dottrina dominante, che soltanto le norme del diritto internazionale generale possono avere carattere di *ius cogens*; e che soltanto un nucleo ristretto di diritti umani è stato incorporato in norme di diritto internazionale generale. Per di più, non vi è neppure coincidenza fra i diritti umani incorporati nel diritto internazionale generale e quelli protetti dallo *ius co-*

---

[72] Vedi Mc Dougal (1980), p. 279; Suy (1983), p. 939; Mosler (1980), p. 19.

[73] Vedi *infra*, Cap. V, parr. 4.3 e 4.5.

[74] Vedi *infra*, Cap. V, parr. 4.4 e 4.5.

gens. Infine, come si è già visto [75], non si può neppure aderire alla tesi che vi sia una coincidenza fra le norme di *ius cogens* e le norme contenenti obblighi *erga omnes* (e tantomeno le norme convenzionali che contengono soltanto obblighi *erga omnes partes*).

In conclusione, la tesi sul carattere cogente di tutte le norme convenzionali sui diritti umani *non* può essere accolta.

8.4. *Tesi sulla natura "costituzionale" dei trattati sui diritti umani. Critica*

Secondo una quarta tesi dottrinale, piuttosto recente, il diritto internazionale dei diritti umani non sarebbe soltanto un settore del diritto internazionale, ma rappresenterebbe una dimensione costituzionale di tale diritto, come tale vincolante sugli Stati anche oltre la loro permanente volontà di essere vincolati. In questo senso i trattati sui diritti umani non sarebbero "normali" trattati fra Stati, ma costituirebbero una forma embrionale di una *costituzione globale*. In altri termini, le norme convenzionali sui diritti umani avrebbero assunto, nell'ordinamento internazionale contemporaneo, una funzione simile a quella svolta dalle norme costituzionali negli ordinamenti statali [76].

La natura "costituzionale" delle norme sui diritti umani si fonderebbe sul loro legame con valori morali fondamentali e sul fatto che gli individui sono destinatari principali di tali norme [77]; ma tale natura "costituzionale" non sarebbe coincidente con quella di *ius cogens*. Quest'ultimo concetto sarebbe più restrittivo e le norme sui diritti umani aventi carattere di *ius cogens* rappresenterebbero solo un esempio limitato ed estremo della natura costituzionale delle norme sui diritti umani, con l'effetto di conferire una supremazia formale delle norme di *ius cogens* sulle altre norme (natura costituzionale in senso formale). Invece, la natura costituzionale di tutte le norme sui diritti umani, qui in esame, avrebbe solo l'effetto di attribuire un carattere di specialità alle norme che regolano l'interpretazione e applicazione dei trattati sui diritti umani (natura costituzionale in senso sostanziale).

La tesi della natura "costituzionale" dei trattati sui diritti umani, a nostro avviso, non si fonda su elementi oggettivi della prassi e della giurisprudenza internazionale. Il richiamo, talora fatto, ad alcune sentenze della Corte europea dei diritti umani, nelle quali la Corte definisce la Convenzione europea come un "constitutional instrument of European public order" [78], può essere spiegato, come si è visto [79], nel quadro del concetto del "carattere oggettivo" degli obblighi sui diritti umani, che tuttavia riguarda *solo alcune* norme convenzionali sui diritti umani inserite in sistemi istituzionalizzati. E comunque tale richiamo non è sufficiente per dimostrare la presunta "natura costituzionale" di tutti i trattati sui diritti umani. Inoltre, come è stato rilevato anche da altri [80], è difficile affermare che le norme convenzionali sui diritti umani, le quali si fondano su una pluralità di sistemi normativi a livello universale e regionale [81], costituiscano "espressione di un potere intrinsecamente

---

[75] Vedi *supra*, Cap. I, par. 7.3.

[76] Vedi Scheinin (2009), pp. 29-31, e gli altri autori citati da Russo (2012), p. 295, nota 28.

[77] Scheinin (2009), p. 30.

[78] Vedi, ad es., ECtHR, *Banković*, par. 80.

[79] Vedi *supra*, par. 8.2.

[80] Russo (2012), p. 295.

[81] Vedi *infra*, Cap. IV.

costituente" e "diano vita ad un unico sistema di tutela dell'individuo". Pertanto la tesi sulla natura "costituzionale" dei trattati sui diritti umani *non* può essere accolta.

Ciononostante, questa tesi ha il pregio di cogliere alcuni aspetti importanti. In primo luogo, come si è già visto, il diritto internazionale dei diritti umani ha avuto un impatto notevole sul processo (sia pure parziale) di progressiva "pubblicizzazione" del diritto internazionale, tramite l'apertura alla tutela di interessi collettivi, solidaristici e comunitari [82]. Questo aspetto "pubblicistico" dei trattati sui diritti umani è rilevante; ma non ci sembra che esso possa essere equiparato addirittura ad una loro funzione di tipo "costituzionale" nell'ordinamento internazionale. In secondo luogo, condividiamo la tesi che i trattati sui diritti umani abbiano un legame con valori morali fondamentali; quantomeno nel senso che essi perseguono lo scopo di "universalizzare" la protezione della persona umana. Ciò significa, a nostro avviso, che il *principio di universalità dei diritti umani* riguarda anche i trattati, e non solo il diritto internazionale generale. Ed infatti, come vedremo meglio in seguito [83], il funzionamento di questo principio spiega alcuni effetti "speciali" dei trattati sui diritti umani, che tendono a favorire la loro continuità e la partecipazione più ampia possibile degli Stati a tali trattati. In terzo luogo, come vedremo subito, condividiamo un altro aspetto della tesi in esame; cioè l'opinione che gli individui siano i destinatari principali dei trattati sui diritti umani.

Tuttavia, come si è detto, nonostante questi aspetti condivisibili, la tesi in oggetto *non* è convincente.

8.5. *Individui come destinatari dei trattati sui diritti umani*

Infine vi è una quinta tesi dottrinale, che serve a spiegare la differenza fra i trattati sui diritti umani e gli altri trattati. Essa sostiene che i trattati sui diritti umani hanno come destinatari principali (o comunque come destinatari accanto agli Stati) gli individui. Questa tesi parte dal presupposto generale che gli individui siano, nella realtà dell'ordinamento internazionale contemporaneo, soggetti o, se si preferisce, *destinatari formali* del diritto internazionale [84]. Ne deriva che i trattati sui diritti umani impongono obblighi agli Stati cui corrispondono sia diritti di altri Stati sia diritti di individui. In altri termini, questi trattati hanno carattere "binario", creando due categorie di destinatari attivi o, se si vuole, due categorie di rapporti giuridici: quello che vincola gli Stati contraenti fra loro (secondo lo schema degli obblighi *erga omnes partes*) e quello che vincola ogni Stato contraente agli individui destinatari della tutela.

Ciò significa che gli Stati parti, dopo avere ratificato i trattati sui diritti umani, subiscono dei limiti al proprio potere di azione in virtù dei diritti conferiti agli individui. In altri termini, il riconoscimento di diritti individuali, conferiti direttamente a livello internazionale dai trattati sui diritti umani, finisce per creare un *regime giuridico di protezione degli individui* che tendenzialmente non può essere modificato unilateralmente dalla volontà degli Stati parti.

---

[82] Vedi *supra*, Cap. I, par. 7.3.

[83] Vedi *infra*, parr. 9 e 10.

[84] Vedi *supra*, Cap. I, par. 7.2 e *infra*, Cap. III, par. 3.2.

A nostro avviso, è questa la tesi più convincente e più decisiva, per spiegare *certi caratteri particolari* dei trattati sui diritti umani rispetto ai trattati internazionali tradizionali, che stabiliscono soltanto obblighi fra Stati o fra organizzazioni internazionali (o fra Stati e organizzazioni internazionali). La presenza degli individui come destinatari diretti e formali delle norme convenzionali sui diritti umani spiega e giustifica, come vedremo, l'esistenza ed il funzionamento di una serie di regole particolari, che derogano o integrano parzialmente le regole tradizionali del diritto dei trattati, con lo scopo di favorire la massima tutela degli individui. Questa tutela dei diritti individuali si concretizza, in pratica, in un regime giuridico che, da una parte, favorisce la stabilità, o quantomeno, la continuità dei trattati sui diritti umani [85] e, dall'altra parte, favorisce un'interpretazione favorevole ai diritti individuali piuttosto che ai diritti statali [86].

In definitiva, questa tesi, che si fonda soprattutto sul fatto che i trattati sui diritti umani creano un regime giuridico di protezione degli individui, è quella che valorizza maggiormente il principio-guida di *preminenza dell'individuo*. Essa trova varie conferme nella giurisprudenza e prassi degli organi internazionali di controllo. Il Comitato dei diritti umani, ad esempio, ha dichiarato che:

> "The rights enshrined in the Covenant belong to the people living in the territory of the State party. The Human Rights Committee has consistently taken the view, as evidenced by its long-standing practice, that once the people are accorded the protection of the rights under the Covenant, such protection devolves with territory and continues to belong to them [...]" [87].

In conclusione, a nostro avviso, la tesi basata sugli individui come destinatari principali dei trattati sui diritti umani è la più adatta, insieme a quella del carattere *omnes partes* degli obblighi, a definire la natura particolare degli obblighi convenzionali sui diritti umani. Ma anche tale tesi (come quella sugli obblighi *erga omnes partes*) non è sufficiente *da sola* per spiegare la "specialità" dei trattati sui diritti umani rispetto agli altri trattati. Infatti i trattati sui diritti umani sono l'esempio principale, ma non l'unico, di trattati che hanno per destinatari formali gli individui.

8.6. *Conclusioni provvisorie: impatto dei principi di preminenza dell'individuo e di universalità dei diritti umani*

L'esame, fin qui condotto, delle varie tesi sulle quali si cerca di fondare la c.d. "specialità" dei trattati sui diritti umani, ci ha portato ad alcune conclusioni provvisorie, che andranno verificate nei paragrafi seguenti.

La prima conclusione è che i trattati sui diritti umani possiedono sempre due caratteristiche importanti: *a*) hanno come destinatari diretti e formali anche (e a mio avviso princi-

---

[85] Tramite regole particolari in materia di riserve, successione nei trattati, cause di estinzione e recesso. V. *infra*, par. 9.

[86] Tramite regole particolari in materia di interpretazione dinamica, di nozioni giuridiche autonome, di obblighi positivi, di effetti "orizzontali" dei diritti umani. V. *infra*, par. 10.

[87] HRCtee, General Comment No. 26, 8 December 1997, par. 3. Il Comitato sembra fondarsi anche su principi quali la buona fede o il riconoscimento di diritti acquisiti o il legame territoriale che si viene a creare fra i trattati sui diritti umani e gli individui. Sulla analogia fra il regime dei diritti quesiti e quello dei trattati sui diritti umani v. Mullerson (1993).

palmente) gli individui; *b*) stabiliscono (nelle loro disposizioni sostanziali) obblighi *erga omnes partes*. Si tratta di caratteristiche che li distinguono dai trattati tradizionali; ma che non appartengono esclusivamente ai trattati sui diritti umani. Inoltre, *alcuni* importanti trattati sui diritti umani, che si inseriscono nel quadro di un'organizzazione internazionale e degli scopi di questa e che dispongono di un meccanismo di garanzia collettiva giurisdizionale o quasi-giurisdizionale, possono essere definiti anche come trattati che creano un regime giuridico "oggettivo"; cioè un *quid pluris* rispetto agli altri trattati sui diritti umani. Non riteniamo che si possa andare oltre questa conclusione; cioè che si possa aderire alle tesi secondo cui tutti i trattati sui diritti umani avrebbero carattere cogente o avrebbero natura "costituzionale".

La seconda conclusione è che anche le norme convenzionali sui diritti umani, come le norme di diritto internazionale generale, sono ispirate, influenzate, e forse addirittura indirizzate, dai due principi-guida generali di cui abbiamo già parlato: *a*) il principio della *preminenza dell'individuo* (che si esprime soprattutto nel fatto che gli individui sono i destinatari attivi principali dei diritti umani); e *b*) il principio dell'*universalità dei diritti umani* (che si esprime soprattutto negli obblighi *erga omnes* e nei regimi giuridici "oggettivi"). Peraltro si deve notare che nel caso delle norme convenzionali sui diritti umani, rispetto alle norme di diritto internazionale generale, si ha un'inversione di importanza dei due principi: quello di preminenza dell'individuo è più rilevante. Ciò è logico, poiché il principio di universalità può giocare solo un ruolo limitato nel diritto internazionale pattizio (con la parziale riserva dei trattati sui diritti umani promossi dalle NU [88]).

Si tratta adesso di vedere se e come questi due principi generali e queste due caratteristiche dei trattati sui diritti umani diano luogo ad alcune regole *particolari*, che integrino o deroghino le regole tradizionali del diritto dei trattati. Cioè, quali siano gli *effetti* concreti dei due principi. Anticipando qui le conclusioni principali, si può dire che gli effetti principali dei due principi sono i seguenti.

In primo luogo, il principio di prevalenza dei diritti individuali tende a creare un regime giuridico di protezione degli individui, che favorisce la *stabilità* e la *continuità* dei trattati sui diritti umani. Questo effetto di stabilità/continuità è rafforzato dal principio del valore universale dei diritti umani, che tende a incoraggiare la più ampia partecipazione possibile da parte degli Stati ai trattati sui diritti umani. In secondo luogo, i due principi producono effetti sulla *interpretazione* dei trattati, nel senso di favorire la maggiore tutela possibile per i diritti individuali, ampliare la loro sfera di applicazione e rafforzare la loro effettività.

Esaminiamo adesso, in maniera più approfondita, questi effetti. Vedremo prima quelli relativi al regime di stabilità e continuità dei trattati sui diritti umani, e poi quelli relativi al regime dell'interpretazione di tali trattati.

9. *Effetti dei due principi sul regime di stabilità e continuità dei trattati*

Da un esame complessivo della prassi applicativa dei trattati sui diritti umani, si ricava l'esistenza di alcune *regole particolari*, che hanno introdotto innovazioni rispetto al

[88] Vedi *infra*, Cap. IV, par. 5.

regime consuetudinario tradizionale del diritto dei trattati, nel senso di incidere sulla stabilità e continuità dei medesimi e sull'ampiezza degli Stati contraenti. Queste regole particolari riguardano: *a*) le riserve; *b*) la successione nei trattati; *c*) le cause di estinzione dei trattati.

9.1. *Riserve*

Un primo esempio di prassi innovativa, rispetto al regime tradizionale del diritto dei trattati, si ha in materia di riserve nei trattati sui diritti umani [89]. Il regime tradizionale sulle riserve, come è noto, si fonda sul parere del 1951 della Corte internazionale di giustizia relativo alla Convenzione delle NU contro il genocidio [90] e sugli artt. 19-23 della Convenzione di Vienna del 1969 sul diritto dei trattati. In estrema sintesi, tale regime prevede che uno Stato può formulare una riserva purché non sia espressamente proibita o implicitamente esclusa dal trattato e purché non sia incompatibile con l'oggetto e lo scopo del trattato [91]. Inoltre la riserva, quando non è autorizzata dal trattato, può essere contestata da un altro Stato contraente, manifestando un'intenzione nettamente contraria [92]; in tale caso lo Stato obiettante può ritenere che il trattato non entri in vigore nei suoi rapporti con lo Stato autore della riserva. La Convenzione di Vienna prevede poi altre norme di dettaglio, che tuttavia non sono ritenute come codificative del diritto internazionale consuetudinario.

Rispetto a questo regime consuetudinario tradizionale, la prassi degli organi internazionali di controllo dei trattati sui diritti umani ha apportato almeno due importanti novità.

In primo luogo, nel regime tradizionale non era chiaro quale criterio prevalesse fra quello, soggettivo, delle obiezioni e delle accettazioni delle riserve da parte degli Stati contraenti, e quello, oggettivo, della contrarietà della riserva allo scopo e oggetto del trattato; né chi potesse decidere sulla sussistenza o meno del criterio oggettivo. La Corte interamericana dei diritti umani, la Commissione e la Corte europea dei diritti umani ed anche il Comitato dei diritti umani hanno rivendicato il proprio potere autonomo di decidere sulla validità o meno delle riserve nei trattati sui diritti umani [93]. Gli organi di Strasburgo hanno fatto derivare la propria competenza a decidere sulla validità delle riserve "dal sistema stesso della Convenzione europea" e dal carattere "oggettivo" degli obblighi in essa contenuti. Il Comitato dei diritti umani ha preso una posizione ancora più radicale, affermando che:

> "it necessarily falls to the Committee to determine whether a specific reservation is compatible with the object and purpose of the Covenant. […] Because of the special character of a human rights treaty, the compatibility of a reservation with the object and purpose of the Covenant must be established objectively, by reference to legal principles, and the Committee is particularly well placed to perform this task" [94].

---

[89] Sul tema vedi, fra gli altri, Sudre (2006), pp. 65-75; Boerefijn (2009); Russo (2012), pp. 1-70.

[90] ICJ, *Reservations to the Convention on the Prevention and Punishment of the Crime of Genocide.*

[91] Art. 19 Convenzione di Vienna.

[92] Art. 20(4)(b) Convenzione di Vienna.

[93] Vedi Conforti (2018), pp. 109-110 e la prassi ivi citata. V. anche Russo (2012), pp. 42-64.

[94] HRCtee, General Comment No. 24, 4 November 1994, par. 18.

In secondo luogo, un'altra novità, ancora più importante, rispetto al regime tradizionale, riguarda le conseguenze della accertata invalidità di una riserva. Gli organi internazionali di controllo dei trattati sui diritti umani, specie per impulso della Corte di Strasburgo [95] e del Comitato dei diritti umani [96], hanno affermato che, una volta dichiarata una riserva invalida, specie per la sua contrarietà all'oggetto e scopo del trattato, l'invalidità non produce l'estraneità dello Stato autore della riserva rispetto al trattato, ma l'invalidità della sola riserva, che dovrà essere considerata come mai apposta. È chiaro che questa soluzione è fortemente innovativa, se non addirittura in conflitto, rispetto al regime tradizionale delle riserve, e che essa limita assai il principio consensualistico tipico del diritto internazionale convenzionale [97].

Come viene giustificata questa soluzione innovativa? La Corte di Strasburgo sembra giustificare la sua posizione sia sulla base di una volontà implicita dello Stato autore della riserva di partecipare comunque alla CEDU, sia sulla base dell'obiettivo di evitare che la tutela prevista dalla CEDU sia sottoposta a limiti che impediscano di conseguire il suo scopo ed oggetto. Una posizione simile ha preso la Corte interamericana dei diritti umani, che fa riferimento all'esigenza di tutelare un "set of higher common values [...] endowed with specific supervisory mechanisms, (that) are applied as a collective guarantee" [98]. Il Comitato dei diritti umani ha assunto una posizione più radicale, poiché ritiene che la regola della eliminazione delle riserve dichiarate invalide sia automaticamente applicabile, senza bisogno di tener conto della implicita volontà dello Stato autore della riserva [99].

A nostro parere, la prassi innovativa qui in esame è influenzata sia dal principio dell'*universalità* dei diritti umani che dal principio di *preminenza dell'individuo*. Infatti, sotto il primo profilo, essa tende a favorire la più ampia partecipazione possibile degli Stati ai trattati sui diritti umani, ponendo limiti al principio consensualistico; mentre, sotto il secondo profilo, essa tende a privilegiare l'interesse degli individui ad usufruire di tutti i diritti garantiti dal trattato rispetto all'interesse degli Stati ad apporre riserve su taluni di tali diritti.

9.2. *Successione nei trattati*

Un secondo esempio di prassi innovativa, rispetto al regime consuetudinario tradizionale del diritto dei trattati, si ha in materia di successione degli Stati nei trattati sui diritti umani [100]. Il regime tradizionale prevede che, per i trattati non localizzabili, si applichi la c.d. regola della *tabula rasa*; cioè che lo Stato "successore" non sia, in linea di principio e salvo alcune specifiche eccezioni, vincolato dai trattati conclusi dallo Stato predecessore.

Rispetto a questo regime tradizionale, la prassi degli organi internazionali di controllo

---

[95] ECtHR, *Belilos*, par. 60; ECtHR, *Weber*, parr. 38-40; ECtHR, *Loizidou (preliminary objections)*, Judgment of 23 March 1995, parr. 90-98.

[96] HRCtee, General Comment No. 24, 4 November 1994; HRCtee, *Kennedy v. Trinidad and Tobago*, par. 6. Vedi anche la prassi citata da Russo (2012), pp. 53-60.

[97] Conforti (2018), p. 110.

[98] IACtHR, *Hilaire v. Trinidad and Tobago (preliminary exceptions)*, parr. 93-94.

[99] HRCtee, General Comment No. 24, 4 November 1994, par. 19. Vedi anche Russo (2012), pp. 56 e 60.

[100] Sul tema vedi, fra gli altri, Sudre (2006), p. 77; Kamminga (2009); Russo (2012), pp. 167-276.

dei trattati sui diritti umani ha apportato una novità, perché essa mostra una chiara tendenza favorevole alla continuità (ovvero alla successione automatica) dei trattati multilaterali sui diritti umani. In questo senso si è pronunciata per prima, sia pure in maniera non netta, la Commissione per i diritti umani, con tre risoluzioni adottate negli anni '90 del secolo scorso [101], con le quali esortava gli Stati di nuova formazione a garantire, nel minor tempo possibile dalla loro indipendenza, la successione nei trattati sui diritti umani, intesa come continuità negli obblighi convenzionali. In una di queste risoluzioni, la Commissione:

> "Reiterates its call to successor States which have not yet done so to confirm to appropriate depositaries that they *continue to be bound* by obligations under international human rights treaties" [102].

Il Comitato dei diritti umani ha adottato in maniera decisa la medesima posizione ed ha affermato più volte, in relazione a casi specifici, che la continuità per gli Stati "successori" negli obblighi assunti dallo Stato predecessore con il Patto sui diritti civili e politici è automatica, perché è legata al diritto degli individui che si trovano sul territorio di tale Stato di conservare la tutela dei diritti umani riconosciuta nel Patto medesimo [103]. Tale posizione è stata poi ribadita, in termini più generali, nel Commento Generale n. 26:

> "[...] once the people are accorded the protection of the rights under the Covenant, such protection devolves with the territory and continues to belong to them, notwithstanding change in government of the State party, including dismemberment in more than one State or State succession or any subsequent action of the State party designed to divest them of the rights guaranteed by the Covenant" [104].

In seguito il Comitato ha mantenuto la medesima posizione. Una simile prassi è stata seguita dal Comitato sull'eliminazione della discriminazione razziale [105]. Anche la Corte europea dei diritti umani ha adottato implicitamente la medesima posizione con riferimento alla successione di Stati nella Convenzione europea, attribuendo alla Repubblica Ceca o alla Slovacchia alcune violazioni della Convenzione compiute dalla Cecoslovacchia come Stato predecessore [106].

Infine, la questione della successione degli Stati nei trattati sui diritti umani è stata dibattuta dinanzi alla Corte internazionale di giustizia nel corso di una controversia sulla *Applicazione della Convenzione sul genocidio* [107]. La Bosnia-Erzegovina sosteneva l'esistenza della regola della successione automatica nei trattati sui diritti umani; mentre la Repubblica federale iugoslava negava l'operatività di tale regola. La Corte non ha preso posi-

---

[101] Vedi le risoluzioni del 5 marzo 1993, del 25 febbraio 1994 e del 24 febbraio 1995, citate da Russo (2012), p. 253.

[102] CmHR, Resolution No. 18 of 24 February 1995 (corsivo aggiunto).

[103] Vedi la prassi del Comitato citata da Russo (2012), pp. 254-259.

[104] HRCtee, General Comment No. 26, 8 December 1997, par. 4.

[105] CteeAT, General Recommendation No. 12, 20 March 1993. Vedi anche la prassi citata da Russo (2012), pp. 259-60.

[106] ECtHR, *Matter v. Slovakia*, par. 52; *Chovancik v. Slovakia*, par. 18; *Konečný v. Czech Republic*, par. 62.

[107] ICJ, *Application of the Convention on the Prevention and Punishment of the Crime of Genocide*, Judgment of 11 July 1996, p. 595.

zione su questa questione, che tuttavia è stata affrontata nelle opinioni separate di alcuni giudici, i quali si sono dichiarati favorevoli alla applicazione della regola della successione automatica nei trattati sui diritti umani [108].

In conclusione, la regola innovativa, in tema di successione degli Stati nei trattati, che prevede una continuità per gli Stati "successori" negli obblighi convenzionali sui diritti umani assunti dagli Stati predecessori, sembra ormai affermata nella prassi. La giustificazione di tale regola riposa soprattutto sulla tesi per cui gli individui sono i destinatari principali dei trattati sui diritti umani e pertanto hanno diritto alla continuità della tutela, indipendentemente dal consenso degli Stati. A livello più generale, ci sembra chiaro che questa regola sia influenzata dal principio-guida della *preminenza dell'individuo* nei trattati sui diritti umani. Anche il principio dell'*universalità* dei diritti umani giuoca un ruolo, poiché la regola della successione automatica favorisce la più ampia partecipazione possibile ai trattati in questione.

9.3. *Cause di estinzione dei trattati*

Infine, un terzo esempio di prassi innovativa, sviluppatasi nei trattati sui diritti umani rispetto al diritto dei trattati tradizionale, si verifica in alcune regole attinenti alle cause di estinzione dei trattati. Si tratta delle regole in tema di grave inadempimento della controparte, di effetti dei conflitti armati e di recesso non previsto nel trattato. Vediamo adesso separatamente, ed in estrema sintesi, queste regole.

9.3.1. *Grave inadempimento della controparte*

L'art. 60 della Convenzione di Vienna sul diritto dei trattati stabilisce che un inadempimento grave (*a material breach*) di un trattato, bilaterale o multilaterale, ad opera di uno degli Stati parti, legittima gli altri Stati parti alla risoluzione o sospensione del trattato, interamente o in parte. Tuttavia il par. 5 dell'art. 60 stabilisce un'eccezione a tale regola:

> "Paragraphs 1 to 3 do not apply to provisions relating to the protection of the human person contained in treaties of a humanitarian character, in particular to provisions prohibiting any form of reprisals against persons protected by such treaties".

La regola generale dell'art. 60 viene considerata come una codificazione del diritto internazionale consuetudinario sia dalla Corte internazionale di giustizia [109] sia dalla dottrina unanime [110]. Anche l'eccezione di cui al par. 5 dell'art. 60, la cui genesi nei lavori preparatori della Convenzione di Vienna è nota [111], viene considerata come facente parte del diritto consuetudinario. Ma si è discusso sul punto se tale eccezione debba essere limitata, secondo un'interpretazione letterale, ai soli trattati di diritto internazionale umanitario oppu-

---

[108] *Ibidem*, Separate Opinions of Judges Shahabuddeen (p.635 ss.), Weeramantry (p. 640 ss.) e Parra-Aranguren (p. 656).

[109] ICJ, *Legal Consequences for States of the Continued Presence of South Africa in Namibia*, par. 94; ICJ, *Gabčikovo-Nagymaros Project*, par. 46.

[110] Peraltro in dottrina è controverso se la regola derivi dal diritto dei trattati o dal diritto della responsabilità internazionale oppure da l'uno o l'altro settore a seconda delle circostanze e del tipo di reazione alla violazione del trattato. Vedi, fra gli altri, Simma (1970); Pisillo Mazzeschi (1984); Sicilianos (1993); Forlati (2005).

[111] Vedi Pisillo Mazzeschi (1984), pp. 147-154.

re se debba essere estesa anche ai trattati sui diritti umani [112]. Questa seconda interpretazione, più estensiva, si è ormai affermata nella prassi internazionale [113].

Ciò conferma che lo scopo della eccezione è quello di mantenere in vita, tramite la deroga alla regola della risoluzione o sospensione per grave inadempimento, quelle disposizioni convenzionali che tutelano i diritti umani degli individui. Anche in questo caso la *continuità* e *stabilità* delle norme sui diritti umani dipende, a nostro avviso, dal fatto che gli individui sono i destinatari principali di tali norme. Pertanto opera il principio-guida della *preminenza dell'individuo*. Ma tali continuità e stabilità favoriscono anche, in via indiretta, un'ampia partecipazione degli Stati ai trattati sui diritti umani e quindi sono collegate anche al principio di *universalità dei diritti umani*.

9.3.2. *Effetti dei conflitti armati*

L'esigenza di garantire la continuità delle norme convenzionali sui diritti umani opera anche nel campo delle regole del diritto dei trattati che disciplinano gli effetti dei conflitti armati sulla estinzione o sospensione dei trattati [114]. Per la verità, il contenuto esatto delle regole consuetudinarie è piuttosto controverso, poiché tali regole sono cambiate nel corso del tempo [115]. In sintesi, sulla base delle opinioni dominanti, si può dire che, fino alla Prima Guerra Mondiale, prevaleva la regola della estinzione dei trattati nei rapporti fra Stati belligeranti. Nel periodo fra le due guerre mondiali, si sono venute affermando alcune eccezioni alla regola dell'estinzione, nel senso che alcuni trattati, come quelli di carattere commerciale, venivano soltanto sospesi ed altri, come quelli di diritto umanitario o costitutivi di regimi permanenti, rimanevano in vigore anche durante i conflitti armati. La prassi del periodo successivo alla Seconda Guerra Mondiale sembra orientata verso un regime generale che favorisce la sospensione (anziché l'estinzione) dei trattati fra Stati belligeranti.

Tuttavia, la prassi ancora più recente, che emerge soprattutto dai lavori di codificazione della materia da parte della Commissione del Diritto Internazionale [116], è orientata a favore di un regime giuridico "misto", che si fonda sulla natura, l'oggetto e lo scopo di ciascun trattato. In sostanza, a seconda del loro contenuto, molti trattati si sospendono, alcuni si estinguono, ed altri ancora restano in vigore fra gli Stati belligeranti. Si noti che la CDI elenca espressamente i trattati sui diritti umani fra quelli che restano in vigore durante i conflitti armati. Secondo la CDI, la regola della "continuità" dei trattati sui diritti umani si ricava chiaramente dalla prassi più recente. E, in effetti, ciò trova conferma anche in due pareri consultivi della CIG [117] e in prese di posizione del Comitato dei diritti umani [118].

---

[112] Sul punto v. Russo (2012), pp. 88-90.

[113] ICJ, *Legal Consequences for States of the Continued Presence of South Africa in Namibia*, par. 122.

[114] Vedi Russo (2012), pp. 106-122.

[115] Vedi la dottrina citata da Russo (2012), pp. 106-109.

[116] Cfr. i lavori della Commissione del diritto internazionale sul tema degli effetti dei conflitti armati sui trattati. Vedi, in particolare, ILC, *Draft articles on the effects of armed conflicts on treaties*, 17 May 2011.

[117] ICJ, *Legality of the Threat or Use of Nuclear Weapons*, par. 24; ICJ, *Legal Consequences of the Construction of a Wall*, par. 106.

[118] HRCtee, General Comment No. 31, 26 May 2004, par. 11.

Pertanto, si può concludere che la regola della continuità dei trattati sui diritti umani si è progressivamente affermata; e che essa ha innovato sia rispetto alla regola generale più antica della estinzione dei trattati durante i conflitti armati sia rispetto a quella più moderna della loro sospensione. A nostro avviso, alla base della regola della continuità in materia di diritti umani, vi sono anche vari motivi di carattere logico-giuridico. In primo luogo, e di nuovo, poiché gli individui sono i destinatari principali dei trattati sui diritti umani, non si vede perché i loro diritti dovrebbero essere travolti da un conflitto che incide soprattutto nei rapporti fra Stati. In secondo luogo, l'interesse collettivo della comunità internazionale nel suo insieme tende a favorire la continuità dei trattati sui diritti umani ed a prevalere sugli interessi individuali degli Stati belligeranti [119]. In definitiva, come si può notare, anche in materia di effetti dei conflitti armati sui trattati, le regole applicabili ai trattati sui diritti umani si ispirano ai due principi-guida della *preminenza dell'individuo* e della *universalità* dei diritti umani.

9.3.3. *Recesso non previsto dal trattato*

Molti trattati, compresi alcuni trattati sui diritti umani, ammettono espressamente la facoltà di recesso per gli Stati parti. In questi casi, ovviamente, la legittimità del recesso non è in discussione, anche se, nella prassi, i casi di recesso di uno Stato da un trattato sui diritti umani, che pure prevedesse la facoltà di recesso, sono stati finora rari e sono stati criticati dagli altri Stati parti nonché dagli organi internazionali di controllo sui diritti umani.

Invece, il problema si pone per i trattati che non prevedono una espressa facoltà di recesso [120]. Fra questi, vi sono anche alcuni importanti trattati sui diritti umani, quali, ad esempio, i due Patti delle NU del 1966. Nel diritto internazionale consuetudinario precedente alla Convenzione di Vienna del 1969, la regola escludeva la facoltà di recesso in mancanza di una previsione nel trattato, nel rispetto del principio generale *pacta sunt servanda*. La Convenzione di Vienna del 1969 contiene una disposizione *ad hoc*, l'art. 56, che conferma, in linea generale, la regola che esclude la possibilità di recesso per i trattati conclusi a tempo indeterminato, che non prevedono tale possibilità, a meno che: *a*) si accerti che le parti intendevano ammettere la possibilità di recesso; o *b*) il diritto di recesso possa essere dedotto dalla natura del trattato. In sostanza la disposizione limita la facoltà di recesso ai casi in cui essa risulti dalla volontà implicita degli Stati oppure dalla natura oggettiva del trattato. Queste due eccezioni costituivano probabilmente, al tempo della Convenzione di Vienna, tentativi di sviluppo progressivo del diritto consuetudinario. L'eccezione più problematica è quella che si fonda sulla natura del trattato.

Si può ritenere che le due eccezioni alla regola tradizionale siano adesso entrate a far parte del diritto internazionale consuetudinario? Probabilmente la risposta è positiva, e pertanto si deve concludere che il diritto consuetudinario ammette adesso dei casi nei quali uno Stato ha facoltà di recedere da un trattato che non prevede espressamente tale facoltà. Ma le due eccezioni dovrebbero essere interpretate in maniera restrittiva. In particolare,

---

[119] Si può anche notare che gli stessi trattati sui diritti umani talora prevedono la possibilità di sospendere alcuni diritti umani, ma non quelli fondamentali, in situazioni di stati di necessità ed emergenza, fra le quali può rientrare un conflitto armato. Ciò può significare che, al di fuori dell'operare di tali clausole espresse, la continuità delle norme sui diritti umani costituisce la regola generale.

[120] Vedi Russo (2012), pp. 137-165.

quella che ammette il recesso quando può essere dedotto dalla natura del trattato dovrebbe essere interpretata nel senso che certi trattati sono rivolti a regolare interessi di natura oggettivamente temporanea [121].

Venendo ai trattati sui diritti umani, che non contemplino espressamente la facoltà di recesso, si deve ritenere che tale facoltà sia esclusa. In primo luogo, ciò è confermato dalla prassi [122]. In secondo luogo, si può notare che l'eccezione fondata sulla volontà implicita delle parti appare impraticabile per i trattati sui diritti umani. La stessa conclusione vale per l'altra eccezione fondata sulla natura del trattato. Infatti, i trattati sui diritti umani non regolano certamente interessi di natura temporanea. Inoltre, come si è detto varie volte, essi hanno come destinatari principali gli individui e proteggono valori universali.

In conclusione, anche in questo caso molti fattori giuridici e logici militano a favore della continuità e stabilità dei trattati sui diritti umani e della partecipazione più ampia possibile a tali trattati da parte degli Stati. Questi fattori giustificano ampiamente la regola contraria alla facoltà di recesso.

10. *Effetti dei due principi-guida sul regime di interpretazione dei trattati*

Passiamo ora ad esaminare gli effetti prodotti dai due principi-guida della *preminenza dell'individuo* e dell'*universalità* dei diritti umani sul regime consuetudinario tradizionale dell'*interpretazione* dei trattati. Come vedremo, la prassi applicativa dei trattati sui diritti umani rivela l'esistenza di alcune regole particolari che presentano aspetti innovativi rispetto alle regole tradizionali del diritto dei trattati. Tali aspetti concernono: *a*) il metodo dinamico ed evolutivo di interpretazione dei trattati sui diritti umani; *b*) il ricorso alle nozioni giuridiche "autonome"; *c*) i concetti di obblighi positivi e di obblighi positivi "procedurali" degli Stati; *d*) la teoria degli "effetti orizzontali" dei diritti umani.

Si noti che i principali sistemi convenzionali sui diritti umani, come vedremo meglio in seguito [123], dispongono di organi e procedure di controllo internazionali di natura giurisdizionale o quasi-giurisdizionale, per verificare il rispetto dei trattati. Pertanto, questi sistemi si sono sviluppati soprattutto tramite la giurisprudenza e la prassi di tali organi di controllo. Per questo motivo, i metodi di interpretazione adottati dagli organi hanno assunto grande importanza, specie quando tali metodi presentano aspetti innovativi.

10.1. *Interpretazione dinamica ed evolutiva*

Innanzitutto, conviene sottolineare che gli organi internazionali di controllo dei trattati sui diritti umani hanno adottato un metodo generale che prevede un'interpretazione *dina-*

---

[121] In questo senso può essere interpretata la sentenza della Corte internazionale di giustizia relativa al progetto *Gabčikovo Nagymaros*, che ha affermato che il carattere permanente del trattato concluso fra Ungheria e Cecoslovacchia escludeva la facoltà di recesso da parte dell'Ungheria. Vedi ICJ, *Gabčikovo-Nagymaros Project*, par. 100.

[122] Vedi la prassi citata da Russo (2012), pp. 149-159. Cfr. anche HRCtee, General Comment No. 26, 8 December 1997, parr. 3-4.

[123] Vedi *infra*, Cap. IV.

mica, teleologica ed evolutiva, allo scopo di conferire la massima *efficacia* possibile ai trattati sui diritti umani, nell'ottica di estendere i diritti degli individui e di non limitare gli obblighi assunti dagli Stati parti.

La Commissione e la Corte europea dei diritti umani hanno mostrato questa tendenza fin dai primi anni del loro funzionamento [124]. Già nella sentenza *Wemhoff* del 1968, la Corte europea ha notato che il Preambolo della CEDU si riferisce non solo alla salvaguardia ma anche allo sviluppo dei diritti umani ed ha affermato un criterio generale di interpretazione della CEDU nei seguenti termini:

> "s'agissant d'un traité normatif, il y a lieu d'autre part de rechercher quelle est l'interprétation la plus propre à atteindre le but et à réaliser l'objet de ce traité et non celle qui donnerait l'étendue la plus limitée aux engagements des Parties" [125].

Anche nella sentenza *Golder* del 1975 [126], la Corte europea, pur riferendosi ai criteri interpretativi dei trattati previsti dalla Convenzione di Vienna del 1969, ha ribadito la sua intenzione di privilegiare una interpretazione *dinamica* e *teleologica* della Convenzione europea. Inoltre la Corte ha affermato numerose volte di voler utilizzare un'interpretazione *evolutiva*, poiché la Convenzione è "uno strumento vivente" [127]; che essa "deve essere interpretata alla luce delle condizioni del tempo contemporaneo" [128]; che essa chiede "di mantenere un approccio dinamico ed evolutivo" [129]. Questo metodo interpretativo da parte della Corte europea è stato in seguito confermato in numerosissimi casi, che non è possibile qui citare. Conviene solo ricordare che, a partire dagli anni 1970, la Corte ha interpretato in maniera dinamica ed evolutiva anche l'ambito di applicazione extra-territoriale della Convenzione [130]; e poi, dai primi anni 2000, ha sviluppato l'importante giurisprudenza innovativa sulle "misure generali" di esecuzione delle sue sentenze e le conseguenze delle c.d. "violazioni strutturali" della Convenzione [131].

Questo metodo generale di interpretazione adottato dagli organi di Strasburgo ha molto influenzato anche altri organi internazionali di controllo dei trattati sui diritti umani. Il Comitato dei diritti umani, ad esempio, ha affermato che il Patto sui diritti civili e politici deve essere interpretato "come uno strumento vivente e che i diritti che esso protegge devono essere applicati nel contesto ed alla luce della situazione del tempo contemporaneo" [132]. In senso simile si sono pronunciati il Comitato per l'eliminazione della discriminazione razziale [133] ed il Comitato europeo dei diritti sociali [134]. Ancora più esplicita è la prassi degli organi della Convenzione americana dei diritti umani. Si pensi, ad esempio, al-

---

[124] Vedi, fra gli altri, Pustorino (1998), pp. 25-81; Sudre (2006), p. 230 ss.

[125] ECtHR, *Wemhoff*, par. 8.

[126] ECtHR, *Golder*, parr. 33-35.

[127] ECtHR, *Tyrer*, par. 31.

[128] ECtHR, *Marckx*, par. 41.

[129] ECtHR, *Stafford*, par. 68; *Goodwin Christine*, par. 74.

[130] V. *infra*, Cap. III, parr. 11 e 12. Vedi anche De Sena (2002), p. 45 ss.

[131] Vedi *infra*, Cap. IV, par. 8.1.2.Vedi anche Pustorino (2019), p. 51; Focarelli (2019), pp. 733-734.

[132] HRCtee, *Judge v. Canada*, par. 10.3.

[133] CteeERD, *Hagan v. Australia*, par. 7.3.

[134] ECteeSR, *FIDH v. France*, par. 27.

l'interpretazione evolutiva data dalla Corte interamericana al diritto di proprietà in vari casi relativi ai diritti dei popoli indigeni [135].

10.2. *Nozioni giuridiche "autonome"*

Un secondo metodo interpretativo, adottato dagli organi internazionali di controllo sui diritti umani (che può anche essere considerato come una specificazione del metodo generale dinamico sopra descritto), consiste nel ricorso alle nozioni giuridiche "autonome"; cioè nel dare ai termini, alle espressioni ed ai concetti giuridici contenuti nel trattato un significato giuridico "comune" ed "autonomo" rispetto ai significati dati negli ordinamenti dei singoli Stati parti del trattato. Ciò al fine di colmare le imprecisioni dei termini contenuti nel trattato, di rimediare alle difformità dei singoli diritti interni degli Stati parti, e di permettere una definizione giuridica uniforme delle disposizioni del trattato e quindi degli obblighi di tutti gli Stati parti [136]. In realtà, questo metodo contribuisce molto anche a rafforzare l'efficacia dei trattati sui diritti umani.

Ovviamente è una regola generale del diritto dei trattati, codificata anche dalla Convenzione di Vienna del 1969 [137], quella che tende ad evitare interpretazioni "unilateralistiche" dei trattati; cioè che una norma contenuta in un trattato possa assumere significati diversi a seconda dello Stato contraente al quale tale norma debba volta per volta applicarsi. Ma tale regola assume una *forza particolare* nei trattati che disciplinano materie di speciale interesse per gli individui, quali gli accordi commerciali, gli accordi di diritto privato uniforme, le convenzioni di diritto internazionale privato e processuale, ed anche i trattati sui diritti umani. Ciò probabilmente è dovuto al fatto che, in tali materie, è più frequente l'intervento dei giudici interni, che potrebbero pregiudicare un'interpretazione uniforme del trattato. Inoltre, l'efficacia della regola è meglio garantita quando il trattato prevede un organo internazionale di controllo, giurisdizionale o quasi-giurisdizionale.

I più importanti sistemi convenzionali sui diritti umani [138] possiedono ambedue le suddette caratteristiche. Ed infatti il metodo interpretativo fondato sulle nozioni giuridiche "autonome" ha assunto in tali sistemi un'importanza particolare; e soprattutto permette agli organi internazionali di controllo di pervenire ad una interpretazione *sostanziale*, e non formale, delle nozioni contenute nei trattati sui diritti umani e di dare loro un significato *estensivo*. In questo modo, si ottiene un risultato più ampio: quello di estendere la sfera di applicazione delle disposizioni dei trattati che tutelano i diritti umani degli individui e di rafforzare, come si è detto, l'*efficacia* del trattato [139].

La Commissione e la Corte europea dei diritti umani hanno fatto ricorso al metodo delle nozioni giuridiche "autonome" fin dai primi anni del proprio funzionamento [140]. Gli organi di Strasburgo hanno usato questo metodo, ad esempio, per interpretare i termini "leg-

---

[135] Vedi, per tutti, IACtHR, *Mayagna (Sumo) Awas Tingni (Merits)*, parr. 146-155.

[136] Cfr. Sudre (2006), p. 234.

[137] Vedi gli artt. 33 e 31(3) della Convenzione di Vienna.

[138] Vedi *infra*, Cap. IV.

[139] Sudre (2006), p. 236.

[140] Vedi Pustorino (1998), pp. 135-144.

ge" e "qualità della legge"[141]; per interpretare la nozione di "vittima" ai sensi dell'art. 34 della Convenzione europea[142]; per interpretare la nozione di "accusa in materia penale"[143] e quella di "diritti o obblighi di carattere civile"[144] in relazione all'art. 6 della Convenzione europea sull'equo processo. Si noti che, specie con riguardo alle ultime due nozioni citate, l'interpretazione "autonoma" ha permesso alla Corte di estendere le garanzie dell'art. 6 ad una vasta serie di materie che, in molti diritti statali, non godevano di tali garanzie. Per fare solo un esempio, si pensi all'estensione del carattere penale a materie quali sanzioni disciplinari militari[145], sanzioni di violazioni del diritto della concorrenza, sanzioni amministrative[146] e numerose sanzioni tributarie[147].

In maniera simile, anche il Comitato dei diritti umani ha applicato il metodo interpretativo del ricorso alle nozioni giuridiche "autonome", sempre nell'ottica di permettere una definizione giuridica uniforme delle disposizioni del Patto sui diritti civili e politici, e di ampliare la sfera di applicazione del Patto nell'interesse della protezione dei diritti umani[148]. Infine, anche gli organi del sistema interamericano dei diritti umani hanno fatto ricorso al medesimo metodo interpretativo.

10.3. *Obblighi positivi ed obblighi positivi "procedurali"*

Un altro elemento innovativo, sviluppato dalla prassi relativa all'interpretazione dei trattati sui diritti umani, è costituito dalla teoria degli obblighi positivi.

Per la verità, si deve premettere che la distinzione fra obblighi negativi e positivi (sulla quale ritorneremo in seguito)[149] si applica alla teoria generale degli obblighi internazionali, e non è quindi specifica del settore della tutela internazionale dei diritti umani. Tuttavia è anche vero che, nei più importanti sistemi convenzionali sui diritti umani, gli organi internazionali di controllo hanno fatto progressivamente un uso via via più ampio della categoria degli obblighi positivi[150], sempre nell'ottica di interpretare in maniera dinamica ed evolutiva le norme convenzionali e di conferire loro la maggiore efficacia possibile. Anche in questa prassi possiamo pertanto vedere l'impatto dei due principi-guida, più volte citati, di *preminenza dell'individuo* e di *universalità* dei diritti umani.

Nel settore dei diritti umani, gli obblighi negativi sono concepiti come obblighi nei quali lo Stato si astiene o non si ingerisce nella sfera dei diritti e delle libertà individuali. Invece, gli obblighi internazionali positivi chiedono allo Stato di intervenire, compiendo

---

[141] ECtHR, *Kruslin*.

[142] Vedi, ad es., ECtHR, *Klass and Others; Norris*.

[143] Vedi, ad es., ECtHR, *Engel and Others; Ozturk*; *Adolf*; *Bloch*.

[144] Vedi, ad es., ECtHR, *König*.

[145] ECtHR, *Engel and Others*.

[146] Vedi, ad es., ECtHR, *Grande Stevens and Others*.

[147] Tuttavia, si deve precisare che talora la Corte europea, nell'interpretare certi concetti non definiti dalla Convenzione europea, cerca di verificare se vi sia un "consenso europeo", da individuare tramite la comparazione delle diverse legislazioni nazionali.

[148] Vedi, ad es., HRCtee, *Gordon C. Van Duzen v. Canada*, par. 10.2; *Wallmann and Others*.

[149] Vedi *infra*, Cap. III, par. 5.1.

[150] Vedi Pisillo Mazzeschi (2008).

certe azioni o certe prestazioni, allo scopo di favorire la realizzazione dei diritti e delle libertà individuali. Ciò detto, si comprende facilmente per quali motivi, nell'evoluzione della tutela internazionale dei diritti umani, gli obblighi positivi degli Stati sono via via cresciuti rispetto agli obblighi negativi. Nel passato, nell'epoca dei diritti umani c.d. di prima generazione, quali i diritti civili e politici, vi era la tendenza a concepire gli obblighi degli Stati specie come obblighi negativi. Solo in un'epoca più recente si è compresa l'importanza degli obblighi positivi anche nel settore dei diritti di prima generazione. Ma è soprattutto con l'importanza acquisita dai diritti umani di seconda e terza generazione che si è meglio compresa l'importanza degli obblighi positivi degli Stati.

Ciò significa che il diritto internazionale contemporaneo non si limita a stabilire regole su ciò che gli Stati non devono fare contro la persona umana, ma anche regole per stabilire ciò che gli Stati devono fare a favore della persona umana. In altri termini, la responsabilità dello Stato per violazione dei diritti umani si realizza non solo quando esso compie un'ingerenza attiva contro un diritto umano degli individui; ma anche quando lo Stato non adotta le misure positive che l'applicazione concreta ed efficace del diritto umano richiede; cioè quando si realizza un'inerzia illecita dei poteri pubblici [151]. È chiaro che ciò ha rappresentato un importante cambiamento di prospettiva nel settore dei diritti umani. D'altra parte, esso appare anche come un aspetto particolare di un fenomeno più generale, che riguarda l'intero sistema del diritto internazionale, e che è stato talora descritto come il passaggio dal diritto internazionale della coesistenza verso il diritto internazionale della cooperazione o della interdipendenza [152].

Questo sviluppo crescente dell'importanza degli obblighi positivi nel settore dei diritti umani, come si è detto sopra, si coglie in maniera molto nitida nella prassi degli organi internazionali di controllo dei trattati sui diritti umani [153]. Già nella decisione *Airey* del 1979 [154], la Corte europea dei diritti umani, a proposito del diritto di accesso alla giustizia, ha sostenuto che la Convenzione europea vuole "protéger des droits non pas théoriques ou illusoires, mais concrets et effectifs" e che ciò richiede "mesures positives" da parte dello Stato "qui ne saurait se borner à demeurer passif". E nella sentenza *Marckx* del medesimo anno, la Corte, a proposito del diritto alla vita privata e familiare, ha affermato che l'art. 8 della Convenzione:

> "[...] ne se contente pourtant pas d'astreindre l'Etat à s'abstenir de pareilles ingérences: à cet engagement plutôt négatif peuvent s'ajouter des obligations positives inhérentes à un 'respect' effectif de la vie familiale. Il en résulte notamment que l'Etat [...] doit agir de manière à permettre aux intéressés de mener une vie familiale normale" [155].

D'altra parte, anche la Corte interamericana dei diritti umani, nel caso *Castillo Petruzzi* del 1999, ha affermato che:

> "[...] as part of the obligation to ensure human rights, the States parties are to adopt laws for effective protection of the rights and freedoms established in the Convention. As the

---

[151] Sudre (2006), p. 240.

[152] Vedi *supra*, Cap. I, par. 7.3.

[153] Cfr. Pisillo Mazzeschi (2008), Capp. III, IV, V.

[154] ECtHR, *Airey v. Ireland*, parr. 24-25.

[155] ECtHR, *Marckx*, par. 31.

Commission pointed out, 'this obligation implies positive action, in that States are obliged to adopt new measures' [...]" [156].

In seguito, anche altri organi internazionali di controllo dei trattati sui diritti umani hanno sviluppato una prassi assai estesa sugli obblighi positivi. Da tale prassi si ricava che gli obblighi positivi in materia di diritti umani comprendono, a loro volta, una serie assai diversificata di obblighi più specifici, che, in base al contenuto delle attività richieste ai poteri pubblici degli Stati, possono comprendere le seguenti categorie [157]: *a*) obbligo di avere una legislazione che rispetti i diritti umani; *b*) obbligo di avere un apparato adeguato di prevenzione delle violazioni dei diritti umani e di adottare misure concrete di prevenzione quando esse sono richieste dalle circostanze; *c*) obbligo di avere un apparato adeguato di indagine sulle violazioni dei diritti umani e di adottare misure concrete di indagine su tali violazioni; *d*) obbligo di avere un apparato adeguato di amministrazione della giustizia per accertare le violazioni dei diritti umani; *e*) obbligo di riparare le violazioni dei diritti umani; *f*) obblighi specifici di adottare atti amministrativi o giurisdizionali o misure concrete per la tutela di certi diritti umani; *g*) obblighi di agire allo scopo di assicurare progressivamente la piena realizzazione di certi diritti umani.

Una categoria particolare di obblighi positivi, che è tipica del settore dei diritti umani, è quella degli obblighi c.d. "*procedurali*" [158]. Essa è stata elaborata soprattutto dalla Commissione e dalla Corte europea dei diritti umani ed è stata ripresa poi da altri organi internazionali di controllo dei trattati sui diritti umani e da una parte della dottrina. Questa categoria riguarda le situazioni nelle quali uno Stato ha l'obbligo di adottare certe misure positive di natura procedurale o strumentale, a carattere preventivo o repressivo, per proteggere certi diritti umani, in particolare il diritto alla vita ed il divieto di tortura e di trattamenti disumani o degradanti. La condotta di omissione dello Stato, che non adotta le misure preventive o repressive volta per volta necessarie secondo la situazione concreta, costituisce una violazione *autonoma* in rapporto alle violazioni sostanziali dei diritti umani sopra indicati, anche se i due tipi di violazioni possono talora coesistere.

D'altra parte, nella violazione degli obblighi c.d. "procedurali", la condotta di omissione dello Stato può essere legata sia a violazioni sostanziali da parte di altri organi dello Stato, sia a violazioni sostanziali da parte di individui, sulla base della teoria degli "effetti orizzontali" dei diritti umani, di cui parleremo in seguito [159]. Ad esempio, uno Stato può violare il suo obbligo "procedurale" di prevenire violazioni del diritto alla vita, sia omettendo le misure preventive di controllo su certe operazioni delle proprie forze di sicurezza o di polizia che hanno provocato una violazione del diritto alla vita [160], sia omettendo le misure preventive di controllo su certe attività pericolose da parte di individui privati, che si sono poi concretizzate in una violazione del diritto alla vita di altre persone private [161]. Lo stesso discorso vale per le misure repressive che lo Stato ha l'obbligo "procedurale" di

---

[156] IACtHR, *Castillo Petruzzi*, par. 202.

[157] Vedi Pisillo Mazzeschi (2008), Capp. III, IV, V. Vedi anche *infra*, Cap. III, par. 5 e Capp. V e VI, *passim*.

[158] Cfr. Pisillo Mazzeschi (2008), pp. 228-230, 393-410 e 414-422; Bestagno (2003), pp. 75-146.

[159] Vedi *infra*, par. 10.4.

[160] Vedi, ad es., ECtHR, *McCann and Others*.

[161] Vedi, ad es., ECtHR, *Osman*.

prendere per catturare, processare e punire sia organi statali sia individui privati, che abbiano violato il diritto alla vita.

10.4. *Teoria degli "effetti orizzontali" dei diritti umani*

Strettamente legata alla teoria degli obblighi positivi degli Stati è quella dei c.d. "effetti orizzontali" dei diritti umani, o meglio di certe norme contenute nei trattati sui diritti umani. Si tratta di norme che impongono agli Stati parti di proteggere gli individui contro le violazioni dei loro diritti umani effettuate da altri individui. L'effetto orizzontale, in sostanza, consiste nell'estendere l'applicazione delle norme sui diritti umani (tipicamente concepite per regolare i rapporti fra Stato e individui) anche ai rapporti fra individui privati. Questo effetto si ispira alla teoria di origine tedesca della *Drittwirkung*, secondo la quale i diritti fondamentali costituzionali devono essere rispettati sia dai poteri pubblici sia dai privati fra di loro [162].

Anche in questo caso, la teoria degli effetti orizzontali delle norme sui diritti umani è stata inizialmente elaborata e sviluppata dalla Commissione e dalla Corte europea dei diritti umani [163], e poi ripresa da altri organi internazionali di controllo [164] e dalla dottrina [165]. In realtà, vi sono molte norme convenzionali sui diritti umani che prevedono espressamente un effetto orizzontale per certi diritti umani. Ad esempio, l'art. 20 del Patto internazionale sui diritti civili e politici impone agli Stati di impedire (evidentemente anche ai privati) la propaganda a favore della guerra e tutti gli appelli all'odio nazionale, razziale o religioso. L'art. 17(2) del medesimo Patto stabilisce che il diritto alla vita privata deve essere protetto dalla legge e che quindi lo Stato deve prevedere una protezione giuridica contro tutte le interferenze nella vita privata delle persone anche da parte di altri individui o enti privati. Al contrario, molte altre disposizioni convenzionali sui diritti umani non prevedono espressamente effetti orizzontali, ma sono state parimenti interpretate dagli organi internazionali di controllo come suscettibili di produrre effetti orizzontali. Un esempio importante è costituito dalle norme convenzionali sul divieto di tortura e di trattamenti disumani o degradanti.

L'importanza degli effetti orizzontali delle norme sui diritti umani è del tutto evidente. L'*efficacia* concreta di un gran numero di diritti umani sarebbe fortemente minacciata se gli Stati non avessero l'obbligo di controllare anche gli abusi contro i diritti umani nella sfera delle relazioni fra individui privati.

La teoria degli effetti orizzontali dei diritti umani è stata spesso accolta come una novità nel diritto internazionale. Ma in realtà, a mio avviso, si tratta, nella maggior parte dei casi, solo di un'applicazione, al nuovo settore dei diritti umani, di una teoria che si era già sviluppata in altri settori più tradizionali del diritto internazionale, come, ad esempio, quello della protezione degli stranieri; cioè la teoria della responsabilità degli Stati in connessione ad atti di individui privati. Secondo tale ultima teoria, oggi pacifica, se un cittadino straniero subisce un'offesa nello Stato territoriale da parte di individui, lo Stato territoriale è responsabile se e quando i propri organi, che nelle circostanze concrete avevano un ob-

---

[162] Vedi, fra gli altri, Sudre (2006), pp. 244-245.

[163] Vedi, fra i primi casi, ECtHR, *Young, James and Webster*; *X and Y v. The Netherlands*.

[164] Per questa prassi vedi Sudre (2006), p. 247.

[165] Vedi Pustorino (1998), pp. 48-50 e gli autori ivi citati.

bligo di prevenire o reprimere l'illecito degli individui nei confronti dello straniero, hanno commesso un'omissione in tali loro obblighi.

In effetti, anche la teoria degli effetti orizzontali dei diritti umani si basa, quasi sempre, sul medesimo presupposto. Quando certe norme sui diritti umani impongono, esplicitamente o implicitamente, obblighi positivi ad effetti orizzontali a carico di uno Stato, la responsabilità di quest'ultimo sorge soltanto se si dimostra che gli organi di tale Stato non hanno adempiuto il loro obbligo di proteggere, con misure preventive o repressive, gli individui destinatari di tali obblighi contro le interferenze illecite da parte di altri individui privati. In questo senso, questa teoria include, nel suo ambito, anche la teoria più restrittiva (perché applicata solo a certi diritti umani) degli obblighi positivi "procedurali" sui diritti umani, sopra esaminata.

Tuttavia, vi è anche una diversa applicazione, più rara, della teoria degli effetti orizzontali dei diritti umani, che non presuppone una condotta omissiva da parte dello Stato responsabile della violazione e quindi la violazione di obblighi positivi. Si tratta della situazione in cui lo Stato è responsabile, per le violazioni dei diritti umani commesse da individui contro altri individui, per aver fornito ai primi i mezzi per realizzare le violazioni; ad esempio, quando il diritto interno dello Stato ha legittimato o addirittura favorito tali violazioni. In questo senso si possono ricordare alcune sentenze della Corte europea dei diritti umani in materia di libertà di associazione [166], di libertà di informazione, di diritto alla vita privata.

In sintesi, la teoria degli effetti orizzontali delle norme sui diritti umani, anche se in parte fondata su concetti già operanti in altri settori del diritto internazionale, ha avuto l'effetto di estendere in maniera molto ampia gli obblighi degli Stati derivanti dai trattati sui diritti umani. Pertanto anch'essa costituisce un metodo di *interpretazione* di tali trattati che si inserisce nel quadro più generale dei due principi-guida *di preminenza dell'individuo* e di *universalità* dei diritti umani.

11. *Limiti ai due principi: le prerogative degli Stati*

Si è visto finora che i trattati sui diritti umani possiedono alcuni caratteri *peculiari* rispetto ad altri trattati internazionali; e che tali caratteri sono influenzati dai due principi-guida della *preminenza dell'individuo* e dell'*universalità* dei diritti umani. Questi due principi hanno favorito lo sviluppo di una prassi applicativa di tali trattati, che ha finito per creare regole innovative, o comunque integrative, rispetto alle regole consuetudinarie tradizionali del diritto dei trattati. Queste regole, da una parte, favoriscono la *stabilità e continuità* dei trattati sui diritti umani [167] e, d'altra parte, incentivano l'*interpretazione* di tali trattati nel senso più favorevole possibile ai diritti degli individui [168].

---

[166] ECtHR, *Young, James and Webster*; *Sigurjónsson*; *VgT Verein gegen Tierfrabriken*; *Pla and Puncernau*; *Sciacca*.

[167] Vedi (*supra*, par. 9) le regole sulle riserve, sulla successione degli Stati nei trattati, sulle cause di estinzione dei trattati.

[168] Vedi (*supra*, par. 10) le regole sulla interpretazione dinamica ed evolutiva, sulle nozioni giuridiche "autonome", sugli obblighi positivi e gli obblighi positivi "procedurali", sugli "effetti orizzontali" dei diritti umani.

Tuttavia, ciò non significa che gli Stati, nel predisporre e poi ratificare i trattati sui diritti umani, abbiano "abdicato" alla propria sovranità e abbiano rinunciato a far valere i propri interessi, per favorire soltanto gli interessi individuali. Una simile conclusione sarebbe utopistica e totalmente fuori dalla realtà. Al contrario, si deve riconoscere che, nei trattati sui diritti umani, vi sono alcuni limiti importanti rispetto al funzionamento dei due principi-guida suddetti. Questi limiti, a mio avviso, possono essere concepiti come una salvaguardia delle *prerogative* degli Stati.

I limiti principali derivano: *a*) dal concetto di *sussidiarietà*, che regola il rapporto fra i trattati sui diritti umani ed i diritti statali; *b*) dalla esistenza nei trattati sui diritti umani di *clausole di restrizione*, che permettono alle autorità nazionali di prendere misure che interferiscono con i diritti garantiti per perseguire certi interessi pubblici; *c*) dalla esistenza in molti trattati sui diritti umani di *clausole di deroga*, che permettono alle autorità nazionali addirittura di sospendere l'esercizio di molti diritti garantiti in casi di guerra o di emergenze pubbliche; *d*) dalla nozione giurisprudenziale del c.d. "*margine di apprezzamento*", che concede agli Stati un certo potere discrezionale nel porre restrizioni o sospensioni ai diritti garantiti.

Vediamo adesso, in sintesi, questi limiti.

11.1. *Sussidiarietà*

Il primo limite è costituito dal concetto (o principio) di sussidiarietà. L'idea della sussidiarietà dei trattati sui diritti umani rispetto ai diritti statali significa, come è noto, che spetta in primo luogo alle autorità nazionali, e specie ai giudici interni, il compito di assicurare l'osservanza dei diritti umani sanciti nei trattati. Pertanto questi trattati hanno carattere sussidiario o, se si vuole, complementare, da un punto di vista sostanziale e procedurale, rispetto ai diritti statali. Del resto, come è stato osservato [169], il concetto stesso di sussidiarietà deriva logicamente dal fatto che uno Stato, che abbia ratificato un trattato, ha l'obbligo primario di assicurarne il suo puntuale rispetto e dal fatto che i mezzi per realizzare concretamente i diritti umani dipendono essenzialmente dai governi nazionali. Pertanto gli Stati assumono la responsabilità primaria per l'osservanza dei trattati sui diritti umani e gli eventuali meccanismi internazionali di controllo subentrano soltanto quando i meccanismi nazionali non hanno funzionato.

In effetti, il principio di sussidiarietà ispira tutti i trattati sui diritti umani, anche se esso ha trovato la sua elaborazione più ampia nel sistema della Convenzione europea dei diritti umani. La giurisprudenza degli organi di Strasburgo ha, fin dai primi anni, stabilito espressamente tale principio. Ad esempio, nel "*Caso linguistico belga*" del 1968, la Corte europea ha affermato che:

> "elle ne saurait se substituer aux autorités nationales compétentes, faute de quoi elle perdrait de vue le caractère subsidiaire du mécanisme international de garantie collective instauré par la Convention" [170].

---

[169] Tomuschat (2014), p. 103.

[170] ECtHR, *Belgian Linguistic Case*, par. 10 ("Interprétation retenue par la Cour").

In maniera ancora più esplicita, nella sentenza *Handyside* del 1976 [171], la medesima Corte ha detto che:

> "le mécanisme de sauvegarde instauré par la Convention revêt un caractère subsidiaire par rapport aux systèmes nationaux de garantie des droits de l'homme".

La giurisprudenza successiva della Corte europea ha confermato molte volte il principio di sussidiarietà [172]. Inoltre, tale principio di sussidiarietà è stato riaffermato in maniera netta nella Dichiarazione di Brighton del 2012 [173] e nel Protocollo n. 15 alla Convenzione del 2013 [174].

Anche la Carta dei diritti fondamentali dell'Unione Europea contiene una disposizione esplicita sul principio di sussidiarietà (art. 51(1)). La Convenzione americana, pur non contenendo una disposizione *ad hoc* su tale principio, prevede, all'art. 2, che la responsabilità primaria per l'attuazione dei diritti umani sia affidata agli ordinamenti interni degli Stati parti. Nel sistema africano di protezione dei diritti umani, il principio c.d. di complementarietà svolge funzioni simili a quelle della sussidiarietà. Inoltre, la Commissione africana dei diritti dell'uomo e dei popoli ha aderito al principio di sussidiarietà, affermando che la responsabilità principale per l'attuazione della Carta africana spetta agli Stati parti [175].

Infine, si deve notare che i trattati più importanti sui diritti umani prevedono la regola del previo esaurimento dei ricorsi interni ed il diritto degli individui vittime di violazioni di ottenere un rimedio interno effettivo. Come vedremo subito, questa regola e questo diritto costituiscono la più netta espressione del principio di sussidiarietà, dal punto di vista procedurale.

11.1.1. *Previo esaurimento dei ricorsi interni*

I trattati sui diritti umani che prevedono procedure di controllo, per l'esame di reclami concernenti violazioni dei diritti ivi garantiti, contengono quasi sempre disposizioni sul previo esaurimento dei ricorsi interni [176]. Esse sono sostanzialmente simili, poiché stabiliscono che gli organi internazionali di controllo prenderanno in esame i reclami soltanto dopo che tutti i ricorsi interni esistenti nello Stato accusato della violazione siano stati esauriti, secondo i principi di diritto internazionale generalmente riconosciuti. Si vedano, ad esempio, l'art. 35(1) della Convenzione europea; l'art. 41(1)(c) del Patto internazionale sui diritti civili e politici e gli artt. 2 e 5(2)(b) del suo Protocollo facoltativo; gli artt. 46(1)(a) e 46(2) della Convenzione americana; gli artt. 50 e 56(5) della Carta africana [177].

---

[171] ECtHR, *Handyside*, par. 48.

[172] Cfr. Tomuschat (2014), p. 103 e la giurisprudenza ivi citata nella nota 46.

[173] Council of Europe, Committee of Ministers, Declaration of Brighton, 20 April 2012, parr. 3, 7-9.

[174] Art. 1 del Protocollo n.15 recante emendamento alla Convenzione per la salvaguardia dei Diritti dell'Uomo e delle Libertà Fondamentali, Strasburgo, 24 giugno 2013.

[175] ACmHPR, *Garreth Anver Prince v. South Africa*, par. 50.

[176] Sul tema in generale vedi Pisillo Mazzeschi (2004a).

[177] Vedi anche gli artt. 11(3) e 14(7)(a) della Convenzione internazionale del 1965 sull'eliminazione di ogni forma di discriminazione razziale; gli artt. 21(1)(c) e 22(5)(b) della Convenzione del 1984 contro la tortura ed altri trattamenti o punizioni crudeli, inumani o degradanti; l'art. 4(1) del Protocollo facoltativo della Convenzione sull'eliminazione di ogni forma di discriminazione nei confronti delle donne.

La prassi degli organi internazionali di controllo di tali trattati ha fatto un'applicazione estesissima di tali regole sull'esaurimento dei ricorsi interni, tanto che, a mio avviso, si può da tale prassi ormai ricavare anche una norma consuetudinaria *ad hoc*, che, pur trovando ispirazione dalla norma consuetudinaria più antica sull'esaurimento dei ricorsi interni in materia di protezione diplomatica, ha in realtà una sua autonomia ed un suo contenuto specifico, e in parte diverso, rispetto alla norma più antica [178].

Comunque, tornando alle regole sul previo esaurimento contenute nei trattati sui diritti umani, non vi è dubbio che esse si ispirino al sopra esaminato principio di *sussidiarietà* di tali trattati rispetto ai diritti statali. A questo proposito, conviene sottolineare il fondamento diverso fra la regola sul previo esaurimento in materia di diritti umani e la regola simile in materia di protezione diplomatica. Quest'ultima regola, più antica, riguarda, come è noto, l'esercizio della protezione diplomatica da parte dello Stato che rivendica l'offesa subìta dal proprio cittadino, persona fisica o giuridica, all'estero; e significa che uno Stato non può esercitare l'azione internazionale (o far valere la responsabilità) a tutela del proprio cittadino, danneggiato da un illecito commesso da un altro Stato, prima che la persona lesa abbia esaurito i ricorsi interni esistenti in tale ultimo Stato senza ottenere la riparazione. La regola, secondo la dottrina e la prassi dominante, si fonda sul principio che gli stranieri sono sottoposti alla sovranità dello Stato territoriale; e quindi sui principi di sovranità, del dominio riservato e della non ingerenza. Lo scopo principale è quello di concedere allo Stato territoriale la possibilità di riparare l'offesa causata allo straniero prima che entrino in gioco i rapporti e le istanze internazionali fra tale Stato e lo Stato nazionale della persona offesa.

Invece, nel settore dei diritti umani, il fondamento della regola del previo esaurimento si sposta decisamente dal principio di sovranità verso quello di *sussidiarietà*. La prassi degli organi internazionali di controllo sui diritti umani ha sempre evitato di menzionare il principio di sovranità ed ha invece spesso citato il principio di sussidiarietà. Questo fatto è assai significativo. In materia di protezione diplomatica, il dominio assoluto del principio di sovranità degli Stati significa che la regola del previo esaurimento è tesa a proteggere soprattutto gli interessi statali, *in primis* quelli dello Stato territoriale ed anche, di riflesso quelli degli altri Stati. Siamo nel quadro di una logica strettamente interstatale e gli interessi dell'individuo straniero offeso all'estero sono del tutto secondari, se non addirittura irrilevanti.

Al contrario, in materia di diritti umani, il principio di sussidiarietà sposta l'ottica generale per interpretare la regola del previo esaurimento. In primo luogo, tale principio non privilegia necessariamente gli interessi statali rispetto a quelli individuali; non opera solo nel quadro di una logica interstatale; non presuppone una separazione netta fra la sfera internazionale e la sfera interna, ma anzi ha proprio lo scopo di coordinare in maniera appropriata le due sfere e non esclude l'idea di una certa continuità fra le medesime. In altri termini, le procedure internazionali sui diritti umani possono essere concepite come una sorta di prosecuzione delle procedure interne: la funzione più importante della regola, in materia di diritti umani, è quella di coordinare in maniera equilibrata ed efficiente il livello dei reclami e delle procedure internazionali con il livello dei ricorsi e delle procedure nazionali. Questa funzione di coordinamento differenzia la regola in materia di diritti umani,

---

[178] Vedi Pisillo Mazzeschi (2004a), *passim* e spec. pp. 38-53.

che assume una natura chiaramente procedurale e non sostanziale [179], dalla regola in materia di protezione diplomatica.

In secondo luogo, il fatto che la regola del previo esaurimento, in materia di diritti umani, si fondi sulla sussidiarietà invece che sulla sovranità, introduce un altro cambiamento generale di prospettiva nell'interpretare gli scopi ed il contenuto della regola. Infatti, nella prassi degli organi internazionali di controllo sui diritti umani, è progressivamente aumentata l'importanza della protezione degli interessi individuali rispetto a quella degli interessi statali. Ciò ha inciso in vari modi sul contenuto della regola, ad esempio sul regime delle eccezioni alla regola, che nella prassi si sono sviluppate in maniera assai più ampia rispetto alle eccezioni alla regola in materia di protezione diplomatica [180]. Le eccezioni (cioè i casi nei quali la vittima è dispensata dall'onere di esaurire i ricorsi interni), nel campo dei diritti umani, sono le seguenti: *a*) inaccessibilità dei ricorsi interni; *b*) inefficacia ed inadeguatezza dei ricorsi interni; *c*) diniego e ritardo di giustizia; *d*) le c.d. circostanze speciali; *e*) misure legislative e prassi amministrative illecite; *f*) violazioni gravi e sistematiche dei diritti umani.

Questa differenza fra le due regole riflette logicamente il fatto che, mentre la protezione diplomatica è un mezzo per la composizione delle controversie fra Stati, le norme e le procedure sui diritti umani mirano soprattutto a proteggere diritti individuali. Quindi gli Stati membri di un trattato sui diritti umani, come si è già detto, devono garantire agli individui la protezione dei diritti riconosciuti nel trattato innanzitutto nel proprio ordinamento interno e dinanzi ai propri tribunali interni. Da ciò deriva un'importante conseguenza: la regola del previo esaurimento in materia di diritti umani non ha soltanto la funzione "negativa" di fare da filtro ai ricorsi dinanzi agli organi internazionali di controllo; ma anche la funzione "positiva" di verificare se il sistema interno dello Stato membro del trattato sui diritti umani si è conformato o meno agli obblighi posti dal trattato. In altri termini, la regola serve anche a controllare l'attuazione interna dei diritti umani ed a garantire agli individui *ricorsi interni effettivi*. La funzione "positiva" della regola del previo esaurimento in materia di diritti umani è stata riconosciuta esplicitamente dai maggiori organi internazionali di controllo dei trattati sui diritti umani [181]. Ancora una volta, emerge chiaramente l'influenza del principio-guida della *preminenza dell'individuo* nei trattati sui diritti umani.

11.1.2. *Diritto ad un ricorso interno effettivo*

Quanto si è appena detto è confermato dal fatto che, nei trattati sui diritti umani, accanto alle disposizioni che impongono all'individuo vittima l'onere di esaurire i ricorsi interni, vi sono quasi sempre anche altre disposizioni, che garantiscono all'individuo il diritto di usufruire di ricorsi effettivi (*effective remedies*), dinanzi ai giudici interni, per far valere la violazione dei diritti umani garantiti dal trattato e per ottenere la riparazione [182]. Si pos-

---

[179] Cfr. Pisillo Mazzeschi (2004a), pp. 81-94.

[180] Cfr. Pisillo Mazzeschi (2004a), cap. IV, pp. 171-194.

[181] Per la giurisprudenza della Corte europea, vedi, ad es., ECtHR, *Aksoy*; *Akdivar and Others*, Judgment of 16 September 1996; *Selmouni*; *Scordino and Others*, Decision of 27 March 2003.

[182] A nostro avviso, il diritto a ricorsi interni effettivi contro la violazione dei diritti umani, adesso assorbito dal diritto di accesso alla giustizia, è ormai protetto anche dal diritto internazionale consuetudinario. V. *infra*, Cap. V, par. 18.

sono citare, ad esempio, l'art. 2(3) del Patto sui diritti civili e politici; l'art. 13 della Convenzione europea; l'art. 25 della Convenzione americana; l'art. 7 della Carta africana; l'art. 47 della Carta dei diritti fondamentali dell'UE; l'art. 6 della Convenzione contro la discriminazione razziale; gli artt. 13 e 14 della Convenzione delle NU contro la tortura.

Come si è già accennato, è chiaro che, in ognuno di questi trattati, la regola del previo esaurimento dei ricorsi interni deve essere strettamente collegata al diritto dell'individuo vittima a disporre di ricorsi interni effettivi. Questo collegamento stretto risulta molto chiaro nella prassi degli organi internazionali di controllo sui diritti umani [183]. Esso significa che lo Stato parte di un trattato sui diritti umani deve adempiere l'obbligo di rispettare tali diritti nel proprio ordinamento giuridico interno e l'obbligo supplementare (e funzionalmente collegato) di fornire agli individui ricorsi interni effettivi, affinché essi possano concretamente far valere tali diritti. Se lo Stato non adempie questi due obblighi, esso non può più avvalersi dello scudo della regola del previo esaurimento. Ciò per tre motivi: *a*) perché si verifica l'eccezione della inaccessibilità o della inefficacia e inadeguatezza dei ricorsi interni; *b*) perché si realizza anche, quantomeno nei casi più gravi, l'eccezione del diniego di giustizia; *c*) perché la regola del previo esaurimento non ha assolto in questo caso la sua funzione "positiva".

In sostanza, il principio di sussidiarietà, in materia di diritti umani, trova attuazione anche nel diritto ad un ricorso interno effettivo. Tuttavia, si deve notare che tale principio, che ha pur sempre lo scopo di dare priorità alle autorità nazionali rispetto a quelle internazionali nel compito di assicurare l'osservanza dei diritti umani sanciti nei trattati, ha subìto negli anni recenti una evoluzione, nel senso di un riequilibrio fra interessi statali e interessi individuali a favore di questi ultimi. In altri termini, oggi il peso della bilancia si sposta dalla difesa degli interessi statali verso la tutela della piena affermazione dei diritti umani. Si potrebbe dire che il peso si sposta dalla funzione "negativa" della regola del previo esaurimento verso la sua funzione "positiva" e verso il rafforzamento del diritto umano dell'individuo ad avere ricorsi interni effettivi. Ne deriva che quest'ultimo diritto va oggi interpretato estensivamente, perché si colloca nel quadro del più ampio diritto umano di accesso alla giustizia, inteso come diritto procedurale fondamentale, necessario per garantire l'efficacia concreta dei diritti umani sostanziali [184].

11.2. *Clausole di restrizione dei diritti garantiti*

Il secondo limite ai due principi-guida di preminenza dell'individuo e di universalità dei diritti umani, che dimostra anch'esso come gli Stati, pur con la ratifica dei trattati sui diritti umani, non abbiano rinunciato a far valere i propri interessi, è costituito dalle c.d. *clausole di restrizione* [185]. Queste clausole sono presenti spesso nei suddetti trattati e riguardano soprattutto i diritti umani c.d. di prima generazione. Esse, in sintesi, permettono alle autorità nazionali di interferire nei diritti protetti, e di restringerne la sostanza, per soddisfare certi interessi pubblici, ritenuti meritevoli di particolare tutela. Pertanto anche

---

[183] Vedi la prassi citata da Pisillo Mazzeschi (2004a), p. 198, note 190, 191, 192.

[184] V. *infra*, Cap. V, par 18.

[185] Sul tema vedi, fra gli altri, De Schutter (2010), pp. 288-364; Sudre (2006), p. 206 ss.; Tomuschat (2014), pp. 104-106.

queste clausole, come il principio di sussidiarietà, mettono in luce in maniera esemplare il rapporto dialettico fra protezione dei diritti individuali e difesa degli interessi pubblici statali.

Le clausole di restrizione non si applicano ad un numero limitato di diritti che vengono talora definiti come "assoluti", con un termine che peraltro rischia di creare qualche confusione e che, a nostro avviso, dovrebbe avere un significato più restrittivo [186]. Ma la maggior parte dei diritti umani gode soltanto di una protezione relativa, poiché gli Stati possono, in certe circostanze, limitare il loro godimento.

Peraltro, si deve avvertire che le clausole di restrizione hanno un contenuto parzialmente diverso nei vari trattati sui diritti umani. Alcune clausole sono formulate in maniera ampia e generica, poiché fanno riferimento al pubblico interesse o all'ordine pubblico dello Stato. Altre, parimenti generiche, proibiscono ogni interferenza "arbitraria" dello Stato con i diritti umani garantiti dal trattato [187]. Ma molte clausole di restrizione sono più precise, poiché stabiliscono quali sono gli obiettivi che lo Stato può perseguire nel sottoporre a limitazioni il diritto umano in questione. Ad esempio, l'art. 8(2) della Convenzione europea, sul diritto al rispetto della vita privata e familiare, stabilisce che:

> "There shall be no interference by a public authority with the exercise of this right except such as is in accordance with the law and is necessary in a democratic society in the interests of national security, public safety or the economic well-being of the country, for the prevention of disorder or crime, for the protection of health or morals, or for the protection of the rights and freedoms of others".

In termini più sintetici, l'art. 18(3) del Patto sui diritti civili e politici, sulla libertà di pensiero, coscienza e religione, recita:

> "Freedom to manifest one's religion or beliefs may be subject only to such limitations as are prescribed by law and are necessary to protect public safety, order, health, or morals or the fundamental rights and freedoms of others".

Se si esamina la prassi degli organi internazionali di controllo dei trattati sui diritti umani, si può ricavare un *metodo*, ampiamente utilizzato, per verificare la legittimità di una restrizione o interferenza dello Stato [188]. Tale metodo procedurale prevede *quattro fasi* logicamente separate e successive [189]. In primo luogo, l'organo di controllo deve accertare l'esistenza di una *ingerenza* (o interferenza), da parte dello Stato, nell'esercizio del diritto umano in questione. Il concetto di ingerenza significa il fatto che il diritto umano in questione sia limitato o ristretto in un qualsiasi modo. Una volta stabilita l'esistenza di un'ingerenza, si deve accertare che essa si fondi su una base legale (*test di legalità*). In terzo luogo, occorre verificare che l'ingerenza persegua uno dei motivi di limitazione legittimi enumerati nella disposizione pertinente del trattato (*test di legittimità*). In quarto luogo, si deve valutare se l'ingerenza sia "necessaria in una società democratica" (*test di necessità*). Questa espressione significa che tale misura deve rispondere ad un *bisogno sociale premi-*

---

[186] Vedi *infra*, Cap. V, par. 4.2.

[187] Vedi, ad esempio, CCPR, artt. 6(1), 9(1) e 17(1).

[188] Vedi Tomuschat (2014), pp. 105-106 e la prassi ivi citata degli organi internazionali di controllo.

[189] Per una delle prime applicazioni di questo metodo v. ECtHR, *Sunday Times*.

nente, cioè "ad una esigenza effettiva in quel particolare contesto sociale, in quel determinato momento storico" [190]. Si deve notare che il test di necessità spesso comprende anche un giudizio di *proporzionalità* della misura di ingerenza. Talora, per maggiore chiarezza, il giudizio di proporzionalità viene tenuto distinto e costituisce allora una quinta fase di verifica. Tale giudizio significa che l'organo di controllo, dopo avere accertato che l'ingerenza risponde ad un bisogno sociale preminente, compie anche una valutazione sulla proporzionalità dell'ingerenza rispetto agli obiettivi che le autorità statali si sono posti.

Come si è detto, le clausole di restrizione riguardano soprattutto i trattati sui diritti umani c.d. di prima generazione. Invece, per quanto riguarda i trattati o le singole norme convenzionali sui diritti umani di seconda generazione (specie i diritti economici, sociali e culturali) e su qualche diritto di terza generazione, il discorso è in parte diverso [191], poiché gli Stati assumono di solito obblighi non immediati, ma "a realizzazione progressiva" [192]; cioè si impegnano a prendere misure allo scopo di raggiungere progressivamente la piena realizzazione dei diritti riconosciuti nel trattato. In questo senso è esemplare l'art. 2(1) del Patto sui diritti economici, sociali e culturali, il quale stabilisce che:

> "Each State Party to the present Covenant undertakes to take steps, individually and through international assistance and co-operation, especially economic and technical, to the maximum of its available resources, with a view to achieving progressively the full realization of the rights recognized in the present Covenant by all appropriate means, including particularly the adoption of legislative measures".

È chiaro che, in relazione ai propri obblighi "a realizzazione progressiva", come vedremo meglio in seguito [193], gli Stati hanno un maggiore margine di discrezionalità e di tempo per ottemperare. Pertanto in questi casi i diritti umani sono sottoposti a maggiori limiti, rispetto a quelli posti dalle clausole di restrizione per quei diritti umani che prevedono obblighi immediati. Ma ciò non significa che gli Stati parti dei trattati, che prevedono obblighi "progressivi" relativi ai diritti umani, non assumano veri e propri obblighi giuridici vincolanti. Infatti tali Stati si impegnano pur sempre "a intraprendere azioni" (*take steps*), "al massimo delle proprie risorse disponibili" e "con tutti i mezzi appropriati", allo scopo di pervenire alla "piena realizzazione" dei diritti umani.

Pertanto, in primo luogo, gli organi internazionali di controllo devono verificare la "adeguatezza" o "ragionevolezza" delle misure prese dagli Stati. Questo requisito è confermato dall'art. 8(4) del Protocollo Opzionale al Patto sui diritti economici, sociali e culturali [194]. In

---

[190] La definizione del termine "necessario" è stata fornita dalla Corte europea nel caso *Handyside*. La Corte ha precisato che l'aggettivo "necessario" non significa "indispensabile", ma non ha neppure significati più blandi come gli aggettivi "ammissibile", "normale", "utile", "ragionevole" o "opportuno". Secondo Tomuschat (2014), p. 105, il test di necessità richiede di dimostrare un "pressing social need" dello Stato.

[191] Vedi Tomuschat (2014), p. 106.

[192] Per gli obblighi "a realizzazione progressiva", vedi *infra*, Cap. III, par. 5.3.

[193] *Infra*, Cap. III, par. 5.3.

[194] Optional Protocol to the International Covenant on Economic, Social and Cultural Rights, 18 June 2008, Art. 8(4): "When examining communications under the present Protocol, the Committee shall consider the reasonableness of the steps taken by the State Party in accordance with part II of the Covenant. In doing so, the Committee shall bear in mind that the State Party may adopt a range of possible policy measures for the implementation of the rights set forth in the Covenant".

secondo luogo, gli Stati parti devono rispettare altri obblighi [195]: *a*) non devono adottare misure regressive rispetto all'obiettivo della piena realizzazione del diritto in questione; *b*) non devono rimanere totalmente passivi, cioè non adottare azioni di alcun tipo tese verso l'obiettivo suddetto; *c*) devono utilizzare i mezzi appropriati per raggiungere l'obiettivo; *d*) devono usare ragionevolezza nel bilanciare i mezzi e le risorse usati per l'attuazione del diritto umano in questione con quelli usati per perseguire altri interessi statali primari; *e*) devono assicurare un livello minimo essenziale del diritto umano in questione.

11.3. *Clausole di deroga ai diritti garantiti*

Il terzo limite ai due principi generali più volte menzionati, che gioca a favore degli interessi statali, è costituito dalle c.d. *clausole di deroga*, che sono presenti nei più importanti trattati di carattere generale sui diritti umani [196]. Si tratta di disposizioni che prevedono la possibilità che uno Stato parte possa derogare a molti dei diritti garantiti, *rectius* sospendere tali diritti, quando esso si trovi in uno stato di emergenza pubblica o addirittura di guerra. Ma la facoltà di deroga è soggetta, come vedremo, ad una serie di condizioni di procedura e di sostanza. Le clausole di deroga non devono essere confuse con le clausole di restrizione, né con il concetto dei diritti stabiliti da norme di *ius cogens* (o cogenti o imperative o perentorie) [197].

La norma più celebre, che costituisce l'esempio cui altre norme si sono ispirate, è contenuta nell'art. 15 della Convenzione europea [198]. L'art. 15 stabilisce, in sintesi, che uno Stato parte, in caso di guerra o in caso di altra emergenza pubblica che minacci la vita della nazione, può adottare misure in deroga ai diritti previsti nella Convenzione, nella misura in cui la situazione lo richieda e purché le misure non contrastino con gli altri obblighi del diritto internazionale. Sono esclusi dalla possibilità di deroga alcuni diritti espressamente specificati. Infine, l'art. 15 stabilisce una procedura, per cui lo Stato, che esercita la deroga, deve informare il Consiglio d'Europa sulle misure prese e sulla loro cessazione. La Corte europea può controllare il rispetto di questa norma.

Disposizioni simili sono l'art. 4 del Patto sui diritti civili e politici, l'art. 27 della Convenzione americana, l'art. F (Parte V) della Carta sociale europea (riveduta), l'art. 4 della Carta araba. Invece, non vi sono clausole di deroga in altri trattati sui diritti umani, ad esempio nel Patto sui diritti economici, sociali e culturali e nella Carta africana. Ciò forse non impedisce ad uno Stato parte di questi trattati di invocare, se ricorrono le condizioni stabilite dal diritto internazionale generale, lo stato di necessità come circostanza di esclusione dell'illecito [199].

---

[195] Su questi obblighi vedi Pisillo Mazzeschi (2008), pp. 429-489.

[196] Sulle clausole di deroga vedi, fra gli altri, Higgins (1976-77); Ergec (1987); McDonald (1997); Svensson-McCarthy (1998); Viarengo (2005); Cataldi (2006); Id. (2012); Id. (2019); Sommario (2018).

[197] Per questi concetti vedi anche *infra*, Cap. V, par. 4.

[198] Art. 15: "1. In time of war or other public emergency threatening the life of the nation any High Contracting Party may take measures derogating from its obligations under this Convention to the extent strictly required by the exigencies of the situation, provided that such measures are not inconsistent with its other obligations under international law […]".

[199] Così Kälin, Künzli (2009), p. 143.

Qual è lo scopo di queste clausole di deroga? È quello di evitare che gli Stati sospendano i diritti umani con troppa libertà o discrezionalità, ricorrendo al generico stato di necessità del diritto internazionale generale, e quello di delimitare e regolare più specificamente i presupposti e le condizioni, procedurali e sostanziali, che gli Stati devono rispettare per poter sospendere l'applicazione dei diritti umani; e ciò sotto il controllo di organi internazionali giurisdizionali o quasi-giurisdizionali. Si tratta, in sintesi, di trovare un giusto bilanciamento fra sicurezza degli Stati e rispetto dei diritti umani. In effetti, esiste una prassi, anche se non particolarmente ampia, di applicazione di clausole di deroga da parte degli Stati. Ad esempio, nel quadro della Convenzione europea, si sono avvalsi nel tempo della facoltà di deroga, *ex* art. 15, diversi Stati, fra i quali la Francia, la Grecia, il Regno Unito, la Turchia. Molte di tali deroghe sono state motivate dall'esigenza di fronteggiare fenomeni di terrorismo o di movimenti separatisti.

Le questioni giuridiche principali sollevate dalle clausole di deroga sono tre: *a*) qual è il presupposto per la deroga; *b*) quali sono le condizioni procedurali che lo Stato deve rispettare quando chiede la deroga; *c*) quali sono le condizioni sostanziali che legittimano la deroga.

La prima questione riguarda, in sostanza, la definizione precisa del concetto di "emergenza pubblica". Nel sistema della Convenzione europea dei diritti umani, gli organi di Strasburgo hanno dato una definizione di tale concetto fin dagli anni 1960 [200], stabilendo che esso significa una situazione di emergenza che costituisca una minaccia, attuale o imminente, alla vita organizzata della comunità dello Stato. Il pericolo deve essere eccezionale, nel senso che le misure normali permesse dalla Convenzione per il mantenimento della sicurezza e dell'ordine pubblico devono essere inadeguate per fronteggiare la situazione. Questa definizione iniziale del concetto di "emergenza pubblica" non ha subìto grandi cambiamenti nella prassi successiva dinanzi agli organi di Strasburgo; ma vi è stata una certa tendenza ad interpretarla in maniera più estensiva.

Infatti, per molti anni la deroga *ex* art. 15 non poteva essere invocata per scopo solo preventivo, ma richiedeva l'esistenza di una violenza già scatenata sul territorio dello Stato o comunque un pericolo attuale o imminente su tale territorio. Invece, recentemente la Corte di Strasburgo ha interpretato in maniera più ampia il concetto di pericolo imminente, poiché, nel caso *A. and Others v. UK* del 2009 [201], ha affermato che la paura di un attacco terroristico è giustificata dalla semplice esistenza del terrorismo internazionale di Al-Qaeda, anche se tale organizzazione non ha effettuato alcun attacco nel Regno Unito, poiché lo Stato può legittimamente proteggere la sua popolazione da futuri pericoli.

Un altro punto interessante, nella definizione del concetto di "emergenza pubblica", riguarda la dimensione spaziale. L'art. 15 della Convenzione europea sembra richiedere che l'emergenza, per consentire la deroga ai diritti umani, debba interessare soltanto il territorio dello Stato che chiede la deroga medesima. Ma la prassi ha esteso quasi subito l'ambito territoriale dell'emergenza: ad esempio, nel caso *Lawless*, la Commissione e poi la Corte ammisero che le operazioni terroristiche dell'IRA, pur avendo prodotto effetti concreti solo in Irlanda,

---

[200] ECmHR, *Lawless v. Ireland*, Report of 12 April 1960; ECtHR, *Lawless v. Ireland (No. 3)*, Judgment of 1 July 1961; ECtHR, *Greek case*.

[201] ECtHR, *A. and Others v. UK*, par. 216.

erano destinate a produrre conseguenze anche nel Regno Unito[202]. Anche nel sopra citato caso *A. and Others v. UK*, la Corte ha stabilito che l'emergenza del terrorismo internazionale giustificava misure di deroga prese nel Regno Unito, anche se la minaccia non si era concretamente manifestata nel territorio britannico[203]. In sostanza, sembra sufficiente che l'emergenza abbia la probabilità di produrre *effetti* nel territorio dello Stato che chiede la deroga.

Recentemente, si è verificato un ulteriore ampliamento della dimensione spaziale del concetto di emergenza pubblica, tale da comportare una vera e propria efficacia extraterritoriale dell'art. 15. Tale disposizione, secondo un'interpretazione letterale, sembra richiedere che l'emergenza, per consentire la deroga, debba interessare, direttamente o indirettamente (cioè mediante i possibili effetti) soltanto il territorio dello Stato che chiede la deroga medesima. Invece, di recente, sia l'Alta Corte di Giustizia britannica[204], sia la Corte di Strasburgo[205] hanno affermato che uno Stato può invocare l'art. 15 anche quando l'emergenza si realizza in un territorio estero nel quale tale Stato svolge operazioni militari, quali quelle intraprese dal Regno Unito in Afghanistan nella fase post-bellica o quelle condotte in Iraq durante il conflitto armato internazionale.

Inoltre, mentre nei casi più risalenti gli organi di Strasburgo avevano affermato che l'emergenza doveva "colpire tutta la popolazione" dello Stato che chiede la deroga, in alcuni casi successivi (specie relativi alla Turchia) essi hanno ammesso che l'emergenza possa riguardare solo una parte del territorio e quindi della popolazione di uno Stato. Naturalmente anche le misure di deroga devono allora avere effetti limitati a quella parte del territorio[206].

Quanto al Patto sui diritti civili e politici, l'art. 4 ha una formulazione piuttosto simile all'art. 15 della Convenzione europea, poiché parla di "public emergency which threatens the life of the nation". Tuttavia il Comitato dei diritti umani, nel suo Commento Generale n. 29 del 2001, tende a dare un'interpretazione più restrittiva del concetto di pubblica emergenza, poiché sottolinea che:

> "Not every disturbance or catastrophe qualifies as a public emergency which threatens the life of the nation [...] During armed conflict, whether international or non-international, rules of international humanitarian law become applicable and help [...] to prevent the abuse of a State's emergency powers. The Covenant requires that even during an armed conflict measures derogating from the Covenant are allowed only if and to the extent that the situation constitutes a threat to the life of the nation".

La seconda delle questioni principali, sollevate dalle clausole di deroga, riguarda le condizioni procedurali che lo Stato deve rispettare. Le misure di emergenza devono essere dichiarate in maniera ufficiale dallo Stato che chiede la deroga, rispettando le disposizioni specifiche previste nel trattato in questione, ed una notifica della deroga deve essere data all'organo internazionale stabilito in tale trattato. Ad esempio, l'art. 15(3) della Convenzione europea prevede che ogni Stato parte, che si avvalga del diritto di deroga, debba te-

---

[202] ECmHR, *Lawless v. Ireland*; ECtHR, *Lawless v. Ireland (No. 3)*, parr. 27-30 e 36.

[203] ECtHR, *A. and Others v. UK*, par. 180.

[204] High Court of Justice, *Serdar Mohammed*, parr. 155-158.

[205] ECtHR, *Hassan v. UK*, par. 101 ss.

[206] Vedi, ad es., ECmHR, *France, Norway, Denmark, Sweden and The Netherlands v. Turkey*; ECtHR, *Sakik and Others* v. *Turkey*.

nere pienamente informato il Segretario Generale del Consiglio d'Europa delle misure che ha preso e delle loro motivazioni. Inoltre, dovrà anche informare il Segretario Generale quando tali misure derogatorie hanno cessato di operare e le disposizioni della Convenzione vengono di nuovo interamente applicate. In maniera assai simile, l'art. 4(3) del Patto sui diritti civili e politici stabilisce che ogni Stato parte, che voglia esercitare il diritto di deroga, debba immediatamente informare gli altri Stati parti, tramite l'intermediazione del Segretario Generale delle NU, circa le disposizioni del Patto che intende derogare e le relative motivazioni. Un'altra comunicazione dovrà essere inviata sulla data in cui lo Stato cessa la deroga. Una norma analoga è contenuta nell'art. 27(3) della Convenzione americana.

Tuttavia, per la verità, le disposizioni convenzionali sopra citate hanno il difetto di tacere sulle conseguenze a carico dello Stato per le sue mancate comunicazioni e informazioni. Probabilmente si deve ritenere che le misure di deroga adottate siano illegittime e che nasca una responsabilità dello Stato verso gli altri Stati contraenti e verso gli organi delle convenzioni, per violazione delle convenzioni medesime.

La terza questione principale, quella più complessa, riguarda le condizioni sostanziali che legittimano la deroga. Tali condizioni sono sostanzialmente simili, anche se non identiche, nei vari trattati sopra indicati. Per motivi di sintesi, esamineremo soprattutto quelle previste nella Convenzione europea.

Ai sensi dell'art. 15 della Convenzione, la prima condizione richiesta, forse la più importante, è che le misure derogatorie prese dallo Stato rispettino i principi di *necessità* e di *proporzionalità*. Ciò deriva dalla lettera dell'art. 15 che parla di "measures ... to the extent strictly required by the exigencies of the situation". A mio avviso, si deve distinguere fra i concetti di necessità e di proporzionalità, che sono diversi anche se strettamente collegati [207]. Il primo concetto significa che vi deve essere un rapporto di stretta necessità delle misure adottate rispetto alla situazione di emergenza. In altri termini, lo Stato deve dimostrare che misure diverse e meno severe non erano sufficienti per fronteggiare la situazione di emergenza. Il requisito della proporzionalità invece significa che, una volta stabilito che certe misure derogatorie sono necessarie, la loro applicazione concreta deve essere proporzionata, cioè le misure non devono essere eccessive rispetto allo scopo di fronteggiare l'emergenza. In altri termini, vi deve essere un nesso di proporzionalità fra le misure concrete di esercizio di poteri eccezionali e le esigenze concrete poste dalla singola situazione di emergenza.

La seconda condizione, che per la verità è sostenuta specie in dottrina, è quella della *durata limitata* nel tempo delle misure derogatorie. Si dice che di solito lo stato di emergenza non si protrae in maniera indefinita nel tempo e che quindi anche le misure derogatorie dovrebbero essere temporanee e provvisorie. Dal carattere temporaneo delle misure, la dottrina deduce anche un obbligo dello Stato in questione di tenere sotto continuo controllo le misure di emergenza vigenti, per un processo di adattamento continuo [208]. Tutta-

---

[207] Invece vari autori non distinguono fra necessità e proporzionalità. Anche nella prassi, la distinzione talora non è netta.

[208] Vedi, ad es., Cataldi (2012), pp. 558-559. L'obbligo dello Stato di tenere sotto controllo le misure derogatorie risulta, implicitamente, anche da alcune decisioni della Corte europea (v. spec. ECtHR, *Ireland v. UK*; *Brannigan and McBride*). Inoltre, dal carattere temporaneo dello stato di emergenza e delle misure in deroga, la

via, recentemente la Corte di Strasburgo ha messo in discussione il limite della temporaneità delle misure, affermando che dalla sua giurisprudenza non risulta esplicitamente tale limite, anche se la proporzionalità delle risposte può essere legata alla durata dell'emergenza [209]. La Corte ha aggiunto che vi è la possibilità che un'emergenza pubblica continui per molti anni.

La terza condizione, che è invece espressamente prevista nei trattati sopra citati, è che le clausole di deroga non possono operare per i *diritti umani "inderogabili"*. L'art. 15(2) della Convenzione europea contiene un elenco delle disposizioni che non possono essere in nessun caso sospese, perché prevedono diritti inderogabili in stati di emergenza [210]. Si tratta del diritto alla vita, con una eccezione; del divieto di tortura e di pene o trattamenti inumani o degradanti; del divieto di schiavitù e di servitù; del principio di irretroattività della legge penale. A questo elenco sono stati in seguito aggiunti il divieto della pena di morte e il principio *ne bis in idem*. Ma la lista dei diritti inderogabili della Convenzione europea è più limitata rispetto a quella contenuta nell'art. 4 del Patto sui diritti civili e politici [211], che prevede anche il divieto di discriminazione, il divieto di incarcerazione per debiti contrattuali, il diritto al riconoscimento come persona dinanzi alla legge, e la libertà di pensiero, coscienza e religione. Ancora più estensiva è la lista dei diritti inderogabili contenuta nell'art. 27 della Convenzione americana [212]. Inoltre la dottrina ritiene che altri diritti umani debbano essere implicitamente considerati come inderogabili, ad esempio il diritto ad un ricorso interno effettivo. Pertanto si pone il problema di identificare con esattezza quali diritti umani siano inderogabili in stati di emergenza secondo il diritto internazionale generale; e la prassi e giurisprudenza non sono univoche a questo riguardo [213].

La quarta condizione, anch'essa espressamente prevista nei trattati sopra citati, è che le misure in deroga non devono essere in conflitto con gli altri *obblighi derivanti dal diritto internazionale* [214]. Ciò significa, secondo un'interpretazione concorde, che le misure in deroga devono rispettare non solo i limiti previsti dal trattato in questione, ma anche gli eventuali limiti previsti da altre norme di diritto internazionale applicabili allo Stato. Quindi lo Stato deve rispettare, anche in caso di emergenza, gli altri trattati sui diritti umani ed i trattati di diritto internazionale umanitario dei quali sia contraente [215], nonché le norme di diritto internazionale generale [216]. Per quanto riguarda, in particolare, il rispetto del diritto

---

dottrina deduce anche che l'art. 15 non è per sua natura adatto a regolare situazioni in cui uno Stato reitera spesso nel tempo le dichiarazioni di deroga. Infatti molti Stati membri della Convenzione europea hanno contestato la prassi della Turchia che, negli anni 1980, aveva reiterato molte volte nel tempo le dichiarazioni di deroga. Nel 1985, sulla base di un ricorso presentato da 5 Stati contro la Turchia, la Commissione convenne che il continuo ricorso a misure *ex* art. 15 snaturava la partecipazione dello Stato alla Convenzione (ECmHR, *France, Norway, Denmark, Sweden and The Netherlands v. Turkey*).

[209] ECtHR, *A. and Others v. UK*, par. 178.

[210] Si noti che questo concetto di "inderogabilità in stati di emergenza" non corrisponde al concetto di inderogabilità/imperatività delle norme di *ius cogens*. Su questo punto vedi *infra*, Cap. V, parr. 4.3 e 4.5.

[211] ECHR, art. 4, parr. 1 e 2.

[212] ACHR, art. 27, parr. 1 e 2.

[213] Vedi *infra*, Cap. V, par. 4.3.

[214] Cfr. ECHR, art. 15(1); CCPR. art. 4; ACHR, art. 27(1).

[215] Secondo Kälin, Künzli (2009), p. 146, sono particolarmente rilevanti le liste dei diritti umani contenute nell'art. 75 del Protocollo Addizionale I e nell'art. 4 del Protocollo Addizionale II alle Convenzioni di Ginevra.

[216] Sulle norme di diritto internazionale generale in materia di diritti umani, v. *infra*, Cap. V, par. 4.4.

internazionale umanitario, conviene sottolineare che è sorto di recente il problema se tale diritto possa interagire anche in maniera diversa, e in un certo senso opposta, con l'art. 15 della Convenzione europea; cioè ampliando, anziché limitando, il diritto degli Stati di sospendere certi diritti umani. In altri termini, in giurisprudenza si è posta la questione se il diritto internazionale umanitario possa autorizzare uno Stato, in situazioni di conflitti armati internazionali o anche interni, ad adottare misure che non rispettano certi diritti tutelati dalla Convenzione europea (specie il diritto alla libertà personale), misure che invece non sarebbero consentite dalla Convenzione medesima in tempo di pace; e se lo Stato possa adottare tali misure senza bisogno di notificare una deroga *ex* art. 15. Una risposta positiva, che trova la sua base sul carattere speciale del diritto internazionale umanitario rispetto ai diritti umani, è stata data dalla Corte di Strasburgo[217]. Invece una risposta negativa, a mio avviso più convincente, è stata data dalla Alta Corte di Giustizia Britannica[218].

La quinta condizione, sulla quale però non vi è accordo in dottrina, è che le misure derogatorie rispettino il *divieto generale di discriminazione*[219]. In realtà, questa condizione è espressamente prevista da alcuni trattati, quali il Patto sui diritti civili e politici e la Convenzione americana; ma non da altri, quali la Convenzione europea. Si pone pertanto il problema se il divieto di discriminazione si applichi o meno nei trattati che non lo prevedono espressamente come limite per le misure derogatorie. Gli autori che rispondono in modo affermativo sostengono che tale divieto fa parte del diritto internazionale generale[220]; e che pertanto la condizione che le misure derogatorie devono rispettare il divieto di discriminazione sarebbe già compresa, in maniera implicita, in quella del rispetto degli obblighi internazionali dello Stato. Ci sembra che questa tesi possa essere accolta.

Infine, alcuni autori sostengono che vi è una sesta condizione sostanziale richiesta, per legittimare la deroga; e cioè che nello Stato che chiede la medesima esistano adeguate *garanzie giuridiche*, e specie procedure giudiziarie, di controllo contro possibili abusi nell'applicazione delle misure derogatorie. Nella giurisprudenza della Corte europea, vi sono alcuni casi nei quali la Corte ha dato importanza a tali garanzie[221]; ed anche il Commissario per i diritti umani del Consiglio d'Europa ha assunto una posizione simile, nella opi-

---

[217] ECtHR, *Hassan*. In questa sentenza, che riguardava comportamenti di militari britannici in Iraq durante un conflitto armato internazionale, la Corte ha affermato che il fatto che il Regno Unito non avesse presentato una deroga formale *ex* art. 15 non impediva di interpretare l'art. 5 della Convenzione europea, in tema di libertà personale, tenendo conto del contesto del conflitto armato in Iraq e del diritto internazionale umanitario; e che quindi misure di detenzione che non sarebbero state giustificate in tempo di pace lo erano invece in tempo di conflitto armato. Quindi ha concluso che l'art. 5 non era stato violato.

[218] High Court of Justice, *Serdar Mohammed*. L'Alta Corte di Giustizia britannica, in questo caso che riguardava comportamenti di militari britannici in Afghanistan nella fase post-bellica, ha invece respinto con forza l'idea che, in tempo di conflitto armato, il diritto internazionale umanitario possa derogare l'art. 5 della Convenzione europea. La Corte ha detto che l'art. 5, che proibisce l'arresto e la detenzione salvo certi casi elencati, è una norma specifica, che non consente una deroga da parte del diritto umanitario. Ha respinto inoltre la tesi che, durante un conflitto armato, il diritto umanitario, come diritto speciale, possa derogare la Convenzione europea. Quindi la Corte ha concluso che l'art. 5 era stato violato.

[219] Vedi, ad es., Kälin, Künzli (2009), p. 145; De Schutter (2010), p. 547 ss. L'art. 4 del Patto prevede espressamente che le misure derogatorie non devono comportare discriminazione. Così anche l'art. 27(2) della Convenzione americana.

[220] Sul divieto di discriminazione vedi *infra*, Cap. V, par. 21.

[221] Vedi, ad es., ECtHR, *Aksoy; Brannigan and McBride*.

nione relativa alla deroga comunicata dal Regno Unito nel 2001 in relazione alla sua legislazione antiterrorismo. Tuttavia, a mio parere, la prassi in supporto di questa sesta condizione è troppo esigua, per concludere che essa sia prevista dal diritto internazionale generale.

In conclusione, le clausole di deroga hanno il merito di stabilire regole procedurali e sostanziali piuttosto precise, per legittimare le misure derogatorie dei diritti umani prese dagli Stati. Tuttavia esse presentano anche alcuni aspetti critici. Il primo riguarda i meccanismi per controllare che le misure derogatorie rispettino le condizioni procedurali e sostanziali per la loro legittimità. Infatti, i meccanismi previsti di solito operano solo *a posteriori* ed in via incidentale, quando viene presentato un ricorso agli organi internazionali giudiziari o quasi-giudiziari di controllo previsti da ciascun trattato. Sarebbe invece preferibile un meccanismo internazionale di controllo continuo ed efficace ogni volta che uno Stato comunica che intende avvalersi delle clausole di deroga.

Il secondo aspetto critico deriva dal fatto che tali clausole sono state pensate per fronteggiare eventi eccezionali di emergenza e non funzionano bene quando uno Stato si trova spesso in una situazione emergenziale[222]. Inoltre, dopo gli attentati terroristici dell'11 settembre 2001, molti Stati hanno adottato misure anti-terrorismo destinate a durare nel tempo, a prescindere da emergenze immediate e concrete. Tali misure di lunga durata, come si è già detto, non si prestano bene a rientrare nell'ambito di applicazione delle clausole di deroga previste dai principali trattati sui diritti umani, anche se la Corte di Strasburgo sembra recentemente propensa ad ammettere la loro legittimità. Tutto ciò induce a pensare che forse sia venuto il tempo di rivedere ed aggiornare il funzionamento delle clausole di deroga ai diritti umani.

11.4. *Margine di apprezzamento degli Stati*

Infine, il quarto limite, che tende anch'esso a favorire gli interessi statali, è costituito dal c.d. "margine di apprezzamento" degli Stati, che, per certi aspetti, potrebbe anche essere considerato come una espressione o conseguenza del principio di sussidiarietà[223].

La dottrina (o nozione) del margine di apprezzamento è stata sviluppata, per prima, dalla giurisprudenza della Commissione e Corte europea dei diritti umani ed è stata in seguito ripresa da altri organi internazionali di controllo, quali soprattutto la Commissione africana sui diritti dell'uomo e dei popoli. Anche la prassi del Comitato dei diritti umani in alcuni casi, non molto frequenti, ha applicato implicitamente tale nozione[224]. Invece, quest'ultima gioca un ruolo assai limitato nella giurisprudenza della Corte interamericana dei diritti umani. L'importanza della dottrina in esame nel quadro del sistema della Convenzione europea è stata recentemente confermata, poiché essa è stata espressamente recepita nel Preambolo della Convenzione tramite il Protocollo n. 15 del 24 giugno 2013[225]. Pertanto faremo riferimento soprattutto al sistema della Convenzione europea.

---

[222] Ad esempio, nel caso della Turchia.

[223] Tuttavia a me sembra che sia preferibile trattare separatamente la nozione di margine di apprezzamento, poiché essa ha caratteristiche proprie ed una propria autonomia rispetto al principio di sussidiarietà, pur avendo con quest'ultimo un legame.

[224] Vedi la prassi citata da Tomuschat (2014), p. 109.

[225] Protocollo n. 15 recante emendamento alla Convenzione europea per la salvaguardia dei Diritti dell'Uomo e delle Libertà fondamentali, art. 1.

La nozione del margine di apprezzamento rileva soprattutto per i diritti umani che sono soggetti a clausole di restrizione o di deroga da parte degli Stati. Infatti, tramite tale nozione, agli Stati viene concessa una certa misura di potere discrezionale nel porre restrizioni o addirittura deroghe ai diritti umani garantiti dai trattati. In linea più generale, la dottrina in esame serve a definire, in maniera flessibile, il rapporto fra le misure riservate all'autonomia nazionale e la competenza degli organi internazionali circa la propria funzione di controllo dei trattati sui diritti umani. In altri termini, essa serve a trovare un difficile equilibrio fra l'autonomia nazionale e le norme internazionali convenzionali, che sono, in linea di principio, comuni per tutti gli Stati contraenti.

Quali sono le motivazioni che stanno alla base della nozione del margine di apprezzamento?

In primo luogo, gli organi internazionali di controllo sui diritti umani sono spesso chiamati a giudicare su *controversie di natura delicata*, che possono toccare elementi di base della filosofia costituzionale di uno Stato[226], oppure investire la sicurezza stessa di uno Stato. Quindi nasce il problema di chi debba prendere la decisione finale quando, sulla base di una clausola di restrizione oppure di deroga, uno Stato abbia concretamente preso misure limitative o addirittura sospensive di uno o più diritti umani. Ciò anche se gli organi internazionali di controllo, con una clausola di stile piuttosto ovvia, hanno sempre affermato che la misura restrittiva o la misura sospensiva adottata dallo Stato rimane sotto il loro controllo.

In secondo luogo, vi è una motivazione di *natura pratica o funzionale*[227]; cioè il fatto che le autorità nazionali hanno la migliore conoscenza delle circostanze concrete e delle condizioni e necessità locali di applicazione del trattato sui diritti umani in questione. La Corte europea, ad esempio, nel caso *Handyside*, ha affermato, a proposito di una restrizione ad una libertà, che:

> "grâce à leurs contacts directs et constants avec les forces vives de leur pays, les autorités de l'Etat se trouvent en principe mieux placés que le juge international pour se prononcer"[228].

La Corte ha ribadito spesso tale concetto[229].

Anche la Commissione africana ha espresso un concetto simile, se non più ampio, quando ha affermato che lo Stato:

> "has direct and continuous knowledge of its society, its needs, resources, economic and political situation, legal practices, and the final balance that needs to be struck between the competing and sometimes conflicting forces that shape its society"[230].

In terzo luogo, il margine di apprezzamento risponde ad un'esigenza ideologica, legata al principio del *pluralismo* tipico di una "società democratica"[231]. Questa motivazione è particolarmente forte nel quadro della Convenzione europea. Il principio del pluralismo richiede che la Corte di Strasburgo presti attenzione alle diversità esistenti fra gli Stati europei che

---

[226] Cfr. Tomuschat (2014), p. 107.

[227] Cfr. Sudre (2006), p. 217.

[228] ECtHR, *Handyside*, par. 48.

[229] Vedi la giurisprudenza citata da Tomuschat (2014), p. 107, nota 75.

[230] ACmHPR, *Garreth Anver Prince v. South Africa*, par. 51.

[231] Cfr. Sudre (2006), pp. 217-219.

sono parti della Convenzione, specie alle diversità delle loro culture giuridiche[232], delle loro tradizioni culturali[233] e dei fattori storici e politici propri di ciascuno Stato[234]. In altri termini, la Convenzione europea non può imporre una "uniformità assoluta"[235] delle legislazioni nazionali o una concezione uniforme europea di certi concetti, come ad esempio la morale[236], o il significato della religione nella società[237] o il diritto all'aborto[238].

Infine, una quarta ed ultima motivazione, che è emersa talora dalla giurisprudenza della Corte europea, è costituita dalla *legittimazione democratica delle autorità nazionali*, che può giustificare, specie in relazione a certi diritti umani, una restrizione al potere di controllo della Corte a favore del margine di apprezzamento statale[239].

Da queste quattro motivazioni, che stanno alla base della nozione del margine di apprezzamento, derivano anche i *criteri* che la Corte europea, e gli altri organi internazionali di controllo, hanno di solito usato, per decidere se riconoscere o meno un margine di apprezzamento allo Stato nelle singole controversie; ed anche, in caso positivo, per decidere se il margine di apprezzamento statale debba essere "ampio" oppure "ristretto".

Un primo criterio, il più importante nel quadro della Convenzione europea, è costituito dalla assenza o presenza di un denominatore comune ai sistemi giuridici nazionali. L'assenza di un denominatore comune ai sistemi giuridici nazionali amplia il margine di apprezzamento dello Stato. Ciò vale, specialmente, per questioni sociali che presentano caratteristiche tipiche nazionali e che spesso riguardano aspetti di etica o di morale[240]. Si può fare l'esempio della concessione di diritti genitoriali ai transessuali[241], o del diritto di accesso all'adozione da parte degli omosessuali[242], o dei simboli religiosi nelle scuole[243]. Al contrario, la presenza di principi giuridici o di interpretazioni comuni fra gli Stati parti restringe il margine di apprezzamento dello Stato accusato dell'ingerenza. In altri termini, se vi è un ampio consenso europeo sul contenuto di un diritto umano, non vi è motivo per lasciare un margine di apprezzamento, cioè un potere discrezionale di autonomia, allo Stato. Si può fare l'esempio del diritto di uguaglianza fra figli legittimi e naturali[244], o della protezione delle fonti giornalistiche[245].

Un secondo criterio è quello della natura del diritto in esame o delle specifiche questioni giuridiche in gioco. Gli organi internazionali di controllo concedono agli Stati un margine di apprezzamento, o comunque un margine "ampio", quando il diritto in esame incide

---

[232] Vedi ECtHR, *Sunday Times*, par. 61, dove si afferma che la Corte non può "négliger les caractéristiques de fond et de procédure (des) droits internes respectifs".

[233] Vedi ECtHR, *Casado Coca*, par. 54.

[234] Vedi ECtHR, *Gitonas*, par. 39.

[235] ECtHR, *Sunday Times*, par. 61.

[236] ECtHR, *Handyside*, par. 48.

[237] ECtHR, *Otto-Preminger-Institut*, par. 50.

[238] ECtHR, *Open Door v. Ireland*, par. 63.

[239] ECtHR, *Hatton*, par. 97.

[240] Vedi la giurisprudenza citata da Tomuschat (2014), p. 108, nota 77 e da Sudre (2006), p. 222.

[241] ECtHR, *X, Y and Z v. UK*.

[242] Vedi ECtHR, *Fretté*, par. 41.

[243] Vedi ECtHR, *Leyla Şahin*, parr. 109-110; *Lautsi and Others*.

[244] ECtHR, *Marckx*.

[245] ECtHR, *Goodwin*.

su aspetti di etica o di moralità, con particolare riguardo alla morale sessuale, aspetti che peraltro tendono anche a variare da Stato a Stato o ad avere carattere contingente piuttosto che permanente[246]. Lo stesso vale quando le questioni giuridiche in gioco sono assai tecniche e complesse oppure quando hanno carattere prevalente di politica giuridica, come, ad esempio, la concorrenza sleale[247] o la politica urbanistica[248]. Si noti anche che, quando si tratta di applicare la nozione del margine di apprezzamento in materia di deroghe (e non di restrizioni) ai diritti umani, la tendenza è sempre quella di concedere agli Stati un margine di apprezzamento ampio[249], poiché viene in gioco la valutazione sullo stato di emergenza pubblica e sulla sicurezza dello Stato, questioni sulle quali l'autonomia statale viene considerata prevalente rispetto alla uniformità delle norme convenzionali per tutti gli Stati parti. Al contrario, gli organi di controllo tendono a negare il margine di apprezzamento, o ad applicare un margine "ristretto", quando il diritto soggetto ad ingerenza statale incide sulla sfera intima e privata dell'individuo o sulla sua identità[250], considerati evidentemente come valori sui quali le norme convenzionali debbono prevalere rispetto all'autonomia statale. Lo stesso vale quando è in gioco un diritto che è strettamente legato al concetto di democrazia o di stato di diritto, come, ad esempio, la libertà di espressione o di informazione su temi di pubblico interesse[251]. Anche in questi casi la necessità di garantire standard uniformi e comuni fra tutti gli Stati parti del trattato deve evidentemente prevalere.

Tuttavia, si deve notare che la giurisprudenza sul margine di apprezzamento della Corte europea e degli altri organi internazionali di controllo sui diritti umani non sempre è convincente; e talora l'applicazione del margine di apprezzamento a favore dello Stato autore dell'ingerenza non appare giustificata.

Su un piano più generale, a mio parere, si può concludere che la teoria del margine di apprezzamento è stata per molti anni uno strumento utile di flessibilità nel rapporto fra autonomia nazionale e controllo internazionale. In passato, essa era giustificata come mezzo per riconoscere le diversità fra gli Stati parti ed il loro difficile progresso verso standard più uniformi in materia di diritti umani. Ma adesso, dopo molti anni di funzionamento dei sistemi di tutela internazionale dei diritti umani, sembra giunto il momento in cui gli organi internazionali di controllo (*in primis* la Corte europea) dovrebbero imporre agli Stati in maniera più netta e coraggiosa i suddetti standard uniformi ed evitare di rimettere nelle mani dei governi la decisione sulla legittimità o meno di una restrizione o una deroga ai diritti umani. In altri termini, il progresso dei diritti umani richiede l'ampliamento della sfera in cui tali diritti devono divenire patrimonio comune degli Stati[252]. La dottrina del margine di apprezzamento, specie se applicata in maniera "ampia", costituisce un serio ostacolo verso questo progresso e alimenta il relativismo in materia di diritti umani[253].

---

[246] Questo criterio è messo in evidenza da Sudre (2006), p. 221.

[247] ECtHR, *Markt Intern Verlag GmbH and Klaus Beermann*.

[248] ECtHR, *Sporrong and Lönnroth*.

[249] Vedi Svensson-McCarthy (1998), spec. pp. 313-319 e 324-325.

[250] Vedi la giurisprudenza citata da Sudre (2006), p. 220 e da Tomuschat (2014), p. 108, nota 78.

[251] Vedi la giurisprudenza citata da Tomuschat (2014), p. 109, note 87, 88 e 89.

[252] Ciò vale ancor più nel quadro di sistemi regionali di tutela dei diritti umani, laddove vi è maggiore omogeneità fra gli Stati parti.

[253] Vedi anche Benvenisti (2018).

Sezione III

FONTI PREVISTE DA ACCORDI

12. *Gli atti giuridicamente vincolanti delle organizzazioni internazionali*

Le fonti previste da accordi (talora denominate anche fonti di terzo grado) attualmente più importanti sono costituite dagli *atti giuridicamente vincolanti delle organizzazioni internazionali*. In realtà, come è noto, nella maggior parte dei casi le organizzazioni internazionali non hanno poteri normativi, ma solo quelli di emanare raccomandazioni o altri atti giuridicamente non vincolanti (*soft law*) o di predisporre progetti di trattati. Vi sono però alcuni casi, piuttosto eccezionali, nei quali tali organizzazioni sono dotate del potere di adottare atti vincolanti. Questi ultimi, quando sono atti "organici", cioè emanati da organi autorizzati dal trattato istitutivo dell'organizzazione, prendono di solito (ma non sempre) il nome di "decisioni" e sono considerati come fonti "previste da accordi". Le ipotesi più importanti di atti vincolanti delle organizzazioni internazionali si hanno nel quadro delle Nazioni Unite e dell'Unione Europea. Altri esempi si trovano nell'ambito di alcuni Istituti Specializzati, nel WTO e nella NATO.

La Carta delle NU prevede che l'Assemblea Generale può prendere decisioni *ex* art. 17, relative all'approvazione del bilancio ed alla ripartizione delle spese fra Stati membri. Il Consiglio di Sicurezza, *ex* art. 94(2) della Carta, può decidere misure per obbligare uno Stato condannato da una sentenza della Corte internazionale di giustizia a rispettare la decisione di condanna. Inoltre, ed è l'ipotesi più importante, il Consiglio di Sicurezza può prendere decisioni *ex* art. 41 della Carta; cioè adottare "misure non implicanti l'uso della forza armata" e imporre la loro osservanza a tutti gli Stati membri.

Nel sistema dell'Unione Europea, gli atti giuridicamente vincolanti adottati dalle Istituzioni, che possono essere considerati come fonti previste da accordi, sono la regola, anziché l'eccezione. I più importanti fra tali atti sono, come è noto, i regolamenti, le decisioni e le direttive[254], denominati di solito come "atti normativi tipici" di diritto derivato dell'UE. Vi sono poi i c.d. "atti atipici" dell'UE, quali, ad esempio, le decisioni adottate dal Consiglio nel quadro della Politica Estera e di Sicurezza Comune[255].

Inoltre, come si è detto, alcuni Istituti Specializzati delle NU hanno il potere di adottare atti vincolanti nei confronti degli Stati membri; ma specie su questioni di natura tecnica e specialistica. Il Trattato istitutivo dell'ICAO autorizza il Consiglio ad emanare, a maggioranza di due terzi, in forma di "allegati" o "annessi", una serie di atti relativi al traffico aereo (denominati standard internazionali o pratiche raccomandate), che entrano in vigore per tutti gli Stati membri dopo un certo periodo, a meno che la maggioranza degli Stati membri non abbia notificato al Consiglio la propria opposizione[256]. Il Trattato istitutivo

---

[254] TFEU, art. 288.

[255] TEU, artt. 28 e 29.

[256] Convention on International Civil Aviation, 7 December 1944, artt. 37-38. In pratica, gli annessi diventano quasi sempre vincolanti per tutti gli Stati membri.

del WHO prevede [257] che l'Assemblea possa adottare, a maggioranza di due terzi, "regolamenti" in materia di sanità, che vincolano tutti gli Stati membri, eccettuati quegli Stati che notifichino al Segretario generale del WHO il loro rifiuto entro un termine predeterminato [258]. Lo Statuto dell'ILO prevede che gli Stati membri devono sottoporre i progetti di convenzioni predisposti dall'Organizzazione alle proprie autorità interne per la ratifica entro un certo termine [259]. Al di fuori degli Istituti Specializzati, esempi di atti vincolanti si trovano nello Statuto dell'Organizzazione Mondiale del Commercio (WTO) [260] e in quello della NATO [261].

Ciò premesso, si tratta adesso di vedere se il diritto internazionale dei diritti umani abbia influito su queste fonti del diritto internazionale. Si prenderanno in esame soltanto le fonti più importanti: le decisioni vincolanti del Consiglio di Sicurezza *ex* art. 41 della Carta delle NU e gli atti di diritto derivato dell'UE.

12.1. *Le decisioni del Consiglio di Sicurezza delle Nazioni Unite*

Ai sensi del Capitolo VII della Carta delle NU, il Consiglio di Sicurezza (CdS), prima di prendere decisioni *ex* art. 41, deve accertare l'esistenza di "una minaccia alla pace, di una violazione della pace o di un atto di aggressione" (art. 39). Dopo tale accertamento, il CdS può, fra l'altro, decidere quali misure "non implicanti l'uso della forza armata" (ad esempio, interruzione delle relazioni economiche, embargo commerciale, blocco di beni e di conti correnti) debbano essere adottate dai Membri delle NU contro lo Stato o gli Stati responsabili di uno o più dei suddetti illeciti internazionali [262]. Si parla comunemente, a questo proposito, delle "sanzioni" del CdS.

Un primo effetto del diritto internazionale dei diritti umani su queste norme consiste nel fatto che, negli anni recenti, il CdS ha ritenuto varie volte, talora con un notevole grado di discrezionalità, che le violazioni gravi e ripetute dei diritti umani, anche all'interno di uno Stato, possano costituire una "minaccia alla pace", e quindi giustificare la sua adozione di decisioni ai sensi dell'art. 41. Pertanto, le decisioni vincolanti del CdS possono esse-

---

[257] Constitution of the World Health Organization, 22 July 1946, art. 21.

[258] *Ibidem*, art. 22. Inoltre gli Stati membri hanno l'obbligo di sottoporre i progetti di accordi predisposti dal WHO ai propri organi interni competenti per la ratifica entro un dato termine.

[259] Anche il Trattato istitutivo dell'ITU, che ha subìto varie modifiche nel tempo, prevede che gli organi possano adottare "regolamenti" e progetti di convenzioni. Le revisioni periodiche dei regolamenti amministrativi, adottate a maggioranza semplice, vincolano tutti gli Stati membri, salvo che questi non manifestino la loro opposizione al momento dell'adozione o entro un certo termine successivo. Nel 1992 è stata adottata una "costituzione", completata poi da una "convenzione" e due "regolamenti amministrativi".

[260] Lo Statuto del WTO prevede che la Conferenza Ministeriale o il Consiglio generale possono adottare, a maggioranza di tre quarti, decisioni vincolanti, con le quali tali organi forniscono una interpretazione vincolante delle norme dello Statuto e degli annessi o anche dispensano, in casi eccezionali e per un tempo limitato, uno Stato membro dall'osservanza degli obblighi stabiliti in tali norme. Vedi Marrakesh Agreement Establishing the World Trade Organization, art. IX (2) e (3).

[261] North Atlantic Treaty, Washington, 4 April 1949, art. 9. Cfr. Focarelli (2015), p. 474.

[262] L'art. 41 elenca le seguenti misure, a titolo esemplificativo: un'interruzione totale o parziale delle relazioni economiche e delle comunicazioni ferroviarie, marittime, aeree, postali, telegrafiche, radio ed altre, e la rottura delle relazioni diplomatiche. Nella prassi sono frequenti anche altri tipi di misure.

re usate come sanzioni contro violazioni gravi dei diritti umani [263].

Un secondo effetto dei diritti umani si è verificato dopo la fine della guerra fredda, quando il CdS ha cominciato ad adottare sempre più spesso "misure non implicanti l'uso della forza armata", specie sanzioni economiche, contro vari Stati. Allora si è compreso che tali sanzioni potevano produrre gravi danni, ed anche violazioni di diritti umani fondamentali e di altri diritti di natura economica e sociale, alle popolazioni degli Stati colpiti dalle sanzioni ed alle popolazioni di Stati terzi che tenessero con i primi rapporti commerciali. In altri termini, le sanzioni economiche, oltre a rivelarsi non sempre efficaci contro gli Stati da esse colpiti, hanno spesso finito per violare di fatto diritti umani di individui e gruppi di individui. Per rimediare a questa situazione, non è stato sufficiente introdurre "esenzioni umanitarie" nelle misure sanzionatorie.

Pertanto, il CdS ha iniziato ad adottare le c.d. "sanzioni mirate o intelligenti" (*targeted* o *smart sanctions*) [264]; cioè misure dirette contro singoli individui o gruppi di individui espressamente nominati, ad esempio, autorità governative anche in carica, presunti terroristi o organizzazioni terroristiche, gruppi di insorti, individui che violano misure di embargo sulle armi, ed anche individui che vengano qualificati da uno speciale Comitato delle sanzioni come responsabili di azioni che minaccino la pace e la sicurezza. Le sanzioni "mirate" inoltre contengono una "clausola di decadenza", che stabilisce la loro estinzione automatica dopo un certo termine, se non vengono espressamente rinnovate. Infine, esse di solito concernono singoli settori (embargo su armi, diamanti, petrolio, congelamento di certi beni o di conti correnti). Tuttavia, anche le sanzioni "mirate" hanno talora violato, o rischiato di violare, certi diritti umani degli individui colpiti, quali, ad esempio, il diritto ad un equo processo o il diritto alla vita privata.

In conclusione, si può affermare che il diritto internazionale dei diritti umani ha prodotto certi effetti sulle decisioni del CdS *ex* artt. 39 e 41 della Carta delle NU, sia ampliando il potere di intervento del CdS tramite un'interpretazione estensiva del concetto di "minaccia alla pace", sia, in senso opposto, introducendo alcuni limiti a tale potere di intervento a tutela dei diritti umani, tramite la prassi delle sanzioni "mirate". Questi effetti non hanno, certamente, prodotto modifiche strutturali sulle decisioni vincolanti del CdS; ma hanno introdotto alcuni interessanti elementi di "peculiarità" rispetto al normale funzionamento di tali decisioni.

12.2. *Gli atti di diritto derivato dell'Unione Europea*

Veniamo adesso agli atti normativi di diritto derivato dell'UE. Conviene premettere subito che il diritto internazionale dei diritti umani ha esercitato un'importante influenza su tali atti. Infatti, come è noto, i Trattati CEE, CECA e CEEA non contenevano alcuna disposizione volta a garantire che gli atti comunitari rispettassero i diritti umani (denomi-

---

[263] È vero peraltro, come è stato notato (Conforti (2015), p. 446), che la grande discrezionalità di cui gode il CdS nel decidere quando ricorrano i presupposti per il suo intervento ai sensi del cap. VII, fa sì che il sistema sanzionatorio ivi previsto, compreso l'art. 41, abbia carattere *sui generis*, perché non garantisce in ogni caso una sanzione contro le suddette violazioni.

[264] Vedi Focarelli (2015), pp. 457-460.

nati come "diritti fondamentali" nel linguaggio del diritto comunitario e poi dell'UE)[265]. Pertanto, in una prima fase del processo di integrazione europea, fino alla fine degli anni '60 del secolo scorso, tale assenza di riferimenti ai diritti umani nei trattati comunitari aveva condotto la giurisprudenza della Corte di giustizia a rifiutare di prendere in considerazione, nella valutazione della legittimità di un atto comunitario, eventuali violazioni dei diritti fondamentali[266].

Tuttavia, in seguito, a partire dai primi anni '70, anche per la pressione esercitata dalle corti costituzionali italiana e tedesca[267], la Corte di giustizia ha progressivamente elaborato nel tempo, tramite la propria giurisprudenza, una forma "comunitaria" di tutela dei diritti umani[268]. Infatti la Corte ha iniziato ad affermare la propria competenza ad accertare eventuali violazioni dei diritti umani da parte delle Istituzioni, sulla base dell'argomento per cui i diritti fondamentali fanno parte dei principi generali del diritto comunitario[269]. Tali principi sui diritti fondamentali, secondo la Corte, si ricavano dalle tradizioni costituzionali comuni degli Stati membri e dai trattati internazionali sui diritti umani cui tali Stati hanno aderito, con particolare riguardo per la Convenzione europea dei diritti umani. Questa giurisprudenza, piuttosto creativa, della Corte di giustizia ha costituito un progresso importante, perché ha di fatto inserito la tutela dei diritti umani nel diritto comunitario (ora dell'UE). Tuttavia essa presentava alcuni difetti: *a*) quello di svilupparsi lentamente ed in maniera sporadica per via "pretoria"; *b*) quello di lasciare un margine di incertezza circa l'individuazione esatta dei diritti umani facenti parte del diritto comunitario; *c*) quello di richiamare solo in via indiretta i trattati sui diritti umani, compresa la Convenzione europea. In sostanza, mancava un catalogo scritto e dettagliato dei diritti umani facenti parte del diritto comunitario.

L'evoluzione successiva è nota: in un primo tempo, la suddetta giurisprudenza della Corte di giustizia è stata richiamata dall'art. 6 del Trattato sull'Unione Europea (TUE), nella sua versione originale[270]. Poi, si è coltivato il progetto di rendere la Convenzione europea direttamente applicabile nel diritto comunitario mediante un'adesione formale della Comunità Europea a tale Convenzione. Arenatosi tale progetto a causa di un primo parere negativo della Corte di giustizia[271], si è deciso di predisporre un autonomo catalogo di diritti fondamentali. Questo si è finalmente realizzato con la Carta dei diritti fondamentali dell'UE, proclamata una prima volta a Nizza nel 2000; ma poi divenuta obbligatoria con il Trattato di Lisbona del 2007. Attualmente, l'art. 6(1) del TUE stabilisce che tale Carta "ha lo stesso valore giuridico dei trattati".

---

[265] Sul rispetto dei diritti umani nel diritto dell'UE vedi, per tutti, Villani (2017), pp. 48-60.

[266] Vedi, ad es., ECJ, *Stork*.

[267] Vedi Corte costituzionale italiana, *Frontini*, sent. n. 183 del 18 dicembre 1973; Bundesverfassungsgericht, "*Solange I*", ord. 29 maggio 1974.

[268] Daniele (2014), p. 185; Villani (2017), p. 49.

[269] La svolta nella giurisprudenza della Corte di giustizia si verifica con le note sentenze *Stauder*, *Internationale Handelsgesellschaft*, *Nold* e *Hauer*.

[270] Trattato sull'Unione Europea, art. 6(2): "L'Unione rispetta i diritti fondamentali quali sono garantiti dalla Convenzione europea per la salvaguardia dei diritti dell'uomo e delle libertà fondamentali, firmata a Roma il 4 novembre 1950, quali risultano dalle tradizioni costituzionali comuni degli Stati membri, in quanto principi generali del diritto comunitario".

[271] ECJ, *Accession by the Community*, Opinion 2/94.

Ciò premesso, quali sono i risultati di questo lungo processo di progressiva affermazione dei diritti umani nell'ordinamento giuridico dell'UE, specie con riferimento agli atti normativi tipici di diritto derivato? In primo luogo, i diritti fondamentali dell'uomo appartengono ai principi generali di diritto dell'UE. Tali diritti sono ricavabili dalle tradizioni costituzionali comuni degli Stati membri e dai trattati sui diritti umani ratificati da tali Stati, e comprendono oggi anche i diritti enunciati dalla Carta dei diritti fondamentali dell'UE che siano innovativi rispetto ai primi. Le Istituzioni europee sono obbligate al rispetto di tali diritti; e pertanto gli atti normativi delle Istituzioni emanati in loro violazione sono illegittimi e possono essere annullati dalla Corte di giustizia.

In secondo luogo, i diritti fondamentali suddetti sono obbligatori anche nei confronti degli Stati membri, quando si tratti di materie che rientrano nell'ambito di applicazione del diritto dell'UE [272]. Pertanto, nel quadro di tali materie, la Corte di giustizia può accertare l'infrazione di uno Stato membro per una sua condotta nazionale in violazione dei diritti fondamentali, ad esempio, per una normativa di origine interna che violi la libertà di espressione nel contesto della libera circolazione dei lavoratori subordinati.

In terzo luogo, si è posto il problema della eventuale responsabilità degli Stati membri dell'UE quando essi violano i diritti fondamentali tramite attività poste in essere per eseguire atti delle Istituzioni dell'UE, ad esempio, per eseguire un regolamento o una direttiva. Questo problema è sorto dinanzi alla Corte europea dei diritti umani ed è stato affrontato in numerose sentenze. Fra queste, è particolarmente importante la sentenza del 2005 nel caso *Bosphorus* [273]. La Corte di Strasburgo ha distinto fra due categorie di casi. Nella prima categoria, rientrano i casi nei quali gli Stati membri si limitano ad eseguire gli atti dell'UE, senza usufruire di alcuna discrezionalità. In queste circostanze, la Corte europea non ritiene che il suo intervento sia in linea di principio necessario, poiché i diritti fondamentali possono essere tutelati dai meccanismi di controllo del diritto dell'UE, che sono equivalenti (salvo la possibilità di prova contraria in casi eccezionali). La seconda categoria comprende, invece, i casi nei quali gli Stati membri godono di un certo margine di discrezionalità nell'eseguire gli atti dell'UE. In queste circostanze, la Corte europea afferma che lo Stato che viola diritti fondamentali deve essere ritenuto responsabile ai sensi della Convenzione europea. Ciò appare logico, perché in questi casi lo Stato ha violato i propri obblighi derivanti dalla Convenzione, senza che ciò gli fosse imposto dal diritto dell'UE.

Più recentemente, la Corte di Strasburgo sembra voler estendere il proprio controllo sugli atti degli Stati membri posti in esecuzione del diritto dell'UE, interpretando restrittivamente la presunzione di protezione equivalente stabilita nel caso *Bosphorus*. Nella sentenza *M.S.S. c. Belgio e Grecia*, del 2011 [274], la Corte ha condannato il Belgio per violazione dell'art. 3 della Convenzione europea per il fatto di aver rinviato il ricorrente verso la Grecia, paese competente ad esaminare la domanda di asilo secondo il c.d. Regolamento Dublino; ha ritenuto la Grecia paese "non sicuro" nonostante la presunzione contraria sancita dal sistema Dublino; ha sostenuto che le autorità del Belgio avrebbero dovuto agire di

---

[272] Vedi, ad es., ECJ, *Wachauf*, par. 19.

[273] ECtHR, *Bosphorus*.

[274] ECtHR, *M.S.S. v. Belgium and Greece*, parr. 338-340.

conseguenza; ed ha affermato che la presunzione di protezione equivalente non si applicava al caso di specie.

In conclusione, non vi è dubbio che la materia dei diritti umani, originariamente estranea al diritto comunitario (ora dell'UE), abbia oggi acquistato un ruolo importante in tale diritto ed abbia prodotto alcuni effetti importanti anche sulle sue fonti. Infatti, i diritti umani: *a*) hanno portato ad un forte ampliamento del contenuto dei principi generali del diritto dell'UE; *b*) vengono in rilievo, in quanto principi generali, come criteri interpretativi delle altre fonti del diritto dell'UE[275]; *c*) inoltre (e questo è il punto che qui più interessa) operano come parametro di legittimità per gli atti normativi delle Istituzioni; *d*) infine, servono anche come parametro di legittimità per i comportamenti degli Stati membri nelle ipotesi sopra descritte. In sostanza, si può affermare che i diritti umani hanno introdotto molti elementi di "specialità" rispetto al tradizionale funzionamento delle fonti del diritto dell'Unione Europea, compresi gli atti normativi di diritto derivato.

13. *Conclusioni*

L'esame fin qui condotto delle più importanti fonti previste da accordi, anche se limitato alle decisioni del CdS *ex* art. 41 della Carta ed agli atti di diritto derivato dell'UE, dimostra che il diritto internazionale dei diritti umani ha esercitato un impatto significativo anche su queste fonti. In relazione alle decisioni vincolanti del CdS, vi è stato un processo di ampliamento dell'ambito della loro applicazione e, al contempo, un processo di limitazione e controllo del loro contenuto. Quanto agli atti di diritto derivato dell'UE, il controllo della loro conformità con i principi generali sui diritti umani e con la Carta dei diritti fondamentali è diventato un fattore di grande importanza. Esso ha inciso anche su quelle condotte degli Stati membri, che sono imposte dall'esecuzione degli atti normativi dell'UE.

Come si è detto sopra, questo impatto non ha prodotto vere e proprie modifiche strutturali sulle fonti previste da accordi; ma alcuni interessanti effetti, o elementi di "specialità" o "peculiarità", rispetto al normale funzionamento di tali fonti. Si può sostenere che anche questi effetti sono stati in ultima analisi prodotti dall'influenza dei principi-guida della *preminenza* dell'individuo e della *universalità* dei diritti umani? Ci sembra che la risposta sia positiva, specie con riferimento al primo principio: infatti il valore della tutela dei diritti dell'individuo/persona umana ha finito per incidere sui poteri normativi di importanti organi e/o istituzioni delle Nazioni Unite e dell'Unione Europea. In altri termini, il "nuovo" valore della dignità umana ha portato ad un *riequilibrio*, anche nei poteri e nelle funzioni delle organizzazioni internazionali, rispetto al "tradizionale" valore della cooperazione fra Stati.

---

[275] Vedi Daniele (2014), p. 203; Villani (2017), p. 55.

Sezione IV

SOFT LAW

14. *La varietà degli atti di* soft law

Si sono esaminate finora, con riferimento ai diritti umani, le vere e proprie fonti normative (consuetudine, principi generali di diritto *in foro domestico*, principi del diritto internazionale, *ius cogens*, trattati e fonti previste da accordi). Ma si deve notare che, in aggiunta a queste fonti, esiste una moltitudine di atti internazionali sui diritti umani che sono stati adottati come "raccomandazioni", cioè atti esortativi ma non vincolanti, e che pertanto non possono essere inquadrati fra le fonti. Questi atti prendono, di solito, il nome di "risoluzioni" o "dichiarazioni" o "atti finali di conferenze"; e talora, quando sono formulati in forma particolarmente solenne dall'Assemblea Generale delle NU, sono denominati "dichiarazioni di principi". Nel loro complesso, essi vengono qualificati come "*soft law*", per indicare appunto che non sono giuridicamente vincolanti, in contrapposizione alla "*hard law*".

Nel settore dei diritti umani, a livello universale, conviene ricordare le numerose risoluzioni o dichiarazioni adottate dall'Assemblea Generale delle NU, dalla (*ex*) Commissione sui diritti umani, dal Consiglio dei diritti umani. A livello regionale, si possono citare varie dichiarazioni dell'Organizzazione degli Stati Americani (OAS)[276], del Consiglio d'Europa[277] e del Parlamento europeo. Si devono aggiungere alcuni atti non vincolanti emanati da organizzazioni non governative o da iniziative private[278]. Infine, anche alcuni accordi fra Stati non aventi natura obbligatoria vengono definiti, da alcuni autori[279], come *soft law* o comunque come atti di valore simile a quello di una raccomandazione: ad esempio, l'Atto di Helsinki adottato nel 1975 da 35 Stati[280], contenente anche il c.d. terzo cesto (*basket*) sulla cooperazione nel campo umanitario. Il terzo cesto è stato poi ampliato per comprendere anche la c.d. "dimensione umana" della CSCE (ora OSCE), espressione che comprende, ma non esaurisce, quella di "diritti umani"[281]. Peraltro, non è sempre facile stabilire se e quando gli impegni OSCE degli Stati relativi alla "dimensione umana" siano giuridicamente obbligatori.

Si noti che alcune delle suddette raccomandazioni hanno carattere generale, cioè si occupano in linea tendenzialmente generale dei diritti umani internazionali; mentre altre hanno carattere settoriale o particolare, perché intendono stabilire regole o standard di

---

[276] Vedi, ad esempio, la Dichiarazione americana dei diritti e doveri dell'uomo del 1948.

[277] Tali dichiarazioni sono di solito predisposte dalla Assemblea Parlamentare e adottate dal Comitato dei Ministri in forma di raccomandazione agli Stati membri.

[278] Vedi, ad esempio, la Dichiarazione islamica e la Dichiarazione di Helsinki sui Principi etici per la ricerca medica che coinvolge i soggetti umani, adottata in occasione della diciottesima Assemblea Generale della World Medical Association (WMA) nel 1964 ad Helsinki in Finlandia.

[279] Cfr. Sudre (2006), p. 173.

[280] Come è noto, da tale atto hanno preso avvio prima la Conferenza sulla Sicurezza e Cooperazione in Europa (CSCE) e poi l'Organizzazione per la Sicurezza e la Cooperazione in Europa (OSCE).

[281] Vedi Ronzitti (2016), pp. 343-346.

comportamento degli Stati in relazione a specifiche categorie di persone (ad esempio, donne, fanciulli, rifugiati, minoranze, popoli indigeni, disabili, lavoratori migranti, ecc.) o a specifici diritti o situazioni critiche di violazioni (ad esempio, divieto di genocidio, di discriminazione razziale, di *apartheid*, di tortura, di sparizioni forzate, ecc.).

15. *Il valore di tali atti*

Ciò premesso, si pongono *due problemi* giuridici principali: *a*) quello del valore giuridico, in generale, della *soft law*; e *b*) quello di un suo eventuale valore "speciale" o "particolare" in materia di diritti umani.

Il primo problema riguarda il valore, *rectius* gli *effetti giuridici,* degli atti di *soft law*. Si tratta di una questione molto trattata in dottrina; e pertanto converrà riassumerla in maniera assai sintetica. Si può parlare di almeno quattro effetti prodotti dagli atti di *soft law* nel quadro del diritto internazionale. Un primo effetto, di carattere morale e politico piuttosto che giuridico, è dato dal fatto che la *soft law* induce gli Stati a conformarsi ad essa, anche se essi non hanno un obbligo giuridico di farlo [282]. In particolare, le raccomandazioni emanate dalle organizzazioni internazionali producono un effetto "esortativo". In effetti, nel settore dei diritti umani, le Nazioni Unite e le organizzazioni regionali sui diritti umani hanno spesso perseguito il percorso strategico di emanare in un primo tempo una dichiarazione o una raccomandazione, per raccogliere il consenso degli Stati su atti non vincolanti, e di passare successivamente alla predisposizione di trattati che riprendono e specificano in maggior dettaglio, ed in maniera vincolante, il contenuto degli atti di *soft law*.

Un secondo effetto riguarda la funzione di interpretazione e rilevazione del diritto internazionale. Le regole di *soft law* possono aiutare le corti e gli altri organi internazionali di controllo, i giudici statali e gli operatori giuridici più in generale, nella rilevazione e interpretazione del contenuto di norme internazionali, scritte e non scritte. Nella funzione interpretativa del diritto scritto, la *soft law* può essere usata come ausilio sia del metodo c.d. oggettivistico [283] sia del metodo c.d. soggettivistico [284].

Un terzo effetto può consistere nella codificazione del diritto internazionale generale. In altri termini, talora certi atti di *soft law* riproducono, o riproducono in parte, specificando meglio per iscritto, norme di diritto internazionale generale. Come è noto, l'effetto di codificazione si verifica, in maniera significativa, per le c.d. "dichiarazioni di principi" dell'Assemblea Generale delle NU. Tuttavia, per tutti gli atti di *soft law*, l'effetto codificativo va verificato volta per volta, confrontando il contenuto della *soft law* con quello del diritto internazionale generale. Alcuni esempi di atti di *soft law* in tema di diritti umani, che sono adesso ritenuti riproduttivi del diritto internazionale consuetudinario, sono la Dichiarazione universale dei diritti umani, relativamente ad una parte dei diritti ivi enunciati [285]; la Dichiarazione delle NU del 1960 sull'indipendenza dei popoli coloniali, con ri-

---

[282] Focarelli (2013), p. 78.

[283] Perché può aiutare a stabilire lo scopo e l'oggetto della norma internazionale.

[284] Perché può aiutare a stabilire l'intenzione degli Stati durante i lavori preparatori delle norme convenzionali e di quelle di terzo grado.

[285] Vedi *infra*, Cap. IV, par. 3.

guardo alla norma sull'autodeterminazione esterna dei popoli; la Dichiarazione delle NU del 1963 sull'eliminazione di ogni forma di discriminazione razziale; la Dichiarazione delle NU del 1975 sulla protezione di tutte le persone dalla tortura e da altre pene o trattamenti crudeli, inumani o degradanti.

Infine, il quarto effetto prodotto dalla *soft law*, che è forse il più interessante, è quello di contribuire, talora in maniera assai importante, allo sviluppo progressivo del diritto internazionale (cioè di *hard law*)[286]. Questo effetto non va confuso (anche se è in qualche misura connesso) con il primo effetto sopra citato, di carattere soltanto morale e politico, poiché esso presenta un carattere giuridico. In che modo la *soft law* può contribuire allo sviluppo progressivo del diritto internazionale, e specie di quello generale? Per quanto riguarda il diritto internazionale consuetudinario, in primo luogo la *soft law*, se deriva da un *consenso* generalizzato di Stati o di organizzazioni internazionali, può esprimere l'elemento dell'*opinio iuris ac necessitatis*, che può rafforzarsi con il tempo, specie se accompagnato da altre e successive manifestazioni di *opinio iuris*. In secondo luogo, la *soft law*, derivando pur sempre da atti giuridici approvati da Stati o da organizzazioni internazionali, può esprimere anche l'elemento della *diuturnitas*, poiché oggi è opinione dominante che questo elemento sia costituito non solo da prassi "materiale" ma anche da prassi "verbale"[287]. Naturalmente, occorre cautela nel valutare l'impatto della *soft law* sulla *diuturnitas*, poiché si dovrà verificare che quest'ultima sia rilevabile anche da una prassi uniforme e costante degli Stati "esterna" rispetto agli atti di *soft law*. Per quanto riguarda, invece, i principi generali del diritto internazionale, come si è visto[288], la *soft law* può giocare un ruolo ancora più importante, quando da essa sia desumibile con sicurezza un consenso generale della comunità internazionale nel suo insieme su alcuni di tali principi.

Venendo al secondo problema (quello di un eventuale valore giuridico "particolare" della *soft law* in materia di diritti umani), ci sembra che la risposta sia in termini quantitativi piuttosto che qualitativi. In altre parole, i suddetti quattro effetti della *soft law* sono particolarmente forti e significativi nel settore dei diritti umani, per i motivi che abbiamo già esposto parlando delle consuetudini e dei principi generali del diritto internazionale[289]. La carenza di una significativa prassi interstatale classica e di controversie interstatali in materia di diritti umani, e la spinta esercitata dai principi-guida di *preminenza dell'individuo* e di *universalità* dei diritti umani, inducono l'interprete ad attribuire un'importanza particolare agli elementi dell'*opinio iuris* e del consenso generale della comunità internazionale. Ciò finisce anche per rivalutare molto il ruolo della *soft law* nel settore dei diritti umani.

---

[286] Tomuschat (2014), pp. 45-46.

[287] Vedi *supra*, par. 3.1.

[288] Vedi *supra*, par. 5.

[289] Vedi *supra*, parr. 3 e 5.

Capitolo III

GLI OBBLIGHI INTERNAZIONALI

1. *Introduzione: importanza di una teoria sugli obblighi internazionali relativi ai diritti umani*

L'esame delle fonti internazionali dei diritti umani è importante, dal punto di vista dei concetti generali sul diritto internazionale dei diritti umani, perché ci dà informazioni sui metodi di produzione normativa e di conoscenza dei diritti umani. Tuttavia, tale esame non ci dice nulla su altri aspetti concettuali e pratici importanti, che attengono soprattutto agli obblighi che derivano dal diritto internazionale dei diritti umani. In particolare: chi sono i titolari attivi e passivi di tali obblighi? Qual è il contenuto e la natura (spesso assai diversa) dei singoli obblighi? Qual è il loro ambito di applicazione "spaziale"? Trovare una risposta a queste domande è importante, soprattutto nell'ottica della violazione dei diritti umani e della relativa responsabilità internazionale. Si tratta infatti di capire chi è obbligato al rispetto dei diritti umani e nei confronti di chi (ambito di applicazione "personale" degli obblighi); cosa deve fare in concreto il titolare passivo dell'obbligo per rispettare un determinato diritto umano e quando si verifica la sua violazione (contenuto e natura dell'obbligo); infine, entro quali limiti spaziali il titolare dell'obbligo deve rispettarlo (ambito di applicazione "spaziale").

Tutte queste questioni richiedono di affrontare ed esaminare una vera e propria teoria degli obblighi internazionali relativi ai diritti umani. Per la verità, in maniera piuttosto sorprendente, la dottrina specialistica dei diritti umani non si è occupata a fondo di questo tema ed ha finora condotto su di esso soprattutto delle indagini di carattere descrittivo, e non di carattere teorico-sistematico. Inoltre, come vedremo, anche quando essa ha tentato un inquadramento più concettuale del tema, ha voluto costruire, a nostro avviso erroneamente, una teoria particolare ed autonoma degli obblighi internazionali sui diritti umani [1], che, anche se ha avuto un certo successo, è criticabile e non presenta alcun collegamento con la teoria generale del diritto e del diritto internazionale.

D'altra parte, una teoria generale degli obblighi internazionali è piuttosto carente anche nella dottrina generalista del diritto internazionale, poiché sono pochissimi e assai risalenti gli studi che trattano in maniera sistematica ed organica l'insieme delle problematiche attinenti a questo argomento. In realtà, il discorso sugli obblighi internazionali ha avuto un qualche sviluppo, sia pure insufficiente, non tanto nel quadro di studi di carattere generale oppure sulle fonti, quanto piuttosto in alcuni studi sulla responsabilità internazionale degli

---

[1] Vedi *infra*, par. 4.4.

Stati; e specie in quelli dedicati al c.d. elemento oggettivo dell'illecito, costituito appunto dalla violazione di un obbligo internazionale. Ma ciò ha una sua logica, se solo si riflette sul fatto che, per indagare a fondo sull'illecito internazionale, occorre preliminarmente chiarire bene la natura e l'ambito di applicazione dei vari obblighi internazionali cui gli Stati sono vincolati.

Questa conclusione è evidente per quanto riguarda l'ambito di applicazione "personale" e "spaziale" degli obblighi. Ma vale anche in relazione alla natura ed al contenuto degli obblighi. Infatti il contenuto esatto del comportamento richiesto dal diritto internazionale volta per volta allo Stato (e quindi anche l'eventuale accertamento circa la sua violazione) dipende non tanto da una certa norma primaria, quanto da ciascuno specifico obbligo posto da tale norma. In altri termini, ciascuna norma primaria del diritto internazionale può imporre allo Stato una serie di obblighi di natura e struttura diversa, alla cui violazione corrispondono forme diverse di responsabilità. Ciò è vero anche in materia di diritti umani: ad esempio, la norma sul diritto umano alla vita[2] comprende al suo interno una serie di obblighi aventi natura e caratteristiche assai diverse fra loro. Lo stesso vale, per fare un altro esempio, per la norma sul diritto al cibo[3] o per quella sul diritto al rispetto della vita privata[4]. Pertanto, ai fini della responsabilità dello Stato, le distinzioni davvero utili vanno fatte non fra diverse categorie di diritti umani, bensì fra diverse categorie di obblighi.

In conclusione, una teoria degli obblighi internazionali relativi ai diritti umani è necessaria, sia per motivi teorici e sistematici, sia per motivi pratici. Ma si può parlare anche per questi obblighi (così come si è fatto per le fonti) di una loro "specialità" rispetto ai tradizionali obblighi del diritto internazionale? La risposta, come vedremo, è solo in parte positiva. È positiva per quanto riguarda l'ambito di applicazione "personale" degli obblighi ed il loro ambito di applicazione "spaziale". Invece, a mio avviso, la risposta è negativa per quanto riguarda la natura e le forme degli obblighi sui diritti umani.

Ciò premesso, esamineremo prima la questione dell'ambito di applicazione "personale" degli obblighi sui diritti umani; poi la tematica, più complessa, circa il contenuto e la natura di tali obblighi; ed infine il problema del loro ambito di applicazione "spaziale" (territoriale ed extraterritoriale).

---

[2] Vedi *infra*, Cap.V, par. 7.

[3] Vedi *infra*, Cap.V, par. 10.

[4] Vedi *infra*, Cap. VI, par. 2.

Sezione I
AMBITO DI APPLICAZIONE PERSONALE DEGLI OBBLIGHI

2. *Titolari degli obblighi*

La prima questione che si pone è quella di stabilire quali siano i titolari passivi degli obblighi internazionali relativi ai diritti umani; cioè a quali enti tali obblighi si impongano.

2.1. *Stati*

È evidente che gli obblighi internazionali sui diritti umani si impongono prima di tutto, e soprattutto, agli Stati. I diritti umani nascono, anche a livello di diritti statali, come un limite all'esercizio, potenzialmente abusivo, del potere di sovranità dello Stato sui propri sudditi, che si accompagna al monopolio da parte dello Stato dell'uso della forza. Pertanto i diritti umani sono inizialmente, e tuttora in gran parte, concepiti come diritti dei singoli nei confronti dello Stato. Da ciò deriva anche il fatto che le violazioni dei diritti umani, dovute all'esercizio abusivo di potere da parte dello Stato, costituiscono violazioni particolarmente gravi del diritto e differiscono radicalmente dalle violazioni del diritto penale o civile commesse da privati contro altri privati [5].

Il fatto che i titolari degli obblighi internazionali sui diritti umani siano normalmente, e soprattutto, gli Stati risulta chiaramente anche dalle disposizioni di carattere generale contenute nei principali trattati sui diritti umani. L'art. 1 della Convenzione europea dei diritti umani stabilisce che gli *Stati parti* riconoscono i diritti e libertà contenuti nella Convenzione ad ogni persona soggetta alla loro giurisdizione. L'art. 2(1) del Patto sui diritti civili e politici stabilisce che ciascuno degli *Stati parti* del Patto si impegna a rispettare e garantire a tutti gli individui, che si trovino sul suo territorio e siano sottoposti alla sua giurisdizione, i diritti riconosciuti nel Patto. L'art. 2(1) del Patto sui diritti economici, sociali e culturali stabilisce che ciascuno degli *Stati parti* si impegna ad operare, al fine di assicurare progressivamente la piena attuazione dei diritti riconosciuti nel Patto. Le disposizioni generali contenute in altri trattati sui diritti umani hanno un simile contenuto.

Pertanto la responsabilità di adempiere gli obblighi internazionali relativi ai diritti umani grava innanzitutto sugli Stati. Ma qual è il concetto di Stato come destinatario passivo di obblighi internazionali e come possibile responsabile della loro violazione? Una prima risposta, di carattere assai generale, deriva dal fatto che, nel diritto internazionale, lo Stato è preso in considerazione come Stato-governo o Stato-organizzazione e non come Stato-comunità [6]. Pertanto gli obblighi dello Stato gravano, in linea di principio, su tutti gli organi che compongono l'organizzazione dello Stato.

---

[5] Kälin, Künzli (2009), p. 78.

[6] Vedi, per tutti, Conforti (2018), pp. 13-14.

Tuttavia, adesso una risposta più precisa alla suddetta domanda deriva dalle norme consuetudinarie sulla responsabilità internazionale degli Stati che disciplinano l'elemento soggettivo dell'illecito internazionale (cioè l'attribuzione allo Stato della condotta internazionalmente illecita). Come è noto, queste norme sono regolate in dettaglio dal Progetto di articoli sulla responsabilità degli Stati adottato dalla Commissione del Diritto Internazionale (CDI) nel 2001 [7], che, pur non essendo giuridicamente vincolante, viene comunemente riconosciuto come largamente rappresentativo del diritto internazionale consuetudinario. Tale Progetto, sul quale non ci possiamo qui soffermare, stabilisce che sono attribuibili ad uno Stato non solo i comportamenti dei suoi individui-organi che agiscono nell'esercizio ufficiale delle funzioni (organi *de iure*) [8], ma anche altri comportamenti, come quelli di organi che agiscono *ultra vires* [9] o di individui che agiscono come organi *de facto* [10] o sotto la direzione o il controllo di un altro Stato [11].

2.2. *Organizzazioni internazionali*

Negli anni recenti, si è posto sempre di più il problema se gli obblighi internazionali relativi al rispetto dei diritti umani si impongano non solo agli Stati, ma anche alle organizzazioni internazionali [12]. Ciò è dovuto al fatto che gli Stati tendono oggigiorno a delegare una serie di funzioni sempre più importanti alle organizzazioni internazionali, quali, ad esempio, il potere di adottare atti vincolanti nei confronti degli Stati membri [13]; il potere di organizzare missioni di *peace-keeping* o *peace-enforcing* o addirittura di amministrazione di territori; o il potere di finanziare, organizzare ed anche amministrare progetti operativi o missioni di aiuto e di soccorso in territori statali. Nell'esercizio di questi poteri, può darsi che le organizzazioni internazionali violino il diritto internazionale, specie nel campo dei diritti umani.

Si potrebbe replicare che le organizzazioni internazionali non sono titolari di obblighi in materia di diritti umani, perché quasi tutti i trattati sui diritti umani sono stati firmati e ratificati soltanto da Stati [14]. Tuttavia, si tratta di un'obiezione piuttosto formalistica, poiché, se gli Stati parti di un trattato istitutivo di un'organizzazione internazionale sono vincolati da un certo trattato sui diritti umani, è difficile sostenere che l'organizzazione, in quanto ente che persegue per definizione la cooperazione fra gli Stati parti, possa ignorare tale trattato.

In ogni caso, anche qualora si volesse ammettere che le organizzazioni internazionali non sono vincolate dai trattati sui diritti umani dei quali non sono formalmente parti contraenti, si dovrebbe pur sempre concludere che le organizzazioni internazionali, quando

---

[7] ILC, *Draft Articles on Responsibility of States for Internationally Wrongful Acts*, 1 August 2001.

[8] Artt. 4 e 5.

[9] Art. 7.

[10] Art. 9.

[11] Art. 8.

[12] Su questo tema vedi, fra gli altri, Kälin, Künzli (2009), pp. 85-93; Focarelli (2013), pp. 338-342; Tomuschat (2014), pp. 120-129. Cfr. anche, di recente, sulla responsabilità dell'Unione Europea per violazione dei diritti umani, Carli (2019), pp. 137-218.

[13] Vedi *supra*, Cap. II, par. 12.

[14] Per un'eccezione, vedi la Convenzione del 2006 sui diritti delle persone disabili.

hanno personalità internazionale, sono vincolate dal diritto internazionale generale in materia di diritti umani, che si applica a tutti i membri della comunità internazionale nel suo insieme. Non ci sembra da condividere invece la tesi che vorrebbe vincolare le organizzazioni internazionali soltanto al rispetto dei diritti umani aventi carattere di *ius cogens*.

Ciò premesso, le norme sulla responsabilità internazionale delle organizzazioni internazionali, comprese quelle che disciplinano l'elemento soggettivo dell'illecito internazionale, sono state recentemente oggetto di un progetto di codificazione della CDI: il Progetto di articoli sulla responsabilità delle organizzazioni internazionali, adottato dalla CDI nel 2011 [15]. Questo Progetto tende a seguire le linee generali del Progetto del 2001 sulla responsabilità degli Stati. Anche se non tutte le norme di dettaglio del Progetto del 2011 hanno forse acquisito natura consuetudinaria, non si può dubitare sull'esistenza del principio generale, enunciato nell'art. 3, per il quale ogni illecito internazionale commesso da un'organizzazione internazionale comporta la sua responsabilità internazionale.

2.3. *Individui*

In base alle regole sulla responsabilità degli Stati, ed in particolare quelle sull'attribuzione della condotta illecita, le persone o i gruppi di persone che hanno la qualità di privati non sono vincolati dagli obblighi internazionali sui diritti umani, eccetto che in quelle situazioni, piuttosto eccezionali, nelle quali tali persone agiscono come organi *de facto* o sotto la direzione o il controllo di uno Stato o quando uno Stato riconosce e adotta successivamente i loro comportamenti. Ma, in realtà, in questi casi, i comportamenti delle persone o gruppi di persone sono attribuiti allo Stato [16] e comportano la responsabilità di quest'ultimo. Pertanto non si può parlare, in senso proprio, di obblighi internazionali che gravano direttamente su tali persone.

Ma ci si può chiedere se, in deroga a questa regola generale, vi siano nel diritto internazionale alcune situazioni nelle quali gli individui o i gruppi privati siano direttamente vincolati da obblighi internazionali sui diritti umani e rispondano essi stessi a livello internazionale per la violazione di tali obblighi.

Allo stato attuale, quantomeno nel diritto internazionale generale, ciò si verifica soltanto per gli obblighi che derivano agli individui dal *diritto internazionale penale*; e cioè in relazione ai divieti di crimini internazionali individuali (genocidio, crimini contro l'umanità, crimini di guerra, aggressione) [17]. In questo caso si può parlare di veri e propri obblighi internazionali che gravano sugli individui, e la cui violazione crea responsabilità penale individuale a livello internazionale. Forse si può ritenere che, a titolo di sviluppo progressivo del diritto internazionale, vi sia una tendenza a considerare anche il terrorismo internazionale (nonostante le perduranti difficoltà di una sua definizione precisa) come un crimine internazionale individuale. Una conferma potrebbe derivare dal fatto che vi è una tendenza di molti Stati, nel diritto internazionale contemporaneo, a ritenere lecita la legittima difesa contro gruppi di terroristi, anche qualora la loro condotta non sia attribuibile ad uno Stato. Pertanto, se questo sviluppo si concretizzerà, si potrà

---

[15] ILC, *Draft Articles on Responsibility of International Organizations*, 3 June 2011.

[16] Vedi *supra*, par. 2.1.

[17] Vedi *infra*, Cap. V, par. 9.

parlare anche di obblighi internazionali di individui e gruppi di individui relativi al crimine di terrorismo internazionale. Si deve inoltre tener conto del fatto che, comunque, il compimento di atti terroristici si traduce spesso nella commissione di illeciti che sono a loro volta configurabili quali crimini internazionali, specie crimini contro l'umanità, come nel caso di sterminio.

Vi sono poi alcune situazioni nelle quali gli individui privati sono *indirettamente* vincolati da obblighi sui diritti umani derivanti dal diritto internazionale [18]. Ciò si verifica quando un trattato internazionale obbliga gli Stati parti ad adottare normative interne che puniscano penalmente le violazioni di quei diritti umani che sono contenuti nel trattato in questione. Si possono citare, ad esempio, l'art. 4 della Convenzione del 1965 sull'eliminazione di tutte le forme di discriminazione razziale e l'art. 4 della Convenzione del 1984 contro la tortura. Ma, in realtà, gli obblighi per gli individui derivano dalle norme statali emesse in esecuzione del trattato e non direttamente dal diritto internazionale. Lo stesso può dirsi per le situazioni nelle quali uno Stato, per adempiere il proprio obbligo di prevenire e reprimere le violazioni di diritti umani protetti dal diritto internazionale generale o dal diritto convenzionale, emana norme interne di diritto civile o amministrativo per eseguire tali obblighi. Anche in questo caso, gli obblighi per gli individui privati derivano direttamente dalle norme nazionali e solo in via indiretta dal diritto internazionale.

3. *Titolari dei diritti*

3.1. *Stati*

È chiaro che agli obblighi sui diritti umani assunti da uno Stato, sulla base del diritto internazionale, corrispondono *diritti* di altri Stati al rispetto di tali obblighi. Si tratta dei rapporti interstatali tipicamente regolati dal diritto internazionale, che operano pacificamente anche nel settore dei diritti umani. Infatti, i trattati sui diritti umani sono stipulati dagli Stati, che si impegnano tra loro al rispetto dei medesimi; le norme di diritto internazionale generale sui diritti umani (siano esse regole consuetudinarie o principi generali di diritto o principi del diritto internazionale) obbligano tutti gli Stati e li impegnano tra loro al rispetto di tali norme; infine, le decisioni vincolanti delle organizzazioni internazionali sui diritti umani obbligano ed impegnano tra loro gli Stati cui tali atti sono diretti.

Ciò premesso, si possono realizzare tre situazioni nelle quali uno o più Stati possono far valere il proprio diritto al rispetto degli obblighi internazionali sui diritti umani assunti da un altro Stato. La prima situazione, piuttosto rara in pratica, si verifica quando l'obbligo sul rispetto dei diritti umani ha soltanto carattere reciproco. Si potrebbe fare l'esempio di un trattato bilaterale che preveda per ambedue gli Stati parti l'obbligo di estradare o giudicare (*aut dedere aut iudicare*) un individuo accusato di una grave violazione dei diritti umani. Se lo Stato che detiene il colpevole non intende processarlo, l'altro Stato ha il diritto di ottenere l'estradizione.

La seconda situazione, assai più frequente, si verifica quando i trattati sui diritti umani

[18] Kälin, Künzli (2009), p. 83.

stabiliscono obblighi *erga omnes partes*. Come si è già detto [19], in questo caso ogni Stato parte assume gli obblighi previsti dal trattato in maniera solidale nei confronti di tutti gli altri Stati parti. Pertanto, ciascuno di questi ha un diritto [20] al rispetto degli obblighi convenzionali da parte dello Stato accusato della loro violazione. In alcuni di questi trattati, come si vedrà meglio in seguito [21], tale diritto può essere fatto valere anche tramite forme di garanzia collettiva, cioè per mezzo di ricorsi interstatali dinanzi a corti od altri organi internazionali di controllo sui diritti umani.

Infine, la terza situazione si realizza quando vi sono norme di diritto internazionale generale sui diritti umani, che stabiliscono obblighi *erga omnes*, cioè obblighi di ciascuno Stato nei confronti di tutti gli altri Stati della comunità internazionale. Questi ultimi hanno tutti il diritto al rispetto di tali obblighi da parte dello Stato accusato della violazione.

3.2. *Individui*

A nostro avviso, non vi è dubbio che, agli obblighi sui diritti umani assunti dagli Stati, in base al diritto internazionale, corrispondono non solo diritti di altri Stati, ma anche, e direi soprattutto, diritti degli individui. In altri termini, i destinatari attivi *principali* dei diritti umani sono gli individui e, per certi diritti umani, gruppi di individui, quali popoli, minoranze e popoli indigeni. Del resto la stessa definizione più comune dei diritti umani è quella di diritti di cui sono titolari tutti gli esseri umani [22].

Peraltro, se vogliamo essere più teorici, possiamo ricordare quanto abbiamo già detto; e cioè che, proprio grazie all'impulso innovatore della teoria dei diritti umani internazionali, oggi la dottrina dominante ammette che il diritto internazionale contemporaneo regola *formalmente e direttamente* (cioè senza bisogno di essere recepito o incorporato dal diritto interno di uno Stato) anche alcuni rapporti fra Stati ed individui ed alcuni rapporti interindividuali. Ne deriva che gli individui sono adesso destinatari diretti di alcune norme internazionali (primarie, secondarie e terziarie), nonché di diritti ed obblighi internazionali. Ovviamente, affinché la singola norma internazionale possa creare diritti od obblighi per un individuo, essa deve avere le idonee caratteristiche (essere indirizzata anche all'individuo ed essere immediatamente applicabile). Queste caratteristiche non vanno confuse con quelle, ulteriori, che la norma internazionale deve avere per creare a favore dell'individuo un diritto giustiziabile dinanzi ai giudici interni [23].

Quasi tutte le norme internazionali sui diritti umani costituiscono esempi tipici di norme che impongono obblighi ad uno Stato cui corrispondono sia diritti di altri Stati sia diritti di individui. In questo senso, si può dire che esse hanno carattere "binario"; cioè che creano due categorie di destinatari attivi. Naturalmente, ciò non significa che gli individui abbiano a disposizione contro lo Stato destinatario passivo dell'obbligo tutte le garanzie (norme secondarie e terziarie) di attuazione di cui invece dispongono gli Stati destinatari attivi dell'obbligo (sia quelli lesi che quelli "indirettamente" lesi).

---

[19] Vedi *supra*, Cap. I, parr. 7.3.1 e 7.4.1.

[20] Ma, secondo alcuni autori, un mero interesse giuridico.

[21] Vedi *infra*, Cap. IV, parr. 8.1, 11 e 12.

[22] Focarelli (2013), p. 122.

[23] Su questo punto vedi Pisillo Mazzeschi (2008), pp. 256-267.

Come è noto, questa conclusione non è accolta da una parte, ormai minoritaria, della dottrina, la quale continua a ritenere che gli individui non siano soggetti del diritto internazionale né destinatari diretti delle norme internazionali sui diritti umani. Queste norme dovrebbero essere costruite come norme che si dirigono soltanto agli Stati, i quali si obbligano, nei loro ordinamenti interni, ad accordare determinati diritti agli individui. Solo nel quadro degli ordinamenti interni statali, e sempre che tali ordinamenti recepiscano le norme internazionali, gli individui diverrebbero titolari dei diritti umani riconosciuti dalle norme internazionali. In altri termini, gli individui sarebbero soltanto "beneficiari di fatto" delle norme sui diritti umani.

Questa teoria appare oggi formalistica e non convincente. Prendiamo, per esempio, in esame una norma internazionale primaria sui diritti umani: il divieto di tortura *ex* art. 3 della Convenzione europea dei diritti umani. Non vi è alcuna difficoltà logica a ritenere che tale norma crei direttamente un obbligo di ciascuno Stato parte della Convenzione non solo nei confronti di tutti gli altri Stati parti, ma *anche nei confronti degli individui* sottoposti alla giurisdizione di tutti gli Stati parti; e che quindi tali individui siano destinatari o titolari diretti, e non meri "beneficiari di fatto", del diritto di non subire tortura, *che viene conferito loro direttamente dal diritto internazionale*. In realtà, questa conclusione è quella più naturale e spontanea, se solo si riflette sul fatto che l'obbligo degli Stati di non commettere tortura viene assunto in via principale proprio per proteggere l'individuo.

Una conferma di ciò è data dal fatto che l'individuo, che abbia subito una tortura *ex* art. 3 della Convenzione europea, può adire la Corte di Strasburgo ed ottenere una sentenza che dichiari che il suo diritto è stato violato. Si potrebbe obiettare che il medesimo individuo non può far valere una violazione del divieto di tortura (che non è contenuto in una norma *self-executing*) dinanzi ai giudici interni di uno Stato che non abbia provveduto ad adeguare il proprio ordinamento interno a tale divieto (come l'Italia fino ai tempi più recenti); e quindi non disponga di un diritto giustiziabile dinanzi ai giudici interni. Ma ciò non significa che il diritto internazionale non abbia conferito all'individuo il diritto in questione; significa solo che lo Stato che non ha attuato tale diritto nel proprio ordinamento interno ha violato il diritto internazionale.

Un discorso simile si può fare anche per *alcune* norme internazionali secondarie sui diritti umani, per esempio, quelle relative alla riparazione dell'illecito. Se uno Stato viola una norma primaria sui diritti umani che sia diretta *anche* nei confronti dell'individuo, nulla impedisce di ritenere che lo Stato commetta un illecito e incorra in responsabilità internazionale *anche nei confronti dell'individuo* vittima; e che quest'ultimo possa usufruire di certi diritti derivanti da norme internazionali secondarie, specie il diritto alla riparazione dell'illecito. Questa conclusione ha trovato una conferma esplicita nella Risoluzione adottata il 16 dicembre 2005 dall'Assemblea generale delle Nazioni Unite sul diritto a un ricorso e alla riparazione per le vittime di violazioni gravi dei diritti umani e del diritto umanitario[24].

Infine, anche nel caso delle norme internazionali terziarie (che stabiliscono forme o garanzie di accertamento giurisdizionale o quasi-giurisdizionale del diritto internazionale), nulla impedisce di ritenere che gli individui possano essere destinatari diretti di *alcune* di

---

[24] *Basic Principles and Guidelines on the Right to a Remedy and Reparation for Victims of Gross Violations of International Human Rights Law and Serious Violations of International Humanitarian Law*, GA Res. 60/147, 16 December 2005. Vedi anche *supra*, Cap. I, par. 7.4.3.

tali norme. Gli esempi più evidenti sono dati dai diritti di ricorso che gli individui hanno contro gli Stati dinanzi a organi internazionali di controllo, quali la Corte europea dei diritti umani, la Commissione interamericana sui diritti umani, il Comitato dei diritti umani, il Comitato delle Nazioni Unite contro la tortura, e altri *Treaty Bodies* o organi simili. Una conferma che gli individui possano essere titolari di diritti derivanti da norme internazionali terziarie si trova, da ultimo, nell'art. 33(2) (e nel relativo commento) del Progetto della Commissione del diritto internazionale delle Nazioni Unite sulla responsabilità degli Stati adottato nel 2001 [25]; nonché, in maniera ancora più esplicita, nell'art. 16 (e nel relativo commento) del Progetto della medesima Commissione sulla protezione diplomatica approvato nel 2006, che riconosce agli individui il diritto:

> "to resort under international law to actions or procedures other than diplomatic protection to secure redress for injury suffered as a result of an internationally wrongful act [...]" [26].

3.3. *Popoli, minoranze e popoli indigeni*

Per i gruppi di individui, costituiti da popoli, minoranze e popoli indigeni, valgono, in linea di principio, le stesse conclusioni sopra indicate per gli individui. Ma si deve notare che le norme sui diritti umani formalmente indirizzate a queste categorie sono meno numerose, e talora più "deboli", rispetto alle norme formalmente indirizzate agli individui [27].

Da ciò deriva che popoli, minoranze e popoli indigeni sono destinatari soltanto di un numero limitato di diritti umani aventi carattere giuridicamente vincolante; specie dal punto di vista del diritto internazionale generale.

Sezione II

CONTENUTO E NATURA DEGLI OBBLIGHI. VARIE CATEGORIE E LORO VALIDITÀ

Dopo aver esaminato l'argomento dei titolari attivi e passivi degli obblighi relativi ai diritti umani, conviene affrontare il tema del contenuto e della natura di tali obblighi. Ma, prima, conviene fare due premesse sul problema più ampio circa l'inquadramento concettuale degli obblighi internazionali sui diritti umani.

La prima premessa è che, a mio avviso, una teoria sugli obblighi relativi ai diritti umani non deve essere confinata dentro il settore specifico ed angusto del diritto internazionale dei diritti umani, ma deve invece essere collocata nel quadro di una *teoria generale* sugli

---

[25] ILC, *Draft Articles on Responsibility of States for Internationally Wrongful Acts*, 1 August 2001, art. 33(2): "This part is without prejudice to any right, arising from the international responsibility of a State, which may accrue directly to any person or entity other than a State". Vedi anche, in maniera simile, ILC, *Draft Articles on Responsibility of International Organizations*, 3 June 2011, art. 33(2).

[26] ILC, *Draft Articles on Diplomatic Protection*, 8 August 2006, art. 16.

[27] Vedi *infra*, Cap. V, par. 24; Cap. VI, parr. 17, 18 e 19.

obblighi internazionali. Infatti, è nostra ferma convinzione che gli obblighi internazionali degli Stati in materia di diritti umani non abbiano natura diversa rispetto ad altri obblighi internazionali degli Stati. Essi hanno la particolarità di dirigersi, come destinatari attivi, non solo ad altri Stati, ma anche ad individui, che diventano titolari di veri e propri diritti derivanti dal diritto internazionale; ma tale particolarità non è oggigiorno esclusiva del settore dei diritti umani. D'altra parte, sono errate, a mio avviso, quelle tendenze dottrinali a separare ed isolare il settore dei diritti umani (per esempio, con le teorie dei regimi *self-contained*) rispetto al resto del diritto internazionale[28]. Al contrario il settore normativo dei diritti umani deve essere inquadrato nell'intero sistema del diritto internazionale, con il quale interagisce e con il quale deve essere armonizzato.

La seconda premessa è che la teoria degli obblighi internazionali (e pertanto anche degli obblighi relativi ai diritti umani) deve comprendere una vasta serie di categorie e di distinzioni giuridiche, che sono diverse a seconda del punto di osservazione. Ad esempio, nell'ottica dei destinatari attivi degli obblighi si possono identificare le categorie degli obblighi reciproci e degli obblighi *erga omnes*; nell'ottica dell'attuazione interna degli obblighi si può parlare di obblighi *self-executing* o *non self-executing*; nell'ottica dell'accertamento giudiziario degli obblighi, si può parlare di obblighi giustiziabili o non giustiziabili; e così via. Alcune di queste categorie sono state già trattate.

In questa sede, dovendo affrontare la questione del contenuto e della natura degli obblighi sui diritti umani, conviene privilegiare l'ottica relativa al modo di adempimento o di violazione degli obblighi nell'ordinamento internazionale. In altri termini, l'aspetto ora più interessante è quello di comprendere *il contenuto del comportamento* richiesto dal diritto internazionale volta per volta allo Stato e quindi di comprendere quando si ha una violazione. È chiaro che tale comportamento dipende non dal contenuto generale della norma primaria, né dal diritto umano protetto da tale norma; bensì da *ciascuno specifico obbligo* imposto dalla norma. E dalla natura e struttura di tale obbligo. In altri termini, ciascuna norma primaria può imporre allo Stato una serie di obblighi di natura e struttura diverse, alla cui violazione corrispondono forme diverse di responsabilità. Ciò è vero anche in materia di diritti umani: ciascun diritto umano può imporre allo Stato uno spettro di obblighi di natura e struttura diversa. Ai fini della responsabilità, *le distinzioni utili non sono fra categorie di diritti, ma fra categorie di obblighi*.

Da queste premesse, deriva che non ritengo convincenti né utili quelle tesi dottrinali sugli obblighi relativi ai diritti umani che si basano su una sistemazione fatta per categorie di diritti[29]; né quelle tesi dottrinali che si basano su categorie soltanto descrittive di obblighi, oppure che mancano di rigore giuridico e di un'impostazione teorica adeguata.

Ciò detto, esaminiamo comunque, in maniera critica, le teorie più note, che propongono categorie di obblighi di carattere descrittivo o comunque categorie non adeguate. Proporremo in seguito le categorie che ci sembrano invece utili e aventi valore concettuale-sistematico.

---

[28] Vedi *supra*, Cap. I, par. 6.

[29] Vedi, ad es., Mowbray (2004).

4. *Categorie solo descrittive e di scarso valore concettuale-sistematico*

4.1. *Obblighi relativi ai diritti di prima, seconda, terza e quarta generazione. Critica*

Nel settore dei diritti umani, la distinzione che è stata utilizzata per molto tempo ed è tuttora più celebre è quella fra diritti umani di prima, di seconda e di terza generazione (o dimensione). Di conseguenza, una parte della dottrina ha anche sviluppato una parallela distinzione fra obblighi relativi ai diritti umani di prima, seconda e terza generazione. Come è noto, sono di solito considerati di prima generazione i diritti civili e politici; di seconda generazione i diritti economici, sociali e culturali; e di terza generazione certi diritti, di solito di natura collettiva (o di solidarietà), come il diritto allo sviluppo, alla pace, ad un ambiente salubre, allo sfruttamento delle risorse economiche. Altri diritti umani di natura collettiva, sviluppatisi più recentemente, come il diritto alla democrazia, ad un buon governo, alla sicurezza umana, sono classificati talora come di terza e talora come di quarta generazione. Infine, sono considerati come di quarta generazione certi nuovi diritti emergenti, ancora in fase di affermazione a livello internazionale, che sono legati allo sviluppo delle biotecnologie, della genetica e dell'informatica.

Questa distinzione fra diverse generazioni di diritti umani ha una base soprattutto storica e socio-politica: i diritti civili e politici furono i primi ad affermarsi a livello internazionale e nel quadro delle Nazioni Unite grazie alla spinta dei Paesi occidentali; i diritti economici, sociali e culturali furono i secondi a svilupparsi a livello internazionale grazie specie alla pressione dei Paesi socialisti; mentre i diritti umani della terza generazione sono di formazione più recente e sono dovuti soprattutto ai Paesi in via di sviluppo. Più difficile è, invece, ricondurre i diritti umani di quarta generazione ad un particolare gruppo "politico" di Stati.

Tuttavia, la medesima distinzione ha assunto fin dall'inizio anche una funzione più tecnico-giuridica, perché da essa si sono tratte anche varie conseguenze di carattere giuridico. Le più note riguardano la distinzione fra diritti civili e politici, da una parte, e diritti economici, sociali e culturali, dall'altra parte. Specie in passato, molti giuristi ritenevano che i due gruppi di diritti avessero una natura assai diversa, sotto vari profili.

Primo: si diceva che i diritti civili e politici avevano natura negativa perché richiedevano un'astensione da parte dello Stato, mentre i diritti economici, sociali e culturali avevano natura positiva perché richiedevano un'azione da parte dello Stato. Secondo: si sosteneva che i diritti di prima generazione avevano carattere obbligatorio e immediatamente precettivo, mentre i diritti di seconda generazione avevano carattere solo programmatico. In altri termini, il godimento dei primi diritti si poteva realizzare subito, con la mera presenza di certe norme negli ordinamenti interni statali; mentre il godimento dei secondi presupponeva che lo Stato intervenisse, con misure non solo legislative, ma anche amministrative, organizzative e tecniche, che richiedevano costi particolari ed un'attuazione graduale nel tempo. Terzo: si diceva che i diritti di prima generazione erano formulabili in termini più precisi, mentre quelli di seconda generazione erano più vaghi e generici. Quarto: come logica conseguenza, i diritti di prima generazione erano ritenuti "giustiziabili" dinanzi ai giudici interni, una volta inseriti nell'ordinamento statale; mentre i diritti di seconda generazione non erano considerati "giustiziabili". Quinto: anche le misure di controllo a livello internazionale dovevano essere diverse: mentre per i diritti civili e politici si poteva prevedere anche una forma di controllo quasi-giurisdizionale sulle singole violazioni; per i diritti economici, sociali e culturali era possibile solo un controllo di carattere politico-diplomatico sui rapporti di carattere generale sottoposti dagli Stati.

In realtà, con il tempo, molte di queste distinzioni si sono dimostrate inesatte; ed attualmente si tende a riconoscere che non vi sono differenze così nette fra i due gruppi di diritti. Ad esempio, oggi si sostiene che alcuni tra i diritti economici, sociali e culturali si prestano ad essere garantiti anche dinanzi ai giudici interni; che, d'altra parte, i diritti politici e molti diritti civili non sono precettivi senza un intervento dell'apparato statale; che la immediatezza o gradualità della realizzazione dei diritti dipende dalle preesistenti strutture statali più che dalla natura dei diritti medesimi; ed infine che le misure internazionali di controllo quasi-giurisdizionale possono funzionare sia per l'una che per l'altra categoria di diritti.

Per quanto riguarda poi i diritti di terza e di quarta generazione, la dottrina di solito ritiene che essi siano per ora troppo vaghi e generici per dar luogo a veri e propri obblighi vincolanti per gli Stati ed a veri e propri diritti per gli individui. Pertanto, essi non avrebbero né carattere precettivo né carattere meramente programmatico, ma sarebbero addirittura sprovvisti di forza normativa e sarebbero solo programmi di azione di natura politica. Tuttavia, come vedremo in seguito [30], anche questa conclusione non è sempre valida.

Cosa possiamo concludere circa la distinzione fra diritti di prima, seconda, terza e quarta generazione e circa la parallela distinzione fra i relativi obblighi?

A nostro parere, si tratta di una distinzione che è utile da un punto di vista storico e socio-politico, come avevamo già detto. Tuttavia, da un punto di vista giuridico, si tratta di una distinzione che ha valore solo descrittivo e che non presenta molta utilità concettuale e sistematica. Tanto è vero che i giuristi, per precisare le differenze fra le suddette categorie, ricorrono ad altre distinzioni, come quelle sopra indicate, fra norme precettive, norme programmatiche e impegni senza forza normativa, oppure fra diritti giustiziabili e non giustiziabili, oppure fra diritti precisi e diritti vaghi, ecc. ecc. Inoltre, è chiaro che la distinzione in oggetto, essendo fondata soprattutto su ragioni storiche, non è destinata a restare sempre netta nei suoi caratteri essenziali ed anzi tali caratteri tendono a variare nel tempo.

Infine, la distinzione in oggetto è ancora meno utile se viene trasferita dal piano dei diritti a quello degli obblighi e della loro violazione. Infatti, come si è già detto, non è vero che a certe categorie o a certe generazioni di diritti umani corrispondano sempre obblighi aventi la medesima natura; al contrario, ciascun diritto umano può imporre allo Stato una *varietà* di obblighi di natura diversa. Per fare solo un esempio, il diritto alla vita privata e familiare, che appartiene alla prima generazione dei diritti umani, impone allo Stato sia obblighi negativi, sia obblighi positivi immediati di risultato [31], sia obblighi positivi immediati di *due diligence* [32], sia infine obblighi "a realizzazione progressiva" nel tempo [33].

---

[30] Vedi, ad es., certi aspetti del diritto ad un ambiente sano: *infra*, Cap. VI, par. 20.2.

[31] Ad esempio, emanare leggi per proteggere i rapporti fra genitori e figli illegittimi o adottare un provvedimento di ammissione di uno straniero per motivi di riunione familiare.

[32] Ad esempio, prendere misure di prevenzione per ridurre fenomeni di inquinamento dannosi per la vita privata delle persone.

D'altra parte, il diritto al lavoro, che appartiene alla seconda generazione dei diritti umani, può imporre allo Stato sia obblighi negativi[34], sia obblighi positivi immediati di risultato[35], sia infine obblighi "a realizzazione progressiva"[36]. In altri termini, la circostanza che sia in discussione un diritto di prima generazione, come il diritto alla vita privata e familiare, oppure un diritto di seconda generazione, come il diritto al lavoro, non ci dice nulla di per sé circa le differenze nel modo con cui lo Stato deve adempiere al correlativo obbligo e quindi non ci dice nulla neppure sulla natura e struttura della responsabilità dello Stato in caso di violazione.

In conclusione, la distinzione fra obblighi relativi ai diritti appartenenti a diverse generazioni ha carattere descrittivo e non ci aiuta a determinare il contenuto esatto dei vari obblighi relativi ai diritti umani.

4.2. *Obblighi precisi e obblighi vaghi. Critica*

Una seconda distinzione fra obblighi, che viene talora usata sia nella teoria generale del diritto, sia nel diritto internazionale globalmente considerato, sia infine in relazione al settore specifico del diritto internazionale dei diritti umani, è quella fra obblighi precisi ed obblighi vaghi. Essa fa riferimento alla precisione o meno con cui viene descritto in termini normativi il contenuto del singolo obbligo.

Questa distinzione viene spesso associata, più o meno esplicitamente, alla distinzione fra obblighi negativi e positivi ed a quella fra obblighi relativi ai diritti umani di prima, seconda e terza (o quarta) generazione. Si tratta tuttavia, a mio parere, di generalizzazioni che possono avere solo qualche elemento di verità; ma che spesso si rivelano inesatte ed approssimative. Infatti, può accadere spesso che un obbligo negativo abbia un contenuto più preciso rispetto ad un obbligo positivo; ma ciò non si verifica sempre. Si pensi, ad esempio, al contenuto piuttosto vago dell'obbligo negativo dello Stato di non interferire in maniera arbitraria o illegittima nella vita privata di una persona, ai sensi dell'art. 17 del Patto sui diritti civili e politici, ed invece al contenuto piuttosto preciso dell'obbligo positivo dello Stato di garantire un equo salario ed una eguale remunerazione per un lavoro di eguale valore, ai sensi dell'art. 7(a)(i) del Patto sui diritti economici, sociali e culturali.

Parimenti, può verificarsi frequentemente che un diritto umano di prima generazione abbia un contenuto più preciso di un diritto umano di seconda generazione e che questo, a sua volta, sia più preciso di un diritto umano di terza generazione. Ma anche questa conclusione si rivela talora inesatta. Ad esempio, il diritto alla vita ed il diritto alla libertà di espressione, ai sensi degli artt.6 e 19 del Patto sui diritti civili e politici, che sono diritti di prima generazione, non sono più precisi del diritto di aderire ai sindacati, ai sensi dell'art. 8 del Patto sui diritti economici, sociali e culturali, che è un diritto di seconda generazione. Anche il diritto di essere informato su modifiche ambientali che possano causare danni si-

---

[33] Sulle distinzioni fra obblighi negativi, obblighi positivi immediati di risultato, obblighi positivi immediati di *due diligence* ed obblighi "a realizzazione progressiva", vedi *infra*, par. 5.

[34] Ad esempio, permettere la libertà di associazione sindacale.

[35] Ad esempio, emanare legislazione sulla parità di retribuzione fra i sessi.

[36] Ad esempio, eliminare la discriminazione *de facto* fra i sessi in materia di lavoro.

gnificativi all'ambiente (che può essere considerato come un diritto di terza generazione) è più preciso rispetto ad alcuni diritti di prima o di seconda generazione.

In realtà, si deve concludere che la distinzione fra obblighi precisi ed obblighi vaghi dipende da tutta una serie complessa di fattori. Alcuni di questi fattori hanno natura contingente. Ad esempio, è chiaro che il processo di negoziazione e di redazione di un trattato sui diritti umani, o di una singola norma di un trattato sui diritti umani, può portare a formulare disposizioni e singoli obblighi di carattere più o meno preciso, a seconda dell'accordo esistente fra i negoziatori, del grado di compromesso necessario, dell'opportunità di lasciare più o meno spazio ad un'interpretazione evolutiva della norma, e così via. Altri fattori hanno carattere storico. Ad esempio, molti diritti civili e politici, nel momento in cui sono stati riconosciuti a livello internazionale, avevano già alle spalle una lunga storia nel diritto costituzionale interno di molti Stati ed anche una lunga evoluzione giurisprudenziale nei diritti statali. Ciò ha certamente favorito il loro grado di precisione normativa.

Anche a livello internazionale, è chiaro che, se certi obblighi sui diritti umani vengono introdotti per la prima volta in un trattato, il loro livello di precisione sarà di solito inferiore rispetto ad altri obblighi che possono appoggiarsi su trattati preesistenti. Ciò spiega, ad esempio, come molte disposizioni del Patto sui diritti civili e politici siano più circostanziate e più precise rispetto a disposizioni corrispondenti contenute nella Convenzione europea dei diritti dell'uomo. Sempre a livello internazionale, l'esistenza di organi di controllo giurisdizionale o quasi giurisdizionale sulle singole violazioni dei diritti umani tende, tramite la continua interpretazione data da tali organi, a rendere più preciso il significato di certi diritti. Anche sotto questo profilo, è chiaro che l'elaborazione giurisprudenziale dei diritti civili e politici, che si è verificata nel sistema della Convenzione europea, della Convenzione americana e del Patto sui diritti civili e politici, ha favorito il processo di precisazione di tali diritti rispetto a quelli economici, sociali e culturali.

In definitiva, pertanto, si può concludere che la distinzione fra obblighi precisi ed obblighi vaghi è anch'essa di natura descrittiva e non teorico-sistematica. Ma soprattutto tale distinzione non è rigorosa e netta, perché è chiaro che esiste tutta una gamma o uno spettro continuo di livelli diversi di precisione di una norma o di un obbligo, e non una vera e propria dicotomia fra categorie di obblighi qualitativamente diversi.

4.3. *Obblighi senza costi e obblighi costosi. Critica*

Un'altra distinzione fra obblighi, che viene talora usata specie in materia di diritti umani, è quella fra obblighi senza costo ed obblighi costosi, con riferimento alle misure di attuazione degli obblighi che ogni Stato deve prendere nel proprio ordinamento interno per realizzare pienamente il rispetto dei diritti umani.

Anche questa distinzione viene spesso collegata a quella fra obblighi negativi e positivi, nel senso che l'attuazione dei primi sarebbe senza costo mentre l'attuazione dei secondi sarebbe costosa. Oppure viene accostata all'altra distinzione, fra obblighi relativi ai diritti umani di prima, seconda e terza (o quarta) generazione, nel senso che l'attuazione dei diritti umani di prima generazione sarebbe senza costo, mentre quella dei diritti umani di seconda e terza generazione sarebbe costosa. In effetti, vi è qualche elemento di verità in queste opinioni. Infatti può ammettersi che spesso l'attuazione di obblighi negativi comporta meno spese rispetto a quella di obblighi positivi. Né si può negare che l'attuazione di molti obblighi legati ai diritti economici comporti più spese rispetto a quella di molti obblighi legati ai diritti civili. Tuttavia, si tratta di generalizzazioni di massima e non di una regola assoluta; e non si può escludere che avvenga talora il contrario.

Ma, soprattutto, la critica che si deve fare alla distinzione in oggetto è che essa non rappresenta affatto una vera e propria dicotomia fra due categorie di obblighi diversi; e pertanto ha scarso valore teorico-sistematico. E ciò per vari motivi. Primo: l'attuazione di quasi tutti i diritti umani richiede allo Stato di impiegare certe risorse economiche, se non altro per stabilire o mantenere una struttura istituzionale adeguata. Pertanto è difficile configurare obblighi sui diritti umani che siano senza costo per lo Stato. Secondo: è evidente che l'attuazione di ciascun singolo obbligo relativo a ciascun diritto umano può implicare costi diversi per lo Stato. Pertanto non vi è una vera e propria dicotomia fra obblighi senza costo ed obblighi costosi, ma piuttosto uno spettro continuo di situazioni più o meno costose. Terzo: il costo più o meno elevato nell'attuazione dei diritti umani varia evidentemente da Stato a Stato, poiché dipende in larga misura dalle strutture istituzionali, giuridiche, amministrative e di altra natura già esistenti in ciascuno Stato, nel momento in cui esso deve adempiere a quel particolare obbligo internazionale relativo ai diritti umani.

In definitiva, si può concludere che la distinzione fra obblighi senza costo ed obblighi costosi è imprecisa e non è utile ai fini della ricostruzione di una teoria giuridica e sistematica sugli obblighi internazionali.

4.4. *Obblighi di rispettare, di proteggere e di realizzare i diritti umani. Critica*

Infine si deve criticare, a mio avviso, anche la classificazione di obblighi sui diritti umani che è attualmente la più popolare in dottrina ed è stata usata anche dal Comitato sui diritti economici, sociali e culturali, dalla Commissione africana e dall'Alto Commissario delle NU per i diritti umani: quella, originariamente proposta da alcuni studiosi[37], e poi sostenuta con qualche variante da altri specialisti dei diritti umani, che distingue fra obblighi di rispettare (*to respect*), obblighi di proteggere (*to protect*) e obblighi di realizzare (*to fulfil*) i diritti umani. Il Comitato dei diritti economici, sociali e culturali tende anche a distinguere, nel quadro dell'obbligo di realizzare i diritti umani, tre diversi sottolivelli: l'obbligo di facilitare (*to facilitate*) tale realizzazione, l'obbligo di provvedere (*to provide*) ad essa e l'obbligo di promuoverla (*to promote*). Si noti che tale distinzione, nota come "tipologia in tre parti" (*tripartite typology*), è stata studiata ed elaborata soprattutto con riferimento ai diritti economici, sociali e culturali; ma che, nelle intenzioni dei suoi sostenitori, intende applicarsi a tutti i diritti umani.

Non è facile descrivere in poche parole il contenuto esatto di ciascuna di tali categorie e sottocategorie; anche perché talora esse assumono, in dottrina, significati parzialmente diversi. Tuttavia, con uno sforzo di sintesi, si può affermare che l'obbligo di rispettare (*to respect*) i diritti umani ha carattere prevalentemente negativo e proibisce allo Stato di agire in modo tale da incidere direttamente e negativamente sui diritti e le libertà riconosciuti agli individui; cioè in modo tale da negare o limitare l'accesso ai diritti umani. Ma esso

[37] Vedi, specialmente, Shue (1980); Eide (1984).

può avere talora anche carattere positivo, ad esempio quando impone allo Stato di riconoscere e registrare i diritti di proprietà di certi individui.

Invece, l'obbligo di proteggere (*to protect*) i diritti umani ha carattere prevalentemente positivo ed impone allo Stato di prendere una serie di misure, di carattere legislativo, amministrativo o di altra natura, per *prevenire* che individui terzi possano violare diritti o libertà di altri individui. Ed anche per reprimere quelle violazioni che non sia stato possibile prevenire. Pertanto tale obbligo sembra corrispondere, in linea di massima, alla categoria degli obblighi positivi con effetti orizzontali, che abbiamo già esaminato [38].

L'obbligo di realizzare (*to fulfil*) i diritti umani è il più difficile da definire. In linea di massima, si può dire che esso ha carattere positivo ed impone allo Stato di prendere delle misure di più vasta portata e di carattere più programmatico; in particolare di creare attivamente le condizioni tese al raggiungimento di certi risultati nella forma di una più effettiva realizzazione di diritti o libertà riconosciuti. Quanto poi, ai suoi tre sottolivelli, si può dire che l'obbligo di facilitare (*to facilitate*) la realizzazione dei diritti umani richiede agli Stati di impegnarsi attivamente in attività intese ad assistere gli individui nel godimento dei diritti umani ed a rafforzare le loro capacità di accedere alle risorse utili per tale godimento e di utilizzarle. L'obbligo di provvedere (*to provide*) alla realizzazione dei diritti umani richiede invece agli Stati di fornire ed assicurare direttamente il godimento di un certo diritto, quando gli individui o i gruppi di individui sono incapaci, per motivi al di fuori del loro controllo, di raggiungere direttamente tale godimento con i mezzi a propria disposizione. Infine, l'obbligo di promuovere (*to promote*) la realizzazione dei diritti umani richiede agli Stati di prendere una serie di azioni diverse di carattere promozionale, quali lo studio e la ricerca sui diritti umani, la diffusione di informazioni su tali diritti ai propri cittadini, la gestione di programmi di addestramento (*training*) ai diritti umani, l'aiuto alla gente nel compiere scelte ben informate sul godimento dei diritti umani, ed azioni simili.

Come si è detto, questa distinzione in tre grandi categorie di obblighi, ma se si vuole anche in cinque categorie se si considerano i tre sottolivelli dell'obbligo di realizzare, viene adesso sostanzialmente condivisa da vari studiosi specialisti dei diritti umani, anche se talora la terminologia e certe sfumature sono diverse da autore ad autore. Non vale la pena di entrare nel merito delle differenze fra le varie tesi dottrinali; e conviene piuttosto dare una valutazione della distinzione accolta dal Comitato sui diritti economici, sociali e culturali, la quale finisce sostanzialmente per riassumere e conglobare le varie tesi dottrinali sopraindicate.

A nostro avviso, il pregio della distinzione fra obblighi di rispettare, di proteggere e di realizzare (nei suoi tre sottolivelli) i diritti umani sta nel fatto di avere superato le precedenti dicotomie piuttosto rozze ed approssimative; e soprattutto nel fatto di avere chiarito che ciascun diritto umano può imporre uno spettro di obblighi di diversa natura, e quindi che la condotta dello Stato, specie nell'ottica della responsabilità, va valutata sulla base del singolo e specifico obbligo che è stato violato.

Tuttavia, questa distinzione presenta anche quattro gravi difetti. In primo luogo, essa resta una distinzione di carattere meramente descrittivo, poiché si limita a raggruppare in maniera piuttosto approssimativa certi comportamenti possibili dello Stato in relazione ai

[38] Vedi *supra*, Cap. II, par. 10.4.

diritti umani, senza approfondire il contenuto, la natura giuridica e la struttura degli obblighi. Ad esempio, dire che lo Stato ha l'obbligo di rispettare (*to respect*) i diritti umani delle persone è, per certi aspetti, un concetto del tutto ovvio e, per altri aspetti, un concetto confuso quando intende ricomprendere sia obblighi negativi che positivi. Parimenti, dire che lo Stato ha l'obbligo di proteggere (*to protect*) i diritti umani, tramite la prevenzione delle loro violazioni da parte di individui privati, non dice nulla, da un punto di vista della teoria giuridica, sulla struttura e sulla natura di tale tipologia di obblighi. Infine, dire che lo Stato ha l'obbligo di realizzare (*to fulfil*) i diritti umani, tramite una serie di impegni (o sottocategorie di obblighi) di natura assai diversa volti a facilitare (*to facilitate*), o promuovere (*to promote*) tale realizzazione oppure a supplire (*to provide*) alle incapacità di realizzazione da parte degli individui, non dice nulla di importante e di giuridicamente significativo circa la struttura, il contenuto o la natura di tale obbligo di realizzazione; e cioè circa i comportamenti concretamente richiesti allo Stato per il suo esatto adempimento. In altri termini, l'obbligo di realizzare resta assai vago e generico, e finisce per comprendere anche impegni che non hanno carattere vincolante (ad esempio, quello di informare e istruire le persone in materia di diritti umani).

In secondo luogo, la distinzione ha il difetto di essere ritagliata su misura solo sui diritti umani; ed è quindi del tutto scollegata dalla teoria generale degli obblighi nel diritto internazionale. Ciò costituisce un limite assai grave, poiché pone la materia dei diritti umani in isolamento rispetto agli altri settori del diritto internazionale ed alla teoria generale del diritto. Naturalmente, è ovvio che questo secondo difetto si collega al primo, poiché una distinzione fra obblighi che ha carattere meramente descrittivo non è in grado di contribuire ad una teoria generale degli obblighi internazionali.

In terzo luogo, la distinzione in questione non è così innovativa come sembrerebbe a prima vista, poiché essa rispecchia, sia pure in modo approssimativo, vecchie categorie di obblighi già note e consolidate. L'obbligo di rispettare (*to respect*) corrisponde, in massima parte, alla categoria degli obblighi negativi [39]. L'obbligo di proteggere (*to protect*) sembra avere un contenuto assai limitato, perché corrisponde agli obblighi positivi di prevenzione rispetto ad atti di privati (o obblighi positivi con "effetti orizzontali") [40]. L'obbligo di realizzare (*to fulfil*), invece, ha un contenuto assai ampio perché cerca di unificare in una vasta categoria (che però resta disomogenea) una serie di obblighi e di obiettivi politici non vincolanti che riguardano soprattutto la realizzazione dei diritti umani di seconda e terza generazione.

Infine, la distinzione in oggetto, nonostante riproponga in gran parte vecchie categorie di obblighi, ha il difetto di non essere completa, perché trascura alcuni obblighi importanti: ad esempio, gli obblighi degli individui-organi di rango superiore di prevenire e reprimere le violazioni dei diritti umani commesse da individui-organi di rango inferiore [41], gli obblighi di *due diligence* [42], e gli obblighi "a realizzazione progressiva" [43].

In conclusione, la distinzione fra obblighi di rispettare, obblighi di proteggere e obbli-

---

[39] Vedi *infra*, par. 5.1.

[40] Vedi *supra*, Cap. II, par. 10.4.

[41] Vedi, ad esempio, *infra*, Cap. V, parr. 7.3.2, 7.3.3, 8.3.2 e 8.3.3.

[42] Vedi *infra*, par. 5.2.

[43] Vedi *infra*, par. 5.3.

ghi di realizzare i diritti umani, nonostante il favore crescente di cui gode in dottrina ed anche nella prassi di alcuni organi di controllo, difetta di rigore giuridico e non può essere qui accolta per individuare vere e proprie categorie giuridiche di obblighi.

5. *Categorie utili e aventi valore concettuale-sistematico*

Come si è visto, tutte le distinzioni fra categorie di obblighi internazionali che abbiamo esaminato finora, e che si applicano al settore specifico dei diritti umani, presentano notevoli difetti ed appaiono prevalentemente descrittive, piuttosto approssimative e giuridicamente non rigorose. Conviene pertanto concentrare adesso la nostra attenzione su quelle distinzioni fra categorie di obblighi che hanno il merito di operare per l'intero ordinamento internazionale, che sono del tutto applicabili anche nel settore dei diritti umani, e che hanno valore giuridico e concettuale-sistematico.

A mio avviso, le distinzioni più utili, sempre nell'ottica del contenuto e natura degli obblighi e del loro modo di adempimento, sono le seguenti: *a*) la distinzione fra obblighi negativi e positivi; *b*) quella fra obblighi di risultato e di *due diligence*; *c*) quella fra obblighi immediati ed obblighi "a realizzazione progressiva".

5.1. *Obblighi negativi e positivi*

La prima distinzione utile è quella fra obblighi internazionali negativi e positivi. La loro rispettiva definizione, sia nel diritto internazionale generale che nel settore dei diritti umani, è nota ed è sufficiente qui richiamarla in estrema sintesi.

Per obblighi internazionali negativi si intendono gli obblighi nei quali lo Stato (o un altro ente titolare di obblighi internazionali) si astiene da certe azioni; cioè obblighi di non fare o di non ingerenza. Nel settore dei diritti umani, gli obblighi negativi si configurano soprattutto come obblighi di astensione rispetto alla sfera dei diritti e delle libertà individuali. Si tratta di una categoria che ha il suo campo di applicazione classico in molti diritti "fondamentali" [44] (diritto alla vita, divieti di tortura e di schiavitù, diritto alla libertà e sicurezza della persona, ecc.) ed in molti diritti civili e politici. Tuttavia, non si può escludere che vi siano obblighi negativi anche in relazione ad alcuni diritti economici, sociali e culturali: per esempio, l'obbligo dello Stato di garantire il diritto di sciopero, la libertà di formare sindacati, la libertà di ricerca scientifica, la libertà dei genitori di scegliere l'educazione per i propri figli.

Per obblighi internazionali positivi, invece, si intendono gli obblighi nei quali allo Stato (o ad altro ente) si richiede di compiere certe azioni o certe prestazioni; cioè obblighi di fare o di intervento. Nel settore dei diritti umani, gli obblighi positivi si configurano soprattutto come obblighi dello Stato di favorire il raggiungimento dei diritti e delle libertà individuali. Il campo di applicazione degli obblighi positivi, inizialmente limitato, si è via via allargato e si estende adesso ai diritti umani di prima, seconda e terza generazione.

La distinzione fra obblighi negativi e positivi funziona nello stesso modo ed egualmen-

---

[44] Vedi *infra*, Cap. V.

te bene sia per il diritto internazionale in generale che per il settore dei diritti umani. Del resto tale distinzione è ormai ampiamente utilizzata anche dalla prassi e dalla giurisprudenza internazionale [45]. Ciò è logico perché si tratta di una distinzione che appartiene alla stessa teoria generale del diritto. Peraltro, si deve notare che essa è solo una distinzione di carattere molto generale; e che pertanto è possibile, all'interno di ciascuna delle due grandi categorie, configurare altre distinzioni ed altre categorie più specifiche. È appena il caso di ricordare che alla dicotomia fra obblighi negativi e positivi corrisponde, in caso di loro violazione, la dicotomia fra illeciti commissivi (e responsabilità per azione) ed illeciti omissivi (e responsabilità per omissione).

5.2. *Obblighi di risultato ed obblighi di* due diligence

Una seconda distinzione utile, sia nel diritto internazionale generale che nel settore dei diritti umani, è quella fra obblighi di risultato ed obblighi di *due diligence* (o di mezzi o di condotta) [46]. Parliamo adesso di obblighi immediati (cioè che operano subito), che distingueremo in seguito dagli obblighi "a realizzazione progressiva".

Si deve sottolineare che qui non si intende in alcun modo richiamare la distinzione fra obblighi di comportamento specifico e obblighi di risultato elaborata in passato da una parte della dottrina italiana [47], che attiene soprattutto al modo con cui l'obbligo internazionale richiede di essere eseguito a livello interno da parte dello Stato [48]. Al contrario, si vuole fare riferimento alla distinzione, assai diversa anche se terminologicamente simile, che è molto usata nel diritto civile degli Stati di tradizione romanistica ed è applicabile anche nel diritto internazionale, dove ha un'origine antica [49] ma si è consolidata solo negli anni più recenti. Da ultimo, anche la Corte internazionale di giustizia, nel caso *Bosnia e Erzegovina c. Serbia e Montenegro,* in relazione all'obbligo della Serbia di prevenire il genocidio, ha parlato espressamente di obbligo di mezzi o di condotta, nonché di obbligo di usare i "*best efforts*" nelle attività di prevenzione e di standard di *due diligence* [50].

Per comprendere meglio la distinzione in oggetto, si deve notare che, sulla base della teoria generale del diritto, in ogni obbligo rileva sia la condotta dell'obbligato sia il risultato di quella condotta; tuttavia i due elementi possono avere un peso assai diverso e quindi talora l'obbligo viene individuato attraverso il risultato e talora attraverso la condotta dell'obbligato. Ciò caratterizza due categorie diverse di obblighi: si ha un obbligo di risultato quando la norma impone che dal comportamento dell'obbligato derivi un risultato; si ha

---

[45] Vedi Pisillo Mazzeschi (2008), Capp. III, IV e V. Vedi anche *supra*, Cap. II, par. 10.3.

[46] Vedi Pisillo Mazzeschi (1989); Id. (2008); Id. (2018a). Recentemente, vedi Cassella (dir. publ.) (2018).

[47] Vedi soprattutto Ago (1938), p. 178 ss.; Id. (1939), p. 415 ss.; Id. (1977), parr. 2-46.

[48] L'obbligo di comportamento specifico stabilisce il modo di esecuzione interna che esso richiede (esecuzione che può realizzarsi tramite attività normativa o amministrativa o giurisdizionale). Invece, l'obbligo di risultato non specifica il modo di esecuzione interna richiesta, ma lascia lo Stato libero di scegliere i mezzi e le attività di esecuzione appropriati per conseguire lo scopo finale voluto dall'obbligo. Sul punto vedi Pisillo Mazzeschi (2008), pp. 271-282; Id. (2018a), pp. 326-327.

[49] Questa origine risale probabilmente al celebre arbitrato nel caso *Alabama* del 1872. Cfr. *Alabama claims of the United States of America v. Great Britain.*

[50] ICJ, *Application of the Convention on the Prevention and Punishment of the Crime of Genocide*, Judgment of 26 February 2007, parr. 428-438, spec. 430-432.

invece un obbligo di *due diligence* (o di mezzi o di condotta) quando la norma impone un certo comportamento in sé stesso, a prescindere dagli esiti del medesimo. Per l'obbligo di risultato, l'inadempimento deriva dall'assenza del risultato promesso; mentre, per l'obbligo di *due diligence*, l'inadempimento risulta dal fatto che l'obbligato non ha usato la diligenza richiesta dalle circostanze. In altri termini, l'obbligo di risultato è un obbligo di "riuscire", mentre l'obbligo di *due diligence* è un obbligo di "sforzarsi", di usare i "*best efforts*" per ottenere il risultato.

La giustificazione teorica della distinzione riposa soprattutto sull'idea che le due categorie di obblighi sono condizionate da un'*alea* diversa. Nel caso degli obblighi di risultato, la realizzazione dell'oggetto dell'obbligo non incontra difficoltà inerenti alla sua natura, e cioè non comporta un'alea particolare. Al contrario, nel caso degli obblighi di *due diligence*, la realizzazione dello scopo dell'obbligo è per sua natura aleatoria e quindi presuppone uno sforzo particolare di diligenza dell'obbligato ed il gioco favorevole di certi fattori oggettivi di rischio. In definitiva, è il carattere di per sé aleatorio o meno del risultato voluto dalla norma che spiega perché certi obblighi impongano solo di "sforzarsi", mentre altri obblighi impongano di "riuscire".

Tutto ciò vale non solo nella teoria generale del diritto, ma anche nel diritto internazionale. Infatti lo Stato, tramite i suoi organi, è concretamente in grado, in certi casi, di tenere un comportamento, attivo o passivo, che garantisce di impedire, salvo la presenza di certe cause di esclusione dell'illecito, il fatto lesivo nei confronti di altri Stati ed eventualmente anche di individui. Invece, in altri casi, lo Stato può solo tenere, rispetto al fatto lesivo, un comportamento che, seppure di solito sufficiente per impedire il fatto lesivo, non può in assoluto garantire tale risultato, poiché esso dipende anche da fattori fortemente aleatori. Per esempio, in materia di protezione degli stranieri, mentre il diritto internazionale può imporre agli organi statali un obbligo (negativo e di risultato) di astenersi dall'uso improprio di armi contro gli stranieri, non può richiedere loro di prevenire ogni uso improprio di armi contro gli stranieri da parte di individui privati né di assicurare sempre la cattura dei responsabili; ma deve limitarsi a richiedere a tali organi un comportamento positivo di *due diligence*, cioè di usare i "*best efforts*" nelle loro attività di prevenzione e repressione.

La distinzione in oggetto ha notevoli conseguenze, teoriche e pratiche. Una prima conseguenza è che l'elemento "diligenza" è presente nel contenuto di certi obblighi internazionali, mentre è assente nel contenuto di altri obblighi. Ciò caratterizza in maniera diversa la struttura ed il contenuto di due categorie di obblighi internazionali, e caratterizza in maniera diversa anche il modo della loro violazione e quindi il rispettivo regime di responsabilità.

Una seconda conseguenza è che, per la vittima della violazione, è più facile dimostrare la violazione di un obbligo di risultato che non di un obbligo di *due diligence*. Nel primo caso, infatti, per dimostrare la presenza dell'elemento oggettivo dell'illecito, cioè la violazione dell'obbligo, è sufficiente dimostrare che il risultato voluto dall'obbligo non è stato raggiunto. E, poiché in questo caso la regola violata indica quasi sempre chiaramente tale risultato, la violazione appare di solito evidente. Nel secondo caso, invece, la vittima deve dimostrare la mancanza di *due diligence* da parte del presunto autore dell'illecito; cioè la difformità fra la condotta concretamente tenuta da costui e quella richiesta dallo standard di *due diligence*. Si tratta allora di determinare il contenuto della condotta tenuta e di quella astrattamente richiesta dalla norma ed il problema è assai più delicato. In altri termini, il rapporto fra condotta tenuta e violazione dell'obbligo (o, se si vuole il rapporto di causalità) è più difficile da provare.

Una terza conseguenza della distinzione attiene ai rapporti fra diligenza e colpa. Si tratta di un argomento complesso, che non è possibile qui approfondire. In estrema sintesi, e limitandosi al diritto internazionale, si può dire che il concetto positivo di diligenza può essere, per molti aspetti, considerato correlativo a quello negativo di colpa (in senso stretto), cioè che la mancanza di diligenza equivale alla colpa; ma che vi sono almeno due elementi di differenza. Primo, mentre la colpa conserva di solito una connotazione psicologico-soggettiva, o quantomeno in parte soggettivistica, la *due diligence* rappresenta uno standard di comportamento oggettivo; e quindi una sorta di "colpa oggettivizzata". Secondo, e questa differenza è più rilevante, mentre la colpa viene di solito concepita come un elemento (necessario o meno a seconda delle varie teorie) dell'illecito dello Stato, e quindi nel quadro delle norme secondarie sulla responsabilità, invece la diligenza è un elemento contenuto nelle norme primarie, o *rectius* negli obblighi primari.

La prassi degli organi internazionali di controllo dei trattati sui diritti umani dimostra che la distinzione fra obblighi di risultato e di *due diligence* è molto importante, se si vuole comprendere bene il contenuto esatto degli obblighi assunti dagli Stati e di conseguenza accertare con sicurezza in quali casi essi abbiano commesso una violazione di tali obblighi [51].

Infine, conviene ribadire che, parlando di obblighi di risultato e di *due diligence*, abbiamo finora fatto riferimento ad obblighi precettivi e immediati: cioè obblighi che lo Stato deve eseguire immediatamente ed in tutti i loro elementi. Tuttavia, vi sono anche obblighi relativi ai diritti umani che hanno una natura diversa da quelli fin qui esaminati, nel senso che essi non sono immediatamente e completamente precettivi. Per spiegare la loro natura, occorre utilizzare altre categorie giuridiche.

5.3. *Obblighi immediati ed obblighi "a realizzazione progressiva"*

Una terza distinzione utile, pertanto, è quella fra obblighi immediati (di risultato o di *due diligence*) ed obblighi "a realizzazione progressiva". In realtà questa distinzione è stata studiata poco nel diritto internazionale. Il Comitato sui diritti economici, sociali e culturali parla talora di obblighi "progressivi", ma non ha sviluppato bene tale concetto. Più di recente, un tentativo di chiarire la distinzione è stato effettuato dall'Alto Commissario delle NU per i diritti umani.

A nostro parere, la distinzione fra obblighi immediati ed obblighi "a realizzazione progressiva" può richiamarsi alla distinzione, molto conosciuta nel diritto costituzionale di numerosi Stati, fra norme precettive e norme programmatiche. Per la verità, anche nel diritto internazionale si parla talora di norme programmatiche, proprio in relazione alle norme sui diritti economici, sociali e culturali; ma il concetto che prevale è quello per cui le norme programmatiche non avrebbero effetti vincolanti, ma soltanto meri effetti esortativi. In altri termini, si tende, a nostro avviso erroneamente, a contrapporre il concetto di norma programmatica a quello di norma vincolante.

Invece, se si adotta il concetto corretto e attuale di norma programmatica che si è af-

[51] Su tale prassi vedi Pisillo Mazzeschi (2008), Capp. III, IV e V.

fermato nel diritto costituzionale comparato, le conclusioni devono essere diverse. La norma programmatica ha alcuni effetti vincolanti ed è capace di creare veri e propri obblighi per i suoi destinatari; ma non degli obblighi precettivi ed immediati, bensì degli obblighi che si realizzano appunto progressivamente nel tempo, ma anche capaci, durante il percorso verso la loro piena attuazione, di produrre alcuni effetti giuridici. Più in particolare, le corti costituzionali hanno individuato i seguenti effetti prodotti dalle norme costituzionali programmatiche in materia di diritti sociali. Primo: un effetto giuridico di tipo "negativo" di tali norme è quello di poter invalidare le leggi che eventualmente si ponessero in assoluto contrasto con esse. Secondo: un effetto giuridico di tipo "positivo" è dato dal principio di ragionevolezza. Ciò significa che il legislatore, nel determinare l'attuazione dei diritti sociali, deve usare la dovuta ragionevolezza nel bilanciare tale attuazione con gli altri interessi primari garantiti dalla Costituzione e con le necessità del bilancio. Terzo: i diritti sociali, anche se previsti da norme programmatiche, non possono essere compressi al punto tale da intaccare certi "obblighi minimi essenziali".

Ritornando al diritto internazionale, ed al settore dei diritti umani, il concetto di obblighi "a realizzazione progressiva" trova una conferma normativa in vari trattati o singole norme convenzionali sui diritti economici, sociali e culturali. L'art. 2(1) del Patto sui diritti economici, sociali e culturali (che è la norma fondamentale del Patto) stabilisce che ogni Stato parte

> "undertakes to take steps [...] to the maximum of its available resources, with a view to achieving progressively the full realization of the rights recognized in the present Covenant, by all appropriate means [...]".

L'art. 26 della Convenzione americana sui diritti umani (dedicato ai diritti economici, sociali e culturali) è intitolato "progressive development", e stabilisce che gli Stati parti devono adottare misure

> "with a view to achieving progressively [...] the full realization of the rights implicit in the economic, social, educational, scientific, and cultural standards"

stabiliti nella Carta dell'OAS. Norme simili si trovano nell'art. 4(2) della Convenzione delle NU sui diritti delle persone disabili; nell'art. 4 della Convenzione delle NU sui diritti del fanciullo; nell'art. 1 del Protocollo di San Salvador. Formule analoghe sono contenute anche in molte disposizioni più specifiche del Patto sui diritti economici, sociali e culturali [52], nella Carta sociale europea (riveduta) [53] e, sia pure in maniera più implicita, in alcuni principi in materia di solidarietà contenuti nella Carta dei diritti fondamentali dell'UE [54].

Ciò detto, conviene adesso precisare meglio la natura dell'obbligo "a realizzazione progressiva" e la disciplina giuridica di tale obbligo e delle sue violazioni.

Quanto al primo aspetto, il concetto di "realizzazione progressiva" dei diritti umani si può ricavare dall'affermazione fatta dal Comitato sui diritti economici, sociali e culturali, secondo la quale l'art. 2(1) del Patto impone allo Stato "to move as expeditiously and ef-

---

[52] Vedi, ad es., gli artt. 6(2), 11(1), 12(2), 15(2).

[53] Vedi, ad es., gli artt. 2(1), 3(4), 12(3) della Parte II.

[54] Vedi, ad es., gli artt. 31(1), 33(1), 35, 36.

fectively as possible" verso lo scopo della piena realizzazione dei diritti umani [55]. A nostro avviso, è questo, in definitiva, il vero e proprio contenuto dell'obbligo "a realizzazione progressiva": lo Stato deve produrre uno sforzo continuo e protratto nel tempo, teso a raggiungere un determinato obiettivo, deve *procedere* verso tale obiettivo. L'Alto Commissario delle NU per i diritti umani ha espresso lo stesso concetto quando ha detto che gli Stati devono

> "undertake targeted measures to move as expeditiously and effectively as possible towards the full realization of economic, social and cultural rights" [56].

Si tratta, a mio parere, di un *obbligo generale e complesso*, per la cui realizzazione nel tempo lo Stato deve adempiere tutta una serie, più o meno numerosa, di *obblighi più specifici*, come, per esempio, quello di legiferare, quello di adottare provvedimenti giurisdizionali o amministrativi, quello di adottare misure finanziarie, tecniche, educative, promozionali, sociali. Questi obblighi più specifici possono avere natura diversa e quindi configurarsi talora come obblighi di risultato e talora come obblighi di *due diligence*; e non si può escludere che talora questi obblighi si impongano allo Stato come immediati, durante il percorso verso la piena realizzazione dell'obiettivo finale da raggiungere.

Quanto alla disciplina giuridica degli obblighi "a realizzazione progressiva", si può notare che tutte le norme convenzionali sui diritti umani che contengono tali obblighi prevedono anche dei *criteri giuridici* che regolano le forme, i modi ed i tempi con cui gli Stati devono operare per il loro adempimento; e che quindi pongono limiti alla discrezionalità degli Stati. In estrema sintesi, tali criteri sono i seguenti: *a*) gli Stati devono utilizzare tutti i "mezzi appropriati" (cioè le misure adeguate, ragionevoli ed effettive) per raggiungere l'obiettivo richiesto; *b*) gli Stati devono usare anche le "proprie risorse disponibili", economiche, umane e tecniche, bilanciando ragionevolmente le risorse destinate ai diritti umani e quelle destinate ad altri interessi statali primari.

Da ciò deriva che saranno illeciti i comportamenti dello Stato contrari ai vari obblighi specifici ed ai criteri giuridici che fanno parte integrante dell'obbligo generale "a realizzazione progressiva". Ad esempio, un illecito si verifica: *a*) se lo Stato adotta *misure regressive* rispetto all'obiettivo della progressiva attuazione di un diritto; *b*) se lo Stato rimane *totalmente passivo* e non adotta misure di alcun tipo verso l'obiettivo dell'attuazione del diritto umano in questione; *c*) se lo Stato, pur procedendo verso l'obiettivo della realizzazione progressiva di un certo diritto umano, non utilizza i *mezzi appropriati* o le *risorse disponibili* (secondo il criterio di ragionevolezza) per raggiungere tale obiettivo; *d*) se lo Stato non rispetta l'*obbligo minimo* di soddisfare il livello essenziale del diritto umano che si è impegnato a realizzare progressivamente.

Queste diverse ipotesi di violazioni degli obblighi "a realizzazione progressiva" trovano una conferma, specie nel settore dei diritti economici, sociali e culturali, nella prassi degli organi internazionali di controllo sui diritti umani [57].

---

[55] CteeESCR, General Comment No. 3, 14 December 1990, par. 9.

[56] *Report of the United Nations High Commissioner for Human Rights*, E/2007/82, 25 June 2007, par. 76.

[57] Cfr. Pisillo Mazzeschi (2008), Cap. V. Vedi anche *supra*, Cap. II, par. 11.2.

5.4. *Distinzione fra obblighi giuridici e obiettivi politici non vincolanti*

Infine, è possibile che alcune disposizioni, contenute in atti internazionali relativi ai diritti umani, non creino veri e propri obblighi giuridici a carico degli Stati destinatari di tali disposizioni, ma che esse producano soltanto impegni o obiettivi politici di carattere non vincolante.

Ciò si verifica soprattutto per un numero limitato di diritti umani di natura collettiva (o di solidarietà), appartenenti alla terza ed alla quarta generazione [58]. Questi diritti sono contenuti in una serie di atti internazionali di natura diversa, ma di solito non giuridicamente vincolanti, quali risoluzioni o dichiarazioni di principi dell'Assemblea Generale delle NU, risoluzioni del Consiglio (e prima della Commissione) dei diritti umani, e dichiarazioni finali di conferenze internazionali. Ma talora essi sono contenuti anche in atti internazionali a carattere vincolante, quali, ad esempio, la Carta africana dei diritti dell'uomo e dei popoli.

Fra i diritti umani di natura collettiva, come si è già visto [59], si citano di solito il diritto allo sviluppo, quello allo sfruttamento delle risorse naturali, quello alla pace, quello ad un ambiente sano, quello alla democrazia, quello ad un buon governo, e quello alla sicurezza umana. Di questi diritti parleremo in seguito [60].

6. *Conclusioni sul contenuto e la natura degli obblighi relativi ai diritti umani*

Conviene ora tirare alcune conclusioni sulle varie distinzioni esaminate fra categorie di obblighi internazionali relative ai diritti umani. La prima conclusione è che la distinzione fra obblighi negativi e positivi, anche se in certi casi può risultare non del tutto netta, è comunque una distinzione che si è ormai affermata saldamente sia nel diritto internazionale generale sia nel settore dei diritti umani, e che presenta validità teorica ed utilità pratica. Tuttavia ambedue le categorie sono assai vaste e generiche, e comprendono al loro interno sottocategorie di obblighi di natura e struttura diverse. In particolare, la categoria degli obblighi positivi indica solo che lo Stato deve in qualche modo attivarsi per adempiere all'obbligo, ma non indica le forme ed i modi precisi per l'adempimento dei singoli obblighi positivi e di conseguenza le forme ed i modi della loro eventuale violazione. Pertanto, la distinzione fra obblighi negativi e positivi può costituire solo un punto di partenza.

La seconda conclusione riguarda quelle distinzioni fra obblighi internazionali che sono state elaborate specie in materia di diritti umani, ma con la pretesa che esse avessero validità più generale nell'ordinamento internazionale. Noi le abbiamo definite come distinzioni "descrittive", perché ci sembra che esse siano accomunate dal difetto di avere scarso valore tecnico-giuridico e concettuale-sistematico. Esse possono soltanto fornire una descrizione, apparentemente semplice ed efficace ma in realtà assai approssimativa, di certi caratteri (storici, economici o di altro tipo) tendenzialmente prevalenti in certi obblighi internazionali. Anche la distinzione fra obblighi di rispettare (*to respect*), di proteggere (*to protect*) e di realizzare (*to fulfil*) i diritti umani, che ha avuto recentemente successo presso la

[58] Su questo argomento vedi, ad es., Tomuschat (2014), pp. 149-154.

[59] Vedi *supra*, par. 4.1.

[60] Vedi *infra*, Cap. VI, parr. 19-20.

dottrina specializzata nei diritti umani, è, a nostro avviso, assai insoddisfacente dal punto di vista tecnico-giuridico e teorico, e non è in realtà innovativa rispetto ad alcune distinzioni più risalenti.

La terza conclusione, invece, conferma la validità, sia sul piano teorico-sistematico sia su quello della prassi concretamente operante nel diritto internazionale in generale e nel settore specifico dei diritti umani, delle categorie degli obblighi (immediati) di risultato, degli obblighi (immediati) di *due diligence* e degli obblighi "a realizzazione progressiva". Si tratta delle categorie più utili per comprendere il contenuto esatto dei vari obblighi e, quindi, i modi ed i tempi per il loro esatto adempimento ad opera degli Stati e degli altri enti titolari degli obblighi medesimi.

Pertanto, utilizzeremo queste categorie di obblighi quando, nei Capitoli V e VI, esamineremo i singoli diritti umani.

Sezione III

AMBITO DI APPLICAZIONE SPAZIALE DEGLI OBBLIGHI

7. *Premessa*

Il tema dell'ambito di applicazione "spaziale" degli obblighi internazionali degli Stati relativi ai diritti umani è importante [61], perché serve a chiarire gli spazi, e di conseguenza anche le persone e le situazioni concrete, che cadono sotto la protezione delle norme sui diritti umani; e, quindi, serve anche a chiarire quando la condotta di uno Stato sia legittima e quando, invece, essa costituisca una violazione dei diritti umani capace di generare la responsabilità internazionale dello Stato.

In realtà, la locuzione "applicazione spaziale" degli obblighi sui diritti umani non viene di solito usata; ma si preferiscono quelle, più tecniche, di "applicazione territoriale" o di "applicazione giurisdizionale" di tali obblighi. Ma questi due ultimi concetti non sono identici. Il termine "territoriale" ha un significato preciso e piuttosto restrittivo: esso si riferisce al potere di governo (o, in termini più tradizionali, di dominio o di imperio) dello Stato sul proprio territorio. Invece, il termine "giurisdizionale", inteso nel senso giuridico anglosassone di "*jurisdiction*", indica l'autorità di governo dello Stato in senso più lato, cioè che comprende il potere esecutivo, legislativo e giudiziario, e che si estende non solo al territorio statale, ma anche talora al di fuori del territorio, includendo tutti gli spazi, gli oggetti e le persone sui quali lo Stato esercita, *de iure* o *de facto*, un'autorità o controllo effettivo. Si pensi, ad esempio, alle missioni diplomatiche e consolari dello Stato all'estero, o alle missioni ed alle occupazioni militari dello Stato in territori esteri. Pertanto, per evitare confusioni terminologiche, preferiamo usare la locuzione più ampia "giurisdizione spaziale".

---

[61] Su questo argomento vedi, per tutti, De Sena (2002); Clapham, Kamminga (2004).

Gli Stati, in linea di principio, quando assumono obblighi in materia di diritti umani, si impegnano a rispettarli sia all'interno del proprio territorio sia in altri spazi sui quali esercitano la propria autorità di governo o "giurisdizione" (*jurisdiction*). Tuttavia, il problema dell'ambito di applicazione "spaziale" degli obblighi sui diritti umani è piuttosto complesso, poiché, nella realtà attuale, si possono verificare varie situazioni di incerta e controversa soluzione, specie quando gli Stati si trovano ad operare fuori dal proprio territorio, talora insieme ad altri Stati o nel quadro di organizzazioni internazionali. Inoltre, non è facile ricostruire norme di diritto internazionale generale sull'ambito di applicazione "spaziale" degli obblighi degli Stati relativi ai diritti umani, poiché i trattati multilaterali più importanti contengono su questo punto regole simili ma non identiche; ed anche la prassi degli organi internazionali di controllo sui diritti umani non è del tutto uniforme. Ciononostante, come vedremo, ci sembra che alcune regole generali possano essere stabilite.

8. *Le disposizioni dei trattati sul proprio ambito di applicazione "spaziale"*

I principali trattati sui diritti umani stabiliscono per gli Stati parti, in maniera esplicita o implicita, l'obbligo di rispettare i diritti stabiliti nel trattato nei confronti di tutti gli individui, cittadini o stranieri, che sono presenti nel proprio territorio. È questa la situazione più semplice. Si potrebbero definire tali obblighi dello Stato come "territoriali" in senso stretto. Tuttavia, durante i lavori preparatori di tali trattati, si pose il problema se gli obblighi convenzionali di ciascuno Stato dovessero applicarsi anche a comportamenti o atti *compiuti* al di fuori del territorio oppure *aventi effetti* al di fuori del territorio. E si decise di inserire alcune disposizioni *ad hoc* per determinare l'ambito di applicazione "spaziale" dei trattati[62]. Queste disposizioni non hanno tutte la medesima formulazione; ma di solito esse determinano tale ambito utilizzando in maniera cumulativa i due concetti di "territorio" e di "giurisdizione" (*jurisdiction*) oppure usando il solo concetto di "giurisdizione", inteso in senso ampio.

Fra i trattati che utilizzano i due concetti si può citare il Patto internazionale sui diritti civili e politici, che adotta una formula precisa, poiché stabilisce, all'art. 2(1), che ogni Stato parte si impegna a rispettare e assicurare i diritti riconosciuti nel Patto "to all individuals within its territory and subject to its jurisdiction". Il Comitato dei diritti umani ha interpretato questa espressione nel senso che essa comprende anche obblighi "extraterritoriali"; cioè che il Patto si applica anche ad azioni ed atti compiuti da uno Stato parte in territori esteri, purché sotto il controllo effettivo dello Stato[63]. Anche la Corte internazionale di giustizia ha avvalorato tale interpretazione del Patto, nel suo parere del 2004 sul *Muro in Palestina*[64] e nella sua sentenza del 2005 sulle *Attività armate sul territorio del Congo*[65]. La Convenzione delle NU del 1984 contro la tortura adotta una formula simile a quella del Patto, ma meno precisa, poiché, all'art. 2(1), stabilisce che ogni Stato parte deve prendere misure per prevenire atti di tortura "in any territory under its jurisdiction".

---

[62] Cfr. Tomuschat (2014), p. 94.

[63] HRCtee, *Celiberti*; *Lopez Burgos*; *Pereira Montero*. Vedi anche Focarelli (2013), p. 123.

[64] ICJ, *Legal Consequences of the Construction of a Wall*, parr. 109-113.

[65] ICJ, *Armed Activities on the Territory of the Congo*, Judgment of 19 December 2005, par. 216.

Invece, altri trattati utilizzano soltanto il concetto di "giurisdizione". La Convenzione europea dei diritti umani stabilisce, all'art. 1, che gli Stati parti "shall secure to everyone within their jurisdiction the rights and freedoms" previsti nella Convenzione. Ma in realtà, come vedremo meglio in seguito, nella giurisprudenza degli organi di controllo della Convenzione, il concetto di "jurisdiction" dello Stato è stato interpretato in maniera assai ampia e comprende diversi obblighi extraterritoriali dello Stato medesimo. La Convenzione americana sui diritti umani usa una terminologia simile, poiché all'art. 1(1) stabilisce che gli Stati parti si impegnano a rispettare i diritti e libertà riconosciuti dalla Convenzione e ad assicurare "to all persons subject to their jurisdiction" il libero e pieno esercizio di tali diritti e libertà. Anche in questo caso, il termine "jurisdiction" è stato interpretato in senso ampio [66]. In maniera simile, la Convenzione del 1989 sui diritti del fanciullo prevede che gli Stati parti devono rispettare ed assicurare i diritti previsti nella convenzione "to each child within their jurisdiction" [67].

Infine, vi sono altri trattati sui diritti umani che, per determinare il loro ambito di applicazione "spaziale", non fanno riferimento né alla nozione di "territorio" né a quella di "giurisdizione". Si possono ricordare, in questo senso, il Patto internazionale sui diritti economici, sociali e culturali [68]; la Carta africana dei diritti dell'uomo e dei popoli; e la Convenzione del 1965 contro la discriminazione razziale. Tuttavia, si deve ritenere che anche in questi casi l'ambito di applicazione "spaziale" del trattato sia da interpretarsi in maniera estensiva. Questa interpretazione trova conferma anche nella posizione presa dalla Corte internazionale di giustizia nel caso relativo alla *Applicazione della Convenzione contro la discriminazione razziale*. Infatti la Corte, nella sua ordinanza del 15 ottobre 2008, dopo aver constatato che non vi è una restrizione di carattere generale nella applicazione territoriale della Convenzione né uno specifico limite territoriale negli articoli della Convenzione di cui si lamenta la violazione, ha affermato:

> "the Court consequently finds that these provisions of CERD generally appear to apply, like other provisions of instruments of that nature, to the actions of a State party when it acts beyond its territory" [69].

Pertanto, ci sembra si possa concludere che gli Stati parti dei trattati sui diritti umani devono rispettare i diritti ivi previsti nei confronti degli individui che sono nel proprio territorio o sotto la propria "giurisdizione". Tuttavia, si tratta adesso di vedere come questo principio generale debba essere interpretato ed applicato in maniera più specifica.

---

[66] Vedi i casi citati da Focarelli (2013), p. 124.

[67] CRC, art. 2(1).

[68] Per quanto riguarda il Patto sui diritti economici, sociali e culturali, la Corte internazionale di giustizia, nella sua opinione del 9 luglio 2004 sul *Muro in Palestina* ha detto che il Patto "guarantees rights wich are essentially territorial". Ma questa opinione è stata criticata in dottrina: De Shutter (2010), p. 124; Ssenyonio (2009), pp. 42-46.

[69] ICJ, *Application of the International Convention on the Elimination of All Forms of Racial Discrimination*, Order of 15 October 2008, par. 109.

9. *Tre forme diverse di "competenza spaziale" dello Stato in materia di diritti umani*

Per esaminare come l'ambito di applicazione "spaziale" dei trattati sui diritti umani sia stato interpretato nei vari contesti o situazioni che si possono presentare nella realtà, distingueremo, per motivi sistematici, fra *tre forme diverse di competenza* che possono essere esercitate dallo Stato (o fra tre categorie di obblighi dello Stato).

In primo luogo, viene in rilievo il principio di *competenza territoriale*; cioè gli obblighi dello Stato relativi ad atti di possibili violazioni dei diritti umani che *si verificano ed hanno effetti* nel territorio nazionale. Come si è detto, è pacifico che lo Stato sia obbligato a rispettare nel proprio territorio i diritti umani di tutte le persone. Tuttavia, ci chiederemo se questa regola generale subisca delle eccezioni quando lo Stato non ha un controllo effettivo sul proprio territorio (o su una parte del medesimo) e quando gli agenti di uno Stato commettono violazioni dei diritti umani nel territorio di un altro Stato senza che quest'ultimo ne sia a conoscenza o comunque non abbia potuto prevenire le violazioni.

In secondo luogo, si dovrà prendere in esame la c.d. "*giurisdizione extraterritoriale*" dello Stato; cioè gli obblighi statali relativi ad atti di suoi individui-organi che operano in territorio estero (o in spazi non soggetti alla sovranità di alcuno Stato) e possono ivi commettere violazioni dei diritti umani. Nell'ambito dell'ampia categoria della "giurisdizione extraterritoriale", si possono distinguere due situazioni diverse: *a*) quella in cui contingenti militari o altri agenti dello Stato, di solito nel quadro di missioni militari o di *peace-building* o di *State-building*, occupano un territorio straniero o esercitano un controllo effettivo su parti di un territorio straniero; *b*) quella in cui agenti statali operano in territorio estero, senza avere un controllo effettivo di tale territorio, ed ivi commettono violazioni dei diritti umani. Come vedremo, in questa seconda situazione, la questione della giurisdizione extraterritoriale dello Stato viene esaminata tramite il concetto giuridico di "autorità e controllo esercitati da parte di agenti statali" (*State agent authority and control*).

In terzo luogo, si dovrà considerare la "*giurisdizione con effetti extraterritoriali*"; cioè gli obblighi dello Stato relativi ad atti compiuti nel territorio nazionale, ma che producono effetti contrari ai diritti umani fuori dal territorio nazionale. Questa situazione si può realizzare quando atti legislativi, amministrativi o giudiziari di uno Stato, compiuti ed eseguiti nel territorio nazionale, oppure comportamenti concreti di individui-organi dello Stato, anch'essi compiuti nel territorio nazionale, provocano violazioni dei diritti umani di persone che si trovino in territorio estero[70]. Si pensi, ad esempio, ad un provvedimento dello Stato che confisca nel proprio territorio beni appartenenti ad uno straniero o ad un provvedimento di estradizione che comporti la violazione dei diritti di una persona in territorio estero[71].

Esaminiamo adesso, in maniera separata e più analitica, queste tre forme di "competenza spaziale" dello Stato relative ai diritti umani.

---

[70] Kälin, Künzli (2009), pp. 141-142.

[71] Vedi, ad es., ECtHR, *Soering v. UK*. Cfr. *infra*, Cap. V, par. 8.3.1.

10. *Competenza territoriale: obblighi e responsabilità dello Stato per atti compiuti nel proprio territorio*

10.1. *La regola generale fondata sulla sovranità territoriale*

Come si è già detto, non vi è dubbio che gli Stati debbano rispettare i propri obblighi (di diritto internazionale generale o pattizio) relativi ai diritti umani nel territorio nazionale e che essi siano responsabili, in linea di principio, per le violazioni di tali diritti che si verificano nel territorio nazionale, purché ovviamente le violazioni siano attribuibili allo Stato secondo le regole sull'attribuzione dell'illecito internazionale. Del resto gli Stati, in base al principio della sovranità territoriale, godono di un pieno potere di governo, salvo i limiti dettati dal diritto internazionale, sul proprio territorio e sulla comunità umana ivi presente. Pertanto, anche quando i trattati sui diritti umani definiscono il proprio ambito di applicazione "spaziale" con riferimento al solo concetto di "*jurisdiction*", questo concetto, come si è visto, certamente ricomprende anche quello di "territorio".

La stessa regola generale vale anche per gli obblighi dello Stato relativi ad atti di possibili violazioni dei diritti umani che si verifichino a bordo di navi o aerei aventi la nazionalità dello Stato. Si potrebbe parlare, in questi casi, di giurisdizione "*quasi-territoriale*". Comunque, al di là della terminologia, è chiaro che il potere esclusivo di governo dello Stato, e la sua conseguente responsabilità, si applicano pacificamente anche in queste circostanze.

Ciò premesso, si tratta adesso di vedere se questa regola generale subisca delle eccezioni.

10.2. *Incapacità dello Stato di controllare il proprio territorio*

Una prima eccezione può realizzarsi quando lo Stato è incapace di esercitare il proprio potere di governo, o comunque ha perso il controllo effettivo, sul territorio nazionale o su una parte di esso. Questa situazione può verificarsi, ad esempio, quando le forze armate di un altro Stato hanno occupato il territorio nazionale, o quando un movimento insurrezionale ha ottenuto un controllo pieno ed effettivo su una parte del territorio nazionale, o quando forze armate autorizzate dal Consiglio di Sicurezza delle NU hanno occupato di fatto una parte del territorio nazionale. La giurisprudenza degli organi internazionali di controllo dei trattati sui diritti umani sembra favorevole a questa eccezione; ma con qualche cautela. La prassi più significativa è quella del sistema della Convenzione europea e del sistema interamericano dei diritti umani.

La Corte europea dei diritti umani ritiene che esista una presunzione *relativa* che lo Stato territoriale eserciti il potere di governo ed il controllo sugli eventi che si verificano nel proprio territorio; ma che tale presunzione non operi quando si dimostri che lo Stato è concretamente incapace di esercitare i suoi poteri di governo sul proprio territorio o su parti di esso.

Una prima decisione della Corte su questo tema, anche se non esplicita, si trova nella sentenza *Loizidou* del 23 marzo 1995 [72], in cui la Corte ha stabilito che la responsabilità di

[72] ECtHR, *Loizidou*, Judgment of 23 March 1995, parr. 62-64.

uno Stato parte può sorgere quando, in conseguenza di un'azione militare, esso eserciti un controllo effettivo su un'area al di fuori del proprio territorio nazionale; e che ciò comporta l'obbligo di rispettare in tale area i diritti umani stabiliti dalla Convenzione. Questa conclusione è stata poi ribadita nella sentenza *Loizidou* del 18 dicembre 1996 [73]. Ma la prima sentenza della Corte che affronta, in maniera esplicita, la questione dell'incapacità dello Stato di controllare una parte del proprio territorio, è quella del 10 maggio 2001 nel caso *Cyprus v. Turkey* [74]. In tale sentenza la Corte affermò che, poiché la Turchia aveva un controllo effettivo globale sul territorio di Cipro del Nord, tale Stato aveva anche la responsabilità di assicurare il rispetto dei diritti della Convenzione europea in tale territorio [75]. Dalla decisione si deduce anche che, viceversa, il Governo di Cipro non aveva tale responsabilità. Infatti, secondo la Corte:

> "Having regard to the applicant Government's [Cyprus] continuing inability to exercise their Convention obligations in northern Cyprus, any other finding would result in a regrettable vacuum in the system of human-rights protection in the territory in question by removing from individuals there the benefit of the Convention's fundamental safeguards and their right to call a High Contracting Party to account for violation of their rights in proceedings before the Court" [76].

Questa sentenza prende una posizione netta, nel senso che la "giurisdizione" di uno Stato non si estende al suo intero territorio nazionale se, in alcune parti di tale territorio, lo Stato è di fatto incapace di esercitare il suo controllo ai fini della tutela effettiva dei diritti umani [77].

Tuttavia, la Corte di Strasburgo, pochi anni dopo, in un caso simile, ha preso una posizione più prudente e flessibile. Nella sentenza del 2004 sul caso *Ilaşcu*, la Corte ha affermato che il Governo moldavo, unico governo legittimo della Repubblica di Moldavia secondo il diritto internazionale, non esercitava più l'autorità di governo nella parte del suo territorio caduta sotto il controllo effettivo del movimento separatista denominatosi Repubblica Moldava di Transnistria; ma che esso non cessava di avere "giurisdizione" sul territorio occupato ed aveva pur sempre l'obbligo di prendere le misure possibili per tutelare i diritti garantiti dalla Convenzione. Infatti, la Corte prima ha riconosciuto che il Governo moldavo:

> "does not exercise authority over part of its territory, namely that part which is under the effective control of the [Moldavian Republic of Transdniestra]" [78]

ma poi ha aggiunto che:

> "even in the absence of effective control over the Transdniestrian region, Moldova still has a positive obligation under Article 1 of the Convention to take the diplomatic, economic,

---

[73] ECtHR, *Loizidou*, Judgment of 18 December 1996, parr. 52-57.

[74] ECtHR, *Cyprus v. Turkey*, par. 78.

[75] *Ibidem*, par. 77: "It follows that, in terms of Article 1 of the Convention, Turkey's "jurisdiction" must be considered to extend to securing the entire range of substantive rights set out in the Convention and those additional Protocols which she has ratified, and that violations of those rights are imputable to Turkey".

[76] *Ibidem*, par. 78.

[77] Cfr. De Schutter (2010), p. 133.

[78] ECtHR, *Ilaşcu and Others*, par. 330.

judicial or other measures that it is in its power to take and are in accordance with international law to secure to the applicants the rights guaranteed by the Convention"[79].

Infine, la Corte ha spiegato che, in tale situazione, l'ambito di applicazione della "giurisdizione" del Governo legittimo viene ridotto:

> "Where a Contracting State is prevented from exercising its authority over the whole of its territory by a constraining *de facto* situation [...] it does not thereby cease to have jurisdiction within the meaning of Article 1 of the Convention over that part of its territory temporarily subject to a local authority sustained by rebel forces of by another State. Nevertheless such a factual situation *reduces* the scope of that jurisdiction, in that the undertaking given by the State under Article 1 must be considered by the Court only in the light of the Contracting State's positive obligations towards persons within its territory"[80].

Pertanto, si può concludere che, secondo la Corte di Strasburgo, quando lo Stato che ha l'autorità legittima su un territorio non ha la capacità di esercitare poteri concreti di controllo sul territorio od una parte di esso, la sua "giurisdizione" e relativa responsabilità sulle violazioni dei diritti umani ivi verificatesi non si presumono; ma si può comunque dimostrare che lo Stato aveva il potere di influire sulla tutela dei diritti umani delle persone sottoposte al controllo concreto di un altro Stato o altre entità para-statali[81].

Anche la Commissione e la Corte interamericana dei diritti umani hanno esaminato situazioni nelle quali uno Stato sosteneva di essere incapace di esercitare un controllo effettivo su parti del proprio territorio, e che pertanto non poteva essere ritenuto responsabile delle violazioni dei diritti umani verificatesi in tali porzioni del territorio[82]. Un esempio è dato dal caso *Ituango Massacres*[83]. Il Governo colombiano sosteneva che i massacri denunciati erano stati commessi da gruppi paramilitari in un territorio che non poteva di fatto essere controllato dall'esercito governativo. La Corte interamericana, con una sentenza del 2006, ha riconosciuto che i gruppi paramilitari avevano commesso incursioni armate ed ucciso civili indifesi; ma ha ritenuto che vi fosse responsabilità della Colombia per atti di omissione, acquiescenza e collaborazione da parte di individui-organi colombiani. Anche la Commissione interamericana, in alcuni rapporti sulla situazione dei diritti umani in Colombia[84], ha raggiunto simili conclusioni.

In conclusione, ci sembra che la prassi degli organi internazionali di controllo sui diritti umani abbia adottato una soluzione equilibrata, che si fonda soprattutto sul criterio del *controllo effettivo del territorio*, come un elemento chiave del principio di sovranità territoriale. Si tratta di un criterio che non ha carattere assoluto, bensì relativo; e che richiede pertanto di essere volta per volta adattato alle circostanze specifiche e concrete di ogni singolo caso.

---

[79] *Ibidem*, par. 331.

[80] *Ibidem*, par. 333 (corsivo aggiunto).

[81] In questo senso vedi anche Focarelli (2012-2013), vol. I, p. 457. Sul caso *Ilaşcu* vedi anche Nigro (2005).

[82] Sulla giurisprudenza del sistema interamericano, cfr. De Schutter (2010), pp. 138-141.

[83] IACtHR, *Ituango Massacres v. Colombia*.

[84] IACmHR, *Annual Report 1996*, 14 March 1997; *Report of the Human Rights Situation in Colombia*, 26 February 1999, Chapter IV. Su questi rapporti vedi anche De Schutter (2010), pp. 139-141.

10.3. *Incapacità dello Stato di controllare violazioni di diritti umani commesse nel proprio territorio da agenti stranieri*

Secondo una parte della dottrina, una seconda eccezione, alla regola generale fondata sulla responsabilità dello Stato per atti compiuti nel proprio territorio, potrebbe verificarsi quando in tale territorio sono state commesse violazioni dei diritti umani da parte di individui-organi stranieri, senza che lo Stato territoriale avesse di fatto e concretamente la possibilità di conoscere le violazioni e/o di esercitare una prevenzione delle medesime. Si pensi, ad esempio, agli atti di rapimenti, uccisioni o *extraordinary renditions* operati nel territorio di uno Stato da parte di agenti di servizi segreti stranieri. La dottrina in esame ritiene che questa eccezione sia fondata sulla medesima logica di quella appena esaminata. Anche in queste circostanze verrebbe in rilievo la incapacità dello Stato territoriale di esercitare un controllo effettivo; *ma non genericamente sul territorio, bensì su certe persone e certe situazioni*. Si dice che lo Stato territoriale, poiché perde *de facto* il controllo su tali persone o situazioni, non è direttamente responsabile per le violazioni [85].

Tuttavia, a mio avviso, questa eccezione è problematica e non può essere assimilata a quella precedente. Infatti, in queste circostanze, non si può sostenere che viene meno il principio della sovranità territoriale e che lo Stato ha perso il controllo effettivo del proprio territorio. Ciò che viene in rilievo è un'altra questione; e cioè la concreta *capacità dello Stato territoriale di prevenire illeciti* (violazioni dei diritti umani) da parte di individui stranieri presenti nel proprio territorio. Per di più, nell'esempio che abbiamo fatto di abusi commessi da parte di agenti di servizi segreti stranieri, le violazioni sono commesse non da individui privati, ma da individui-organi di Stati esteri, che, per via della loro qualifica, sono di solito soggetti a maggior controllo da parte dello Stato territoriale.

Pertanto, il problema va riportato nel quadro degli obblighi positivi di *due diligence* dello Stato relativi ai diritti umani; e, più esattamente, dell'obbligo di adottare misure concrete volte a prevenire le violazioni dei diritti umani [86]. Ne deriva che *non si può parlare di una eccezione* alla regola generale fondata sulla responsabilità dello Stato territoriale. Anzi, poiché tale Stato dovrebbe esercitare un elevato grado di diligenza nel controllare le azioni di agenti stranieri nel proprio territorio, mi sembra che su tale Stato ricada l'onere di provare che, nelle circostanze concrete di ogni caso, esso era nella assoluta impossibilità di prevenire le violazioni dei diritti umani commesse dagli agenti esteri nel proprio territorio. Altrimenti, lo Stato incorre in responsabilità per omissione.

11. *Giurisdizione "extraterritoriale": obblighi e responsabilità dello Stato per atti compiuti in territorio estero*

Si tratta ora di prendere in esame la c.d. "giurisdizione extraterritoriale" dello Stato in materia di diritti umani; cioè gli obblighi dello Stato relativi ad atti di suoi agenti che operano all'estero e possono ivi commettere violazioni dei diritti umani. Ci sembra che solo in

---

[85] Così Kälin, Künzli (2009), p. 132.

[86] Vedi Pisillo Mazzeschi (2008), pp. 282-290 e 390-414.

questo caso si possa correttamente parlare di "giurisdizione extraterritoriale" e che essa debba essere tenuta separata dalla giurisdizione "con effetti extraterritoriali", che tratteremo in seguito [87].

Peraltro, come si era già accennato [88], nell'ambito del tema della "giurisdizione extraterritoriale", si deve distinguere fra due contesti diversi: *a*) quello in cui uno Stato occupa il territorio di un altro Stato o comunque esercita un controllo effettivo su tale territorio [89]; *b*) quello in cui gli agenti di uno Stato agiscono nel territorio di un altro Stato senza occupare o controllare tale territorio [90]. Come vedremo, il secondo contesto può, a sua volta, comprendere diverse situazioni.

11.1. *Occupazione o controllo effettivo di un territorio straniero*

Anche nel mondo contemporaneo, nonostante il principio che vieta l'uso della forza, si verificano casi nei quali uno Stato (talora insieme ad altri Stati o nel quadro di missioni autorizzate da organizzazioni internazionali) *occupa* militarmente il territorio (o parte del territorio) di un altro Stato oppure, senza raggiungere gli estremi dell'occupazione, esercita comunque un *controllo effettivo* su tale territorio. Si pensi, ad esempio, all'occupazione israeliana dei territori palestinesi, all'occupazione del Kuwait da parte dell'Iraq nel 1991, all'occupazione dell'Iraq da parte degli USA e di altri Stati nel 2003, al controllo di Cipro del Nord da parte della Turchia.

È pacifico che il concetto di "giurisdizione" dello Stato, ai fini dell'applicabilità dei suoi obblighi relativi ai diritti umani, si estende, in linea di principio, a coprire queste situazioni. È irrilevante il fatto che l'occupazione sia legittima o meno ai sensi del diritto internazionale. Questa regola è, del resto, quella *inversamente corrispondente* alla regola, già esaminata [91], che esenta da responsabilità lo Stato territoriale quando è incapace di controllare effettivamente il proprio territorio.

La prassi internazionale conferma questa forma di "giurisdizione extraterritoriale". Nel quadro della Convenzione europea dei diritti umani, due casi importanti e classici, che hanno affrontato il problema della "giurisdizione extraterritoriale" nel caso di controllo di un territorio straniero, sono i già citati casi *Loizidou*. Nella sentenza del 1995, la Corte di Strasburgo ha detto:

> "[...] the Court recalls that, although Article 1 (art. 1) sets limits on the reach of the Convention, the concept of 'jurisdiction' under this provision is not restricted to the national territory of the High Contracting Parties [....] the responsibility of a Contracting Party may also arise when as a consequence of military action – whether lawful or unlawful – it exercises effective control of an area outside its national territory. The obligation to secure, in such an area, the rights and freedoms set out in the Convention derives from the fact of

---

[87] Vedi *infra*, par. 12.
[88] Vedi *supra*, par. 9.
[89] Vedi *infra*, par. 11.1.
[90] Vedi *infra*, par. 11.2.
[91] Vedi *supra*, par. 10.2.

such control whether it be exercised directly, through its armed forces, or through a subordinate local administration" [92].

Quindi, nella successiva sentenza *Loizidou* del 1996, la Corte ha affermato:

> "It is not necessary to determine whether [...] Turkey actually exercises detailed control over the policies and actions of the authorities of the 'TRNC'. It is obvious from the large number of troops engaged in active duties in northern Cyprus [...] that her army exercises *effective overall control* over that part of the island. Such control [...] entails her responsibility for the policies and actions of the 'TRNC' [...] Those affected by such policies or actions therefore come within the 'jurisdiction' of Turkey for the purposes of Article 1 of the Convention (art. 1). Her obligation to secure to the applicant the rights and freedoms set out in the Convention therefore extends to the northern part of Cyprus" [93].

Pertanto, per la Corte, il principale criterio-guida, per determinare la "giurisdizione" dello Stato *ex* art. 1 della Convenzione, è quello del controllo effettivo complessivo (*effective overall control*) che lo Stato esercita su un territorio straniero, a prescindere dall'esistenza o meno della sovranità formale su tale territorio. Questa posizione è stata in seguito confermata anche nella già citata sentenza *Ilaşcu* del 2004, dove la Corte ha dichiarato:

> "The Court has accepted that in exceptional circumstances the acts of Contracting States performed outside their territory, or which produce effects there, may amount to exercise by them of their jurisdiction within the meaning of Article 1 of the Convention [...] It is not necessary to determine whether a Contracting Party actually exercises detailed control over the policies and actions of the authorities in the area situated outside its national territory, since even *overall control* of the area may engage the responsibility of the Contracting Party concerned" [94].

Si deve anche notare che, negli anni più recenti, la Corte europea ha mostrato la tendenza ad ampliare il concetto di *overall control* che uno Stato esercita su un territorio straniero. In questo senso si possono citare i casi *Catan*, del 2012, e *Chiragov*, del 2015. Nel caso *Catan*, la Corte ha sostenuto che uno Stato può esercitare un controllo su un territorio straniero, sia direttamente, tramite le proprie forze armate, sia indirettamente, tramite un'amministrazione locale subordinata, delle cui azioni lo Stato resta comunque responsabile. Per la Corte inoltre:

> "It is a question of fact whether a Contracting State exercises effective control over an area outside its own territory. In determining whether effective control exists, the Court will primarily have reference to the strength of the State's military presence in the area [...] Other indicators may also be relevant, such as the extent to which its military, *economic and political support* for the local subordinate administration provides it with influence and control over the region" [95].

---

[92] ECtHR, *Loizidou*, Judgment of 23 March 1995, par. 62.

[93] ECtHR, *Loizidou*, Judgment of 18 December 1996, par. 56 (corsivo aggiunto).

[94] ECtHR, *Ilaşcu and Others*, parr. 314-315 (corsivo aggiunto).

[95] ECtHR, *Catan and Others v. Moldova and Russia*, parr. 106-107 (corsivo aggiunto). In senso simile vedi anche ECtHR, *Chiragov and Others v. Armenia*, parr. 167-168.

Come si può notare, la Corte ha ampliato la nozione di controllo del territorio da parte di uno Stato estero, stabilendo che questo può derivare non solo da un'occupazione militare, ma anche dall'influenza che tale Stato può esercitare, da un punto di vista politico ed economico, su un'area geografica appartenente ad un altro Stato [96].

La tesi di fondo della Corte europea, fondata sul criterio-guida dell'*overall control* sul territorio straniero, è condivisa dai *Treaty Bodies* delle NU. Il Comitato dei diritti umani ha affermato che le norme del Patto sui diritti civili e politici sono applicabili nei territori palestinesi occupati da Israele sulla base dei principi del diritto internazionale [97]; e che le medesime norme sono applicabili nei territori del Kuwait occupati dall'Iraq nel 1991 [98]. Il Comitato sui diritti economici, sociali e culturali ha espresso la medesima posizione sulla applicabilità del relativo Patto ai territori palestinesi sotto il controllo effettivo di Israele [99]. Una giurisprudenza simile emerge dal sistema interamericano dei diritti umani [100].

Infine, la conferma più autorevole viene dalla Corte internazionale di giustizia. Nel suo parere del 2004 sul *Muro in Palestina*, la Corte ha affermato che:

> "[...] the territories occupied by Israel have for over 37 years been subject to its territorial jurisdiction as the occupying Power. In the exercise of the powers available to it on this basis, Israel is bound by the provisions of the International Covenant on Economic, Social and Cultural Rights" [101].

La Corte ha raggiunto la medesima conclusione in relazione agli obblighi che vincolano Israele in base al Patto sui diritti civili e politici ed alla Convenzione sui diritti del fanciullo [102]. La Corte ha in seguito ribadito questa posizione, in termini più generali, nella sua sentenza del 2005 nel caso delle *Attività armate sul territorio del Congo*, laddove ha detto che:

> "[...] international human rights instruments are applicable 'in respect of acts done by a State in the exercise of its jurisdiction outside its own territory', particularly in occupied territories" [103].

11.2. *Atti di agenti statali che operano in territorio estero senza controllo effettivo del medesimo. Il concetto di* "State agent authority and control".

Il secondo contesto da esaminare è quello che si verifica quando gli agenti di uno Stato operano nel territorio di un altro Stato *senza che vi sia occupazione o controllo effettivo di tale territorio*, ed ivi commettono violazioni dei diritti umani. La questione circa l'esistenza o meno della giurisdizione "extraterritoriale" del primo Stato viene di solito valuta-

---

[96] Cfr. Ronzitti (2016), p. 326.

[97] HRCtee, Concluding Observations: *Israel* (1999), par. 10; Concluding Observations: *Israel* (2003), par. 11.

[98] HRCtee, Concluding Observations: *Iraq* (1991), par. 652.

[99] CteeESCR, Concluding Observations: *Israel*, 23 May 2003, par. 31.

[100] Vedi, ad es., IACmHR, *Salas and Others v. USA*.

[101] ICJ, *Legal Consequences of the Construction of a Wall*, par. 112.

[102] *Ibidem*, par. 113.

[103] ICJ, *Armed Activities on the Territory of the Congo*, Judgment of 19 December 2005, par. 216.

ta con il c.d. criterio della "*State agent authority and control*"; cioè esaminando se gli agenti statali che agivano all'estero potevano esercitare, o hanno di fatto esercitato, un controllo effettivo *su certe persone* (quelle colpite dalle violazioni dei diritti umani) o *su certe circostanze concrete* (quelle nelle quali si sono verificate le violazioni dei diritti umani).

È quindi una situazione assai diversa da quella del controllo effettivo di un territorio; ed essa è assai più problematica e controversa, sia in dottrina che nella prassi. Infatti, anche in questa fattispecie il criterio-guida è quello del *controllo effettivo* esercitato dallo Stato tramite i suoi individui-organi; ma questo criterio, mentre è applicabile in maniera non troppo difficile rispetto ad un territorio o ad una parte di esso, presenta maggiori difficoltà se si cerca di utilizzarlo e di precisarlo con riferimento a certe persone o a certe circostanze concrete.

In particolare si pongono due problemi. Il primo è se, in questo contesto, la responsabilità dello Stato derivi solo dalle norme internazionali sull'attribuzione allo Stato della condotta degli individui-organi ai fini dell'illecito, oppure se, per accertare tale responsabilità, occorra procedere in due fasi distinte fra loro: *a*) prima, si debba risolvere il problema dell'attribuzione allo Stato della condotta dei suoi agenti; *b*) poi, si debba stabilire se la violazione dei diritti umani si è verificata sotto la "giurisdizione" dello Stato [104]. Questo problema sarà affrontato in seguito [105].

Il secondo problema è quello di comprendere meglio come debba essere utilizzato il criterio-guida del controllo effettivo: si deve valutare volta per volta, *per ogni singolo caso* che sia regolato dal criterio della "*State agent authority and control*", il grado di controllo esercitato dagli agenti statali [106], oppure si deve distinguere fra *situazioni diverse*, in ciascuna delle quali il suddetto criterio di controllo funziona in maniera differente? Questa seconda soluzione, a mio parere, è quella adottata dalla giurisprudenza. Più in particolare, da essa si ricava che l'indagine sulla responsabilità dello Stato si configura in maniera diversa a seconda che questa possa derivare: *a*) da atti compiuti da suoi agenti diplomatici e consolari in territorio estero; *b*) da atti compiuti all'estero dai propri agenti su persone in stato di custodia o detenzione; *c*) da altre categorie di atti compiuti all'estero da propri agenti [107]. Vediamo adesso separatamente queste tre situazioni.

11.2.1. *Atti di agenti diplomatici e consolari*

Come si è già detto, la prima situazione non dà luogo ad incertezze. Per la prassi, lo Stato è responsabile per violazioni dei diritti umani dovute ad atti o omissioni di propri agenti diplomatici o consolari [108]. Si può dire che il criterio del controllo effettivo dello Stato è dato per assodato, con una presunzione di carattere assoluto [109]. Oppure, si può so-

---

[104] Questa problematica è bene evidenziata da De Schutter (2010), spec. p. 147; e da Focarelli (2012-2013), p. 457. In realtà, i problemi dell'attribuzione della condotta e quello della giurisdizione extraterritoriale sono concettualmente distinti, anche se talora tendono in concreto a coincidere.

[105] Vedi *infra*, par. 11.2.3.

[106] In questo senso vedi Kälin, Künzli (2009), p. 134.

[107] Per una simile distinzione in sottocategorie vedi ECtHR, *Al-Skeini and Others.*

[108] Vedi, ad es., HRCtee, *El Ghar*, parr. 7.1 ss.

[109] Cfr. ECtHR, *Al Skeini and Others*, par. 134, dove però non sembra che la presunzione sia assoluta.

stenere che queste situazioni sono comprese nella giurisdizione "quasi-territoriale" dello Stato in materia di diritti umani [110], in analogia con la regola sulla giurisdizione dello Stato su navi ed aerei aventi la sua nazionalità.

11.2.2. *Atti di agenti statali su persone in stato di custodia o detenzione*

La seconda situazione è più difficile da risolvere; ma un aiuto viene dalla prassi, che non è univoca, ma è sufficientemente uniforme. Nel complesso, essa indica che lo Stato ha "giurisdizione extraterritoriale" ed è responsabile per violazioni dei diritti umani commesse dai propri agenti all'estero nei confronti di persone che sono in stato di arresto, custodia o detenzione. Questa soluzione deve essere senz'altro approvata, perché è indubbio che lo Stato, tramite i propri agenti (militari o carcerari o di polizia o di sicurezza), esercita concretamente un controllo effettivo sulle persone che sono assoggettate a forme di detenzione. Pertanto, in questo caso, la soddisfazione del criterio della "*State agent authority and control*" deve darsi per *presunta*; ma probabilmente si tratta di una presunzione relativa e non assoluta.

La Corte europea dei diritti umani ha adottato tale soluzione in varie sentenze, fra le quali si segnalano quelle rese nei casi *Öcalan*, *Issa*, *Al-Saadoon*, *Medvedyev*, *Al-Jedda* e *Al-Skeini*. Nel caso *Öcalan*, del 2005, la Corte ha detto che:

> "[...] directly after being handed over to the Turkish officials by the Kenyan officials, *the applicant was effectively under Turkish authority* and therefore within the 'juridiction' of that State for the purpose of Article 1 of the Convention, even though in this instance Turkey exercised its authority outside its territory" [111].

Nel caso *Issa* [112], del 2004, il ricorso si basava sull'arresto illegittimo, la detenzione, i maltrattamenti e poi l'uccisione di alcuni cittadini iracheni durante un'operazione militare condotta dall'esercito turco nel Nord dell'Iraq nel 1995. La Corte di Strasburgo ha ritenuto che, nonostante l'ampiezza dell'operazione militare, la Turchia non avesse esercitato un controllo effettivo globale sull'intera area del Nord dell'Iraq; e che pertanto non fossero applicabili i principi che la Corte aveva utilizzato nei casi *Loizidou* [113]. Tuttavia, la Corte ha anche affermato che, qualora fosse stato stabilito che i soldati turchi avevano preso in custodia i cittadini iracheni, prima di maltrattarli ed ucciderli, costoro sarebbero stati soggetti alla "giurisdizione extraterritoriale" della Turchia *sulla base dell'autorità e controllo esercitato su di loro dai soldati*. Nel caso *Al-Saadoon and Mufdhi* [114], del 2009, la Corte ha ritenuto che due cittadini iracheni detenuti in prigioni militari controllate dalle truppe britanniche in Iraq ricadessero nella "giurisdizione" del Regno Unito, che esercitava un controllo totale ed esclusivo sui prigionieri. Nel caso *Medvedyev* [115], agenti francesi avevano esercitato pieno ed esclusivo controllo su una nave ed il suo equipaggio intercettati in acque internazionali. Nel caso *Al-Jedda*, del 2011, la Corte europea ha confermato i criteri

---

[110] Cfr. UK High Court of Justice, *Al-Skeini and Others*, par. 270.

[111] ECtHR, *Öcalan*, Judgment of 12 May 2005, par. 91 (corsivo aggiunto).

[112] ECtHR, *Issa and Others*, parr. 72-81.

[113] ECtHR, *Loizidou*, Judgments of 23 March 1995, 18 December 1996 and 28 July 1998.

[114] ECtHR, *Al-Saadoon and Mufdhi*, Decision of 30 June 2009, par. 88.

[115] ECtHR, *Medvedyev and Others v. France*.

usati nei casi precedenti, stabilendo che il ricorrente, che era stato internato dalle forze britanniche in una struttura di detenzione in Iraq controllata solo da tali forze, ricadeva nella "giurisdizione" del Regno Unito. Nelle parole della Corte:

> "The internment took place within a detention facility in Basra City, controlled exclusively by British forces, and the applicant was therefore within the authority and control of the United Kingdom throughout [...] The decision to hold the applicant in internment was made by the British officer in command of the detention facility [...] In conclusion, the Court agrees [...] that the internment of the applicant was attributable to the United Kingdom and that during his internment the applicant fell within the jurisdiction of the United Kingdom for the purposes of Article 1 of the Convention" [116].

In questo contesto, è molto importante anche il caso *Al-Skeini*, che nasce da fatti più complessi e che ha dato luogo ad alcune sentenze divergenti dei giudici inglesi e ad una sentenza della Corte europea dei diritti umani. Il caso nasce dal ricorso dei parenti di alcuni cittadini iracheni uccisi in Iraq nell'area che era soggetta ad occupazione da parte del Regno Unito. Cinque di loro erano stati uccisi in incidenti con le truppe militari britanniche, mentre un sesto era deceduto mentre era detenuto in una prigione militare delle truppe britanniche. In una prima sentenza, del 2004, la *High Court of Justice* del Regno Unito ha deciso che le morti dei cinque iracheni derivanti da operazioni militari non rientravano nella "giurisdizione" del Regno Unito. Al contrario, la "giurisdizione extraterritoriale" di tale Stato sussisteva in relazione al cittadino iracheno deceduto in prigione. Secondo la Corte:

> "[...] it is not at all straining the examples of extra-territorial jurisdiction [...] to hold that a British military prison, operating in Iraq with the consent of the Iraqi sovereign authorities, and containing arrested suspects, falls within even a narrowly limited exception exemplified by embassies, consulates, vessels and aircraft, and [...] a prison" [117].

Questa decisione, che conferma in maniera nitida il criterio della "*State agent authority and control*" sulle persone detenute, è stata sostanzialmente confermata dalla *Court of Appeal* in una sentenza del 2005 [118]. Ma, successivamente, la *House of Lords*, nel 2007, ha deciso in senso diverso, affermando che l'*Human Rights Act* del 1998, che ha dato esecuzione nel Regno Unito alla Convenzione europea, non intende avere applicazione extraterritoriale, in particolare per quanto riguarda la condotta di forze britanniche impegnate in operazioni di mantenimento della pace all'estero [119].

Infine, è intervenuta la Corte europea dei diritti umani, con la sentenza *Al-Skeini* del 2011 [120], che ha dato una soluzione diversa rispetto alle tre sentenze dei giudici britannici, poiché ha ritenuto che la "giurisdizione" del Regno Unito, *ex* art. 1 della Convenzione europea, sussistesse in relazione a *tutti* i cittadini iracheni uccisi nel corso delle operazioni di sicurezza condotte dai soldati britannici nell'area e nel periodo in questione. Ma ciò, come

---

[116] ECtHR, *Al-Jedda v. UK*, parr. 85-86.

[117] UK High Court of Justice, *Al-Skeini and Others*, par. 287.

[118] UK Court of Appeal, *Al-Skeini and Others*.

[119] House of Lords, *Al-Skeini and Others*.

[120] ECtHR, *Al-Skeini and Others v. UK*.

vedremo, usando un criterio diverso rispetto a quello del controllo sulle persone detenute, o, se si vuole, dando un'interpretazione più estensiva al concetto di "*State agent authority and control*".

Tornando adesso al criterio del controllo effettivo sulle persone custodite o detenute, si può affermare che anche la prassi di altri organi internazionali di controllo sui diritti umani adotta tale criterio. Il Comitato dei diritti umani ritiene che lo Stato abbia "giurisdizione" e sia responsabile per violazioni dei diritti umani commesse dai propri agenti su persone in stato di custodia o di detenzione. Si possono ricordare i due casi *Lopez Burgos* [121] e *Celiberti de Casariego* [122], decisi nello stesso giorno. Il sig. Lopez Burgos era stato prima detenuto per alcuni mesi in Uruguay e poi accettato come rifugiato in Argentina, dove era stato rapito da membri delle forze di sicurezza dell'Uruguay e segretamente detenuto a Buenos Aires per circa due settimane. In seguito era stato clandestinamente trasferito di nuovo in Uruguay, dove era stato detenuto in una prigione segreta per tre mesi. Il Comitato dei diritti umani ha affermato che, laddove l'art. 1 del Patto sui diritti civili e politici parla di "individui soggetti alla giurisdizione" di uno Stato, esso non si riferisce al "luogo dove si è realizzata la violazione", ma al "rapporto fra l'individuo e lo Stato" [123]. Di recente, il Comitato ha confermato la sua posizione nel suo Commento Generale n. 36, relativo al diritto alla vita:

> "Given that the deprivation of liberty brings a person within a State's effective control, States parties must respect and protect the right to life of all individuals arrested or detained by them, even if held outside their territory" [124].

La Commissione e la Corte interamericana dei diritti umani adottano la medesima posizione. Nel caso *Coard* [125], la Commissione interamericana ha deciso che gli USA avevano violato la Dichiarazione e la Convenzione americana, poiché le forze armate statunitensi, dopo aver invaso Grenada, avevano detenuto illegalmente e maltrattato alcuni cittadini di Grenada.

Vi sono infine dei casi nei quali gli atti degli agenti statali su persone in stato di custodia o detenzione non si verificano sul territorio di altri Stati, bensì in spazi non soggetti alla sovranità di alcuno Stato, in particolare in alto mare. Ci sembra che le due situazioni possano essere assimilate. La Commissione interamericana, ad esempio, nel caso *Haitian Interdiction* [126], doveva decidere circa la legittimità della prassi degli USA di intercettare barche di migranti haitiani in alto mare e di rimpatriare costoro ad Haiti, in possibile violazione dei loro diritti di non discriminazione e di asilo in altri Stati. La Commissione interamericana ha deciso che il divieto di *refoulement ex* art. 33(1) della Convenzione di Ginevra del 1951 ha applicazione extraterritoriale e che gli USA avevano violato anche il diritto di asilo stabilito dall'art. XXVII della Dichiarazione americana dei diritti e doveri dell'uomo. Una situazione simile, più recentemente, si è verificata nel noto caso *Hirsi*, del

---

[121] HRCtee, *Lopez Burgos v. Uruguay*, par. 12.3.

[122] HRCtee, *Celiberti de Casariego*, par. 10.1.

[123] HRCtee, *Lopez Burgos*, par. 12.2.

[124] HRCtee, General Comment No. 36, 3 September 2019, par. 63.

[125] IACmHR, *Coard et al.*, par. 57.

[126] IACmHR, "*Haitian Interdiction*", Decisions of 13 October 1993 and of 13 March 1997.

2012[127], nel quale alcune navi militari italiane avevano intercettato in alto mare migranti irregolari e li avevano trasferiti a bordo, riportati in Libia e consegnati alle autorità libiche. La Corte europea ha condannato l'Italia, fra l'altro, per violazione dell'art. 3 della Convenzione europea e non ha manifestato dubbi circa la "giurisdizione" dell'Italia sui migranti, ai sensi dell'art. 1 della Convenzione.

In realtà, a noi sembra che questi casi rientrino in quella che abbiamo definito come giurisdizione "quasi territoriale", piuttosto che "extraterritoriale", dello Stato. In ogni caso, è chiaro che si tratta anche di atti di agenti statali su persone in stato di custodia o detenzione.

11.2.3. *Altri atti extraterritoriali di agenti statali*

Esaminiamo adesso la terza situazione sopra indicata: quella relativa alla "giurisdizione extraterritoriale" e responsabilità dello Stato per atti di suoi agenti che non rientrino nelle categorie già discusse. In altri termini, si tratta di una situazione di carattere *residuale*. Si pensi, ad esempio, ad atti compiuti da forze militari o altri organi statali durante missioni di *peace-keeping* o di *peace-building* (nelle quali non vi sia un "*effective overall control*" sul territorio); oppure a funzioni esecutive o giudiziarie esercitate da organi di uno Stato nel territorio di un altro Stato con il consenso di quest'ultimo; oppure ad atti isolati di individui-organi statali all'estero, quali uccisioni, rapimenti ed altri abusi (senza l'esercizio di un controllo effettivo su persone detenute). In questi casi la prassi internazionale non è uniforme.

Un'interpretazione estensiva della "giurisdizione extraterritoriale" dello Stato sembra essere quella accolta dal Comitato dei diritti umani, il quale tende ad applicare la nozione della "*State agent authority and control*" a tutti i casi nei quali una persona è soggetta al potere o al controllo effettivo da parte di agenti statali, *a prescindere dalle circostanze nelle quali tale potere si è stabilito ed è esercitato*. Infatti, già nel suo Commento Generale n. 31 del 2004, a proposito dell'art. 2(1) del Patto sui diritti civili e politici, il Comitato scrive:

> "[…] a State party must respect and ensure the rights laid down in the Covenant to anyone within the power or effective control of that State Party […] This principle also applies to those within power or effective control of the forces of a State Party acting outside its territory, *regardless of the circumstances in which such power or effective control was obtained*, such as forces constituting a national contingent of a State Party assigned to an international peace-keeping or peace-enforcement operation"[128].

Questa posizione è stata ribadita, e con maggiore ampiezza, dal Comitato nel suo Commento Generale n. 36 del 2018[129].

---

[127] ECtHR, *Hirsi Jamaa and Others*.

[128] HRCtee, General Comment No. 31, 26 May 2004, par. 10 (corsivo aggiunto).

[129] HRCtee, General Comment No. 36, 3 September 2019, par. 63: "In light of article 2, paragraph 1, of the Covenant, a State party has an obligation to respect and to ensure the rights under article 6 of all persons who are within its territory and all persons subject to its jurisdiction, that is, all persons over whose enjoyment of the right to life it exercises power or effective control. This includes persons located outside any territory effectively controlled by the State whose right to life is nonetheless impacted by its military or other activities in a direct and reasonably foreseeable manner".

Anche la Commissione e la Corte interamericana dei diritti umani sembrano voler applicare un concetto estensivo della "*State agent authority and control*". Ad esempio, nel caso *Ecuador c. Colombia*, la Commissione interamericana ha deciso che la Colombia aveva esercitato la propria "giurisdizione extraterritoriale", *ex* art. 1(1) della Convenzione americana, quando i propri militari avevano fatto delle incursioni nel territorio dell'Ecuador, allo scopo di catturare o uccidere membri del movimento insurrezionale delle FARC. La Commissione ha affermato:

"[...] the Inter-American Commission has considered that it has competence *ratione loci* with respect to a State for acts occurring on the territory of another State, when the alleged victims were subjected to the authority and control of its agents. There would otherwise be a legal *lacuna* in the protection of those individuals' human rights that the American Convention seeks to protect, which would run counter to the object and purpose of this instrument. Thus, the following is essential for the Commission in determining jurisdiction: the exercise of authority over persons by agents of a State even if not acting within their territory, without necessarily requiring the existence of a formal, structured and prolonged legal relation in terms of time to raise the responsibility of a State for acts committed by its agents abroad" [130].

La Corte interamericana ha espresso la stessa posizione nel suo parere consultivo del 15 novembre 2017, avente per oggetto danni ambientali transfrontalieri subiti dalla Colombia [131].

Più prudente appare invece, quantomeno in un primo tempo, l'atteggiamento della Corte europea dei diritti umani. Nel notissimo caso *Bankovic*, la Corte doveva giudicare se gli Stati membri della NATO avessero violato il diritto alla vita di alcune persone che erano rimaste uccise da un missile lanciato da parte delle forze della NATO sugli edifici della radio e della televisione serba a Belgrado nell'aprile 1999. Nella sua sentenza del 2001, la Corte ha affermato che talora atti extraterritoriali possono cadere nella sfera di applicazione della Convenzione europea; ma che la "giurisdizione" degli Stati parti *ex* art. 1 è *essenzialmente territoriale*, mentre tutti gli altri titoli di giurisdizione sono di carattere *eccezionale*:

"The Court is of the view [...] that Article 1 of the Convention must be considered to reflect its ordinary and essentially territorial notion of jurisdiction, other bases of jurisdiction being exceptional and requiring special justification in the particular circumstances of each case" [132].

Quindi la Corte ha respinto gli argomenti dei ricorrenti secondo cui gli Stati membri della NATO, tramite i bombardamenti, avevano stabilito la loro "giurisdizione" sulle vittime. Questa sentenza ha generato numerose critiche.

---

[130] IACmHR, *Ecuador v. Colombia*, parr. 98-99.

[131] IACtHR, *The Environment and Human Rights* (*Medio Ambiente y Derechos Humanos*). La Corte ha affermato che: "[...] los Estados tienen la obligación de evitar daños ambientales transfronterizos que pudieran afectar los derechos humanos de personas fuera de su territorio. A efectos de la Convención Americana, cuando ocurre un daño transfronterizo que afecte derechos convencionales, se entiende que las personas cuyos derechos han sido vulnerados se encuentran bajo la jurisdicción del Estado de origen si existe una relación de causalidad entre el hecho que se originó en su territorio y la afectación de los derechos humanos de personas fuera de su territorio" (par. 101).

[132] ECtHR, *Banković and Others*, par. 61.

Tuttavia, nella sua successiva giurisprudenza, la Corte di Strasburgo, pur tenendo ferma l'idea che la "giurisdizione" degli Stati *ex* art. 1 della Convenzione europea è essenzialmente territoriale [133], ha in pratica finito per estendere la sfera di applicazione dei titoli di giurisdizione "eccezionali". In primo luogo, la Corte ha riconosciuto l'esercizio della "giurisdizione extraterritoriale" da parte di uno Stato contraente quando, con il consenso o l'acquiescenza del governo del territorio estero in questione, esso esercita tutti o alcuni dei pubblici poteri normalmente esercitati da quel governo [134]. In secondo luogo, la Corte ha *ampliato l'interpretazione* del concetto di "*State agent authority and control*" sulle persone. Infatti, nella già citata sentenza *Al-Skeini* del 2011, la Corte ha stabilito che il Regno Unito aveva esercitato in Iraq alcuni dei pubblici poteri normalmente esercitati da uno Stato sovrano, che giustificavano la sua "giurisdizione extraterritoriale". In particolare:

> "[...] the United Kingdom assumed authority and responsibility for the maintenance of security in south-east Iraq. In these exceptional circumstances, the Court considers that the United Kingdom, through its soldiers engaged in security operations in Basra during the period in question, exercised authority and control over individuals killed in the course of such security operations, so as to establish a jurisdictional link between the deceased and the United Kingdom for the purposes of Article 1 of the Convention" [135].

Un'interpretazione ancora più estensiva si ricava dalla sentenza del 2014 nel caso *Jaloud* [136]. Il ricorso riguardava la morte di un cittadino iracheno, ucciso in Iraq nel 2004 per un incidente verificatosi ad un posto di blocco tenuto da militari olandesi. Il Governo olandese sosteneva di non essere responsabile per gli eventi, poiché non era fra le "potenze occupanti" ai sensi della risoluzione 1483 del Consiglio di Sicurezza delle NU. Ma la Corte ha respinto tale argomento ed ha affermato che sussisteva la "giurisdizione" dei Paesi Bassi sulle persone che passavano attraverso il posto di blocco. Secondo la Corte:

> "[...] Mr Azhar Sabah Jaloud met his death when a vehicle in which he was a passenger was fired upon while passing through a checkpoint manned by personnel under the command and direct supervision of a Netherlands Royal Army officer. The checkpoint had been set up in the execution of SFIR's mission [...] to restore conditions of stability and security conducive to the creation of an effective administration in the country. The Court is satisfied that the respondent Party exercised its "jurisdiction" within the limits of its SFIR mission and for the purpose of asserting authority and control over persons passing through the checkpoint. That being the case, the Court finds that the death of Mr Azhar Sabah Jaloud occurred within the "jurisdiction" of the Netherlands, as that expression is to be construed within the meaning of Article 1 of the Convention" [137].

In definitiva, a nostro avviso, la Corte di Strasburgo ha finito per allinearsi all'interpretazione estensiva del criterio di "*State agent authority and control*" data dal Comitato dei diritti umani e dalla Commissione e la Corte interamericane.

---

[133] Vedi, ad es., ECtHR, *Al-Skeini and Others*, par. 131.

[134] Vedi, ad es., ECtHR, *Gentilhomme, Schaff-Benhadji and Zerouki.*

[135] ECtHR, *Al-Skeini and Others*, par. 149.

[136] ECtHR, *Jaloud.*

[137] *Ibidem*, par. 152.

In conclusione, in relazione al problema complessivo della giurisdizione e responsabilità dello Stato per atti di suoi agenti che operano in territorio estero, senza controllo effettivo del medesimo, ci sembra che si possa dare la seguente risposta. Nelle situazioni degli atti di agenti diplomatici o consolari e degli atti commessi da agenti statali contro persone in stato di custodia o detenzione, la sussistenza del criterio della "*State authority and control*" deve essere *presunta*. Invece, nella terza situazione (residuale) da ultimo descritta, il grado del controllo effettivo degli agenti statali sulle persone e sulle circostanze deve essere valutato in ogni singolo caso concreto.

Quanto al secondo problema che ci eravamo posti [138], quello dei rapporti fra le regole sull'attribuzione allo Stato della condotta dei suoi individui-organi e le regole sulla giurisdizione "extraterritoriale" dello Stato, a nostro avviso, la soluzione è chiara. Affinché gli atti degli individui-organi statali che operano all'estero, senza controllo del territorio, producano violazioni dei diritti umani e sussista la competenza degli organi internazionali di controllo a decidere sui ricorsi individuali delle vittime, occorrono ambedue le condizioni: *a*) che gli atti degli agenti siano attribuibili allo Stato secondo le regole classiche sull'attribuzione dell'illecito internazionale; *b*) che vi sia "giurisdizione extraterritoriale" dello Stato in materia di diritti umani.

12. *Giurisdizione "con effetti extraterritoriali": obblighi e responsabilità dello Stato per atti compiuti nel proprio territorio ma con effetti all'estero*

Conviene adesso prendere in considerazione la terza forma di competenza "spaziale" dello Stato in materia di diritti umani, quella che può essere definita come giurisdizione "con effetti extraterritoriali". Si tratta, cioè, di comprendere se, ed eventualmente quando, uno Stato, nell'ambito dei suoi obblighi in materia di diritti umani, possa essere responsabile per atti da esso compiuti *nel territorio nazionale*, ma che producono effetti contrari ai diritti umani fuori dal territorio nazionale. In linea di principio, la giurisdizione "con effetti extraterritoriali" è possibile. La Corte europea dei diritti umani, ad esempio, ha dichiarato che:

> "[...] acts of Contracting States performed outside their territory, *or which produce effects there*, may amount to exercise by them of their jurisdiction within the meaning of Article 1 of the Convention" [139].

Tuttavia, non è facile stabilire esattamente quando lo Stato sia responsabile per un esercizio del suo potere di governo con effetti extraterritoriali. A mio avviso, è utile la distinzione fra obblighi negativi ed obblighi positivi, unita al criterio-guida del *controllo effettivo*.

Partendo da queste basi, un primo punto è piuttosto chiaro: uno Stato ha l'obbligo (negativo) di astenersi dal violare i diritti umani di persone che si trovano fuori del territorio nazionale, sempre che le persone siano soggette al controllo [140], o comunque al potere di governo, di tale Stato. In primo luogo, tali violazioni potrebbero derivare da *azioni* concre-

---

[138] Vedi *supra*, par. 11.2.

[139] ECtHR, *Ilaşcu and Others*, par. 314 (corsivo aggiunto).

[140] Cfr. Kälin, Künzli (2009), p. 141.

te, da parte di agenti statali, che violano i diritti umani di persone all'estero. Si può pensare, ad esempio, ad un soldato o un agente di polizia di uno Stato che spara contro uno straniero che sta cercando di attraversare la frontiera.

In secondo luogo, le violazioni potrebbero derivare da *leggi o decisioni amministrative o giudiziarie* dello Stato che colpiscono persone all'estero. Ad esempio, nel caso *Gueye*, il Comitato dei diritti umani doveva decidere sul ricorso di molti cittadini senegalesi e residenti in Senegal, che avevano prestato servizio militare nell'esercito francese, e la cui pensione era inferiore rispetto a quella di cittadini francesi nelle medesime condizioni. Il Comitato ha ritenuto che la legislazione francese costituisse una discriminazione in violazione del Patto, anche se i ricorrenti non erano normalmente soggetti alla "giurisdizione" della Francia:

> "The Committee recalls that the authors are not generally subject to French jurisdiction, except that they rely on French legislation in relation to the amount of their pension rights" [141].

In sostanza, quando lo Stato ha certi poteri di controllo o di governo nei confronti di persone che si trovano all'estero, deve astenersi da esercitare questi poteri violando i diritti umani di tali persone. Vi è un rapporto fra i poteri di controllo dello Stato ed i suoi obblighi. Si tratta di un concetto che richiama, per certi aspetti, quello, sopra esaminato, della "*State agent authority and control*".

Una situazione simile si verifica quando certe decisioni amministrative o giudiziarie dello Stato, ad esempio provvedimenti di estradizione o espulsione o respingimento di persone, possono condurre o contribuire alla violazione dei diritti umani di tali persone in un altro Stato; cioè quando gli effetti negativi si producono all'estero. In questo senso, un *leading case* è il già citato caso *Soering* [142].

Ma lo Stato ha anche obblighi positivi di questo carattere? Ad esempio, lo Stato ha l'obbligo di esercitare *due diligence* per prevenire, da parte di individui privati, violazioni dei diritti umani di persone che si trovano all'estero? Oppure, lo Stato ha addirittura obblighi di assistenza e cooperazione internazionale con Stati terzi, per aiutare tali Stati a realizzare nel proprio territorio certi diritti economici, sociali e culturali? [143]

Il Comitato dei diritti economici, sociali e culturali, in alcuni dei suoi Commenti Generali [144], ha sostenuto che gli Stati parti del Patto dovrebbero proteggere il godimento, in altri Stati parti, dei diritti contenuti nel Patto medesimo anche tramite misure di prevenzione delle violazioni ad opera di terze parti private "if they are able to influence these third parties by way of legal or political means, in accordance with the Charter of the United Nations [...]". Alcuni autori, appoggiando questa posizione del Comitato, sostengono che gli Stati contraenti del Patto sui diritti economici, sociali e culturali dovrebbero controllare le attività degli attori privati, specie delle imprese multinazionali aventi la propria nazionalità, allo scopo di assicurare che tali imprese non violino i diritti umani in Stati esteri.

---

[141] HRCtee, *Gueye et al.*, par. 9.4.

[142] ECtHR, *Soering v. UK.*

[143] Questi aspetti sono approfonditi da De Schutter (2010), pp. 162-178.

[144] CteeESCR, General Comment No. 14, 11 August 2000, par. 39; General Comment No. 15, 20 January 2003, par. 31.

Tuttavia, la prassi degli altri organi internazionali di controllo dei trattati sui diritti umani e la dottrina prevalente non aderiscono a questa interpretazione estensiva della giurisdizione "con effetti extraterritoriali". L'argomento principale è quello per cui gli obblighi positivi extraterritoriali degli Stati in materia di diritti umani finora si sono affermati in situazioni nelle quali lo Stato esercita un controllo effettivo sulle persone o sulle situazioni concrete. Ed il criterio del controllo effettivo sembra mancare nelle situazioni sopra indicate [145]. Non sembra che tale criterio possa essere soddisfatto dal concetto (suggerito dal Comitato dei diritti economici, sociali e culturali) della capacità di influenza, con mezzi politici, che uno Stato può esercitare su attori privati che agiscono all'estero.

---

[145] Vedi Kälin, Künzli (2009), p. 141 e, più dubitativo, De Schutter (2010), p. 162.

Capitolo IV

I SISTEMI CONVENZIONALI SUI DIRITTI UMANI: TRATTATI, ORGANI E PROCEDURE

1. *Introduzione*

Si è già detto che la teoria dei diritti umani si è imposta a livello internazionale, in maniera generalizzata e non soltanto settoriale, dopo la Seconda Guerra Mondiale; e che si è realizzato progressivamente un "sistema internazionale di tutela dei diritti umani" [1]. Con questo termine, si intende di solito far riferimento ad un insieme di norme, di organi e di procedure, regolate dal diritto internazionale convenzionale, che sono state sviluppate soprattutto da parte di alcune organizzazioni internazionali, allo scopo di proteggere i diritti umani [2].

In realtà, nell'ambito di questa generale evoluzione normativa, conviene distinguere fra un sistema di tutela dei diritti umani di carattere "universale" (*rectius* tendenzialmente universale), promosso e realizzato dalle Nazioni Unite [3], ed alcuni sistemi di carattere "regionale". Fra i secondi spiccano per importanza il sistema europeo, quello interamericano e quello africano. Il sistema europeo di tutela dei diritti umani, come vedremo [4], è assai complesso, perché si compone di norme e meccanismi di garanzia che si sono venuti creando nel quadro di tre diverse organizzazioni internazionali: il Consiglio d'Europa (CdE), l'Unione Europea (UE) e l'Organizzazione per la Sicurezza e la Cooperazione in Europa (OSCE).

In questo capitolo, cercheremo di tracciare un quadro sintetico di tali sistemi convenzionali nell'ottica prevalente dei trattati, degli organi e delle procedure che compongono tali sistemi; e quindi senza per ora approfondire il contenuto dei diritti umani in essi protetti [5]. Questa parte, che potremmo definire come "istituzionale", del diritto internazionale dei diritti umani, viene di solito svolta con molta ampiezza nei manuali dedicati a tale diritto. Invece, a noi sembra che essa possa essere trattata in maniera sintetica, poiché ha carattere più descrittivo che concettuale.

---

[1] Vedi *supra*, Cap. I, par. 3.

[2] In questo senso vedi, ad es., Novak (2003), p. 67.

[3] Ed anche da alcuni Istituti Specializzati delle Nazioni Unite. Vedi *infra*, parr. 7.1 e 7.2.

[4] Vedi *infra*, Sez. II.

[5] Sul contenuto dei diritti umani vedi *infra*, Capp. V e VI.

Sezione I

IL SISTEMA DELLE NAZIONI UNITE

2. *La Carta delle Nazioni Unite*

Alla Conferenza di San Francisco del 1945, emerse un consenso fra gli Stati partecipanti sulla inclusione di disposizioni sui diritti umani nella Carta delle NU, anche se durante la Conferenza si confrontarono su tale punto posizioni differenti, sostenute da gruppi diversi di Stati, che resero necessario raggiungere un compromesso [6].

Nella Carta, il rispetto dei diritti umani figura nel Preambolo e nell'art. 1(3), fra i fini generali delle NU. L'art. 55(c) contiene una norma di natura programmatica, che impegna le NU a promuovere il rispetto e l'osservanza universale dei diritti umani senza discriminazioni. L'art. 56 stabilisce che gli Stati si impegnano ad agire, collettivamente o singolarmente, in cooperazione con l'organizzazione, per raggiungere i fini dell'art. 55. Tuttavia, tale disposizione non impone ad ogni singolo Stato un obbligo specifico, immediato e precettivo, di agire individualmente per garantire i diritti umani. Gli artt. 13, 62, 68 e 76 conferiscono all'Assemblea Generale (AG) ed al Consiglio Economico e Sociale (ECOSOC) la competenza ad occuparsi di questioni relative ai diritti umani. Infine, la Carta proclama il diritto dei popoli all'autodeterminazione, ma solo come principio programmatico per l'organizzazione (artt. 1(2) e 55).

Pertanto, nella Carta le disposizioni sui diritti umani sono poche e generiche. Inoltre i poteri degli organi delle NU sono soggetti al limite generale del dominio riservato (art. 2(7)), che poteva essere interpretato in modo da restringere molto tali poteri in materia di diritti umani. Tuttavia, prima l'AG e l'ECOSOC e poi anche altri organi principali delle NU hanno intrapreso, con l'aiuto di una serie di organi sussidiari, molte azioni tese alla tutela dei diritti umani. Occorreva, in primo luogo, un'azione di natura normativa, per precisare il contenuto dei diritti umani e per passare dagli obblighi generici e programmatici della Carta verso una serie di obblighi più precisi e vincolanti. In secondo luogo, occorreva un'azione di natura istituzionale, per creare anche dei meccanismi di controllo sui comportamenti degli Stati [7].

L'azione delle NU in un primo tempo si è limitata prevalentemente a predisporre progetti di trattati e raccomandazioni generiche; ma è in seguito divenuta più coraggiosa, chiamando gli Stati a rispondere della propria condotta, quantomeno nei casi di gravi violazioni dei diritti umani. In tal modo, hanno progressivamente acquistato maggior valore normativo anche le norme della Carta sui diritti umani, e specie l'art. 55.

---

[6] Cassese (2003-2004), vol. II, pp. 87-88.

[7] *Ibidem*, pp. 88-89.

3. *La Dichiarazione universale dei diritti dell'uomo*

La Dichiarazione Universale del 1948 [8] nasce dall'idea di approvare un documento internazionale sui diritti dell'uomo che, non essendo un trattato con obblighi dettagliati e vincolanti, potesse essere accettato più facilmente da parte di tutti gli Stati membri delle NU, ispirati da tradizioni giuridiche e concezioni politiche e ideologiche assai diverse. Era quindi necessario trovare un accordo capace di unificare le suddette differenze. Il tentativo ebbe successo, anche se la Dichiarazione fu approvata con l'astensione di alcuni Stati.

Dal punto di vista del contenuto, la Dichiarazione è costituita da un Preambolo e da 30 articoli. Nel Preambolo si indicano gli scopi e gli ideali della Dichiarazione; quindi negli artt. 1 e 2 si stabiliscono i concetti di libertà, uguaglianza e fratellanza ed il principio di non discriminazione nel godimento dei diritti riconosciuti; negli articoli da 3 a 5 si affermano i diritti essenziali della persona (diritto alla vita, alla libertà e sicurezza, divieto di schiavitù e di tortura); negli articoli da 6 a 21 i classici diritti civili e politici di matrice liberale; negli articoli da 22 a 27 alcuni diritti economici, sociali e culturali; infine negli articoli da 28 a 30 le modalità di godimento ed i limiti dei diritti elencati. In realtà, prevale nel complesso la concezione occidentale dei diritti umani, con maggiore spazio dato ai diritti civili e politici e minore importanza per i diritti economici, sociali e culturali. Non viene incluso il diritto all'autodeterminazione dei popoli.

Dal punto di vista della sua natura giuridica, la Dichiarazione, adottata con una risoluzione dell'AG, è un atto non vincolante. Tuttavia, con il passare del tempo, alcuni autori hanno sostenuto che essa, essendo strettamente legata alla Carta delle NU, avrebbe in un certo senso concretizzato l'impegno da parte degli Stati membri di promuovere il rispetto dei diritti umani (art. 56 della Carta) e che quindi una violazione dei diritti elencati nella Dichiarazione costituirebbe una violazione della Carta. Altri hanno sostenuto la tesi che la Carta e la Dichiarazione, insieme a successive risoluzioni e dichiarazioni delle NU ed alla prassi degli Stati, avrebbero finito per incorporare i diritti elencati nella Dichiarazione nel diritto internazionale consuetudinario. A nostro avviso, queste due tesi non sono convincenti. Tuttavia, si deve ammettere che *alcuni* dei diritti proclamati nella Dichiarazione sono con il tempo entrati a far parte del diritto internazionale generale [9]. Inoltre, si deve riconoscere che la Dichiarazione, pur con i suoi limiti, rimane uno strumento fondamentale, che ha formulato un insieme universalmente riconosciuto di valori per la comunità internazionale e ha dato un impulso assai importante al processo di formazione progressiva del diritto internazionale dei diritti umani.

4. *Evoluzione nel tempo dell'azione delle Nazioni Unite: le varie generazioni di diritti umani*

L'azione delle NU in materia di diritti umani si è evoluta progressivamente, con riferimento sia alle norme che ai meccanismi di garanzia. Questa evoluzione è dovuta alle mag-

---

[8] Universal Declaration of Human Rights (UDHR), 10 December 1948.

[9] Vedi *supra*, Cap. II, parr. 3-7 e *infra*, Cap. V, par. 4.4.

gioranze politiche (che sono cambiate nel tempo) dei gruppi di Stati che hanno sostenuto, specie nell'AG, tale azione. In proposito si suole distinguere fra quattro fasi storiche *diverse* alle quali corrispondono quattro c.d. "generazioni" di diritti umani [10].

Nella prima fase, che va dall'adozione della Carta fino alla fine degli anni '50, si assiste al predominio degli Stati occidentali ed alla loro concezione dei diritti umani, che tende a privilegiare i diritti civili e politici, che non è favorevole al principio di autodeterminazione dei popoli, che favorisce la predisposizione di trattati sui diritti umani con norme precise e dettagliate e l'adozione di meccanismi internazionali di controllo per verificare il rispetto delle norme. Si parla, in questo senso, di una prima generazione di diritti umani.

La seconda fase, che va dalla fine degli anni '50 fino a circa la metà degli anni '70, è caratterizzata dalla maggiore importanza assunta dal gruppo degli Stati socialisti, che esercitano anche un'influenza su molti Stati in via di sviluppo. Questo gruppo introduce nelle NU una concezione socialista dei diritti umani, che tende a favorire i diritti economici e sociali, che dà molta importanza al principio di autodeterminazione dei popoli, che non favorisce la predisposizione di trattati con norme precise né l'adozione di meccanismi di garanzia internazionali. Si parla, in proposito, di una seconda generazione di diritti umani.

La terza fase storica, che va dalla metà degli anni '70 fino all'inizio degli anni '90, vede consolidarsi la concezione dei diritti umani dei Paesi in via di sviluppo (PVS). Essi tendono a rafforzare, per motivi politici, economici e culturali, l'autorità dello Stato o di leader dotati di poteri assoluti, e non conoscono la contrapposizione, di matrice tipicamente occidentale, fra libertà individuale e potere dello Stato. La loro concezione dei diritti umani tende (come quella socialista) a privilegiare i diritti economici e sociali; pone in primo piano l'esigenza di modificare radicalmente il sistema economico internazionale come priorità rispetto alla tutela dei diritti umani; è interessata a combattere politiche di discriminazione razziale e di *apartheid*; e preferisce promuovere la tutela dei diritti umani con strumenti di *soft law*. La concezione dei diritti umani dei PVS apporta anche novità significative, favorendo la creazione di nuovi diritti di natura collettiva (i c.d. diritti umani di terza generazione), quali il diritto allo sviluppo, alla pace, ad un ambiente sano, allo sfruttamento delle risorse naturali ed i diritti dei popoli indigeni. Ma molti di questi diritti hanno un carattere piuttosto generico e sono difficilmente inquadrabili in diritti con effetti vincolanti e giustiziabili [11].

Infine, negli ultimi anni, si può parlare di una quarta generazione di diritti umani, che vede lo sviluppo di alcuni nuovi diritti collettivi, quali il diritto alla democrazia, ad un buon governo ed alla sicurezza umana. Inoltre, stanno emergendo anche alcuni diritti legati alle innovazioni scientifiche e tecnologiche (specie nel campo delle biotecnologie, della genetica e dell'informatica). Ma anche molti di questi diritti costituiscono obiettivi politici non vincolanti, più che diritti veri e propri.

In questo periodo, si assiste anche ad una sorta di "riconciliazione" fra le precedenti concezioni dei diritti umani, poiché le NU, con alcune importanti risoluzioni, hanno più volte affermato solennemente che tutti i diritti umani sono universali, indivisibili, interdipendenti e strettamente legati fra loro, su una base di uguaglianza e con la medesima im-

---

[10] Cfr., fra gli altri, Cassese (2003-2004), vol. II, pp. 88-93. Vedi anche *supra*, Cap. III, par. 4.1.

[11] Vedi *supra*, Cap. III, par. 5.4 ed *infra*, Cap. VI, par. 19.

portanza. In realtà, come vedremo [12], queste affermazioni hanno una natura "politica" più che strettamente giuridica. Inoltre, e ciò è più importante, si è ormai consolidato un nucleo essenziale di diritti umani fondamentali, che sono riconosciuti da tutti gli Stati e che fanno ormai parte del diritto internazionale generale [13].

5. *Trattati promossi dalle Nazioni Unite. Organi e procedure di controllo (*Treaty-Bodies *o* Treaty-Procedures*)*

Come si è già detto, un primo tipo di azione delle NU, necessaria per lo sviluppo di un sistema universale di tutela dei diritti umani, richiedeva di tradurre i principi generali della Dichiarazione Universale in norme internazionali giuridicamente vincolanti. Questa azione, di carattere normativo, è stata perseguita in due modi diversi. Da una parte, occorreva predisporre trattati a vocazione universale di *contenuto generale*, cioè tendenzialmente comprensivi di tutti i diritti umani. Dall'altra parte, era opportuno redigere altri trattati, sempre a vocazione universale, ma di *carattere settoriale*, cioè adottati per la tutela di diritti specifici o per la protezione di certe categorie di persone particolarmente deboli.

Inoltre, non bastava avere un apparato normativo; ma occorreva anche poter disporre di organi e procedure per controllare, a livello internazionale, l'attuazione delle norme convenzionali da parte degli Stati. Ed in effetti, le NU hanno proceduto a creare, in maniera graduale, un complesso di organi e procedure internazionali di controllo sul rispetto dei suddetti trattati: i c.d. *Treaty-Bodies* o *Treaty-Procedures.*

5.1. *Trattati a carattere generale: i Patti internazionali del 1966*

Il primo obiettivo (quello di disporre di trattati sui diritti umani di contenuto generale) è stato in gran parte raggiunto, dopo lunghi negoziati, con l'adozione dei due Patti internazionali sui diritti umani, approvati dall'AG nel 1966 ed entrati in vigore nel 1976. Essi intendono, in sostanza, specificare in maggiore dettaglio e tradurre in norme vincolanti i principi della Dichiarazione Universale.

Come è noto, l'idea iniziale era quella di predisporre un unico trattato, che si occupasse sia dei diritti di prima generazione che di quelli di seconda generazione. Ma essa fu presto abbandonata e si scelse di negoziare due trattati separati, poiché all'epoca prevalse l'idea che vi fosse una netta distinzione fra i due gruppi di diritti: si pensava che i diritti civili e politici richiedessero agli Stati obblighi negativi di astensione dall'interferire nelle libertà e diritti individuali e quindi fossero anche *self-executing* e giustiziabili dinanzi ai giudici interni; e che, al contrario, i diritti economici, sociali e culturali richiedessero agli Stati obblighi positivi, e spesso addirittura un'azione graduale di attuazione, e quindi non fossero *self-executing* e giustiziabili. Di conseguenza, si riteneva che anche i meccanismi di controllo internazionali dovessero essere diversi.

Pertanto furono predisposti e poi approvati due trattati separati: il Patto sui diritti civili

[12] Vedi *infra*, Cap. V, par. 2.

[13] Vedi *infra*, Cap. V, parr. 3 e 4.

e politici ed il Patto sui diritti economici, sociali e culturali. I due Patti hanno ad oggi raggiunto un numero di ratifiche assai elevato e pertanto costituiscono un notevole successo da parte delle NU.

5.1.1. *Il Patto sui diritti civili e politici*

Il Patto sui diritti civili e politici [14] contiene tutti i diritti che derivano dal modello liberaldemocratico di tradizione occidentale, riprendendo e specificando sia la Dichiarazione Universale del 1948 sia la Convenzione europea dei diritti umani del 1950.

Nel Preambolo, si dichiara che la tutela dei diritti deriva dalla dignità inerente ad ogni persona umana. Peraltro, il Patto si apre, all'art. 1, stabilendo il diritto dei popoli all'autodeterminazione ed alla libera disposizione delle loro ricchezze e risorse naturali. La Parte II contiene alcuni principi generali: molto importante è l'art. 2, che stabilisce che gli Stati parti si impegnano a garantire a tutti gli individui presenti nel proprio territorio e soggetti alla propria "giurisdizione" i diritti enunciati nel Patto senza discriminazioni (par. 1); e che poi richiede ai medesimi Stati di adottare tutte le misure legislative o di altro genere necessarie a dare attuazione concreta a tali diritti (par. 2). L'art. 3 afferma il principio di uguaglianza fra uomo e donna.

La Parte III del Patto contiene, in primo luogo, i diritti essenziali oggetto di protezione: il diritto alla vita (art. 6), alla libertà dalla tortura e dalla schiavitù (artt. 7 e 8), alla libertà e sicurezza personale (art. 9), il divieto di arresti arbitrari (artt. 10 e 11), il diritto al giusto processo ed altri diritti giudiziari (artt. 14 e 15). Quindi seguono i classici diritti civili, quali il diritto alla personalità (art. 16), il diritto alla vita privata e familiare (art. 17), le libertà di pensiero, coscienza e religione (art. 18), le libertà di espressione (art. 19), di associazione e di riunione (art. 21). Inoltre, nel catalogo sono previsti anche altri diritti, quali il diritto di entrare nel proprio paese e di lasciarlo (art. 12), la protezione per la famiglia ed i bambini (artt. 23 e 24), il diritto di partecipazione alla vita politica (art. 25), ed alcuni diritti delle minoranze (art. 27). L'art. 26 ribadisce i principi di uguaglianza e di non discriminazione. I diritti previsti nel Patto possono essere limitati in situazioni di emergenza, ma sulla base di procedure ben definite (art. 4). Ma alcuni diritti vengono indicati come inderogabili anche in situazioni di emergenza.

La Parte IV del Patto stabilisce una procedura di controllo sul rispetto del medesimo, istituendo il Comitato dei diritti umani [15] e determinando le funzioni di tale organo. Il Comitato è composto da 18 individui, competenti nel campo dei diritti umani, che sono eletti e servono nelle loro capacità personali e non come rappresentanti di uno Stato. Il Comitato esercita le proprie funzioni tramite quattro procedure tipiche, le quali, come vedremo, sono state in sostanza riprese anche da altri *Treaty-Bodies*. Conviene descriverle in maniera sintetica.

La prima procedura consiste nell'esame dei rapporti periodici trasmessi dagli Stati contraenti. Il rapporto viene discusso con i rappresentanti dello Stato in questione e, al termine, il Comitato predispone a sua volta un documento, che contiene delle "osservazioni conclusive", nelle quali si indicano gli sviluppi positivi, i punti critici e si emettono le rac-

[14] International Covenant on Civil and Political Rights (CCPR), 16 December 1966.

[15] Human Rights Committee (HRCtee).

comandazioni opportune nei confronti dello Stato sottoposto ad esame. In realtà, le conclusioni del Comitato non sono vincolanti né sono assistite da sanzioni; tuttavia esse esercitano un'importante funzione di pressione politico-diplomatica sugli Stati che sono stati sottoposti a monitoraggio [16].

La seconda procedura si realizza tramite l'esame di presunte violazioni dei diritti contenuti nel Patto da parte di uno Stato contraente su richiesta di un altro Stato contraente (c.d. ricorsi interstatali). Ma finora questa procedura è rimasta in pratica inoperante.

La terza procedura, che è stata istituita con il Protocollo Opzionale al Patto [17], è quella più interessante e più efficace. Essa consiste nell'esame di presunte violazioni di diritti da parte di uno Stato contraente su istanza di individui o gruppi di individui che dichiarino di aver subito una violazione (c.d. ricorsi individuali). Questa procedura ha prodotto una prassi importante del Comitato dei diritti umani, che ha finito per attribuire ad esso una funzione quasi-giurisdizionale. Infatti il Comitato esamina il caso concreto, decide se vi è stata o meno una violazione di una o più disposizioni del Patto e, in caso affermativo, raccomanda allo Stato di adottare misure di riparazione, che nella realtà vengono quasi sempre eseguite da parte dello Stato. Pertanto, la procedura non si conclude con una vera e propria sentenza di condanna, ma con dei pareri (*views*), che sono motivati e che sono molto simili, anche nella forma e nel contenuto, a vere e proprie sentenze.

Infine, il Comitato ha sviluppato una quarta funzione, che consiste nella prassi di predisporre dei commenti generali (*General Comments*) sulle disposizioni del Patto, per fornire agli Stati contraenti un'interpretazione autorevole sul loro significato.

5.1.2. *Il Patto sui diritti economici, sociali e culturali*

Il Patto sui diritti economici, sociali e culturali [18] contiene un'ampia serie di diritti c.d. di "seconda generazione" [19], e pertanto costituisce una notevole innovazione rispetto alla Dichiarazione Universale, che prevedeva un numero assai limitato di diritti di questa natura. La medesima conclusione vale anche se facciamo un confronto con la Convenzione europea dei diritti umani.

Anche il Patto sui diritti economici, sociali e culturali si apre, all'art. 1, riconoscendo il diritto dei popoli all'autodeterminazione ed alla libera disposizione delle loro ricchezze e risorse naturali. La Parte II del Patto, in analogia con quella del Patto sui diritti civili e politici, contiene alcuni principi generali. Ma si deve sottolineare che, per quanto riguarda la natura degli impegni richiesti agli Stati parti, la formulazione di questo Patto è assai diversa. Ciò risulta in maniera netta dall'art. 2(1) del Patto, che definisce, in via generale, la natura di tali impegni, che abbiamo già definito come "obblighi a realizzazione progressiva" [20]. Infatti tale disposizione stabilisce che ciascuno Stato parte si impegna ad operare, con il massimo delle risorse di cui dispone, al fine di assicurare *progressivamente* con tutti i mezzi appropriati la piena attuazione dei diritti riconosciuti nel Patto:

---

[16] Su questo punto vedi anche Zappalà (2011), p. 45.

[17] Optional Protocol to the International Covenant on Civil and Political Rights, 16 December 1966. Questa procedura opera soltanto per gli Stati che hanno aderito a questo Protocollo Opzionale.

[18] International Covenant on Economic, Social and Cultural Rights (CESCR), 16 December 1966.

[19] Vedi *supra*, par. 4 e Cap. III, par. 4.1.

[20] Vedi *supra*, Cap. III, par. 5.3.

"Each State Party to the present Covenant undertakes to take steps, individually and through international assistance and co-operation, especially economic and technical, to the maximum of its available resources, with a view to achieving progressively the full realization of the rights recognized in the present Covenant by all appropriate means, including particularly the adoption of legislative measures" [21].

La Parte III del Patto contiene l'ampio e dettagliato catalogo dei diritti economici, sociali e culturali riconosciuti. In sintesi essi sono: il diritto al lavoro (art. 6), il diritto al godimento di giuste e favorevoli condizioni di lavoro (art. 7), il diritto di formare (e aderire a) sindacati ed il diritto di sciopero (art. 8), il diritto alla sicurezza sociale (art. 9), il diritto alla protezione della famiglia (art. 10), il diritto ad uno standard adeguato di vita (art. 11), il diritto al godimento del massimo standard possibile di salute fisica e mentale (art. 12), il diritto all'educazione (artt. 13 e 14), ed il diritto di partecipare alla vita culturale del paese e di godere dei benefici e libertà delle attività scientifiche e artistiche (art. 15).

Nella parte IV del Patto, si stabilisce una procedura di controllo sul rispetto e l'attuazione dei diritti stabiliti dal medesimo, che è affidata al Consiglio economico e sociale delle NU (ECOSOC). Tale procedura in origine non prevedeva né ricorsi interstatali né ricorsi individuali; ma solo un sistema di rapporti da parte degli Stati all'ECOSOC. Tuttavia, nel 1985, l'ECOSOC ha istituito il Comitato sui diritti economici, sociali e culturali [22], composto da 18 esperti indipendenti, che ha gradualmente sviluppato una procedura di esame dei rapporti trasmessi dagli Stati contraenti, simile a quella adottata dal Comitato dei diritti umani; nonché la prassi di predisporre *General Comments* sulla interpretazione delle disposizioni del Patto. Infine, più recentemente, con il Protocollo Opzionale al Patto del 2008 [23], al Comitato è stata data la competenza a ricevere (e decidere su) comunicazioni individuali e comunicazioni interstatali. Pertanto, attualmente le funzioni del Comitato sui diritti economici, sociali e culturali sono simili a quelle del Comitato dei diritti umani.

5.2. *Trattati a carattere settoriale*

Come si è già rilevato, il secondo obiettivo normativo delle NU, ai fini dello sviluppo di un sistema universale di tutela dei diritti umani, era quello di predisporre una serie di trattati di carattere settoriale, per la tutela di diritti specifici o per la protezione di certe categorie di persone particolarmente deboli. Questo obiettivo è stato raggiunto solo parzialmente ed è stato condizionato dalle priorità che sono state via via privilegiate dai vari gruppi di Stati che esercitavano un predominio in seno all'AG. In realtà, le Nazioni Unite hanno promosso o adottato un ampio numero di trattati attinenti alla protezione dei diritti umani [24]. Tuttavia, si ricorderanno qui soltanto quelli *principali*, in ordine cronologico. Conviene notare che quasi tutti questi trattati sono stati preceduti da una dichiarazione di principi dell'Assemblea Generale delle NU. Si deve anche premettere che ciascuno di questi trattati, con l'eccezione dei due meno recenti, prevede un comitato di esperti indipen-

---

[21] Sugli obblighi "a realizzazione progressiva" vedi *supra*, Cap. III, par. 5.3.

[22] Committee on Economic, Social and Cultural Rights (CteeESCR).

[23] Optional Protocol to the International Covenant on Economic, Social and Cultural Rights, 18 June 2008.

[24] Vedi https://www.ohchr.org/EN/ProfessionalInterest/Pages/UniversalHumanRightsInstruments.aspx.

denti (*human rights treaty-body*), incaricato del controllo internazionale sull'applicazione del trattato da parte degli Stati contraenti.

5.2.1. *La Convenzione sul genocidio*

Fra i trattati a carattere settoriale, va citata, innanzitutto, la Convenzione del 1948 per la prevenzione e repressione del crimine di genocidio [25]. Dopo la Seconda Guerra Mondiale, come reazione allo sterminio di milioni di ebrei e di membri di altri gruppi etnici e religiosi durante l'Olocausto nazista, le Nazioni Unite decisero di dedicare al genocidio una convenzione *ad hoc*. Il contenuto della Convenzione sarà approfondito in seguito [26] e qui viene solo sintetizzato.

La Convenzione dichiara che il genocidio, commesso in tempo di pace o di guerra, è un crimine secondo il diritto internazionale, che gli Stati parti si impegnano a prevenire ed a punire (art. 1). Il reato di genocidio ed altri reati ad esso collegati sono definiti negli artt. 2 e 3 della Convenzione. Le persone responsabili di tali reati devono essere punite "sia che esse siano governanti costituzionalmente responsabili o che siano funzionari pubblici o individui privati" (art. 4). Inoltre, gli Stati parti si impegnano ad adottare le norme interne, specie penali, per attuare la Convenzione. La competenza a processare le persone accusate di genocidio spetta ai tribunali dello Stato nel cui territorio il reato è stato commesso (art. 6) [27]. Peraltro, la Convenzione tiene conto della possibilità che le persone accusate di genocidio possano essere processate da un tribunale internazionale penale "che abbia giurisdizione rispetto agli Stati contraenti che avranno accettato tale giurisdizione" (art. 6) [28].

Per quanto riguarda le misure di controllo e di garanzia, la Convenzione è piuttosto debole. Essa prevede che ogni Stato contraente possa invitare gli organi competenti delle NU a prendere ogni misura appropriata per prevenire e reprimere atti di genocidio (art. 8). Infine, l'art. 9 prevede la possibilità di sottoporre alla Corte internazionale di giustizia le controversie fra gli Stati contraenti relative all'interpretazione, applicazione o esecuzione della Convenzione. In effetti, come vedremo meglio in seguito [29], a partire dagli anni 1990, specie il conflitto armato nella *ex* Jugoslavia ha prodotto alcune controversie in materia di genocidio dinanzi alla Corte internazionale di giustizia.

5.2.2. *La Convenzione di Ginevra sui rifugiati*

Un'altra convenzione molto importante a carattere settoriale, promossa dalle NU, è la Convenzione di Ginevra del 1951 relativa allo status dei rifugiati [30], in seguito completata

[25] Convention on the Prevention and Punishment of the Crime of Genocide (CPPCG), 9 December 1948. La Convenzione fa parte, in senso stretto, del diritto internazionale penale; ma, in senso lato, può essere considerata anche come attinente al diritto internazionale dei diritti umani.

[26] Vedi *infra*, Cap. V, par. 9.1.

[27] Tuttavia oggi si ritiene che sul crimine di genocidio vi sia la c.d. giurisdizione universale, cioè la competenza dei giudici di tutti gli Stati a processare i responsabili.

[28] In realtà, questa possibilità si è poi verificata dopo molti anni con la creazione dei Tribunali internazionali penali ad hoc e della Corte penale internazionale. Vedi *infra*, Cap. V, par. 9.

[29] Vedi *infra*, Cap. V, par. 9.1. Vedi anche, da ultimo, ICJ, *Application of the Convention (The Gambia v. Myanmar)*, Order of 23 January 2020.

[30] Convention relating to the Status of Refugees (CSR), Geneva, 28 July 1951.

dal Protocollo di New York del 1967[31]. La questione della tutela dei rifugiati si pose all'attenzione della comunità internazionale a causa dei grandi flussi di profughi che si erano verificati dopo la Seconda Guerra Mondiale. Il contenuto della Convenzione di Ginevra sarà approfondito in seguito[32] e qui viene sintetizzato.

Il capitolo I regola l'ambito di applicazione soggettivo e oggettivo della Convenzione ed i principi di base sul trattamento dei rifugiati. Trascurando adesso l'ambito di applicazione geografico e temporale della Convenzione, si deve notare che è molto importante la definizione del termine "rifugiato" contenuta nell'art. 1: sono considerati come "rifugiati" tutti coloro che, per un timore ben fondato di essere perseguitati per motivi di razza, religione, nazionalità, appartenenza ad un particolare gruppo sociale o di opinioni politiche, sono al di fuori del proprio Stato nazionale e non possono o non vogliono avvalersi della protezione di tale Stato[33]. Il capitolo II della Convenzione prevede alcune disposizioni sul regime giuridico del rifugiato (artt. 12-16), al quale viene riconosciuta una serie di diritti in materia di status personale, di proprietà, di associazione e di accesso alla giustizia. Il capitolo III disciplina le sue attività lavorative (artt. 17-19); il capitolo IV (artt. 20-24) prevede diritti in materia di assistenza sociale (alloggio, istruzione, sicurezza sociale ecc.); il capitolo V (artt. 25-34) si occupa degli aspetti amministrativi e fiscali relativi al rifugiato. Molto importanti sono gli artt. 32 e 33 in materia di espulsione e di *non-refoulement*, sui quali ritorneremo in seguito[34].

La Convenzione di Ginevra non prevede misure internazionali di controllo o di garanzia sulla sua attuazione da parte degli Stati. Tuttavia, una forma di controllo sul trattamento dei rifugiati viene svolta, di fatto, dall'Alto Commissario delle NU per i Rifugiati.

5.2.3. *La Convenzione contro la discriminazione razziale*

Alla base dell'azione delle NU per la tutela internazionale dei diritti umani vi è sempre stata la lotta contro la discriminazione fra esseri umani[35]. Fra le forme di discriminazione, quella per motivi di razza è la più grave ed odiosa. Pertanto non sorprende che la necessità di condannare i fenomeni di discriminazione razziale abbia indotto le NU a promuovere un importante trattato multilaterale: la Convenzione internazionale sull'eliminazione di ogni forma di discriminazione razziale del 1965[36].

La Convenzione proibisce non solo la discriminazione razziale in senso stretto, ma anche ogni distinzione fondata sulla razza, il colore, la nascita, l'origine nazionale o etnica, che abbia lo scopo o l'effetto di pregiudicare il godimento dei diritti umani (art. 1(1)). Gli obblighi principali degli Stati contraenti sono contenuti negli artt. 2 e 5. Ai sensi dell'art. 2, gli Stati si impegnano, fra l'altro: ad astenersi da qualsiasi atto o pratica di discriminazione razziale; a non incoraggiare o difendere tale forma di discriminazione; a prendere misure

---

[31] Protocol relating to the Status of Refugees (PSR), New York, 31 January 1967.

[32] Vedi *infra*, Cap. VI, par. 15.

[33] Article 1(A): "For the purposes of the present Convention, the term "refugee" shall apply to any person who: [...] owing to well-founded fear of being persecuted for reasons of race, religion, nationality, membership of a particular social group or political opinion, is outside the country of his nationality and is unable, or owing to such fear, is unwilling to avail himself of the protection of that country [...]".

[34] Vedi *infra*, Cap. VI, parr. 13, 14 e 15.

[35] Vedi *infra*, Cap. V, parr. 21-23.

[36] International Convention on the Elimination of All Forms of Racial Discrimination (CERD), 21 December 1965.

efficaci per abrogare o modificare prassi, leggi o regolamenti che abbiano l'effetto di creare discriminazione razziale. Secondo l'art. 5, gli Stati parti si impegnano a proibire ed eliminare la discriminazione razziale ed a garantire a tutte le persone l'uguaglianza nel godimento di una serie di diritti civili, politici, economici, sociali e culturali, che vengono specificati.

Le procedure di controllo della Convenzione sono affidate al Comitato sulla eliminazione della discriminazione razziale [37], composto da 18 esperti indipendenti, che hanno il compito di esaminare: *a*) i rapporti periodici degli Stati parti; *b*) i ricorsi interstatali; *c*) i ricorsi individuali (solo nei confronti degli Stati che hanno accettato questa competenza del Comitato). L'applicazione pratica di queste procedure non si discosta in maniera significativa da quella del Comitato dei diritti umani e degli altri *Treaty-Bodies*. Si noti anche che la Convenzione attribuisce alla Corte internazionale di giustizia, su richiesta di uno Stato parte, la competenza a risolvere controversie fra gli Stati contraenti relative alla interpretazione ed applicazione della Convenzione medesima.

5.2.4. *La Convenzione contro l'*apartheid

Negli anni 1960 si era diffuso in Sudafrica un sistema di *apartheid*, contro il quale le Nazioni Unite avevano condotto una lunga lotta. Ma ciò aveva portato il fenomeno all'attenzione della comunità internazionale ed occorreva anche una risposta di carattere normativo, che si realizzò con l'adozione della Convenzione internazionale sulla soppressione e la punizione del crimine di *apartheid* del 1973 [38].

La Convenzione ha lo scopo di sopprimere e di punire le pratiche di *apartheid*. Essa dichiara che l'*apartheid* è un crimine contro l'umanità e che gli atti derivanti da politiche o pratiche di *apartheid* sono crimini che violano i principi del diritto internazionale (art. I). L'art. II definisce, in maniera dettagliata, il crimine di *apartheid*. L'art. III è una disposizione-chiave della Convenzione, perché stabilisce che la responsabilità internazionale penale si applicherà a individui, a membri di organizzazioni o di istituzioni ed a rappresentanti dello Stato che commettono il reato; ma anche a coloro che partecipano, incitano o cospirano oppure favoriscono, incoraggiano o cooperano nella commissione del reato. Le persone accusate del reato possono essere processate da ogni Stato parte che possa avere la competenza su tali persone o da un tribunale internazionale penale che possa avere giurisdizione rispetto a quelli Stati che l'abbiano accettata (art. V). Si tratta, come si vede, di una formula simile a quella usata nella Convenzione contro il genocidio.

5.2.5. *La Convenzione contro la discriminazione nei confronti delle donne*

Il principio di non discriminazione fra uomini e donne è contenuto nella Carta delle NU (artt. 8 e 55), nella Dichiarazione Universale (artt. 2 e 16), nel Patto sui diritti civili e politici (artt. 2, 3, 23, 26) ed in molti altri trattati sui diritti umani, alcuni dei quali specificamente dedicati a certi diritti delle donne [39]. Tuttavia, la discriminazione contro le donne

[37] Committee on the Elimination of Racial Discrimination (CteeERD).

[38] International Convention on the Suppression and Punishment of the Crime of *Apartheid* (CSPCA), 30 November 1973.

[39] Vedi, ad es., Convention on the Political Rights of Women, 20 December 1952; Convention on the Nationality of Married Women, 20 February 1957; Convention on Consent to Marriage, Minimum Age for Marriage and Registration of Marriages, 7 November 1962.

è un fenomeno comune ed universale e le Nazioni Unite hanno ritenuto che fosse necessario rafforzare la lotta contro di essa e promuovere una convenzione *ad hoc*, tesa a garantire l'uguaglianza fra uomini e donne nella sfera politica, civile, economica e sociale. Questa azione ha prodotto la Convenzione del 1979 sull'eliminazione di ogni forma di discriminazione nei confronti delle donne[40].

La Convenzione cerca di eliminare la discriminazione contro le donne, che viene definita come ogni distinzione, esclusione o restrizione fatta sulla base del sesso, che abbia l'effetto o lo scopo di pregiudicare o annullare il godimento da parte delle donne dei diritti umani nel campo politico, economico, sociale, culturale o civile (art. 1). Gli Stati parti si impegnano a perseguire senza indugio una politica di eliminazione della discriminazione contro le donne e, a tal fine, si impegnano ad adottare una serie di leggi e di altre misure, comprese sanzioni, per assicurare l'attuazione pratica del principio di uguaglianza di genere (art. 2). Inoltre, la Convenzione contiene una serie di disposizioni molto dettagliate, che prevedono obblighi positivi degli Stati parti volti ad eliminare la discriminazione contro le donne nella vita politica e pubblica (artt. 7-9), nella vita economica, sociale e culturale (artt. 10-14), e nel loro regime giuridico, familiare e matrimoniale (artt. 15-16).

Le procedure di controllo sono affidate al Comitato sulla Eliminazione della Discriminazione contro le Donne[41], composto di 23 persone indipendenti. In origine, il Comitato aveva solo il compito dell'esame dei rapporti periodici presentati dagli Stati parti. Tuttavia, con l'adozione del Protocollo facoltativo alla Convenzione[42], entrato in vigore nel 2000, si è prevista una procedura di ricorsi individuali ed anche una procedura di inchiesta nei confronti degli Stati in seguito ad informazioni ricevute su violazioni gravi e sistematiche della Convenzione. Nel quadro della procedura di ricorsi individuali, il Comitato può indicare anche misure urgenti di carattere cautelare.

5.2.6. *La Convenzione contro la tortura*

La tortura costituisce una delle più gravi violazioni dei diritti umani ed è stata ufficialmente messa al bando dagli Stati fin dal secolo XIX. Nel mondo contemporaneo, nessuno Stato ammetterà di praticare o tollerare la tortura nel proprio territorio o negli spazi sotto la propria "giurisdizione". Tuttavia, è noto, e risulta da molti rapporti di organizzazioni non governative, che pratiche di tortura persistono in molti Stati. Per questo motivo, negli anni 1970, le Nazioni Unite ritennero che la lotta contro la tortura richiedesse misure speciali, fra le quali l'adozione di una convenzione *ad hoc*. Nel 1984, l'Assemblea Generale ha adottato la Convenzione contro la tortura ed altri trattamenti o punizioni crudeli, inumani o degradanti[43].

L'art. 1 della Convenzione prevede una definizione restrittiva, e piuttosto controversa[44],

---

[40] Convention on the Elimination of All Forms of Discrimination against Women (CEDAW), 18 December 1979.

[41] Committee on the Elimination of Discrimination against Women (CteeEDAW).

[42] Optional Protocol to the Convention on the Elimination of All Forms of Discrimination against Women (CEDAW-OP), 6 October 1999.

[43] Convention against Torture and Other Cruel, Inhuman or Degrading Treatment or Punishment (CAT), 10 December 1984.

[44] Cfr. Nowak (2003), p. 88.

di "tortura", poiché essa: *a*) è limitata agli atti inflitti da (o su istigazione, consenso o acquiescenza di) un pubblico ufficiale o altra persona che agisca in una veste ufficiale; *b*) deve essere un atto intenzionale; *c*) non può essere commessa senza scopo (ad esempio, per sadismo), ma deve avere lo scopo di ottenere informazioni o confessioni o altri scopi espressamente previsti; *d*) non comprende le sofferenze o il dolore risultanti "unicamente da sanzioni legittime". La Convenzione contiene poi una serie di obblighi per gli Stati parti, che comprendono obblighi di prevenzione (art. 2), di repressione (artt. 5-7 e 12), e di riparazione per le vittime (artt. 13-14). Ma l'obiettivo più importante della Convenzione è quello della repressione penale della tortura: tutti gli Stati contraenti si obbligano a riconoscere gli atti di tortura nel proprio ordinamento interno come reati ed a prevedere per essi pene appropriate (art. 4). Inoltre, la Convenzione prevede il principio della c.d. "giurisdizione universale" sugli atti di tortura (artt. 5(2) e 7(1)). Infine, si deve notare che molti degli obblighi degli Stati contraenti, e specie gli obblighi di prevenzione, si applicano anche a quegli atti di trattamenti o punizioni crudeli, inumani o degradanti che non costituiscono tortura (art. 16).

Le procedure internazionali di controllo sull'attuazione degli obblighi previsti dalla Convenzione sono affidate, innanzitutto, al Comitato contro la tortura[45], composto da 10 esperti indipendenti. Essi hanno la competenza ad esaminare i rapporti periodici degli Stati parti ed a decidere sui ricorsi interstatali ed i ricorsi individuali. Il Comitato può anche procedere ad un'inchiesta confidenziale nei confronti di uno Stato quando abbia ricevuto informazioni su presunte pratiche di tortura. Esiste anche un Sottocomitato sulla prevenzione della tortura, che opera secondo gli obiettivi e i principi enunciati nella Carta delle Nazioni Unite, nonché secondo le norme delle Nazioni Unite relative al trattamento delle persone private della loro libertà. Tale organo è composto da 25 membri ed esercita tre diverse funzioni[46]. In primo luogo, i membri effettuano visite presso i luoghi ove si trovano, o potrebbero trovarsi, persone private della loro libertà ed inviano raccomandazioni agli Stati Parti relativamente alla tutela di tali individui. In secondo luogo, al Sottocomitato spetta l'attuazione di alcuni meccanismi di prevenzione, prevalentemente attraverso attività di consulenza e assistenza verso gli Stati, anche al fine di costituire eventuali "meccanismi di prevenzione nazionali"[47]. Infine, il Sottocomitato coopera per la prevenzione della tortura in generale, con gli organi e con i meccanismi pertinenti delle Nazioni Unite, nonché con istituzioni o organizzazioni internazionali, regionali e nazionali, il cui obiettivo sia potenziare la protezione delle persone dalla tortura e da altri trattamenti o punizioni crudeli, inumani o degradanti.

5.2.7. *La Convenzione sui diritti del fanciullo*

Le Nazioni Unite hanno sempre riconosciuto la necessità di predisporre una protezione speciale per l'infanzia e per i fanciulli, poiché questi ultimi sono soggetti deboli, esposti frequentemente a sfruttamento, violenza, disattenzione ed a varie forme di discriminazione e di esclusione. I diritti del fanciullo sono enunciati già nella Dichiarazione universale

---

[45] Committee against Torture (CteeAT).

[46] Cfr. Optional Protocol to the Convention against Torture (CAT-OP), 18 December 2002, art. 11.

[47] Si tratta di organismi con poteri di visita per la prevenzione della tortura e delle altre pene o trattamenti crudeli, inumani o degradanti. Vedi CAT-OP, art. 3.

(artt. 25(2) e 26), in una Dichiarazione di principi dell'AG del 1959 [48] e nei due Patti internazionali [49]; ma occorreva una protezione più generalizzata. Finalmente, dopo anni di negoziati, l'Assemblea Generale delle NU adottò, nel 1989, la Convenzione sui diritti del fanciullo [50]. Essa è stata ratificata da quasi tutti gli Stati del mondo.

La Convenzione definisce il fanciullo come "ogni essere umano di età inferiore ai 18 anni, a meno che la maggiore età sia ottenuta prima secondo il diritto applicabile al fanciullo" (art. 1). Con l'adesione alla Convenzione, gli Stati contraenti assumono l'obbligo di attribuire ai fanciulli posti sotto la propria "giurisdizione" i diritti previsti dalla Convenzione (art. 2); e cioè una serie molto ampia di diritti civili, politici, economici, sociali e culturali, senza alcuna discriminazione. Il principio-guida della Convenzione è quello del "*best interests of the child*"; cioè la regola per cui, in tutte le azioni che riguardano i fanciulli, i migliori interessi del fanciullo dovranno essere la primaria considerazione. Quindi la Convenzione cerca di soddisfare tutti i diversi bisogni dei fanciulli [51], stabilendo non solo speciali garanzie per la loro protezione (ad esempio da abusi, sfruttamento economico e sessuale, violenza in famiglia ed a scuola); ma anche tutelando i fanciulli nello sviluppo della propria identità e nella loro partecipazione alla vita sociale. Infine, impone agli Stati parti numerosi obblighi positivi, per assicurare ai fanciulli adeguati standard di vita e accesso all'istruzione, alla sicurezza sociale, ecc.

Si noti che, per rafforzare la protezione dei fanciulli, sono stati adottati nel 2000 due protocolli opzionali: il Protocollo facoltativo concernente la vendita di fanciulli, la prostituzione e la pornografia minorile [52] ed il Protocollo facoltativo concernente il coinvolgimento dei fanciulli nei conflitti armati [53].

Le procedure di monitoraggio della Convenzione del 1989 sono affidate al Comitato sui diritti del fanciullo [54], che consiste di 18 esperti indipendenti che hanno la funzione di esaminare i rapporti periodici degli Stati parti. Dal 2014, con l'entrata in vigore del terzo Protocollo facoltativo sulle procedure di comunicazione [55], il Comitato ha competenza a ricevere ricorsi individuali riguardanti la violazione della Convenzione e dei due Protocolli facoltativi del 2000, nonché a svolgere inchieste nel caso di accuse per violazioni gravi o sistematiche dei diritti sanciti da questi strumenti.

5.2.8. *La Convenzione sui diritti dei lavoratori migranti*

Nel 1990, l'Assemblea Generale delle NU ha adottato la Convenzione internazionale sulla protezione dei diritti di tutti i lavoratori migranti e dei membri delle loro fami-

---

[48] Dichiarazione dei diritti del fanciullo, ris. 1386 del 20 novembre 1959.

[49] CCPR, art. 24 e CESCR, artt. 10(3) e 13.

[50] Convention on the Rights of the Child (CRC), 20 November 1989.

[51] Vedi Nowak (2003), p. 93.

[52] Optional Protocol to the Convention on the Rights of the Child on the sale of children, child prostitution and child pornography, 25 May 2000.

[53] Optional Protocol to the Convention on the Rights of the Child on the involvement of children in armed conflicts, 25 May 2000.

[54] Committee on the Rights of the Child (CteeRC).

[55] Optional Protocol to the Convention on the Rights of the Child on a communications procedure, 19 December 2011.

glie[56]. Il termine "lavoratore migrante" si riferisce ad una persona che è impegnata, sta per essere impegnata o è stata impegnata, in un'attività remunerata in uno Stato del quale essa non ha la nazionalità (art. 2(1)). Il principio-guida della Convenzione è quello di non discriminazione: gli Stati contraenti si impegnano ad assicurare a tutti i lavoratori migranti ed ai membri delle loro famiglie tutti i diritti contenuti nella Convenzione senza alcuna discriminazione (art. 7). Quindi la Convenzione stabilisce una serie assai dettagliata di diritti civili, politici[57], economici, sociali e culturali per tali persone. Fra tali diritti sono molto importanti, a nostro avviso, il diritto di accesso alla giustizia in condizioni di uguaglianza rispetto ai cittadini dello Stato in questione (art. 18) e le numerose garanzie procedurali in caso di espulsione (artt. 22 e 23).

Per le procedure internazionali di controllo, la Convenzione ha stabilito un apposito Comitato[58], composto di esperti indipendenti, che ha la competenza (obbligatoria) ad esaminare i rapporti periodici e quella (facoltativa) ad esaminare ricorsi interstatali e individuali. Tuttavia, si deve notare che finora la Convenzione non ha avuto un alto numero di ratifiche, in confronto con gli altri trattati sui diritti umani promossi dalle Nazioni Unite.

5.2.9. *La Convenzione sui diritti delle persone disabili*

Un'altra categoria di soggetti deboli, che necessita di una protezione speciale, è costituita dalle persone disabili. Nel 2006 è stata adottata la Convenzione relativa ai diritti delle persone con disabilità[59]. Lo scopo è quello di assicurare il pieno godimento di tutti i diritti umani da parte delle persone disabili, che vengono definite come:

> "those who have long-term physical, mental, intellectual or sensory impairments which in interaction with various barriers may hinder their full and effective participation in society on an equal basis with others"[60].

La Convenzione, con una disposizione interessante e originale (art. 3), stabilisce che essa si fonda su alcuni principi generali, quali il rispetto per la dignità e autonomia delle persone, la non discriminazione, la piena ed effettiva partecipazione ed inclusione nella società, il rispetto per le differenze, l'uguaglianza di opportunità, l'accessibilità, l'uguaglianza fra uomini e donne, il rispetto per le capacità evolutive dei fanciulli disabili. Quindi la Convenzione contiene il solito elenco dettagliato di diritti civili, politici, economici, sociali e culturali che gli Stati devono rispettare nei confronti dei soggetti destinatari.

Per l'applicazione ed il controllo internazionale della Convenzione, viene istituito il Comitato sui diritti delle persone con disabilità[61], che ha competenza ad esaminare i rapporti periodici degli Stati parti. Il Protocollo facoltativo alla Convenzione[62], adottato nel

---

[56] International Convention on the Protection of the Rights of All Migrant Workers and Members of Their Families (CMW), 18 December 1990.

[57] Per i lavoratori migranti regolari: vedi artt. 41 e 42 CMW.

[58] Committee on the Protection of the Rights of All Migrant Workers and Members of Their Families (CteeMW).

[59] Convention on the Rights of Persons with Disabilities (CRPD), 13 December 2006.

[60] Art. 1 CRPD.

[61] Committee on the Rights of Persons with Disabilities (CteeRPD). Cfr. art. 34 CRPD.

[62] Optional Protocol to the Convention on the Rights of Persons with Disabilities, 13 December 2006.

2006, prevede la competenza del Comitato ad esaminare ricorsi da parte di individui o gruppi di individui contro uno Stato parte ritenuto responsabile di una violazione della Convenzione.

5.2.10. *La Convenzione contro le sparizioni forzate*

Infine, si deve ricordare la Convenzione internazionale per la protezione di tutte le persone da sparizioni forzate del 2006[63], che costituisce il più recente trattato settoriale sui diritti umani adottato dalle Nazioni Unite e dotato di un organo internazionale di controllo indipendente.

La Convenzione definisce, in maniera piuttosto laboriosa, il concetto di sparizione forzata (art. 2). In sintesi, si tratta di varie forme di privazione della libertà, che vengono tenute nascoste e che sono compiute da agenti statali o da persone che agiscono con l'autorizzazione, aiuto o acquiescenza dello Stato. Il diritto di non subire sparizione forzata è assoluto e inderogabile. Infatti, secondo l'art. 1, nessuno deve essere soggetto a sparizione forzata e nessuna circostanza eccezionale, sia essa uno stato di guerra o il pericolo di guerra o altra emergenza pubblica, può giustificare una sparizione forzata. Inoltre, la Convenzione stabilisce che una pratica estesa e sistematica di sparizioni forzate costituisce un crimine contro l'umanità. Quindi la Convenzione prevede una serie di obblighi degli Stati parti, volti specie alla repressione di tali atti criminosi: gli Stati devono investigare (art. 3); devono avere norme penali adeguate (artt. 4 e 6); devono prevedere pene adeguate (art. 7); devono esercitare la propria giurisdizione sui responsabili (artt. 9-10); devono processare o estradare i medesimi (artt. 11 e 13).

Ai fini del controllo internazionale sulla Convenzione, viene istituito il Comitato sulle sparizioni forzate[64], che ha la competenza (obbligatoria) ad esaminare i rapporti degli Stati e la competenza (facoltativa) ad esaminare ricorsi individuali e interstatali.

6. *Organi e procedure di controllo fondati sulla Carta delle Nazioni Unite (*Charter-Bodies *o* Charter-Procedures*)*

In aggiunta agli organi internazionali di controllo che sono stati stabiliti da trattati sui diritti umani promossi dalle NU (*Treaty-Bodies*), fin qui esaminati, esistono anche, nell'ambito delle NU, alcuni organi ed alcune procedure che trovano il loro fondamento nella Carta delle NU, e che pertanto sono denominati *Charter-Bodies* o *Charter-Procedures*. Pertanto, il meccanismo di tutela di diritti umani dei *Charter-Bodies* si affianca a quello dei *Treaty-Bodies*. Nell'ambito dei *Charter-Bodies*, si può fare una distinzione fra quelli specializzati nei diritti umani[65] e quelli (come gli organi principali delle NU) che hanno competenze più ampie, fra le quali anche quella della tutela dei diritti umani[66].

---

[63] International Convention for the Protection of All Persons from Enforced Disappearance (CPPED), 20 December 2006.

[64] Committee on Enforced Disappearances (CteeED). Cfr. art. 26 CPPED.

[65] Vedi *infra*, parr. 6.1, 6.2 e 6.3.

[66] Vedi *infra*, par. 6.4.

6.1. *Consiglio dei diritti umani*

Attualmente il più importante fra i *Charter-Bodies* è il Consiglio dei diritti umani [67], che è stato istituito nel 2006 con la risoluzione 251/60 dell'AG, come organo sussidiario di quest'ultima, e che ha sostituito la precedente Commissione per i diritti umani [68]. Essa era un organo di Stati, che aveva importanti funzioni nel campo della predisposizione di norme ed il compito di controllare il rispetto dei diritti umani da parte degli Stati membri, tramite due procedure di controllo su casi di violazioni gravi e ripetute dei diritti umani [69] ed un sistema di procedure speciali per territorio (c.d. *country procedures*) e per aree tematiche (c.d. *thematic procedures*).

Il Consiglio dei diritti umani è stato creato per rafforzare il sistema di controllo delle NU in materia di diritti umani e per sostituire la Commissione, che era stata accusata di essere poco efficiente e "politicizzata". Esso è un organo composto da 47 Stati, eletti dall'AG, con una ripartizione fra i cinque gruppi regionali del sistema ONU. Il mandato degli Stati è triennale e non immediatamente rinnovabile. In realtà il Consiglio ha ereditato le funzioni principali della vecchia Commissione, ma con qualche significativa novità. In primo luogo, ha uno status più elevato, poiché è un organo sussidiario dell'AG e non dell'ECOSOC. In secondo luogo, la procedura elettiva dei suoi membri e la sua composizione hanno subìto alcuni cambiamenti. In terzo luogo, l'AG ha il potere di sospendere uno Stato membro del Consiglio che abbia commesso gravi e sistematiche violazioni dei diritti umani. Infine, il Consiglio si riunisce molto più frequentemente rispetto alla precedente Commissione e può convocarsi anche in sessioni speciali per trattare problemi urgenti in tema di diritti umani. Il Consiglio, per eseguire il proprio mandato, si avvale di alcune procedure e di alcuni organi sussidiari. Esso ha mantenuto certe procedure che venivano esercitate dalla Commissione per i diritti umani, anche se rivedute ed aggiornate; ed ha inoltre istituito una nuova procedura di controllo, la c.d. *Universal Periodic Review*.

6.1.1. Universal Periodic Review

In effetti, la novità più significativa del Consiglio riguarda l'istituzione della *Universal Periodic Review*, che ha lo scopo di verificare periodicamente che tutti gli Stati membri delle NU rispettino i diritti umani. In sintesi, questo meccanismo prevede che ogni Stato debba presentare un rapporto sulla situazione dei diritti umani nel proprio ordinamento interno. Su tale rapporto possono pervenire i commenti di tutti gli Stati membri, che formano un elenco di osservazioni e di raccomandazioni alle quali lo Stato sotto controllo deve rispondere. Il Consiglio poi esamina e discute i rapporti relativi agli Stati sotto controllo e presenta osservazioni sulla situazione dei diritti umani in tali Stati. Due cicli di rapporti si sono già conclusi e il terzo è attualmente in corso (2017-2021). Questo nuovo meccanismo ha introdotto delle novità importanti, ma ha il difetto strutturale, essendo sostanzialmente gestito dagli Stati e non da organi indipendenti, di non prevedere sanzioni efficaci per le violazioni dei diritti umani. In sostanza, esso costituisce un meccanismo di pressione e sollecitazione politico-diplomatica nei confronti degli Stati, più che un meccanismo giuridico.

---

[67] Human Rights Council (HRC).

[68] United Nations Commission on Human Rights (CmHR).

[69] Cfr. le risoluzioni 1235(XLII) e 1503(XLVIII) dell'ECOSOC.

6.1.2. *Procedure speciali (*Special Procedures*)*

Le due procedure della vecchia Commissione per i diritti umani, denominate "*country procedures*" e "*thematic procedures*", sono state sostanzialmente mantenute dal Consiglio dei diritti umani e sono adesso denominate "*special procedures*". Le procedure speciali sono guidate da esperti indipendenti in materia di diritti umani, aventi il mandato di fornire consulenza su tali diritti da una prospettiva tematica o specifica per Paese. Esse costituiscono un elemento centrale delle *Charter-Procedures* e coprono tutti i diritti umani: civili, culturali, economici, politici e sociali. Sono formate da un individuo (denominato "relatore speciale" o "esperto indipendente") o da un gruppo di lavoro composto da cinque membri, uno per ciascuno dei cinque raggruppamenti regionali delle Nazioni Unite [70]. I relatori speciali, gli esperti indipendenti e i membri dei gruppi di lavoro sono nominati dal Consiglio dei diritti umani e prestano servizio a titolo personale.

Con il supporto dell'Alto Commissariato delle Nazioni Unite per i diritti umani, le procedure speciali hanno le seguenti funzioni: *a*) effettuare visite negli Stati; *b*) agire su singoli casi di presunte violazioni e su problemi di natura più ampia, inviando comunicazioni agli Stati; *c*) condurre studi tematici e convocare consultazioni di esperti, contribuendo allo sviluppo di norme internazionali sui diritti umani; *d*) impegnarsi nella difesa e sensibilizzazione dell'opinione pubblica e fornire consulenza per la cooperazione tecnica [71].

6.1.3. *Procedura di ricorsi (*Complaint Procedure*)*

Anche la c.d. *complaint procedure*, che veniva già esercitata dalla Commissione per i diritti umani [72], è stata mantenuta in vigore da parte del Consiglio dei diritti umani. Essa può essere avviata sulla base di comunicazioni presentate da individui, gruppi di individui o anche ONG; ma non si applica a violazioni singole di diritti umani, bensì solo a situazioni che sembrano rivelare "a consistent pattern of gross and reliably attested violations of human rights". In realtà, questa procedura, che ha avuto qualche successo nel passato, ha perso oggi molto del suo significato [73].

6.1.4. *Comitato consultivo (*Advisory Committee*)*

Infine si può ricordare che il Consiglio dei diritti umani ha alcuni organi sussidiari, fra i quali si distingue, per importanza, il Comitato Consultivo (*Advisory Committee*), composto di 18 esperti indipendenti. Questo organo mette a disposizione del Consiglio dei diritti umani le proprie competenze, prevalentemente sotto forma di studi e ricerche in tema di promozione e protezione dei diritti umani. Il Comitato può inoltre avanzare, nell'ambito del piano di lavoro definito dal Consiglio, ulteriori proposte di ricerca.

6.2. *Alto Commissario per i diritti umani*

L'Alto Commissario per i diritti umani, creato nel 1993, ha la funzione di promuovere

---

[70] Africa, Asia, America Latina e Caraibi, Europa orientale e gruppo occidentale.

[71] Le procedure speciali riferiscono annualmente al Consiglio per i diritti umani e, talora, anche all'Assemblea Generale.

[72] Istituita con la risoluzione 1503 (XLVIII) dell'ECOSOC.

[73] Cfr. Novak (2003), p. 109.

il rispetto dei diritti umani e può fare raccomandazioni, prestare consulenza, assistenza tecnica e cooperazione. È a capo dell'ufficio dell'Alto Commissariato, che svolge attività di assistenza, coordinamento e supporto logistico ed operativo per il Consiglio dei diritti umani e per i *Treaty-Bodies*. Fra le varie funzioni assegnate all'Alto Commissario, la più importante è quella che gli permette

> "to play an active role in removing the current obstacles [...] to the full realization of all human rights and in preventing the continuation of human rights violations throughout the world" [74].

Questo linguaggio, assai ampio e generale, può consentire all'Alto Commissario di assumere un ruolo attivo nella prevenzione delle violazioni dei diritti umani [75]; e, in effetti, egli è intervenuto varie volte personalmente quando si trattava di attirare l'attenzione su casi di gravi violazioni dei diritti umani.

6.3. *Altri* Charter-Bodies *specializzati nei diritti umani*

Vi sono altri organi internazionali di controllo sul rispetto dei diritti umani che sono fondati sulla Carta delle NU. Diversamente da quelli finora esaminati, questi organi hanno carattere settoriale, nel senso che si occupano di specifici diritti umani o di certe categorie di persone. Fra di essi, conviene ricordare la Commissione sullo status delle donne [76], la Commissione sulla prevenzione dei crimini e sulla giustizia criminale [77], l'Alto Commissario delle NU per i rifugiati [78], la ex Commissione sugli insediamenti umani, oggi assorbita dal Consiglio governativo di UN-Habitat [79], il Forum permanente sulle questioni indigene [80], il Consulente speciale sulla prevenzione del genocidio [81], il Consulente speciale sulla responsabilità di proteggere [82].

---

[74] GA Res. 48/141, par. 4(f).

[75] Cfr. Buergenthal *et al.* (2004), p. 121.

[76] Commission on the Status of Women. È un organismo dedicato alla promozione dell'uguaglianza di genere ed alla promozione delle donne.

[77] Commission on Crime Prevention and Criminal Justice. È una delle commissioni operative dell'ECOSOC e rappresenta il principale organo di elaborazione delle politiche in seno all'ONU in materia di prevenzione del crimine e giustizia penale.

[78] United Nations High Commissioner for Refugees (UNHCR). È l'agenzia delle Nazioni Unite specializzata nella gestione dei rifugiati, cui fornisce protezione internazionale ed assistenza materiale, perseguendo anche soluzioni durevoli per la loro condizione.

[79] Commission on Human Settlements. Era una delle commissioni operative dell'ECOSOC, dal 2002 incorporata nel Consiglio governativo del Programma UN-Habitat.

[80] Permanent Forum on Indigenous Issues. È un organo consultivo del Consiglio Economico e Sociale, che ha il compito di trattare questioni relative agli indigeni, incluse quelle relative ai diritti umani.

[81] Special Adviser on the Prevention of Genocide. Ha il compito di fornire consulenza al Segretario Generale sulle materie relative al suo mandato, attraverso attività di allerta preventiva e di mediazione, anche in collaborazione con organizzazioni regionali e sub-regionali, finalizzate ad aumentare la capacità dell'ONU di analizzare e gestire le informazioni riguardanti genocidio e crimini contro l'umanità.

[82] Special Adviser on the Responsibility to Protect. Ha il compito di svolgere attività di allerta preventiva con riferimento a situazioni di genocidio, crimini di guerra, pulizia etnica e crimini contro l'umanità; lavora al fine di sviluppare gli aspetti concettuali, operativi e politici relativi al concetto di "responsabilità di proteggere"

6.4. *Organi principali delle Nazioni Unite e loro compiti relativi ai diritti umani*

Come si è già detto, anche gli organi principali delle NU hanno, fra le loro ampie funzioni, quella di affrontare questioni relative ai diritti umani. Tuttavia, poiché tali organi non sono specializzati nei diritti umani, saranno qui esaminati in maniera assai sintetica.

6.4.1. *Assemblea Generale*

L'Assemblea Generale (AG), ai sensi dell'art. 13 della Carta, può, fra l'altro, iniziare studi e fare raccomandazioni allo scopo di:

"[...] assisting in the realization of human rights and fundamental freedoms for all without distinction as to race, sex, language or religion"[83].

In pratica, l'AG può tenere discussioni pubbliche su questioni generali che concernono certi diritti umani, ma anche su situazioni critiche di rispetto dei diritti umani in uno Stato specifico. Essa può adottare risoluzioni o dichiarazioni di principi, e può anche formulare appelli per sollecitare lo Stato interessato a cessare le violazioni dei diritti umani ad esso contestate. Inoltre, l'AG può negoziare direttamente ed approvare trattati in materia di diritti umani, che dovranno poi essere ratificati dagli Stati. Nell'ambito dell'AG, è la sua Terza Commissione quella che di solito si occupa di questioni relative ai diritti umani e che, ogni anno, tiene una discussione su tali questioni, basandosi sui rapporti ricevuti dall'Alto Commissario e da altri organi specializzati sui diritti umani.

6.4.2. *Consiglio Economico e Sociale*

Il Consiglio Economico e Sociale (ECOSOC) ha competenze specifiche in materia di diritti umani *ex* artt. 62(2)[84] e 68 della Carta ed ha in passato predisposto vari strumenti normativi sui diritti umani. Tuttavia, attualmente, si occupa più di coordinare le iniziative di altri organismi, con particolare riguardo ai diritti economici e sociali, ed il suo ruolo in materia di diritti umani è divenuto poco significativo.

6.4.3. *Segretario Generale*

Il Segretario Generale non ha, sulla base della Carta delle NU, una competenza in materia di diritti umani. Tuttavia, egli può esercitare le sue funzioni autonome di conciliazione, buoni uffici e mediazione in casi di controversie fra Stati ed anche di crisi interne ad uno Stato, in materia di diritti umani. Inoltre, ha una competenza indiretta, poiché, nell'organizzare le operazioni di *peace-keeping* o *peace-enforcing* o *peace-building*, deve accertarsi che tali operazioni avvengano nel rispetto dei diritti umani. Infine, il Segretario Generale ha nominato alcuni suoi rappresentanti speciali[85] ed ha intrapreso una iniziativa, per

---

e promuoverne l'attuazione, in collaborazione con gli Stati membri, la società civile e il sistema delle Nazioni Unite; inoltre, la sua azione è finalizzata ad aumentare la capacità dell'ONU di prevenire il compimento di tali crimini e sapervi rispondere in maniera adeguata.

[83] Art. 13(1)(b).

[84] Art. 62(2): "It may make recommendations for the purpose of promoting respect for, and observance of, human rights and fundamental freedoms for all".

[85] Lo Special Representative for Children and Armed Conflict, lo Special Representative on Sexual Violence in Conflict, lo Special Representative on Violence Against Children.

rispondere alle gravi e diffuse violazioni dei diritti umani, denominata "*Human Rights Up Front Initiative*".

6.4.4. *Consiglio di Sicurezza*

Anche il Consiglio di Sicurezza (CdS) non ha, secondo la Carta delle NU, una competenza esplicita per la protezione dei diritti umani. Tuttavia, con il passare degli anni, le funzioni di mantenimento della pace (che sono quelle tipiche del CdS) e quelle di tutela dei diritti umani si sono venute avvicinando, tanto che le gravi e sistematiche violazioni dei diritti umani possono essere talora considerate come una "minaccia alla pace", ai sensi dell'art. 39 della Carta [86], e quindi rientrare nelle competenze del Consiglio di Sicurezza. E, in realtà, il Consiglio di Sicurezza ha avuto concretamente modo di intervenire in situazioni di violazioni gravi di diritti umani, che costituivano una minaccia per la pace, sia con misure non implicanti l'uso della forza *ex* art. 41 della Carta [87], sia autorizzando Stati o gruppi di Stati ad interventi armati, sia con operazioni di *peace-keeping*, di *peace-enforcing* e di *peace-building*. Infine, il Consiglio ha utilizzato il Capitolo VII della Carta come fondamento giuridico per creare il Tribunale internazionale penale per la ex Jugoslavia [88] ed il Tribunale internazionale penale per il Ruanda [89].

6.4.5. *Corte internazionale di giustizia*

La Corte internazionale di giustizia non ha una giurisprudenza molto ampia in materia di diritti umani, perché gli individui non hanno la facoltà di adire la Corte e, d'altra parte, perché non sono frequenti le controversie fra Stati che riguardano le violazioni dei diritti umani [90]. Ciò nonostante, la Corte ha emesso alcune importanti sentenze ed alcuni pareri consultivi in materia di diritti umani.

Fra le sentenze meno recenti, si possono ricordare: quella del 1970 nel caso *Barcelona Traction* [91], dove la Corte enunciò la celebre distinzione fra obblighi reciproci ed obblighi *erga omnes*, indicando fra i secondi quelli relativi ad alcuni diritti umani fondamentali; la sentenza del 1980 nel caso del *Personale diplomatico degli USA a Teheran* [92], dove la Corte dichiarò che la detenzione illegittima di persone è incompatibile con i principi fondamentali della Dichiarazione Universale; la sentenza del 1986 nel caso delle *Attività militari in Nicaragua* [93], dove la Corte si chiese se certe azioni degli USA fossero conformi a principi fondamentali di diritto umanitario. Più recentemente, la Corte ha emesso decisioni su questioni di diritti umani nei casi *LaGrand* (2001) [94] e

---

[86] Cfr. Novak (2003), pp. 129-130.

[87] Fra gli esempi di misure adottate *ex* art. 41 della Carta, si possono ricordare le sanzioni economiche prese contro Iraq, Somalia, Haiti, *ex* Jugoslavia, Timor Est, Sierra Leone, Afghanistan.

[88] International Criminal Tribunal for the Former Yugoslavia (ICTY). Vedi *infra*, Cap. V, par. 9.

[89] International Criminal Tribunal for Rwanda (ICTR). Vedi *infra*, Cap. V, par. 9.

[90] Vedi *supra*, Cap. II, par. 3. Cfr. anche Kälin, Künzli (2009), pp. 264-265.

[91] ICJ, *Barcelona Traction*, par. 33.

[92] ICJ, *United States Diplomatic and Consular Staff*, par. 91.

[93] ICJ, *Military and Paramilitary Activities*, Judgment of 27 June 1986, par. 220.

[94] ICJ, *LaGrand*, par. 126.

Avena (2004)[95] (in maniera indiretta); nel caso sulla *Legalità dell'uso della forza* del 2004[96]; nei casi sulle *Attività armate nel territorio del Congo*[97]; nei casi sulla *Applicazione della Convenzione sul genocidio*[98]; infine nei casi sulla *Applicazione della Convenzione contro la discriminazione razziale*[99].

Fra i pareri consultivi della Corte, si possono citare: quello del 1975 sul *Sahara Occidentale*[100]; quello del 1951 sulle *Riserve alla Convenzione sul genocidio*[101]; quello del 1996 sulla *Legalità delle armi nucleari*[102]; infine il parere del 2004 sulla *Costruzione di un muro nei territori palestinesi occupati*[103].

7. *Istituti Specializzati e conferenze sui diritti umani*

In aggiunta ai meccanismi di garanzia sopra indicati, che funzionano nel quadro delle NU, vi sono altre organizzazioni internazionali, legate al sistema delle NU, i c.d. Istituti Specializzati, che hanno competenze in materia di diritti umani ed hanno sviluppato procedure di controllo sul rispetto dei medesimi. Qui ricorderemo soltanto i principali, fra tali Istituti, che sono l'Organizzazione internazionale del lavoro (ILO) e l'Organizzazione delle Nazioni Unite per l'educazione, la scienza e la cultura (UNESCO). Infine, meritano un cenno le conferenze sui diritti umani che vengono organizzate dalle NU.

7.1. *Organizzazione internazionale del lavoro*

L'Organizzazione internazionale del lavoro (ILO) si concentra sui diritti umani relativi al diritto al lavoro ed alle condizioni di lavoro, inclusi i diritti sindacali ed i diritti di sciopero e di sicurezza sociale. Cerca di tutelare tali diritti attraverso la predisposizione di progetti di convenzioni e l'adozione di raccomandazioni. Gli Stati membri dell'ILO, che hanno l'obbligo di sottoporre i progetti di convenzioni agli organi competenti per la ratifica (ma non l'obbligo di ratificarli), devono presentare rapporti sulla sorte dei medesimi e sulle convenzioni che hanno ratificato.

L'ILO ha istituito varie procedure di controllo e comitati di esperti, per monitorare il rispetto dei principi e degli standard in materia di lavoro contenuti nelle numerose convenzioni e raccomandazioni adottate dall'Organizzazione. In primo luogo, vi è un Comitato di esperti, composto da 20 persone indipendenti, che esamina i rapporti degli Stati e, qualora

---

[95] ICJ, *Avena*, par. 124.

[96] ICJ, *Legality of Use of Force*, par. 41 ss.

[97] ICJ, *Armed Activities on the Territory of the Congo*, Judgment of 19 December 2005, par. 181 ss.; *Ibidem*, Judgment of 3 February 2006.

[98] ICJ, *Application of the Convention on the Prevention and Punishment of the Crime of Genocide*, Judgment of 26 February 2007; *Ibidem*, Judgment of 3 February 2015; *Ibidem*, Order of 23 January 2020.

[99] ICJ, *Application of the International Convention on the Elimination of All Forms of Racial Discrimination*, Order of 15 October 2008; *Ibidem*, Judgment of 1 April 2011.

[100] ICJ, *Western Sahara.*

[101] ICJ, *Reservations to the Convention on the Prevention and Punishment of the Crime of Genocide.*

[102] ICJ, *Legality of the Threat or Use of Nuclear Weapons*, parr. 24, 29.

[103] ICJ, *Legal Consequences of the Construction of a Wall*, par. 89 ss.

riscontri problemi, può fare "osservazioni" allo Stato interessato. In secondo luogo, vi è un Comitato sulla applicazione delle convenzioni e delle raccomandazioni, composto da rappresentanti dei governi, dei datori di lavoro e dei lavoratori. L'ILO ha anche sviluppato delle procedure di ricorsi (*complaint procedures*). Fra queste, è importante una procedura che è riservata alla libertà di associazione: il Comitato dell'ILO sulla libertà di associazione riceve ricorsi direttamente da lavoratori o associazioni di lavoratori, li esamina e, se riscontra una violazione, può chiedere allo Stato interessato di continuare a fare rapporti sulla questione o rinviare il caso al Comitato di esperti o alla Commissione di conciliazione e di inchiesta sulla libertà di associazione.

7.2. *Organizzazione delle Nazioni Unite per l'educazione, la scienza e la cultura*

L'UNESCO ha il mandato di promuovere l'istruzione, la scienza e la cultura e, nel quadro di tale mandato, può esercitare un'azione di protezione dei diritti umani. In effetti, predispone progetti di convenzioni e adotta raccomandazioni sui diritti umani che sono collegati alle materie dei suoi mandati. Anche in questo caso, gli Stati membri devono sottoporre i progetti di convenzioni ai propri organi interni competenti per la ratifica. Fra le convenzioni che sono state promosse dall'UNESCO e attinenti ai diritti umani, le più note sono la Convenzione del 1960 contro la discriminazione nell'educazione [104], la Convenzione del 1954 per la protezione della proprietà culturale in caso di conflitto armato [105], e la Convenzione del 2005 sulla protezione e promozione della diversità delle espressioni culturali [106].

L'UNESCO ha istituito alcune procedure di controllo. La più interessante è una procedura di ricorsi (*complaint procedure*) aperta a individui e ONG, la quale però ha carattere confidenziale. La vittima o altra persona, che sia a conoscenza della violazione di un diritto umano relativo all'educazione, la scienza o la cultura, può presentare un reclamo all'UNESCO. Il reclamo viene esaminato dal Comitato sulle convenzioni e trasmesso al Governo interessato, che può replicare. Le parti possono essere sentite dal Comitato. Infine, quest'ultimo può proporre allo Stato di prendere specifiche misure. In alternativa, il Direttore Generale dell'UNESCO può condurre consultazioni allo scopo di raggiungere una soluzione amichevole. In realtà, questa procedura, anche se presenta alcuni caratteri quasi-giurisdizionali, privilegia una soluzione diplomatico-conciliativa della controversia.

7.3. *Conferenze sui diritti umani*

La prima conferenza mondiale sui diritti umani è stata organizzata dalle Nazioni Unite a Teheran nel 1968, per celebrare il ventesimo anniversario della Dichiarazione Universale. La seconda conferenza, di particolare rilievo, si tenne a Vienna nel 1993 e produsse, come documento finale, la celebre *Vienna Declaration and Programme of Action of the World Conference on Human Rights*, che presentava un piano comune per rafforzare i diritti umani in tutto il mondo. La Conferenza di Vienna, dopo un'ampia discussione, dichia-

[104] Convention against Discrimination in Education, 14 December 1960.

[105] Convention for the Protection of Cultural Property in the Event of Armed Conflict, 14 May 1954.

[106] Convention on the Protection and Promotion of the Diversity of Cultural Expressions, 20 October 2005.

rò anche il principio della universalità, indivisibilità e interdipendenza di tutti i diritti umani [107]. In seguito, le conferenze sui diritti umani organizzate dalle Nazioni Unite sono divenute più frequenti; ma si sono, volta per volta, concentrare su temi più specifici. Si possono citare, fra le altre, la *International Conference on Population Development* (Cairo, 1994), la *World Conference on Women* (Beijing, 1995), la *World Conference against Racism, Racial Discrimination, Xenophobia and Related Intolerance* (Durban, 2001), la *World Conference on Indigenous Peoples* (New York, 2010) e la *World Conference on Disaster Risk Reduction* (Sendai, 2015).

In realtà, i risultati finali di queste conferenze consistono di solito in dichiarazioni o altri documenti che non hanno carattere giuridicamente vincolante. Tuttavia, le conferenze hanno giocato un ruolo nel formare e sviluppare i programmi delle Nazioni Unite nel settore dei diritti umani.

Sezione II

IL SISTEMA EUROPEO DEI DIRITTI UMANI

8. *Consiglio d'Europa*

Le norme ed i meccanismi di garanzia sul rispetto dei diritti umani che esistono a livello regionale sono spesso più progrediti ed efficaci rispetto a quelli tendenzialmente universali sopra esaminati. Ciò dipende da una maggiore omogeneità di carattere politico, culturale e sociale degli Stati, che favorisce una loro concezione comune dei diritti umani e quindi anche la possibilità di meccanismi di controllo più efficaci. Conviene adesso esaminare in maniera sintetica tali sistemi regionali.

Come è noto, il sistema più avanzato di tutela regionale dei diritti umani è quello creato nel quadro del Consiglio d'Europa (CdE). I risultati maggiori conseguiti dal CdE sono stati la conclusione della Convenzione europea dei diritti dell'uomo del 1950, la Carta sociale europea del 1961 (riveduta nel 1996), la Convenzione europea contro la tortura del 1987, la Convenzione-quadro per la protezione delle minoranze nazionali del 1995 ed il Commissario europeo per i diritti umani istituito nel 1999.

8.1. *La Convenzione europea dei diritti dell'uomo*

La Convenzione europea dei diritti dell'uomo (CEDU) è notissima [108] e quindi possiamo limitarci ai suoi aspetti essenziali. La Convenzione è stata firmata a Roma nel 1950 ed è entrata in vigore nel 1953. Ad essa possono aderire gli Stati membri del Consiglio d'Europa. La Convenzione si compone di due parti: la prima, di carattere sostanziale, elenca i

---

[107] Ma, per una critica, vedi *infra*, Cap. V, parr. 1 e 2.

[108] Ed è oggetto di manuali specifici e di corsi universitari *ad hoc*.

diritti garantiti, la seconda parte, di natura procedurale, stabilisce gli organi ed i meccanismi di garanzia. Peraltro, si deve notare che, nel tempo, la Convenzione è stata integrata e modificata da 16 protocolli addizionali, che hanno aumentato i diritti garantiti (i c.d. Protocolli aggiuntivi) e modificato i meccanismi di garanzia (i c.d. Protocolli emendativi).

Le modifiche più importanti sono quelle che hanno trasformato il meccanismo di garanzia. In origine, esso era assai complesso e si fondava, fino al 1998, su tre organi: la Commissione e la Corte europea dei diritti umani ed il Comitato dei Ministri del Consiglio d'Europa. La Commissione poteva esaminare sia ricorsi interstatali, presentati da uno Stato parte contro un altro Stato parte, sia ricorsi individuali, presentati da individui privati contro uno Stato parte. Essa decideva sulla ammissibilità del ricorso e, in caso positivo, istruiva il medesimo ed esperiva un tentativo di composizione amichevole della controversia. Se il tentativo non riusciva, la Commissione redigeva un rapporto (esprimendosi sulle eventuali violazioni della Convenzione) e lo trasmetteva al Comitato dei Ministri del Consiglio d'Europa. Quindi, in presenza di certe condizioni, sia la Commissione che uno Stato membro potevano portare il caso dinanzi alla Corte europea, che decideva sull'esistenza o meno di violazioni della Convenzione.

Questo sistema è stato radicalmente riformato con il Protocollo n. 11, entrato in vigore nel 1998, che ha istituito una Corte unica e permanente, che ha in sostanza assunto le funzioni che prima erano svolte dalla Commissione e dalla (precedente) Corte. Dinanzi alla (nuova) Corte, ogni persona, fisica o giuridica, può presentare un ricorso direttamente e senza filtri. In effetti, è proprio la possibilità di ricorsi individuali dinanzi ad un organo giurisdizionale che costituisce il fulcro centrale su cui si fonda il sistema della Convenzione europea. Esso, in sostanza, riconosce all'individuo un vero e proprio diritto di azione a livello internazionale, per far valere i diritti riconosciuti dalla Convenzione [109]. Si noti che il diritto di ricorso individuale, che prima era previsto da una clausola opzionale, è ora automaticamente obbligatorio per tutti gli Stati membri. Altre modifiche importanti sono state introdotte con il Protocollo n. 14, entrato in vigore nel 2010, che ha snellito la procedura dinanzi alla Corte.

Si deve anche sottolineare il fatto che la Convenzione contiene obblighi *erga omnes partes*. Una conseguenza è che ogni Stato parte può presentare un ricorso contro un altro Stato parte, che abbia commesso un'eventuale violazione della Convenzione, anche se il primo Stato non abbia subìto una lesione diretta dalla violazione [110], ad esempio anche qualora l'individuo vittima della violazione non sia un proprio cittadino. Ciò significa che i ricorsi interstatali riposano sul "concetto di garanzia collettiva, da parte degli Stati contraenti, dei diritti e libertà definiti dalla Convenzione" [111].

8.1.1. *I diritti garantiti*

Per quanto riguarda la parte sostanziale della Convenzione europea, l'art. 1 stabilisce l'obbligo generale degli Stati contraenti di riconoscere i diritti ivi garantiti "ad ogni persona soggetta alla loro giurisdizione". Abbiamo già visto come questa disposizione, che definisce l'ambito di applicazione spaziale della Convenzione, abbia dato luogo ad una giuri-

---

[109] Cfr. Zagrebelsky *et al.* (2019), p. 30.

[110] Cfr. Ronzitti (2016), p. 324.

[111] Vedi, ad es., ECmHR, *Austria v. Italy*.

sprudenza interessante ed a interpretazioni non sempre univoche da parte degli organi di Strasburgo [112].

Quanto all'elenco dei diritti tutelati, essi appartengono, per lo più, alla c.d. prima generazione dei diritti umani, composta da diritti fondamentali e da diritti civili e politici. Ciò dipende dal fatto che la Convenzione si ispira sia alla tradizione occidentale dei diritti umani sia, per l'epoca in cui è stata redatta, alla Dichiarazione Universale. Non si possono qui enumerare tutti i diritti garantiti dalla Convenzione europea e dai suoi Protocolli aggiuntivi. Fra essi, si possono ricordare il diritto alla vita (art. 2), il divieto di tortura (art. 3), il divieto di schiavitù e lavori forzati (art. 4), il diritto alla libertà e sicurezza (art. 5), il diritto ad equo processo (art. 6), il diritto al rispetto della vita privata e familiare (art. 8), le libertà di pensiero, di espressione, di riunione e associazione (artt. 9, 10 e 11), il divieto di discriminazione (art. 14), il diritto di proprietà (art. 1 del Protocollo n. 1). Molti di questi diritti non sono assoluti, ma subiscono limitazioni, e numerosi diritti possono essere derogati in situazioni di guerra o di emergenza nazionale (art. 15). Il contenuto di questi diritti sarà approfondito in seguito [113].

Si devono inoltre sottolineare due concetti importanti. In primo luogo, la giurisprudenza degli organi di Strasburgo ha chiarito che i diritti previsti non impongono agli Stati solo obblighi negativi di astensione, ma anche obblighi positivi di azione. In secondo luogo, le norme sostanziali della Convenzione europea si indirizzano formalmente non solo agli Stati parti, ma anche direttamente agli individui, conferendo loro veri e propri diritti sul piano internazionale. Pertanto, in base alla Convenzione, gli individui hanno numerosi diritti umani sostanziali ed il diritto di farli valere dinanzi ad un giudice internazionale.

8.1.2. *Organi e procedure*

La parte procedurale della Convenzione europea è quella più interessante e più innovativa; ed infatti essa ha avuto un'influenza anche su altri sistemi regionali di protezione dei diritti umani, quali il sistema interamericano e quello africano.

La Corte si compone di un numero di giudici pari a quello degli Stati parti della Convenzione. Essi siedono a titolo individuale e sono indipendenti rispetto agli Stati parti. La Corte si articola in quattro formazioni di giudizio: *a*) Giudice unico; *b*) Comitati di tre giudici; *c*) Camere di sette giudici; *d*) Grande Camera di 17 giudici. Queste formazioni hanno competenze diverse, di importanza sempre crescente [114].

La Corte, come si è sopra accennato, è competente ad esaminare, in via contenziosa, sia i ricorsi interstatali (art. 33) che i ricorsi individuali (art. 34) [115]. Questi ultimi possono esser presentati da singoli individui, da gruppi di individui o da organizzazioni non governative; ma tali soggetti devono dimostrare di essere "vittime" della violazione di uno dei diritti garantiti dalla Convenzione o dai Protocolli aggiuntivi. La questione talora è complessa. La Corte ha dimostrato in passato un atteggiamento restrittivo, che sembra ora voler

---

[112] Vedi *supra*, Cap. III, parr. 10, 11 e 12. Cfr. anche Ronzitti (2016), pp. 324-326.

[113] Vedi *infra*, Capp. V e VI.

[114] Vedi ECHR, artt. 26-31.

[115] La Corte ha anche una funzione consultiva: essa può, su richiesta del Comitato dei Ministri, dare un parere consultivo su questioni relative all'interpretazione della Convenzione e dei suoi protocolli.

rivedere, per i ricorsi provenienti da organizzazioni che rappresentano interessi collettivi, ma che non sono direttamente colpite dalla violazione. D'altra parte, sono di solito ritenuti ammissibili i ricorsi presentati da vittime indirette, quali i familiari della vittima "diretta", o da vittime potenziali, ad esempio quando il ricorrente lamenta che lo Stato ha adottato una legge che, pur non essendo ancora stata applicata nei suoi confronti, ha molte probabilità di essere applicata in futuro e di recargli un pregiudizio diretto [116].

La procedura contenziosa può essere distinta in tre fasi principali: *a*) quella di ricevibilità (o ammissibilità) del ricorso; *b*) quella di esame, indagine sui fatti e tentativo di composizione amichevole della controversia; *c*) quella della decisione con sentenza.

Nella prima fase, che funziona come una sorta di filtro preliminare, la Corte decide sulla ricevibilità dei ricorsi (art. 35). La principale condizione di ricevibilità è data dal previo esaurimento dei ricorsi interni da parte dell'individuo ricorrente o da parte dell'individuo vittima della violazione fatta valere dallo Stato ricorrente. Della regola del previo esaurimento abbiamo già parlato [117]. Altra condizione di ricevibilità è che il ricorso sia stato presentato entro 6 mesi dalla data di notifica della decisione interna finale [118]. Inoltre, nei ricorsi individuali, si richiede che il ricorso non sia anonimo, non riguardi una questione già presentata alla Corte o ad altro organo internazionale di controllo, non sia manifestamente infondato, non costituisca un abuso del diritto di ricorso. Infine, una condizione di ricevibilità che è stata aggiunta recentemente è quella secondo cui il ricorrente deve aver subìto un significativo pregiudizio (*significant disadvantage*) [119].

Se il ricorso è ammissibile, si apre una seconda fase della procedura, nella quale la Corte esamina il caso con i rappresentanti delle parti e può condurre indagini, nelle quali gli Stati contraenti si impegnano a prestare collaborazione. Peraltro, in qualsiasi stadio della procedura, la Corte si mette a disposizione delle parti con lo scopo di raggiungere una soluzione amichevole della controversia (art. 39). Se la conciliazione riesce, il ricorso è stralciato dal ruolo e la soluzione raggiunta è riportata in una decisione, che viene trasmessa al Comitato dei Ministri, che sorveglia la sua esecuzione.

Se la soluzione amichevole non viene raggiunta, si apre la terza fase della procedura, nella quale la Corte decide nel merito con una sentenza, che ha la funzione di accertare se vi sia stata o meno una violazione della Convenzione o dei protocolli addizionali. Si tratta di una sentenza di mero accertamento, che si limita a decidere sulla conformità o meno della misura presa dallo Stato con la Convenzione [120]. Se la Corte stabilisce che vi è stata una violazione, essa può accordare alla parte lesa una "equa soddisfazione" (art. 41) [121], che può consistere in un risarcimento monetario del danno morale e materiale o in una *restitutio in integrum*. Le sentenze della Corte sono obbligatorie per gli Stati membri (art. 46), anche se esse non sono direttamente esecutive negli ordinamenti interni e quindi la-

---

[116] Vedi, ad es., ECtHR, *Dudgeon v. UK*.

[117] Vedi *supra*, Cap. II, par. 11.1.1.

[118] Il termine sarà ridotto a 4 mesi quando entrerà in vigore il Protocollo n. 15 alla Convenzione europea.

[119] Questa condizione di ricevibilità è stata inserita nel Protocollo n. 14; ed è talora criticata in dottrina. Vedi, ad es., Citroni, Scovazzi (2013), pp. 97-99.

[120] Vedi Ronzitti (2016), p. 332.

[121] Il termine "equa soddisfazione" è piuttosto inconsueto nel diritto internazionale; ma equivale in sostanza al termine "riparazione".

sciano allo Stato condannato un certo margine di discrezionalità nel decidere le misure interne di esecuzione.

Tuttavia, recentemente la Corte di Strasburgo ha sviluppato, tramite una interessante giurisprudenza, nuove tipologie di sentenze. In primo luogo, la Corte, nei c.d. casi di "violazioni strutturali" della Convenzione europea, non si limita a stabilire se lo Stato abbia violato la Convenzione, ma indica allo Stato le misure, anche legislative, che dovrebbero essere adottate per evitare ripetute o continue violazioni. Si parla, a questo proposito, di "sentenze-pilota" della Corte e di "misure generali" che essa stabilisce a carico dello Stato. In secondo luogo, la Corte ha talora emesso sentenze che stabiliscono "misure individuali", cioè che non lasciano margine di apprezzamento agli Stati sulla loro attuazione (ad esempio, la revisione di un determinato processo penale); e talora anche sentenze-monito, nelle quali la Corte, pur non accertando una violazione, avverte lo Stato che in futuro potrebbe cambiare la propria posizione [122].

Conviene anche ricordare che, durante il procedimento contenzioso, la Corte può adottare "misure provvisorie" di natura cautelare, che hanno lo scopo di evitare al ricorrente un danno grave e irreparabile; cioè un danno che non potrebbe essere poi evitato al momento della emanazione della sentenza (ad esempio l'espulsione di una persona verso un Paese nel quale rischia di subire atti di tortura).

Il controllo sull'esecuzione delle sentenze della Corte spetta al Comitato dei Ministri del Consiglio d'Europa. Il Protocollo n. 14 ha rafforzato tale ruolo del Comitato, poiché ha creato una sorta di "giudizio per inadempimento" delle sentenze. Se lo Stato soccombente non adempie, il Comitato dei Ministri può rivolgersi alla Corte per far dichiarare tale inadempienza [123]; e, in caso affermativo, la Corte rinvia di nuovo la questione al Comitato dei Ministri, perché "consideri le misure da prendere" (art. 46 (5)). In realtà, non vengono precisate le misure che il Comitato può adottare; ma, in teoria, un persistente inadempimento di una sentenza della Corte potrebbe anche comportare una sospensione dello Stato dal Consiglio d'Europa, *ex* art. 3 del suo Statuto [124].

8.2. *La Carta sociale europea*

Poiché la Convenzione europea dei diritti dell'uomo si occupava solo marginalmente dei diritti economici, sociali e culturali, il Consiglio d'Europa predispose la Carta sociale europea, firmata nel 1961, e successivamente integrata da tre protocolli. Inoltre, nel 1996, è stata adottata una nuova versione della Carta, denominata Carta sociale europea riveduta.

La Carta è uno strumento giuridico originale, che presenta un carattere flessibile e differenziato fra i vari Stati membri. Infatti, vi è una distinzione fra la Parte I della Carta, che contiene 31 diritti e principi, formulati in maniera molto generale, e la Parte II, che comprende 31 articoli più dettagliati, ciascuno dei quali contiene vari paragrafi numerati. Ogni Stato contraente si impegna a considerare la Parte I della Carta come una dichiarazione

---

[122] Su queste due tipologie di sentenze vedi Pustorino (2019), pp. 50-54.

[123] Vedi la risoluzione del 7 dicembre 2017, con la quale il Comitato dei ministri, dopo aver intimato all'Azerbaigian di eseguire la sentenza nel caso *Mikayil Mammadov*, ha adito la Corte per far valere la mancata esecuzione della sentenza.

[124] Cfr. Citroni, Scovazzi (2013), p. 102.

degli obiettivi che esso perseguirà con tutti i mezzi appropriati. Inoltre, si impegna a vincolarsi ad almeno 6 fra 9 articoli della Parte II, che vengono espressamente indicati; ed anche ad un numero addizionale di articoli o di paragrafi della Parte II, a sua scelta, purché il numero totale di articoli o di paragrafi cui esso si vincola non sia inferiore a 16 articoli o 63 paragrafi. Questo sistema conferma che la Parte I della Carta non contiene obblighi immediatamente precettivi e vincolanti; e che ad ogni Stato è lasciata una libertà piuttosto ampia nello scegliere gli obblighi vincolanti contenuti nella Parte II. Questo meccanismo favorisce un'adesione più generalizzata da parte degli Stati del Consiglio d'Europa, che hanno situazioni interne assai diverse nel campo economico e sociale.

Il catalogo dei diritti protetti comprende, in sintesi, il diritto al lavoro, nelle sue varie specificazioni; il diritto alla salute; il diritto all'assistenza medica e sociale; i diritti di protezione economica della famiglia, delle donne e dei minori; il diritto alla non discriminazione; il diritto all'abitazione.

Conviene inoltre accennare ai meccanismi di garanzia. Vi sono due procedure di controllo, che si fondano, in maniera tradizionale, sulla presentazione di rapporti periodici ad opera degli Stati parti. Ma vi è anche, dal 1998, una procedura più interessante, di natura quasi-giurisdizionale, che consiste nella presentazione di reclami collettivi da parte di organizzazioni internazionali di datori di lavoro e di lavoratori, o di certe organizzazioni non governative, o di organizzazioni nazionali di datori di lavoro e di lavoratori dello Stato accusato della violazione della Carta. I reclami sono istruiti dal Comitato europeo dei diritti sociali [125] (un organo di esperti indipendenti), che decide prima sulla ricevibilità e poi eventualmente sul merito. Quindi il Comitato predispone un rapporto con le sue conclusioni circa la violazione o meno della Carta e lo trasmette al Comitato dei Ministri, che rivolge allo Stato che abbia commesso una violazione una raccomandazione e controlla l'osservanza della medesima.

8.3. *Altri trattati sui diritti umani del Consiglio d'Europa*

Il Consiglio d'Europa ha adottato numerosi trattati che si occupano, in maniera più o meno diretta, di diritti umani, con riferimento, ad esempio, ai diritti dei fanciulli, dei lavoratori migranti, dei rifugiati, delle vittime di reati. Qui di seguito esamineremo, in breve, solo quelli che riteniamo più significativi.

8.3.1. *La Convenzione europea per la prevenzione della tortura*

Come si è visto, la Convenzione delle NU contro la tortura del 1984 si concentra soprattutto sulla repressione degli atti di tortura e di trattamenti o punizioni inumani o degradanti. Nel quadro del Consiglio d'Europa, invece, si è ritenuto che fosse importante creare un regime giuridico volto alla prevenzione di tali atti. Su questa base, il Consiglio d'Europa ha adottato, nel 1987, la Convenzione europea per la prevenzione della tortura e dei trattamenti o punizioni inumani o degradanti [126]. Questa Convenzione si fonda sul presupposto che il maggior rischio di essere sottoposti a tali abusi si verifica durante l'arresto e la

---

[125] European Committee of Social Rights (ECteeSR).

[126] European Convention for the Prevention of Torture and Inhuman or Degrading Treatment or Punishment (ECPT), 26 November 1987.

detenzione delle persone, da parte di agenti di polizia, di agenti carcerari o di altre autorità dello Stato. Pertanto, essa ha istituito un organo di esperti indipendenti, il Comitato europeo per la prevenzione della tortura e dei trattamenti o punizioni inumani o degradanti [127], che ha il potere di visitare i luoghi di detenzione, per controllare il trattamento dei detenuti (anche tramite colloqui privati) e, se occorre, quello di fare raccomandazioni allo Stato interessato allo scopo di rafforzare la protezione dei detenuti. Il Comitato effettua visite periodiche negli Stati parti della Convenzione, ma può anche organizzare visite *ad hoc*. Inoltre, predispone rapporti, che sono in linea di principio confidenziali; ma che di solito, previo consenso dello Stato interessato, vengono pubblicati.

8.3.2. *La Carta europea per le lingue regionali e minoritarie*

Negli anni 1990, il problema delle minoranze nazionali divenne nuovamente importante in Europa, per il riemergere di numerosi conflitti etnici. La prima risposta da parte del Consiglio d'Europa fu l'adozione, nel 1992, della Carta europea per le lingue nazionali o minoritarie [128]. Lo scopo dell'accordo è quello di proteggere la diversità linguistica e, in particolare, le lingue regionali e minoritarie che hanno una tradizione storica in Europa, nonché di rispettare il diritto di usarle nella vita pubblica e privata. La Carta è strutturata in maniera simile alla Carta sociale europea, poiché prima enuncia una serie di scopi e di principi e poi una serie di misure più specifiche. Ogni Stato parte si impegna a vincolarsi ad un numero minimo di articoli della Carta, che vengono espressamente indicati. Il meccanismo di controllo si limita ad una semplice procedura di rapporti periodici da parte degli Stati.

8.3.3. *La Convenzione quadro europea per la protezione delle minoranze nazionali*

Dopo poco tempo, il Consiglio d'Europa ha adottato, in materia di tutela delle minoranze, un trattato di carattere più generale: la Convenzione quadro europea per la protezione delle minoranze nazionali del 1995 [129]. Essa contiene norme piuttosto vaghe e di natura programmatica, a causa della mancanza di posizioni univoche degli Stati contraenti sulla materia. Anche la nozione di "minoranze nazionali" resta indefinita.

La prima parte della Convenzione enuncia alcuni principi generali; la seconda parte una serie di principi più precisi che riguardano molti aspetti relativi alla protezione delle persone appartenenti a minoranze nazionali, che sono raggruppabili in cinque settori principali: *a*) i diritti relativi alla non discriminazione ed alla protezione dell'identità culturale, linguistica e religiosa (artt. 4-6); *b*) questioni collegate ai diritti linguistici ed all'uso della lingua in pubblico ed in privato (artt. 10-11); *c*) diritti nella sfera educativa (artt. 12-14); *d*) diritti relativi alla partecipazione nella sfera decisionale (art. 15); *e*) questioni relative alla cooperazione transfrontaliera nella promozione dei diritti previsti nella Convenzione. Tuttavia, a questi diritti delle minoranze non corrispondono obblighi positivi precisi da parte degli Stati. La quarta parte della Convenzione istituisce un meccanismo di controllo, affidato al Comitato dei Ministri, assistito da un Comitato consultivo di esperti indipendenti, al quale gli Stati parti presentano rapporti periodici.

---

[127] European Committee for the Prevention of Torture and Inhuman or Degrading Treatment or Punishment. Cfr. art. 1 ECPT.

[128] European Charter for Regional or Minority Languages (ECML), 5 November 1992.

[129] Framework Convention for the Protection of National Minorities (FCPNM), 1 February 1995.

8.3.4. *La Convenzione sui diritti umani e la biomedicina*

Con la Convenzione sui diritti umani e la biomedicina, adottata nel 1997 [130], il Consiglio d'Europa ha cercato di proteggere i diritti umani delle persone dai rischi che possono derivare dai nuovi sviluppi della biomedicina e della biotecnologia. In realtà, già alcuni diritti umani tradizionali, quali il diritto alla vita, il diritto all'integrità personale ed il diritto alla vita privata ponevano dei limiti agli eccessi di interventi della medicina moderna nella dignità delle persone [131]. Tuttavia, si è ritenuto che servissero norme più specifiche. La Convenzione contiene una serie di principi e divieti in materia di bioetica, di ricerca medica, di consenso preventivo e informato dei pazienti, di trapianto di organi, di procreazione assistita e di questioni simili. Tuttavia, alcuni autori hanno rilevato che molte delle disposizioni centrali della Convenzione costituiscono solo nuove formulazioni di principi che erano già insiti nei diritti umani, e specie nel diritto alla vita privata [132].

8.4. *Commissario per i diritti umani del Consiglio d'Europa*

Il Consiglio d'Europa ha istituito, nel 1999, un proprio Commissario per i diritti umani [133]. Il suo mandato è quello di: *a*) promuovere l'effettiva osservanza dei diritti umani e assistere gli Stati membri nell'attuazione delle norme sui diritti umani del Consiglio d'Europa; *b*) promuovere e diffondere l'educazione nel campo dei diritti umani; *c*) individuare lacune e difetti nelle legislazioni e nelle prassi degli Stati membri del Consiglio d'Europa e indirizzare raccomandazioni a tali Stati; *d*) agevolare le attività delle istituzioni nazionali e di altre strutture per i diritti umani; *e*) fornire consulenza e informazioni sulla protezione dei diritti umani nella regione. Le attività di questa istituzione si concentrano su tre aree principali, strettamente correlate: visite nei Paesi e dialogo con le autorità nazionali e la società civile; rendicontazione tematica e consulenza sull'attuazione sistematica dei diritti umani; attività di sensibilizzazione. Il Commissario non può agire in merito a ricorsi individuali, ma può trarre conclusioni e intraprendere iniziative più ampie sulla base di informazioni affidabili sulle violazioni dei diritti umani subìte da singoli [134].

9. *Unione Europea*

I Trattati istitutivi delle Comunità europee contenevano, in origine, solo pochissime norme che si occupavano di diritti umani, ma si trattava solo di diritti strumentali alla realizzazione del mercato comune. Ciò si giustificava per il fatto che le Comunità ave-

---

[130] European Convention for the Protection of Human Rights and Dignity of the Human Being with regard to the Application of Biology and Medicine (ECHRB), 4 April 1997.

[131] Novak (2003), p. 181.

[132] *Ibidem*, p. 183.

[133] Council of Europe Commissioner for Human Rights.

[134] Il Commissario collabora, inoltre, con un'ampia gamma di istituzioni nazionali e internazionali, nonché con meccanismi di monitoraggio dei diritti umani. Tra i partner intergovernativi più importanti dell'Ufficio figurano le Nazioni Unite e i suoi Istituti specializzati, l'Unione europea e l'OSCE. L'Ufficio collabora anche con le principali ONG, università e gruppi di riflessione sui diritti umani.

vano una natura prevalentemente economica; e che si riteneva, a quel tempo, che le Istituzioni comunitarie non potessero avere occasione di incidere sui diritti umani delle persone.

Tuttavia, a partire dalla fine degli anni '60 del secolo scorso, la tutela dei diritti umani si è lentamente e gradualmente affermata nel diritto comunitario (ora dell'UE), per via giurisprudenziale, per merito della Corte di giustizia. Essa, sotto la spinta di alcune sentenze delle Corti costituzionali italiana e tedesca che rivendicavano il controllo sulle norme comunitarie contrastanti con i principi costituzionali, ha affermato che la protezione dei diritti umani faceva parte degli obiettivi della Comunità. Più in particolare, la Corte di giustizia, a partire dai celebri casi *Stauder*, *Internationale Handelsgesellschaft* e *Nold*[135], ha affermato che i diritti fondamentali fanno parte dei principi giuridici generali dell'ordinamento comunitario e che tali principi sui diritti umani possono essere ricavati: *a*) dalle tradizioni costituzionali comuni degli Stati membri; *b*) dai trattati sui diritti umani di cui gli Stati membri sono parti, con particolare riguardo per la Convenzione europea dei diritti umani. Tuttavia, questa azione della Corte di giustizia, pur avendo il grande merito di colmare una lacuna dell'ordinamento comunitario, aveva il limite di far progredire i diritti fondamentali solo per via giurisprudenziale e quindi in maniera lenta e frammentaria, e quello di poter stabilire, tramite il rinvio alle tradizioni costituzionali *comuni* di tutti gli Stati membri, soltanto standard minimi di tutela.

Ma la situazione è in seguito cambiata, mediante l'inserimento di alcune norme esplicite sui diritti umani nei trattati sulla Comunità e sull'Unione Europea che si sono succeduti nel tempo. Un primo progresso importante è stato raggiunto con il Trattato di Maastricht sull'Unione Europea del 1992, che ha stabilito espressamente che l'Unione rispetta i diritti fondamentali quali sono garantiti dalla Convenzione europea e quali risultano dalle tradizioni costituzionali degli Stati membri, in quanto principi generali del diritto dell'Unione. Successivamente, fallita l'ipotesi coltivata dalla Commissione di far aderire le Comunità alla Convenzione europea, a causa di un parere negativo della Corte di giustizia del 1996, il Trattato di Amsterdam del 1997 ha segnato un ulteriore progresso: esso ha stabilito che l'Unione si fonda sul rispetto dei diritti umani; che tale rispetto è un requisito per l'adesione di nuovi Stati; e che la violazione grave di tali diritti da parte di uno Stato membro può essere sanzionata con la sospensione di alcuni suoi diritti.

9.1. *Il quadro normativo attuale*

Dopo l'entrata in vigore, nel 2009, del Trattato di Lisbona del 2007, il quadro giuridico è il seguente. L'art. 2 del Trattato sull'Unione Europea (TUE/TEU) elenca, fra i valori sui quali si fonda l'Unione, il rispetto della dignità umana, della libertà, della democrazia, dell'uguaglianza e dei diritti umani. L'art. 6(3) stabilisce che:

> "I diritti fondamentali, garantiti dalla Convenzione europea per la salvaguardia dei diritti dell'uomo e delle libertà fondamentali e risultanti dalle tradizioni costituzionali comuni agli Stati membri, fanno parte del diritto dell'Unione in quanto principi generali".

---

[135] ECJ, *Stauder* (1969); *Internationale Handelsgesellschaft* (1970); *Nold* (1974).

L'art. 7 del TUE prevede che la violazione grave e persistente da parte di uno Stato membro dei valori di cui all'art. 2 può causare la sospensione dei diritti derivanti allo Stato in questione dall'applicazione dei Trattati [136]. L'art. 49 stabilisce, come requisito per l'adesione di un nuovo Stato europeo all'UE, che tale Stato "rispetti i valori di cui all'articolo 2 e si impegni a promuoverli".

Nel frattempo, si era venuta affermando l'idea che fosse opportuno dotare l'UE di un proprio catalogo scritto di diritti fondamentali. Questa idea si è realizzata, in un primo tempo, con la redazione della Carta dei diritti fondamentali dell'UE e la sua proclamazione, come documento non vincolante, durante il Consiglio europeo di Nizza del 2000. In seguito, con l'entrata in vigore del Trattato di Lisbona, la Carta (con piccoli riadattamenti) ha assunto finalmente lo stesso valore giuridico vincolante dei nuovi Trattati. Ciò è sancito espressamente dall'art. 6(1) del TUE.

La Carta riprende ed aggiorna il catalogo dei diritti della Convenzione europea dei diritti umani, nonché ribadisce tutti i diritti che la giurisprudenza della Corte di giustizia aveva progressivamente individuato per via giurisprudenziale. I diritti stabiliti dalla Carta sono raggruppati, in maniera piuttosto innovativa, sotto sei Titoli denominati: "Dignità", "Libertà", "Uguaglianza", "Solidarietà", "Cittadinanza" e "Giustizia". Tuttavia, si deve notare che l'art. 51 della Carta stabilisce che essa si applica alle Istituzioni dell'Unione ed agli Stati membri "esclusivamente nell'attuazione del diritto dell'Unione" e che essa "non estende l'ambito di applicazione del diritto dell'Unione al di là delle competenze dell'Unione, né introduce competenze o compiti nuovi per l'Unione".

Infine, l'art. 6(2) del TUE sancisce ora l'impegno e la competenza dell'UE di aderire alla Convenzione europea. Ma la Corte di giustizia, con un nuovo parere del 18 dicembre 2014, ha ritenuto che il progetto di accordo elaborato dalla Commissione non fosse compatibile con l'ordinamento dell'Unione Europea.

9.2. *Le competenze della Corte di giustizia in materia di diritti umani*

In questo quadro giuridico, conviene fare un cenno alle competenze della Corte di giustizia in materia di diritti umani. La Corte è certamente competente a tutelare i diritti umani protetti dal diritto dell'UE in relazione agli atti delle Istituzioni. Al contrario, la Corte non può giudicare sulla conformità ai diritti umani di atti o norme degli Stati membri in materie che esulano dal diritto dell'UE [137].

Il problema è invece più complicato per quanto riguarda un possibile sindacato della Corte di giustizia su atti o norme degli Stati membri che *diano attuazione* al diritto dell'UE. Si potrebbe pensare, ad esempio, a ipotesi di rinvii pregiudiziali da parte di giudici statali alla Corte di giustizia per far accertare la compatibilità o meno di norme interne rispetto ai diritti umani protetti dal diritto dell'UE [138]. Si noti che questi casi sono delicati, perché la competenza della Corte di giustizia rischia di porsi in conflitto con quella della Corte europea dei diritti umani. Infatti, quest'ultima Corte si è dichiarata competente, in

---

[136] Vedi anche, in senso simile, TFEU, art. 354.

[137] Vedi, ad es., ECJ, *Meryem Demirel.*

[138] Ronzitti (2016), p. 342.

numerose sentenze, a giudicare sulla conformità alla Convenzione europea degli atti degli Stati membri che siano attuativi del diritto dell'UE.

La Corte di Strasburgo ha cercato di risolvere il problema del possibile conflitto di competenze. Nel già citato caso *Bosphorus*[139], la Corte ha distinto fra: *a*) casi in cui gli Stati membri si limitano ad attuare atti dell'UE; *b*) casi in cui gli Stati membri godono di un certo margine di discrezionalità nell'attuazione del diritto dell'UE. Nella prima categoria di casi, la Corte ritiene che il suo intervento non sia, in linea di principio, necessario, poiché l'UE è capace di tutelare i diritti umani in modo, sostanziale e processuale, almeno equivalente a quello della Convenzione europea[140]. Nella seconda categoria di casi, invece, la Corte di Strasburgo ritiene di avere piena competenza a giudicare sulle eventuali violazioni della Convenzione europea da parte degli Stati nella loro attuazione del diritto dell'UE. Questa situazione, probabilmente, è destinata a cambiare se verrà concluso ed entrerà in vigore il previsto accordo di adesione della UE alla Convenzione europea[141]. Secondo alcuni, i potenziali conflitti fra la Corte di giustizia e la Corte europea dei diritti umani sarebbero destinati ad aumentare.

Un altro problema riguarda la competenza della Corte di giustizia a sindacare, sulla base del rispetto dei diritti umani protetti dal diritto dell'UE, atti comunitari di attuazione di decisioni del Consiglio di Sicurezza delle Nazioni Unite. La questione si è posta nei noti casi *Kadi*[142], dove si discuteva sulla legittimità di un regolamento UE che dava esecuzione a certe decisioni del Consiglio di Sicurezza delle NU che restringevano i diritti di proprietà delle persone incluse nella lista allegata al regolamento del Consiglio n. 881/2002 del 27 maggio 2002, che riguardava certi individui ed enti associati a Osama bin Laden, alla rete Al-Qaeda ed ai Talebani. La Corte di giustizia ha affermato che, anche se la Carta delle NU obbliga gli Stati a rispettare le decisioni del Consiglio di Sicurezza, l'attuazione di tali decisioni nell'ordinamento dell'UE deve rispettare i principi di questo ordinamento, e quindi anche i diritti umani fondamentali.

10. *Organizzazione per la Sicurezza e la Cooperazione in Europa*

L'Organizzazione per la Sicurezza e la Cooperazione in Europa (OSCE) è nata, nella conferenza di Helsinki del 1975, come conferenza diplomatica (CSCE)[143], che in seguito si è dotata di alcuni organi ed ha funzionato per alcuni anni tramite conferenze biennali. Nel 1994, si è trasformata in una organizzazione permanente ed ha assunto il nome attuale di OSCE.

Uno degli scopi principali dell'OSCE è costituito dalla tutela dei diritti umani, che viene definita in senso lato come la "dimensione umana" dell'Organizzazione. Questa espressione ha un significato più ampio di quella di "diritti umani", poiché si applica non solo ai diritti umani in senso stretto, ma anche ai rapporti fra le istituzioni: concetto di democra-

[139] ECtHR, *Bosphorus*, parr. 149-165.

[140] Ma è solo una presunzione relativa. Vedi anche ECtHR, *M.S.S. v. Belgium and Greece*, parr. 338-340.

[141] Vedi, sul punto, Daniele (2014), p. 191.

[142] CFI, *Kadi*; EGC, *Kadi*; ECJ, *Kadi*; ECJ, *European Commission and Others v. Kadi*.

[143] Conference on Security and Co-operation in Europe (CSCE).

zia, istituzioni democratiche, stato di diritto, diritti delle minoranze, disarmo, prevenzione dei conflitti [144]. In effetti, la nozione di "dimensione umana" è oramai diventata autonoma rispetto a quella di "diritti umani", anche se ovviamente i due aspetti sono fra loro collegati. Questa autonomia deriva da diversi fattori: *a*) gli impegni OSCE sono di natura sostanzialmente politica, mentre i diritti umani sono tutelati per lo più da norme vincolanti; *b*) gli impegni OSCE non hanno bisogno di ratifica, diversamente dai trattati sui diritti umani, né di formale esecuzione negli ordinamenti statali; c) i meccanismi di garanzia dell'OSCE operano a livello interstatale e non sono aperti a ricorsi da parte di individui.

Nel quadro dell'OSCE, in effetti, si sono sviluppati anche vari meccanismi di garanzia, fondati soprattutto su procedure di negoziati, mediazione e conciliazione.

Il c.d. "meccanismo della dimensione umana" è una procedura tesa a garantire il rispetto delle disposizioni sui diritti umani contenute nei documenti dell'OSCE. Essa si compone di quattro fasi: una denuncia dell'inosservanza da parte di uno Stato nei confronti di un altro; una replica da parte del secondo Stato ed eventuali incontri bilaterali; un deferimento della questione all'attenzione di tutti gli Stati partecipanti; ed infine una discussione della questione in una riunione della Conferenza sulla dimensione umana dell'OSCE. A partire dal 1991, alla procedura partecipano anche esperti e *rapporteurs*. Tuttavia, questo meccanismo ha perso d'importanza dopo l'istituzione del Consiglio Permanente dell'OSCE [145], nel cui ambito avvengono le discussioni circa l'osservanza dei diritti umani da parte degli Stati.

Nel 1992, l'OSCE ha creato l'ufficio dell'Alto Commissario per le Minoranze Nazionali [146], che ha un compito indipendente di prevenzione dei conflitti, quando le questioni relative alle minoranze possono costituire un pericolo per la pace e la sicurezza internazionale. Le sue funzioni consistono nel c.d. "preallarme" (*early warning*) e nell'azione preventiva (*early action*). L'Alto Commissario può svolgere missioni sul terreno, con il consenso dello Stato territoriale, e quindi predisporre rapporti. Nel 1997, è stato istituito un Rappresentante OSCE sulla libertà dei mezzi di informazione [147].

Infine, nel 1992 è stata firmata la Convenzione di Stoccolma, entrata in vigore nel 1994, che ha creato la Corte di conciliazione e arbitrato dell'OSCE [148]. Tuttavia, ad oggi solo 34 Stati, fra i 57 membri dell'OSCE, hanno ratificato la Convenzione. La Corte ha in realtà una competenza assai ampia, poiché può intervenire in tutte le controversie (fra Stati membri della Corte che siano parti della Convenzione e, in certi casi, anche fra Stati membri della Corte e Stati parti soltanto dell'OSCE), che investano qualsiasi materia; e quindi anche nelle controversie relative al rispetto dei diritti umani. Essa può agire tramite una procedura di conciliazione, talora anche su ricorso unilaterale, oppure tramite una procedura arbitrale. Tuttavia la Corte, per una serie piuttosto complessa di motivi [149], non ha finora deciso alcun caso.

---

[144] Vedi Ronzitti (2016), p. 344.

[145] Permanent Council. Vedi https://www.osce.org/permanent-council.

[146] OSCE High Commissioner for National Minorities. Vedi https://www.osce.org/hcnm.

[147] OSCE Representative on Freedom of the Media. Vedi https://www.osce.org/representative-on-freedom-of-media.

[148] OSCE Court of Conciliation and Arbitration. Vedi https://www.osce.org/cca. Sulle funzioni di conciliazione della Corte vedi, recentemente, Tomuschat, Pisillo Mazzeschi, Thürer (eds.) (2016).

[149] Cfr. Tomuschat, Pisillo Mazzeschi, Thürer (eds.) (2016).

Sezione III
ALTRI SISTEMI REGIONALI SUI DIRITTI UMANI

11. *Il sistema interamericano*

Il sistema interamericano di tutela dei diritti umani nasce, nel 1948, con l'adozione della Carta dell'Organizzazione degli Stati Americani (OAS) e della Dichiarazione americana dei diritti e doveri dell'uomo [150], un documento di carattere non vincolante. Nel 1959 fu istituita la Commissione interamericana dei diritti umani [151], che divenne un organo dell'OAS ed alla quale fu affidato il compito di controllare il rispetto della Dichiarazione americana. La Commissione ha sede a Washington ed è costituita da sette membri, esperti indipendenti che siedono a titolo personale e che sono eletti dall'Assemblea Generale dell'OAS.

Un progresso notevole si è realizzato con l'approvazione, nel 1969, della Convenzione americana sui diritti umani [152], entrata in vigore nel 1978, ratificata dai più importanti Paesi del Sudamerica e dell'area centro-americana (ma non da Canada e Stati Uniti). La Convenzione, nella sua Parte I, stabilisce i diritti umani che gli Stati parti si obbligano a riconoscere, con un catalogo che si ispira in gran parte a quello della Convenzione europea dei diritti umani ed a quello del Patto delle NU sui diritti civili e politici. Il contenuto di molti di questi diritti sarà approfondito in seguito [153]. La Parte II della Convenzione istituisce la Corte interamericana dei diritti umani [154] e regola le sue funzioni. La Corte ha sede a San José (Costa Rica), è costituita da sette giudici, che siedono a titolo personale e sono eletti dagli Stati parti della Convenzione. Ma la Convenzione americana attribuisce anche ulteriori competenze alla Commissione, limitatamente agli Stati contraenti della Convenzione medesima. Successivamente sono stati adottati due protocolli addizionali.

Per quanto riguarda i meccanismi di garanzia del sistema interamericano, essi sono affidati alla Commissione ed alla Corte, con un sistema binario che si ispira a quello (originario) della Convenzione europea. Tuttavia, mentre la Commissione funziona sia come organo dell'OAS che come organo della Convenzione americana, la Corte ha competenza solo nel quadro della Convenzione. In effetti, il sistema interamericano di tutela dei diritti umani si fonda su due diversi regimi giuridici: il primo si è sviluppato dalla Carta dell'OAS e vincola tutti gli Stati membri di questa Organizzazione; il secondo si fonda sulla Convenzione americana e vincola soltanto gli Stati contraenti della medesima. I due regimi interagiscono e si sovrappongono in vari modi, che rendono talora difficile tenerli distinti [155].

---

[150] American Declaration on the Rights and Duties of Man, 2 May 1948.

[151] Inter-American Commission on Human Rights (IACmHR).

[152] (Inter)-American Convention of Human Rights (ACHR).

[153] Vedi *infra*, Capp. V e VI.

[154] Inter-American Court of Human Rights (IACtHR).

[155] Vedi Buergenthal *et al.* (2004), pp. 222-223.

11.1. *La Commissione interamericana*

La Commissione svolge il suo mandato tramite diverse procedure [156]. Conviene distinguere fra quelle che operano rispetto agli Stati membri dell'OAS e quelle che funzionano rispetto agli Stati parti della Convenzione americana.

Rispetto agli Stati membri dell'OAS, la Commissione ha un ruolo più limitato [157]. Essa può, fra l'altro, indirizzare raccomandazioni ai governi, preparare studi e rapporti, richiedere agli Stati rapporti sulle misure che adottano in tema di diritti umani, fornire pareri agli Stati, effettuare visite *in loco* negli Stati. In aggiunta, rispetto agli Stati membri dell'OAS che *non* sono parti della Convenzione americana, la Commissione può ricevere petizioni da individui, che lamentino violazioni ad opera degli Stati membri dell'OAS dei diritti proclamati nella Dichiarazione americana [158]. Questo sistema di petizioni individuali fondato sulla Carta dell'OAS, anche se è stato rafforzato nel tempo [159], rimane debole, perché si conclude con un rapporto della Commissione, che contiene conclusioni e raccomandazioni e viene trasmesso all'Assemblea Generale dell'OAS; ma che non può essere trasmesso alla Corte per instaurare un procedimento contenzioso, né usufruisce di mezzi efficaci di esecuzione contro gli Stati inadempienti.

Invece, rispetto agli Stati parti della Convenzione americana, il ruolo della Commissione è più efficace [160]. Essa ha, in aggiunta alle suddette e preesistenti competenze in quanto organo dell'OAS, alcune funzioni importanti in un meccanismo di ricorsi per violazioni della Convenzione (artt. 44-51). In questo meccanismo, che non va confuso con quello sopra menzionato, la Commissione può esaminare sia ricorsi individuali che ricorsi interstatali. Nei primi, la Commissione riceve comunicazioni da parte di individui o gruppi di individui che lamentino la violazione della Convenzione ad opera di uno Stato contraente (art. 44). Nei secondi, la Commissione riceve, sulla base di una clausola opzionale, comunicazioni nelle quali uno Stato parte accusa un altro Stato parte di aver violato la Convenzione (art. 45).

La procedura è piuttosto complicata. In una prima fase, la Commissione decide sulla ricevibilità del ricorso (artt. 46-47). I requisiti sono simili a quelli esistenti nel sistema della Convenzione europea dei diritti umani: quello principale è dato dal previo esaurimento dei ricorsi interni. Se il ricorso è ricevibile, si apre una seconda fase, in cui la Commissione esamina il ricorso nel merito con un procedimento quasi-giurisdizionale, raccogliendo informazioni, svolgendo indagini ed esaminando le osservazioni delle parti (art. 48). In questa fase, la Commissione cerca anche di facilitare una composizione amichevole della controversia. Se tale composizione riesce, la Commissione redige un rapporto che viene pubblicato (art. 49). Se invece la composizione amichevole non riesce, la Commissione redige un rapporto preliminare di natura confidenziale, che contiene proposte e raccomandazioni, e lo in-

---

[156] Vedi gli artt. 41-51 della Convenzione americana e gli artt. 18-20 dello Statuto della Commissione.

[157] Vedi l'art. 41, lett. a), b), c), d), e), g) della Convenzione americana, che codifica le preesistenti funzioni della Commissione come organo dell'OAS, e l'art. 18 dello Statuto della Commissione.

[158] Vedi art. 20 dello Statuto della Commissione.

[159] Prima la Commissione poteva esaminare soltanto le violazioni di certi diritti umani "preferiti", contenuti nella Dichiarazione americana. Questo limite è stato superato con l'adozione del nuovo Statuto della Commissione.

[160] Vedi l'intero art. 41 e gli artt. 42-51 della Convenzione americana e l'art. 19 dello Statuto della Commissione.

via agli Stati interessati (art. 50). Nel termine di tre mesi dalla trasmissione del rapporto preliminare, se il caso non è stato risolto o sottoposto dalla Commissione medesima o dallo Stato interessato alla Corte interamericana, la Commissione redige un rapporto finale, nel quale espone le sue conclusioni sulla questione, adotta raccomandazioni e fissa un termine entro il quale lo Stato deve prendere le misure per porre rimedio alla situazione (art. 51). Decorso tale termine, la Commissione decide se lo Stato abbia preso le misure adeguate e se pubblicare il proprio rapporto. Come si vede, questa procedura si conclude con un rapporto che non ha valore vincolante oppure con il deferimento del caso alla Corte interamericana.

11.2. *La Corte interamericana*

La Corte interamericana dei diritti umani ha una competenza conteziosa ed una consultiva. In base alla prima, la Corte è competente ad esaminare i ricorsi già sottoposti alla Commissione, su richiesta della Commissione medesima o degli Stati interessati, previa l'accettazione della sua competenza da parte di questi ultimi. Gli individui non possono presentare ricorsi diretti alla Corte; tuttavia, dal 2001, a seguito di una riforma del regolamento, i ricorrenti possono partecipare alle varie fasi del giudizio.

Il procedimento dinanzi alla Corte ha i caratteri di un procedimento giurisdizionale, con una fase orale ed una scritta, sulla base del principio del contradditorio. La sentenza della Corte, che è motivata e può essere accompagnata da opinioni concorrenti o dissenzienti dei singoli giudici, accerta l'esistenza o meno di una violazione della Convenzione americana, e decide anche sulle eventuali misure di riparazione. Essa è definitiva ed inappellabile. L'esecuzione delle sentenze è controllata dalla Corte stessa, che riceve ed esamina rapporti presentati dalle parti e può anche convocare apposite udienze. Quindi essa fa un rapporto annuale all'Assemblea Generale dell'OAS, segnalando eventualmente i casi nei quali uno Stato non abbia eseguito le sue sentenze e formulando al riguardo raccomandazioni. In effetti, la Corte può esercitare un controllo piuttosto incisivo sul rispetto delle proprie sentenze. Come è stato notato [161], questo sistema di controllo sull'esecuzione delle sentenze, essendo affidato in gran parte ad un organo giurisdizionale anziché ad un organo politico, appare più efficace rispetto a quello della Convenzione europea.

Quanto alla competenza consultiva, la Corte, su richiesta degli Stati membri dell'OAS o di alcuni organi di tale organizzazione, può adottare pareri consultivi sull'interpretazione della Convenzione americana o di altri trattati sui diritti umani applicabili negli Stati americani. Inoltre, sempre su richiesta di ogni Stato membro dell'OAS, la Corte può fornire pareri sulla compatibilità di leggi nazionali con la Convenzione e con i suddetti trattati.

12. *Il sistema africano*

12.1. *L'Unione Africana*

In tempi più recenti, anche il continente africano si è dotato di norme e istituzioni sulla tutela dei diritti umani. Nel 1981 è stata adottata, nel quadro dell'Organizzazione per

[161] Pustorino (2019), p. 66.

l'Unità Africana (OAU), oggi sostituita dall'Unione Africana (AU), la Carta africana dei diritti dell'uomo e dei popoli [162]. La Carta si ispira agli altri trattati regionali sui diritti umani, ma si differenzia in parte da essi perché prevede, oltre ai diritti, anche i doveri degli individui e soprattutto i diritti dei popoli. Questi ultimi comprendono il diritto all'uguaglianza; all'autodeterminazione; al libero sfruttamento delle ricchezze e risorse naturali; allo sviluppo economico, sociale e culturale; alla pace e sicurezza nazionale e internazionale; ad un ambiente favorevole allo sviluppo.

La Parte II della Carta istituisce e regola il funzionamento della Commissione africana sui diritti dell'uomo e dei popoli [163]. Nel 1998 è stato adottato un Protocollo addizionale, che ha istituito la Corte africana sui diritti dell'uomo e dei popoli [164]. Un ulteriore sviluppo si è verificato nel 2008, con l'adozione di un Protocollo sullo Statuto della Corte africana di giustizia e dei diritti umani [165].

12.1.1. *La Commissione africana sui diritti dell'uomo e dei popoli*

La Commissione, che è composta da 11 membri che operano a titolo individuale ed ha sede a Banjul (Gambia), ha un mandato assai ampio: può interpretare le disposizioni della Carta, effettuare studi su problemi in materia di diritti umani, organizzare conferenze, diffondere informazioni, indirizzare raccomandazioni agli Stati, formulare norme e principi-guida per le legislazioni nazionali (art. 45 della Carta). Ma, soprattutto, la Commissione esercita le funzioni di controllo sul rispetto della Carta tramite due procedure: *a*) quella, tradizionale, di esame dei rapporti periodici degli Stati parti sulle misure adottate per dare attuazione alla Carta (art. 62); *b*) quella di esame delle comunicazioni relative a violazioni specifiche della Carta (artt. 47-59).

In base a quest'ultima procedura, la Commissione esamina le comunicazioni presentate da uno Stato parte che accusa un altro Stato parte di aver violato le disposizioni della Carta (artt. 47-49). Dopo aver accertato che siano stati esauriti i ricorsi interni (art. 50), la Commissione assume le informazioni che ritiene necessarie e tenta di raggiungere una soluzione amichevole (artt. 51-52). Quindi, essa redige un rapporto che trasmette agli Stati interessati ed all'Assemblea dei Capi di Stato e di Governo, formulando, se crede, le raccomandazioni che ritiene utili (artt. 52-53). La Commissione può anche decidere di esaminare le comunicazioni presentate da soggetti diversi dagli Stati parti (ad esempio, individui, gruppi di individui o organizzazioni non governative) (art. 55), purché esse abbiano certi requisiti di ricevibilità (art. 56). Ma si deve notare che non esiste la condizione che questi ricorsi siano presentati dalla vittima della violazione; ed infatti gran parte dei ricorsi sono stati presentati da organizzazioni non governative. Quando la comunicazione rivela l'esistenza di una serie di violazioni massicce dei diritti umani, la Commissione informa l'Assemblea dei Capi di Stato e di Governo, la quale può richiedere alla Commissione di predisporre un rapporto, con le sue conclusioni e raccomandazioni (art. 58). Come si vede, questa procedura ricalca quella di altri sistemi regionali di tutela dei diritti umani; ma è più debole, poiché le raccomandazioni della Commissione non hanno efficacia vincolante.

---

[162] African Charter on Human and Peoples' Rights (ACHPR).

[163] African Commission on Human and Peoples' Rights (ACmHPR).

[164] African Court on Human and Peoples' Rights (ACtHPR).

[165] Protocol on the Statute of the African Court of Justice and Human Rights, 1 July 2008.

12.1.2. *La Corte africana sui diritti dell'uomo e dei popoli*

La scarsa efficacia dei meccanismi di controllo incentrati sulla Commissione africana ha indotto gli Stati africani ad adottare il Protocollo istitutivo della Corte africana sui diritti dell'uomo e dei popoli. Questa, composta da 11 giudici indipendenti e con sede ad Arusha (Tanzania), ha una competenza consultiva ed una contenziosa.

La Corte, sulla base della sua competenza contenziosa, può esaminare i ricorsi presentati dalla Commissione africana, dallo Stato parte che ha presentato un ricorso alla Commissione, dallo Stato parte contro il quale è stato presentato il ricorso alla Commissione, dallo Stato nazionale della vittima, da tutte le organizzazioni intergovernative africane, ed infine anche da individui e da organizzazioni non governative, ma solo quando lo Stato accusato abbia accettato questa competenza della Corte (artt. 5 e 34 (6) del Protocollo). La competenza *ratione materiae* della Corte è interessante, poiché l'art. 7 del Protocollo stabilisce che la Corte

> "shall apply the provisions of the Charter and any other relevant human rights instruments ratified by the States concerned".

Ciò significa, come è stato notato [166], che la Corte può occuparsi anche di violazioni, da parte di Stati membri, di disposizioni di trattati sui diritti umani di carattere universale, quali i due Patti delle Nazioni Unite del 1966. Ed infatti ciò si è verificato in una recente sentenza del 2018 della Corte resa contro il Mali [167].

La procedura della Corte segue le regole tradizionali degli altri organismi internazionali di controllo sui diritti umani: vi è una fase relativa alla ricevibilità dei ricorsi (art. 6), una fase concernente il tentativo di composizione amichevole della controversia (art. 9), ed infine una fase di accertamento tramite udienze in contraddittorio fra le parti (artt. 10 e 26). Quindi, la Corte emana una sentenza nel merito, che accerta l'esistenza o meno di una violazione e che può ordinare allo Stato condannato le misure appropriate per rimediare alla violazione, compreso un equo risarcimento monetario o un'altra forma di riparazione (artt. 27-28). Le sentenze sono riconosciute come obbligatorie dagli Stati parti del Protocollo. Sulla loro esecuzione sorvegliano la stessa Corte (art. 31) ed il Consiglio dei Ministri dell'UA (art. 29(2)). Tuttavia, non si specificano quali misure sanzionatorie possano essere prese dal Consiglio nel caso in cui uno Stato si rifiuti di rispettare le sentenze della Corte [168].

12.1.3. *La Corte africana di giustizia e dei diritti umani*

Nel 2008, l'Assemblea dei Capi di Stato e di Governo dell'Unione Africana ha adottato un Protocollo, non ancora entrato in vigore [169], sullo Statuto della Corte africana di giustizia e dei diritti umani [170]. Questa Corte dovrebbe diventare l'organo giurisdizionale principale dell'Unione Africana e dovrebbe concentrare su di sé le competenze finora attribuite

---

[166] Pustorino (2019), pp. 67-68.

[167] ACtHPR, *APDF & IHRDA v. Republic of Mali.*

[168] Cfr. Citroni, Scovazzi (2013), p. 108.

[169] È stato finora ratificato da 7 Stati e dovrebbe entrare in vigore al momento della ratifica da parte di 15 Stati.

[170] Vedi *supra*, par. 12.1.

alla Corte africana dei diritti dell'uomo e dei popoli ed alla Corte di giustizia dell'Unione Africana [171]. La nuova Corte dovrebbe dividersi in due sezioni, una con competenza generale e l'altra con competenza sui diritti umani. Essa costituirebbe un organo giurisdizionale internazionale con caratteristiche piuttosto originali, combinando la competenza di una corte generalista di un'organizzazione internazionale con quella di una corte regionale specializzata nei diritti umani. Tuttavia, la sostituzione della Corte africana dei diritti dell'uomo e dei popoli, che sta funzionando bene, potrebbe essere rischiosa. Inoltre, si deve considerare che la nuova Corte, che avrebbe competenza anche sui crimini internazionali, definiti in maniera assai estensiva, potrebbe anche finire per limitare, per gli Stati africani, il ruolo attuale della Corte penale internazionale [172].

12.2. *La Comunità Economica degli Stati dell'Africa Occidentale e la sua Corte di giustizia*

La Comunità Economica degli Stati Africani occidentali (ECOWAS) [173] costituisce un'organizzazione internazionale composta da 15 Stati, che ha istituito, nel 1991, una sua Corte di giustizia [174], che presenta alcuni aspetti interessanti [175]. La Corte ha una competenza consultiva ed una contenziosa. Quest'ultima è assai ampia e comprende, fra l'altro, il potere di accertare i casi di violazione dei diritti umani che si verifichino in ogni Stato membro [176]. La Corte può quindi occuparsi di violazioni dei diritti umani che siano protetti da numerosi strumenti internazionali applicabili agli Stati membri dell'ECOWAS [177]. Inoltre, la Corte può essere adita sia da Stati che da individui o gruppi di individui; e senza il filtro del previo esaurimento dei ricorsi interni [178].

13. *Altre iniziative regionali*

Gli Stati dell'Asia non hanno, per molto tempo, creato strumenti normativi vincolanti e meccanismi di garanzia sulla tutela internazionale dei diritti umani. Ciò è dovuto a vari motivi: la mancanza di omogeneità culturale fra gli Stati asiatici; la contestazione del principio di universalità dei diritti umani da parte di un gruppo di tali Stati [179]; la mancanza di un'organizzazione internazionale regionale di carattere "generalista", comparabile al Consiglio d'Europa o all'Organizzazione degli Stati Americani o all'Unione Africana. Tutta-

---

[171] Cfr. Protocol of the Court of Justice of the African Union, 1 July 2003.

[172] Vedi Aja Agwu (2014).

[173] Economic Community of West African States (ECOWAS).

[174] The ECOWAS Community Court of Justice (CCJ).

[175] Vedi Focarelli (2013), p. 276.

[176] Vedi Supplementary Protocol, 1 May 2005, art. 3(4): "The Court has jurisdiction to determine cases of violation of human rights that occur in any Member State".

[177] Vedi CCJ, *Hadijatou Mani Koraou.*

[178] *Ibidem.*

[179] Si pensi, ad es., alla tesi della prevalenza del diritto islamico (*sharia*) sul diritto internazionale o alla tesi della priorità dei "valori asiatici". Cfr. Novak (2003), p. 253.

via, alcune organizzazioni sub-regionali hanno intrapreso iniziative in materia di diritti umani, che potrebbero rafforzarsi in futuro.

Nell'ambito dell'Organizzazione della Conferenza Islamica (OIC) (prima denominata Conferenza Islamica), un'organizzazione internazionale istituita nel 1969 che comprende 57 Stati membri, è stata adottata, nel 1990, la Dichiarazione del Cairo sui diritti umani nell'Islam [180]. Si tratta di un documento di carattere non vincolante, che si ispira alla Dichiarazione Universale, ma che contiene anche alcuni diritti collettivi dei popoli, quali il diritto di autodeterminazione contro la repressione coloniale ed il diritto ad un ambiente salubre. Tuttavia, si deve notare che, sulla base degli artt. 24 e 25 della Dichiarazione, tutti i diritti e libertà ivi contenuti sono soggetti alla Sharia islamica, che è anche la sola fonte di interpretazione della Dichiarazione medesima [181].

Più interessanti sono le iniziative che sono state intraprese nel quadro della Lega Araba, un'organizzazione internazionale, stabilita nel 1945, che comprende attualmente 22 Stati membri. Il Consiglio della Lega Araba ha adottato, nel 1994, la Carta araba sui diritti umani, che è stata poi riveduta nel 2004 [182] ed è entrata in vigore nel 2008. La Carta è un trattato vincolante, che si ispira in gran parte alla Convenzione europea ed al Patto sui diritti civili e politici; ma contiene anche diritti più "nuovi", quali il diritto allo sviluppo (art. 37) ed il diritto ad uno standard di vita adeguato, che assicuri una vita decorosa, comprensiva di cibo, vestiario, alloggio e un ambiente salubre (art. 38). Peraltro, la Carta attacca il Sionismo, equiparandolo al razzismo e considerandolo come una minaccia alla pace ed alla sicurezza internazionale (Preambolo e art. 2(3)). Infine, essa istituisce un Comitato arabo dei diritti umani (artt. 45-47) [183], con il compito di esaminare i rapporti periodici presentati dagli Stati parti (art. 48).

Per quanto riguarda gli altri Stati dell'Asia, le azioni per la tutela internazionale dei diritti umani sono state finora assai limitate. L'iniziativa più importante è stata intrapresa dalla Associazione delle Nazioni del Sud-Est Asiatico (ASEAN). I Capi di Stato e di Governo degli Stati membri di tale organizzazione hanno adottato, nel 2012, la Dichiarazione dei diritti umani dell'ASEAN [184]. Si tratta, anche in questo caso, di un documento non vincolante, ispirato alla Dichiarazione Universale; ma che contiene anche alcuni diritti umani di "terza generazione", quali il diritto ad uno standard di vita adeguato ed a un ambiente sicuro, pulito e sostenibile (art. 28), il diritto allo sviluppo (artt. 35-37), ed il diritto alla pace (art. 38).

---

[180] Cairo Declaration on Human Rights in Islam, 5 August 1990.

[181] Sul punto vedi anche Tomuschat (2014), pp. 39-40.

[182] Arab Charter on Human Rights (ArCHR), 22 May 2004.

[183] Arab Human Rights Committee.

[184] ASEAN Human Rights Declaration, 18 November 2012.

Capitolo V
I DIRITTI UMANI "FONDAMENTALI"

1. *Introduzione: una classificazione dei diritti umani*

L'ultima parte di questo libro (Capitoli V e VI) si occupa del contenuto sostanziale dei diritti umani internazionali. Tuttavia, data l'impossibilità, per motivi di spazio, di fornire un quadro completo e approfondito del contenuto di tutti i diritti umani [1], abbiamo fatto una scelta metodologica, che cerca di conciliare le esigenze di completezza sistematica di un manuale con la necessità di non limitarsi ad un riassunto superficiale dell'argomento. Pertanto cercheremo di dare un quadro complessivo del contenuto dei diritti umani nel diritto internazionale, ma di approfondire soltanto un numero limitato di diritti, che siano importanti e rappresentativi del quadro complessivo.

Questa scelta richiede anche, per motivi sistematici, di classificare, in qualche modo, i diritti umani sulla base di categorie. Premesso che la nostra è una decisione in gran parte soggettiva e discrezionale, abbiamo deciso di adottare una grande *bipartizione* fra: *a*) diritti umani che definiamo come "fondamentali", e *b*) altri diritti umani. Spiegheremo in seguito i motivi che giustificano questa soluzione.

Inoltre, all'interno di ciascuna di queste due grandi categorie, abbiamo individuato alcune sottocategorie (o gruppi) di diritti umani, sulla base soprattutto della *funzione di protezione* esercitata dal gruppo di diritti in questione, cioè della natura delle attività umane che ciascun gruppo mira a proteggere [2]. Questa *classificazione*, che ha solo lo scopo di dare un ordine logico e sistematico ai singoli diritti umani, ci sembra più idonea rispetto ad altre più tradizionali, come quella fra diverse generazioni storiche di diritti umani. Pertanto, all'interno della categoria dei "diritti umani fondamentali", distingueremo fra: *a*) protezione della vita e dell'integrità fisica della persona; *b*) protezione dei suoi *basic needs*; *c*) protezione della sua libertà e sicurezza; *d*) protezione giudiziaria essenziale della persona; *e*) protezione della sua identità essenziale; *f*) protezione della identità dei popoli. Parimenti, all'interno della categoria degli "altri diritti umani", distingueremo fra: *a*) protezione della vita privata e familiare; *b*) protezione delle attività intellettuali e culturali; *c*) protezione delle attività politiche; *d*) protezione delle attività economiche; *e*) protezione delle libertà di movimento; *f*) protezione di diritti umani collettivi.

---

[1] Infatti, la scelta più frequente, nei manuali sui diritti umani, è quella di rinunciare ad occuparsi del contenuto dei singoli diritti umani. Ma ciò costituisce, a mio avviso, una notevole lacuna. Fra le eccezioni a tale scelta, si devono ricordare: Weissbrodt, de la Vega (2007), Kälin, Künzli (2009), Focarelli (2013), Pustorino (2019).

[2] Per l'adozione di queste sotto-categorie mi sono ispirato a Kälin, Künzli (2009), che hanno adottato categorie simili, in una maniera a mio avviso molto convincente.

Tuttavia, queste nostre scelte pongono tre problemi in ordine successivo: *a*) è possibile distinguere fra categorie diverse di diritti umani oppure si deve ritenere che tutti i diritti umani formino un complesso unitario e indivisibile[3]? *b*) se è possibile distinguere fra categorie di diritti umani, è anche ammissibile stabilire una gerarchia fra categorie diverse? *c*) infine, si giustifica una categoria di diritti umani “fondamentali” e qual è, eventualmente, il suo contenuto? Si tratta di problemi importanti, che conviene affrontare prima di procedere a commentare il contenuto sostanziale dei diritti umani.

Sezione I

DISTINZIONI FRA CATEGORIE DI DIRITTI UMANI

2. *Il problema della gerarchia nell'ambito dei diritti umani*

Nel quadro delle Nazioni Unite, specie a partire dagli anni Novanta, si è venuta affermando l'idea che i diritti umani costituiscano una categoria unica e *unitaria* di diritti[4], che hanno caratteristiche comuni e, soprattutto, che essi hanno pari dignità giuridica in base ai principi di universalità, indivisibilità e interdipendenza dei medesimi. Questi principi sono stati affermati solennemente nella Dichiarazione di Vienna del 1993 e in successivi strumenti internazionali sui diritti umani adottati nell'ambito delle Nazioni Unite. Una conseguenza importante di questa impostazione è la *mancanza di una gerarchia normativa* nel quadro dei diritti umani internazionali.

Tuttavia, se in un'ottica di “politica normativa” l'idea della unitarietà e della pari dignità di tutti i diritti umani è comprensibile e forse strategicamente utile, si deve riconoscere che, da un punto di vista più strettamente giuridico e concettuale, questa idea non è convincente, poiché in realtà i diritti umani si differenziano fra loro sotto molteplici aspetti[5].

Queste differenze sono state sempre messe in luce dalla dottrina, che ha via via identificato diverse categorie di diritti umani, ed anche di obblighi relativi ai diritti umani, adottando diverse prospettive, alcune delle quali sono state già descritte. La distinzione più celebre è quella fra diritti civili e politici, da una parte, e diritti economici, sociali e culturali, dall'altra parte. In un'ottica prevalentemente storica, questa distinzione è stata in parte ripresa e assorbita da quella fra diritti umani di prima, seconda, terza e quarta generazione. Da un altro punto di vista, cioè in relazione ai destinatari dei diritti, si è spesso distinto fra diritti umani individuali e collettivi[6]. Altre distinzioni sono state proposte fra diritti giustiziabili e non giustiziabili[7], oppure fra diritti “assoluti” e non assoluti, oppure fra diritti “inderogabili” e derogabili, oppure fra diritti “fondamentali” e non fondamentali. Si è an-

---

[3] Sul punto vedi, fra gli altri, Tomuschat (2014), p. 136 ss.

[4] Cfr. Focarelli (2013), p. 128.

[5] *Ibidem*.

[6] Questi ultimi diritti sono in gran parte coincidenti con i diritti umani di terza generazione.

[7] In passato questa distinzione tendeva a coincidere con quella fra diritti di prima e di seconda generazione.

che visto che varie categorie, in parte simili, sono state proposte dalla dottrina anche in relazione agli obblighi degli Stati relativi ai diritti umani [8].

Se riflettiamo sulle distinzioni dottrinali sopra indicate, possiamo concludere che, se alcune di esse appaiono oggi superate, altre conservano senza dubbio una loro validità. È, ad esempio, innegabile che alcuni diritti umani siano "giustiziabili" ed altri non lo siano; che alcuni diritti umani si prestino ad essere attuati immediatamente dagli Stati mentre altri richiedano piuttosto un'attuazione progressiva; che alcuni diritti umani non ammettano né restrizioni né limiti né eccezioni e siano quindi "assoluti" ed altri invece ammettano restrizioni, limiti ed eccezioni da parte degli Stati; che alcuni diritti umani siano inderogabili anche in stati di guerra o pubblica emergenza ed altri invece non lo siano; che alcuni diritti umani, essendo stabiliti da norme di *ius cogens*, abbiano un grado gerarchico superiore, o quantomeno una forza di resistenza normativa maggiore, rispetto ad altri; e così via. Come si vede, si tratta di differenze giuridicamente importanti, che *smentiscono* l'idea della unitarietà e dell'uguale valore giuridico di tutti i diritti umani.

Una volta ammessa la possibilità di operare distinzioni fra categorie diverse di diritti umani, si tratta adesso di giustificare la nostra scelta di operare una ripartizione fra due grandi categorie e di approfondire il discorso sulla categoria dei diritti umani "fondamentali".

3. *La categoria dei diritti umani "fondamentali"*

Nel diritto internazionale, nel primo periodo di sviluppo storico dei diritti umani, l'espressione "diritti fondamentali" non aveva un preciso significato giuridico e non si riferiva ad una categoria autonoma e unitaria di diritti umani. Ciò probabilmente per l'influenza dei diritti statali, dove fin dai secoli XVIII e XIX, le espressioni "diritti fondamentali" o "diritti inviolabili" o "diritti inalienabili" della persona umana venivano usate in maniera equipollente, per indicare un gruppo essenziale di diritti riconosciuti alla persona umana in quanto tale [9].

Infatti, adeguandosi a questa terminologia piuttosto imprecisa, nei primi anni di sviluppo del diritto internazionale dei diritti umani, l'espressione "diritti fondamentali", sia pure non frequentemente usata, veniva di solito per essere equiparata semplicemente all'espressione "diritti umani" o "diritti dell'uomo", molto più utilizzate. Talora, per rafforzare il concetto, si usava l'endiadi "diritti dell'uomo e libertà fondamentali", come nella Convenzione europea dei diritti dell'uomo del 1950. Anche nel diritto dell'Unione Europea, i diritti umani sono stati sempre definiti come "diritti fondamentali" [10], preferendosi evidentemente utilizzare la terminologia più tipica delle costituzioni statali piuttosto che quella del diritto internazionale [11].

---

[8] Vedi *supra*, Cap. III, par. 4.

[9] Vedi De Sena, Saccucci (2007), p. 376.

[10] Vedi la giurisprudenza della Corte di giustizia e lo stesso titolo della Carta dei diritti fondamentali dell'Unione Europea.

[11] Ma si noti che, nei diritti statali, i diritti fondamentali sono di solito protetti a livello costituzionale e quindi usufruiscono di un rango gerarchico superiore, o comunque di una tutela rafforzata sul piano delle fonti interne, rispetto a tutti gli altri diritti delle persone. Vedi De Sena, Saccucci (2007), p. 377.

Tuttavia, lasciando ora da parte questi usi terminologici impropri o imprecisi del termine "diritti fondamentali", ci si deve chiedere se questo termine possa avere un contenuto autonomo e sostanziale; cioè se si possa affermare che alcuni diritti umani siano più fondamentali rispetto ad altri.

In realtà, l'idea di una gerarchia di importanza fra i diritti umani è stata spesso sostenuta, anche se con terminologie e talora contenuti diversi [12]. Ad esempio, Henry Shue ha affermato che esiste un numero limitato di "*basic rights*" che prevalgono sui "*non-basic rights*", ed ha individuato, nella prima categoria, il diritto alla sicurezza fisica, il diritto alla sussistenza ed il diritto alla libertà [13]. Altri autori privilegiano i diritti civili rispetto a tutti gli altri. Altri ancora hanno parlato di diritti umani "fondamentali" [14], o di un "nucleo fondamentale e irrinunciabile" [15] o di un "nocciolo duro" dei diritti umani, con riferimento ai soli diritti che proteggono la vita e l'integrità fisica delle persone. Un'altra parte della dottrina, specie recentemente, utilizza il concetto di "*core rights*" [16]; ed anche la Corte europea dei diritti umani usa, in alcuni suoi documenti ufficiali, la distinzione fra "*core rights*" e "*other rights and freedoms*" [17].

In queste tesi, non ci sembra tanto importante la terminologia (*fundamental rights, basic rights, core rights*), quanto l'idea di una *bipartizione* fra i diritti umani sulla base della loro importanza. Pertanto, riteniamo sia corretto, quantomeno come ipotesi di partenza, fare una ripartizione (adottando la terminologia più semplice e diretta) fra "diritti umani fondamentali" ed "altri diritti umani". Il termine "diritti fondamentali" ci sembra il più semplice e diretto, e quindi preferibile ad altri termini, quale ad esempio quello di "*core rights*", che, come vedremo, ha un significato assai incerto.

Ma quali sono i criteri distintivi della categoria dei diritti "fondamentali"? In altri termini, quali diritti umani sono compresi in questa categoria? Premesso che la risposta a queste domande ha carattere relativo poiché deriva da una nostra scelta soggettiva, esamineremo qui di seguito, in maniera critica, alcune possibili tesi, per poi proporre la conclusione che ci sembra più convincente ed utile dal punto di vista giuridico.

4. *I possibili criteri distintivi della categoria dei diritti "fondamentali"*

4.1. *Il criterio dei diritti ritenuti "essenziali" o "preminenti" nel quadro dei trattati sui diritti umani. Critica*

Secondo alcuni, il criterio per individuare i diritti umani "fondamentali" si potrebbe dedurre soprattutto dalla giurisprudenza e prassi di alcuni organi di controllo sui diritti

---

[12] Sul tema della gerarchia fra i diritti umani vedi, fra gli altri, Shue (1980); Meron (1986); Sudre (1995); Carrillo Salcedo (1997); Iovane (2000); De Frouville (2004); De Wet, Vidmar (eds.) (2012); Cassese (2012); Scheinin (2013).

[13] Shue (1980), p. 18 ss.

[14] De Sena, Saccucci (2007), p. 378.

[15] Conforti (2015), p. 214.

[16] Vedi, ad es., Scheinin (2013).

[17] Vedi, ad esempio, gli *Annual Reports* della Corte.

umani. In particolare, la Corte europea dei diritti umani, nella propria giurisprudenza, ha talora riconosciuto un carattere "essenziale" o "preminente" a certi diritti umani, che pure non avevano natura inderogabile in stati di emergenza né erano stabiliti da norme imperative (di *ius cogens*). Si tratta, soprattutto, del diritto all'integrità fisica, del diritto alla libertà ed alla sicurezza della persona, della libertà di espressione, della libertà di pensiero, di coscienza e di religione, del diritto a libere elezioni e del diritto ad un processo equo.

Tuttavia, a parte i primi due diritti, gli altri sono tutti diritti di prima generazione, legati a valori tipicamente occidentali ed al concetto di società democratica. Pertanto non ci sembra che questo criterio, del resto piuttosto vago, di "essenzialità" o "preminenza" di tali diritti rispetto a tutti gli altri, possa essere utilizzato per individuare la categoria dei diritti "fondamentali" che deve evidentemente operare a livello universale.

Anche il Comitato dei diritti umani ha talora parlato di diritti "di profonda importanza", ad esempio con riferimento al diritto alla libertà personale ed ai diritti delle minoranze. Ma anche questa prassi, peraltro piuttosto limitata, non appare di per sé significativa ai fini della ricostruzione di una categoria universale di diritti umani "fondamentali".

4.2. *Il criterio dei diritti "assoluti". Critica*

Un altro criterio, talora suggerito per individuare la categoria dei diritti umani "fondamentali", è quello dei diritti "assoluti". L'uso di questa terminologia non è univoco; a nostro avviso, si dovrebbe parlare di diritti "assoluti" soltanto per quei diritti umani che non sono soggetti né a clausole di restrizione né a limiti né ad eccezioni.

In realtà, vi è un numero assai limitato di diritti umani, che possono essere definiti come "assoluti"; ed essi comprendono alcuni diritti assai importanti. Ma esistono diritti altrettanto importanti (nel senso che la loro violazione costituisce un grave attentato alla dignità umana) che purtuttavia consentono eccezioni e restrizioni. Ad esempio, fra i diritti "assoluti" si possono annoverare il divieto di genocidio, il divieto di tortura e di trattamento inumano, e il divieto di schiavitù. Ma non può essere considerato come "assoluto" il diritto alla vita, perché esso ammette limiti (ad esempio, l'uso letale della forza in certe circostanze) ed anche eccezioni nel diritto internazionale generale (la pena di morte non è ovunque vietata). Ed è difficile sostenere che il diritto alla vita sia inferiore, come importanza, rispetto al divieto di trattamento inumano o al divieto di schiavitù. In altri termini, se si ammette la categoria dei diritti umani "fondamentali", è difficile giustificare il fatto che il diritto alla vita non appartenga a tale categoria. Un discorso simile si può fare per il divieto di discriminazione, che, pur essendo un diritto che sta alla base della tutela internazionale dei diritti umani, e quindi "fondamentale", ammette restrizioni.

Da ciò si deduce che il criterio dei diritti "assoluti", anche se è utile per individuare una categoria di diritti che ha certe caratteristiche, non è idoneo ad identificare la categoria dei diritti umani "fondamentali" [18].

---

[18] Una simile conclusione è raggiunta da Scheinin, per escludere che il criterio dei diritti assoluti serva per identificare la categoria dei "core rights". Cfr. Scheinin (2013), pp. 531-532.

4.3. *Il criterio dei diritti definiti come "inderogabili in stati di emergenza". Critica*

Come si è già visto, i più importanti trattati sui diritti umani individuano, di solito in maniera esplicita, alcuni diritti che non possono essere derogati dagli Stati neppure nelle situazioni di guerra, di pubblico pericolo o di altra emergenza che metta in pericolo la sicurezza o la vita della nazione.

Conviene chiarire subito che la categoria dei diritti "inderogabili in stati di emergenza" non coincide con la categoria dei diritti "assoluti": i motivi che stanno alla base delle due categorie sono diversi e la prima categoria è più ampia della seconda. Né vi è coincidenza, nonostante la terminologia ingannevole, fra i diritti "inderogabili in stati di emergenza" ed i diritti contemplati da norme imperative (di *ius cogens*) del diritto internazionale generale. Anche in questo caso si deve ritenere che i motivi che giustificano il carattere di "inderogabilità in stati di emergenza" sono diversi da quelli sui quali si fonda la natura imperativa di certe norme. Ciò è stato riconosciuto anche dal Comitato dei diritti umani che, nel suo Commento Generale n. 29, ha affermato che la "inderogabilità convenzionale" di certi diritti umani non coincide con la natura imperativa delle norme che li contemplano.

Ciò premesso, si deve anche notare che la categoria dei "diritti inderogabili in stati di emergenza" non è ben definita, poiché il catalogo di tali diritti contenuto nei trattati sui diritti umani non è univoco. Ciò si desume anche solo dall'esame dei tre principali trattati sui diritti umani aventi carattere generale. L'art. 15 della Convenzione europea considera inderogabili il diritto alla vita (salvo in caso di uccisioni derivanti da atti leciti di guerra), il divieto di tortura e di trattamenti o punizioni inumane o degradanti, il divieto di schiavitù o servitù, il divieto di irretroattività della legge penale. L'art. 4 del Patto sui diritti civili e politici considera anch'esso inderogabili i suddetti diritti; ma aggiunge anche il divieto di imprigionamento per inadempimenti contrattuali, il diritto di riconoscimento come persona dinanzi alla legge e perfino la libertà di pensiero, coscienza e religione. Quanto all'art. 27 della Convenzione americana dei diritti umani, esso amplia molto la categoria dei diritti inderogabili nelle situazioni sopra descritte, perché, oltre ai diritti indicati come inderogabili nella Convenzione europea, include anche il diritto ad una personalità giuridica, la libertà di coscienza e religione, i diritti della famiglia, il diritto ad un nome, i diritti dei fanciulli, il diritto ad una nazionalità, il diritto di partecipazione politica, ed infine le garanzie giurisdizionali essenziali per la protezione dei suddetti diritti. Inoltre, sia il Patto sui diritti civili e politici che la Convenzione americana considerano come inderogabile il divieto di discriminazione, perché prevedono che, anche nelle situazioni di guerra o di pubblica emergenza, lo Stato non possa prendere misure che comportino discriminazione per motivi di razza, colore, sesso, lingua, religione o origine sociale.

L'esame di queste convenzioni rivela che vi sono differenze significative fra di esse circa il catalogo dei diritti considerati come inderogabili, e che, tenendo conto delle date in cui esse sono state firmate, vi è una tendenza ad ampliare nel tempo tale catalogo. Inoltre, si deve sottolineare il fatto che gli organi di controllo delle suddette convenzioni hanno manifestato un orientamento interpretativo tendente ad ampliare ulteriormente la categoria dei diritti inderogabili. Ad esempio, la Corte europea dei diritti umani sembra ritenere inderogabili, nell'ambito della Convenzione europea, anche il diritto ad un ricorso effettivo ed il divieto di discriminazione. Il Comitato dei diritti umani, nel suo Commento Generale n. 29 del 2001, sembra ritenere almeno parzialmente inderogabili anche il divieto di deportazioni di massa, il rispetto di alcune garanzie del giusto processo (*fair trial*) e della libertà personale. La Corte interamericana include fra i diritti inderogabili, nel quadro della Convenzione americana, anche il diritto all'*habeas corpus*, il diritto ad un ricorso effettivo ed alcune garanzie del giusto processo.

Quali conclusioni si possono ricavare da questo quadro normativo e interpretativo?

A livello di diritto internazionale convenzionale, il fatto che la lista dei diritti inderogabili in stati di emergenza non sia coincidente nelle tre convenzioni citate, né in altri trattati sui diritti umani, non costituisce un problema. È chiaro che ciascuno Stato sarà obbligato a rispettare le disposizioni sulla inderogabilità previste nei trattati che esso ha ratificato. Nel caso di ratifica di più trattati lo Stato dovrà applicare la disposizione che prevede un maggior numero di diritti inderogabili; cioè quella più favorevole ai diritti degli individui [19].

Quanto invece al diritto internazionale generale, ci sembra da escludere che si siano formate norme consuetudinarie, che abbiano recepito un elenco preciso dei diritti "inderogabili in stati di emergenza", viste le notevoli diversità che emergono dal diritto convenzionale. Tutt'al più, si può supporre che vi sia un consenso generalizzato degli Stati sul catalogo minimo di tali diritti stabilito dall'art. 15 della Convenzione europea.

In definitiva, a nostro avviso, il criterio della "inderogabilità in stati di emergenza" non può servire per identificare la categoria dei diritti umani "fondamentali".

4.4. *Il criterio dei diritti stabiliti dal diritto internazionale generale*

Per dare un contenuto alla categoria dei diritti umani "fondamentali", un criterio più valido di quelli finora discussi è quello dei diritti umani che si sono affermati nel diritto internazionale generale. Come abbiamo già detto, il principio di universalità dei diritti umani può dirsi *veramente* realizzato, da un punto di vista giuridico, soltanto per quei diritti umani che, in virtù di norme consuetudinarie, di principi di diritto generalmente riconosciuti *in foro domestico* o di principi del diritto internazionale, godono del consenso o riconoscimento da parte dell'intera comunità internazionale.

Ma quali sono in concreto questi diritti umani? Si deve ammettere che non è facile individuare con precisione quali diritti umani si siano effettivamente affermati nel diritto internazionale generale. Ciò dipende da vari fattori: *a*) la nota difficoltà di rilevare il diritto non scritto; *b*) l'accresciuta difficoltà di rilevazione nel settore dei diritti umani, dove la prassi interstatale non è abbondante; *c*) la diversità delle tesi esistenti sul modo di rilevazione della consuetudine e sull'importanza (se non addirittura sull'esistenza) dei principi generali di diritto *in foro domestico* e dei principi del diritto internazionale.

Questi fattori spiegano perché la dottrina non offra una risposta univoca alla suddetta domanda e perché anche istituzioni ed organi internazionali autorevoli possano pervenire a risposte diverse. Basti confrontare il catalogo, piuttosto restrittivo, dei diritti umani protetti dal diritto internazionale generale che si ricava dal *Restatement of the Foreign Relations Law of the United States* [20] con quello, assai più estensivo, che risulta dai Commenti Generali del Comitato dei diritti umani [21].

---

[19] Vedi Cataldi (2007), p. 384.

[20] *Restatement of the Foreign Relations Law of the United States*, 1986, adopted and promulgated by the American Law Institute, 14 May 1986 (ALI Publ., Washington 1987), par. 702.

[21] Vedi, ad es., HRCtee, General Comment No. 24, 4 November 1994, par. 8.

Nonostante queste difficoltà, cercheremo, nell'esaminare i singoli diritti umani, di esprimere la nostra opinione sul fatto se essi siano o no riconosciuti dal diritto internazionale generale[22]. In ogni caso, ci preme adesso riaffermare che i diritti umani protetti dal diritto internazionale generale possono essere definiti come *effettivamente* universali; che per questo motivo essi possono essere considerati più importanti rispetto agli altri diritti umani; e che pertanto essi sono i più adatti a rappresentare la categoria dei diritti umani "fondamentali". Riprendendo un'immagine che avevamo proposto nel Capitolo I, questi diritti, nel rapporto fra universalismo e multiculturalismo rappresentato da due cerchi concentrici, configurano il cerchio più piccolo.

Ma si può anche ritenere che i diritti umani riconosciuti dal diritto internazionale generale, oltre a possedere un'importanza particolare, si pongano anche su un *livello gerarchico superiore* rispetto agli altri diritti umani? In altri termini, si può mettere in discussione il "mito onusiano" della mancanza di gerarchia fra i diritti umani? Per rispondere a questa domanda, si deve riprendere il discorso sul ruolo dello *ius cogens* in materia di diritti umani.

4.5. *Il criterio dei diritti stabiliti da norme o principi di* ius cogens

Un altro criterio, che è stato talora suggerito per identificare la categoria dei diritti umani "fondamentali", è rappresentato dallo *ius cogens*. Secondo questo criterio, i diritti umani protetti dallo *ius cogens* dovrebbero essere definiti come "fondamentali"[23].

A nostro avviso, si può usare questa definizione, purché si chiarisca che i diritti umani tutelati dallo *ius cogens* sono non soltanto "fondamentali", ma *anche* "imperativi"; cioè hanno, *come ulteriore caratteristica*, gli elementi tipici di tutte le norme internazionali imperative: l'inderogabilità e la prevalenza gerarchica.

Il discorso generale sullo *ius cogens* è complesso e non può essere qui affrontato. Ai nostri fini, ci limitiamo a ricordare che le norme e principi di *ius cogens*, esprimendo alcuni valori *essenziali, fondamentali ed inderogabili* dell'intera comunità internazionale[24], indicano la tendenza del diritto internazionale contemporaneo a stabilire una scala normativa di valori al cui vertice si pongono appunto tali norme[25]. A nostro avviso, questa scala di valori si applica anche nel settore dei diritti umani; e pertanto le norme di *ius cogens* hanno formato una gerarchia normativa anche nel quadro dei diritti umani. L'idea di una *gerarchia normativa* nei diritti umani internazionali può essere oggi affermata alla luce non solo degli sviluppi generali del diritto internazionale, ma anche di quelli verificatisi nel settore stesso della tutela internazionale dei diritti umani. Basti ricordare quanto abbiamo già detto in relazione all'impatto che la teoria dei diritti umani ha esercitato sul diritto internazionale[26] e sulla progressiva affermazione di una natura "pubblicistica" o "costituzionalistica" di tale diritto.

Ma, a questo punto, si pongono due domande: quali sono i diritti umani protetti dallo *ius cogens*? E vi è coincidenza fra questa categoria e quella dei diritti umani stabiliti dal

---

[22] Vedi anche *infra*, parr. 4.4 e 4.5.

[23] De Sena, Saccucci (2007), p. 378.

[24] Vedi *supra*, Cap. I, parr. 7.3.2 e 7.4.2.

[25] Vedi, per tutti, Cassese (2006), p. 199.

[26] Vedi *supra*, Cap. I, par. 7.

diritto internazionale generale? Anche su questo punto la dottrina è divisa; e si possono distinguere, in sintesi, due tesi generali.

Secondo un primo gruppo di autori, le due categorie tendono sostanzialmente a coincidere e comprendono un nucleo assai ristretto di diritti umani [27]. In sostanza questo nucleo viene identificato, o descritto, tramite il concetto del "divieto di *gross violations* dei diritti umani". Per la verità, tale concetto non è sempre interpretato in maniera univoca; ma di solito intende riferirsi al divieto di violazioni *gravi, sistematiche ed organizzate* di diritti umani fondamentali (e di principi fondamentali del diritto internazionale umanitario [28]). La "gravità" riguarda il particolare attentato alla dignità della persona, la "sistematicità" attiene al numero delle vittime ed alla durata della violazione, ed infine l'"organizzazione" significa che le violazioni presuppongono quasi sempre un disegno messo in opera da uno Stato o da un ente o gruppo di persone organizzato [29]. Partendo da questa impostazione, questa dottrina di solito include, nella categoria delle *gross violations*, i divieti di genocidio, di crimini contro l'umanità e di crimini di guerra; di pratiche di tortura, di trattamenti o punizioni disumani, di schiavitù e tratta degli schiavi, di discriminazione razziale e *apartheid*; nonché la violazione del diritto di autodeterminazione dei popoli. Tuttavia, alcuni autori tendono ad ampliare questo catalogo, aggiungendo i divieti di privazione arbitraria della libertà e di lavori forzati [30] o il divieto generale di discriminazione [31].

Un secondo gruppo di studiosi sostiene, invece, che non vi è coincidenza fra le due categorie di diritti umani. Ma ciò non dipende dal catalogo dei diritti protetti dallo *ius cogens*, che viene ritenuto, grosso modo, uguale a quello sopra indicato; bensì dal catalogo dei diritti stabiliti dal diritto internazionale generale, che sarebbe più ampio del primo [32]. In altri termini, secondo questa tesi, il diritto internazionale generale protegge non solo tutti i diritti umani riconosciuti come di *ius cogens*, ma *anche ulteriori diritti*; e vieta violazioni che non hanno necessariamente carattere "grave", "sistematico" ed "organizzato", ma possono anche consistere in abusi singoli, isolati e commessi nei confronti di singoli individui. In sostanza, la categoria dei diritti umani regolati dal diritto internazionale generale andrebbe al di là del "divieto di *gross violations*". Su questa base, ad esempio, sarebbero vietati anche singoli atti di tortura o di trattamento inumano o di uccisione arbitraria o di privazione arbitraria della libertà o di discriminazione razziale o di privazione di un diritto di sussistenza o di diniego di accesso alla giustizia [33].

A nostro avviso, questa seconda tesi è più convincente; e cercheremo di precisarla meglio quando esamineremo i singoli diritti umani. Per adesso, conviene ribadire che l'ade-

---

[27] Vedi, ad es., Conforti (2018), pp. 216-217; Cassese (2006), pp. 205-206.

[28] Cfr. Cassese (2006), p. 206.

[29] Vedi Iovane (2007), p. 675.

[30] Conforti (2018), p. 216.

[31] Cassese (2006), p. 205. Vedi anche Pustorino (2019), pp. 23-24, che tende ad estendere ulteriormente l'ambito applicativo dello *ius cogens* in materia di diritti umani.

[32] Vedi, ad es., Tomuschat (2014), pp. 42-45; Kälin, Künzi (2009), pp. 68-71.

[33] Alcuni autori aggiungono altri diritti, quali il diritto di proprietà o alcuni diritti sociali o perfino quei diritti umani che sono inclusi nella Dichiarazione Universale, ma non sono stati ripresi dal Patto sui diritti civili e politici. Vedi, ad es., Pustorino (2019), p. 24; Tomuschat (2014), pp. 42-44 e la dottrina ivi citata. Ci sembra che queste opinioni tendano ad estendere troppo il catalogo dei diritti umani riconosciuti dal diritto internazionale generale.

sione a questa tesi significa, come avevamo anticipato, che vi è un gruppo (non molto ampio, ma neppure esiguo) di diritti umani "fondamentali", che è costituito da quelli protetti dal diritto internazionale generale; e che, all'interno di questo gruppo, vi è un nucleo più ristretto di diritti umani che sono anche "imperativi", cioè che possiedono le caratteristiche ulteriori e aggiuntive della "inderogabilità" e della "superiorità gerarchica", che sono proprie in via generale dello *ius cogens*.

5. *I concetti di* "core rights", "core content" *e* "core obligations"

In tempi recenti, alcuni organi internazionali di controllo dei trattati sui diritti umani ed alcuni autori hanno iniziato ad utilizzare le nozioni di *core rights*, *core content* dei diritti umani e *core obligations*. Conviene tenere distinti i tre concetti, anche se talora vengono confusi.

Il concetto di *core rights* è usato per "definire alcuni diritti umani come superiori o più fondamentali rispetto ad altri diritti umani"[34]. Se la nozione ha solo questo significato generico, essa può anche essere accettata, poiché si tratta soltanto di una questione terminologica: il termine *core rights* può, per alcuni, essere migliore rispetto al termine "diritti fondamentali", che noi riteniamo invece preferibile[35].

Tuttavia, il vero problema è dato dal fatto che i sostenitori del concetto di *core rights* non hanno chiarito il contenuto esatto di tale concetto; cioè quali siano i caratteri giuridici distintivi della categoria dei *core rights* e quali diritti umani siano compresi in tale categoria. La Corte europea dei diritti umani utilizza la nozione di *core rights* soltanto in alcuni documenti[36] ai fini di tenerli separati dagli altri diritti; i *core rights* sono quelli regolati dagli artt. 2, 3, 4, e 5 della Convenzione europea. Ma la Corte non approfondisce gli elementi distintivi della categoria. La dottrina non mostra di avere idee più precise. Un autore[37], ad esempio, analizza e poi respinge i tre criteri che potrebbero essere usati per identificare la categoria dei *core rights*: *a*) quello dei diritti che derivano dalla dignità della persona umana; *b*) quello dei diritti "assoluti"; *c*) quello dei diritti "inderogabili in stati di emergenza". E poi contesta l'idea di una gerarchia fra i diritti umani e, in sostanza, anche il concetto stesso di *core rights*.

In conclusione, la categoria dei *core rights* rimane per ora assai incerta e indefinita sia in dottrina che nella prassi; e pertanto non può essere accolta nel presente libro.

Il concetto di *core content* (contenuto essenziale) dei diritti umani va tenuto separato e distinto da quello di *core rights*. La questione del *core content* consiste nel chiedersi se, all'interno dei diritti umani o di alcuni diritti umani, è possibile identificare un contenuto essenziale ed inviolabile[38]. Si tratta di un problema importante, che non può essere ridotto ad una semplice questione terminologica. Tuttavia, a nostro avviso, il concetto di *core content* non è convincente.

---

[34] Scheinin (2013), p. 527.

[35] Vedi *supra*, par. 3.

[36] Vedi, ad es., ECtHR, *Annual Report 2017, Overview of the Court's case-law*.

[37] Scheinin (2013).

[38] *Ibidem*, p. 532.

Un primo elemento di forte perplessità riguarda l'idea stessa che un diritto umano possa essere scomposto o frazionato in due o più contenuti; e che quindi possano coesistere, all'interno di un diritto, un contenuto "essenziale" ed uno o più contenuti "non essenziali". A noi sembra che questa idea debba essere sgombrata da due confusioni concettuali.

In primo luogo, non si deve confondere il discorso dei contenuti di un diritto con quello, assai diverso, delle norme che regolano un diritto. Infatti, è possibile che un certo diritto umano sia regolato da norme diverse, non solo pattizie come è ovvio, ma anche talora consuetudinarie. E che tali norme abbiano un contenuto diverso. Ad esempio, come vedremo meglio in seguito, la norma sul diritto alla vita della Convenzione europea dei diritti umani esclude adesso l'eccezione della pena di morte, mentre la norma sul diritto alla vita del Patto sui diritti civili e politici prevede tale eccezione. Oppure, per fare un altro esempio, la norma generale sul diritto ad un cibo adeguato, che emerge dai trattati sui diritti umani, è diversa dalla norma che vieta di privare il cibo indispensabile alla sussistenza delle persone, che invece emerge dai trattati di diritto internazionale umanitario.

In secondo luogo, non si deve confondere il discorso dei contenuti di un diritto con quello degli obblighi, corrispondenti al diritto, che una norma può prevedere. È chiaro, come si è già visto, che una certa norma che regola un determinato diritto umano può stabilire un'ampia pluralità di obblighi, anche di natura diversa, a carico di uno Stato.

Un secondo elemento di perplessità, sul concetto di *core content* dei diritti umani, deriva, anche in questo caso, dal fatto che tale concetto è assai incerto e indefinito, sia nella prassi che in dottrina. Innanzitutto, non sono chiari gli elementi che caratterizzano tale concetto. In particolare, non si comprende se il *core content* dei diritti umani abbia il carattere della "assolutezza", cioè non sia soggetto ad eccezioni, limiti o restrizioni; oppure abbia il carattere della "inderogabilità in stati di emergenza"; oppure addirittura il carattere di *ius cogens*.

Il Comitato dei diritti umani, che è l'organo internazionale di controllo che ha maggiormente utilizzato il concetto di *core content*, mostra incertezze su questo punto. Nei suoi Commenti Generali n. 27 e n. 31, il Comitato ha utilizzato la nozione di "essenza" (*essence*) di un diritto umano ed ha affermato che le *restrizioni* a tale diritto non possono mai pregiudicare tale "essenza" [39]. Invece, nel suo Commento Generale n. 34, il Comitato, parlando della libertà di opinione e di espressione, ha affermato che, anche se la libertà di opinione non è elencata dal Patto fra i diritti inderogabili in stato di emergenza, ci possono essere elementi in tale diritto che non sono soggetti a *deroghe* [40]. Ma poi ha detto che:

> "Paragraph 1 of Article 19 requires protection of the right to hold opinion without interference. This is a right to which the Covenant permits no *exception or restriction*" [41].

Nel Commento Generale n. 32, il Comitato sembra sostenere che, in certi casi, il diritto ad un giusto processo non può subire né deroghe in stati di emergenza né restrizioni. Infatti, prima si afferma che:

---

[39] HRCtee, General Comment No. 27, 2 November 1999, par. 13; General Comment No. 31, 26 May 2004, par. 6.

[40] HRCtee, General Comment No. 34, 12 September 2011, par. 5.

[41] *Ibidem*, par. 9 (corsivo aggiunto).

> "States derogating from normal procedures required under article 14 in circumstances of a public emergency should ensure that such derogations do not exceed those strictly required by the exigencies of the actual situation" [42].

E poi si aggiunge:

> "The failure of a State party to establish a competent tribunal to determine such rights and obligations or to allow access to such a tribunal in specific cases would amount to a violation of article 14 if […] the access left to an individual would be limited to an extent that would undermine the very essence of the right" [43].

Pertanto, sembra che, per il Comitato dei diritti umani, il *core content* di un diritto umano sia quel contenuto minimo essenziale che non è soggetto né a restrizioni né a deroghe in stati di emergenza.

Invece, la Carta dei diritti fondamentali dell'UE utilizza il concetto di *core content* soltanto con riferimento al suo carattere "assoluto". Infatti, l'art. 52(1) della Carta stabilisce che:

> "Any *limitation* on the exercise of the rights and freedoms recognised by this Charter must be provided for by law and respect the *essence* of those rights and freedoms" [44].

In secondo luogo, non è chiaro se il concetto di *core content* si debba applicare a tutti i diritti umani [45] oppure soltanto ad alcuni diritti. La prima soluzione è contraddittoria: un diritto umano che è già di per sé "assoluto" (ad esempio, il divieto di tortura) non ha certo bisogno di un *core content* "assoluto". Similmente, un diritto umano che è già di per sé "inderogabile in stati di emergenza" non ha bisogno di un *core content* con i medesimi caratteri. Lo stesso discorso si può fare per un diritto umano che sia di *ius cogens*: non ha molto senso ritenere, ad esempio, che il divieto di genocidio abbia un suo *core content*.

In conclusione, il concetto di *core content* è concettualmente confuso e non è stato chiarito dai suoi sostenitori nei suoi elementi essenziali. Pertanto, non può essere qui accolto.

Veniamo infine al concetto di *core obligations*. La questione qui si sposta dal campo dei diritti umani di una persona a quello degli obblighi degli Stati che corrispondono a tali diritti. Essa consiste nel chiedersi se si possano identificare alcune *core obligations* o *minimum core obligations*, cioè degli obblighi relativi ai diritti umani che siano "more burning, more immediate, or more compelling" [46] rispetto ad altri obblighi. La nozione di *core obligations* è stata introdotta nel diritto internazionale dei diritti umani a partire dagli anni 1980, specie in relazione ai diritti economici, sociali e culturali. Nei c.d. Principi di Limburg [47] si raccomandava che gli Stati, senza riguardo per il loro livello di sviluppo economico, assumessero gli obblighi di "ensure respect for minimum subsistence rights". In se-

---

[42] HRCtee, General Comment No. 32, 23 August 2007, par. 6.

[43] *Ibidem*, par. 18.

[44] Corsivi aggiunti.

[45] Questa sembra essere l'opinione di Scheinin (2013), pp. 532-535.

[46] Scheinin (2013), p. 536.

[47] *Limburg Principles on the Implementation of the International Covenant on Economic, Social and Cultural Rights*, Maastricht, 2-6 June 1985.

guito la dottrina ha sviluppato il concetto che a ciascun diritto umano corrisponda un "absolute minimum entitlement" [48] e la nozione di "minimum core obligations" [49].

Va subito detto che il concetto di *core obligations* è, in linea teorica, più corretto rispetto a quello di *core content* sopra esaminato. Infatti, come si è detto, è concepibile, ed anzi assai frequente, che ad un unico diritto umano corrisponda una pluralità di obblighi ed anche che alcuni di questi siano più immediati o più vincolanti rispetto ad altri.

Il concetto di *core obligations* è stato finora utilizzato soprattutto dal Comitato dei diritti economici, sociali e culturali. Come abbiamo già detto [50], il Patto sui diritti economici, sociali e culturali prevede a carico degli Stati parti, per l'attuazione dei diritti ivi contenuti, soprattutto obblighi "a realizzazione progressiva" [51]. Ciò tuttavia non esclude l'esistenza di alcuni obblighi di natura diversa. E in effetti il Comitato ESCR ha cercato di identificare questi ultimi obblighi che vengono appunto definiti come *core obligations* o *minimum core obligations*. Ad esempio, nel suo Commento Generale n. 3 [52], il Comitato sostiene che gli Stati hanno un "minimum core obligation" che consiste nell'assicurare "satisfaction of, at the very least, minimum essential levels of each of the rights". Quindi offre gli esempi del cibo essenziale, di una tutela primaria della salute, di un alloggio di base o delle forme più elementari di educazione [53]. Altri Commenti Generali successivi hanno ripreso questo concetto. Ad esempio, nel Commento Generale n. 12, dedicato al diritto al cibo, il Comitato ha affermato che:

> "The right to adequate food will have to be realized progressively. However, States have a *core obligation* to take the necessary action to mitigate and alleviate hunger as provided for in paragraph 2 of article 11, even in times of natural or other disasters [...]" [54].

Ma quali sono le caratteristiche esatte delle *core obligations*? Il loro carattere più importante sembra essere l'*immediatezza*. Se le norme sui diritti economici, sociali e culturali richiedono, di solito, agli Stati obblighi progressivi, tali norme possono anche, in via eccezionale, richiedere agli Stati di adempiere immediatamente alcuni obblighi minimi essenziali relativi al diritto in questione. Vi sono altri effetti delle *core obligations*? Un autore [55] ha sostenuto che le *core obligations* sono giustiziabili, non consentono agli Stati di prendere misure regressive e non consentono agli Stati di invocare la scusa della mancanza di risorse. Questa tesi non convince: a mio parere, il primo di questi effetti non opera per tutte le *core obligations*; mentre gli altri due effetti operano per tutti gli obblighi "a realizzazione progressiva" [56] e non per le sole *core obligations*.

In conclusione, il concetto di *core obligations* è l'unico, fra i tre qui esaminati, che può essere accolto. Ma esso funziona, come una sorta di eccezione, soltanto nel quadro di dirit-

---

[48] Alston (1987), p. 352.

[49] Vedi, ad es., Scheinin (2013); Forman (2016a); Id. (2016b).

[50] Vedi *supra*, Cap. III, par. 5.3.

[51] Vedi Pisillo Mazzeschi (2008), pp. 290-297 e 429-489.

[52] CteeESCR, General Comment No. 3, 14 December 1990.

[53] *Ibidem*, par. 10.

[54] CteeESCR, General Comment No. 12, 12 May 1999, par. 6 (corsivo aggiunto).

[55] Scheinin (2013), pp. 536-538.

[56] Vedi Pisillo Mazzeschi (2008), pp. 445-484.

ti umani che prevedono di solito obblighi "a realizzazione progressiva", e l'unico suo carattere rilevante è quello di essere un obbligo *immediato*.

6. *Conclusioni*

Sulla base di quanto detto finora, ci sembra giustificata la nostra scelta di adottare una bipartizione generale fra la categoria dei diritti umani "fondamentali" e quella degli altri diritti umani. Per noi, i diritti umani "fondamentali" sono quelli riconosciuti dal diritto internazionale generale. Fra di essi vi è poi un nucleo più ristretto di diritti umani, che sono stabiliti da norme o principi di carattere imperativo; ed hanno quindi anche le caratteristiche tipiche dello *ius cogens*.

In questo Capitolo, esamineremo i diritti umani "fondamentali" e, nel Capitolo VI, gli altri diritti umani. All'interno delle due categorie, distingueremo i diritti sulla base delle sottocategorie che abbiamo già indicato[57].

Sezione II

PROTEZIONE DELLA VITA E DELL'INTEGRITÀ FISICA DELLA PERSONA

Nel quadro dei diritti umani "fondamentali", conviene esaminare, innanzitutto, un primo gruppo di diritti che ha lo scopo di tutelare la vita e l'integrità fisica delle persone. Non vi è dubbio che questo scopo abbia carattere preminente nel sistema di tutela internazionale dei diritti umani; e che pertanto i diritti appartenenti a questo gruppo meritino di essere trattati in maniera piuttosto ampia. Essi comprendono: *a*) il diritto alla vita; *b*) il divieto di tortura e di trattamenti o pene inumani o degradanti; *c*) il divieto di crimini internazionali. Quest'ultimo divieto comprende, a sua volta, alcune sottocategorie.

7. *Diritto alla vita*

7.1. *Norme*

Il diritto alla vita è previsto dalla Dichiarazione universale dei diritti dell'uomo in termini molto generali. L'art. 3 proclama che:

> "Everyone has the right to life [...]".

Invece le principali convenzioni sui diritti umani contengono disposizioni più specifiche. La Convenzione europea, all'art. 2, afferma:

---

[57] Vedi *supra*, par. 1.

"1. Everyone's right to life shall be protected by law. No one shall be deprived of his life intentionally save in the execution of a sentence of a court following his conviction of a crime for which this penalty is provided by law.

2. Deprivation of life shall not be regarded as inflicted in contravention of this Article when it results from the use of force which is no more than absolutely necessary: (a) in defence of any person from unlawful violence; (b) in order to effect a lawful arrest or to prevent the escape of a person lawfully detained; (c) in action lawfully taken for the purpose of quelling a riot or insurrection".

Si noti che il par. 1 enuncia il diritto alla vita e regola i casi in cui si può privare la vita in esecuzione di una pena di morte. Il par. 2, invece, stabilisce che la privazione della vita è legittima quando la morte risulta da un ricorso alla forza resosi assolutamente necessario in alcune circostanze che vengono espressamente indicate.

Il Patto sui diritti civili e politici non contiene una disposizione altrettanto specifica su questo ultimo punto, poiché l'art. 6 si limita a stabilire che "No one shall be arbitrarily deprived of his life" [58]. D'altra parte, il Patto contiene disposizioni sulla pena di morte più elaborate e complesse rispetto a quella della CEDU. Il diritto alla vita è previsto anche dall'art. 4 della Convenzione americana [59], dall'art. 4 della Carta africana, dagli artt. 5-7 della Carta araba e dall'art. 2 della Carta dei diritti fondamentali dell'UE. Vi sono poi al-

---

[58] CCPR, art. 6:

"1. Every human being has the inherent right to life. This right shall be protected by law. No one shall be arbitrarily deprived of his life.

2. In countries which have not abolished the death penalty, sentence of death may be imposed only for the most serious crimes in accordance with the law in force at the time of the commission of the crime and not contrary to the provisions of the present Covenant and to the Convention on the Prevention and Punishment of the Crime of Genocide. This penalty can only be carried out pursuant to a final judgement rendered by a competent court.

3. When deprivation of life constitutes the crime of genocide, it is understood that nothing in this article shall authorize any State Party to the present Covenant to derogate in any way from any obligation assumed under the provisions of the Convention on the Prevention and Punishment of the Crime of Genocide.

4. Anyone sentenced to death shall have the right to seek pardon or commutation of the sentence. Amnesty, pardon or commutation of the sentence of death may be granted in all cases.

5. Sentence of death shall not be imposed for crimes committed by persons below eighteen years of age and shall not be carried out on pregnant women.

6. Nothing in this article shall be invoked to delay or to prevent the abolition of capital punishment by any State Party to the present Covenant".

[59] ACHR, art. 4:

"1. Every person has the right to have his life respected. This right shall be protected by law and, in general, from the moment of conception. No one shall be arbitrarily deprived of his life.

2. In countries that have not abolished the death penalty, it may be imposed only for the most serious crimes and pursuant to a final judgment rendered by a competent court and in accordance with a law establishing such punishment, enacted prior to the commission of the crime. The application of such punishment shall not be extended to crimes to which it does not presently apply.

3. The death penalty shall not be reestablished in states that have abolished it.

4. In no case shall capital punishment be inflicted for political offenses or related common crimes.

5. Capital punishment shall not be imposed upon persons who, at the time the crime was committed, were under 18 years of age or over 70 years of age; nor shall it be applied to pregnant women.

6. Every person condemned to death shall have the right to apply for amnesty, pardon, or commutation of sentence, which may be granted in all cases. Capital punishment shall not be imposed while such a petition is pending decision by the competent authority".

cuni trattati sui diritti umani di carattere specifico, che contengono norme in tema di pena di morte[60].

Si deve sottolineare il fatto che tutte queste norme stabiliscono il concetto base per cui nessuno può essere arbitrariamente privato della vita. È questo il nucleo essenziale e comune di tutte le norme convenzionali sul diritto alla vita. Dalla prassi dei vari organi internazionali di controllo dei trattati suddetti si desume che non sono ritenute arbitrarie le uccisioni che derivano dall'uso legittimo della forza, che risponda anche ai requisiti di necessità e proporzionalità. Su questo aspetto ritorneremo in seguito.

A nostro avviso, questo nucleo essenziale delle norme pattizie sul diritto alla vita, cioè il *divieto di uccisioni arbitrarie*, si è affermato non solo nel diritto internazionale convenzionale, ma anche nel diritto internazionale generale. Invece ci sembra dubbio che tale divieto sia divenuto parte dello *ius cogens*. Naturalmente il discorso cambia quando si verificano violazioni gravi, sistematiche ed organizzate di tale divieto: siamo allora nel campo delle *gross violations* di un diritto umano fondamentale e quindi nell'ambito di applicazione dello *ius cogens*.

7.2. *Contenuto del diritto*

Il diritto alla vita viene spesso considerato come un diritto umano "supremo"[61] o un diritto tutelato da una delle norme più fondamentali[62] o il diritto che costituisce il valore preminente nella gerarchia dei diritti umani[63]. Inoltre è di solito incluso tra i diritti inderogabili anche in situazioni di emergenza, ma soltanto in tempo di pace[64]. Tuttavia non si tratta di un diritto umano "assoluto", perché ammette limiti e due eccezioni: *a*) l'esecuzione della pena di morte legittimamente inflitta; *b*) l'uccisione che si verifica nel corso di un conflitto armato secondo le regole del diritto internazionale umanitario.

7.2.1. *Eccezioni: pena di morte e conflitti armati*

La prima eccezione al diritto alla vita è costituita dalla pena di morte, che è di solito consentita nei trattati sui diritti umani. Ciò perché la pena di morte era ed è ancora prevista in numerosi Stati ed era quindi necessario regolarla e inquadrarla entro alcuni limiti giuridici[65]. Infatti, nei principali trattati sui diritti umani la pena di morte è subordinata ad una serie di condizioni, sostanziali, procedurali e personali che valgono per gli Stati che non hanno abolito tale pena[66].

Queste condizioni sono bene specificate nell'art. 6 del Patto sui diritti civili e politici: *a*) la pena di morte può essere imposta soltanto per i crimini più gravi; *b*) tali crimini devono essere stabiliti secondo il diritto in vigore al tempo in cui sono stati commessi (principio della irretroattività del diritto penale); *c*) il diritto che prevede la pena di morte non

---

[60] Vedi, ad es., CRC, art. 37.

[61] HRCtee, General Comment No. 6, 30 April 1982, par. 1.

[62] ECtHR, *McCann and Others*, par. 147.

[63] Vedi ECtHR, *Streletz, Kessler and Krenk*, par. 72.

[64] Cfr. Focarelli (2013), p. 131.

[65] Cfr. Zagrebelsky *et al.* (2016), p. 156.

[66] Cfr. Focarelli (2013), p. 134.

deve essere in contrasto con gli altri diritti umani stabiliti nel Patto (ad esempio, il divieto di trattamento inumano); *d*) la pena di morte può essere stabilita soltanto da una sentenza definitiva resa da un tribunale competente; *e*) la persona condannata alla pena di morte deve avere il diritto di chiedere il perdono o una commutazione della sentenza; *f*) la pena di morte non può essere imposta a persone di età inferiore a 18 anni e non può essere eseguita su donne in stato di gravidanza. Condizioni simili, anche se non identiche e non così dettagliate, sono previste anche in altri trattati sui diritti umani [67].

Tuttavia, si deve notare che, negli anni più recenti, si è verificata una chiara tendenza verso l'abolizione della pena di morte. In primo luogo, la pena di morte è stata abolita in alcuni protocolli addizionali. Nel sistema della Convenzione europea, la pena di morte è stata abolita prima, in tempo di pace, dal Protocollo n. 6 del 1983 e poi, in ogni circostanza e quindi anche in tempo di guerra, dal Protocollo n. 13 del 2002. Anche il Protocollo n. 2 al Patto sui diritti civili e politici ed il Protocollo n. 2 alla Convenzione americana hanno abolito la pena di morte. In secondo luogo, la Corte di Strasburgo ha prima affermato che la pena di morte doveva ritenersi come un trattamento inumano vietato dall'art. 3 della Convenzione europea [68] e poi ha sostenuto che l'art. 2 della Convenzione debba oggi essere interpretato nel senso di proibire la pena di morte in ogni circostanza [69]. In terzo luogo, vi sono alcune norme convenzionali che vietano agli Stati che hanno abolito la pena di morte di reintrodurla nei propri ordinamenti giuridici [70]. Infine, anche il Comitato dei diritti umani e la Corte interamericana considerano l'abolizione della pena di morte come un progresso nel godimento del diritto alla vita ed incoraggiano gli Stati verso tale abolizione [71].

La seconda eccezione al diritto alla vita è costituita da quelle uccisioni che si verifichino durante i conflitti armati nel rispetto delle norme di diritto internazionale umanitario [72]. Tuttavia anche questa eccezione è cambiata nel tempo. Infatti, nel diritto internazionale tradizionale si riteneva che il diritto alla vita, tutelato dai trattati sui diritti umani, non si applicasse in situazioni di conflitti armati. Secondo questa tesi, in tempo di pace gli individui sarebbero tutelati dal diritto internazionale dei diritti umani, mentre in tempo di conflitti armati tale protezione si indebolirebbe perché gli individui sarebbero tutelati soltanto dal diritto internazionale umanitario. E, secondo quest'ultimo, la perdita della vita attribuibile ad atti legittimi di guerra non è illegittima. In altri termini, durante i conflitti armati, il diritto internazionale umanitario derogherebbe *in toto*, in quanto *lex specialis*, al diritto internazionale dei diritti umani.

Ma questa tesi appare oggi superata. Nel diritto internazionale contemporaneo, questi due settori normativi si sono ravvicinati ed hanno subìto reciproche influenze e convergenze, cosicché la loro distinzione non è più così netta come in passato, né è così chiaro il funzionamento del principio di specialità. In particolare, la tendenza della prassi è quella di ritenere che certi diritti umani fondamentali, fra i quali il diritto alla vita, operino anche

[67] Vedi ECHR, art. 2(1); ACHR, art. 4(2-5); ArCHR, artt. 6 e 7; CRC, art. 37(a).

[68] ECtHR, *Öcalan*, 12 May 2005, par. 165.

[69] ECtHR, *Al-Saadoon and Mufdhi*, Judgment of 2 March 2010, par. 120.

[70] In questo senso vedi l'art. 4(3) ACHR.

[71] HRCtee, General Comment No. 6, 30 April 1982, par. 6; Id., Concluding Observations: *Suriname* (2004), par. 10; IACtHR, *The Right to Information on Consular Assistance*, par. 134 ss.

[72] Sul tema vedi, per tutti, Kälin, Künzli (2009), p. 284 ss.

durante i conflitti armati. Ciò è stato confermato anche dalla Corte internazionale di giustizia nel parere sulla *Legalità delle armi nucleari*[73] e nel parere sulla *Costruzione di un muro nel territorio palestinese*[74].

La conseguenza principale di questo approccio è che quelle privazioni della vita che sono proibite dal diritto internazionale umanitario (ad esempio, uccisioni di feriti o prigionieri, o uccisioni derivanti da attacchi indiscriminati) costituiscono *anche* violazioni del diritto alla vita secondo il diritto internazionale dei diritti umani. Da un punto di vista pratico, ciò permette alle vittime o ai parenti delle vittime di presentare ricorsi agli organi internazionali di controllo dei trattati sui diritti umani. In questo senso, si possono ricordare le sentenze della Corte europea dei diritti umani nei casi *Isayeva and Others*[75], *Isayeva*[76], *Khatsiyeva and Others*[77], relativi al conflitto armato in Cecenia.

7.2.2. *Ambito di applicazione del diritto: l'inizio e la fine della vita*

Sempre in relazione al contenuto del diritto alla vita, si pone il problema di definire l'ambito di applicazione del diritto, specie in relazione ad una serie di questioni collegate all'inizio ed alla fine della vita.

In relazione all'inizio della vita, una questione importante riguarda la posizione del nascituro rispetto al diritto alla vita e la legittimità o meno dell'aborto[78]. La Convenzione europea, il Patto sui diritti civili e politici e la Carta africana non fanno alcun riferimento al tema dell'aborto. Invece, la Convenzione americana contiene una disposizione (art. 4(1)), secondo cui il diritto alla vita deve essere protetto "from the moment of conception". La questione è affrontata in maniera più specifica dal Protocollo alla Carta africana relativo ai diritti della donna in Africa, del 2003, che, all'art. 14(2), obbliga gli Stati parti ad autorizzare l'aborto in alcuni casi, come lo stupro, l'incesto o le situazioni di rischio per la salute fisica o mentale della madre, o per la vita della madre o del feto.

Nella prassi degli organi internazionali di controllo dei trattati sui diritti umani la questione dell'aborto viene in rilievo sia dal punto di vista del possibile diritto alla vita del feto, sia da quello della tutela del diritto alla vita della madre, che potrebbe essere messo a rischio se essa fosse costretta a partorire. La Commissione e la Corte europea hanno dovuto decidere vari ricorsi riguardanti l'aborto[79]. Sulla questione della titolarità del diritto alla vita da parte del nascituro, tali organi non si sono voluti pronunciare in maniera astratta, prendendo atto della mancanza di un consenso degli Stati parti della Convenzione europea. Pertanto hanno riconosciuto agli Stati un margine di discrezionalità[80]. Tuttavia, in alcuni casi hanno escluso che il feto abbia un diritto assoluto alla vita, tale da comportare un di-

---

[73] ICJ, *Legality of the Threat or Use of Nuclear Weapons*, par. 25.

[74] ICJ, *Legal Consequences of the Construction of a Wall*, par. 106.

[75] ECtHR, *Isayeva, Yusupova and Bazayeva v. Russia*, parr. 168-200.

[76] ECtHR, *Isayeva v. Russia*, parr. 172-201.

[77] ECtHR, *Khatsiyeva and Others v. Russia*, parr. 129-140.

[78] Sul tema vedi Citroni, Scovazzi (2013), p. 308 ss.; Focarelli (2013), pp. 134-136; Kälin, Künzli (2009), pp. 294-295; Zagrebelski *et al.* (2019), p. 165 ss.

[79] Vedi, in particolare, per un dettagliato esame di tale giurisprudenza, Citroni, Scovazzi (2013), pp. 312-317.

[80] Vedi ECmHR, *W.P. v. United Kingdom*, parr. 12-24; ECtHR, *Vo v. France*, parr. 84-85.

vieto all'aborto perfino in caso di pericolo di vita della futura madre [81]. La Corte europea ha toccato il tema dell'aborto anche in casi di ricorsi da parte di donne cui era stato negato l'aborto terapeutico e che facevano valere violazioni di diritti diversi rispetto al diritto alla vita, ad esempio il divieto di trattamento disumano o degradante o il diritto al rispetto della vita privata: si possono citare i casi *Tysiac c. Polonia* [82], *R.R. c. Polonia* [83], *P. e S. c. Polonia* [84].

Anche la Corte di giustizia dell'UE si è pronunciata sulla questione [85]; ma non ha preso posizione circa la titolarità del diritto alla vita da parte del feto; e quindi ha lasciato a ciascuno Stato la libertà di regolare l'aborto. Il Comitato dei diritti umani sembra aver preso una posizione un po' più netta a favore del diritto alla vita ed alla salute delle donne. Infatti, in alcuni casi il Comitato ha osservato che il divieto di aborto non può essere assoluto e che deve ammettere eccezioni a tutela del diritto alla vita delle donne; ed anche che normative nazionali che vietino certi aborti terapeutici sono contrarie al Patto sui diritti civili e politici [86]. La Commissione interamericana, nonostante l'art. 4 della Convenzione americana, sopra citato, dichiari che il diritto alla vita deve essere protetto fin dal momento del concepimento, ha concluso che tale formula ha carattere generale e non impedisce agli Stati di derogarvi, legalizzando l'aborto in casi eccezionali [87].

Per quanto riguarda, invece, la fine della vita, vengono in rilievo questioni relative all'eutanasia ed al c.d. "suicidio assistito". In realtà, tali questioni non sono regolate espressamente dai principali trattati generali sui diritti umani. Il problema interpretativo che si pone è se il diritto alla vita includa anche il diritto della persona a decidere di porre fine alla propria vita.

La Corte europea dei diritti umani ha risposto in senso negativo, affermando che dal diritto alla vita non si può dedurre il diritto a morire [88]; ma ha riconosciuto la legittimità ai sensi della Convenzione europea di normative statali che ammettono forme di suicidio assistito purché accertino la volontà espressa dalla persona. In alcuni casi, la Corte ha ritenuto applicabile alla questione l'art. 8 della Convenzione, sul diritto alla vita privata [89]. Nel complesso la Corte, pur osservando che non vi è concordanza fra gli Stati membri sul tema del suicidio assistito, non sembra escludere che legislazioni statali in materia possano essere compatibili con la Convenzione in presenza di certe situazioni specifiche e di adeguate garanzie per evitare abusi [90].

Il Comitato dei diritti umani si è occupato del tema dell'eutanasia con riferimento ad una proposta di legge olandese su eutanasia e suicidio assistito. Nelle sue osservazioni

---

[81] ECmHR, *H. v. Norway.*

[82] ECtHR, *Tysiąc v. Poland.*

[83] ECtHR, *R.R. v. Poland.*

[84] ECtHR, *P. and S. v. Poland.*

[85] ECJ, *Brüstle*; *The Society for the Protection of Unborn Children.*

[86] HRCtee, Concluding Observations: *Chile* (1999), par. 15; Concluding Observations: *Guatemala* (2001); *Queenan v. Canada*, par. 4.2; *Huamán v. Peru*, parr. 6.4-6.6; *V.D.A. v. Argentina*, par. 9.2.

[87] IACmHR, *Baby Boy Case.*

[88] ECtHR, *Pretty v. UK.*

[89] ECtHR, *Haas v. Switzerland*, parr. 51, 55 e 61; *Koch v. Germany*, parr. 65-72.

[90] Cfr. Focarelli (2013), p. 136.

conclusive del 2001 sui Paesi Bassi[91], il Comitato ha affermato che gli Stati hanno un margine di discrezionalità in materia. Tuttavia, quando uno Stato offre protezione giuridica ad atti intesi deliberatamente a porre fine ad una vita umana, si devono prendere le più rigorose precauzioni nello stabilire i casi in cui tali atti non siano punibili, al fine di proteggere il diritto alla vita.

7.3. *Obblighi*

Il tema degli obblighi che incombono sugli Stati (e sugli altri titolari degli obblighi relativi ai diritti umani)[92] per la protezione del diritto alla vita è di grande importanza; e quindi verrà trattato con una certa ampiezza. Distingueremo fra obblighi negativi e varie categorie di obblighi positivi (di prevenzione, di repressione e di riparazione). Nel trattare questi obblighi positivi, adotteremo le categorie concettuali che abbiamo proposto nel Capitolo III: obblighi immediati di risultato, obblighi immediati di *due diligence* ed obblighi "a realizzazione progressiva"[93]. Si deve fin d'ora premettere che molte delle osservazioni che faremo sugli obblighi relativi al diritto alla vita costituiranno un modello, con le opportune varianti, quando esamineremo gli obblighi relativi ad altri diritti umani.

7.3.1. *Obblighi negativi*

Il diritto alla vita impone, prima di tutto, allo Stato obblighi negativi. Il primo obbligo dello Stato è quello di astenersi dal compiere, per mezzo dei propri individui-organi, un'uccisione arbitraria. Si potrebbe definire come un divieto di uso arbitrario o eccessivo della forza "letale" (cioè che può causare la morte). L'uso della forza letale, da parte di agenti di polizia, di agenti delle forze di sicurezza, di agenti carcerari o di altri organi statali, è giustificato in certe circostanze, come quelle indicate dall'art. 2(1) della Convenzione europea. Ma tale uso della forza, per non essere arbitrario o eccessivo, deve rispettare i criteri di necessità e di proporzionalità; cioè deve essere necessario per raggiungere lo scopo e non deve superare i mezzi idonei e necessari per conseguire tale scopo. In altri termini, vi deve essere un nesso di proporzionalità fra lo scopo ed i mezzi usati per la sua realizzazione[94].

Nella giurisprudenza della Corte europea, il *leading case* è il caso *McCann*[95] nel quale i ricorrenti contestavano la legittimità, ai sensi della Convenzione europea, di un'operazione anti-terrorismo condotta a Gibilterra da forze militari di sicurezza britanniche, in cui avevano perso la vita alcuni parenti dei ricorrenti. In relazione all'uso della forza, i giudici affermarono che esso deve essere strettamente proporzionato al raggiungimento di uno degli obiettivi previsti dall'art. 2 della Convenzione europea. La Corte ritenne che i militari inglesi avessero agito ragionevolmente, reputando che fosse necessario sparare ai sospetti per impedire che attivassero un ordigno piazzato in un'auto. Ciò nonostante, poiché l'identità dei tre terroristi era nota alle autorità britanniche e, pertanto, sarebbe stato

---

[91] HRCtee, Concluding Observations: *Netherlands* (2001).

[92] Vedi *supra*, Cap. III, par. 2.

[93] *Ibidem*, par. 5.

[94] Più in generale, sul principio di proporzionalità nel diritto internazionale, vedi Cannizzaro (2000).

[95] ECtHR, *McCann and Others*.

possibile arrestarli preventivamente una volta entrati in Gibilterra, la Corte concluse che l'uso della forza non era "assolutamente necessario" e che l'uccisione dei tre sospetti costituiva una violazione dell'art. 2.

L'uso eccessivo della forza da parte di agenti di polizia è stato ritenuto contrario all'art. 2 anche nei casi *Makaratzis*[96], *Nachova*[97], *Nikolova and Velichkova*[98], *Saoud*[99] e *Alikaj*[100]. Invece, nel caso *Ramsahai*[101], la Corte ha ritenuto che l'uccisione di una persona da parte di un agente di polizia fosse «no more than absolutely necessary»[102]. Alle stesse conclusioni è giunta la Corte nel caso *Giuliani*[103], che trae origine dalle violente manifestazioni di protesta contro il G8, tenutosi a Genova nel luglio 2001. Giuliani era uno dei manifestanti; nella concitazione degli eventi egli, dopo aver impugnato un estintore, si era avvicinato a una jeep con a bordo tre carabinieri. Uno di questi aveva estratto la propria pistola e sparato dei colpi in direzione del finestrino posteriore del mezzo, colpendo a morte la vittima. I giudici di Strasburgo affermarono che le autorità italiane non avevano violato l'obbligo di fare tutto ciò che fosse ragionevolmente possibile per garantire un livello di sicurezza adeguato rispetto all'esecuzione di operazioni potenzialmente implicanti l'uso di forza letale, come quelle occorse nella fattispecie. In particolare, il possesso e l'uso della pistola dalla quale partirono i colpi che uccisero Giuliani, da parte di un carabiniere, furono ritenuti legittimi, così come l'uso della forza letale fu reputato «absolutely necessary in defence of any person from unlawful violence»[104].

In sostanza, nella giurisprudenza della Commissione e Corte europee, l'uso eccessivo della forza può violare il diritto alla vita, anche quando lo scopo di tale uso è legittimo e la conseguenza letale non è intenzionale[105]. Inoltre, l'esistenza di altri modi per raggiungere lo scopo perseguito con l'uso della forza esclude che il ricorso alla forza letale sia necessario e proporzionato[106].

Anche la prassi del Comitato dei diritti umani conferma che il diritto alla vita, *ex* art. 6 del Patto, consiste, innanzitutto, nel diritto di non essere ucciso arbitrariamente dalle autorità dello Stato. Nel caso *Guerrero*[107], ad esempio, il Comitato ha condannato la Colombia per l'uccisione di presunti malviventi da parte di agenti di polizia. Nel 1978 la polizia fece irruzione in una casa a Bogotá, dove credeva che fosse stato rinchiuso un ambasciatore che era stato precedentemente rapito. L'ambasciatore non fu trovato, ma la polizia si nascose

---

[96] ECtHR, *Makaratzis*, par. 55.

[97] ECtHR, *Nachova and Others*, Judgment of 6 July 2005, parr. 71-74, 96 e 107.

[98] ECtHR, *Nikolova and Velichkova.*

[99] ECtHR, *Saoud.*

[100] ECtHR, *Alikaj and Others.*

[101] ECtHR, *Ramsahai and Others*, par. 288.

[102] Ramsahai aveva rubato uno scooter dopo aver minacciato con una pistola il legittimo proprietario. In seguito era fuggito ed era stato inseguito da alcuni agenti della polizia. Una volta raggiunto, egli aveva estratto la pistola e l'aveva puntata contro un poliziotto che, in risposta, gli aveva sparato al collo, uccidendolo.

[103] ECtHR, *Giuliani and Gaggio.*

[104] *Ibidem*, par. 194.

[105] Vedi Zagrebelsky *et al.* (2016), p. 152 ed i casi ivi citati.

[106] *Ibidem.*

[107] HRCtee, *Suarez de Guerrero*, parr. 13.2-13.3.

comunque nella casa aspettando l'arrivo dei rapitori. Sette persone entrarono in seguito nell'appartamento e furono uccise con colpi di arma da fuoco dai poliziotti. Il *modus operandi* degli agenti, che non dettero alcun avvertimento preventivo alle vittime e, di conseguenza, la possibilità per loro di arrendersi o dare spiegazioni della loro presenza, portò il Comitato a giudicare l'uccisione, sebbene "legittima" ai sensi del diritto colombiano, come arbitraria, non necessaria e sproporzionata e pertanto contraria all'art. 6 del Patto. Secondo il Comitato, anche un tentato omicidio può causare la violazione dell'art. 6. Nel caso *Chongwe*[108] il ricorrente ha contestato l'autorizzazione, senza un legittimo motivo, da parte di autorità della Colombia, all'uso di forza letale, che avrebbe potuto causare la sua morte. Il Comitato ha ritenuto che lo Stato avesse violato l'art. 6.

La giurisprudenza degli organi interamericani sui diritti umani segue criteri simili, in relazione al diritto alla vita tutelato dall'art. 4 della Convenzione americana. Si noti che gran parte dei casi relativi al diritto alla vita decisi dalla Corte interamericana riguarda violazioni massicce perpetrate da organi dello Stato ed esecuzioni sommarie e indiscriminate nei confronti di individui sottoposti alla sua giurisdizione. Si possono citare, fra gli altri, i casi *Paniagua Morales*[109], *Barrios Altos*[110], *The Street Children*[111], *Montero-Aranguren*[112]. In realtà, la giurisprudenza della Corte è assai interessante, perché essa ha precisato con un certo dettaglio i criteri della necessità del ricorso alla forza e della proporzionalità dei mezzi impiegati. Inoltre, come vedremo in seguito, la Corte ha anche approfondito il contenuto degli obblighi positivi di repressione dello Stato con riferimento al diritto alla vita[113].

Un altro obbligo negativo dello Stato, relativo al diritto alla vita, consiste nel fatto che lo Stato non può respingere, espellere o estradare una persona verso un Paese nel quale essa rischi seriamente di essere privata della vita. Questo obbligo, a mio avviso, deriva (o comunque è stato influenzato) dal c.d. principio di *non-refoulement*. Di questo principio parleremo più diffusamente in seguito, a proposito dei diritti di movimento degli stranieri e della protezione dei richiedenti asilo e dei rifugiati[114]. Qui è sufficiente notare che questo principio trova origine nell'art. 33 della Convenzione di Ginevra del 1951 sullo status dei rifugiati, che vieta agli Stati parti di respingere i rifugiati verso le frontiere di un Paese dove la loro vita o libertà sarebbero minacciate per una serie specifica di motivi di discriminazione[115]. Ma il principio si è poi affermato nel diritto consuetudinario; ha esteso il suo ambito soggettivo di applicazione dai soli rifugiati a tutti gli stranieri; ed il suo ambito oggettivo non solo al respingimento in senso stretto, ma anche all'espulsione ed all'estradizione degli stranieri.

Infine (ed è questo il punto che qui più interessa) il principio si è ampliato anche sotto

---

[108] HRCtee, *Chongwe*.

[109] IACtHR, *Paniagua Morales and Others*.

[110] IACtHR, *Barrios Altos*, Judgment of 14 March 2001.

[111] IACtHR, *The "Street Children"*, Judgment of 19 November 1999.

[112] IACtHR, *Montero-Aranguren et al.*, parr. 67-74.

[113] Vedi *infra*, par. 7.3.3.

[114] Vedi *infra*, Cap. VI, parr. 13, 14 e 15.

[115] Il divieto di respingimento ammette un'eccezione quando il rifugiato costituisca un pericolo per la sicurezza dello Stato di rifugio (art. 33, par. 2, della Convenzione di Ginevra).

l'aspetto delle cause che ostano al respingimento, poiché adesso protegge non solo dai pericoli derivanti dagli specifici motivi di discriminazione elencati nella Convenzione di Ginevra, ma anche dal rischio di subire gravi violazioni del diritto alla vita e del diritto di non subire torture o trattamenti inumani o degradanti. Ciò deriva dal fatto che il principio di *non-refoulement* ha avuto nel tempo un impatto sui suddetti diritti, che sono stati via via interpretati in maniera più evolutiva. In particolare, il diritto alla vita, nella prassi degli organi internazionali di controllo dei trattati sui diritti umani, è stato con il tempo interpretato nel senso che uno Stato ha l'obbligo negativo di non respingere (né espellere né estradare) una persona verso un Paese nel quale essa rischi seriamente, *per qualsiasi motivo*, di essere arbitrariamente privata della vita [116].

In sostanza, il principio di *non-refoulement* ed il diritto alla vita si sono reciprocamente integrati.

Come vedremo [117], uno sviluppo simile ha interessato anche il divieto di tortura e di trattamenti inumani e degradanti.

7.3.2. *Obblighi positivi di prevenzione*

Il rispetto del diritto alla vita impone allo Stato anche una serie numerosa di obblighi positivi, di prevenzione, di repressione e di riparazione.

Cominciando dai primi, si deve subito notare che l'obbligo *generale* dello Stato di prevenire violazioni del diritto alla vita delle persone è molto importante e che esso si compone, a sua volta, di una pluralità di obblighi più specifici. Sintetizzando, lo Stato ha: *a*) l'obbligo di avere un apparato normativo adeguato di prevenzione delle violazioni; *b*) l'obbligo di avere un apparato amministrativo per lo stesso scopo; *c*) l'obbligo di adottare le misure concrete, volta per volta richieste, per la prevenzione [118].

La distinzione fra questi tre obblighi diversi è stata bene evidenziata dalla Corte europea nel celebre caso *Osman* del 1998 [119]. I ricorrenti, Mrs. Osman ed il figlio Ahmet, si lamentavano del fatto che la polizia di Londra non aveva protetto la vita di Mr. Osman e di Ahmet di fronte al pericolo costituito da un insegnante di Ahmet, che aveva sviluppato una forma di ossessione verso quest'ultimo. In effetti l'insegnante aveva poi, durante una sparatoria, ucciso Mr. Osman, ferito Ahmet ed ucciso anche una terza persona. La Corte europea ha concluso che, nel caso di specie, non era stata provata la responsabilità della polizia e quindi non vi era stata violazione dell'art. 2. Tuttavia, nella sentenza, la Corte fa delle osservazioni assai interessanti circa gli obblighi di prevenzione dello Stato; e, più in particolare, distingue fra tre obblighi diversi: quello di avere delle norme penali di deterrenza dei reati contro le persone; quello di avere un apparato di esecuzione di tali norme allo scopo di prevenire, sopprimere e sanzionare le violazioni delle medesime; ed infine l'obbligo aggiuntivo delle autorità statali, in certe circostanze, di prendere misure preventive di

[116] In aggiunta, gli Stati che hanno abolito la pena di morte, ad esempio gli Stati parti della Convenzione europea, hanno anche l'obbligo di non respingere uno straniero verso un Paese nel quale egli rischi di essere sottoposto alla pena di morte.

[117] Vedi *infra*, par. 8.3.1.

[118] Sull'approfondimento di queste tre categorie di obblighi di prevenzione vedi Pisillo Mazzeschi (2008), pp. 334-344 e 390-414.

[119] ECtHR, *Osman v. UK*.

carattere operativo per proteggere un individuo, la cui vita sia a rischio di subire atti criminali da parte di un altro individuo. Infatti, secondo la Corte:

"[...] the State's obligation in this respect extends beyond its primary duty to secure the right to life by putting in place effective criminal-law provisions to deter the commission of offences against the person backed up by law-enforcement machinery for the prevention, suppression and sanctioning of breaches of such provisions. [...] Article 2 of the Convention may also imply in certain well-defined circumstances a positive obligation on the authorities to take preventive operational measures to protect an individual whose life is at risk from the criminal acts of another individual" [120].

Conviene adesso esaminare separatamente questi tre obblighi di prevenzione, perché essi hanno caratteristiche diverse.

7.3.2.1. *Obbligo di avere un apparato normativo di prevenzione.* – L'obbligo dello Stato di avere (o dotarsi di) un apparato normativo (specie penale ma anche di altra natura) che sia idoneo, in linea generale ed astratta, a prevenire violazioni del diritto alla vita, è un obbligo immediato di risultato [121]. Infatti, lo Stato è certamente in grado di garantire il risultato di adottare, modificare o abrogare le leggi e non si può limitare ad un semplice sforzo di diligenza in tale direzione.

La giurisprudenza della Corte europea contiene, oltre al citato caso *Osman*, altri casi interessanti, che confermano in maniera chiara l'esistenza di tale obbligo dello Stato. Nei tre casi *Güleç*, *Oğur* e *Akkoç* [122], ad esempio, la Corte ha stabilito che la legislazione penale e di procedura penale turca, relativa ai crimini nei quali erano implicati militari o forze dell'ordine, non garantiva una procedura indipendente ed efficace e quindi essa violava l'obbligo dello Stato di proteggere la vita delle persone ai sensi dell'art. 2 della Convenzione europea. Nel già citato caso *Makaratzis* [123], gli agenti di polizia, che avevano sparato contro un automobilista che aveva violato dei posti di blocco e che erano stati accusati di impiego non autorizzato di armi da fuoco, erano stati assolti sulla base di una legge greca del 1943. Ma, secondo la Corte europea, la Grecia, non avendo fissato le direttive né i limiti all'impiego della forza armata necessari per orientare correttamente tale impiego, aveva violato l'obbligo positivo di proteggere la vita delle persone previsto dall'art. 2 della Convenzione europea. Si può ricordare anche il caso *Mastromatteo* [124], nel quale il figlio del ricorrente era stato ucciso da criminali che erano stati provvisoriamente rilasciati dalle prigioni italiane, in regime di libertà provvisoria, sulla base di certe leggi miranti a facilitare la reintegrazione sociale dei detenuti. La Corte europea si è chiesta se la legislazione italiana violasse l'obbligo positivo dello Stato di garantire una protezione sufficiente alla società circa eventuali attentati contro la vita delle persone; ma ha concluso per la non violazione dell'art. 2 della Convenzione europea. Per l'obbligo dello Stato di avere una legisla-

---

[120] *Ibidem*, par. 115.

[121] Cfr. Pisillo Mazzeschi (2008), p. 311 ss.

[122] ECtHR, *Güleç v. Turkey*; *Oğur v. Turkey*; *Akkoç v. Turkey*.

[123] ECtHR, *Makaratzis v. Greece*.

[124] ECtHR, *Mastromatteo v. Italy*.

zione civile per risarcire i danni da omicidio colposo, si può citare il caso *Calvelli e Ciglio* [125], relativo alla responsabilità professionale dei medici.

Anche la giurisprudenza della Corte e Commissione interamericane conferma che lo Stato ha l'obbligo di avere un apparato normativo di prevenzione, che deriva dall'art. 2 della Convenzione americana. Ad esempio, nel caso *Castillo Petruzzi*, la Corte interamericana ha affermato:

> "The general duty under Article 2 of the American Convention implies the adoption of measures of two kinds: on the one hand, elimination of any norms and practices that in any way violate the guarantees provided under the Convention; on the other hand, the promulgation of norms and the development of practices conductive to effective observance of those guarantees" [126].

Principi simili sono stati affermati in altre sentenze, ad esempio nei già citati casi *Barrios Altos* e *The "Street Children"*.

Infine, anche il Comitato dei diritti umani, sia pure in linea più generale, ha affermato che l'obbligo generale, imposto agli Stati parti dall'art. 2(2) del Patto sui diritti civili e politici, richiede che gli Stati adattino il proprio diritto interno per attuare i diritti protetti. Infatti, il Comitato ha affermato che:

> "[...] unless Covenant rights are already protected by their domestic laws or practices, States Parties are required on ratification to make such changes to domestic laws and practices as are necessary to ensure their conformity with the Covenant" [127].

7.3.2.2. *Obbligo di avere un apparato amministrativo di prevenzione*. – Il secondo obbligo positivo di prevenzione, a carico dello Stato, è quello di avere un apparato amministrativo adeguato, in linea generale ed in astratto, a prevenire violazioni del diritto alla vita delle persone, siano tali violazioni commesse da individui-organi statali o da individui privati. Si pensi, soprattutto, all'apparato di polizia e di sicurezza, ma anche a quello penitenziario e quello sanitario. Si tratta, anche in questo caso, di un obbligo di risultato.

Conviene, in primo luogo, citare alcuni casi che concernono l'*apparato di polizia e di sicurezza* dello Stato. Nella giurisprudenza degli organi della Convenzione europea, si possono ricordare, oltre il già citato caso *Osman*, i casi *Mahmut Kaya* [128] e *Akkoç* [129]. In ambedue i casi, alcune persone erano state uccise da sconosciuti nella regione del sud est della Turchia ed i parenti avevano accusato le autorità turche di aver violato il diritto alla vita. La Corte europea ha rilevato, fra l'altro, che vi erano delle carenze strutturali nel sistema di protezione penale nella regione del sud est della Turchia nel periodo in cui era avvenuto l'omicidio; che tale sistema non era efficace e che il governo in linea generale non aveva istituito appropriate misure di protezione in tale area. Pertanto, la Corte ha accertato la violazione di un obbligo generale di risultato riguardante l'apparato statale di

---

[125] ECtHR, *Calvelli and Ciglio v. Italy*, parr. 49-51.

[126] IACtHR, *Castillo Petruzzi et al.*, par. 207.

[127] In questo senso vedi anche HRCtee, General Comment n. 31, 26 May 2004, par. 13.

[128] ECtHR, *Mahmut Kaya v. Turkey*.

[129] ECtHR, *Akkoç v. Turkey*.

prevenzione. Ancora più nette sono le affermazioni della Corte nel caso *Perk*, relativo alla protezione del diritto alla vita durante certe operazioni antiterrorismo. Sull'obbligo degli Stati di avere un apparato amministrativo di prevenzione, la Corte ha affermato:

> "L'obligation de l'Etat […] implique le devoir primordial d'assurer le droit à la vie en mettant en place un cadre juridique et administratif propre à dissuader de commettre des atteintes contre la personne et s'appuyant sur un mécanisme d'application conçu pour en prévenir, réprimer et sanctionner les violations" [130].

Nella giurisprudenza del sistema interamericano dei diritti umani, l'esistenza di un obbligo generale dello Stato di *avere* un adeguato apparato amministrativo di prevenzione delle violazioni dei diritti umani è confermata in maniera netta. Esemplari sono, a questo riguardo, le seguenti identiche affermazioni fatte dalla Corte interamericana dei diritti umani nei casi *Velásquez Rodríguez* [131] e *Godínez Cruz* [132]:

> "The second obligation of the States Parties is to "ensure" the free and full exercise of the rights recognized by the Convention to every person subject to its jurisdiction. This obligation implies the duty of the States parties to organize the governmental apparatus and, in general, all the structures through which public power is exercised, so that they are capable of juridically ensuring the free and full enjoyment of human rights".

Nella prassi degli organi internazionali di controllo sui diritti umani, vi sono anche alcuni casi che riguardano le carenze strutturali dell'*apparato carcerario* dello Stato. La Corte interamericana ha ritenuto che, in alcuni casi, le carenze oggettive e strutturali delle carceri o di altri istituti di detenzione di un certo Stato costituissero una violazione del diritto alla vita tutelato dalla Convenzione americana. Ad esempio, nel caso *"Juvenile Reeducation Institute"* [133], la Corte ha accertato tali violazioni da parte del Paraguay, poiché il suddetto Istituto di rieducazione non costituiva una infrastruttura adeguata per ospitare gli internati, aveva una sovrappopolazione carceraria, celle insalubri e servizi igienici insufficienti ed infine non forniva alimentazione e cure mediche adeguate [134]. Pertanto la Corte ha concluso che:

> "… las condiciones de detención infrahumanas y degradantes a que se vieron expuestos todos los internos del Instituto, conlleva necesariamente una afectación en su salud mental, repercutiendo desfavorablemente en el desarrollo psíquico de su vida e integridad personal" [135].

Infine, vi sono alcuni casi che riguardano le carenze strutturali dell'*apparato sanitario* dello Stato. Essi si rinvengono specie nella giurisprudenza della Corte europea dei diritti umani. Si può citare, ad esempio, il caso *Cyprus v. Turkey* del 2001 [136]. Cipro sosteneva dinanzi alla Corte, fra l'altro, che le autorità turche di Cipro del Nord avevano omesso di

---

[130] ECtHR, *Perk and Others v. Turkey*, par. 54.

[131] IACtHR, *Velásquez Rodríguez v. Honduras.*

[132] IACtHR, *Godínez Cruz v. Honduras.*

[133] IACtHR, *"Juvenile Reeducation Institute" v. Paraguay.*

[134] *Ibidem*, parr. 165-166.

[135] *Ibidem*, par. 168.

[136] ECtHR, *Cyprus v. Turkey*, Judgment of 10 May 2001.

fornire adeguati servizi medici a molte centinaia di ciprioti greci e maroniti che ancora vivevano nella parte settentrionale di Cipro, in tal modo violando il diritto alla vita *ex* art. 2 della Convenzione europea. La Corte ha concluso per l'assenza di violazione dell'art. 2; ma, sia pure con cautela, ha detto che uno Stato può essere responsabile di violazione del diritto alla vita, se il suo apparato sanitario omette di fornire ad un individuo quelle cure mediche suscettibili di salvare la vita che lo Stato ha promesso di rendere generalmente disponibili [137]. In una sentenza successiva, nel già citato caso *Calvelli e Ciglio* [138], la Corte di Strasburgo ha affermato che, anche quando le cure mediche sono affidate a servizi privati, lo Stato mantiene una funzione di controllo e che gli obblighi positivi dello Stato *ex* art. 2 della Convenzione europea [139] richiedono allo Stato di imporre agli ospedali di adottare misure appropriate per la protezione delle vite dei pazienti. In sostanza, si va affermando, nella giurisprudenza della Corte europea, un obbligo dello Stato di avere un apparato sanitario, che garantisca quantomeno un livello minimo di tutela preventiva del diritto alla vita.

7.3.2.3. *Obbligo di adottare misure concrete di prevenzione.* – Infine, il terzo obbligo positivo di prevenzione, a carico dello Stato, probabilmente il più importante, è quello di adottare le misure concrete che sono volta per volta ed in ogni singola situazione richieste, per prevenire violazioni del diritto alla vita. Questo è un tipico obbligo di *due diligence*, poiché gran parte delle attività di prevenzione richieste alle singole autorità statali, in certe circostanze concrete, non sono per loro natura idonee a garantire un risultato certo, ma sono invece soggette ad alea. Pertanto, di solito, l'obbligo dello Stato è solo un obbligo di usare la *due diligence* o i suoi "*best efforts*" per raggiungere un certo risultato, in questo caso prevenire la violazione del diritto alla vita. Ciò vale sia per le attività di prevenzione che lo Stato deve compiere per impedire violazioni del diritto alla vita da parte di agenti statali, sia, in maniera ancora più evidente, per le attività di prevenzione tese ad impedire tali violazioni da parte di persone private [140].

La prassi degli organi internazionali di controllo relativa all'obbligo di prevenire violazioni del diritto alla vita è molto ricca ed essa attiene soprattutto ai seguenti aspetti: *a*) prevenzione rispetto ad atti criminali di individui privati; *b*) prevenzione e controllo sull'uso letale della forza da parte di agenti statali; *c*) prevenzione di gravi danni alla salute.

Il primo aspetto, cioè l'obbligo dello Stato di adottare misure preventive per proteggere la vita degli individui da *atti criminali compiuti da altri individui*, si colloca, da un punto

---

[137] Secondo la Corte: "[…] an issue may arise under Article 2 of the Convention where it is shown that the authorities of a Contracting State put an individual's life at risk through the denial of health care which they have undertaken to make available to the population generally" (par. 219).

[138] ECtHR, *Calvelli and Ciglio v. Italy.*

[139] *Ibidem*, par. 49.

[140] Vedi HRCtee, General Comment No. 31, 26 May 2004, par. 8: "[…] the positive obligations on States Parties to ensure Covenant rights will only be fully discharged if individuals are protected by the State, not just against violations of Covenant rights by its agents, but also against acts committed by private persons or entities [...] There may be circumstances in which a failure to ensure Covenant rights [...] would give rise to violations by States Parties of those rights, as a result of States Parties' permitting or *failing to take appropriate measures or to exercise due diligence to prevent*, punish, investigate or redress the harm caused by such acts by private persons or entities" (corsivo aggiunto).

di vista giuridico sistematico, nel quadro della classica responsabilità dello Stato in relazione ad atti di privati, laddove l'omissione degli organi statali di prendere misure di prevenzione si collega, con un rapporto di causalità, alle lesioni materialmente commesse da individui privati. È questo uno dei settori in cui, tradizionalmente, gioca un ruolo importante la carenza di *due diligence,* da parte degli organi statali, nel compiere quelle attività di prevenzione che erano richieste dalle circostanze concrete.

Nella maggior parte dei casi, le attività di prevenzione devono essere effettuate dalle *forze di polizia* dello Stato. Nella giurisprudenza della Convenzione europea, il *leading case* in questa materia è il già citato caso *Osman*. Nella sentenza, la Corte europea ha stabilito che l'art. 2 della Convenzione, richiedendo di adottare anche misure positive, non solo impone allo Stato di avere una legislazione penale ed un apparato di prevenzione, ma:

> "may also imply in certain well-defined circumstances a positive obligation on the authorities *to take preventive operational measures* to protect an individual whose life is at risk from the criminal acts of another individual" [141].

Quindi la Corte ha precisato e limitato il contenuto di tale obbligo di prevenzione, con delle affermazioni importanti, che sono state successivamente riprese in altri casi, e che meritano di essere riportate:

> "[f]or the Court [...] such an obligation must be interpreted in a way which does not impose an impossible or disproportionate burden on the authorities. Accordingly, not every claimed risk to life can entail for the authorities a Convention requirement to take operational measures to prevent that risk from materializing [...] In the opinion of the Court [...] it must be established to its satisfaction that the authorities knew or ought to have known at the time of the existence of a real and immediate risk to the life of an identified individual or individuals from the criminal acts of a third party and that they *failed to take measures within the scope of their powers* which, judged reasonably, might have been expected to avoid that risk [...] it is sufficient for an applicant to show that the authorities *did not do all that could be reasonably expected of them to avoid* a real and immediate risk to life of which they have or ought to have knowledge" [142].

L'obbligo delle forze di polizia di proteggere le persone sottoposte a minacce per la loro vita è stato ripreso dalla Corte europea anche nei casi *Kaya*, *Kiliç* e *Akkoç* [143]. In questi casi, come si è già visto, la Corte europea ha rilevato che vi erano carenze strutturali nell'apparato statale penale di prevenzione, ma ha accertato che le autorità turche avevano violato *anche* un obbligo più specifico di diligenza nelle misure di prevenzione richieste dalle circostanze concrete.

Si deve notare che l'obbligo di prevenire lesioni del diritto alla vita da parte di atti criminali compiuti da terzi non incombe solo sulle forze di polizia, ma anche su altre autorità dello Stato. In particolare, le *autorità carcerarie* hanno la responsabilità di proteggere la vita dei detenuti in certe situazioni di rischio reale ed imminente, dovute ad esempio al pe-

---

[141] ECtHR, *Osman v. UK*, par. 115 (corsivo aggiunto).
[142] *Ibidem*, par. 116.
[143] ECtHR, *Kaya v. Turkey*; *Kiliç v. Turkey*; *Akkoç v. Turkey*.

ricolo di atti criminali da parte di altri detenuti [144]. Una situazione simile si è verificata nel caso *Edwards* [145], nel quale la Corte di Strasburgo ha riaffermato i principi sull'obbligo di prevenzione già stabiliti nel caso *Osman*, ma aggiungendo che tale obbligo è più pregnante quando è a favore di persone sotto custodia dello Stato [146].

Il secondo aspetto della prassi, relativa all'obbligo di prevenire violazioni del diritto alla vita, comprende casi nei quali si è lamentata una privazione arbitraria della vita ad opera di *forze di sicurezza*, che abbiano fatto un uso improprio della forza letale. Si tratta, di solito, di operazioni anti-terrorismo o di operazioni di contrasto a rivolte o sommosse e, talora, anche di operazioni militari condotte da uno Stato nel quadro di una guerra civile. In questi casi, come è evidente, non si tratta di responsabilità dello Stato in relazione ad atti di privati, ma di responsabilità "diretta" dello Stato derivante dalla condotta, attiva o omissiva, delle stesse forze di sicurezza che hanno agito o dalla omissione di misure di prudenza e di cautela da parte degli organi superiori che hanno pianificato ed organizzato tali operazioni. In realtà, la condotta delle forze di sicurezza dovrebbe essere tenuta distinta da quella degli organi superiori; ma la prassi degli organi di controllo dei trattati sui diritti umani tende spesso a confondere le due condotte ed a riportarle nel quadro concettuale della carenza di *due diligence*.

Per quanto riguarda le *operazioni anti-terrorismo*, il *leading case*, nella giurisprudenza della Corte europea dei diritti umani, è il già citato caso *McCann*, relativo ad un'operazione anti-terrorismo condotta da forze militari di sicurezza britanniche. La sentenza è celebre perché la Corte ha enunciato per la prima volta in maniera netta il principio che il diritto alla vita richiede, per la sua tutela effettiva, l'obbligo positivo dello Stato di adottare tutte le misure idonee a prevenire le lesioni al diritto medesimo. La Corte ha riscontrato la violazione di tale obbligo, a causa della mancanza di diligenza, sia nel controllo e nell'organizzazione dell'operazione di sicurezza sia nelle modalità concrete con cui l'azione è stata condotta:

> "[t]heir reflex action in this vital respect lacks the degree of caution in the use of firearms to be expected from law enforcement personnel in a democratic society, even when dealing with dangerous terrorist suspects, and stands in marked contrast to the *standard of care* reflected in the instructions in the use of firearms by the police which had been drawn to their attention [...] This failure by the authorities also suggests *a lack of appropriate care* in the control and organisation of the arrest operation" [147].

Un altro esempio assai noto, in cui la Corte europea ha riscontrato una violazione dell'obbligo di prevenire lesioni al diritto alla vita, in relazione ad operazioni anti-terrorismo condotte da forze statali di sicurezza, è dato dal caso *Ergi* [148]. Anche in questo caso, la

---

[144] Si noti che le autorità carcerarie hanno l'obbligo di proteggere la vita dei detenuti anche di fronte a pericoli derivanti da gravi problemi di salute. Vedi ECtHR, *Velikova v. Bulgaria* e *Anguelova v. Bulgaria*.

[145] ECtHR, *Edwards Paul and Audrey v. UK*, parr. 54-55.

[146] *Ibidem*, par. 56: "In the context of prisoners, the Court has had previous occasions to emphasize that persons in custody are in a vulnerable position and that the authorities are under a duty to protect them. It is incumbent on the State to account for any injuries suffered in custody, which obligation is particularly stringent where that individual dies".

[147] ECtHR, *McCann and others v. UK*, par. 212 (corsivo aggiunto).

[148] ECtHR, *Ergi v. Turkey*, parr. 79-81 e 86.

Corte di Strasburgo ha ritenuto che vi fosse stata una negligenza nella pianificazione e condotta delle operazioni delle forze di sicurezza [149].

Nel caso di operazioni statali di *contrasto a rivolte o sommosse*, si applicano i medesimi principi. Si può ricordare, ad esempio, la sentenza della Corte interamericana dei diritti umani nel caso *Neira Alegría* [150], dove si discuteva, fra l'altro, circa la proporzionalità nell'uso della forza da parte delle autorità militari peruviane nel contrastare una rivolta nel carcere "San Juan Bautista". La Corte ha ritenuto che la forza usata fosse sproporzionata rispetto al pericolo concreto ed inoltre che nessuna misura precauzionale fosse stata messa in opera per ridurre il costo di vite umane nella soppressione della rivolta [151].

Infine, sono assai interessanti alcuni casi che riguardano vere e proprie *operazioni militari* condotte da uno Stato durante una guerra civile. Al riguardo sono celebri i casi *Isayeva, Yusupova and Bazayeva v. Russia* [152] e *Isayeva v. Russia* [153], concernenti attacchi di aerei militari russi contro civili durante il conflitto armato in Cecenia. La Corte europea dei diritti umani ha ritenuto che la Russia avesse violato l'art. 2 della Convenzione sul diritto alla vita, poiché le operazioni militari non erano state pianificate e controllate con la diligenza dovuta per minimizzare ogni rischio per la vita della popolazione civile. La Corte, fra l'altro, ha affermato:

> "[...] it is necessary to examine whether the operation was planned and controlled by the authorities so as to minimise, to the greatest extent possible, recourse to lethal force. The authorities must take *appropriate care* to ensure that any risk to life is minimised. The Court must also examine whether the authorities were not *negligent* in their choice of action" [154].

Il terzo aspetto della prassi qui in esame riguarda casi nei quali si è discusso sugli obblighi dello Stato di prevenire, tramite misure concrete, gravi danni alla *salute* delle persone, suscettibili di causare la loro morte. Nella giurisprudenza della Corte di Strasburgo, due esempi interessanti sono dati dai casi *Velikova* [155] e *Anguelova* [156], ambedue relativi alla morte di persone arrestate o detenute da autorità di polizia che hanno omesso di fornire o di richiedere cure mediche urgenti per tali persone. Nelle due sentenze, la Corte ha stabilito che le autorità erano state negligenti e che il loro comportamento omissivo aveva violato l'obbligo dello Stato di proteggere la vita delle persone in sua custodia. Infine, si

---

[149] Si trattava di un agguato antiterrorismo condotto nel 1993 nel Sud Est della Turchia, durante il quale la figlia del ricorrente era stata casualmente uccisa da un colpo di arma da fuoco. In particolare, la Corte ha detto: "[..] the responsibility of the State is not confined to circumstances where there is significant evidence that misdirected fire from agents of the State has killed a civilian. It may also be engaged where they *fail to take all feasible precautions* in the choice of means and methods of a security operation [...] Having regard to the above considerations, the Court finds that the Turkish authorities failed to protect Havva Ergi's right to life on account of *the defects in the planning and conduct* of the security forces' operation" (corsivi aggiunti).

[150] IACtHR, *Neira Alegría et al. v. Peru.*

[151] *Ibidem*, par. 62.

[152] ECtHR, *Isayeva, Yusupova and Bazayeva v. Russia*, Judgment of 24 February 2005.

[153] ECtHR, *Isayeva v. Russia*, Judgment of 24 February 2005.

[154] *Ibidem*, par. 175 (corsivo aggiunto).

[155] ECtHR, *Velikova v. Bulgaria.*

[156] ECtHR, *Anguelova v. Bulgaria.*

può ricordare anche il caso *L.C.B. v. UK*, che riguarda la possibile omissione da parte delle autorità del Regno Unito di prevenire il rischio alla salute di una persona per la sua partecipazione a certi esperimenti nucleari. Dinanzi alla Corte di Strasburgo, la ricorrente sosteneva che il Governo del Regno Unito aveva violato il diritto alla vita, poiché aveva mancato di avvisare il proprio padre circa il possibile rischio alla salute causato dalla sua partecipazione a certi esperimenti nucleari condotti dalla Royal Air Force in un'isola del Pacifico; ed aveva mancato di monitorare i livelli di radiazione cui costui era stato esposto. La Corte, pur ritenendo che, nel caso di specie, non vi fosse stata violazione dell'art. 2 della Convenzione europea, ha affermato che:

> "The Court's task is [...] to determine whether, given the circumstances of the case, the State did all that could have been required of it to prevent the applicant's life from being avoidably put at risk" [157].

7.3.3. *Obblighi positivi di repressione*

Come si è già detto, la protezione effettiva del diritto alla vita richiede allo Stato non solo attività e doveri di prevenzione, ma anche di repressione delle violazioni. Nel quadro dell'obbligo *generale* di repressione a carico dello Stato, si possono distinguere due obblighi più specifici, in ordine logico successivo: *a*) quello di investigare sulle presunte violazioni del diritto alla vita; *b*) quello di processare e punire i responsabili. Questi due obblighi sono spesso definiti, nel linguaggio degli organi di controllo dei trattati sui diritti umani, come obblighi positivi "procedurali" [158], e sono ritenuti necessari per assicurare il rispetto degli obblighi definiti come "sostanziali".

L'importanza di questi due obblighi è confermata con chiarezza dalla Risoluzione 60/147 dell'Assemblea Generale delle NU del 16 dicembre 2005, che ha adottato una serie di Principi e linee guida sui diritti delle vittime di gravi violazioni dei diritti umani e del diritto umanitario [159]. Il principio I stabilisce, fra l'altro, che:

> "The obligation to respect, ensure respect for and implement international human rights law [...] includes, inter alia, the duty to: [...] investigate violations effectively, promptly, thoroughly and impartially and, where appropriate, take action against those allegedly responsible in accordance with domestic and international law".

Esaminiamo separatamente l'obbligo di investigare e quello di processare e punire, in relazione al diritto alla vita.

7.3.3.1. *Obbligo di investigare*. – L'obbligo dello Stato di investigare ha lo scopo di stabilire i fatti relativi alla presunta violazione del diritto alla vita e di identificare, ricercare e catturare gli eventuali colpevoli. Esso comprende, a sua volta, due obblighi più specifici che hanno natura diversa: *a*) l'obbligo dello Stato di avere un apparato amministrativo e giudiziario adeguato per indagare sulle violazioni del diritto alla vita; *b*) l'obbligo dello

---

[157] ECtHR, *L.C.B. v. UK*, par. 36.

[158] Vedi *supra*, Cap. II, par. 10.3.

[159] *Basic Principles and Guidelines on the Right to a Remedy and Reparation for Victims of Gross Violations of International Human Rights Law and Serious Violations of International Humanitarian Law*, GA Res. 60/147 of 16 December 2005, Annex, Art. II (3)(b).

Stato di adottare le misure concrete ed effettive di indagine, che siano volta per volta richieste dalle circostanze.

L'obbligo dello Stato di possedere un apparato amministrativo e giudiziario di investigazione ed indagine, capace in astratto di raggiungere lo scopo sopra indicato, è un obbligo positivo immediato e di risultato. Infatti, nel mondo contemporaneo, ogni Stato deve avere tale apparato e non può certo limitarsi ad uno sforzo di diligenza per ottenerlo.

La giurisprudenza della Corte europea dei diritti umani comprende molti casi nei quali viene in evidenza questo obbligo a carico degli Stati. Fra gli altri, si possono ricordare i casi *Güleç*, *Oğur*, *Akkoç*, *Perk*[160]. In tutti questi casi, nei quali era convenuta la Turchia, la Corte ha concluso che lo Stato turco aveva violato il proprio obbligo di investigare sulle circostanze ed i responsabili di certe uccisioni, a causa di una carenza istituzionale di indipendenza da parte degli organi di investigazione. Tale mancanza di indipendenza non è stata ritenuta dalla Corte come un fattore contingente, ma come un fattore strutturale dell'apparato statale. Nel caso *Oğur*, ad esempio, la Corte ha detto:

> "At all events, serious doubts arise as to the ability of the administrative authorities concerned to carry out an independent investigation, as required by Article 2 of the Convention. The Court notes that the investigating officer appointed by the governor was a gendarmerie lieutenant-colonel and, as such, was subordinate to the same chain of command as the security forces he was investigating [...]"[161].

Anche nel caso *Kelly*[162], la Corte europea ha affermato che le autorità statali che conducono le indagini devono essere indipendenti da un punto di vista istituzionale ed anche pratico.

La giurisprudenza del sistema interamericano dei diritti umani conferma, in vari casi, l'esistenza dell'obbligo dello Stato di avere un apparato amministrativo e giudiziario di inchiesta adeguato. Si possono ricordare, ad esempio, le già citate sentenze della Corte interamericana nei casi *Velásquez Rodríguez*[163] e *Godínez Cruz*[164] e la decisione del 1996 della Commissione interamericana nel caso *Garay Hermosilla*[165]. Infine, nella prassi del Comitato dei diritti umani, si può ricordare il caso *Rodríguez*[166].

Il secondo obbligo specifico dello Stato, nel quadro delle attività di indagine, è quello di adottare, volta per volta, le misure concrete tese ad investigare sulle violazioni del diritto alla vita. Infatti, è chiaro che lo Stato non può limitarsi ad avere un idoneo apparato di inchiesta; ma deve farlo funzionare quando occorre ed in maniera rapida ed efficiente, tanto più quando si è verificata una violazione del diritto alla vita. Questo è di solito un obbligo di *due diligence*, perché normalmente le attività concrete volte ad indagare sui fatti, e ricercare e catturare le persone colpevoli delle violazioni, sono sottoposte ad alea quanto al loro risultato. Pertanto allo Stato sono richiesti solo i suoi "*best efforts*" nelle attività di indagine.

---

[160] ECtHR, *Güleç v. Turkey*, par. 77; *Oğur v. Turkey*, par. 88; *Akkoç v. Turkey*, parr. 87-88; *Perk and Others v. Turkey*, par. 55.

[161] ECtHR, *Oğur*, par. 91.

[162] ECtHR, *Kelly and Others v. UK*, parr. 95 e 114.

[163] IACtHR, *Velásquez Rodríguez v. Honduras*.

[164] IACtHR, *Godínez Cruz v. Honduras*.

[165] IACmHR, *Garay Hermosilla et al. v. Chile*.

[166] HRCtee, *Rodríguez v. Uruguay*.

Sull'obbligo di adottare misure concrete di indagine in seguito a violazioni del diritto alla vita, gli organi della Convenzione europea dei diritti umani hanno sviluppato una abbondante giurisprudenza. Il primo esempio importante è dato dal già citato caso *McCann*. La Corte europea ha enunciato il principio che l'obbligo dello Stato di garantire il diritto alla vita, per essere effettivo, implica anche un obbligo procedurale di indagare per accertare eventuali violazioni di tale diritto:

> "The obligation to protect the life [...] requires by implication that there should be some form of effective official investigation when individuals have been killed as a result of the use of force by, *inter alios*, agents of the State" [167].

In alcuni casi successivi, la Corte ha precisato che l'obbligo dello Stato di indagare sussiste anche quando vi è incertezza sulla responsabilità di agenti statali nell'uccisione [168] e quando i responsabili sono semplici individui privati [169]. La Corte ha poi precisato bene il contenuto e la natura dell'obbligo di indagare nel caso *Kelly*:

> "The investigation must also be effective in the sense that it is capable of leading to a determination of whether the use of force used in such cases was or was not justified in the circumstances [...] and to the identification and punishment of those responsible. This is not an obligation of result, but of means. The authorities must have taken the reasonable steps available to them to secure the evidence concerning the incident [...] [170].

Anche la Commissione e la Corte interamericane hanno sviluppato un'ampia giurisprudenza sull'obbligo di indagare circa violazioni del diritto alla vita. Essa riprende i principi applicati dagli organi di Strasburgo. Gli esempi più noti sono dati, ancora una volta, dai casi *Velásquez Rodríguez* e *Godínez Cruz*. Nei due casi, la Corte interamericana ha fatto le seguenti puntuali osservazioni:

> "The duty to investigate, like the duty to prevent, is not breached merely because the investigation does not produce a satisfactory result. Nevertheless, it must be undertaken in a serious manner and not as a mere formality pre-ordinated to be ineffective. An investigation must have an objective and be assumed by the State as its own legal duty, not as a step taken by private interests that depends upon the initiative of the victim or his family or upon their offer of proof, without an effective search for the truth by the government [...]" [171].

Questi principi sono stati poi ripresi dalla Corte in diversi casi successivi.

Infine, si possono trarre le medesime conclusioni dalla prassi del Comitato dei diritti umani in materia di obblighi di indagare sulle violazioni del diritto alla vita. Si possono citare i casi *Mojica*, *Laureano* e *Bautista de Arellana* [172].

---

[167] ECtHR, *McCann and Others v. UK*, par. 161.

[168] ECtHR, *Ergi v. Turkey*, par. 82.

[169] ECtHR, *Yaşa v. Turkey*, par. 100.

[170] ECtHR, *Kelly and Others v. UK*, par. 96. Vedi anche ECtHR, *Mahmut Kaya v. Turkey*, par. 108.

[171] IACtHR, *Velásquez Rodríguez*, par. 177; *Godínez Cruz*, par. 188.

[172] HRCtee, *Mojica v. Dominican Republic*, par. 5.5; *Laureano v. Peru*, par. 8.3; *Bautista de Arellana v. Colombia*, par. 8.6.

7.3.3.2. *Obbligo di processare e punire*. – Qualora le indagini sulle violazioni del diritto alla vita e sulla ricerca dei presunti colpevoli abbiano avuto un esito, lo Stato ha l'obbligo di sottoporre a processo ed eventualmente punire i responsabili o presunti responsabili. È questo il naturale coronamento dell'obbligo generale di repressione. A mio avviso, si tratta di un obbligo positivo immediato e di risultato. Infatti ogni Stato deve avere un apparato giurisdizionale che sia idoneo a garantire l'accertamento delle violazioni dei diritti umani e l'amministrazione della giustizia penale, sia in linea generale ed astratta sia nei singoli casi concreti [173]. Pertanto, la sottoposizione a processo dei responsabili delle violazioni del diritto alla vita, siano essi individui-organi statali o individui privati, non può essere un'attività sottoposta ad alea.

Inoltre, si noti che l'obbligo dello Stato di processare e punire i colpevoli costituisce non solo un obbligo "procedurale", che serve a garantire l'effettività del diritto sostanziale alla vita; ma è anche strettamente connesso all'obbligo dello Stato di garantire alle vittime accesso alla giustizia per l'accertamento delle violazioni. Questa stretta connessione risulta anche dalla già citata Risoluzione 60/147 dell'Assemblea Generale delle NU, la quale, subito dopo aver indicato l'obbligo degli Stati di agire contro i responsabili delle gravi violazioni dei diritti umani, proclama anche il loro obbligo di attribuire alle vittime "equal and effective access to justice" [174].

L'esistenza dell'obbligo di processare e punire i presunti responsabili di violazioni del diritto alla vita è confermata, in maniera chiara, dalla prassi degli organi internazionali di controllo [175].

7.3.4. *Obblighi positivi di riparazione*

Infine, lo Stato ha l'obbligo di dare la riparazione alle vittime delle violazioni del diritto alla vita.

Questo obbligo costituisce il completamento necessario degli altri obblighi dello Stato che abbiamo fin qui descritto: quelli di prevenzione, quelli di indagine e quelli di accertamento giurisdizionale e di punizione dei colpevoli. È chiaro che, in caso di difetto di prevenzione delle uccisioni arbitrarie, l'identificazione dei responsabili attraverso le attività di indagine e l'accertamento delle violazioni attraverso la funzione giurisdizionale non hanno, in sé stesse, molto senso se, alla fine, si omette di dare la riparazione alle vittime delle violazioni e/o ai loro parenti.

Questa conclusione è inevitabile, anche da un punto di vista strettamente giuridico, se si crede, come noi crediamo, che gli individui siano oggi destinatari diretti delle norme internazionali sui diritti umani, comprese le norme secondarie in materia di riparazione dell'illecito [176]. Da ciò deriva che gli individui vittime delle violazioni dei diritti umani hanno un vero e proprio diritto alla riparazione, che deriva *direttamente* dal diritto internazionale [177].

---

[173] Vedi Pisillo Mazzeschi (2008), pp. 352-365.

[174] *Basic Principles and Guidelines on the Right to a Remedy and Reparation for Victims of Gross Violations of International Human Rights Law and Serious Violations of International Humanitarian Law*, Principle VII, par. 11.

[175] Vedi Bestagno (2003), pp. 200-214 e la prassi ivi citata.

[176] Vedi *supra*, Cap. I, par. 7.2; Cap. II, par. 8.5; Cap. III, par. 3.2.

[177] Vedi Pisillo Mazzeschi (2004b); Bartolini (2009). Cfr. anche ICJ, *Legal Consequences of the Construction of a Wall*, parr. 147, 152-153.

Questa conclusione trova conferma nei già citati Principi e linee guida sui diritti delle vittime di gravi violazioni dei diritti umani e del diritto umanitario. Il Principio VII (*Victims' rights to remedies*), stabilisce che i rimedi per tali violazioni comprendono, fra l'altro:

> "[...] the victim's right to the following as provided for under international law:
> a) Equal and effective right to justice
> b) Adequate, effective and prompt reparation for harm suffered
> c) Access to relevant information concerning violations and reparation mechanisms".

Ciò premesso, si tratta adesso di determinare la natura dell'obbligo di riparare le violazioni del diritto alla vita. Su questo punto è difficile dare una risposta unitaria, perché la riparazione, nell'illecito internazionale in generale, così come in materia di violazione dei diritti umani, può prendere tre forme differenti: *a*) il risarcimento monetario; *b*) la restituzione in forma specifica (*restitutio in integrum*); *c*) la soddisfazione.

L'obbligo dello Stato responsabile della violazione di dare il risarcimento monetario ai parenti delle vittime e, eventualmente, ad altri Stati, è certamente un obbligo immediato e di risultato, poiché il pagamento di una somma di denaro non è sottoposto ad alea.

Invece, la situazione è più complessa per quanto riguarda la restituzione in forma specifica; cioè il ripristino della situazione di fatto e di diritto esistente prima della violazione. La restituzione è la forma di riparazione in linea di principio preferibile e prioritaria nell'illecito internazionale; ma, nel caso di violazione del diritto alla vita, essa è purtroppo impossibile. Si potrebbe forse ipotizzare come una forma particolare di restituzione l'abrogazione di una legge che preveda la pena di morte od un provvedimento amministrativo che cancelli l'erogazione della pena di morte comminata ad una persona. In questi casi, l'obbligo dello Stato di riparare una violazione del diritto alla vita si configurerà come un obbligo di risultato.

Infine, vi è l'obbligo dello Stato di riparare l'illecito tramite la soddisfazione. Quest'ultima è una forma di riparazione specie dei danni morali, e può consistere, nel diritto internazionale, nel riconoscimento della violazione, in espressioni di rammarico o di scuse ufficiali o in altre modalità appropriate alle circostanze [178]. La soddisfazione può configurarsi come obbligo di risultato oppure di *due diligence* a seconda dei casi [179]. Si noti che la soddisfazione, che nel diritto internazionale tradizionale interstatale non ha grande importanza, può invece esercitare una funzione di rilievo nelle violazioni dei diritti umani, e specie di diritti fondamentali come il diritto alla vita. Infatti, i parenti delle vittime di privazioni arbitrarie della vita possono essere interessati, più che ad un risarcimento monetario dei danni, a forme di soddisfazione morale.

In questo senso, è assai interessante la giurisprudenza della Corte interamericana, che ha preso l'abitudine di imporre allo Stato ritenuto responsabile di violazioni del diritto alla vita una serie dettagliata di misure di soddisfazione, quali, ad esempio, la presentazione

---

[178] Vedi ILC, *Draft Articles on Responsibility of States for Internationally Wrongful Acts*, 1 August 2001, art. 37.

[179] Il pagamento di una somma simbolica di denaro, ad esempio, è un obbligo di risultato, mentre l'obbligo dello Stato di ricercare i corpi delle vittime o quello di prendere le misure appropriate per impedire che gli illeciti si ripetano sono obblighi di *due diligence*. Vedi Pisillo Mazzeschi (2008), pp. 370-372 e 423-424 e la giurisprudenza ivi citata.

ufficiale di scuse da parte dello Stato responsabile [180], la pubblicazione della sentenza che condanna lo Stato su giornali di grande diffusione [181], la costruzione di statue o altri monumenti commemorativi in ricordo delle vittime [182], la dedica di una scuola o di un ospedale alla memoria delle vittime [183], ed altri atti simbolici di questo genere. In questi casi, la soddisfazione si configura come un obbligo di risultato.

8. *Divieto di tortura e di trattamenti o pene inumani o degradanti*

8.1. *Norme*

Il divieto di tortura e di trattamenti o pene inumani o degradanti è enunciato dall'art. 5 della Dichiarazione universale dei diritti dell'uomo nei seguenti termini:

"No one shall be subjected to torture or to cruel, inhuman or degrading treatment or punishment".

Una formula del tutto simile è contenuta nell'art. 3 della Convenzione europea, nell'art. 5(2) della Convenzione americana e nell'art. 4 della Carta dei diritti fondamentali dell'UE. Anche la Carta africana (art. 5) contiene il medesimo divieto. L'art. 7 del Patto sui diritti civili e politici stabilisce un divieto analogo e aggiunge che

"[…] no one shall be subjected without his free consent to medical or scientific experimentation".

Più complessa è la norma contenuta nella Carta araba (art. 8), che prevede anche gli obblighi degli Stati parti di prevenire e reprimere tali abusi e di fornire riparazione per le vittime. Il divieto in oggetto è stabilito non solo dai suddetti trattati generali sui diritti umani, ma anche da alcuni trattati settoriali, fra i quali sono assai importanti la Convenzione delle NU contro la tortura ed altri trattamenti o punizioni crudeli, inumani o degradanti del 1984 [184], che vincola oltre 150 Stati; e la Convenzione europea per la prevenzione della tortura e dei trattamenti inumani e degradanti del 1987 [185].

Inoltre la tortura è vietata da altri trattati sui diritti umani di carattere settoriale (ad esempio la Convenzione sui diritti del fanciullo [186]) e da numerose norme internazionali di diritto internazionale umanitario [187] e di diritto internazionale penale [188]. Naturalmente si

---

[180] IACtHR, *Bámaca-Velásquez*, par. 84; *Barrios Altos*, Judgment of 30 November 2001, par. 44.

[181] IACtHR, *Cantoral Benavides*, Judgment of 3 December 2001, par. 79; *Bámaca-Velásquez*, par. 84.

[182] IACtHR, *The "Street Children"*, Judgment of 26 May 2001, par. 103.

[183] IACtHR, *Trujillo-Oroza*, par. 122; *Aloeboetoe et al.*, Judgment of 10 September 1993, par. 116.

[184] Convention against Torture and Other Cruel, Inhuman or Degrading Treatment or Punishment, 10 December 1984.

[185] European Convention for the Prevention of Torture and Inhuman or Degrading Treatment or Punishment (ECPT), 26 November 1987.

[186] CRC, art. 37.

[187] Vedi, ad es., GCI, art. 3; GCIII, artt. 13, 17, 87, 89, 99.

[188] Vedi, ad es., Rome Statute, artt. 7(1)(f), 8(2)(a)(ii).

devono tenere concettualmente distinti i trattati sui diritti umani da quelli di diritto internazionale penale [189].

Pertanto il divieto di tortura e di trattamenti o pene inumani o degradanti è fermamente stabilito nel diritto internazionale convenzionale. Ma si ritiene comunemente che tale divieto sia sancito anche da una norma di diritto internazionale generale [190]. Più difficile è stabilire se tale norma abbia anche la natura di *ius cogens*. La giurisprudenza internazionale sembra orientata a favore del carattere cogente del divieto di tortura e di trattamenti o pene inumani, non solo nel caso di pratiche di abusi ma anche quando si tratti di atti isolati [191]. Più incerta ci sembra la natura cogente del divieto di trattamenti o pene degradanti.

8.2. *Contenuto del divieto*

Venendo adesso al contenuto ed alla natura del divieto di tortura e di trattamenti o pene inumani o degradanti (e del relativo diritto di non subire tali abusi), conviene notare subito che esso ha carattere assoluto, perché non ammette eccezioni, restrizioni o limiti, neppure in ragione di altri diritti umani potenzialmente in conflitto, quale ad esempio l'esigenza di proteggere la vita di un individuo.

Inoltre, il divieto in oggetto è inderogabile in stati di emergenza; cioè non può essere sospeso dallo Stato neppure in stati di guerra, di emergenza, di sicurezza nazionale o di pericolo pubblico. Ciò è stabilito espressamente dalle norme della Convenzione europea (art. 15(2)), della Convenzione americana (art. 27(2)) e del Patto sui diritti civili e politici (art. 4(2)). Queste norme, prevedendo clausole di deroga dei diritti in casi di emergenze pubbliche, escludono espressamente il divieto in oggetto dal funzionamento di dette clausole.

Questi due caratteri, di "assolutezza" e di "inderogabilità in stati di emergenza", del divieto in questione risultano anche dalla giurisprudenza internazionale [192]. Si può ricordare, fra le altre, la sentenza della Corte interamericana nel caso *Bueno Alves* [193].

Ciò premesso, si tratta ora di approfondire la nozione giuridica di "tortura" e le sue differenze con le altre nozioni di "trattamenti o pene inumani o degradanti".

8.2.1. *La nozione di tortura*

Il Patto sui diritti civili e politici ed i trattati regionali sui diritti umani, come si è visto, proibiscono la tortura ma non contengono una definizione precisa o dettagliata di tale nozione. Ciò dipende, probabilmente, sia dal carattere generale di tali trattati sia dal fatto che

---

[189] I primi impongono il divieto di tortura ad uno Stato nei confronti di individui e di altri Stati (obblighi *erga omnes*) e la loro violazione produce responsabilità internazionale dello Stato. Invece, le norme di diritto internazionale penale impongono il divieto di tortura agli individui, e la loro violazione produce responsabilità internazionale penale degli individui medesimi.

[190] Secondo alcuni autori da una consuetudine e, secondo altri, da un principio generale di diritto riconosciuto *in foro domestico*.

[191] Vedi ICTY, *Furundžija*, par. 153; ECtHR, *Al-Adsani*, par. 61; House of Lords, "*Pinochet III*", pp. 198-199; Id., *Jones and Mitchell*, par. 43; ICJ, *Questions relating to the Obligation to Prosecute*, par. 99.

[192] Cfr. Citroni, Scovazzi (2013), pp. 325-328 e le sentenze ivi citate.

[193] IACtHR, *Bueno Alves v. Argentina*, par. 76.

si è preferito non congelare la nozione nel tempo, per evitare di escludere una sua interpretazione dinamica [194].

Invece, la già citata Convenzione delle NU contro la tortura del 1984 contiene una definizione giuridica dettagliata del concetto di tortura. L'art. 1(1) di questa Convenzione stabilisce:

> "For the purpose of this Convention, the term 'torture' means any act by which severe pain or suffering, whether physical or mental, is intentionally inflicted on a person for such purposes as obtaining from him or a third person information or a confession, punishing him for an act he or a third person has committed, or intimidating or coercing him or a third person, or for any reason based on discrimination of any kind, when such pain or suffering is inflicted by or at the instigation of or with the consent or acquiescence of a public official or other person acting in an official capacity. It does not include pain or suffering arising only from, inherent in or incidental to lawful sanctions".

In sintesi, da questa definizione si ricava che la tortura consiste nel fatto che un individuo-organo statale, o un privato con istigazione, consenso o acquiescenza di un individuo-organo statale, infligge intenzionalmente una grave sofferenza fisica o mentale ad una persona per una serie di scopi specifici; con esclusione delle sofferenze che sono la conseguenza inevitabile di una pena legittima. Si noti che questa definizione, limitando la tortura solo ad atti commessi, istigati o tollerati da organi statali, è assai restrittiva dal punto di vista degli autori della violazione.

Invece, è più ampia la nozione di tortura che emerge complessivamente dalla prassi del Comitato dei diritti umani e degli organi di controllo dei trattati regionali sui diritti umani, poiché tale nozione comprende anche atti di tortura commessi da parte di privati [195]. Nella stessa direzione si muove il diritto internazionale penale, e specie la giurisprudenza dei Tribunali per la ex Iugoslavia e per il Ruanda [196]. Anche la definizione di tortura contenuta nello Statuto della Corte Penale Internazionale non limita la tortura agli atti commessi da agenti statali. Tuttavia, questa tendenza ad un'interpretazione estensiva non va sopravvalutata, perché può derivare anche dalla diversa funzione del diritto internazionale penale, che ha per scopo la punizione degli individui e non degli Stati.

In ogni caso, secondo la prassi internazionale, affinché operi il divieto di tortura, è necessario superare una soglia minima di gravità nella sofferenza inflitta alla vittima. La giurisprudenza della Corte europea dei diritti umani definisce la tortura come un trattamento particolarmente crudele, con il quale si infligge alla vittima una sofferenza grave [197]. Peraltro, in tale giurisprudenza si può notare un'evoluzione, nel senso che la Corte ha abbassato nel tempo la soglia minima di gravità richiesta per integrare la nozione di tortura [198]. Ciò è dovuto ad una interpretazione dinamica della Convenzione europea, che induce ad una

---

[194] Cfr. Zagrebelsky *et al.* (2016), p. 161, con riferimento all'art. 3 della Convenzione europea dei diritti umani.

[195] Vedi Kälin, Künzli (2009), p. 321.

[196] Vedi, ad es., ICTY, *Kunarac*, Judgment of 22 February 2001, par. 496; *Kvočka*, Judgment of 2 November 2001, parr. 137-141, ed altre sentenze citate da Focarelli (2013), p. 89.

[197] Vedi, ad es., ECtHR, *Labita v. Italy*, par. 113 s.; *Cestaro v. Italy*, parr. 164-176.

[198] Zagrebelski *et al.* (2016), p. 162.

crescente protezione dei diritti umani fondamentali. Nel 1978, ad esempio, la Corte, nel caso *Ireland v. UK*[199], non seguendo il rapporto della Commissione, decise che certe tecniche di interrogatorio impiegate dalle forze di sicurezza britanniche contro detenuti accusati di atti di terrorismo in Irlanda[200] non costituissero tortura, ma solo trattamento inumano e degradante. Adesso la Corte qualificherebbe, probabilmente, tali abusi come atti di tortura. Si consideri, ad esempio, che la Corte nel 1999, nel caso *Selmouni*, ha caratterizzato come tortura una serie di maltrattamenti compiuti da agenti francesi contro uno straniero in stato di custodia prima della deportazione; ed ha affermato che:

> "certain acts which were classified in the past as "inhuman and degrading treatment" as opposed to "torture" could be classified differently in the future"[201].

Ed ha proseguito:

> "the increasingly high standard being required in the area of protection of human rights and fundamental liberties correspondingly and inevitably requires greater firmness in assessing breaches of the fundamental values of democratic societies"[202].

Anche la Corte interamericana dei diritti umani ha mostrato una simile tendenza all'interpretazione dinamica del concetto di tortura. Nel caso *Cantoral Benavides*, ad esempio, la Corte ha citato con approvazione gli sviluppi giurisprudenziali della Corte europea ed ha detto:

> "[...] according to international standards for protection, torture can be inflicted not only via physical violence, but also through acts that produce severe physical, psychological or moral suffering in the victim [...] International jurisprudence has been developing the notion of psychological torture"[203].

Infine, il Comitato dei diritti umani ha ritenuto che costituisse un trattamento inumano equivalente a tortura la mancanza di cure mediche o psichiatriche per dei prigionieri, che aveva causato grave sofferenza[204].

8.2.2. *Differenze fra tortura e trattamenti o pene inumani o degradanti*

Come si è visto, i trattati sui diritti umani di solito contengono una norma unica che proibisce la tortura, i trattamenti o pene inumani ed i trattamenti o pene degradanti. Tuttavia, le differenze fra le tre ipotesi, ed anche fra il concetto di pena e quello di trattamento, non sono definite espressamente e si devono ricavare dalla prassi degli organi internazionali di controllo, che non sempre è chiara ed univoca. La dottrina, per definire tali diffe-

---

[199] ECtHR, *Ireland v. UK*, parr. 165-168.

[200] Esse consistevano nel tenere i detenuti incappucciati, nel sottoporli a rumori assordanti, nel tenerli in piedi contro il muro con il peso del corpo gravante sulle dita delle mani, nel privarli del sonno, nella riduzione di cibo ed acqua.

[201] ECtHR, *Selmouni v. France*, par. 101.

[202] *Ibidem*, par. 101 ss.

[203] IACtHR, *Cantoral Benavides*, Judgment of 18 August 2000, parr. 100-102. Vedi anche IACtHR, *Maritza Urrutia*, parr. 91 ss.

[204] HRCtee, *Rouse v. The Philippines*, par. 7.8.

renze, ha ricavato dalla prassi due modelli interpretativi: *a*) quello che si fonda sui livelli di gravità della sofferenza inflitta; *b*) quello che si fonda sullo scopo perseguito da coloro che violano il divieto [205].

Il modello fondato sui livelli di gravità della sofferenza inflitta alla vittima è quello più tradizionale. Secondo questo approccio, la tortura è la più grave forma di abuso, che comporta una condotta particolarmente dura e crudele da parte dell'autore, e che produce un livello elevato di sofferenza per la vittima. Il trattamento inumano è una forma meno grave di abuso, che tuttavia può essere qualificato come inumano poiché produce pur sempre una sofferenza fisica o mentale per la vittima. Si può dire che costituisce un abuso che si pone ad un livello intermedio fra tortura e trattamento degradante. Infine, il trattamento degradante si pone al livello più basso di gravità. Esso consiste in una condotta che produce l'effetto di degradare o umiliare profondamente la vittima, talora, ma non sempre, anche di fronte ad altre persone. In sostanza, in questa ipotesi, la sofferenza della vittima consiste soprattutto nella degradazione e svilimento della sua dignità. La Corte europea, nel caso *Pretty*, ha detto:

> "Where treatment humiliates or debases an individual, showing a lack of respect for, or diminishing, his or her human dignity, or arouses feelings of fear, anguish or inferiority capable of breaking an individual's moral and physical resistance, it may be characterised as degrading [...]" [206].

Questo modello tradizionale di distinzione fra le tre forme di abusi, che risale al caso *Ireland v. UK* [207], è stato mantenuto fermo, specie dalla Corte europea. Ad esempio, nel caso *Aksoy*, la Corte ha affermato:

> "In order to determine whether any particular form of ill-treatment should be qualified as torture, the Court must have regard to the distinction drawn in Article 3 [...] between this notion and that of inhuman or degrading treatment. As it has remarked before, this distinction would appear to have been embodied in the Convention to allow the special stigma of "torture" to attach only to deliberate inhuman treatment causing very serious and cruel suffering [...] [208].

Tuttavia, il modello interpretativo basato sui livelli di gravità della sofferenza della vittima non è esente da problemi, soprattutto perché spesso è difficile distinguere fra tali livelli [209] e perché diversi criteri possono essere usati per qualificare la gravità dell'abuso e della sofferenza inflitta [210].

Il secondo modello interpretativo, per distinguere fra tortura, trattamenti o pene inumani e trattamenti o pene degradanti, si fonda sullo scopo perseguito dagli autori degli abusi. Secondo questa tesi [211], la tortura, oltre ad essere una condotta che produce una grave sofferenza fisica o mentale, deve essere: *a*) deliberata; e *b*) avere uno degli scopi previsti dal-

---

[205] Vedi, in particolare, Kälin, Künzli (2009), pp. 322-325.

[206] ECtHR, *Pretty v. UK*, par. 52.

[207] ECtHR, *Ireland v. UK*, par. 167.

[208] ECtHR, *Aksoy v. Turkey*, par. 63.

[209] Kälin, Künzli (2009), p. 323.

[210] Focarelli (2013), p. 139.

[211] Vedi Rodley (1999), pp. 29 e 75; Kälin, Künzli (2009), p. 323.

l'art. 1 della Convenzione del 1984 contro la tortura; cioè soprattutto quello di forzare la volontà della vittima per ottenere informazioni o confessioni o per punirla. Il trattamento o pena degradante, invece, ricorre quando lo scopo è quello di umiliare o degradare la vittima. Infine il trattamento inumano resta un concetto più generico, che copre gli abusi che producono grave sofferenza fisica o mentale: *a*) causata in circostanze non coperte dalla tortura[212] oppure *b*) che deriva da punizioni illegittime. Questo secondo modello interpretativo è applicato soprattutto dal Comitato contro la tortura[213] e dalla giurisprudenza più recente della Corte interamericana[214].

Ma vi sono anche alcuni organi internazionali di controllo, come il Comitato dei diritti umani, che preferiscono non attribuire grande importanza alla distinzione fra le tre forme di abusi e limitarsi a stabilire se vi sia stata o meno violazione della pertinente norma del trattato. In effetti, dal punto di vista pratico, questa posizione ha un senso poiché i tre abusi comportano le medesime conseguenze giuridiche. Tuttavia, resta il fatto che la distinzione è importante da un punto di vista teorico e che, per la vittima ed i suoi familiari, può avere un valore morale significativo che lo Stato responsabile e gli autori materiali degli abusi siano colpiti dallo stigma forte della tortura piuttosto che da quello più debole dei trattamenti o pene inumani o degradanti.

Infine, si deve sottolineare il fatto che non tutti i casi di maltrattamenti o di comportamenti che causano dolori e sofferenze alle persone costituiscono violazioni dei divieti di tortura e di trattamenti o pene inumani o degradanti. La prassi degli organi internazionali di controllo è chiara sul punto che, per tali violazioni, si deve raggiungere un certo livello di gravità o di intensità della sofferenza causata. Questo livello non può essere prestabilito in generale ed in astratto; ma deve essere valutato in ogni caso concreto. Possono rilevare la durata del maltrattamento, gli effetti dannosi provocati, l'età e la salute della vittima, ed altre circostanze.

8.2.3. *Ambito di applicazione materiale del divieto: principali abusi proibiti nella prassi*

Non è possibile fare un elenco di tutti gli abusi ed i maltrattamenti che sono suscettibili di essere qualificati come tortura o come trattamenti o pene inumani o degradanti. Si possono solo indicare, in sintesi, le principali categorie di situazioni che ricorrono nella prassi degli organi di controllo dei trattati sui diritti umani. Come vedremo, molte di queste situazioni riguardano maltrattamenti nei confronti di soggetti "vulnerabili", come prigionieri, malati di mente, donne.

Una prima categoria è costituita dai maltrattamenti dei *detenuti* e delle persone in stato di arresto o di custodia. Le persone detenute in carcere conservano, ovviamente, i propri diritti umani, salvo quelli che sono necessariamente limitati dalla condizione stessa di detenzione[215]. La detenzione di per sé non può essere considerata un maltrattamento illegittimo; ma possono essere vietate certe condizioni della detenzione. Le condizioni del carce-

---

[212] Ad esempio, gravi maltrattamenti di detenuti o malati di mente.

[213] Sul punto vedi Novak, McArthur (2008), p. 51.

[214] Vedi, ad es., IACtHR, *Bueno Alves*, par. 78 ss.

[215] Vedi, ad es., ECtHR, *Hirst v. UK (No. 2)*, parr. 69-70.

re, quali, ad esempio, l'insufficiente spazio o luce nelle celle o la ventilazione delle medesime, può costituire trattamento inumano o degradante [216]. Le perquisizioni personali dei detenuti ad opera delle guardie carcerarie possono dar luogo a trattamenti degradanti. L'isolamento assoluto, e talora anche quello relativo, può costituire trattamento inumano. La carenza di cure mediche, per i detenuti malati o disabili o con disturbi mentali, può dar luogo a trattamenti inumani o degradanti [217]. L'alimentazione forzata del detenuto, quando non risulta necessaria per la sua sussistenza, può costituire tortura. L'esecuzione di misure disciplinari in carcere, se si realizza con un uso della forza sproporzionato, può costituire trattamento inumano.

La prassi degli organi internazionali di controllo sui diritti umani è assai ricca in materia di trattamento dei detenuti [218]. Fra le sentenze più importanti, si può citare quella nel caso *Torreggiani*, dove la Corte europea ha affermato che i detenuti possono aver bisogno di una protezione speciale, per la loro situazione di soggezione all'autorità dello Stato; e che pertanto le autorità statali hanno:

> "une obligation positive qui consiste à s'assurer que tout prisonnier est détenu dans des conditions qui sont compatibles avec le respect de la dignité humaine, que les modalités d'exécution de la mesure ne soumettent pas l'intéressé à une détresse ou à une épreuve d'une intensité qui excède le niveau inévitable de souffrance inhérent à la détention […]" [219].

Una seconda categoria di situazioni è quella relativa agli abusi nei confronti delle persone *malate di mente*. Anche queste persone sono particolarmente vulnerabili e quindi richiedono una protezione speciale, perché sono esposte a maggiori pericoli di essere sottoposte a trattamenti inumani o degradanti. Infatti, sono stati adottati alcuni strumenti internazionali, sia pure di carattere non vincolante, per la tutela di queste persone, ad esempio i Principi per la protezione delle persone malate di mente e per il miglioramento della salute mentale, adottati dall'Assemblea Generale delle NU con la risoluzione 46/119 del 1991 [220]. La prassi degli organi di controllo dei trattati sui diritti umani conferma questa impostazione [221]. La Corte europea ha dovuto affrontare molti casi concernenti il trattamento dei malati di mente ed ha sempre affermato che, per queste persone, è necessario un particolare livello di attenzione nel valutare l'esistenza di una violazione dell'art. 3 della Convenzione europea. Fra le varie sentenze [222], si può ricordare quella nel caso *Keenan* [223], dove il Regno Unito fu condannato per la mancanza di una sorveglianza ed un'assistenza psichiatrica adeguata nei confronti di una persona mentalmente malata e con tendenze suicide.

---

[216] Vedi, ad es., ECtHR, *Sulejmanovic v. Italy*, par. 43; *Torreggiani and Others v. Italy*, par. 78.

[217] Vedi, ad es., ECtHR, *Cara-Damiani v. Italy*, parr. 69-78.

[218] Per un esame approfondito della prassi, vedi Citroni, Scovazzi (2013), pp. 353-382.

[219] ECtHR, *Torreggiani and Others*, par. 65.

[220] *Principles for the protection of persons with mental illness and the improvement of mental health care*, Res. 46/119 of 17 December 1991.

[221] Vedi ancora Citroni, Scovazzi (2013), pp. 382-388.

[222] Vedi ECtHR, *Herczegfalvy v. Austria*; *Rivière v. France*; *Filip v. Rumenia*; *Renolde v. France*.

[223] ECtHR, *Keenan v. UK*.

Anche la Corte interamericana ha affermato principi simili [224]. Infine, è interessante un caso deciso dalla Commissione africana [225], che ha dichiarato che la legislazione del Gambia in materia di malati di mente andava abrogata, perché contraria al divieto di trattamenti inumani e degradanti.

Una terza categoria riguarda lo *stupro* e le violenze sessuali [226]. La Corte europea ha ritenuto che lo stupro fosse una forma di tortura fin dalla sentenza del 1997 sul caso *Aydin* [227]. Questa posizione è stata mantenuta anche nella giurisprudenza successiva [228]. Anche la Commissione e Corte interamericane hanno raggiunto le medesime conclusioni in alcuni casi di stupro e di altre forme di violenza sessuale. Si possono citare i casi *Martín de Mejía* [229], *Miguel Castro* [230] e *Masacre de las Dos Erres* [231].

Conforme è la prassi della Commissione africana [232]. Infine, si deve notare che i tribunali penali internazionali hanno sviluppato una giurisprudenza interessante sul reato di stupro, che viene equiparato alla tortura e considerato, quando ne ricorrono le condizioni, come un crimine contro l'umanità. In proposito, si possono ricordare i casi *Akayesu* [233], *Delalić* [234], *Furundžija* [235] e *Kunarac* [236].

Una quarta categoria è costituita da *pene eccessive e punizioni corporali*. La Corte europea ha stabilito, ad esempio, che la pena dell'ergastolo costituisce un trattamento inumano, quando la normativa applicabile escluda ogni possibilità di liberazione della persona condannata [237]; e che una pena manifestamente sproporzionata può costituire una violazione dell'art. 3 della Convenzione europea [238]. Sulla questione delle pene corporali [239], è nota la sentenza del 1978 sul caso *Tyrer* [240], nella quale la Corte europea ha condannato il Regno Unito, stabilendo che la fustigazione di un alunno minorenne, come sanzione per la sua aggressione ad un altro studente, fosse una punizione degradante ai sensi dell'art. 3 della Convenzione europea. La Corte interamericana, nel caso *Caesar* [241], ha affermato che le punizioni corporali sono oggi vietate dal diritto internazionale e che la fustigazione di un adulto, nu-

---

[224] IACtHR, *Ximenes Lopes v. Brasil.*

[225] ACmHPR, *Purohit and Moore v. Gambia.*

[226] Vedi Citroni, Scovazzi (2013), pp. 341-350; Focarelli (2013), pp. 144-145.

[227] ECtHR, *Aydin v. Turkey*, parr. 83-86.

[228] Vedi, ad es., ECtHR, *M.C. v. Bulgaria*; *Maslova and Nalbandov v. Russia*; *D.J. v. Croatia.*

[229] IACmHR, *Raquel Martín de Mejía v. Peru.*

[230] IACtHR, *Miguel Castro v. Peru*, parr. 310-312.

[231] IACtHR, *Masacre de las Dos Erres v. Guatemala*, parr. 139-141.

[232] ACmHPR, *Malawi African Association and Others v. Mauritania*; *Institute for Human Rights and Development in Africa v. Guinea.*

[233] ICTR, *Akayesu*, Judgment of 2 September 1998, parr. 596-598.

[234] ICTY, *Delalić*, Judgment of 16 November 1998, par. 475.

[235] ICTY, *Furundžija*, Judgment of 10 December 1998, parr. 164-186.

[236] ICTY, *Kunarac*, Judgment of 12 June 2002, par. 185.

[237] ECtHR, *Kafkaris v. Cyprus*, parr. 95-99; *Vinter and Others v. UK*, parr. 103-118; *Öcalan v. Turkey (No. 2)*, Judgment of 18 March 2014, parr. 193-207.

[238] ECtHR, *Harkins and Edwards v. UK*, parr. 133-138.

[239] Vedi Focarelli (2013), pp. 140-141.

[240] ECtHR, *Tyrer v. UK*, parr. 30-33.

[241] IACtHR, *Caesar v. Trinidad and Tobago*, par. 20.

do e legato fino al suo svenimento, costituisce una tortura. La Commissione africana, nel caso *Doebbler*[242], ha qualificato la pena della flagellazione come una forma di tortura.

Una quinta categoria di situazioni che ricorrono nella prassi è data dalle c.d. "consegne straordinarie" (*extraordinary renditions*); cioè quelle misure antiterroristiche che consistono nel trasferimento extra-giudiziario di una persona da una giurisdizione a un'altra, al fine di detenzione e interrogatorio al di fuori del normale sistema giuridico[243]. Come è stato efficacemente notato in dottrina, le consegne straordinarie costituiscono "una sorta di circuito segreto di tortura per procura che coinvolge diversi Stati, legati da un rapporto di complicità nell'illecito"[244]: lo Stato che organizza il circuito, quello che consente la cattura della vittima nel proprio territorio, e quello che riceve la vittima e estorce le informazioni con la tortura. È chiaro che le *extraordinary renditions* si risolvono in violazioni di numerosi diritti umani fondamentali, fra i quali, quasi sempre, il divieto di tortura e di trattamenti inumani e degradanti ed i divieti di detenzioni arbitrarie e di sparizione forzata delle persone[245].

Sulla prassi delle *extraordinary renditions* sono stati predisposti rapporti nel quadro del Consiglio d'Europa e delle Nazioni Unite e sono state adottate numerose raccomandazioni da parte di enti ed organizzazioni internazionali[246]. Nella prassi degli organi internazionali di controllo sui diritti umani, si possono ricordare il caso *Alzery*[247], deciso nel 2006 dal Comitato dei diritti umani, ed i casi *Babar Ahmad* e *El Masri*[248] decisi dalla Corte europea. In Italia, un noto esempio di sparizione forzata si è verificato nel caso *Abu Omar*[249], che ha dato luogo a varie pronunce di giudici interni (Corte d'appello di Milano, Cassazione, Corte costituzionale)[250], ad un intervento del Governo italiano che ha opposto il segreto di stato, ed in seguito anche ad una sentenza della Corte europea[251], che ha accertato numerose violazioni dei diritti umani da parte dell'Italia.

Infine, si deve notare che altre pratiche sono state considerate come violazioni del divieto di tortura e trattamenti o pene inumani o degradanti. La *sterilizzazione forzata*, ad esempio, è stata ritenuta dalla Corte di Strasburgo come una violazione dell'art. 3 della Convenzione europea in alcuni casi contro la Slovacchia[252]. Anche le *sparizioni di persone*, accompagnate da carenza di indagini adeguate da parte delle autorità per ritrovare gli scomparsi, possono costituire un trattamento inumano e degradante nei confronti dei familiari degli scomparsi. La Corte europea lo ha affermato, ad esempio, in alcuni casi contro la Turchia e l'Ucraina[253].

---

242 ACmHPR, *Curtis Francis Doebbler v. Sudan*, Decision of 4 May 2003, par. 42.

243 Vedi ECtHR, *Babar Ahmad and Others v. UK*.

244 Citroni, Scovazzi (2013), p. 417.

245 Vedi *infra*, parr. 16 e 17.

246 Per maggiori dettagli vedi Citroni, Scovazzi (2013), pp. 418-422.

247 HRCtee, *Alzery v. Sweden.*

248 ECtHR, *Babar Ahmad and Others v. UK*; *El-Masri v. FYRM.*

249 Sulla vicenda *Abu Omar* vi sono numerosi contributi dottrinali. Vedi Carpanelli (2013) e la dottrina ivi citata a p. 316, note 4 e 5.

250 Vedi, fra le altre, App. Milano, *Courtney et al.*; Id., *Abu Omar et al.*; Cass., *Nasr et al.*; Id., *Medero et al.*; Corte cost., ord. n. 69 del 2013.

251 ECtHR, *Nasr and Ghali v. Italy.*

252 ECtHR, *V.C. v. Slovakia*; *N.B. v. Slovakia.*

253 ECtHR, *Kurt v. Turkey*, par. 134; *Çakici v. Turkey*, par. 98; *Gongadze v. Ukraine*, par. 186.

8.3. *Obblighi*

Le norme internazionali sul divieto di tortura e di trattamenti o pene inumani o degradanti impongono agli Stati numerosi obblighi, che sono simili a quelli, già esaminati, relativi al rispetto del diritto alla vita. Pertanto, si possono distinguere gli obblighi negativi da quelli positivi (di risultato e di *due diligence*). Inoltre, nel quadro degli obblighi positivi, si possono individuare obblighi di prevenzione, di repressione e di riparazione. L'analisi di questi obblighi sarà sintetica, perché gli aspetti concettuali dei medesimi sono già stati esaminati.

8.3.1. *Obblighi negativi*

Lo Stato ha, prima di tutto, l'obbligo negativo di astenersi, per mezzo dei propri individui-organi (anche quando eccedono la propria autorità o contravvengono ad istruzioni)[254], dal compiere atti di tortura o da infliggere trattamenti o pene inumani o degradanti.

Riguardo a tale obbligo, la prassi degli organi di controllo dei trattati sui diritti umani è assai ampia. Nella giurisprudenza della Convenzione europea, un esempio classico di violazione di obblighi negativi da parte di uno Stato è dato dal già citato caso *Ireland v. UK*[255], nel quale le forze di sicurezza britanniche avevano impiegato, nei confronti di detenuti sospettati di far parte dell'IRA, cinque tecniche di interrogatorio che avevano causato sofferenze alle vittime. La Corte europea condannò il Regno Unito per violazione del divieto di trattamenti inumani. Nel più recente caso *Selmouni*[256], nel quale il ricorrente era stato sottoposto ad interrogatori molto violenti da parte delle forze dell'ordine francesi, la Corte ha condannato la Francia per atti di tortura. Nella giurisprudenza del sistema interamericano, si può ricordare la sentenza della Corte interamericana del 1988 nel caso *Velásquez Rodríguez*, nella quale la Corte ha condannato l'Honduras per la violazione degli artt. 7, 5 e 4, letti in connessione all'art. 1(1), della Convenzione americana ed ha affermato che:

> "under international law a State is responsible for the acts of its agents undertaken in their official capacity and for their omissions, even when those agents act outside the sphere of their authority or violate internal law"[257].

In certe circostanze, può essere difficile ottenere prove circa le violazioni di tale obbligo da parte dello Stato. Si pensi, ad esempio, ai maltrattamenti delle persone in stato di detenzione o di custodia. La giurisprudenza degli organi di controllo dei trattati sui diritti umani ha spesso stabilito che in tali casi si ha un'inversione dell'onere della prova: in presenza di segni fisici di maltrattamento delle persone detenute o custodite, spetta allo Stato provare che tali segni non sono attribuibili ai propri individui-organi[258].

L'obbligo degli Stati di non ricorrere alla tortura ed a trattamenti o pene inumani o degradanti è così importante che esso comporta, in certe circostanze, anche un obbligo degli Stati di evitare che tali abusi siano compiuti da altri Stati ed al di fuori del territorio o della

---

[254] Vedi ILC *Draft Articles on Responsibility of States for Internationally Wrongful Acts*, artt. 4-11.

[255] ECtHR, *Ireland v. UK*.

[256] ECtHR, *Selmouni v. France*.

[257] IACtHR, *Velásquez Rodríguez*, par. 170.

[258] Vedi, ad es., ECtHR *Aktaş v. Turkey*, par. 291; IACtHR *Juan Humberto Sánchez v. Honduras*, par. 100. Cfr. anche Kälin, Künzli (2009), p. 334.

"giurisdizione" degli Stati stessi. In altri termini, si è affermato anche l'obbligo negativo degli Stati di non estradare, espellere, respingere, o comunque consegnare una persona ad un altro Stato dove vi sono motivi fondati per ritenere che essa possa subire tali abusi. Come si è già detto[259], questa evoluzione interpretativa del divieto di tortura è stata influenzata dal principio di *non-refoulement* ed ha finito, a sua volta, per integrare tale principio.

Nella giurisprudenza della Convenzione europea, questo obbligo è stato affermato per la prima volta nel noto caso *Soering* del 1989[260]. Il ricorrente, cittadino tedesco, era in carcere nel Regno Unito in attesa di estradizione negli USA, dove sarebbe stato processato nello Stato della Virginia per omicidio aggravato, punibile con la pena di morte. Soering sosteneva che una sua estradizione negli USA avrebbe prodotto la conseguenza di una sua certa condanna ed una sua sottoposizione, nelle carceri della Virginia, alla c.d. sindrome da corridoio della morte (*death row phenomenon*), che doveva essere qualificata come un trattamento inumano e degradante vietato dall'art. 3 della Convenzione. La Corte europea accolse, nella sostanza, tale argomento, affermando che uno Stato parte della Convenzione non deve estradare un individuo se tale misura può produrre, in maniera prevedibile, conseguenze contrarie all'art. 3. Secondo la Corte:

> "[…] It would hardly be compatible with the underlying values of the Convention […] were a Contracting State knowingly to surrender a fugitive to another State where there were substantial grounds for believing that he would be in danger of being subjected to torture […] this inherent obligation not to extradite also extends to cases in which the fugitive would be faced in the receiving State by a real risk of exposure to inhuman or degrading treatment or punishment […]"[261].

I principi affermati dalla Corte europea nel caso *Soering* sono stati in seguito ribaditi molte volte[262]. La Corte li ha applicati anche quando si trattava di espulsione o estradizione di individui sospettati o condannati per atti di terrorismo: le sentenze più note sono quelle nei casi *Chahal*[263] e *Saadi*[264]. Si noti che in tali casi la Corte ha stabilito che il divieto di deportazione si applica in modo assoluto, a prescindere dalla pericolosità dell'individuo, ed ha escluso che si possa operare un bilanciamento fra i rischi potenziali per l'individuo, se fosse deportato, ed i pericoli per l'ordine pubblico derivanti dalla sua presenza nel territorio dello Stato[265]. Conviene inoltre citare la sentenza del 2012 nel caso *Hirsi*[266], nella quale l'Italia è stata condannata per violazione dell'art. 3 della Convenzione europea, per aver respinto dei migranti in mare verso Tripoli, esponendoli al pericolo di essere sottoposti a maltrattamenti in Libia e di essere rimpatriati in Somalia o Eritrea ed ivi sottoposti a tortura.

---

[259] Vedi *supra*, par. 7.3.1.

[260] ECtHR, *Soering v. UK*.

[261] *Ibidem*, par. 88.

[262] Vedi, ad es., ECtHR, *Vilvarajah and Others v. UK*; *N.A. v. UK*.

[263] ECtHR, *Chahal v. UK*.

[264] ECtHR, *Saadi v. Italy*.

[265] Tuttavia questa posizione non è "universalmente" condivisa. La Corte Suprema canadese, ad esempio, nel caso *Suresh*, ha lasciato spazio alla possibilità di attuare il suddetto bilanciamento, sia pure in casi eccezionali. Cfr. Supreme Court of Canada, *Suresh v. Canada*.

[266] ECtHR, *Hirsi Jamaa and Others v. Italy*.

Una prassi conforme a quella della Corte europea è stata sviluppata anche dal Comitato dei diritti umani [267]. Infine, si deve notare che la Convenzione delle NU contro la tortura del 1984 ha espressamente recepito l'obbligo in oggetto, ma limitatamente alla tortura, nell'art. 3(1), secondo il quale:

> "No State Party shall expel, return or extradite a person to another State where there are substantial grounds for believing that he would be in danger of being subjected to torture".

8.3.2. *Obblighi positivi di prevenzione*

Il divieto di tortura e trattamenti o pene inumani o degradanti impone agli Stati un obbligo generale di prevenzione, che si compone, a sua volta, di alcuni obblighi più specifici. Questo concetto è espresso, anche se non in maniera dettagliata, nell'art. 2(1) della Convenzione del 1984 contro la tortura:

> "Each State Party shall take effective legislative, administrative, judicial or other measures to prevent acts of torture in any territory under its jurisdiction".

Pertanto, lo Stato ha, in primo luogo, l'obbligo (immediato e di risultato) di avere (o dotarsi di) un *apparato normativo* di prevenzione, idoneo a prevenire in astratto le violazioni del divieto in oggetto. Ciò significa, soprattutto, introdurre nei propri codici penali i reati di tortura e di trattamenti inumani o degradanti, prevedendo pene adeguate alla gravità di tali reati. Quest'obbligo viene enunciato in maniera chiara dal Comitato dei diritti umani nel suo Commento Generale n. 20 [268] e viene confermato nella giurisprudenza degli organi di controllo: ad esempio, nelle sentenze della Corte europea nei casi *A. c. UK* e *M.C. c. Bulgaria* [269] e nella sentenza della Corte interamericana nel caso *Heliodoro Portugal c. Panama* [270]. Anche l'art. 4 della Convenzione delle NU contro la tortura stabilisce che:

> "1. Each State Party shall ensure that all acts of torture are offences under its criminal law [...]
> 2. Each State Party shall make these offences punishable by appropriate penalties which take into account their grave nature" [271].

In secondo luogo, lo Stato ha l'obbligo (immediato e di risultato) di avere (o dotarsi di) un *apparato amministrativo*, che sia anch'esso idoneo, in astratto, a prevenire le violazioni del divieto in oggetto. Si tratta, soprattutto, dell'apparato di polizia, di quello carcerario e delle forze armate. Questi apparati devono avere il grado di funzionamento e di efficienza richiesto ad ogni Stato moderno, per prevenire atti di tortura o trattamenti inumani o degradanti che possano essere compiuti da parte di agenti statali o da privati. Anche su tale obbligo si può citare il Commento Generale n. 20 del Comitato dei diritti umani, secondo il quale:

---

[267] Vedi, ad es., HRCtee, *Ng v. Canada*; *Maksudov and Others v. Kyrgyzstan and Uzbekistan*; *Kaba v. Canada*; *Warsame v. Canada*. Per un esame approfondito di questi casi, vedi Citroni, Scovazzi (2013), pp. 410-415.

[268] HRCtee, General Comment No. 20, 10 March 1992, par. 8.

[269] ECtHR, *A. v. UK*, parr. 23-24; *M.C. v. Bulgaria*, par. 166.

[270] IACtHR, *Heliodoro Portugal v. Panama*.

[271] L'Italia non ha rispettato questo obbligo di legiferare per molto tempo, nonostante avesse ratificato la Convenzione del 1984. Solo recentemente si è dotata di una normativa in materia: la legge 14 luglio 2017, n. 110.

> "Article 7 should be read in conjunction with article 2, paragraph 3, of the Covenant. In their reports, States parties should indicate how their legal system effectively guarantees the immediate termination of all the acts prohibited by article 7 […]" [272].

In terzo luogo, lo Stato ha l'obbligo di prendere quelle *misure concrete* che sono, volta per volta, richieste per prevenire violazioni del divieto in oggetto. Si tratta di un obbligo di *due diligence*, perché il suo adempimento è soggetto ad alea. Lo Stato deve attivarsi e prendere misure preventive, usando i suoi *best efforts*, per evitare violazioni sia da parte di individui privati sia da parte di individui-organi statali soggetti a controllo da parte di autorità superiori.

Quest'ultimo obbligo trova conferma in un'ampia prassi degli organi internazionali di controllo. Nella giurisprudenza della Corte europea, vi sono molti casi importanti. Alcuni di essi riguardano obblighi di prevenzione che spettano ad autorità statali specifiche rispetto ad atti commessi da individui privati. In questi casi si applicano i principi già indicati dalla Corte nel caso *Osman*, relativo al diritto alla vita [273]. In questo senso si può ricordare, ad esempio, il caso *Z and Others* [274], nel quale alcuni adolescenti si lamentavano del fatto che le autorità inglesi competenti non avevano preso misure per proteggerli contro trattamenti inumani e degradanti che essi subivano da parte dei propri genitori. Altri casi riguardano, invece, illeciti omissivi consistenti nel difetto di prevenzione da parte degli organi statali considerati nel loro complesso. Si possono citare, ad esempio, i casi *Kaya* e *Ilaşcu* [275]. Anche la Corte interamericana ha applicato principi simili in numerosi casi [276].

8.3.3. *Obblighi positivi di repressione*

Lo Stato ha, inoltre, un obbligo generale di repressione rispetto alla violazione del divieto di tortura e trattamenti o pene inumani o degradanti. Anche in questo caso, l'obbligo generale si compone di due obblighi più specifici: *a*) quello di *indagare* in maniera rapida ed efficace, allo scopo di identificare e catturare i colpevoli delle violazioni; *b*) quello di *processare e punire* i colpevoli. Come si è già visto, alcuni di questi obblighi sono di *due diligence* ed altri sono di risultato.

La prassi degli organi internazionali di controllo su questi due obblighi relativi al divieto di tortura è assai ampia. Per la Corte europea, si possono ricordare, fra gli altri, i casi *Assenov*, *Labita*, *Ilhan* e *Sakik* [277]. Nel caso *Assenov*, la Corte ha affermato:

> "where an individual raises an arguable claim that he has been seriously ill-treated by the police or other such agents of the State unlawfully and in breach of Article 3, that provision, read in conjunction with the State's general duty under Article 1 of the Convention […] requires by implication that there should be an effective official investigation. This investigation […] should be capable of leading to the identification and punishment of those responsible […]. If this were not the case, the general legal prohibition of torture and inhu-

---

[272] HRCtee, General Comment No. 20, 10 March 1992, par. 14.

[273] Vedi *supra*, par. 7.3.2.3.

[274] ECtHR, *Z and Others v. UK*.

[275] ECtHR, *Kaya v. Turkey*, parr. 85-101; *Ilaşcu and Others v. Moldova and Russia*, par. 348.

[276] Vedi, ad es., IACtHR, *Velásquez Rodríguez; Godínez Cruz; "Juvenile Reeducation Institute"*.

[277] ECtHR, *Assenov and Others v. Bulgaria*; *Labita v. Italy*; *Ilhan v. Turkey*; *Sakik and Others v. Turkey*.

man and degrading treatment and punishment, despite its fundamental importance [...], would be ineffective in practice"[278].

Conclusioni simili sono state raggiunte da altri organi di controllo. Il Comitato dei diritti umani ha affermato, nel suo Commento Generale n. 20, che ogni denuncia di tortura deve essere oggetto di una indagine completa, rapida e imparziale da parte dello Stato[279]; ed ha poi applicato questo principio in diversi casi[280]. Il Comitato contro la tortura, nel caso *Halimi-Nedzibi*, ha applicato lo stesso principio[281]. Per la Corte interamericana, si possono citare i casi *Velásquez Rodríguez*, *Godínez Cruz*, *Caballero Delgado* e *Vargas Areco*[282]. Per la Commissione africana, si può ricordare la decisione nel caso *Zimbabwe Human Rights NGO Forum*[283].

Infine, con specifico riferimento all'obbligo di eseguire le sentenze di punizione dei responsabili di abusi, è interessante il caso *Bondonga*[284], nel quale il Comitato dei diritti umani ha dichiarato il Congo responsabile di una violazione dell'art. 7 del Patto, perché le autorità congolesi non avevano eseguito la sentenza con cui alcuni militari erano stati condannati, da un tribunale militare congolese, per atti di tortura e di trattamento inumano contro una persona in stato di custodia.

8.3.4. *Obblighi positivi di riparazione*

Infine, lo Stato ha l'obbligo di garantire un accesso alla giustizia ed una adeguata *riparazione* alle vittime di tortura e di trattamenti inumani o degradanti ed ai loro familiari. Come si è già visto, questi due obblighi sono espressamente previsti nei Principi e linee-guida sui diritti delle vittime di gravi violazioni dei diritti umani[285]. Anche il Comitato dei diritti umani, nel suo Commento Generale n. 20, in tema di tortura, afferma che:

> "States may not deprive individuals of the right to an effective remedy, including compensation and such full rehabilitation as may be possible"[286].

Inoltre, il Comitato afferma che gli Stati parti devono indicare come il loro sistema giuridico garantisce alle vittime dei rimedi adeguati[287]; e che, in linea di principio, non sono ammissibili leggi di amnistia per atti di tortura[288].

Nella prassi degli organi internazionali di controllo, la misura di riparazione più comu-

---

[278] ECtHR, *Assenov and Others*, par. 102.

[279] HRCtee, General Comment No. 20, 10 March 1992, par. 14.

[280] Vedi, ad es., HRCtee, *Rodríguez v. Uruguay*.

[281] CteeAT, *M. Qani Halimi-Nedzibi v. Austria*, par. 13.5.

[282] IACtHR, *Velásquez Rodríguez v. Honduras; Godínez Cruz v. Honduras; Caballero Delgado and Santana v. Colombia; Vargas Areco v. Paraguay*.

[283] ACmHPR, *Zimbabwe Human Rights NGO Forum v. Zimbabwe*.

[284] HRCtee, *Basongo Bondonga v. DRC*.

[285] Vedi *supra*, par. 7.3.3.2.

[286] HRCtee, General Comment No. 20, 10 March 1992, par. 15.

[287] *Ibidem*, par. 14: "The right to lodge complaints against maltreatment prohibited by article 7 must be recognized in the domestic law [...] The reports of States parties should provide specific information on the remedies available to victims of maltreatment and the procedure that complainants must follow [...]".

[288] *Ibidem*, par. 15: "Amnesties are generally incompatible with the duty of States to investigate such acts; to guarantee freedom from such acts within their jurisdiction; and to ensure that they do not occur in the future".

ne, per le violazioni del divieto di tortura e trattamenti o pene inumani o degradanti, è, naturalmente, quella del risarcimento monetario, poiché per tali violazioni la *restitutio in integrum* non è possibile.

Tuttavia, per quanto riguarda la riparazione in forma di soddisfazione, è interessante la giurisprudenza degli organi del sistema interamericano. Come si è già visto in relazione al diritto alla vita, la Corte interamericana ha interpretato in maniera innovativa il suo potere di decidere misure di soddisfazione a carico degli Stati condannati per violazioni di diritti umani fondamentali; e ciò vale, ovviamente, anche per le violazioni del divieto di tortura e trattamenti o pene inumani o degradanti. Talora le misure di soddisfazione decise dalla Corte sembrano avere anche la funzione di garanzia di non ripetizione dell'illecito[289].

La Corte, ad esempio, nel caso *González*[290], relativo a stupri e sparizioni di donne, ha deciso che il Messico dovesse adottare, fra l'altro, programmi e sistemi di indagine adeguati in casi di violenza sessuale, una banca dati per identificare le donne scomparse e programmi di sensibilizzazione per la popolazione in tema di violenza contro le donne. Nel caso *Vargas Areco*[291], relativo ad atti di violenza ed uccisione di un minorenne, la Corte ha deciso che il Paraguay dovesse, fra l'altro: prendere tutte le misure necessarie per identificare, processare e punire i responsabili dell'uccisione del ragazzo; fare una cerimonia pubblica per scusarsi e riconoscere le violazioni in presenza della famiglia della vittima e delle autorità civili e militari; apporre una targa commemorativa; assicurare ai familiari un trattamento medico, psicologico e psichiatrico; creare programmi e corsi sui diritti umani per i membri delle forze armate; pubblicare la sentenza della Corte nella gazzetta ufficiale e in un giornale di ampia diffusione nazionale; modificare le proprie leggi sul reclutamento dei minori nelle forze armate per adattarle agli standard internazionali.

9. *Divieto di crimini internazionali*

Nel quadro dei diritti umani fondamentali che hanno lo scopo di proteggere la vita e l'integrità fisica della persona, si può collocare anche il divieto generale di crimini internazionali. Si deve premettere che la categoria dei "crimini internazionali" viene di solito usata nel *diritto internazionale penale*, per riferirsi ad una serie di reati commessi da individui privati o, più spesso, da individui-organi di uno Stato, che costituiscono anche gravi violazioni di diritti umani e del diritto umanitario, e che danno luogo ad una responsabilità penale internazionale di tali persone. In altri termini, per "crimini internazionali" si intende di solito far riferimento ai crimini internazionali *individuali*, alla responsabilità penale internazionale delle persone che commettono tali crimini, ed al regime di repressione penale che esiste dinanzi ai giudici statali e dinanzi ad alcuni tribunali internazionali.

Noi non intendiamo occuparci *direttamente* del diritto internazionale penale, perché si tratta di un settore diverso rispetto a quello della tutela dei diritti umani, anche se ovvia-

---

[289] Vedi ILC *Draft Articles on Responsibility of States for Internationally Wrongful Acts*, art. 30.

[290] IACtHR, *González et al. v. Mexico.*

[291] IACtHR, *Vargas Areco v. Paraguay.*

mente i due settori sono strettamente collegati e complementari nella loro funzione. Ma si deve sottolineare che, molto spesso, gli individui che commettono un crimine internazionale sono individui-organi del proprio Stato o di un'entità a carattere parastatale, come un movimento insurrezionale che controlla un territorio[292]. Infatti solo questi enti sono di solito capaci di produrre quegli attacchi estesi e sistematici contro una popolazione od un gruppo, che caratterizzano le varie categorie di crimini internazionali.

Pertanto, quando vengono commessi crimini internazionali, sorge di solito una duplice responsabilità internazionale: *a*) quella dell'*individuo*, che mira alla sua punizione secondo le regole del diritto internazionale penale; *b*) quella dello *Stato* (o di altro ente titolare di obblighi internazionali sui diritti umani)[293] che ha commesso o non impedito il crimine, che viene regolata dalle norme internazionali sui diritti umani[294] e da quelle sulla responsabilità internazionale dello Stato[295]. *A noi interessa quest'ultimo aspetto*. Di conseguenza, parleremo d'ora in poi di "divieto di crimini internazionali" con riferimento alle *norme che impongono obblighi a carico degli Stati* (o di altri enti titolari di obblighi internazionali sui diritti umani)[296]. Ma, sia pure in maniera indiretta, sarà necessario far riferimento anche alle norme del diritto internazionale penale.

Ciò premesso, conviene ricordare che la categoria dei "crimini internazionali" risale all'Accordo di Londra del 1945[297], con il quale fu istituito il Tribunale militare internazionale di Norimberga per la punizione dei criminali nazisti[298]. All'epoca i crimini internazionali venivano distinti in tre categorie: *a*) crimini di guerra; *b*) crimini contro l'umanità; *c*) crimini contro la pace[299]. Il processo di Norimberga, ed il parallelo processo di Tokio contro i criminali giapponesi, segnarono l'avvio di un nuovo settore del diritto internazionale, denominato in seguito come diritto internazionale penale.

Questo settore, dopo molti anni di sviluppo piuttosto lento, affidato in gran parte alla prassi dei tribunali militari statali, ha avuto un processo di accelerazione a partire dagli anni 1990, con le istituzioni del Tribunale penale internazionale per la ex Jugoslavia[300], del

---

[292] Vedi, per tutti, Conforti (2015), p. 221.

[293] Vedi *supra*, Cap. III, par. 2.

[294] E dalle norme di diritto internazionale umanitario nel caso dei crimini di guerra.

[295] E dalle norme sulla responsabilità internazionale delle organizzazioni internazionali.

[296] Si deve peraltro avvertire che, da un punto di vista terminologico, non è corretto parlare di "crimini internazionali degli Stati", poiché tale espressione non è stata riconosciuta nella prassi e nell'*opinio iuris* della comunità internazionale. Il concetto di "crimini internazionali degli Stati" era stato proposto dal Relatore Speciale Ago nel celebre art. 19 del Progetto di articoli sulla responsabilità degli Stati, adottato in prima lettura dalla Commissione del diritto internazionale nel 1976. Ma in seguito, per l'opposizione da parte di molti Stati, questa espressione è stata eliminata. L'art. 40 del Progetto approvato nel 2001 parla ora di gravi violazioni di obblighi stabiliti da norme imperative di diritto internazionale generale.

[297] Agreement by The Government of The United Kingdom of Great Britain and Northern Ireland, The Government of the United States of America, the Provisional Government of the French Republic and the Government of the Union of Soviet Socialist Republics for the Prosecution and Punishment of the Major War Criminals of the European Axis, London, 8 August 1945, in *UNTS*, vol. 82, p. 279 ss.

[298] Charter of the International Military Tribunal, Annex to the Agreement for the prosecution and punishment of the major war criminals of the European Axis ("London Agreement").

[299] IMT Charter, art. 6.

[300] International Criminal Tribunal for the Former Yugoslavia (ICTY).

Tribunale penale internazionale per il Ruanda[301], della Corte penale internazionale[302] e di altri tribunali internazionali penali c.d. "misti" o "ibridi" o "internazionalizzati"[303]. Le tre categorie originarie di crimini sono state aggiornate, sulla base degli statuti della Corte penale internazionale e degli altri tribunali penali internazionali, che prevedono adesso quattro tipologie di crimini: *a*) il genocidio; *b*) i crimini contro l'umanità; *c*) i crimini di guerra; *d*) i crimini contro la pace (che oggi si risolvono nel crimine di aggressione). In sostanza, il genocidio, che prima veniva inquadrato nei crimini contro l'umanità, ha adesso acquistato una sua autonomia.

Si deve notare che uno Stato, se viola uno dei divieti sopra indicati, commette una grave violazione di diritti umani fondamentali o di norme basilari del diritto umanitario. Quindi, come vedremo, si può anche ritenere, *di solito ma non sempre*, che lo Stato abbia commesso una violazione di obblighi stabiliti da norme di diritto internazionale generale ed aventi carattere di *ius cogens*.

Esaminiamo adesso separatamente le suddette quattro categorie di crimini internazionali.

9.1. *Genocidio*

9.1.1. *Norme*

Probabilmente il genocidio è stato praticato spesso nella storia dell'umanità. Tuttavia il termine giuridico "genocidio", che significa uccisione di un intero gruppo nazionale (*génos* in greco), è stato introdotto nel diritto internazionale per la prima volta nel 1944 dal giurista polacco R. Lemkin[304].

Ma la parola "genocidio" non fu usata nel testo dello Statuto del Tribunale di Norimberga né nella sentenza emessa dal Tribunale[305]. Il genocidio degli ebrei fu punito a Norimberga come "atti di sterminio e persecuzione", che rientravano nella più ampia categoria dei crimini contro l'umanità. Tuttavia, dopo poco tempo, il concetto giuridico di genocidio fu riconosciuto dall'Assemblea Generale delle NU, che, nel 1946, adottò una risoluzione che definiva il genocidio come "a denial of the right of existence of entire groups" ed affermava che il genocidio era un "crime under international law"[306].

Successivamente, il genocidio ha acquistato un'autonomia ed una notevole importanza nella Convenzione per la prevenzione e la repressione del crimine di genocidio del 9 dicembre 1948, di cui abbiamo già parlato in maniera sintetica[307]. La Convenzione costituisce la normativa di riferimento per quanto riguarda il genocidio in generale. Essa considera il genocidio *sia come un crimine penale individuale*, che comporta la responsabilità in-

---

[301] International Criminal Tribunal for Rwanda (ICTR).

[302] International Criminal Court (ICC).

[303] Vedi, ad es., la Corte speciale per la Sierra Leone (SCSL) ed il Tribunale speciale per il Libano (STL).

[304] Lemkin (1944), p. 79.

[305] IMT, *United States et al. v. Goering et al.* Ma l'atto di imputazione del Tribunale di Norimberga faceva riferimento al genocidio: cfr. *Trial of Major War Criminals before the International Military Tribunal, 1945-1946*, Nuremberg 1947, vol. 1, Indictment, Count Three, pp. 43-44. Sulla questione del mancato riferimento al genocidio nel processo di Norimberga vedi anche Barret (2010); Sands (2017), pp. 292, 297, 301, 306.

[306] GA Res. 96(I), 11 December 1946.

[307] Vedi, *supra*, Cap. IV, par. 5.2.1.

ternazionale degli individui che lo hanno perpetrato, *sia come un illecito internazionale dello Stato*, al quale appartengono gli individui-organi che hanno commesso atti di genocidio. Come si è detto, le due forme di responsabilità vanno tenute distinte.

Fra le norme internazionali rilevanti in materia di genocidio, si devono considerare anche le disposizioni contenute negli statuti dei tribunali internazionali penali, anche se esse si riferiscono solo al genocidio come crimine individuale. Le disposizioni più rilevanti sono l'art. 4 dello Statuto del Tribunale internazionale per la ex Jugoslavia, l'art. 2 dello Statuto del Tribunale internazionale per il Ruanda e l'art. 6 dello Statuto della Corte penale internazionale. In realtà, le definizioni del crimine di genocidio contenute in questi statuti riprendono, in maniera identica o molto simile, la definizione contenuta nella Convenzione del 1948.

Infine, si deve notare che il divieto di genocidio è sancito non solo dalle norme convenzionali citate, ma anche da una norma di diritto internazionale generale[308] e di natura imperativa (*ius cogens*). Ciò trova conferma in alcune importanti sentenze della Corte internazionale di giustizia[309].

9.1.2. *Contenuto del divieto*

Il contenuto del divieto di genocidio, anche ai fini del diritto internazionale generale, si ricava soprattutto dalla Convenzione contro il genocidio del 1948. L'art. II della Convenzione definisce i due elementi costitutivi del crimine di genocidio. L'elemento soggettivo consiste nello "intent to destroy, in whole or in part, a national, ethnical, racial or religious group". L'elemento oggettivo consiste nella commissione di uno dei seguenti atti:

> "a) Killing members of the group;
> b) Causing serious bodily or mental harm to members of the group;
> c) Deliberately inflicting on the group conditions of life calculated to bring about its physical destruction in whole or in part;
> d) Imposing measures intended to prevent births within the group;
> e) Forcibly transferring children of the group to another group".

L'elemento più caratteristico del genocidio è pertanto il c.d. dolo specifico; cioè l'intento di distruggere fisicamente (in tutto o in parte) uno dei quattro gruppi protetti. Come si può notare, la Convenzione contiene un'accurata definizione del crimine di genocidio. Sotto certi aspetti la definizione è ampia, perché punisce il crimine commesso sia in tempo di pace che in tempo di guerra; e perché comprende anche atti che non comportano l'uccisione di persone (ad esempio, lesioni gravi). Tuttavia, sotto altri aspetti, la definizione è restrittiva, perché occorre la difficile dimostrazione del dolo specifico e perché essa esclude il c.d. genocidio politico (la distruzione di un gruppo politico avversario) ed il c.d. genocidio culturale (la distruzione dei simboli culturali di un gruppo). La definizione dell'art. II sembra escludere anche la c.d. pulizia etnica; cioè l'espulsione forzata di un gruppo etnico da una certa area geografica, per realizzare una omogeneità etnica locale.

---

[308] Alcuni ritengono che si tratti di una norma consuetudinaria ed altri, invece, di un principio generale del diritto internazionale. Per questa seconda tesi, vedi Pisillo Mazzeschi, Viviani (2018), p. 147.

[309] ICJ, *Armed Activities on the Territory of the Congo*, Judgment of 3 February 2006, par. 64; *Application of the Convention on the Prevention and Punishment of the Crime of Genocide*, Judgment of 26 February 2007, parr. 161-162; *Ibidem*, Judgment of 3 February 2015, parr. 87-88.

Peraltro, si deve sottolineare che la definizione di genocidio contenuta nella Convenzione non prevede che la commissione del crimine si debba realizzare nel quadro di una prassi sistematica o diffusa. Ciò significa che, a differenza dei crimini contro l'umanità [310], il genocidio non richiede di dimostrare l'esistenza di un contesto di violenza diffusa o una politica o piano concertato di genocidio. Tuttavia, nella realtà, gli atti di genocidio raramente costituiscono episodi isolati o sporadici, e di solito fanno parte di un disegno approvato o tollerato dallo Stato [311]. Pertanto, spesso si realizza una duplice responsabilità: quella dello Stato e quella dei suoi individui-organi. Anche l'art. III della Convenzione è importante, poiché esso prevede la punibilità di altri atti connessi alla commissione di atti di genocidio; e cioè: *a*) la concertazione mirante a commettere genocidio; *b*) l'incitamento diretto e pubblico a commetterlo; *c*) il tentativo; *d*) la complicità.

Le definizioni del genocidio contenute negli statuti dei tribunali internazionali penali, come si è già detto, sono molto simili a quella stabilita dalla Convenzione del 1948.

Per quanto riguarda la prassi, conviene distinguere quella relativa al genocidio come *illecito internazionale dello Stato* da quella relativa al genocidio come *crimine penale individuale*.

Quanto al primo aspetto, per molto tempo l'applicazione della Convenzione sul genocidio non ha dato luogo ad una prassi significativa. Solo a partire dagli anni 1990, la Corte internazionale di giustizia è stata adita in relazione ad alcune controversie sull'*Applicazione della Convenzione contro il genocidio* [312]. In una sentenza del 26 febbraio 2007, la Corte ha avuto modo di chiarire alcuni aspetti sul contenuto del divieto di genocidio. La Corte ha precisato il concetto di "gruppo protetto" ai fini del genocidio, sostenendo che il gruppo non può essere definito al negativo, cioè come un insieme di individui che non hanno certe caratteristiche; e che il termine "in parte" deve riferirsi ad una parte significativa del gruppo. Inoltre, la Corte ha affermato che la pratica della pulizia etnica può costituire una forma di genocidio, purché siano rispettati gli elementi costitutivi di questo stabiliti nell'art. II della Convenzione; e cioè che sussista l'intento di distruggere un gruppo e che sia stato commesso uno degli atti indicati nel medesimo art. II. Infine, la Corte, come vedremo, ha approfondito il contenuto degli obblighi statali di prevenzione del genocidio.

Invece, per quanto riguarda il *genocidio come crimine penale individuale*, il diritto internazionale ha compiuto maggiori progressi, tramite la giurisprudenza dei tribunali penali internazionali [313]. Tuttavia, non possiamo qui approfondire la materia perché, come si è detto, essa rileva solo in via indiretta sul genocidio come illecito degli Stati, e quindi sul diritto internazionale dei diritti umani.

---

[310] Vedi *infra*, par. 9.2.

[311] Cassese, Gaeta (2008), p. 189.

[312] Vedi ICJ, *Application of the Convention on the Prevention and Punishment of the Crime of Genocide (Bosnia and Herzegovina v. Yugoslavia), Preliminary Objections*, Judgment of 11 July 1996; *Ibidem, (Bosnia and Herzegovina v. Serbia and Montenegro)*, Judgment of 26 February 2007; *Ibidem (Croatia v. Serbia)*, Judgment of 3 February 2015; *Ibidem, (The Gambia v. Myanmar)*, Order of 23 January 2020.

[313] Vedi, ad es., ICTR, *Akayesu*, Judgment of 2 September 1998; ICTR, *Kayishema et al.*, Judgment of 1 June 2001; ICTY, *Jelisić*, Judgment of 5 July 2001.

9.1.3. *Obblighi*

Il divieto di genocidio impone agli Stati (ed agli altri enti destinatari del divieto) obblighi negativi e positivi, che non sono molto dissimili da quelli che abbiamo già esaminato in relazione al diritto alla vita ed al divieto di tortura.

Volendo sintetizzare, si può dire che il principale obbligo negativo dello Stato è quello di astenersi, tramite i propri individui-organi (che agiscano *de iure* o *ultra vires*) o tramite individui o gruppi che agiscano come organi *de facto* o sotto la direzione o il controllo dello Stato, dal commettere atti di genocidio. In questa materia, come vedremo subito, può essere talora difficile risolvere il problema dell'attribuzione o meno ad uno Stato di atti di genocidio commessi da gruppi armati, di militari o paramilitari, che non sono organi dello Stato, ma che sono sospettati di agire sotto il controllo dello Stato.

I principali obblighi positivi dello Stato sono quelli di prevenire e reprimere atti di genocidio commessi da individui privati o gruppi di individui privati. Nel citato caso *Bosnia-Erzegovina contro Serbia e Montenegro*, la Corte internazionale di giustizia era chiamata ad accertare, fra l'altro, la responsabilità per il massacro di migliaia di persone bosniaco-musulmane che era stato compiuto a Srebrenica nel 1995 da forze militari e paramilitari serbe, che appartenevano alla Repubblica autonoma Srpska (Repubblica serba di Bosnia-Erzegovina). Nella sua sentenza [314], la Corte ha stabilito che gli atti di genocidio non potevano essere attribuiti alla Serbia, poiché le forze militari e paramilitari che avevano compiuto materialmente il genocidio non potevano essere considerate come organi, né *de iure* né *de facto*, della Serbia. Né era stato provato, ad avviso della Corte, un controllo effettivo della Serbia sulle azioni di tali forze, tale da giustificare l'attribuzione di tali azioni alla Serbia. Tuttavia, la Corte ha stabilito che la Serbia era responsabile del genocidio, per violazione dei propri obblighi positivi di prevenzione; cioè perché la Serbia non aveva esercitato la *due diligence* nella prevenzione del massacro [315].

La prudenza della Corte internazionale di giustizia, nel valutare l'elemento del controllo effettivo della Serbia sulle forze militari e paramilitari che avevano compiuto il massacro di Srebrenica, è stata talora criticata in dottrina. Inoltre, si deve notare che il Tribunale internazionale per la ex Iugoslavia, nel valutare la responsabilità penale internazionale *individuale* dei militari che avevano commesso il suddetto massacro, ha invece stabilito che esisteva un controllo globale delle autorità serbe su tali militari.

9.2. *Crimini contro l'umanità*

9.2.1. *Norme*

La categoria dei crimini contro l'umanità venne inserita nell'Accordo di Londra del 1945, che istituiva il Tribunale militare internazionale di Norimberga (IMT), e poi ripresa nell'art. 6, lett. c), dello Statuto del Tribunale. La sua origine è dovuta al fatto che il diritto

---

[314] ICJ, *Application of the Convention on the Prevention and Punishment of the Crime of Genocide*, Judgment of 26 February 2007, parr. 385-450.

[315] In relazione alla mancata prevenzione del massacro di Srebrenica, vedi anche, sulla responsabilità dei Paesi Bassi, The Hague Court of Appeal, *Mehida Mustafić-Mujić et al v. The Netherlands*; Supreme Court, *State of the Netherlands v. Mustafić et al.* Su queste sentenze cfr. anche Pustorino (2019), pp. 111-112.

internazionale dei conflitti armati, già esistente da molto tempo, si applicava soltanto ai rapporti fra belligeranti; e quindi le norme sui crimini di guerra, che erano contenute in tale diritto, non si applicavano ai crimini compiuti dai nazisti tedeschi nei confronti della propria popolazione per motivi politici, religiosi o razziali (ebrei, zingari, comunisti, sindacalisti, ecc.) o della popolazione degli Stati alleati alla Germania. Pertanto, per processare i leader nazisti per tali crimini dinanzi al Tribunale di Norimberga, si doveva superare il diritto internazionale tradizionale.

Nello Statuto del Tribunale, i crimini contro l'umanità venivano definiti come:

> "[...] murder, extermination, enslavement, deportation, and other inhumane acts committed against any civilian population, before or during the war, or persecutions on political, racial or religious grounds [...]"[316].

Inoltre, si stabiliva l'importante precisazione che tali atti o persecuzioni potevano essere giudicati dal Tribunale a prescindere dalla circostanza che essi "abbiano costituito o meno una violazione del diritto interno del paese in cui sono stati commessi"[317]. Tuttavia, tali atti dovevano essere stati "perpetrati nell'esecuzione di uno dei crimini rientranti nella competenza del Tribunale, o in connessione con uno dei siffatti crimini"[318]. Cioè, i crimini contro l'umanità dovevano essere collegati ad un crimine di guerra o un crimine contro la pace. È chiaro che quest'ultima condizione poneva un limite rilevante alla competenza del Tribunale.

In ogni caso, l'aspetto più interessante è dato dal fatto che la categoria dei crimini contro l'umanità costituiva un'innovazione del diritto internazionale. Ciò poneva, da una parte, il problema del rispetto del principio di legalità penale (*nullum crimen, nulla poena sine lege*); ed infatti questa obiezione fu sollevata dagli avvocati dei leader nazisti durante il processo di Norimberga, ma fu superata dal Tribunale. D'altra parte, questa nuova categoria di crimini rappresentava un importante progresso del diritto internazionale, perché significava che tale diritto vietava atti e comportamenti contrari ai valori fondamentali della persona umana, e ciò anche se compiuti senza violare (o addirittura attuando) il diritto interno dello Stato[319].

Dopo il processo di Norimberga, la nozione giuridica di crimini contro l'umanità si è affermata assai rapidamente. Nel 1946, anche il Tribunale militare internazionale di Tokio[320] adottò tale nozione[321]. Inoltre gli Alleati conclusero un accordo[322], nel dicembre 1945, che ampliava la definizione dei crimini contro l'umanità, perché ometteva ogni riferimento o collegamento alla Seconda Guerra Mondiale. Nel 1946, l'Assemblea Generale delle NU adottò una risoluzione[323] con cui riaffermava i principi contenuti nello Statuto e

---

[316] IMT, Charter, art. 6, lett. c).

[317] *Ibidem*.

[318] *Ibidem*.

[319] Cassese, Gaeta (2008), p. 182.

[320] Cfr. Establishment of an International Military Tribunal for the Far East, Special proclamation by the Supreme Commander for the Allied Powers at Tokyo, January 19, 1946; Charter of the International Military Tribunal for the Far East.

[321] IMTFE Charter, art. 5, lett. c).

[322] Control Council Law No. 10, 20 December 1945.

[323] GA Res. 95 (I) of 11 December 1946: *Affirmation of the Principles of International Law recognized by the Charter of the Nuremberg Tribunal*.

nella sentenza del Tribunale di Norimberga. Nel 1950, anche la Commissione del diritto internazionale adottò principi simili [324].

Più recentemente, la nozione è stata riaffermata nel "Progetto di codice sui crimini contro l'umanità e la sicurezza", presentato nel 1996 dalla Commissione del diritto internazionale all'Assemblea Generale delle NU [325]; e poi negli statuti del Tribunale per la ex Iugoslavia [326], del Tribunale per il Ruanda [327] e della Corte penale internazionale [328]. Questi statuti, anche se non sono del tutto uniformi fra loro, hanno ampliato la nozione di crimini contro l'umanità rispetto a quella contenuta nello Statuto del Tribunale di Norimberga. In particolare, dagli statuti del Tribunale per il Ruanda e della Corte penale internazionale, e dalla giurisprudenza del Tribunale per la ex Jugoslavia, risulta che i crimini contro l'umanità possono essere commessi anche in tempo di pace e che non vi è più la necessità del nesso fra tali crimini ed un conflitto armato.

Conviene adesso chiederci se il divieto di crimini contro l'umanità sia sancito da una norma di diritto internazionale generale e, eventualmente, se tale norma abbia natura di *ius cogens*. A nostro avviso, la risposta è positiva ad ambedue le domande. Più in particolare, ci sembra si debba parlare di un principio generale di diritto internazionale, più che di una norma consuetudinaria [329].

Tuttavia, si è già detto che le norme convenzionali in materia *non* sono identiche, specie con riferimento alle singole condotte vietate. Pertanto, si deve concludere che il principio generale sul divieto di crimini contro l'umanità, avendo per sua natura carattere ampio e non dettagliato, ha un contenuto che corrisponde, grosso modo, al *contenuto minimo comune di tutte le norme convenzionali* sopra ricordate. In altri termini, non si può ritenere che il contenuto del principio generale corrisponda, in maniera precisa, al contenuto specifico dell'art. 7 dello Statuto della Corte penale internazionale oppure a quello dell'art. 5 dello Statuto del Tribunale per la ex Jugoslavia. Comunque, il tema del contenuto del divieto generale di crimini contro l'umanità sarà adesso affrontato.

9.2.2. *Contenuto del divieto*

Nel diritto internazionale contemporaneo, i crimini contro l'umanità consistono, nella loro sostanza essenziale, in "attacchi estesi o sistematici, ed aventi carattere intenzionale, contro la popolazione civile". Questo concetto va precisato.

In primo luogo, gli attacchi sono "estesi" quando provocano un numero elevato di vittime; ed essi sono "sistematici" quando non hanno carattere isolato o sporadico, ma fanno parte di una prassi sistematica e diffusa, o di un piano politico approvato o tollerato da uno

---

[324] ILC, *Principles of International Law Recognized in the Charter of the Nuremberg Tribunal and in the Judgment of the Tribunal*, June-July 1950, in *YILC*, 1950, II, par. 97.

[325] ILC, *Draft Code of Crimes against the Peace and Security of Mankind with commentaries, 1996*, in *YILC*, 1996, II (2).

[326] ICTY Statute, art. 5.

[327] ICTR Statute, art. 3.

[328] ICC Rome Statute, art. 7.

[329] Anche in questo caso, come per il genocidio, alcuni sostengono che la norma generale sul divieto di crimini contro l'umanità abbia natura consuetudinaria ed altri, invece, che abbia la natura di un principio di diritto internazionale. A noi sembra preferibile questa seconda opinione, sia per il carattere quasi immediato di formazione della norma, sia per il suo contenuto ampio e piuttosto indeterminato.

Stato o da un'autorità che esercita un controllo di fatto sul territorio dove gli atti vengono perpetrati. Secondo il Tribunale per il Ruanda:

> "The concept of 'widespread' may be defined as massive, frequent, large scale action, carried out collectively with considerable seriousness and directed against a multiplicity of victims. The concept of 'systematic' may be defined as thoroughly organised and following a regular pattern on the basis of a common policy involving substantial public or private resources. There is no requirement that this policy must be adopted formally as the policy of a state. There must however be some kind of preconceived plan or policy"[330].

In secondo luogo, gli attacchi devono essere "intenzionali"; cioè si richiede il c.d. elemento soggettivo (o *mens rea*) del crimine: le condotte vietate devono essere compiute con l'intento di commettere il crimine in questione e la consapevolezza del contesto generale di politica o prassi sistematica di violazioni.

In terzo luogo, per "popolazione civile" si intende un gruppo di persone, aventi qualsiasi nazionalità (compresa quella degli autori del crimine); ma che non siano "combattenti".

In quarto luogo, rilevano le singole condotte materiali che sono vietate (elemento oggettivo o *actus rei*). In realtà, esse sono molteplici e, come si è detto, non sempre identiche nelle diverse norme convenzionali. L'art. 7 dello Statuto della Corte penale internazionale, ad esempio, contiene un elenco di condotte assai più dettagliato di quello dell'art. 6, lett. c), dello Statuto del Tribunale di Norimberga, perché comprende anche i "crimini di genere" e l'*apartheid*. Ciò dipende, ovviamente, dalla maggiore attualità storica del primo.

Infine, si noti che, nei crimini contro l'umanità, il rapporto fra il *crimine penale individuale*, sulla base del diritto internazionale penale, e l'*illecito internazionale dello Stato* (o dell'organizzazione che controlla il territorio) sulla base del diritto internazionale dei diritti umani, è strettissimo, dato che tali crimini si inquadrano in una politica criminale del governo. Tale rapporto spiega anche perché spesso la definizione di un crimine contro l'umanità rinvia a quella contenuta in una norma sui diritti umani[331]. Si pensi, ad esempio, ai divieti di tortura, di *apartheid*, di sparizione forzata di persone, che costituiscono atti vietati nel quadro dei crimini contro l'umanità e, parallelamente, sono regolati da norme sui diritti umani.

9.2.3. *Obblighi*

Il divieto di crimini contro l'umanità (visto qui nell'ottica dei diritti umani e quindi dell'illecito internazionale dello Stato) impone agli Stati obblighi negativi e positivi, in maniera analoga a quelli già esaminati in relazione agli altri diritti umani posti a protezione della vita e dell'integrità fisica della persona.

Si può solo notare che, poiché tali crimini di solito fanno parte di una prassi sistematica e diffusa approvata da uno Stato, vengono in primo piano gli obblighi negativi. Lo Stato deve, innanzitutto, astenersi dal compiere o approvare quegli attacchi estesi e sistematici contro la popolazione civile che costituiscono l'essenza dei crimini contro l'umanità. Tuttavia, come per il genocidio, non si può escludere che talora questi attacchi provengano da enti o gruppi di persone, che controllano ad esempio parte del territorio dello Stato, ma i

---

[330] ICTR, *Akayesu*, Case No. ICTR-96-4-T, Judgment of 2 September 1998, par. 580.

[331] Vedi Focarelli (2013), pp. 305-306.

cui atti non sono attribuibili allo Stato. In questi casi, possono entrare in gioco gli obblighi positivi dello Stato, specie quelli di prevenzione e di repressione.

9.3. *Crimini di guerra*

9.3.1. *Norme*

La categoria dei crimini di guerra viene di solito ricondotta, originariamente, al c.d. codice *Lieber*, una codificazione del diritto di guerra adottata nel 1863 dal Presidente degli USA Lincoln. In seguito, le Convenzioni dell'Aja del 1899 e del 1907 prevedevano la categoria delle "violazioni delle leggi e gli usi di guerra", un concetto ripreso anche da alcuni manuali militari recenti. Tuttavia, questo concetto è troppo ampio per essere utilizzato come nozione giuridica di "crimini di guerra".

In tempi più moderni, la categoria dei crimini di guerra fu inserita nello Statuto del Tribunale di Norimberga, che, dopo aver premesso che i crimini di guerra sono "le violazioni delle leggi e degli usi di guerra", stabiliva che tali violazioni comprendono, fra l'altro:

> "murder, ill-treatment or deportation to slave labour or for any other purpose of civilian population of or in occupied territory, murder or ill-treatment of prisoners of war or persons on the seas, killing of hostages, plunder of public or private property, wanton destruction of cities, towns or villages, or devastation not justified by military necessity"[332].

In realtà lo Statuto del Tribunale di Norimberga continuava ad ispirarsi, in gran parte, alle Convenzioni dell'Aja del 1899 e del 1907. Ma oggi la definizione dei crimini di guerra contenuta in tale Statuto deve essere aggiornata, alla luce degli sviluppi del diritto internazionale umanitario e del diritto internazionale penale, che si sono verificati in tempi più recenti. Basti pensare, per il diritto umanitario, alle quattro Convenzioni di Ginevra del 1949[333] ed ai due Protocolli alle Convenzioni adottati nel 1977[334] e, per il diritto internazionale penale, agli statuti e la prassi dei tribunali penali internazionali e internazionalizzati. Su ciò ritorneremo, in relazione al contenuto del divieto.

Per quanto riguarda il diritto internazionale generale, anche in questo caso si può dire (come per i crimini contro l'umanità) che il divieto dei crimini di guerra è sancito da una norma di diritto internazionale generale e di *ius cogens*; ma che il contenuto di questa norma è più generico e, al tempo stesso, più limitato rispetto al contenuto più dettagliato delle varie norme convenzionali sopra indicate. A nostro avviso, la norma generale sul divieto dei crimini di guerra, vista la sua lunga gestazione storica, ha la natura di consuetudine piuttosto che di principio generale di diritto internazionale.

---

[332] IMT Charter, art. 6, lett. b).

[333] Geneva Convention for the Amelioration of the Condition of the Wounded and Sick in Armed Forces in the Field (GCI); Geneva Convention for the Amelioration of the Condition of the Wounded, Sick and Shipwrecked Members of Armed Forces at Sea (GCII); Geneva Convention relative to the Treatment of Prisoners of War (GCIII); Geneva Convention relative to the Protection of Civilian Persons in Time of War (GCIV).

[334] Protocol Additional to the Geneva Convention of 12 August 1949 (Protection of Victims of International Armed Conflicts) (AP I); Protocol Additional to the Geneva Convention of 12 August 1949 (Protection of Victims of Non-International Armed Conflicts) (AP II).

9.3.2. *Contenuto del divieto*

La questione del contenuto del divieto di crimini di guerra si risolve, in gran parte, in quella di fornire una nozione (o definizione) giuridica precisa di "crimini di guerra". Ma si tratta di un problema difficile, che non ha dato luogo finora ad una soluzione sicura e generalmente condivisa. Comunque si può tentare di fissare alcuni criteri [335].

In primo luogo, i crimini di guerra possono essere commessi solo nel contesto di un *conflitto armato*, internazionale o interno; cioè in un contesto entro il quale si applichi il diritto internazionale umanitario. In secondo luogo, occorre che vi sia un *nesso* fra la condotta criminosa ed il conflitto. In terzo luogo, è anche necessario che la *vittima* (sia essa un combattente o un civile) sia identificabile con il "nemico" o con l'"avversario". Non è invece necessario che l'autore dell'illecito sia un militare o un combattente.

Premessi questi criteri generali, quali sono gli atti illeciti specifici che costituiscono un crimine di guerra? Una definizione importante, che può servire come punto di partenza, è stata fornita dalla Camera d'appello del Tribunale internazionale penale per la ex Jugoslavia nella decisione interlocutoria resa nel 1995 nel caso *Tadić* [336]. Secondo tale decisione, si ha un crimine di guerra quando: *a*) vi è stata una violazione di una norma del diritto dei conflitti armati "posta a tutela di beni fondamentali" e la violazione "causa serie conseguenze per la vittima"; *b*) la norma è consuetudinaria o, se è convenzionale, essa precisa e sviluppa il diritto consuetudinario; *c*) la violazione comporta la responsabilità internazionale dell'individuo che ha tenuto la condotta illecita. In sintesi, da questa decisione si può ricavare che i crimini di guerra consistono in violazioni gravi di norme fondamentali del diritto dei conflitti armati; e tali da comportare anche la responsabilità individuale. Ci sembra che questa definizione, sia pure relativa ai *crimini penali individuali*, si adatti anche agli *illeciti internazionali degli Stati*.

Tuttavia, resta da risolvere il problema di quali siano le suddette norme fondamentali del diritto dei conflitti armati. Si tratta di una questione che richiede un'attività di interpretazione e di rilevazione della prassi da parte dell'interprete. La dottrina distingue fra il regime giuridico dei conflitti armati internazionali e quello dei conflitti armati interni.

In materia di conflitti armati internazionali, rilevano, in primo luogo, le norme sui mezzi e metodi di combattimento (c.d. diritto dell'Aja). Si tratta, in sostanza, di stabilire quali, fra le norme delle Convenzioni dell'Aja del 1899 e del 1907, abbiano prodotto norme che siano consuetudinarie e che diano rilevanza penale a condotte individuali. In secondo luogo, rilevano le norme sulla tutela di coloro che non partecipano, o non partecipano più, alle ostilità: cioè le vittime della guerra (c.d. diritto di Ginevra). Tali norme sono contenute specie nelle quattro Convenzioni di Ginevra del 1949, le quali specificano che certe violazioni sono considerate come "infrazioni gravi", che comportano sanzioni penali. Sono le c.d. "grave breaches" delle Convenzioni di Ginevra.

Per quanto riguarda, invece, il regime giuridico dei conflitti armati interni, si deve notare che solo recentemente si è affermata la tesi che la violazione grave di alcune norme fondamentali di tale regime costituisca un crimine di guerra [337]. L'opinione dominante è

---

[335] Vedi Cassese, Gaeta (2008), pp. 177-179; Henckaerts, Doswald-Beck (2005), Vol. 1: *Rules*.

[336] ICTY, *Tadić*, ICTY-94-1-AR72, Decision of 2 October 1995, parr. 94-136.

[337] See ICTY, *Tadić*, Decision of 2 October 1995, par. 134: "[…] customary international law imposes criminal liability for serious violations of common Article 3, as supplemented by other general principles and rules

che costituiscano crimini di guerra le violazioni gravi dell'art. 3 comune alle quattro Convenzioni di Ginevra del 1949, che stabilisce alcune regole minime di umanità da rispettare durante i conflitti di ogni natura. Ma molti autori affermano che si dovrebbero aggiungere anche le disposizioni principali del Secondo Protocollo alle Convenzioni di Ginevra, espressamente dedicato ai conflitti armati interni [338].

La complessa nozione giuridica di "crimini di guerra" fin qui tracciata trova, in linea di massima, conferma nell'art. 8 dello Statuto della Corte penale internazionale, che tuttavia costituisce una disposizione estremamente dettagliata, che non ha la pretesa di codificare il diritto internazionale consuetudinario. L'art. 8 prevede quattro categorie generali di crimini di guerra e, nel quadro di ciascuna categoria, un elenco dettagliato di atti più specifici. Le quattro categorie generali sono: *a*) le "grave breaches" delle Convenzioni di Ginevra del 1949; *b*) altre gravi violazioni delle leggi e consuetudini applicabili nei conflitti armati internazionali nel quadro stabilito del diritto internazionale; *c*) nei conflitti armati non internazionali, le gravi violazioni dell'art. 3 comune alle Convenzioni di Ginevra del 1949; *d*) altre gravi violazioni delle leggi e consuetudini applicabili nei conflitti armati non internazionali nel quadro stabilito del diritto internazionale.

Un ultimo punto riguarda il c.d. elemento soggettivo dei crimini di guerra. La maggior parte delle disposizioni sopra citate richiede, espressamente o implicitamente, il dolo della persona (individuo-organo dello Stato o individuo privato) che ha commesso il crimine. Tuttavia, salvo che la disposizione non la escluda esplicitamente, sembra che sia sufficiente anche la colpa grave [339].

9.3.3. *Obblighi*

La prassi dimostra che il divieto di crimini di guerra comporta per gli Stati non solo obblighi negativi, ma anche, talora, obblighi positivi. In altri termini, la responsabilità può derivare sia da un'azione che da un'omissione.

Sotto questo secondo aspetto, sono esemplari i casi di responsabilità dei *leader* militari per i crimini di guerra commessi dai loro subordinati [340]. Il *leading case* in materia è costituito dalla sentenza *Yamashita* della Corte Suprema degli USA [341]. Il generale Yamashita, che era a capo delle forze militari giapponesi nelle Filippine dall'ottobre 1944 fino alla fine della Seconda Guerra Mondiale, fu sottoposto a processo per i crimini di guerra commessi da tali forze contro i militari statunitensi, prima dinanzi ad una Commissione militare e poi dinanzi alla Corte Suprema degli USA. Yamashita non era accusato di aver commesso, ordinato o autorizzato gli atti criminali, bensì di aver omesso di prendere le misure appropriate per impedirli. Sia la Commissione militare che la Corte Suprema stabilirono che il generale era responsabile, perché aveva un potere di controllo sui propri militari e non poteva ignorare i loro atti criminali.

---

on the protection of victims of internal armed conflict, and for breaching certain fundamental principles and rules regarding means and methods of combat in civil strife".

[338] Cfr. Abi-Saab, ICTY, *Tadić*, Separate opinion on the defence motion for interlocutory appeal on jurisdiction of 2 October 1995; Cassese, Gaeta (2008), p. 179.

[339] Così Cassese, Gaeta (2008), p. 180.

[340] Vedi, in generale, Viviani (2005), pp. 203-324.

[341] U.S. Supreme Court, *In re Yamashita*.

Anche la prassi dei Tribunali Militari Alleati e dei tribunali interni degli Stati, nonché gli statuti dei tribunali penali internazionali, confermano le regole sulla responsabilità omissiva dei comandanti militari e, più in generale, dei superiori gerarchici. Ad esempio, l'art. 7(3) dello Statuto del Tribunale penale internazionale per la ex Jugoslavia stabilisce:

> "The fact that any of the acts referred to in articles 2 to 5 of the present Statute was committed by a subordinate does not relieve his superior of criminal responsibility if he knew or had reason to know that the subordinate was about to commit such acts or had done so and the superior failed to take the necessary and reasonable measures to prevent such acts or to punish the perpetrators thereof".

Regole assai simili, anche se precisate in maggior dettaglio, sono contenute nell'art. 28 dello Statuto della Corte penale internazionale.

9.4. *Crimini contro la pace. Aggressione*

Anche la categoria dei crimini contro la pace risale all'Accordo di Londra del 1945, che istituiva il Tribunale militare internazionale di Norimberga, ed allo Statuto di tale Tribunale. L'art. 6, lett. a), dello Statuto definiva come "crimini contro la pace" i seguenti atti:

> "planning, preparation, initiation or waging of a war of aggression, or a war in violation of international treaties, agreements or assurances, or participation in a common plan or conspiracy for the accomplishment of any of the foregoing".

Come si vede, tale disposizione non forniva una definizione del crimine di aggressione; ma elencava una serie di atti aggressivi [342]. Anche con riferimento ai crimini contro la pace (come per i crimini contro l'umanità), il Tribunale di Norimberga sostenne che non si trattava di una nozione giuridica nuova e che pertanto essa non violava il principio di legalità dei delitti e delle pene. Il Tribunale anzi affermò che l'aggressione costituiva il più grave dei crimini internazionali; e poi condannò alcuni degli imputati, dopo averli dichiarati colpevoli di aver commesso crimini contro la pace.

In seguito, anche il Tribunale militare internazionale di Tokyo [343] condannò alcuni imputati per crimini contro la pace. Nel 1946, l'Assemblea Generale delle NU adottò la già citata risoluzione, con cui riaffermava i principi contenuti nello Statuto e nella sentenza del Tribunale di Norimberga. In tal modo, come è stato notato [344], gli Stati che all'epoca erano membri delle NU approvarono formalmente la nozione di crimini contro la pace e quella, più specifica, di aggressione. In seguito, le due nozioni hanno finito, in pratica, per coincidere ed ha prevalso, nell'uso, il termine di "aggressione".

Tuttavia, va sottolineato il fatto che il crimine di aggressione ha trovato maggiori difficoltà ad affermarsi, nel diritto internazionale, rispetto alle altre categorie di crimini internazionali. Queste difficoltà hanno riguardato sia l'aggressione come *illecito internazionale dello Stato* sia l'aggressione come *crimine penale individuale*. I motivi delle difficoltà sono chiari. Da una parte, gli Stati più forti (e specie i cinque membri permanenti del CdS)

---

[342] Cfr. Focarelli (2013), p. 310.

[343] IMTFE Statute, art. 5, lett. a).

[344] Cassese, Gaeta (2008), p. 193.

temono che una definizione troppo precisa dell'illecito statale di aggressione possa limitare la discrezionalità del Consiglio di Sicurezza *ex* art. 39 della Carta delle NU [345] e la loro stessa discrezionalità nell'interpretare le norme internazionali sull'uso della forza. Dall'altra parte, una definizione rigorosa del crimine individuale di aggressione potrebbe, in certi casi, portare ad incriminare i supremi *leader* politici e militari degli Stati. In altri termini, si tratta di una materia con un "elevato grado di politicizzazione" [346].

Ciò è dimostrato dagli scarsi progressi normativi che il crimine di aggressione ha conseguito dal tempo dei processi di Norimberga e di Tokio fino ad oggi. Per quanto riguarda l'aggressione come *illecito dello Stato*, lo sviluppo più rilevante è costituito dalla Risoluzione n. 3314 (XXIX) sulla definizione di aggressione adottata dall'Assemblea Generale delle NU nel 1974 [347]. L'art. 3, in particolare, elenca in maniera dettagliata una serie di atti che integrano il concetto di aggressione. Tuttavia, la risoluzione ha due limiti importanti. In primo luogo, stabilisce espressamente che essa non è vincolante per il Consiglio di Sicurezza, che, con la sua discrezionalità, può discostarsi da tale definizione (art. 4). In secondo luogo, essa non prevede che gli atti di aggressione possano creare sia responsabilità internazionale dello Stato che responsabilità penale internazionale di individui; ed anzi sembra riferirsi soltanto alla responsabilità dello Stato [348].

Anche in relazione all'aggressione come *crimine penale individuale*, i progressi non sono stati rilevanti. Negli anni dal 1947 al 1954, la Commissione del diritto internazionale lavorò nel tentativo di adottare un *Codice dei crimini contro la pace e la sicurezza dell'umanità*. Un progetto di codice, completato dalla Commissione nel 1954, conteneva una disposizione (art. 2), che raggruppava tutte le fattispecie criminose e che menzionava anche l'aggressione e la minaccia di aggressione. Ma quel progetto di codice non ebbe alcun seguito. Dopo quasi trent'anni, nel 1981, la Commissione tornò ad occuparsi dell'argomento; ma solo nel 1996 ha completato un *Progetto di Codice dei crimini contro la pace e la sicurezza dell'umanità* [349], che tuttavia non è mai stato approvato dalle Nazioni Unite. In ogni caso, anche in questo documento manca una definizione accurata del crimine penale individuale di aggressione. L'art. 16 del Progetto di Codice, intitolato "Crimine di aggressione", si limita a prevedere che:

> "An individual who, as leader or organizer, actively participates in or orders the planning, preparation, initiation or waging of aggression committed by a State shall be responsible for a crime of aggression".

D'altra parte, il crimine di aggressione non rientra, di solito, nella giurisdizione dei tribunali penali internazionali; con l'eccezione dello Statuto della Corte penale internaziona-

---

[345] UN Charter, art. 39: "The Security Council shall determine the existence of any threat to the peace, breach of the peace, or act of aggression and shall make recommendations, or decide what measures shall be taken in accordance with Articles 41 and 42, to maintain or restore international peace and security".

[346] Così Cassese, Gaeta (2008), p. 196.

[347] AG Res. 3314 (XXIX) of 14 December 1974: *Definition of Aggression*.

[348] Vedi anche AG Res. 2625 (XXV) of 24 October 1970: *Declaration on Principles of International Law Concerning Friendly Relations and Co-operation among States in accordance with the Charter of the United Nations*, secondo la quale: "A war of aggression constitutes a crime against the peace, for which there is responsibility under international law".

[349] ILC, *Draft Code of Crimes against the Peace and Security of Mankind*, 5 July 1996.

le, che prevede che la Corte abbia giurisdizione su tale crimine (art. 5, par. 1). Tuttavia, lo Statuto in origine precisava che la Corte non avrebbe potuto esercitare tale giurisdizione finché non fosse stato adottato un emendamento allo Statuto medesimo, con una definizione di tale crimine. In effetti, nel 2010, si è tenuta in Uganda, a Kampala, una conferenza di revisione dello Statuto, che ha adottato un emendamento che contiene una definizione dell'aggressione. L'art. 8 *bis*, par. 1, stabilisce che:

> "For the purpose of this Statute, 'crime of aggression' means the planning, preparation, initiation or execution, by a person in a position effectively to exercise control over or to direct the political or military action of a State, of an act of aggression which, by its character, gravity and scale, constitutes a manifest violation of the Charter of the United Nations".

Il par. 2 specifica che "atto di aggressione" significa l'uso della forza armata da parte di uno Stato contro la sovranità, l'integrità territoriale o l'indipendenza politica di un altro Stato o in altro modo contrario alla Carta delle NU. Vengono poi elencate alcune condotte specifiche che sono considerate come atti di aggressione dalla Risoluzione n. 3314 del 1974. Come si vede, la definizione dell'art. 8 *bis* riprende, in sostanza, sia pure con qualche variante ed aggiornamento, le definizioni che erano contenute negli statuti del Tribunale di Norimberga [350] e del Tribunale di Tokyo [351].

In conclusione, quantomeno in relazione all'aggressione come illecito internazionale dello Stato, si deve escludere, a nostro parere, che una norma dal contenuto sufficientemente preciso si sia affermata nel diritto internazionale generale [352]. Resta pertanto al Consiglio di Sicurezza delle NU il compito principale di accertare, con un ampio grado di discrezionalità, se e quando un atto di aggressione da parte di uno Stato si sia verificato.

Sezione III

PROTEZIONE DEI *BASIC NEEDS* E DEI DIRITTI DI SUSSISTENZA DELLE PERSONE

Quando si parla, in relazione ai diritti umani, dei *basic needs* della persona, di solito si fa riferimento ai diritti al cibo, all'acqua, all'abitazione, alla salute e, talora, anche al diritto ad un tenore di vita adeguato [353]. Questi diritti vengono anche, talora, definiti come "diritti di sussistenza" (*subsistence rights*) [354]. Ciò perché essi hanno un collegamento con certe condizioni necessarie per l'esistenza delle persone. Tuttavia queste definizioni, anche

[350] IMT Statute, art. 6, lett. a).

[351] IMTFE Statute, art. 5, lett. a).

[352] Così anche Focarelli (2013), pp. 311-312.

[353] Vedi, ad es., Focarelli (2013), pp. 211-213. Non tratteremo qui, invece, il diritto ad un ambiente sano, che ci sembra più pertinente ai diritti umani collettivi. Vedi *infra*, Cap. VI, par. 20.2.

[354] Cfr., ad es., Kälin, Künzli (2009), p. 303 ss.

se in parte pertinenti, rischiano di non essere precise e di creare qualche confusione, se non si fanno due precisazioni.

Innanzitutto, alcuni di questi diritti sono più generali ed altri più particolari ed i rapporti fra di loro sono piuttosto complicati. Ad esempio, il diritto ad un tenore di vita adeguato potrebbe essere considerato come un diritto umano autonomo, ma potrebbe anche essere considerato, per il suo contenuto assai ampio e indeterminato, come un diritto-contenitore (o forse solo come un obiettivo politico non vincolante) che ricomprende i diritti al cibo, all'acqua, all'abitazione e alla salute. Anche il diritto alla salute, che pure ha carattere meno generico rispetto al diritto ad un tenore di vita adeguato, potrebbe essere inteso in senso ampio come comprendente alcuni dei suddetti diritti più specifici, oppure in senso stretto come diritto autonomo. Occorre quindi cautela nel definire l'ambito di applicazione di questi diritti ed i loro rapporti reciproci.

In secondo luogo, e ciò è anche più importante, non ci sembra che i singoli diritti in questione abbiano una natura univoca, tale da poter essere definiti sempre, ed in maniera indifferenziata, come "diritti attinenti ai *basic needs*" oppure come "diritti di sussistenza". A nostro avviso, si deve invece fare una *distinzione terminologica e sostanziale* fra i due gruppi di diritti.

Infatti, i diritti al cibo, all'acqua, all'abitazione ed alla salute riguardano sempre i bisogni primari (*basic needs*) delle persone. Ma, se essi vengono *intesi in senso ampio*, si configurano come diritti economici e sociali, e sono collegati al (o sono aspetti specifici del) *diritto ad un tenore di vita adeguato*. In questo caso, come vedremo, i diritti in oggetto sono regolati da norme che, di solito, non hanno carattere precettivo immediato, ma piuttosto impongono agli Stati obblighi "a realizzazione progressiva" o talora soltanto impegni politici non vincolanti. Pertanto, a proposito di questi diritti *intesi in senso ampio*, è inappropriato, a nostro avviso, parlare di "diritti di sussistenza" e classificarli fra i diritti umani "fondamentali".

Invece, il discorso cambia radicalmente se i diritti al cibo, all'acqua, all'abitazione ed alla salute vengono *intesi in senso stretto*, o meglio quando essi sono attinenti, anziché ad un tenore di vita adeguato, alle *condizioni minime di esistenza e di mantenimento in vita delle persone*. In queste situazioni, tali diritti, seppure autonomi, sono funzionalmente collegati al diritto umano alla vita, che non significa solo il diritto di non essere uccisi arbitrariamente, ma anche il diritto di godere delle condizioni minime necessarie per la sussistenza[355]. Pertanto, in queste ipotesi, i diritti al cibo, all'acqua, all'abitazione ed alla salute possono correttamente essere definiti come *diritti di sussistenza* (o addirittura di *sopravvivenza*) ed essere inquadrati nella categoria dei diritti umani "fondamentali".

Come si può risolvere questa apparente contraddizione fra due modi diversi di intendere e interpretare questi diritti umani? A nostro avviso, come abbiamo già anticipato, non si tratta di individuare contenuti diversi all'interno di ciascun diritto; e cioè di distinguere fra un contenuto "essenziale" (*core content*) ed uno o più contenuti "non essenziali", come invece tende a fare il Comitato sui diritti economici, sociali e culturali. Si deve, invece, riconoscere che esistono norme diverse (ed aventi un contenuto diverso) che regolano ciascuno di questi diritti. Per esempio, in relazione al diritto al cibo, come vedremo, esistono

---

[355] Vedi IACtHR, *The "Street Children"*, Judgment of 19 November 1999, par. 139.

alcune norme, che prevedono il *diritto ad un cibo adeguato al benessere delle persone*, ed altre norme che stabiliscono, in certi casi, il *divieto di privare il cibo indispensabile alla sussistenza delle persone*. Una situazione simile si verifica anche per altri dei diritti umani qui in esame.

Ciò premesso, esamineremo ora separatamente i diritti al cibo, all'acqua, all'abitazione ed alla salute, tenendo presente che a noi interessano soprattutto le norme che li prevedono come diritti "fondamentali". Ma sarà inevitabile prendere in esame anche le norme che li regolano in maniera diversa; e cioè come diritti collegati al diritto ad un tenore di vita adeguato. Non considereremo quest'ultimo come un diritto umano autonomo [356].

10. *Diritto al cibo*

10.1. *Norme*

Il diritto al cibo è previsto da numerose norme convenzionali sui diritti umani; ma anche da alcune norme di diritto internazionale umanitario e di diritto internazionale penale, e forse anche da una norma consuetudinaria in materia di emergenze umanitarie. Da un esame complessivo di queste norme emerge, a nostro avviso, una *differenza* importante: le norme del primo gruppo sono ampie e generiche, e concepiscono quasi sempre il diritto al cibo come un aspetto del diritto ad un tenore di vita adeguato, mentre le norme degli altri tre gruppi sono più precise e specifiche, e intendono il diritto al cibo come una risorsa essenziale per la sussistenza delle persone. In altri termini, si devono distinguere le norme che regolano il *diritto ad un cibo adeguato al benessere delle persone* dalle norme che regolano il *diritto al cibo essenziale per la sussistenza delle persone*.

Nel settore del diritto internazionale dei diritti umani, conviene ricordare, innanzitutto, la Dichiarazione universale, che si occupa del diritto al cibo nell'art. 25(1):

> "Everyone has the right to a standard of living adequate for the health and well-being of himself and of his family, including food, clothing, housing and medical care [...]".

Come si vede, il diritto al cibo viene concepito soltanto come un aspetto particolare del diritto ad un tenore di vita adeguato.

Il Patto sui diritti civili e politici non menziona affatto il diritto al cibo. Invece, il Patto sui diritti economici, sociali e culturali contiene una disposizione importante su tale diritto: l'art. 11. In realtà, il par. 1 dell'art. 11 si limita a riprendere una formula simile a quella della Dichiarazione universale:

> "The States Parties to the present Covenant recognize the right of everyone to an *adequate* standard of living for himself and his family, including *adequate* food, clothing and housing, and to the continuous improvement of living conditions. The States Parties will take appropriate steps to ensure the realization of this right, recognizing to this effect the essential importance of international co-operation based on free consent" [357].

---

[356] Ma vedi, in senso contrario, Focarelli (2013), pp. 211-213.

[357] Corsivi aggiunti.

Come si può notare, questa disposizione parla di cibo "adeguato", come di un diritto specifico e funzionale, insieme ad altri, per realizzare il più ampio diritto ad un "adeguato" tenore di vita. Pertanto, a nostro avviso, si può affermare che questa norma regola il *diritto ad un cibo adeguato al benessere delle persone*.

Per la verità, il par. 2 dell'art. 11 sembra introdurre, rispetto al par. 1, un significato diverso e più "coraggioso" del diritto al cibo, poiché in esso si afferma che gli Stati parti del Patto riconoscono "the fundamental right of everyone to be free from hunger". Ma, dopo questa affermazione del diritto a non soffrire la fame, la disposizione prosegue in maniera assai più cauta, indicando una serie di misure e di programmi, di carattere vago e non vincolante, che gli Stati parti si impegnano a prendere, individualmente e tramite la cooperazione internazionale, allo scopo di migliorare la produzione, conservazione e distribuzione del cibo.

Molti altri trattati sui diritti umani contengono disposizioni sul diritto al cibo; ma quest'ultimo è sempre concepito, sulla falsariga della Dichiarazione universale e del Patto sui diritti economici, sociali e culturali, come il *diritto ad un cibo adeguato al benessere delle persone*. In questo senso è esemplare il Protocollo di San Salvador, il cui art. 12 stabilisce che ciascuno ha il diritto ad una nutrizione adeguata, che garantisca la possibilità di godere il più alto livello di sviluppo fisico, emotivo ed intellettuale[358]. In maniera simile, la Convenzione sui diritti del fanciullo menziona, indirettamente e fugacemente, il diritto al cibo (*rectius* le questioni della nutrizione e della malnutrizione dei fanciulli) nel quadro del diritto del fanciullo al più alto standard di salute (art. 24(2)(c)) e ad uno standard di vita adeguato per il suo sviluppo (art. 27(3)). Norme simili, e piuttosto vaghe e generiche, sono contenute nella Carta araba del 2004 (art. 38) e nella Convenzione sui diritti delle persone disabili del 2006 (art. 28(1)).

Invece, nel settore del diritto internazionale umanitario, si possono trovare norme di diverso tenore. Esse hanno lo scopo di impedire che gli Stati parti dei conflitti armati facciano soffrire la fame alle vittime di tali conflitti (prigionieri, persone civili, ecc.) o addirittura privino costoro del *cibo essenziale per la loro sopravvivenza*. Si possono citare la III Convenzione di Ginevra del 1949 (artt. 20 e 26), la IV Convenzione (art. 55), il I Protocollo Addizionale del 1977 (art. 54) ed il II Protocollo Addizionale (artt. 5(1)(b) e 14). Ad esempio, l'art. 55 della IV Convenzione di Ginevra stabilisce che:

> "[...] the Occupying Power has the duty of ensuring the food and medical supplies of the population; it should, in particular, bring in the *necessary* foodstuffs, medical stores and other articles if the resources of the occupied territory are inadequate [...]"[359].

L'art. 14 del II Protocollo Addizionale prevede che:

> "Starvation of civilians as a method of combat is prohibited. It is therefore prohibited to attack, destroy, remove or render useless, for that purpose, *objects indispensable to the survival* of the civilian population, such as foodstuffs, agricultural areas for the production of foodstuffs, crops, livestock, drinking water installations and supplies and irrigation works"[360].

---

[358] Il par. 2 dell'art. 12 aggiunge: "In order to promote the exercise of this right and eradicate malnutrition, the States Parties undertake to improve methods of production, supply and distribution of food, and to this end, agree to promote greater international cooperation in support of the relevant national policies".

[359] Corsivo aggiunto.

[360] Corsivo aggiunto.

Queste norme non si occupano del cibo adeguato al benessere o ad un buon tenore di vita delle persone, bensì del cibo come risorsa indispensabile alla sopravvivenza (*survival*) delle persone.

Una situazione simile si verifica nel diritto internazionale penale, dove esistono norme che addirittura configurano come un crimine internazionale la privazione, in certe circostanze, di cibo essenziale alla sussistenza o sopravvivenza delle persone. Ad esempio, l'art. 7(2)(b) dello Statuto della Corte penale internazionale considera come crimine contro l'umanità, in quanto sterminio,

> "[...] the intentional infliction of conditions of life, *inter alia* the deprivation of access to food and medicine, calculated to bring about the destruction of part of a population".

Parimenti, l'art. 8(2)(2)(b)(xxv) del medesimo Statuto considera come crimine di guerra:

> "Intentionally using starvation of civilians as a method of warfare [...]".

Infine, vi è un altro settore del diritto internazionale che merita di essere preso in esame: quello che riguarda le emergenze umanitarie, che siano dovute non solo a conflitti armati ma anche a disastri naturali o di altra natura. Infatti, in tempi recenti, si sta affermando l'idea che si sia formata (o sia in via di formazione) una norma di diritto internazionale generale che obbliga gli Stati ad agire in caso di emergenze umanitarie, con attività di assistenza alle vittime, tramite distribuzione di cibo, acqua, alloggi di fortuna, medicine e la prestazione di cure mediche[361]. A questo proposito, alcuni parlano di un "diritto umano all'assistenza umanitaria". Anche in questo ambito, il diritto al cibo si configura come diritto essenziale per la sussistenza delle persone.

In conclusione, come si era detto[362], si deve distinguere fra le norme che si occupano del *diritto ad un cibo adeguato al benessere e tenore di vita* delle persone e le norme che regolano il *diritto al cibo essenziale per la sussistenza* (o *sopravvivenza*) delle persone. È vero che queste ultime norme si trovano nel diritto umanitario e nel diritto internazionale penale; e ciò è del tutto logico, visti gli scopi generali di tali settori normativi. Tuttavia, ci sembra che queste norme possano operare, per *analogia*, anche nel diritto internazionale dei diritti umani, quantomeno in situazioni particolari di emergenza, di carestia o di disastri naturali. In altri termini, in tutti i casi nei quali il cibo è indispensabile per la sussistenza delle persone. Ciò trova conferma anche nell'esistenza della succitata norma consuetudinaria in materia di emergenze umanitarie. Inoltre, si deve ricordare che, come si era già detto[363], nei tempi recenti si è realizzata una notevole convergenza fra il settore dei diritti umani e quelli del diritto umanitario e del diritto internazionale penale, specie in relazione ai diritti fondamentali.

Si può sostenere che le varie norme convenzionali sopracitate sul diritto al cibo abbiano prodotto, con il tempo, anche una norma consuetudinaria? La risposta ci sembra negativa per quanto riguarda il *diritto ad un cibo adeguato al benessere* delle persone: le

---

[361] Sul punto vedi Acconci (2001), p. 33 ss. Cfr. anche Institut de Droit International, Sixteenth Commission, "*Humanitarian Assistance*", Resolution of 2 September 2003, Bruges session; ILC, *Draft articles on the protection of persons in the event of disasters*, 2016, in *YILC*, 2016, II(2).

[362] Vedi *supra*, par. 5.

[363] Vedi *supra*, par. 9; Cap. I, par. 8; Cap. III, par. 11.2.2.

norme pattizie in materia contengono obblighi "progressivi" e impegni politici degli Stati parti che ci sembrano difficilmente estensibili a tutti gli Stati della comunità internazionale.

Invece, si potrebbe dare una risposta positiva, sia pure con qualche cautela, circa l'esistenza di una norma di diritto internazionale generale sul *diritto al cibo essenziale per la sussistenza*. È vero che la prassi, convenzionale e di altra natura, è limitata; ma si potrebbero valorizzare il ruolo dell'*opinio iuris*, la *ratio* di tale norma, il suo stretto legame con la norma sul diritto alla vita, ed infine il recente sviluppo del diritto umano all'assistenza umanitaria. Tutti questi elementi potrebbero indurre a concludere che si sia formato un consenso generalizzato della comunità internazionale sull'esistenza di tale norma generale.

10.2. *Contenuto del diritto*

Anche il discorso sul contenuto del diritto al cibo segue la medesima logica. Infatti, le due tipologie di norme sul diritto al cibo, che abbiamo sopra indicato, hanno un contenuto assai diverso. Le norme sul *diritto ad un cibo adeguato al benessere* delle persone hanno di solito un contenuto assai vago e indeterminato, tanto che molti aspetti di tale contenuto sembrano addirittura carenti di valore giuridico vincolante e precettivo. Invece, le norme sul *diritto al cibo essenziale per la sussistenza* hanno un contenuto più specifico e di carattere precettivo, nonché un ambito di applicazione più ristretto, perché operano in situazioni di conflitti armati o di emergenza o di particolare urgenza.

Tuttavia, si deve avvertire che il Comitato sui diritti economici, sociali e culturali non segue questa impostazione[364]. Il Comitato ha cercato, in alcuni suoi Commenti Generali, di dare una definizione del diritto al cibo[365]; ma, a nostro avviso, in maniera non convincente. Infatti, il Comitato, concentrandosi sull'art. 11 del Patto sui diritti economici, sociali e culturali, si limita a distinguere fra un diritto al cibo adeguato, dal contenuto assai vago e da realizzarsi progressivamente, ed una *core obligation* degli Stati di agire "per mitigare ed alleviare la fame", che deriverebbe dal par. 2 dell'art. 11. In particolare, nel suo Commento Generale n. 12, il Comitato afferma:

> "The right to adequate food is realized when every man, woman and child, alone or in community with others, have physical and economic access at all times to adequate food or means for its procurement. The *right to adequate food* shall therefore not be interpreted in a narrow or restrictive sense which equates it with a minimum package of calories, proteins and other specific nutrients. The *right to adequate food* will have to be realized progressively. However, States have a core obligation to take the necessary action to mitigate and alleviate hunger as provided for in paragraph 2 of article 11, even in times of natural or other disasters"[366].

---

[364] Forse anche perché la norma di riferimento del Comitato è solo l'art. 11 del Patto sui diritti economici, sociali e culturali.

[365] CteeESCR, General Comment No. 12, 12 May 1999; General Comment No. 15, 20 January 2003.

[366] CteeESCR, General Comment No. 12, 12 May 1999, par. 6 (corsivi nel testo).

Da queste parole, la realizzazione effettiva del diritto al cibo appare quantomeno "utopistica". Ed anche la c.d. *core obligation* non è ben definita. Inoltre, nel medesimo Commento, il Comitato parla anche di un *core content* del diritto al cibo, che implicherebbe la disponibilità di cibo sufficiente a soddisfare i bisogni nutritivi delle persone e l'accessibilità a tale cibo[367]. A parte le nostre riserve sul concetto stesso di *core content*[368], si deve notare che anche questa definizione del "contenuto essenziale" del diritto al cibo è troppo vaga ed estensiva.

10.3. *Obblighi*

Il Comitato sui diritti economici, sociali e culturali ha cercato anche di definire gli obblighi degli Stati parti del Patto, in relazione al diritto al cibo[369]; ed ha seguito la sua tradizionale distinzione fra obblighi di rispettare (*to respect*), di proteggere (*to protect*) e di realizzare (*to fulfil*) i diritti umani. Abbiamo già criticato questa tripartizione, perché essa ha debole valore concettuale e scarsa utilità pratica. Al contrario, riteniamo che, anche con riferimento al diritto al cibo, si debbano usare le più volte citate categorie di: *a*) obblighi negativi; *b*) obblighi positivi immediati di risultato; *c*) obblighi positivi immediati di *due diligence*; *d*) obblighi "a realizzazione progressiva".

Ciò premesso, le norme sul *diritto ad un cibo adeguato al benessere* delle persone contengono alcuni programmi di natura politica ed alcuni obblighi "a realizzazione progressiva". Per questi ultimi, valgono gli effetti giuridici che abbiamo già descritto[370].

Invece, le norme sul *diritto al cibo essenziale per la sussistenza* delle persone contengono obblighi immediati. In primo luogo, lo Stato ha l'obbligo *negativo* di non negare l'accesso di individui o gruppi di individui a cibo essenziale che sia già disponibile, ad esempio distruggendo cibo o infrastrutture di approvvigionamento alimentare[371]. Questo divieto rileva soprattutto, ma non solo, durante i conflitti armati[372]. Anche provvedimenti statali di natura legislativa che neghino accesso al cibo essenziale possono entrare a far parte di questo divieto. In secondo luogo, lo Stato ha l'obbligo *positivo* (immediato e di risultato) di fornire cibo essenziale alla popolazione durante periodi di conflitti armati, di carestia o durante disastri umanitari[373]. Infine, lo Stato ha anche l'obbligo *positivo* (immediato e di *due diligence*) di prevenire misure o azioni da parte di privati che abbiano lo scopo di impedire a individui o gruppi di individui l'accesso al cibo essenziale alla sussistenza.

---

367 *Ibidem*, par. 8: "The Committee considers that the core content of the right to adequate food implies: The availability of food in a quantity and quality sufficient to satisfy the dietary needs of individuals, free from adverse substances, and acceptable within a given culture; The accessibility of such food in ways that are sustainable and that do not interfere with the enjoyment of other human rights".

368 Vedi *supra*, par. 5.

369 CteeESCR, General Comment No. 12, 12 May 1999, parr. 14-20.

370 Vedi *supra*, Cap. III, par. 5.3.

371 Kälin, Künzli (2009), p. 306.

372 Vedi AP I, art. 54(2); AP II, art. 14.

373 Secondo Kälin, Künzli (2009), p. 307, questo sarebbe un obbligo di realizzare (*obligation to fulfil*). Come abbiamo già detto più volte, noi siamo contrari a questa categoria di obblighi.

11. *Diritto all'acqua*

11.1. *Norme*

Il discorso sul diritto all'acqua presenta molte analogie con quello, appena svolto, sul diritto al cibo. Infatti, anche il diritto all'acqua è previsto, sia pure in maniera meno frequente, da alcune norme convenzionali sui diritti umani e da alcune norme di diritto internazionale umanitario. E di nuovo emerge una *differenza*: le norme del primo gruppo sono generiche e indeterminate, mentre quelle del secondo gruppo sono più specifiche ed hanno un contenuto più restrittivo. Inoltre, si può ritenere che anche per l'acqua operi la norma di diritto internazionale generale in materia di emergenze umanitarie.

Cominciando con il settore dei diritti umani, si deve notare che il diritto all'acqua non è menzionato dalla Dichiarazione universale, né dal Patto sui diritti civili e politici, né dal Protocollo di San Salvador, né dalla Carta sociale europea. In realtà neppure il Patto sui diritti economici, sociali e culturali prevede esplicitamente tale diritto; ma il relativo Comitato ha affermato che il diritto all'acqua è implicitamente regolato dall'art. 11 del Patto, poiché esso è un diritto "emanating from, and indispensable for, the realization of the right to an adequate standard of living"[374]. Pertanto anche il diritto all'acqua, come quello al cibo, è concepito dal Comitato come un aspetto specifico del più ampio diritto ad un tenore di vita adeguato[375]. In altri termini, si può parlare del *diritto ad un'acqua adeguata al benessere delle persone*.

Questa concezione viene riaffermata in vari trattati sui diritti umani, di carattere settoriale, che sono più precisi perché menzionano esplicitamente il diritto all'acqua. Si possono citare la Convenzione sul divieto di discriminazione contro le donne (art. 14(2)(h)); la Convenzione sui diritti del fanciullo (art. 24(2)(c)); la Convenzione sui diritti delle persone disabili (art. 28(2)(a)); ed alcuni accordi del continente africano sui diritti dei fanciulli e delle donne[376]. Nella Convenzione sul divieto di discriminazione contro le donne, ad esempio, si afferma che gli Stati parti prenderanno le misure appropriate per assicurare alle donne i benefici dello sviluppo rurale e, in particolare, il diritto:

> "To enjoy adequate living conditions, particularly in relation to housing, sanitation, electricity and *water supply* [...]"[377].

Nella Convenzione sui diritti del fanciullo, si richiede agli Stati di combattere la malnutrizione anche "through the provision of adequate nutritious foods and *clean drinking-water*"[378].

Se invece esaminiamo il diritto internazionale umanitario, si osserva che esistono varie norme che configurano il diritto all'acqua in maniera differente. Queste norme, analogamente a quelle sopra esaminate sul diritto al cibo, hanno lo scopo di proibire agli Stati par-

[374] CteeESCR, General Comment No. 15, 20 January 2003, par. 3.

[375] Secondo il Comitato, il diritto all'acqua dovrebbe anche considerarsi implicito nel diritto al cibo e nel diritto alla salute.

[376] African Charter of the Rights and Welfare of the Child (art. 14(2)(c)); Protocol to the African Charter on Human and Peoples' Rights on the Rights of Women in Africa (art. 15(a)).

[377] Art. 14(2)(h) (corsivo aggiunto).

[378] Art. 24(2)(c) (corsivo aggiunto).

ti dei conflitti armati di far soffrire la sete alle vittime di tali conflitti o addirittura di privare costoro dell'*acqua indispensabile per la loro sussistenza*. Si possono citare gli artt. 20, 26 e 46 della III Convenzione di Ginevra del 1949, gli artt. 89 e 127 della IV Convenzione di Ginevra, l'art. 54 del I Protocollo Addizionale e gli artt. 5(1)(b) e 14 del II Protocollo Addizionale. Ad esempio, l'art. 26 della III Convenzione di Ginevra stabilisce che:

"Sufficient drinking water shall be supplied to prisoners of war".

L'art. 5(1)(b) del II Protocollo Addizionale prevede che le persone private della libertà per motivi connessi con il conflitto armato:

"[…] shall, to the same extent as the local civilian population, be provided with food and drinking water […]".

Inoltre, come si è già visto, l'art. 14 del medesimo Protocollo vieta di attaccare o distruggere beni indispensabili alla sussistenza della popolazione civile, fra i quali "le istallazioni e le riserve di acqua potabile".

In conclusione, anche in relazione al diritto all'acqua, come per il diritto al cibo, si può distinguere fra le norme che concernono il *diritto ad un'acqua adeguata al benessere* delle persone e le norme che regolano il *diritto all'acqua essenziale per la sussistenza* (o *sopravvivenza*) delle persone. Queste seconde norme operano in situazioni di conflitti armati e trattano il diritto all'acqua come un "diritto di sussistenza", strettamente connesso con il diritto alla vita. Non ci sembra azzardato sostenere che queste ultime norme possano operare, anche al di fuori dei conflitti armati, in situazioni di emergenze umanitarie, di disastri naturali o di particolare urgenza; e che si sia sviluppata con il tempo anche una norma di diritto internazionale generale avente il medesimo contenuto. Anche in questo caso, come per il diritto al cibo essenziale, questa conclusione è rafforzata dal crescente favore nei confronti di norme che obbligano gli Stati ad agire nelle situazioni di emergenza umanitaria [379].

11.2. *Contenuto del diritto*

Il contenuto del diritto all'acqua cambia a seconda dei due gruppi di norme sopra indicati.

Le norme che si occupano del *diritto ad un'acqua adeguata al benessere* delle persone non hanno un contenuto uniforme. Come si è visto, talora questo diritto emerge solo implicitamente come un aspetto del diritto ad un tenore di vita adeguato. Talora, invece, il diritto è funzionale alle condizioni di vita rurale delle donne, oppure alla protezione sociale dei disabili oppure alla salute dei fanciulli. La difficoltà di dare un contenuto preciso a questo diritto risulta anche dai lavori del Comitato sui diritti economici, sociali e culturali. Il Comitato, ad esempio, nel suo Commento Generale n. 15, parte da una definizione molto ampia e ambiziosa del diritto in oggetto, quando afferma che:

"The human right to water entitles everyone to sufficient, safe, acceptable, physically accessible and affordable water for personal and domestic uses" [380].

---

[379] Vedi *supra*, par. 10.1.

[380] CteeESCR, General Comment No. 15, 20 January 2003, par. 2.

Ma dopo il Comitato, quando deve precisare meglio il contenuto normativo del diritto, si limita ad affermare che esso comprende una serie di "libertà e di diritti" (*freedoms and entitlements*)[381], ai quali corrispondono sia obblighi generali che specifici degli Stati. E passa ad occuparsi di tali obblighi, tralasciando di approfondire il contenuto del diritto ad un'acqua adeguata.

Se invece si esamina il secondo gruppo di norme, cioè quelle che regolano il *diritto all'acqua essenziale per la sussistenza* e che derivano dal diritto umanitario, si nota che il loro contenuto è più preciso, ha carattere vincolante e, al tempo stesso, il loro ambito di applicazione è più limitato, perché esse operano solo in situazioni di conflitti armati o di emergenza. Valgono qui le considerazioni che abbiamo fatto a proposito del diritto al cibo essenziale.

In realtà, anche il Comitato sui diritti economici, sociali e culturali sembra riconoscere, sia pure da un punto di vista diverso dal nostro, che il diritto all'acqua ha anche una dimensione diversa e più "forte" rispetto a quella meramente legata al benessere e tenore di vita delle persone. Infatti, il Comitato, sia pure incidentalmente, ha affermato che tale diritto "is one of the most fundamental conditions for *survival*"[382] e che esso "should also be seen in conjunction with other rights [...] foremost amongst them the right to life and human dignity"[383]. Ma poi questo concetto del collegamento con il diritto alla vita non è stato ulteriormente sviluppato.

11.3. *Obblighi*

Anche in relazione agli obblighi che derivano dal diritto all'acqua, è utile distinguere fra le norme sul *diritto ad un'acqua adeguata al benessere* delle persone, che contengono programmi di carattere politico ed obblighi "a realizzazione progressiva", e le norme sul *diritto all'acqua essenziale per la sussistenza*, che contengono obblighi immediati[384]. Di questi ultimi, si possono fare alcuni esempi. Gli Stati hanno l'obbligo negativo di non impedire accesso di individui o gruppi ad acqua essenziale che è già disponibile; di non distruggere servizi o infrastrutture di acqua essenziale durante conflitti armati o altri stati di emergenza; di non disconnettere o escludere in maniera ingiustificata le persone da servizi di fornitura di acqua essenziale. Inoltre, gli Stati hanno l'obbligo positivo (immediato) di fornire l'acqua essenziale alla popolazione e di prevenire misure da parte di privati che abbiano lo scopo di impedire l'accesso all'acqua essenziale a individui o gruppi di individui.

Nella prassi internazionale, sono significative alcune decisioni della Commissione africana dei diritti dell'uomo e dei popoli[385], che considerano il diritto di non essere privati dell'acqua essenziale nel quadro del diritto alla salute e del diritto ad un ambiente sano rispettivamente protetti dagli artt. 16 e 24 della Carta africana. Nel caso *Free Legal Assi-*

---

[381] *Ibidem*, par. 10.

[382] *Ibidem*, par. 3 (corsivo aggiunto).

[383] *Ibidem*.

[384] Invece, il Comitato sui diritti economici, sociali e culturali, come al solito, distingue fra obblighi di rispettare (*to respect*), di proteggere (*to protect*) e di realizzare (*to fulfil*). CteeESCR, General Comment No. 15, 20 January 2003, parr. 20-29.

[385] Vedi Focarelli (2013), pp. 214-215.

stance Group[386], la Commissione ha affermato che lo Zaire aveva violato l'art. 16 della Carta africana, perché aveva mancato di fornire servizi essenziali per la salute come l'acqua potabile. Nel caso *Social and Economic Rights Action Center v. Nigeria*[387], la Commissione ha ritenuto che la Nigeria avesse violato, fra l'altro, gli artt. 16 e 24 della Carta africana, perché aveva causato direttamente, e comunque non aveva impedito, l'inquinamento delle risorse acquifere nel territorio degli Ogoni.

12. *Diritto all'abitazione*

12.1. *Norme*

Anche il diritto all'abitazione è previsto, in maniera più o meno diretta, da norme sui diritti umani e da norme di diritto internazionale umanitario. E, di nuovo, si tratta di norme che hanno contenuti diversi.

Nei trattati ed altri atti internazionali sui diritti umani, vi è un primo gruppo di norme, piuttosto numeroso, che tratta il diritto all'abitazione come un aspetto particolare del diritto ad un tenore di vita adeguato. Con riferimento a queste norme, si può parlare del *diritto ad un'abitazione adeguata al benessere* delle persone. In questo senso, si possono ricordare l'art. 25(1) della Dichiarazione universale; l'art. 11(1) del Patto sui diritti economici, sociali e culturali; l'art. 38 della Carta araba; l'art. 27(3) della Convenzione sui diritti del fanciullo; l'art. 28 della Convenzione sui diritti dei disabili; e l'art. 14(2)(h) della Convenzione sull'eliminazione della discriminazione contro le donne. Anche l'art. 31 della Carta sociale europea (riveduta), che pure prevede un *autonomo* diritto all'abitazione, lo considera in realtà in maniera non dissimile dalle norme precedenti, poiché lo regola in termini sostanzialmente programmatici. Infatti, l'art. 31 recita:

> "With a view to ensuring the effective exercise of the right to housing, the Parties undertake to take measures designed:
> 1. to promote access to housing of an adequate standard;
> 2. to prevent and reduce homelessness with a view to its gradual elimination;
> 3. to make the price of housing accessible to those without adequate resources".

Un secondo gruppo di norme concepisce nello stesso modo il diritto all'abitazione; ma è complementare rispetto al primo gruppo, perché stabilisce il principio di uguaglianza o di non discriminazione nel godimento del diritto all'abitazione. Si possono citare l'art. 5(e)(iii) della Convenzione contro la discriminazione razziale; l'art. 21 della Convenzione di Ginevra sullo *status* dei rifugiati; e l'art. 43(1)(d) della Convenzione sui diritti dei lavoratori migranti. Ma queste norme adesso non ci interessano, poiché i principi di uguaglianza e di non discriminazione saranno esaminati in seguito[388]. Un terzo gruppo di norme, sempre in materia di diritti umani, si occupa in realtà di diritti diversi dal diritto all'abitazione, che tuttavia possono avere un'incidenza indiretta su tale diritto. Si pensi, ad esempio, alle norme sul diritto alla

---

[386] ACmHPR, *Free Legal Assistance Group and Others*, par. 47.

[387] ACmHPR, *Social and Economic Rights Action Center and Other v. Nigeria*, parr. 50-54.

[388] Vedi *infra*, parr. 21-23.

salute, sul diritto al rispetto della vita privata e familiare, sul diritto di proprietà e sul diritto ad un ambiente sano. Ma anche di tali norme ci occuperemo in seguito [389].

Infine, vi sono le norme di diritto internazionale umanitario sul diritto all'abitazione, che sono quelle per noi rilevanti nell'ottica dei diritti umani "fondamentali". Queste norme, che non sono per la verità numerose, trattano il diritto all'abitazione come un *diritto essenziale per la sussistenza delle persone*. Esemplare, in questo senso, è l'art. 69 del I Protocollo Addizionale alle Convenzioni di Ginevra, che regola i bisogni essenziali nei territori occupati, e secondo cui:

> "[...] la Potenza occupante assicurerà anche, nella misura consentita dai suoi mezzi e senza alcuna distinzione di carattere sfavorevole, la fornitura di [...] alloggi di fortuna, delle altre provviste essenziali per la sussistenza della popolazione civile nel territorio occupato [...]" [390].

Il successivo art. 70 prevede che, quando la fornitura di tali beni sia insufficiente, debbano essere intraprese azioni di soccorso di carattere umanitario. Altre norme pertinenti sono, ad esempio, quelle della IV Convenzione di Ginevra che proibiscono il saccheggio (art. 33) [391], che vietano alla Potenza che occupa un territorio di distruggere immobili che appartengono alla popolazione civile (art. 53), e che impongono a tale Potenza di assicurare beni indispensabili ai bisogni di tale popolazione (art. 55).

Ciò premesso, ci si deve chiedere, anche per il diritto all'abitazione, se le norme convenzionali sopra citate abbiano prodotto anche una norma consuetudinaria. A nostro avviso, la risposta è negativa per quanto riguarda il *diritto ad un'abitazione adeguata al benessere* delle persone; per gli stessi motivi già indicati con riguardo ai diritti ad un cibo e ad un'acqua adeguati [392].

Più difficile è valutare se sul *diritto all'abitazione essenziale per la sussistenza* delle persone si sia sviluppata una norma di diritto internazionale generale, che possa operare quando manchi una norma convenzionale *ad hoc*. Da una parte, si potrebbe dare una risposta positiva, sulla base degli argomenti che abbiamo sopra proposto in relazione ai diritti al cibo ed all'acqua essenziali; e quindi facendo valere la *ratio* della norma, il suo legame con il diritto alla vita ed il crescente consenso circa l'esistenza di un diritto umano all'assistenza umanitaria. Tuttavia, d'altra parte, si deve anche ammettere che, con riguardo al diritto all'abitazione essenziale, il numero delle norme convenzionali è esiguo, e che l'abitazione, rispetto al cibo ed all'acqua, costituisce più raramente un bene indispensabile per la sussistenza o addirittura la sopravvivenza delle persone. Pertanto, nel complesso, ci sembra che si debba escludere la formazione di una norma di diritto internazionale generale.

12.2. *Contenuto del diritto*

Venendo al contenuto dei due principali gruppi di norme sopra indicati, si nota subito

---

[389] Vedi *infra*, par. 13 e Cap. VI, parr. 2, 3, 11 e 20.2.

[390] AP I, art. 69.

[391] Vedi anche AP II, art. 4(2)(g).

[392] Le norme convenzionali sul diritto ad un'abitazione adeguata contengono per lo più obblighi "a realizzazione progressiva" o impegni politici non vincolanti, che non sono estensibili a tutti gli Stati della comunità internazionale.

che le norme che trattano il *diritto ad un'abitazione adeguata al benessere* delle persone hanno un contenuto vago e indeterminato. Anche il Comitato sui diritti economici, sociali e culturali fornisce un'interpretazione ampia ed estensiva di tale contenuto, quando, ad esempio, nel suo Commento Generale n. 4, afferma che:

"[...] the right to housing should not be interpreted in a narrow or restrictive sense which equates it with, for example, the shelter provided by merely having a roof over one's head or views shelter exclusively as a commodity. Rather it should be seen as the right to live somewhere in security, peace and dignity" [393].

Quindi il Comitato aggiunge che l'art. 11(1) del Patto si riferisce non solo all'abitazione, ma a una adeguata abitazione, e che ciò significa:

"[...] adequate privacy, adequate space, adequate security, adequate lighting and ventilation, adequate basic infrastructure and adequate location, with regard to work and basic facilities – all at a reasonable cost" [394].

Questa interpretazione assai estensiva del contenuto del diritto all'abitazione, a nostro parere, può essere accettata soltanto se essa fa riferimento ad un diritto che possa essere realizzato dagli Stati progressivamente in un futuro piuttosto indeterminato, o addirittura se essa contempla, più che un vero e proprio diritto, un programma politico non vincolante per gli Stati. Del resto, il Comitato ha dovuto ammettere che:

"remains a disturbingly large gap between the standards set in article 11(1) [...] and the situation prevailing in many parts of the world" [395].

Ma il discorso cambia se si prende in esame il contenuto delle norme che regolano il *diritto all'abitazione essenziale per la sussistenza* delle persone. Ricordiamo il citato art. 69 del I Protocollo Addizionale, che parla di "alloggi di fortuna" per la popolazione civile nei territori occupati durante i conflitti armati. Qui non è in questione il diritto ad un'abitazione adeguata, con i criteri di riservatezza, spaziosità, sicurezza, illuminazione, ventilazione ed altri simili, che sono stati indicati dal Comitato sui diritti economici, sociali e culturali; bensì l'assai più limitato diritto di avere "un ricovero o un riparo abitativo" (*right to shelter*). Si tratta, ancora una volta, di un diritto di sussistenza, strettamente collegato al diritto alla vita. Ci sembra che a questo diritto ad "un ricovero o riparo abitativo" abbia fatto riferimento, in sostanza, anche la Commissione africana, nel già citato caso *Social and Economic Rights Action Center*, quando ha affermato che:

"[...] the right to shelter obliges the Nigerian Government not to destroy the housing of its citizens and not to obstruct efforts by individuals or communities to rebuild lost homes [...] The government has destroyed Ogoni houses and villages and then, through its security forces, obstructed, harassed, beaten and, in some cases, shot and killed innocent citizens who have attempted to return to rebuild their ruined homes. These actions constitute massive violations of the right to shelter [...]" [396].

---

[393] CteeESCR, General Comment No. 4, 13 December 1991, par. 7.

[394] *Ibidem*.

[395] *Ibidem*, par. 4.

[396] ACmHPR, *Social and Economic Rights Action Center and Other v. Nigeria*, parr. 61-62.

Peraltro, la Commissione ha ritenuto che il diritto in oggetto, anche se non esplicitamente previsto dalla Carta africana, derivi dalla combinazione delle disposizioni della Carta sul diritto alla salute, sul diritto di proprietà e sulla protezione della famiglia[397]. In realtà, anche da questa decisione emerge la difficoltà di poter fondare il *diritto all'abitazione essenziale per la sussistenza* delle persone su una norma di diritto internazionale generale, che possa essere applicata quando manchi una norma convenzionale *ad hoc*. Infatti, la Commissione africana ha preferito dedurre il diritto in questione da altri diritti umani, espressamente previsti dalla Carta africana.

12.3. *Obblighi*

Le varie norme sul diritto di abitazione contengono una serie di obblighi diversi a carico degli Stati. Tralasciando qui gli impegni di carattere politico e gli obblighi "a realizzazione progressiva", per i quali valgono le osservazioni che abbiamo fatto più volte, conviene ricordare gli obblighi principali che corrispondono al *diritto all'abitazione essenziale per la sussistenza* delle persone. In primo luogo, gli Stati hanno l'obbligo *negativo*, derivante dal diritto umanitario, di astenersi dal distruggere o saccheggiare gli immobili della popolazione civile; e l'obbligo negativo di astenersi dall'effettuare evacuazioni o deportazioni forzate che non siano giustificate dalla necessità militare o dalla necessità di salvare la popolazione[398]. In secondo luogo, gli Stati hanno l'obbligo *positivo* (immediato e di solito di *due diligence*) di fornire un alloggio di emergenza alle vittime di conflitti armati e di disastri naturali o umanitari[399].

Il Comitato sui diritti economici, sociali e culturali ritiene che dal diritto all'abitazione derivino *anche altri obblighi* per gli Stati, quali il divieto di non privare arbitrariamente le persone della propria abitazione, tramite sfratti illegali o "evizioni forzate"[400], e l'obbligo di proteggere le persone da ingerenze da parte di privati che tendano a sopprimere il diritto di abitazione. A nostro avviso, tali obblighi esistono; ma non derivano dal diritto all'abitazione, bensì da altri diritti umani, quali il diritto di proprietà[401] ed il diritto al rispetto della vita privata e familiare[402].

13. *Diritto alla salute*

13.1. *Norme*

Il diritto alla salute[403] è previsto da numerose norme internazionali sui diritti umani, ma anche da varie norme di diritto internazionale umanitario, volte a proteggere la salute

---

397 *Ibidem*, par. 60.

398 Cfr. anche Kälin, Künzli (2009), p. 311.

399 *Ibidem*, p. 312.

400 Vedi CteeESCR, General Comment No. 7, 16 May 1997.

401 Vedi *infra*, Cap. VI, par. 11.

402 Vedi *infra*, Cap. VI, parr. 2 e 3.

403 Su tale diritto vedi, fra gli altri, Acconci (2001).

dei combattenti e dei civili coinvolti in conflitti armati. Infine, rileva la norma generale sul diritto all'assistenza umanitaria.

Fra gli strumenti internazionali sulla tutela dei diritti umani, si possono menzionare la Dichiarazione universale (art. 25); il Patto sui diritti economici, sociali e culturali (art. 12); la Convenzione contro la discriminazione razziale (art. 5(e)(iv)); la Convenzione sull'eliminazione della discriminazione contro le donne (art. 12); la Convenzione sui diritti del fanciullo (art. 24); la Convenzione sui diritti delle persone disabili (art. 25); la Carta sociale europea (riveduta) (art. 11); la Carta dei diritti fondamentali dell'UE (art. 35); il Protocollo di San Salvador (art. 10); la Carta africana (art. 16); la Carta araba (art. 39).

Queste disposizioni non sono formulate in maniera uniforme; ma la loro concezione del diritto alla salute è la stessa, e cioè il *diritto delle persone al godimento di un alto livello di salute e di benessere*. La Dichiarazione universale, ad esempio, nell'art. 25(1) già citato, proclama che:

> "Everyone has the right to a standard of living adequate for the health and well-being of himself and of his family, including [...] medical care [...]".

L'art. 12 del Patto sui diritti economici, sociali e culturali prevede, invece, un autonomo diritto alla salute; ed inizia (al par. 1) con una definizione assai estensiva di tale diritto:

> "The States Parties [...] recognize the right of everyone to the enjoyment of the highest attainable standard of physical and mental health".

Ma poi l'art. 12 continua, al par. 2, elencando una serie di misure, dal carattere fortemente programmatico, che gli Stati parti dovrebbero prendere per realizzare pienamente tale diritto. L'art. 24 della Convenzione sui diritti del fanciullo adotta la medesima formula del Patto (*the right to the enjoyment of the highest attainable standard of health*); ma è più elaborato e dettagliato nell'elencare le misure che gli Stati parti dovrebbero prendere. Assai più sintetiche, invece, sono le norme contenute nelle due convenzioni contro la discriminazione, che si limitano a vietare la discriminazione razziale nel diritto alle cure mediche ed alla assistenza sanitaria e la discriminazione contro le donne nel campo della assistenza sanitaria.

Quanto agli strumenti regionali, l'art. 16 della Carta africana è assai sintetico e si limita a riprendere, in sostanza, la formula dell'art. 12, par. 1, del Patto sui diritti economici, sociali e culturali. Ancora più "deboli" appaiono le norme contenute nella Carta sociale europea[404] e nella Carta dei diritti fondamentali dell'UE[405], la quale si limita addirittura a rinviare alle leggi e le prassi dei diritti statali.

Più interessanti sono, invece, le disposizioni contenute nel Protocollo di San Salvador e nella Carta araba. L'art. 10 del Protocollo di San Salvador, dopo la solita formula del par.

---

[404] ESCrev, art. 11 (*The right to protection of health*): "With a view to ensuring the effective exercise of the right to protection of health, the Parties undertake, either directly or in cooperation with public or private organisations, to take appropriate measures designed *inter alia*: 1. to remove as far as possible the causes of ill-health; 2. to provide advisory and educational facilities for the promotion of health and the encouragement of individual responsibility in matters of health; 3. to prevent as far as possible epidemic, endemic and other diseases, as well as accidents".

[405] EUCh, art. 38 (*Health care*): "Everyone has the right of access to preventive health care and the right to benefit from medical treatment under the conditions established by national laws and practices [...]".

1, secondo cui ognuno ha il diritto alla salute, inteso come il godimento del più alto livello di benessere fisico, mentale e sociale, stabilisce, al par. 2, che gli Stati parti "agree to recognise health as a public good"; e che, in particolare, essi si impegnano ad adottare varie misure che hanno un carattere più preciso rispetto a quelle previste dagli altri strumenti internazionali. Fra queste misure, spicca l'adozione di un'*assistenza sanitaria primaria*, cioè un'assistenza sanitaria accessibile per tutti gli individui ed i gruppi nella comunità. Anche la Carta araba, nel suo art. 39, riconosce il diritto di godere del più alto livello raggiungibile di salute fisica e mentale, ed il diritto del cittadino di godere dei servizi di base di assistenza medica e di accedere ai servizi medici senza alcuna discriminazione.

In conclusione, le norme sul diritto alla salute contenute nei trattati sui diritti umani prevedono, di regola, il diritto di tutti gli individui ad un alto livello di salute e, talora, anche una serie di misure programmatiche per la realizzazione progressiva di tale diritto. Soltanto alcuni trattati prevedono il diritto più specifico delle persone di accedere ad un'assistenza sanitaria di base o primaria.

Invece, sono differenti, ancora una volta, le norme del diritto internazionale umanitario e quelle in materia di emergenze e catastrofi naturali.

Nel diritto umanitario, lo scopo non è ovviamente quello di realizzare un alto livello di salute e di benessere per tutte le persone; bensì quello, assai più limitato ma più impellente, di garantire un'*assistenza sanitaria alle persone coinvolte in conflitti armati*, con particolare riguardo per i soggetti più vulnerabili, quali i feriti, i malati, gli infermi, i prigionieri e le donne in stato di gravidanza. In altri termini, si tratta di provvedere ai bisogni primari di cure sanitarie (*basic medical needs*) di tali persone; e pertanto si può parlare di un loro *diritto ad un livello essenziale di assistenza sanitaria.*

In effetti, sono numerose le norme del diritto umanitario che perseguono tale scopo. Si possono qui fare solo alcuni esempi. L'art. 3(2) comune alle quattro Convenzioni di Ginevra stabilisce che "[i] feriti ed i malati saranno raccolti e curati". La III Convenzione di Ginevra prevede molte disposizioni dettagliate per assicurare adeguate cure mediche ai prigionieri di guerra (artt. 29-32). La IV Convenzione di Ginevra stabilisce norme simili per i feriti, i malati, gli infermi e le puerpere (artt. 16-23); e prevede che, nei territori occupati, la Potenza occupante debba assicurare medicinali, servizi sanitari o ospedalieri e, se del caso, azioni di soccorso a favore della popolazione (artt. 55-57 e 59). Il I Protocollo Addizionale contiene molte disposizioni dedicate a curare e proteggere la salute delle vittime dei conflitti armati (artt. 10-15) ed una norma importante dedicata al soccorso della popolazione civile (art. 70). Anche il II Protocollo Addizionale contiene norme sulla protezione dei feriti, malati e naufraghi nei conflitti armati non internazionali (artt. 7-11).

Infine, in tema di catastrofi naturali, vale qui il discorso che abbiamo già fatto (parlando dei diritti al cibo ed all'acqua) circa l'esistenza di una norma di diritto internazionale generale sul *diritto all'assistenza umanitaria.* Anzi, in relazione al diritto alla salute, gli obblighi degli Stati di fornire assistenza umanitaria sono ancora più pertinenti, poiché tali obblighi hanno quasi sempre lo scopo primario di rispondere ad un'emergenza sanitaria.

13.2. *Contenuto del diritto*

Il contenuto del diritto alla salute cambia a seconda dei diversi gruppi di norme sopra descritti.

Le norme degli strumenti internazionali sui diritti umani, come si è visto, tendono a concepire tale diritto come il "diritto di ogni individuo a godere delle migliori condizioni di salute fisica e mentale che sia in grado di conseguire"[406]. Ne consegue che il contenuto di tale diritto è vago e indeterminato. D'altra parte, è chiaro, anche soltanto per ragioni di logica, che il diritto alla salute non può significare il diritto di essere sani, che evidentemente dipende anche da condizioni fisiche personali; ma solo il diritto che lo Stato cerchi di creare le condizioni che favoriscano il migliore standard di salute per le persone sottoposte alla propria giurisdizione[407]. Ciò trova conferma anche nei lavori del Comitato sui diritti economici, sociali e culturali. Il Comitato, nel suo Commento Generale n. 14, dichiara che il diritto alla salute non si limita al diritto all'assistenza sanitaria (*health care*); ma che esso:

"[…] embraces a wide range of socio-economic factors that promote conditions in which people can lead a healthy life, and extends to the underlying determinants of health, such as food and nutrition, housing, access to safe and potable water and adequate sanitation, safe and healthy working conditions, and a healthy environment"[408].

Il Comitato sostiene, poi, che il diritto alla salute:

"[…] contains both freedoms and entitlements. The freedoms include the right to control one's health and body, including sexual and reproductive freedom, and the right to be free from interference, such as the right to be free from torture, non-consensual medical treatment and experimentation. By contrast, the entitlements include the right to a system of health protection which provides equality of opportunity for people to enjoy the highest attainable level of health"[409].

Inoltre, secondo il Comitato, il diritto alla salute, pur avendo una sua autonomia, ha rapporti stretti di interdipendenza con molti altri diritti, quali il diritto alla vita, il divieto di tortura e di trattamenti inumani o degradanti, il diritto alla libertà e sicurezza personale, il diritto al cibo, all'acqua, all'abitazione, ecc. In molti casi, pertanto, vi è una sovrapposizione fra il diritto alla salute ed altri diritti umani.

Invece, le norme di diritto umanitario, quantomeno quelle convenzionali, hanno un contenuto più limitato e più preciso, che viene volta per volta definito dalla singola norma. Tuttavia, dal loro insieme, si può forse trarre un principio generale: cioè che gli Stati parti di un conflitto armato hanno l'obbligo di prestare un'assistenza sanitaria essenziale alle persone coinvolte in conflitti armati, e specie a coloro che non partecipano o non partecipano più alle ostilità. Pertanto queste persone hanno il *diritto ad un livello essenziale di assistenza sanitaria*.

Infine, un diritto di contenuto simile si ricava dalle norme in materia di emergenze umanitarie. Infatti, la norma emergente di diritto internazionale generale, che impone agli Stati un obbligo di assistenza umanitaria in situazioni di disastri o emergenze naturali, ha un contenuto ampio, poiché prevede varie attività di soccorso e assistenza; ma, fra queste,

---

[406] CESCR, art. 12(1).

[407] Kälin, Künzli (2009), p. 313.

[408] CteeESCR, General Comment No. 14, 11 August 2000, par. 4.

[409] *Ibidem*, par. 8.

spicca quella volta a rispondere ai bisogni primari di assistenza medica (*basic medical needs*) delle persone. Pertanto anche in questo caso si può parlare di un diritto delle persone coinvolte in tali emergenze di godere di un livello essenziale di assistenza medica.

13.3. *Obblighi*

Anche per gli obblighi degli Stati, corrispondenti al diritto alla salute, si può fare un discorso simile a quello già fatto in relazione agli altri diritti che proteggono i *basic needs* delle persone.

Il *diritto al godimento di un alto livello di salute e di benessere* non è, in linea di massima, un diritto immediatamente precettivo e giustiziabile, cui possano corrispondere obblighi negativi e obblighi positivi immediati da parte degli Stati. Al contrario, richiede agli Stati programmi politici ed obblighi "a realizzazione progressiva". Inoltre, esso dipende molto dalle risorse economiche e dai mezzi effettivi a disposizione di ciascuno Stato e quindi presuppone diversi standard di tutela della salute nei diversi paesi[410]. Tuttavia, si deve notare che alcune norme convenzionali, sopra citate, obbligano gli Stati ad adottare a favore di tutti gli individui un'assistenza sanitaria primaria (art. 10 Protocollo di San Salvador) o servizi di base di assistenza medica (art. 39 Carta araba). Forse tali obblighi potrebbero essere configurati come obblighi positivi immediati di *due diligence*. Ma non si può ritenere che obblighi simili si impongano a tutti gli Stati in virtù di una norma di diritto internazionale generale.

Quanto, invece, agli obblighi corrispondenti al *diritto ad un livello essenziale di assistenza sanitaria* (nelle situazioni di conflitti armati o di emergenze umanitarie), essi hanno, in linea di massima, il carattere della immediatezza. Ad esempio, gli Stati hanno l'obbligo negativo di non distruggere, durante conflitti armati, strutture sanitarie esistenti, e di non impedire alle persone l'accesso a tali strutture. Hanno inoltre i numerosi obblighi positivi immediati, sia di risultato che di *due diligence*, che sono precisati nelle varie disposizioni sopra citate delle Convenzioni di Ginevra e dei Protocolli Addizionali. Basti ricordare, fra gli altri, l'obbligo della Potenza occupante di assicurare medicinali e servizi sanitari a favore della popolazione civile.

14. *Diritto ad un ambiente sano (rinvio)*

Il diritto umano ad un ambiente sano si configura, per certi aspetti, come un diritto individuale, ma, per altri aspetti più rilevanti, come un diritto collettivo. Sarà quindi trattato in seguito[411].

---

[410] Cfr. CESCR, art. 12(1): "[...] the right of everyone to the enjoyment of the *highest attainable* standard of physical and mental health" (corsivo aggiunto).

[411] Vedi *infra*, Cap. VI, par. 20.2.

Sezione IV
PROTEZIONE DELLA LIBERTÀ E SICUREZZA DELLA PERSONA

Finora abbiamo parlato dei diritti umani che hanno lo scopo di tutelare la vita e l'integrità fisica delle persone [412] e di quelli che hanno lo scopo di proteggere i bisogni primari e talora la sussistenza stessa delle persone [413]. Non vi è dubbio che questi scopi abbiano carattere preminente nel quadro del diritto internazionale dei diritti umani. Ma un altro obiettivo preminente è quello di proteggere la *libertà e sicurezza* delle persone. Esso è affidato ad alcuni diritti di origine assai antica e che appartengono alla prima generazione dei diritti umani. I più importanti sono quelli che derivano dal divieto di schiavitù, servitù e lavori forzati e dal divieto di arresti o detenzioni arbitrarie. Più recentemente, si sono aggiunte norme sul divieto di sparizione forzata delle persone.

15. *Divieto di schiavitù, servitù e lavori forzati*

15.1. *Norme*

Il divieto di schiavitù, di servitù e di lavori forzati è previsto da numerosi strumenti internazionali sui diritti umani. La Dichiarazione universale proclama solennemente, all'art. 1, che "All human beings are born free and equal in dignity and rights" e, all'art. 4, stabilisce che:

> "No one shall be held in slavery or servitude; slavery and the slave trade shall be prohibited in all their forms".

I principali trattati generali sui diritti umani prevedono disposizioni che completano il divieto di schiavitù e servitù con il divieto di lavori forzati o obbligatori; e che hanno un contenuto più specifico e dettagliato rispetto a quello della Dichiarazione universale. Si possono ricordare l'art. 8 del Patto sui diritti civili e politici, l'art. 4 della Convenzione europea [414], l'art. 6 della Convenzione americana, l'art. 5 della Carta dei diritti fondamentali

---

[412] Vedi *supra*, parr. 7, 8 e 9.

[413] Vedi *supra*, parr. 10, 11, 12 e 13.

[414] ECHR, art. 4 (*Prohibition of slavery and forced labour*): "1. No one shall be held in slavery or servitude. 2. No one shall be required to perform forced or compulsory labour. 3. For the purpose of this article the term 'forced or compulsory labour' shall not include:

a. any work required to be done in the ordinary course of detention imposed according to the provisions of Article 5 of this Convention or during conditional release from such detention;

b. any service of a military character or, in case of conscientious objectors in countries where they are recognised, service exacted instead of compulsory military service;

c. any service exacted in case of an emergency or calamity threatening the life or well-being of the community;

d. any work or service which forms part of normal civic obligations".

dell'UE, l'art. 10 della Carta araba. La Carta africana, invece, si limita a proibire la schiavitù ed il commercio degli schiavi (art. 5)[415].

Vi sono poi dei trattati settoriali che si occupano di questi diritti; si possono citare: la Convenzione sulla schiavitù ed il commercio degli schiavi del 1926[416]; la Convenzione supplementare relativa all'abolizione della schiavitù, della tratta degli schiavi e degli istituti o pratiche analoghi alla schiavitù del 1956[417]; la Convenzione ILO n. 29 del 1930 sul lavoro forzato[418]; la Convenzione ILO n. 105 del 1957 sull'abolizione del lavoro forzato[419]; il Protocollo addizionale del 2000 alla Convenzione di Palermo, relativo alla tratta di persone[420]; la Convenzione europea del 2005 contro la tratta di esseri umani[421].

Infine, si deve notare che la riduzione in schiavitù è considerata come un crimine contro l'umanità ed è punita dallo Statuto della Corte penale internazionale[422]. Pertanto, quando pratiche di riduzione in schiavitù, schiavitù sessuale o prostituzione forzata sono messe in opera nel quadro di un "attacco esteso o sistematico" diretto contro la popolazione civile, in esecuzione di un piano da parte di un governo o di un gruppo, i responsabili sono perseguibili in base al diritto internazionale penale[423]. La riduzione in schiavitù può costituire anche un crimine di guerra[424].

Dalle numerose norme internazionali che vietano ogni forma di schiavitù o servitù e dall'*opinio iuris* della comunità internazionale, si deduce che tale divieto è divenuto oggetto di una norma consuetudinaria del diritto internazionale e che tale norma ha la natura di *ius cogens*[425]. Non ci sembra, invece, che il divieto di lavori forzati o obbligatori abbia il carattere di norma perentoria.

15.2. *Contenuto dei divieti*

Le forme storiche di schiavitù, cioè di individui che sono oggetto di proprietà di altri individui, che non hanno personalità o capacità giuridica, e che possono essere ridotti a oggetti sfruttabili e commerciabili, sono oramai scomparse. Tuttavia, le norme internazionali sopra indicate non hanno perso il loro significato, poiché sopravvivono nel mondo forme moderne di schiavitù o di servitù e di lavori forzati. Si pensi, ad esempio, alla tratta di esseri umani, specie di donne e fanciulli, a scopo di sfruttamento sessuale; alla prostitu-

---

[415] Vedi anche CRPD, art. 27(2); CMW, art. 11; ESCrev, art. 1(2).

[416] Convention to Suppress the Slave Trade and Slavery of 25 September 1926.

[417] Supplementary Convention on the Abolition of Slavery, the Slave Trade, and Institutions and Practices Similar to Slavery of 7 September 1956.

[418] ILO Forced Labour Convention of 28 June 1930 (No. 29).

[419] ILO Abolition of Forced Labour Convention of 25 June 1957 (No. 105).

[420] Protocol to Prevent, Suppress and Punish Trafficking in Persons Especially Women and Children of 15 November 2000, supplementing the UN Convention against Transnational Organized Crime.

[421] European Convention on Action against Trafficking in Human Beings of 16 May 2005. Si noti che la tratta di esseri umani (*human trafficking*) va distinta dal traffico di migranti (*migrant smuggling*), anche se i due fenomeni sono spesso connessi.

[422] Rome Statute, art. 7(1)(c) e (g).

[423] Vedi Kälin, Künzli (2009), p. 423.

[424] Cfr. Rome Statute, art. 8(2)(b)(xxii) ed (e)(vi).

[425] Vedi, fra gli altri, Zagrebelsky *et al.* (2016), p. 172.

zione forzata; alle pratiche dei matrimoni forzati; allo sfruttamento del lavoro minorile; all'uso dei bambini soldato.

Per chiarire il contenuto delle norme in oggetto, conviene definire meglio le nozioni di schiavitù, servitù e lavori forzati, premettendo che queste nozioni sono state interpretate in maniera dinamica ed evolutiva dagli organi internazionali di controllo dei trattati sui diritti umani.

La *schiavitù* è definita, nell'art. 1(1) della Convenzione del 1926, come:

> "[…] the status or condition of a person over whom any or all of the powers attaching to the right of ownership are exercised".

Questa definizione è stata considerata dal Tribunale penale internazionale per la ex Jugoslavia come quella valida anche per il diritto consuetudinario. Invece, lo Statuto della Corte penale internazionale definisce la schiavitù come:

> "[…] the exercise of any or all the powers attaching to the right of ownership over a person and includes the exercise of such power in the course of trafficking in persons, in particular women and children"[426].

Questa disposizione pone il problema dei rapporti fra la nozione di schiavitù e quella di *tratta* di esseri umani. Nello Statuto della Corte penale internazionale, la seconda nozione viene, in pratica, ad essere ricompresa nella prima. Anche la Corte europea dei diritti umani, ad esempio nel caso *Rantsev*[427], ha equiparato la tratta di esseri umani alla riduzione in schiavitù ed ha applicato ad essa l'art. 4 della Convenzione europea. Il Comitato dei diritti umani[428] ha ritenuto che la tratta delle donne e la prostituzione forzata, anche se non espressamente previste dall'art. 8 del Patto sui diritti civili e politici, violino in realtà tale disposizione. Tuttavia, più spesso si ritiene che il concetto di tratta di esseri umani abbia una sua specificità e debba essere trattato separatamente rispetto al divieto di schiavitù, specie nell'ottica della repressione penale. Ad esempio, la Carta dei diritti fondamentali dell'UE, all'art. 5, proibisce espressamente la tratta di esseri umani. L'Unione Europea ha anche adottato la Direttiva 2011/36, sulla prevenzione e repressione della tratta di esseri umani e la protezione delle vittime[429], che specifica il concetto di tratta e quello di sfruttamento.

Il concetto di *servitù*, invece, si riferisce a persone che non hanno perduto la propria capacità giuridica; ma che devono sottoporre il loro lavoro o i loro servizi alla volontà discrezionale di un'altra persona. La citata Convenzione supplementare del 1956 definisce la servitù come la condizione di una persona:

> "[…] who is by law, custom or agreement bound to live and labour on land belonging to another person and to render some determinate service to such other person, whether for reward or not, and is not free to change his status"[430].

---

[426] Rome Statute, art. (2)(c).

[427] ECtHR, *Rantsev v. Cyprus and Russia*, parr. 281-282.

[428] HRCtee, General Comment No. 28, 29 March 2000, par. 12.

[429] Directive 2011/36/EU of the European Parliament and of the Council of 5 April 2011 on preventing and combating trafficking in human beings and protecting its victims.

[430] Supplementary Convention on the Abolition of Slavery, the Slave Trade, and Institutions and Practices Similar to Slavery, art. 1(b).

Inoltre, questa Convenzione equipara alla servitù una serie di pratiche che vengono elencate in maniera dettagliata, quali, ad esempio, la servitù per debiti, le prassi matrimoniali di sfruttamento delle donne, le prassi di sfruttamento del lavoro di minori. Anche la Corte europea dei diritti umani ritiene che la servitù sia una nozione vicina, ma non identica, a quella di schiavitù [431]. La Corte, nella sentenza *Siliadin* [432], ha stabilito che erano contrarie all'art. 4 della Convenzione certe situazioni di lavoro domestico di minori immigrati, equiparate alla servitù.

Quanto alla nozione di *lavori forzati od obbligatori*, essa si ricava specie dalla Convenzione ILO n. 29 del 1930, che parla di:

> "all work or service which is exacted from any person under the menace of any penalty and for which the said person has not offered himself voluntarily" [433].

Peraltro, anche questa nozione è stata poi interpretata in senso estensivo dagli organi di controllo dei trattati sui diritti umani. Ad esempio, la Corte europea ha affermato che la minaccia di rimpatriare immigrati assunti come lavoratori domestici può, in certi casi, costituire un'ipotesi di lavoro forzato [434]. La Corte interamericana dei diritti umani, nel caso *Ituango Massacres*, ha ritenuto che le condizioni di lavoro cui erano stati costretti alcuni pastori in Colombia, obbligati a lavorare in luoghi lontani da casa e minacciati di morte in caso di fuga, costituivano lavori forzati [435].

Infine, si deve notare che i divieti di schiavitù e di servitù sono assoluti, cioè non ammettono limiti o eccezioni; ed inoltre sono inderogabili anche in situazioni di emergenza [436]. Invece, il divieto di lavori forzati od obbligatori prevede alcune eccezioni ed è derogabile, come vedremo qui di seguito.

15.2.1. *Deroghe ed eccezioni al divieto di lavori forzati o obbligatori*

Il divieto di lavori forzati o obbligatori è derogabile in stati di emergenza. Ciò si deduce, ad esempio, dagli artt. 8(3)(a) e 4(4) del Patto sui diritti civili e politici; dagli artt. 4(2) e 15(2) della Convenzione europea; e dagli artt. 6 e 27 della Convenzione americana.

Inoltre, il divieto in oggetto non è assoluto, perché prevede eccezioni. Nei principali trattati sui diritti umani queste eccezioni sono elencate esplicitamente [437]; ed esse sono costituite da: *a*) lavori o servizi normalmente imposti a individui regolarmente detenuti o in libertà condizionata; *b*) servizi di carattere militare e, laddove è ammessa l'obiezione di coscienza, servizi imposti per legge agli obiettori di coscienza; *c*) servizi imposti in situazioni di crisi o disastri o calamità, che minacciano la vita o il benessere della comunità nazionale; *d*) lavori o servizi che facciano parte dei normali doveri civici.

Il contenuto esatto di queste eccezioni solleva alcuni problemi di interpretazione, per la soluzione dei quali si deve far riferimento alla prassi degli organi internazionali di control-

---

[431] ECtHR, *Seguin v. France*.

[432] ECtHR, *Siliadin v. France*, parr. 89 e 148.

[433] ILO Forced Labour Convention, art. 2.

[434] ECtHR, *C.N. v. UK*, parr. 69 e 81.

[435] IACtHR, *Ituango Massacres v. Colombia*, parr. 154-166.

[436] Vedi ECHR, art. 15(2); CCPR, art. 4(2); ACHR, art. 27(2).

[437] Vedi, ad es., CCPR, art. 8(3)(c); ECHR, art. 4(3); ACHR, art. 6(3).

lo. Il Comitato dei diritti umani, ad esempio, ha ritenuto che il lavoro effettuato durante la detenzione possa ritenersi "normalmente richiesto" se ha per scopo principale la reintegrazione dei detenuti [438]. La Convenzione europea non prevede un diritto all'obiezione di coscienza; ma la Carta dei diritti fondamentali dell'UE riconosce tale diritto sulla base delle leggi nazionali che ne disciplinano l'esercizio. In relazione ai servizi di carattere militare, la Corte europea ha ritenuto, nel caso *Chitos* [439], che il ricorrente, cittadino greco che aveva prestato servizio nell'esercito per venti anni ed era stato richiamato per servire per altri nove anni a pena di versare una tassa, fosse vittima di un lavoro forzato, non soggetto all'eccezione dei servizi di carattere militare.

Quanto ai doveri civici, il Comitato dei diritti umani ha ritenuto che essi siano "normali" se non sono misure eccezionali, se non hanno uno scopo o effetto punitivo, e se sono previsti dalla legge per adempiere ad uno scopo legittimo secondo il Patto [440]. Gli organi di Strasburgo hanno affermato che rientrano fra i doveri civici quello di un dentista che in Norvegia deve svolgere la sua professione come servizio pubblico per un periodo di due anni; e quello imposto dalla legge austriaca, ad avvocati e notai, di prestare assistenza giuridica gratuita ai soggetti affetti da malattie mentali [441].

15.3. *Obblighi*

I divieti di schiavitù, servitù e lavori forzati comportano, per gli Stati, una serie di obblighi simili a quelli di cui abbiamo già parlato in relazione al diritto alla vita, al divieto di tortura ed al divieto di crimini internazionali.

Pertanto, in sintesi, gli Stati hanno, innanzitutto, l'obbligo negativo di astenersi da tali abusi e di non adottare norme che li consentano. In secondo luogo, gli Stati sono soggetti ad una serie di obblighi positivi (immediati) di prevenzione, di repressione e di riparazione, tesi ad assicurare una efficace protezione contro la violazione di tali divieti da parte di privati. In particolare, gli Stati devono avere (o fornirsi di) adeguati apparati normativi e amministrativi di prevenzione e devono prendere misure concrete di prevenzione quando è necessario. Inoltre, devono avere un adeguato apparato amministrativo e giudiziario di repressione [442] ed hanno l'obbligo concreto di investigare per identificare i responsabili delle violazioni, e l'obbligo di processare e punire costoro [443]. Gli Stati hanno anche l'obbligo di dare una riparazione alle vittime delle violazioni. Come si è già visto, alcuni di questi obblighi sono di risultato ed altri di *due diligence*. Questi obblighi positivi sono bene riassunti dal Comitato dei diritti umani nelle sue *Osservazioni conclusive sulla Polonia* del 2016 [444]. Infine, secondo alcuni autori [445], i divieti in oggetto imporrebbero agli Stati anche

---

[438] Vedi HRCtee, *Radosevic v. Germany*, par. 7.3.

[439] ECtHR, *Chitos v. Greece*.

[440] HRCtee, *Faure v. Australia*, par. 7.5. Cfr. anche Kälin, Künzli (2009), p. 425.

[441] ECmHR, *Iversen v. Norway*; ECtHR, *Graziani-Weiss v. Austria*, parr. 41-42. Cfr. anche Focarelli (2013), p. 153.

[442] Vedi, ad es., Slavery Convention, art. 6; Supplementary Slavery Convention, art. 6.

[443] Vedi, ad es., ECtHR, *C.N. v. UK*, parr. 69 e 81.

[444] HRCtee, Concluding Observations: *Poland* (2016), par. 28.

[445] Kälin, Künzli (2009), p. 422.

alcuni obblighi positivi non immediati, quali, ad esempio, quelli relativi alla riabilitazione e reintegrazione sociale delle vittime.

16. *Divieto di arresti o detenzioni arbitrari*

16.1. *Norme*

La protezione della liberta e sicurezza della persona richiede che ogni individuo sia affrancato non solo da schiavitù, servitù e lavori forzati, ma anche da poteri esercitati in maniera arbitraria o illegittima da parte dello Stato (o di altri enti titolari di obblighi sui diritti umani). Ciò implica necessariamente il divieto di arresti o detenzioni arbitrari. In effetti, tale divieto risale, nella storia, ai primi documenti nazionali sui diritti umani, quali la *Magna Charta* del 1215, l'*Habeas Corpus Act* del 1679, il *Bill of Rights* del 1689 [446].

Nel diritto internazionale dei diritti umani, il legame stretto fra la tutela della libertà e sicurezza personale ed il divieto di arresti o detenzioni arbitrari è molto evidente [447]. La Dichiarazione universale prevede, all'art. 3, che:

> "Everyone has the right to [...] liberty and security of person".

e, all'art. 9, che:

> "No one shall be subjected to arbitrary arrest, detention or exile".

Il Patto sui diritti civili e politici ribadisce in maniera ancora più esplicita tale legame. L'art. 9(1) del Patto stabilisce che:

> "Everyone has the right to liberty and security of person. No one shall be subjected to arbitrary arrest or detention. No one shall be deprived of his liberty except on such grounds and in accordance with such procedure as are established by law".

Il divieto di arresti o detenzioni arbitrari viene, inoltre, previsto dall'art. 5 della Convenzione europea; dall'art. 7 della Convenzione americana; dall'art. 6 della Carta africana; dall'art. 14 della Carta araba. Altre norme rilevanti sono l'art. 6 della Carta dei diritti fondamentali dell'UE; l'art. 37(b) della Convenzione sui diritti del fanciullo; l'art. 16 della Convenzione sui diritti dei lavoratori migranti; l'art. 14 della Convenzione sui diritti delle persone disabili; l'art. 7(1) della Dichiarazione sui diritti dei popoli indigeni.

Il *nucleo* essenziale del divieto di arresti o detenzioni arbitrari è definito molto bene dal suddetto art. 9(1) del Patto sui diritti civili e politici. Ma si deve notare che il Patto medesimo e molte delle altre norme sopra citate prevedono non solo il divieto di arresti o detenzioni arbitrari, ma anche una serie di *garanzie procedurali* per i detenuti o arrestati e di *diritti accessori* a loro favore, che sono strettamente collegati al divieto principale. In particolare, si prevede: *a*) il loro diritto di essere prontamente informati dei motivi della detenzione; *b*) il loro diritto di ricorrere ad un giudice, perché decida sulla legalità della deten-

---

[446] Vedi *supra*, Cap. I, par. 2.1.

[447] Per la dottrina sul divieto di detenzione arbitraria, vedi, *e.g.*, Cornelisse (2010); Favuzza (2018).

zione ed ordini il rilascio se la detenzione non ha fondamento giuridico; *c*) il loro diritto ad un indennizzo se la detenzione è illegale. Inoltre: *d*) coloro che sono stati arrestati o detenuti in base ad un'accusa penale hanno diritto di essere giudicati entro un termine ragionevole o di essere liberati.

È chiaro che tali garanzie procedurali e diritti accessori sono importanti, perché rafforzano il divieto principale. Tuttavia, poiché qui ci occupiamo dei diritti umani "fondamentali", ci limiteremo ad esaminare il solo divieto di arresti o detenzioni arbitrari. A nostro parere, questo divieto è previsto, oltre che da norme convenzionali, anche da una norma consuetudinaria. Ciò si ricava dalla prassi secolare sul divieto, dalla concordanza delle norme convenzionali sui diritti umani e dalla prassi degli organi internazionali di controllo. Ciò non vale, invece, per le garanzie procedurali ed i diritti accessori rispetto al divieto generale, che hanno natura troppo dettagliata per essere oggetto di una norma consuetudinaria; e quindi non rientrano nella nostra definizione dei diritti umani "fondamentali".

La tesi secondo cui il divieto generale di detenzione arbitraria è imposto da una norma consuetudinaria, ed avente per di più carattere di *ius cogens*, è sostenuta anche dal *Working Group on Arbitrary Detention*, creato nel 1991 dalla (allora) Commissione sui diritti umani delle NU [448], e tuttora attivo. A supporto della natura consuetudinaria della regola, il *Working Group* cita, fra l'altro, la sentenza della Corte internazionale di giustizia nel caso del *Personale diplomatico e consolare a Teheran* [449].

16.2. *Contenuto del divieto*

Come si è già accennato, il divieto in oggetto ha il seguente contenuto: nessuno può essere arrestato, detenuto, o comunque privato della propria libertà, in maniera arbitraria o illegale. Spesso si parla sinteticamente di detenzione "arbitraria", comprendendo nella nozione anche la detenzione "illegale".

Il primo aspetto da chiarire riguarda la nozione di "privazione di libertà". Essa deve essere interpretata in senso ampio; e pertanto comprende tutte le privazioni della libertà fisica di movimento di una persona che, per loro natura, grado, modalità, durata ed effetti, si distinguano dalle semplici limitazioni alla libertà di circolazione che cadono sotto la disciplina della libertà di movimento delle persone [450]. Pertanto, le forme nelle quali si può realizzare la "privazione di libertà" sono molteplici e non si limitano ad arresti o detenzioni relativi a procedimenti penali; ma possono comprendere situazioni quali gli arresti domiciliari, le perquisizioni personali, il ricovero in ospedali psichiatrici, la detenzione in centri di identificazione ed espulsione, l'obbligo dei migranti di restare in zone di transito di aeroporti, gli arresti o reclusioni a titolo di pene disciplinari dei militari, l'esilio in piccole isole senza possibilità di contatti sociali, ecc. [451]. Il Comitato dei diritti umani, nel suo Commento Generale n. 8, con riferimento agli scopi della detenzione, ha affermato che l'art. 9 del Patto:

---

[448] Vedi HRC, *Report of the Working Group on Arbitrary Detention*, UN Doc. A/HCR/22/44 of 24 December 2012. Per un commento vedi Bufalini (2013).

[449] ICJ, *United States Diplomatic and Consular Staff in Tehran*, par. 91.

[450] Vedi Focarelli (2013), p. 154. Sulle libertà di movimento delle persone vedi *infra*, Cap. VI, parr. 12-16.

[451] Vedi la prassi citata da Kälin, Künzli (2009), pp. 443-444 e da Favuzza (2019), *passim*.

"[...] is applicable to all deprivations of liberty, whether in criminal cases or in other cases such as, for example, mental illness, vagrancy, drug addiction, educational purposes, immigration control, etc."[452].

Il secondo aspetto da esaminare riguarda la nozione di "legalità/illegalità". In primo luogo, per essere consentita, la privazione della libertà deve essere legittima in base alle norme procedurali e sostanziali del diritto statale. In secondo luogo, essa è legale se si fonda su una delle giustificazioni che sono ammesse dal diritto internazionale dei diritti umani. Su questo punto, ad esempio, è molto chiaro l'art. 5 della Convenzione europea, che elenca in maniera specifica una serie di situazioni che giustificano la privazione della libertà[453]. Tuttavia, gli altri trattati sui diritti umani non contengono tale elenco specifico; e pertanto si deve far ricorso alla prassi degli organi internazionali di controllo di tali trattati, per individuare i motivi internazionalmente legittimi di privazione della libertà. In terzo luogo, la privazione della libertà è illegale quando essa è la conseguenza dell'esercizio, da parte di un individuo, dei suoi diritti umani fondamentali[454] o quando rappresenta una violazione del principio di non discriminazione.

Un altro aspetto importante riguarda la nozione di "arbitrarietà", intesa ora *in senso stretto* come distinta dalla nozione di "illegalità". Una privazione della libertà può essere arbitraria, anche se è, o è stata, legale. Il concetto di arbitrarietà si riferisce ad elementi di irragionevolezza, imprevedibilità ed ingiustizia[455], o al fatto che la detenzione, pur essendo giustificata da un motivo giuridicamente legittimo, finisce per violare altri diritti umani del detenuto[456], specie alcuni suoi diritti umani fondamentali, o al fatto che essa è collegata ad una grave violazione del diritto all'equo processo, o al fatto che essa si prolunga per un periodo eccessivo o discrezionale[457].

Vi è, inoltre, il problema se il divieto di arresti o detenzioni arbitrari abbia carattere di "inderogabilità in stati di emergenza". Qualche dubbio potrebbe derivare dal fatto che, nei trattati sui diritti umani, le disposizioni su tale divieto non sono espressamente indicate fra quelle "inderogabili in stati di emergenza". Tuttavia, ciò non è decisivo poiché, come si è visto, tale concetto non è univoco né è ben definito in tali trattati. In realtà, l'opinione preferibile è che il divieto di arresti o detenzioni arbitrarie non sia derogabile in stati di emergenza. Anche il Comitato dei diritti umani sembra condividere questa conclusione, poiché

---

[452] HRCtee, General Comment No. 8, 30 June 1982, par. 1.

[453] Queste situazioni, fra l'altro, riguardano: a) chi è detenuto regolarmente in seguito ad una condanna da parte di un tribunale competente; b) chi è in regolare stato di arresto o detenzione per violazione di un provvedimento legittimo adottato da un tribunale; c) chi è stato arrestato o detenuto per essere tradotto dinanzi all'autorità giudiziaria competente quando vi sono ragioni plausibili per sospettare che abbia commesso un reato; d) la detenzione regolare di un minore, decisa per sorvegliare la sua educazione; e) la detenzione regolare di una persona per prevenire la propagazione di una malattia contagiosa, di un alienato, di un alcolizzato, di un tossicomane o di un vagabondo; f) l'arresto o la detenzione regolare di una persona per impedirle di penetrare irregolarmente nel territorio o di una persona contro la quale è in corso un procedimento d'espulsione o di estradizione.

[454] Secondo il Working Group on Arbitrary Detention, tali diritti umani sono quelli previsti dagli artt.7, 13, 14, 18, 19, 20 e 21 della Dichiarazione universale.

[455] Cfr. Kälin, Künzli (2009), p. 445.

[456] Cfr. Focarelli (2013), p. 155.

[457] Vedi HRCtee, *A. v. Australia*, parr. 9.2-9.4; *C. v. Australia*, par. 8.2; *Baban et al. v. Australia*, par. 7.2.

ha affermato che certi aspetti essenziali del diritto alla libertà personale sono inderogabili [458]. Alla stessa conclusione è pervenuto il *Working Group on Arbitrary Detention*. Ma si deve notare che questa inderogabilità non si estende alle garanzie procedurali ed ai diritti accessori rispetto al divieto.

Infine, conviene ricordare che la questione della “derogabilità in stati di emergenza” non va confusa con quella del carattere cogente o imperativo della norma sulla detenzione arbitraria; né con quella della assolutezza del divieto. Invece, il *Working Group on Arbitrary Detention* fa una certa confusione fra i tre diversi concetti.

16.3. *Obblighi*

Il divieto di arresti o detenzioni arbitrari impone agli Stati, prima di tutto, obblighi negativi. Essi riguardano, in maniera particolare, certi individui-organi dello Stato, quali agenti di polizia e di sicurezza, militari ed agenti carcerari. Ma sono importanti anche gli obblighi positivi, che rilevano specie nelle attività di prevenzione, a carico di organi superiori (ad esempio, capi di polizia, dirigenti di carceri, militari di grado elevato), di abusi da parte di organi inferiori a loro sottoposti; e nelle attività di prevenzione, a carico di agenti statali, di abusi da parte di individui privati. Infine, non si devono trascurare gli obblighi positivi di repressione degli abusi e quelli di riparazione a favore delle vittime.

17. *Divieto di sparizioni forzate delle persone*

17.1. *Norme*

La pratica delle c.d. “sparizioni forzate” delle persone ad opera degli Stati costituisce una forma gravissima e assai evidente di detenzione arbitraria, che tuttavia può essere trattata separatamente poiché ha acquistato una sua autonomia nella prassi contemporanea. Tale pratica consiste nella privazione *in maniera segreta* della libertà di una persona da parte di *agenti statali* o di persone autorizzate dallo Stato. Spesso tale persona viene poi uccisa. La pratica, seguita in passato in America Latina, è stata di recente ripresa, in forma ancora più grave, con le già ricordate “*extraordinary renditions*”, condotte nel quadro delle misure anti-terroristiche adottate da alcuni Stati [459].

I trattati generali sui diritti umani non menzionano espressamente il divieto di “sparizioni forzate”; ma gli organi internazionali di controllo di tali trattati ritengono che tali abusi costituiscano violazioni del divieto di arresti o detenzioni arbitrari. In effetti, la prassi del Comitato dei diritti umani, della Corte interamericana e della Corte europea è assai

---

[458] Vedi HRCtee, General Comment No. 29, 31 August 2001, parr. 11 e 13. Per la verità il Comitato sembra riferirsi al concetto di cogenza (*ius cogens*) più che a quello di inderogabilità in stati di emergenza. Ma sembra dell’opinione che il primo concetto ricomprenda il secondo. Invece, per la nostra distinzione fra i due concetti vedi *supra*, parr. 4.3 e 4.5.

[459] Vedi *supra*, par. 8.2.3.

ampia[460]. In diversi casi, tali organi hanno ritenuto che la prassi delle sparizioni forzate costituisse anche una violazione del divieto di tortura e trattamento inumano o degradante. Si possono ricordare, tra le altre, le sentenze della Corte europea nei casi *Kurt*, *El-Masri* e *Nasr and Ghali*[461], la sentenza della Corte interamericana nel caso *Morales Zegarra*[462], e la decisione del Comitato dei diritti umani nel caso *Sarma*[463].

Vi sono, inoltre, alcuni importanti trattati recenti che si occupano specificamente del divieto di sparizioni forzate. Essi sono la Convenzione interamericana del 1994 sulla sparizione forzata delle persone[464] e la Convenzione delle NU del 2006 per la protezione di tutte le persone dalla sparizione forzata[465]. Infine, si deve notare che l'art. 7(2)(i) dello Statuto della Corte penale internazionale considera la sparizione forzata come un crimine contro l'umanità, quando è commessa nel quadro di un attacco diffuso o sistematico contro la popolazione civile.

Per quanto riguarda il diritto internazionale generale, si deve ritenere che il divieto di sparizioni forzate, in quanto forma gravissima di privazione arbitraria della libertà delle persone, sia protetto da una norma generale e di carattere cogente.

17.2. *Contenuto del divieto*

La citata Convenzione delle NU del 2006, all'art. 2, definisce la sparizione forzata come:

> "the arrest, detention, abduction or any other form of deprivation of liberty by agents of the State or by persons or groups acting with the authorization, support or acquiescence of the State, followed by a refusal to acknowledge the deprivation of liberty or by concealment of the fate or whereabouts of the disappeared person, which place such a person outside the protection of the law".

Una definizione assai simile è contenuta nell'art. 7(2)(i) dello Statuto della Corte penale internazionale.

Pertanto, la nozione di "sparizione forzata" è precisa e dettagliata; ed anche il contenuto del relativo divieto è chiaro. Si deve ritenere che esso abbia carattere assoluto e che sia inderogabile anche in stati di emergenza.

17.3. *Obblighi*

Per gli obblighi che si impongono agli Stati in relazione al divieto di "sparizioni forzate", valgono le considerazioni sopra svolte a proposito del divieto di arresti o detenzioni arbitrari, con la precisazione che vanno esclusi gli obblighi statali di prevenzione e repres-

---

[460] Per un esame accurato di tale prassi, vedi Citroni, Scovazzi (2013), pp. 286-308.

[461] ECtHR, *Kurt v. Turkey*, par. 124; *El-Masri v. The Former Yugoslav Republic of Macedonia*, parr. 191-193, 206, 223, 240-242, 262; *Nasr and Ghali v. Italy*, parr. 298-303.

[462] IACmHR, *Romer Morales Zegarra et al. v. Peru*, par. 62.

[463] HRCtee, *Sarma v. Sri Lanka*.

[464] Inter-American Convention on the Forced Disappearance of Persons, 9 June 1994.

[465] International Convention for the Protection of All Persons from Enforced Disappearance (CPPED), 20 December 2006.

sione relativi ad atti di privati individui, salvo il caso che in tali atti vi sia l'aiuto o acquiescenza dello Stato [466].

Sezione V

PROTEZIONE GIUDIZIARIA ESSENZIALE DELLA PERSONA

Uno degli scopi più antichi dei diritti umani, come si è visto, è quello di tutelare l'individuo dai poteri esercitati in maniera arbitraria o illegittima da parte di autorità statali. La realizzazione di questo scopo richiede che l'individuo possa disporre di strumenti di protezione giudiziaria a livello interno e, auspicabilmente, anche a livello internazionale.

Inoltre, da un punto di vista più ampio, si consideri che l'esistenza negli Stati di un adeguato apparato di amministrazione della giustizia, idoneo ad accertare le eventuali violazioni dei diritti umani, è strettamente e funzionalmente necessaria per raggiungere lo scopo generale del rispetto dei diritti umani. Infatti, è chiaro che non è sufficiente che lo Stato cerchi di prevenire le violazioni dei diritti umani, ed eventualmente di investigare per scoprire e catturare i responsabili, se poi la carenza di un idoneo apparato di amministrazione della giustizia non permette di accertare in maniera imparziale le violazioni, di punire i responsabili e di fornire la riparazione alle vittime.

Di conseguenza, si sono storicamente sviluppati numerosi diritti umani che attengono alla protezione giudiziaria delle persone. Alcuni di essi sono assai precisi e dettagliati. Ma qui prenderemo in esame solo i diritti che ci sembrano "fondamentali": *a*) il diritto di accesso alla giustizia (inteso in senso lato); *b*) il diritto delle vittime alla riparazione; *c*) i diritti degli imputati che derivano dal principio di legalità penale.

18. *Diritto di accesso alla giustizia*

18.1. *Norme e loro evoluzione storica*

Il diritto di accesso alla giustizia è un concetto difficile e controverso; ed esso, nel diritto internazionale dei diritti umani, viene inteso con significati diversi, talora restrittivi e talora estensivi. Ciò è probabilmente dovuto anche al fatto che i trattati sui diritti umani, come vedremo, non usano di solito questo termine; ma piuttosto quelli di diritto ad un "rimedio effettivo" (*effective remedy*) oppure ad un "equo processo" (*fair trial*) oppure ad una "protezione giudiziaria" (*judicial protection*). In realtà, questi diversi termini intendono significare, quantomeno in origine, concetti diversi, i quali tuttavia nel tempo si sono venuti ravvicinando. In particolare, a nostro avviso, nel diritto internazionale consuetudinario, il concetto di diritto ad un rimedio effettivo e quello di diritto ad un equo processo

---

[466] Ciò perché gli atti di privati individui non possono, da soli, costituire una pratica di "sparizioni forzate".

sono adesso ricompresi nel più ampio diritto ad una *protezione giudiziaria essenziale*, che può anche essere denominato, per semplicità e per via di una terminologia più ricorrente, come diritto di *accesso alla giustizia* (in senso lato).

Questo processo storico può essere ricavato se solo si esaminano, in ordine temporale, le disposizioni pertinenti dei maggiori strumenti internazionali sui diritti umani. La Dichiarazione universale distingue fra diritto ad un rimedio interno effettivo (art. 8) e diritto ad un equo processo (artt. 10 e 11). Secondo l'art. 8:

> "Everyone has the right to an effective remedy by the competent national tribunals for acts violating the fundamental rights granted him by the constitution or by law".

Invece, secondo l'art. 10:

> "Everyone is entitled in full equality to a fair and public hearing by an independent and impartial tribunal, in the determination of his rights and obligations and of any criminal charge against him".

Anche la Convenzione europea distingue nettamente fra il diritto ad un rimedio interno effettivo (art. 13) ed il diritto ad un equo processo (art. 6). La seconda norma è assai dettagliata, mentre la prima norma è sintetica e dispone:

> "Everyone whose rights and freedoms as set forth in this Convention are violated shall have an effective remedy before a national authority notwithstanding that the violation has been committed by persons acting in an official capacity".

La medesima distinzione fra i due diritti è adottata dal Patto sui diritti civili e politici, che contiene disposizioni assai dettagliate sia sul rimedio effettivo (art. 2(3)) sia sull'equo processo (art. 14). Anche la Convenzione americana tratta separatamente i due diritti (artt. 8 e 25). Ma si deve notare che qui il diritto ad un rimedio effettivo (art. 25) è denominato come "diritto alla protezione giudiziaria" ed ha un contenuto più ampio rispetto al diritto analogo dei precedenti trattati sui diritti umani. Infatti l'art. 25 parla del diritto di ogni persona ad un ricorso "pronto ed effettivo" dinanzi "ad una corte o tribunale competente" per la protezione contro atti che violano i suoi diritti fondamentali, riconosciuti "dalla costituzione o le leggi dello Stato interessato o dalla Convenzione americana".

I trattati settoriali sui diritti umani, invece, contengono di solito disposizioni sul diritto ad un rimedio effettivo, ma non sul diritto ad un equo processo. Si possono ricordare, fra gli altri, l'art. 6 della Convenzione contro la discriminazione razziale del 1965 [467] e gli artt. 13 e 14 della Convenzione contro la tortura del 1984 [468].

Da queste norme si ricava che, in questa prima fase storica, il diritto ad un rimedio effettivo ha un contenuto *limitato*. Esso significa il diritto di una persona, che ritiene di essere vittima di una violazione di un proprio *diritto umano* contenuto in un trattato [469], di *agire* dinanzi ad un'*autorità statale* (giurisdizionale o di altra natura), per ottenere una decisione; e ciò anche se la presunta violazione sia stata commessa da un individuo-organo dello Stato. Ma la garanzia del rimedio effettivo *non è autonoma* rispetto alla violazione

---

[467] CERD, art. 6.

[468] CAT, artt. 13 e 14.

[469] Fa eccezione, come si è visto, l'art. 25 ACHR.

dei diritti umani. Per di più, queste norme non garantiscono che il rimedio abbia carattere giurisdizionale in senso stretto: in esse di solito gli Stati parti dei trattati si limitano a prendere un impegno a "sviluppare" in futuro le possibilità di un rimedio giurisdizionale[470]. Inoltre, il diritto ad un rimedio effettivo non comprende le garanzie attinenti alla fase della procedura, né la garanzia di una riparazione per la vittima nel caso di accertata violazione. In sostanza, in questa fase storica, il diritto ad un rimedio effettivo ha carattere piuttosto elementare.

Invece, il diritto ad un equo processo è per certi aspetti più restrittivo, ma per molti altri più ampio rispetto al diritto ad un rimedio effettivo. È più restrittivo, perché non attiene alla fase di inizio e di conclusione del procedimento, ma solo alla fase intermedia della procedura. Ma è più ampio, perché non si limita ai procedimenti attinenti alla violazione dei diritti umani, ma *si estende a tutti i processi* in materia civile, penale e (talora) amministrativa. In altri termini, le garanzie dell'equo processo sono *autonome* rispetto alla violazione dei diritti umani. Inoltre, le norme convenzionali sull'equo processo richiedono di solito che l'autorità nazionale abbia carattere *giurisdizionale in senso stretto*, sia precostituita per legge, e sia indipendente ed imparziale. Infine, tali norme prevedono alcuni principi generali di natura processuale, quali la parità delle armi, la durata ragionevole del processo, oltre ad una serie assai dettagliata di garanzie di carattere più specifico per i processi penali. Ed infatti, le norme convenzionali sull'equo processo sono molto più lunghe e dettagliate rispetto a quelle sul rimedio effettivo. Basti confrontare gli artt. 6 e 13 della Convenzione europea o gli artt. 14 e 2(3) del Patto sui diritti civili e politici.

Conviene aggiungere che, in questa fase storica, la dottrina, quando parla di accesso alla giustizia in materia di diritti umani, tende di solito a riferirsi al diritto ad un rimedio effettivo e non al diritto ad un equo processo. E quindi essa adotta un'interpretazione *restrittiva* della nozione di accesso alla giustizia.

Tuttavia, al di là di queste differenze fra i due diritti, vi sono anche delle analogie significative, poiché ambedue i diritti impongono allo Stato di possedere un apparato di amministrazione della giustizia che rispetti certi requisiti o standard minimi di funzionamento stabiliti dal diritto internazionale. Ed infatti, per effetto di queste analogie, in una fase storica più recente, i due diritti si sono ravvicinati e reciprocamente completati. Ciò risulta nitidamente dai più recenti trattati sui diritti umani. La Carta africana, ad esempio, contiene una sola disposizione (art. 7), che contiene regole sul diritto ad un rimedio interno effettivo e sul diritto ad un equo processo[471]. Anche la Carta araba prevede il diritto di tutte le persone ad un rimedio giuridico dinanzi ad organi giurisdizionali indipendenti (art. 12) e regole dettagliate sul giusto processo (artt. 13 e 16). Ancora più significativo è l'art. 47 della Carta dei diritti fondamentali dell'UE (*Right to an effective remedy and to a fair trial*), che stabilisce:

> "Everyone whose rights and freedoms guaranteed by the law of the Union are violated has the right to an effective remedy before a tribunal in compliance with the conditions laid down in this Article.
>
> Everyone is entitled to a fair and public hearing within a reasonable time by an independent and impartial tribunal previously established by law. Everyone shall have the possibility of being advised, defended and represented".

---

[470] Vedi CCPR, art. 2(3)(b); ACHR, art. 25(2)(b).

[471] Vedi il par. 1 (a) sul rimedio effettivo ed i parr. 1 (b), (c) e (d) e 2 sul giusto processo.

Come si può notare, in questi trattati, risulta bene la complementarietà fra i due diritti, che si rafforzano l'uno con l'altro. Inoltre, si nota un ampliamento del contenuto del diritto ad un rimedio interno effettivo, perché tale diritto diventa *autonomo* rispetto alla violazione dei diritti umani contenuti nel trattato in oggetto, e perché esso richiede che il ricorso sia deciso da un'*autorità giurisdizionale* in senso stretto.

Pertanto, a nostro parere, si può concludere che, nei trattati sui diritti umani, la distinzione fra il diritto ad un rimedio effettivo ed il diritto ad un equo processo sussiste ancora; ma che i due diritti tendono a integrarsi. Anche la prassi degli organi internazionali di controllo di tali trattati tende sempre di più a rivalutare e ad ampliare l'interpretazione del primo diritto, a sfumare le differenze fra i due diritti e ad interpretarli in maniera fra di loro complementare. Da tale prassi emerge quindi l'idea che, nel diritto internazionale contemporaneo, il diritto di accesso alla giustizia debba essere inteso in senso *estensivo*, in maniera tale da ricomprendere quantomeno i *contenuti essenziali* del diritto ad un rimedio effettivo e del diritto ad un equo processo. Si potrebbe parlare di una nozione "ampia" e moderna di accesso alla giustizia.

Conviene adesso chiederci se questa nozione si sia affermata anche nel diritto internazionale generale.

18.1.1. *Una norma consuetudinaria sull'accesso alla giustizia?*

Questa nozione ampia di accesso alla giustizia, a nostro avviso, si è ormai consolidata nel diritto internazionale consuetudinario. Ciò si ricava dall'insieme dei sistemi convenzionali sui diritti umani, dalla prassi degli organi internazionali di controllo e dall'*opinio iuris* della comunità internazionale. In base a questa norma consuetudinaria, il diritto di accesso alla giustizia *comprende* il diritto di agire dinanzi ad un'autorità giurisdizionale, che sia predeterminata dalla legge, che sia indipendente e imparziale, che adotti le garanzie minime procedurali del processo equo, che garantisca una decisione in tempi ragionevoli, e che assicuri che la decisione possa essere concretamente eseguita. Questa conclusione è bene riassunta nelle seguenti parole del giudice Cançado Trindade:

> "[...] the right of access to justice *lato sensu* comprises not only the formal access to justice (the right to institute legal proceedings) by means of an effective remedy, but also the guarantees of the due process of law (with equality of arms, conforming the *procès équitable*), up to the judgment (as the *prestation juridictionnelle*), with its faithful execution, with the provision of the reparation due" [472].

Una ulteriore conferma, circa l'esistenza di questa nozione ampia e moderna di accesso alla giustizia, quantomeno per le gravi violazioni dei diritti umani, si trova anche nella più volte citata Risoluzione 60/147 dell'Assemblea Generale delle NU in tema di Principi sui diritti delle vittime di gravi violazioni dei diritti umani e del diritto umanitario [473]. L'art. VII proclama che, fra i diritti delle vittime, vi è un "equal and effective access to justice". L'art. VIII, intitolato "Access to Justice", stabilisce che:

---

[472] ICJ, *Jurisdictional Immunities of the State*, Dissenting Opinion of Judge Cançado Trindade, par. 221. Si noti che Cançado Trindade fa rientrare nel diritto di accesso alla giustizia anche il diritto della vittima di ottenere, in caso di esito positivo della procedura, la riparazione. Su questo punto ritorneremo, *infra*, par. 19.

[473] *Basic Principles and Guidelines on the Right to a Remedy and Reparation for Victims of Gross Violations of International Human Rights Law and Serious Violations of International Humanitarian Law*, Annex, 16 December 2005.

> “A victim of a gross violation of international human rights law or a serious violation of international humanitarian law shall have equal access to an effective judicial remedy as provided for under international law [...] Obligations arising under international law to secure the right to access to justice and fair and impartial proceedings shall be reflected in domestic laws [...]”.

La natura consuetudinaria del diritto di accesso alla giustizia, per violazione dei diritti umani, è attestata anche dal fatto che, nel diritto internazionale dei diritti umani, si è affermata la regola consuetudinaria che richiede all’individuo vittima di esperire il previo esaurimento dei ricorsi interni prima che egli possa adire le istanze internazionali [474]. Questa regola ha, come corollario necessario, l’obbligo dello Stato autore della presunta violazione di offrire ricorsi interni adeguati ed effettivi, cui corrisponde, evidentemente, il diritto dell’individuo vittima. Pertanto, anche tramite l’affermazione della suddetta norma sull’esaurimento dei ricorsi interni, si è venuto affermando il diritto ad una tutela giurisdizionale effettiva per violazione dei diritti umani.

Inoltre, su un piano più generale, conviene ribadire che l’obbligo dello Stato di avere un adeguato apparato di amministrazione della giustizia, al quale possano accedere le vittime delle violazioni dei diritti umani, è funzionalmente necessario per la protezione dei diritti umani. E del resto, questo obbligo statale ha radici antiche, perché esso riprende e riproduce, in sostanza, nel settore dei diritti umani, il tradizionale obbligo consuetudinario dello Stato di proteggere gli stranieri, che abbiano subito offese nel proprio territorio, anche tramite l’accesso ai propri tribunali; cioè l’obbligo di non compiere un “diniego di giustizia” nel trattamento degli stranieri. È logico che l’obbligo consuetudinario in tema di accesso alla giustizia a favore degli stranieri si sia poi riprodotto, *mutatis mutandis*, anche a favore delle vittime di violazioni dei diritti umani.

Infine, si può ritenere che la norma consuetudinaria sul diritto di accesso alla giustizia abbia il carattere di *ius cogens*? Qualche elemento della prassi sembrerebbe tendere in questa direzione: ad esempio, la Corte di giustizia dell’UE, nella già citata sentenza *Kadi* del 2008 [475], ha ritenuto che tale diritto fosse irrinunciabile anche in presenza di una risoluzione del Consiglio di Sicurezza che di fatto lo limita. Tuttavia, a nostro avviso, la risposta è in generale negativa, eccetto che quando l’individuo chiede accesso alla giustizia per far valere la violazione di diritti umani che sono protetti dallo *ius cogens*, ad esempio atti di tortura o crimini contro l’umanità. In questo caso, la natura cogente del diritto umano sostanziale si deve estendere logicamente anche al diritto umano procedurale di accesso alla giustizia. Su questo punto ritorneremo più avanti [476].

18.2. *Contenuto del diritto*

Il contenuto del diritto di accesso alla giustizia, nel diritto consuetudinario, è già stato sopra indicato nelle sue linee essenziali. Ma restano da chiarire alcune questioni circa il suo ambito di applicazione.

---

[474] Vedi Pisillo Mazzeschi (2004a).

[475] ECJ, *Kadi*.

[476] Vedi *infra*, par. 18.3.2.

La prima questione è se tale diritto, sia pure inteso in senso ampio, operi soltanto nel caso di violazione di diritti umani oppure anche nel caso di violazioni di altri diritti, ad esempio stabiliti dal diritto civile, penale o amministrativo interno dello Stato in questione. Si è visto che il diritto ad un rimedio interno effettivo, anche se ha allargato con il tempo il suo campo di applicazione, si riferisce *soltanto alla violazione di diritti umani* (stabiliti dal diritto internazionale o dalle costituzioni o leggi interne dello Stato). Invece, le garanzie dell'equo processo sono *autonome* rispetto alla violazione dei diritti umani. Quale delle due impostazioni ha finito per prevalere nella norma consuetudinaria sull'accesso alla giustizia?

A nostro avviso, sulla base della prassi degli organi internazionali di controllo sui diritti umani e delle considerazioni sopra svolte, si deve ritenere che il diritto di accesso alla giustizia, *nel diritto internazionale consuetudinario*, operi soltanto nel caso di violazione dei diritti umani. Cioè che esso non costituisca un diritto umano individuale autonomo ed a sé stante; ma piuttosto un *diritto procedurale* che esiste solo nella misura in cui vi sia un diritto umano sostanziale da far valere dinanzi ad un giudice[477]. Si dovrebbe quindi parlare, per essere precisi, di *diritto di accesso alla giustizia per violazione dei diritti umani*[478].

La seconda questione è se il diritto di accesso alla giustizia, come diritto umano individuale, operi solo dinanzi ai giudici interni oppure anche dinanzi ai giudici o altre istanze internazionali[479]. La risposta cambia a seconda che si faccia riferimento al diritto consuetudinario oppure al diritto convenzionale. Per quanto riguarda il diritto consuetudinario, è evidente che non si può parlare di un diritto individuale di accesso alla giustizia dinanzi a tutti i tribunali internazionali ed a tutti gli organi di controllo quasi-giurisdizionali esistenti nell'ambito del diritto internazionale. Infatti, è noto che molte di queste istanze non sono aperte a ricorsi da parte di individui. Invece, la risposta è diversa dal punto di vista del diritto convenzionale. Molti trattati sui diritti umani, come si è visto[480], prevedono propri meccanismi di controllo, giurisdizionale o quasi-giurisdizionale e, fra essi, sono sempre più numerosi quelli che prevedono un accesso diretto da parte di individui che sono vittime di violazioni dei diritti umani contemplati dal trattato. In questi casi, si deve ritenere applicabile, anche a livello internazionale, il diritto umano individuale di accesso alla giustizia[481].

Tuttavia, si deve sottolineare che questa limitata capacità di accesso dell'individuo a rimedi processuali internazionali non significa che il suo Stato nazionale non possa far valere il proprio diritto ed *anche* il diritto del proprio cittadino dinanzi a tribunali o altri organi internazionali di controllo contro lo Stato autore della violazione, invocando le norme sulla responsabilità internazionale degli Stati. Ciò risulta chiaro, fra l'altro, dalla giurisprudenza della Corte internazionale di giustizia, che, ad esempio nei noti casi *LaGrand* e

---

[477] In questo senso, sia pure in relazione ad un concetto meno ampio di accesso alla giustizia, vedi Francioni (2007), pp. 30-33.

[478] In altri termini, non ci sembra che il carattere autonomo del diritto ad un equo processo nei sistemi convenzionali si sia esteso anche al diritto internazionale consuetudinario.

[479] Anche su questo punto v. Francioni (2007), p. 41 ss.

[480] Vedi *supra*, Cap. IV.

[481] Vedi anche la citata Risoluzione 60/147 dell'AG delle NU, Annex, art. VIII (12): "An adequate, effective and prompt remedy for gross violations of international human rights law or serious violations of international humanitarian law should include all available and appropriate international processes in which a person may have legal standing [...]".

Avena[482], ha chiarito che lo Stato nazionale della vittima può far valere contemporaneamente sia i propri diritti sia i diritti individuali[483].

Infine, quanto alla natura del diritto di accesso alla giustizia, conviene osservare che esso non ha, in linea di massima, carattere "inderogabile in stati di emergenza". Non ha neppure carattere assoluto, perché ammette certe eccezioni o limiti, come vedremo. Tuttavia, a nostro avviso, esso può diventare un diritto umano assoluto ed anche inderogabile in stati di emergenza, quando è funzionalmente collegato a diritti umani sostanziali con carattere di *ius cogens*. Esaminiamo adesso più a fondo queste questioni.

18.3. *Deroghe e limiti*

18.3.1. *Deroghe in stati di emergenza*

Abbiamo già trattato, in linea generale, il tema delle clausole di deroga nei trattati sui diritti umani[484]. Si tratta ora di riprendere la questione con riferimento specifico al diritto di accesso alla giustizia[485]. Ciò è giustificato dal fatto che il tema è controverso ed è oggetto di una prassi interessante. Inoltre, si tratta di una tematica attuale, poiché la crescita del terrorismo internazionale in questo secolo ha indotto molti Stati ad adottare misure eccezionali, che sospendono, in virtù di tali clausole di deroga, molti diritti umani di carattere sostanziale. Ci si deve ora chiedere se sia legittima anche la sospensione del diritto umano procedurale di accesso alla giustizia.

Come si è già visto, i trattati sui diritti umani che contengono clausole di deroga ai diritti umani, in situazioni di guerra o di emergenza pubblica, prevedono di solito una esplicita lista di diritti che sono esclusi dalla possibilità di deroga[486]. Ma tali trattati non sono uniformi circa il carattere derogabile o meno del diritto di accesso alla giustizia. Tale diritto, ad esempio, non è incluso nella lista dell'art. 15(2) della Convenzione europea, né in quella dell'art. 4(2) del Patto sui diritti civili e politici. Invece, la Convenzione americana, pur non includendo il diritto alla protezione giudiziaria *ex* art. 25 nella lista dei diritti non derogabili dell'art. 27(2), espressamente stabilisce che non possono essere sospese "le garanzie giuridiche essenziali per la protezione di tali diritti". Pertanto, la Convenzione americana stabilisce un nesso funzionale fra i diritti considerati inderogabili e la loro protezione giudiziaria: se un diritto umano non può essere derogato neppure in stati di emergenza perché ha carattere fondamentale, anche la protezione giudiziaria di tale diritto deve essere sempre garantita e non può essere sospesa. La Carta araba prevede un livello ancora più alto di garanzia per il diritto di accesso alla giustizia: nella lista dei diritti non derogabili *ex*

---

[482] ICJ, *LaGrand*, p. 466 ss.; *Avena*, p. 121 ss.

[483] Vedi anche la citata Risoluzione 60/147 dell'AG delle NU, Annex, art. VIII (12)(d): "[States should:] Make available all appropriate legal, diplomatic and consular means to ensure that victims can exercise their right to remedy for gross violations of international human rights law or serious violations of international humanitarian law".

[484] Vedi *supra*, Cap. II, par. 11.3.

[485] Sul tema vedi anche Francioni (2007), pp. 43-47.

[486] Si possono ricordare l'art. 15 (2) della Convenzione europea, l'art. 4(2) del Patto sui diritti civili e politici, l'art. 27 (2) della Convenzione americana e l'art. 4(2) della Carta araba. Invece, l'art. F della Carta sociale europea (riveduta) prevede la possibilità di deroghe ai diritti da essa previsti in situazioni di guerra o di emergenza pubblica, ma non contiene una lista dei diritti non derogabili.

art. 4(2) viene incluso il diritto ad un equo processo *ex* art. 13 (ma non il diritto ad un ricorso interno effettivo *ex* art. 12). Inoltre, con una formula simile a quella della Convenzione americana, la Carta araba stabilisce che non possono essere sospese "le garanzie giuridiche richieste per la protezione" dei diritti non derogabili.

Nonostante questa mancanza di uniformità fra i vari trattati, la prassi applicativa degli organi internazionali di controllo sembra orientata ad accogliere quella soluzione più garantista che è esplicitamente prevista dalla Convenzione americana e dalla Carta araba. Più in particolare, da tale prassi si ricavano tre criteri: *a*) il criterio dell'*importanza* dei diritti sostanziali collegati al diritto di accesso alla giustizia: quanto più importanti sono tali diritti tanto meno è possibile la sospensione delle loro garanzie giudiziarie. Di solito, se i diritti sostanziali sono inderogabili in stati di emergenza, non si possono sospendere le loro garanzie giudiziarie; *b*) il criterio di preservare comunque, anche in stati di emergenza, le garanzie giuridiche *essenziali*, quali l'accesso ad un rimedio effettivo e l'*habeas corpus*; *c*) infine, anche in relazione ai diritti umani derogabili, va rispettato il criterio della *proporzionalità* e del bilanciamento fra le limitazioni all'accesso alla giustizia e l'interesse alla protezione della pubblica sicurezza: le restrizioni al funzionamento del sistema giudiziario non devono andare oltre ciò che è strettamente necessario per fronteggiare l'emergenza.

Questi tre criteri sono stati accolti esplicitamente dalla Corte interamericana, nei suoi due pareri consultivi del 1987 sugli *Stati di emergenza* e sull'*Habeas Corpus*[487]. La Corte ha affermato che:

> "[...] the declaration of a state of emergency-whatever its breadth or denomination in internal law – cannot entail the suppression or ineffectiveness of the judicial guarantees that the Convention requires the States Parties to establish for the protection of the rights not subject to derogation or suspension by the state of emergency"[488].

Inoltre, ha aggiunto che:

> "the 'essential' judicial guarantees which are not subject to derogation, according to Article 27(2) of the Convention, include habeas corpus (Art. 7(6)), amparo, and any other effective remedy before judges or competent tribunals (Art. 25(1))"[489].

Infine, secondo la Corte, anche in relazione ai diritti sostanziali derogabili si deve applicare il criterio della proporzionalità[490].

Anche il Comitato dei diritti umani ritiene che le garanzie giuridiche essenziali debbano essere rispettate in stati di emergenza. Nel suo Commento Generale n. 29, ha affermato che, anche se l'accesso alla giustizia non è compreso nella lista dei diritti inderogabili *ex* art. 4(2) del Patto sui diritti civili e politici:

---

[487] IACtHR, *States of Emergency*; Id., *Habeas Corpus in Emergency Situations*.

[488] IACtHR, *Judicial Guarantees in States of Emergency*, par. 25.

[489] *Ibidem*, par. 1 del dispositivo.

[490] *Ibidem*, par. 21: "From Article 27(1) [...] comes the general requirement that in any state of emergency there be appropriate means to control the measures taken, so that they are proportionate to the needs and do not exceed the strict limits imposed by the Convention or derived from it".

"the State Party must comply with the fundamental obligation under article 2, paragraph 3, of the Covenant to provide a remedy that is effective"[491].

La giurisprudenza della Corte europea conferma questo approccio generale. La Corte ha ritenuto applicabile il diritto ad un rimedio effettivo, anche in situazioni di conflitto armato, quando la vittima lamentava la violazione di diritti umani fondamentali, quali il diritto alla vita[492] o il divieto di tortura[493]. Secondo la Corte, quanto più grave è la violazione del diritto sostanziale, tanto più è importante tutelare il diritto della vittima di avere accesso a garanzie giudiziarie per far valere la violazione.

18.3.2. *Restrizioni e limiti. Conflitto fra il diritto di accesso alla giustizia e le immunità internazionali*

Si è detto sopra che il diritto di accesso alla giustizia ammette, in linea di massima, restrizioni o limiti; ma non quando è funzionalmente collegato a diritti umani sostanziali di carattere "fondamentale". Approfondiamo adesso questo tema, che è di grande attualità.

Il diritto di accesso alla giustizia può essere assoggettato a varie restrizioni, derivanti, per lo più, dalla necessità di proteggere interessi pubblici propri degli ordinamenti interni. Vi possono essere limiti alla competenza giurisdizionale dello Stato del foro, oppure l'ostacolo del carattere non giustiziabile della controversia, oppure restrizioni derivanti da teorie seguite da alcuni Stati, come quella dell'*act of state* o del *forum non conveniens*[494]. Vi possono essere, poi, limiti derivanti dall'ordinamento internazionale. Recentemente, ad esempio, si è posto il problema del possibile conflitto fra il diritto di accesso alla giustizia e le misure sanzionatorie adottate dal Consiglio di Sicurezza delle NU nella lotta contro il terrorismo internazionale[495].

Non è qui possibile esaminare tutti questi limiti. Tratteremo quello che, a nostro avviso, è il limite più importante al diritto di accesso alla giustizia, dal punto di vista delle vittime della violazione dei diritti umani. Esso è dato dalle immunità internazionali; cioè dalle immunità dalla giurisdizione dello Stato del foro di cui godono, in base al diritto internazionale, gli Stati esteri, i loro individui-organi, le organizzazioni internazionali ed i loro funzionari. Infatti, per effetto di tali immunità, la vittima di una violazione non può agire dinanzi ai propri tribunali interni contro tali enti o soggetti che siano ritenuti responsabili della violazione. In realtà, le norme internazionali che regolano le immunità internazionali hanno un contenuto tra loro parzialmente diverso e talora anche controverso (specie le immunità degli individui-organi statali[496]). Ma, nel complesso, semplificando, si può dire che tutte queste norme hanno la comune caratteristica di costituire un limite al diritto di accesso alla giustizia. Questo limite al diritto *procedurale* della vittima si può risolvere spesso anche in un limite ai diritti umani *sostanziali* che la vittima vuol far valere in giudi-

---

[491] HRCtee, General Comment No. 29, 31 August 2001, par. 14.

[492] Vedi, ad es., ECtHR, *Isayeva v. Russia*, parr. 226-230.

[493] Vedi, ad es., ECtHR, *Ilaşcu and Others v. Moldova and Russia*, parr. 475-482. In realtà, qui la Corte ha riscontrato una violazione, non dell'art. 13, bensì dell'art. 34 della Convenzione europea, relativo al diritto individuale di ricorso alla Corte medesima.

[494] Vedi Francioni (2007), pp. 42-43.

[495] Vedi, ad es., ECtHR, *Bosphorus and Others*; CFI, *Kadi*; *Yusuf*; EGC, *Kadi*; ECJ, *Kadi*; *European Commission v. Kadi*.

[496] Vedi Pisillo Mazzeschi (2014c).

zio, poiché, secondo un principio generale di giustizia, non esiste un diritto sostanziale effettivo in mancanza di rimedi per la sua violazione [497]. Pertanto, è chiaro che esiste un'*antinomia potenziale*, nel diritto internazionale contemporaneo, fra le norme internazionali sulle immunità (di Stati, organi statali, organizzazioni internazionali e funzionari internazionali), da una parte, e le norme internazionali sui diritti umani sostanziali e quelle sull'accesso alla giustizia per violazione di tali diritti, dall'altra parte.

Tuttavia, questa antinomia potenziale non crea problemi particolarmente difficili da risolvere in due ipotesi. La prima ipotesi si verifica quando l'individuo vittima, per superare lo sbarramento dell'immunità dinanzi ai tribunali del foro, ha la possibilità di azionare *mezzi di ricorso alternativi ed effettivi* per far valere la violazione ed ottenere giustizia [498]. Si tratta, cioè, di usare il criterio c.d. della "protezione equivalente". In questi casi, si può sostenere che l'antinomia potenziale fra norme sulle immunità e norme (sostanziali e procedurali) sui diritti umani non si risolve in un vero e proprio conflitto concreto ed effettivo. In altri termini, il diritto della vittima di accesso alla giustizia, ed i diritti umani sostanziali che intende far valere, non sono pregiudicati, o quantomeno non lo sono in maniera sostanziale, dalle norme sulle immunità.

La seconda ipotesi si verifica quando l'antinomia fra le norme sulle immunità e le norme sui diritti umani viene risolta a favore delle prime norme, poiché esse prevalgono, sulla base del criterio di specialità, sulle seconde norme. Ciò avviene, a nostro avviso, quando le norme sui diritti umani non tutelano diritti "fondamentali" della persona. Si pensi, ad esempio, all'ipotesi in cui uno Stato estero, tramite una nazionalizzazione, violi il diritto di proprietà di un cittadino italiano; cioè un diritto umano che non ha carattere "fondamentale". In questo caso, anche qualora vi fosse un conflitto concreto fra il diritto dell'individuo di convenire in giudizio lo Stato estero dinanzi ai tribunali italiani e la norma sull'immunità giurisdizionale degli Stati per atti *iure imperii*, si ritiene che quest'ultima norma debba prevalere, perché essa si configura come speciale, sia nei confronti della norma (sostanziale) sul diritto di proprietà, sia nei confronti della norma (procedurale) sull'accesso alla giustizia in relazione al diritto di proprietà.

Invece, il discorso cambia e l'antinomia fra norme sulle immunità e norme sui diritti umani crea un problema difficile da risolvere quando: *a*) si verifica un *conflitto concreto ed effettivo* fra i due gruppi di norme (perché l'accesso alla giustizia non è garantito neppure dalla regola della "protezione equivalente"); e inoltre: *b*) le norme sui diritti umani tutelano diritti riconosciuti come "fondamentali" o addirittura cogenti (di *ius cogens*) dalla comunità internazionale. In sostanza, queste due condizioni cumulative si verificano quando le norme sulle immunità impediscono *totalmente* agli individui vittime di adire la giustizia contro Stati, organi statali, organizzazioni internazionali o funzionari internazionali che siano accusati di avere commesso violazioni di diritti umani "fondamentali" o addirittura cogenti [499].

---

[497] Vedi Pisillo Mazzeschi (2012), pp. 317-320 e 323-325. Vedi anche Corte Costituzionale, sentenza n. 238 del 22 ottobre 2014.

[498] Quando, ad es., tale individuo può convenire in giudizio uno Stato estero presso i tribunali di tale Stato o esperire un'azione contro un'organizzazione internazionale presso un tribunale amministrativo interno di tale ente o presentare un ricorso contro un agente diplomatico straniero dinanzi ai giudici dello Stato nazionale di quest'ultimo.

[499] Per la nostra distinzione fra la categoria dei diritti umani fondamentali e quella, più restrittiva, dei diritti umani cogenti vedi *supra*, parr. 4.4 e 4.5.

Come è noto, recentemente alcune sentenze molto importanti hanno affrontato e risolto questo problema in modi assai diversi. Si possono ricordare, ad esempio, le tre sentenze della *House of Lords* nel caso *Pinochet*[500]; la sentenza della medesima *House of Lords* nel caso *Jones and Mitchell*[501]; la decisione della Corte di Cassazione francese nel caso *Gheddafi*[502]; la sentenza della Corte di Cassazione italiana nel caso *Ferrini*[503]; la sentenza della Corte Suprema del Canada nel caso *Kazemi*[504]; le decisioni della Corte europea dei diritti umani nei casi *Waite and Kennedy*[505], *Al-Adsani*[506], *Stichting Mothers of Srebrenica*[507] e *Jones*[508]; le sentenze della Corte internazionale di giustizia nel caso *Arrest Warrant*[509] e nel caso delle *Immunità giurisdizionali dello Stato*[510]; ed infine la sentenza della Corte costituzionale italiana n. 238/2014[511], nella quale la Corte ha rifiutato l'esecuzione interna della sentenza della Corte internazionale di giustizia nel caso delle *Immunità giurisdizionali*, perché ritenuta in conflitto con i diritti umani fondamentali protetti dalla Costituzione italiana. Questo problema ha anche provocato un ampio dibattito nella dottrina internazionalistica, che ha mantenuto anch'essa posizioni diverse.

Quali sono le soluzioni proposte dalla dottrina e dalla giurisprudenza per risolvere il problema di questo conflitto?

In linea molto generale, si è manifestata una contrapposizione fra una concezione tradizionale e "stato-centrica" del diritto internazionale, fondata sul ruolo centrale della sovranità statale e dell'ordine interstatuale, che si è dimostrata tendenzialmente contraria a porre limiti alle classiche norme sulle immunità internazionali, e, dall'altra parte, una concezione più moderna e "umano-centrica" del diritto internazionale, tendente ad attribuire un ruolo centrale alla protezione della persona umana, che si è dimostrata propensa a porre sempre maggiori limiti alle immunità internazionali, quando esse siano suscettibili di pregiudicare la tutela dei diritti umani fondamentali.

Più in particolare, nel quadro di questa contrapposizione generale fra concezioni teoriche di fondo, ed anche scelte ideologiche assai diverse dal punto di vista dei valori ed interessi degni di maggior protezione, si possono distinguere varie tesi giuridiche portate a sostegno dell'una o dell'altra concezione generale.

Nel quadro della concezione "stato-centrica", una prima tesi, di carattere radicale, è quella secondo cui le clausole in materia di "giurisdizione", contenute nei trattati sui diritti umani[512],

---

[500] House of Lords, "*Pinochet I*", Judgment of 25 November 1998; "*Pinochet II*", Judgment of 15 January 1999; "*Pinochet III*", Judgment of 24 March 1999.

[501] House of Lords, *Jones and Mitchell v. Saudi Arabia.*

[502] Cour de Cassation, *Khadafi.*

[503] Corte di Cassazione, *Ferrini c. Repubblica Federale di Germania.*

[504] Supreme Court of Canada, *Kazemi Estate v. Islamic Republic of Iran.*

[505] ECtHR, *Waite and Kennedy v. Germany.*

[506] ECtHR, *Al-Adsani v. UK.*

[507] ECtHR, *Stichting Mothers of Srebrenica et al. v. The Netherlands.*

[508] ECtHR, *Jones and Others v. UK.*

[509] ICJ, *Arrest Warrant.*

[510] ICJ, *Jurisdictional Immunities of the State.*

[511] Corte Costituzionale, sentenza n. 238 del 22 ottobre 2014.

[512] Quali, ad es., l'art. 1 della Convenzione europea, l'art. 1 della Convenzione americana e l'art. 2 del Patto sui diritti civili e politici.

andrebbero interpretate nel senso di ritenere che i ricorsi contro Stati esteri o organi di Stati esteri non sono soggetti alla "giurisdizione" dello Stato del foro a causa del funzionamento delle norme internazionali sulle immunità [513]. Ma questa tesi non convince, perché, fra l'altro, non spiega perché le immunità dovrebbero prevalere sugli obblighi di rispettare i diritti umani e le garanzie giudiziarie per la loro violazione [514].

Una seconda tesi, anch'essa favorevole alle immunità, è quella che nega alla radice la possibilità di un conflitto fra le norme sulle immunità e quelle sui diritti umani. Il conflitto non potrebbe esistere perché i due gruppi di norme si occuperebbero di materie diverse: le prime avrebbero carattere procedurale ed il loro accertamento sarebbe preliminare rispetto alle seconde norme, che avrebbero carattere sostanziale. Come è noto, questo argomento è stato sostenuto anche dalla Corte internazionale di giustizia, nella sentenza sulle *Immunità giurisdizionali dello Stato* [515]. A mio avviso, questa tesi è assai formalistica e non convince, perché contrasta con il già menzionato principio generale secondo cui un diritto sostanziale non esiste in assenza di rimedi processuali per la sua violazione. È chiaro che alle vittime delle violazioni dei diritti umani fondamentali interessa, in concreto, avere un accesso alla giustizia per ottenere una decisione e la riparazione del pregiudizio subito. Pertanto i diritti umani fondamentali si legano, *funzionalmente e necessariamente*, al diritto di accesso alla giustizia in caso di loro violazione. In termini parzialmente diversi, alla tesi in esame si potrebbe obiettare che essa trascura il fatto che le immunità sono in conflitto non solo con i diritti umani sostanziali, ma anche e soprattutto con il diritto procedurale di accesso alla giustizia collegato a tali diritti. Pertanto si realizza comunque un conflitto fra gruppi di norme aventi la medesima natura procedurale.

Una terza tesi, più ragionevole, parte dalla premessa che le norme internazionali sulle immunità siano ben radicate nella prassi internazionale. Pertanto il problema si risolverebbe solo nello stabilire se si sia formata, *nel quadro del diritto internazionale delle immunità*, una nuova regola consuetudinaria che stabilisca un'eccezione (la c.d. *human rights exception*) a tali immunità, tale da permettere ai giudici nazionali di esercitare la propria giurisdizione nel caso di violazioni dei diritti umani fondamentali, e specie di crimini internazionali. Tuttavia, i fautori di questa tesi sostengono che questa presunta *human rights exception* non è sorretta da una prassi sufficiente. Pertanto si dovrebbe escludere, sulla base della prassi e non di un argomento logico, che un conflitto possa esistere fra le norme sulle immunità, da una parte, e le norme sostanziali e procedurali sui diritti umani fondamentali, dall'altra parte [516].

A mio avviso, anche questa tesi non convince per due motivi principali. Il primo è che essa ha il difetto di fondarsi su un metodo "tradizionale" di rilevazione delle norme consuetudinarie, che è sorpassato per vari motivi: *a*) perché favorisce l'elemento *diuturnitas* rispetto all'elemento *opinio iuris*; *b*) perché dà importanza fondamentale ad un esame quantitativo ed aritmetico della *diuturnitas*; *c*) perché, nella rilevazione della *diuturnitas*,

---

[513] Vedi Voyiakis (2003), p. 309 ss.

[514] Francioni (2007), p. 49.

[515] ICJ, *Jurisdictional Immunities of the State*, par. 93.

[516] Questa tesi è sostenuta dalla Corte internazionale di giustizia nel caso delle *Immunità giurisdizionali dello Stato*, dalla Corte suprema del Canada nel caso *Kazemi* e dalla Corte europea dei diritti umani nel caso *Jones and Others*.

va indietro nel tempo e non favorisce gli sviluppi più recenti; *d*) infine, perché dà più importanza alla giurisprudenza internazionale rispetto alla giurisprudenza statale in materia di immunità. Il secondo motivo è che questa tesi si fonda su un metodo interpretativo assai restrittivo, perché richiede che l'interprete debba limitarsi a cercare una eventuale *human rights exception* soltanto all'interno del settore normativo delle immunità. In tal modo si finisce per considerare il regime giuridico delle immunità come una sorta di regime *self-contained*, che pretende di ricercare solo dentro sé stesso al fine di stabilire la regola generale e l'eccezione. Al contrario, noi riteniamo che le norme sulle immunità non dovrebbero essere interpretate in isolamento e soltanto nel quadro del loro proprio regime giuridico; ma dovrebbero essere interpretate tramite un confronto con le norme ed i principi contenuti in altri settori del diritto internazionale. In sostanza, poiché l'ordinamento giuridico internazionale ha un carattere unitario, nulla impedisce di confrontare norme derivanti da settori diversi e di fornire, in tal modo, una interpretazione "sistematica" del diritto internazionale. Da quest'ottica (come vedremo) lo *ius cogens* può costituire un criterio gerarchico molto utile al fine di risolvere conflitti fra norme consuetudinarie appartenenti a settori diversi.

Passiamo ora alla seconda concezione generale sopra esposta; cioè quella "umanocentrica", propensa a giustificare una deroga alle norme sulle immunità internazionali, oppure ad interpretare restrittivamente tali norme, nel caso in cui esse siano in *conflitto concreto ed effettivo* con le norme sui diritti umani fondamentali.

Nel quadro di questa concezione, sono state proposte numerose tesi. Non possiamo qui esaminarle tutte. Ci limitiamo a ricordare che, secondo una tesi più radicale, ogni Stato sarebbe libero di regolare a sua discrezione l'eventuale conflitto fra immunità e diritti umani, poiché le immunità non sarebbero regolate dal diritto internazionale consuetudinario, ma solo dalle varie legislazioni interne al fine di disciplinare le relazioni esterne del singolo Stato [517]. Secondo altre tesi più moderate, la "*human rights exception*" alle immunità potrebbe essere giustificata come una rinuncia implicita da parte degli Stati rinvenuta nell'adesione alla Carta delle NU o ai trattati sui diritti umani [518]; oppure come l'esercizio di una contromisura da parte dello Stato del foro [519]; oppure come conseguenza del principio di giurisdizione universale sui crimini internazionali [520]; oppure tramite lo strumento dello *ius cogens* [521]. Infine, vi è anche la tesi secondo cui l'interprete dovrebbe, volta per volta, decidere il conflitto fra immunità e diritti umani fondamentali sulla base di un bilanciamento fra gli interessi, i valori ed i principi in gioco. A nostro avviso, queste due ultime tesi sono quelle più convincenti, e su di esse conviene approfondire il discorso.

Secondo la tesi che si fonda sullo *ius cogens*, lo strumento normativo principale, per risolvere i *veri e propri conflitti* fra le norme internazionali sulle immunità, da una parte, e

---

[517] Vedi, ad es., Brownlie (2008), pp. 323-333, che esprime scetticismo sulla condizione giuridica delle immunità nel diritto internazionale consuetudinario o generale. Questa tesi trova tuttora corrispondenza nella prassi di alcuni Stati di *common law*. Sul punto cfr. Francioni (2007), pp. 49-50.

[518] Gergen (1995-96), pp. 783-787.

[519] Bianchi (1997), p. 414 ss.

[520] Gergen (1995-96), p. 792 ss.; Bianchi (1997), p. 427. Vedi anche ILA, *Final Report on the Exercise of Universal Jurisdiction in Respect of Gross Human Rights Offences, Report of the 69th Conference held in London*, 25-29 July 2000, London, 2000, p. 416.

[521] Vedi, ad es., Bianchi (1999), p. 265; Kamto (2002), pp. 526-529; Robertson (1999), pp. 408-409; Van Alebeek (2000), p. 49.

le norme internazionali sulla tutela dei diritti umani fondamentali, dall'altra parte, è fornito dal fatto che questo secondo gruppo di norme appartiene allo *ius cogens*, concepito come una fonte *gerarchicamente superiore*, o comunque dotata di forza di resistenza superiore, rispetto alle norme consuetudinarie di carattere dispositivo, quali le norme sulle immunità. Pertanto, i giudici dello Stato del foro possono legittimamente derogare alle immunità ed esercitare la propria giurisdizione su Stati esteri e organizzazioni internazionali accusati di violazioni di diritti umani fondamentali o su organi di Stati esteri e funzionari internazionali accusati delle medesime violazioni o di crimini internazionali. Nella giurisprudenza, questa tesi è stata sostenuta varie volte. Si possono ricordare, ad esempio, le sentenze della Corte di Cassazione italiana nei casi *Ferrini*[522], *Milde*[523] e in altri casi; l'opinione dissidente di sei giudici nella sentenza *Al-Adsani* della Corte europea dei diritti umani[524]; le opinioni di due Lords nella sentenza *Pinochet III*[525]; le opinioni dissidenti di due giudici nella sentenza *Arrest Warrant* della Corte internazionale di giustizia[526]; l'opinione separata del giudice *ad hoc* Dugard nella sentenza *Armed Activities on the Territory of the Congo* della medesima Corte[527]; l'opinione dissidente del giudice Cançado Trindade nella sentenza *Jurisdictional Immunities* della stessa Corte[528].

Ma si devono sottolineare due punti importanti. Il primo, già evidenziato, è che le norme sulle immunità possono confliggere non solo con le norme sostanziali sui diritti umani fondamentali, ma anche, ed anzi *più direttamente*, con la norma procedurale sull'accesso alla giustizia per le vittime delle violazioni, quando non è rispettata la regola della "protezione equivalente". Il secondo punto è che la norma consuetudinaria sull'accesso alla giustizia, quando è collegata alla violazione di quei diritti umani che sono protetti dallo *ius cogens*, diventa anch'essa una norma di *ius cogens*; e quindi, in caso di vero e proprio conflitto, prevale sulle norme sulle immunità internazionali che non hanno natura cogente. Questa conclusione ci sembra inevitabile, anche da un punto di vista meramente logico. Infatti, se il divieto di violare certi diritti umani è stabilito da una norma di *ius cogens*, ne consegue logicamente che la norma sull'accesso alla giustizia per violazioni di tale divieto è anch'essa una norma di *ius cogens,* perché è funzionalmente e necessariamente collegata alla prima. In altri termini, la natura imperativa, per la comunità internazionale, della necessità di reprimere le violazioni di *alcuni* diritti umani fondamentali non avrebbe alcuna concreta efficacia se l'accesso alla giustizia per le vittime di tali violazioni non fosse protetto da norme aventi la medesima natura imperativa. Nella giurisprudenza, questa tesi è stata sostenuta dalla Corte interamericana nella sua sentenza nel caso *Goiburù*[529]; dal Pre-

---

522 Corte di Cassazione, *Ferrini*, parr. 9.1 e 11.

523 Corte di Cassazione, *Milde*, par. 3.

524 ECtHR, *Al-Adsani v. UK*, Joint Dissenting Opinion of Judges Rozakis, Caflish, Costa, Wildhaber, Cabral Barreto and Vajić.

525 House of Lords, "*Pinochet III*", Opinion of Lord Browne-Wilkinson, par. 198; Opinion of Lord Hope of Craighead, par. 247.

526 ICJ, *Arrest Warrant*, Dissenting Opinion of Judge Al-Khasawneh, par. 7; Dissenting Opinion of Judge *ad hoc* van den Wyngaert, parr. 27-28.

527 ICJ, *Armed Activities*, Judgment of 3 February 2006, Separate Opinion of Judge *ad hoc* Dugard, parr. 3-14.

528 ICJ, *Jurisdictional Immunities*, Dissenting Opinion of Judge Cançado Trindade, parr. 117-120, 214-220 e 288-299.

529 IACtHR, *Goiburù et al. v. Paraguay*, par. 131.

sidente del Tribunale Speciale per il Libano nella sua ordinanza del 2010 nel caso *El-Sayed*[530] e da alcuni giudici della Corte europea nel caso *Al-Dulimi*[531].

Concludendo su questo punto, riteniamo che l'utilizzazione dello *ius cogens* come criterio gerarchico, per risolvere conflitti fra norme consuetudinarie sulle immunità e norme consuetudinarie sui diritti umani fondamentali, debba essere approvata. Un vantaggio è che fornisce una soluzione chiara per tali conflitti ed assicura certezza giuridica. Un altro vantaggio è che finalmente dà sostanza all'idea che le norme di *ius cogens*, incorporando valori essenziali ed irrinunciabili della comunità internazionale, dovrebbero prevalere su norme consuetudinarie che non hanno natura imperativa. Tuttavia, si deve riconoscere che la prassi internazionale, anche se spesso ammette in astratto l'esistenza dello *ius cogens* nel diritto internazionale contemporaneo, ha finora mostrato scarsa volontà di applicare tale concetto in pratica, specie per risolvere antinomie fra norme consuetudinarie.

Infine, conviene ricordare la tesi secondo cui il conflitto fra immunità internazionali e diritti umani fondamentali dovrebbe essere risolto sulla base di un *bilanciamento* fra valori e principi in gioco. Questa tesi è stata sostenuta specie in relazione alle immunità giurisdizionali di individui-organi di Stati esteri, ma anche in relazione alle immunità di Stati esteri e di organizzazioni internazionali.

Con riguardo alle immunità degli individui-organi stranieri, il criterio del bilanciamento fra principi è stato esplicitamente proposto dai giudici Higgins, Kooijmans e Buergenthal nella loro opinione separata congiunta nella sentenza *Arrest Warrant*[532] della Corte internazionale di giustizia[533]. Un criterio simile ha ispirato, anche se in maniera meno esplicita, le opinioni di alcuni Lords nelle sentenze *Pinochet I* e *Pinochet III* della *House of Lords*[534].

Il criterio del bilanciamento è stato sostenuto anche in relazione alle immunità di Stati esteri. Nella sua opinione dissidente nella sentenza *Jurisdictional Immunities of the State* della Corte internazionale di giustizia, il giudice Yusuf ha affermato che, quando le immunità giurisdizionali confliggono con i diritti fondamentali protetti dal diritto dei diritti umani o dal diritto umanitario, un bilanciamento fra questi differenti valori è necessario, e che oggi l'uso da parte di uno Stato dell'immunità per impedire l'accesso alla giustizia ed il diritto ad un rimedio effettivo può essere considerato un abuso (*misuse*) dell'immunità[535]. Argomenti simili sono stati usati anche dalla Corte di Cassazione italiana nella sen-

---

[530] STL, *El-Sayed*, par. 29.

[531] ECtHR, *Al-Dulimi and Montana*, Concurring Opinion of Judge Pinto de Albuquerque, joined by Judges Hajiyev, Pejchal and Delov, parr. 33-37.

[532] ICJ, *Arrest Warrant*, Joint Separate Opinion of Judges Higgins, Kooijmans and Buergenthal, parr. 70-79.

[533] Questi giudici hanno criticato il fatto che la maggioranza dei giudici della Corte non ha bilanciato in maniera appropriata gli interessi che sottostanno all'esercizio della giurisdizione e quelli che sottostanno all'eccezione all'immunità. Essi hanno anche detto che la norma sull'immunità evolve nel tempo e che ciò rende ancora più necessario il test del bilanciamento. *Ibidem*, par. 75.

[534] Vedi nella sentenza "*Pinochet I*" le opinioni di Lord Steyn (par. 115) e di Lord Nicholls of Birkenhead (par. 110); e nella sentenza "*Pinochet III*" le opinioni di Lord Hutton (parr. 225, 262, 265), di Lord Phillips (par. 290) e di Lord Browne-Wilkinson (par. 65). Essi hanno escluso la possibilità che l'immunità funzionale dei Capi di Stato potesse coprire atti di tortura e simili gravi crimini internazionali, poiché tali atti non possono mai essere considerati dal diritto internazionale come atti compiuti nell'esercizio delle funzioni ufficiali di un Capo di Stato.

[535] ICJ, *Jurisdictional Immunities of the State*, Dissenting Opinion of Judge Yusuf, parr. 28-30 e 37.

tenza *Ferrini*[536] e, sia pure con risultati diversi, dalle corti supreme di Grecia e Polonia nelle sentenze rese nei casi *Margellos*[537] e *Natoniewski*[538].

Anche in relazione alle immunità delle organizzazioni internazionali, alcuni elementi della prassi internazionale sembrano usare il test del bilanciamento. Anche se non in maniera esplicita, questo criterio è stato usato dalla Corte di Strasburgo in una serie di note decisioni (*Waite & Kennedy*[539], *Beer & Regan*[540], *Naletilić*[541]), nelle quali la Corte ha bilanciato l'immunità delle organizzazioni internazionali con il diritto di accesso alla giustizia per la vittima. Ma la Corte ha recentemente abbandonato questo approccio (*Mothers of Srebrenica*[542]) e si è dimostrata riluttante a limitare le immunità.

A nostro parere, il criterio del bilanciamento dei principi e valori è un tentativo interessante di affrontare il problema generale dei conflitti normativi e quello specifico dei conflitti fra immunità internazionali e diritti umani fondamentali. Esso, richiedendo all'interprete di valutare il relativo "peso" delle norme in conflitto in ciascun caso concreto, offre il vantaggio della flessibilità rispetto al criterio gerarchico dello *ius cogens*. D'altra parte, tuttavia, tale metodo è oggi sostenuto solo da una parte della dottrina e della prassi internazionale; ed è esposto alla critica di coloro che temono la discrezionalità interpretativa dei giudici e preferiscono la certezza del diritto.

18.4. *Obblighi*

Al diritto di accesso alla giustizia (previsto dalla norma consuetudinaria) corrispondono numerosi obblighi da parte degli Stati. Di essi abbiamo già parlato con riferimento ad altri diritti umani "fondamentali"; e quindi sarà sufficiente un breve richiamo.

Lo Stato ha l'obbligo di possedere, e di far funzionare, un adeguato apparato di amministrazione della giustizia, allo scopo di *accertare* le violazioni dei diritti umani; e l'obbligo che tale apparato garantisca un "accesso effettivo" a tutte le vittime di tali violazioni verificatesi nell'ambito della propria "giurisdizione". L'adeguatezza va misurata con i criteri che abbiamo sopra esposto: esistenza di giudici predeterminati dalla legge, loro indipendenza e imparzialità, loro potere di decidere sulla base del diritto ed in tempi ragionevoli, garanzie procedurali essenziali del processo equo. Si tratta di obblighi positivi immediati e di risultato, perché ogni Stato contemporaneo deve essere in grado di garantire un tale sistema di giustizia sulla base di uno standard internazionale. Questi obblighi tendono all'accertamento giudiziale delle violazioni dei diritti umani, e devono essere tenuti distinti dagli obblighi volti ad indagare sulle violazioni ed a punire i colpevoli (obblighi di repressione).

Naturalmente, le singole norme convenzionali che regolano il diritto di accesso alla giustizia (nelle sue forme del rimedio interno effettivo e dell'equo processo) prevedono di solito una serie di obblighi più dettagliati; ma che rispondono al medesimo scopo generale.

---

[536] Corte di Cassazione, *Ferrini*. Sul punto vedi De Sena, De Vittor (2005), pp. 89-116.

[537] Greek Supreme Court, *Margellos and Others v. Federal Republic of Germany*. Vedi De Sena (2016), p. 1020.

[538] Polish Supreme Court, *Natoniewski v. Federal Republic of Germany*.

[539] ECtHR, *Waite and Kennedy*, parr. 63-68.

[540] ECtHR, *Beer and Regan*, parr. 48-49, 53, 57-58.

[541] ECtHR, *Naletilić*, par. 1 b).

[542] ECtHR, *Stichting Mothers of Srebrenica and Others*, parr. 161-165.

19. *Diritto alla riparazione*

19.1. *Norme*

Il diritto dell'individuo alla riparazione, a seguito della violazione dei suoi diritti umani, è, a nostro avviso, autonomo rispetto al diritto di accesso alla giustizia, anche se i due diritti sono ovviamente collegati. La tesi opposta, che ha autorevoli seguaci [543], sostiene invece che il diritto di accesso alla giustizia (per violazione dei diritti umani) comprende già nel suo contenuto il diritto alla riparazione (in caso di accertamento della violazione). In realtà, questa tesi ha il merito di far comprendere che, per l'individuo-vittima, è inutile ottenere l'accesso alla giustizia se poi, una volta accertato l'illecito, egli non può ottenere la riparazione.

Tuttavia, per vari motivi, ci sembra più corretta la distinzione fra diritto di accesso alla giustizia (come diritto procedurale) e diritto alla riparazione (come diritto sostanziale). In primo luogo, nei trattati sui diritti umani, le disposizioni sulla riparazione sono sempre separate e diverse rispetto a quelle sul rimedio effettivo e sul giusto processo. In secondo luogo, anche la prassi degli organi internazionali di controllo sui diritti umani conferma questa separazione. Infine, anche l'Assemblea Generale delle NU ritiene di dover distinguere, nell'ambito dei diritti delle vittime di violazioni dei diritti umani, fra "effective access to justice" e "adequate, effective and prompt reparation for harm suffered" [544].

Ciò premesso, si può notare che il diritto alla riparazione è previsto in numerose disposizioni contenute nei trattati sui diritti umani. Si possono ricordare: gli artt. 5(5) e 41 della Convenzione europea, l'art. 3 del suo Settimo Protocollo, gli artt. 9(5) e 14(6) del Patto sui diritti civili e politici, gli artt. 10 e 63(1) della Convenzione americana, l'art. 27(1) del Protocollo del 1998 alla Carta africana, l'art. 14(7) della Carta araba, l'art. 6 della Convenzione sull'eliminazione della discriminazione razziale, l'art. 14 della Convenzione delle NU contro la tortura.

In realtà, queste norme hanno un contenuto diverso. Una prima differenza è che alcune di esse prevedono una *riparazione generale*, cioè in relazione a tutte le violazioni della pertinente convenzione. Un celebre esempio è dato dall'art. 41 della Convenzione europea, secondo cui:

> "If the Court finds that there has been a violation of the Convention or the Protocols thereto, and if the internal law of the High Contracting Party concerned allows only partial reparation to be made, the Court shall, if necessary, afford just satisfaction to the injured party".

Una norma simile, ma più precisa e dettagliata, è contenuta nell'art. 63(1) della Convenzione americana [545]. Anche le disposizioni sopra citate del Protocollo alla Carta africana, della Convenzione sull'eliminazione della discriminazione razziale e della Convenzione contro la tortura appartengono a questa categoria di norme. Invece, altre norme hanno

---

[543] ICJ, *Jurisdictional Immunities of the State*, Dissenting Opinion of Judge Cançado Trindade, par. 221.

[544] *Basic Principles and Guidelines on the Right to a Remedy and Reparation for Victims of Gross Violations of International Human Rights Law and Serious Violations of International Humanitarian Law*, Annex, Art. VII.

[545] ACHR, art. 63(1): "If the Court finds that there has been a violation of a right of freedom protected by this Convention, the Court shall rule that the injured party be ensured the enjoyment of his right or freedom that was violated. It shall also rule, if appropriate, that the consequences of the measure or situation that constituted the breach of such right or freedom be remedied and that fair compensation be paid to the injured party".

carattere più particolare, perché stabiliscono una *riparazione specifica*, cioè soltanto in relazione a certe violazioni del trattato, ad esempio un arresto o una detenzione illegittimi oppure una condanna penale in seguito annullata[546].

Una seconda differenza consiste nel fatto che, nei sistemi convenzionali che dispongono di un organo di controllo *giurisdizionale*, le norme sulla riparazione stabiliscono un obbligo *internazionale* di riparazione dello Stato verso l'individuo vittima, poiché prevedono che la riparazione dovuta dallo Stato all'individuo sia decisa espressamente con una *sentenza* dell'organo internazionale di controllo. Invece, nei sistemi convenzionali che dispongono di organi di controllo *quasi-giurisdizionali*, le norme sulla riparazione si limitano a stabilire l'obbligo dello Stato di fornire la riparazione nel proprio diritto interno.

Tuttavia, e questo è un punto importante, la prassi degli organi internazionali di controllo ha finito, in pratica, per attenuare molto queste differenze.

Sotto un primo aspetto, anche laddove il trattato non conteneva una norma sulla *riparazione generale*, gli organi di controllo hanno deciso misure di riparazione in seguito all'accertamento di *qualsiasi violazione dei diritti* contenuti nel trattato[547]. Un caso paradigmatico è dato dal Comitato dei diritti umani, che (in relazione ai ricorsi individuali per le violazioni del Patto sui diritti civili e politici) si è attribuito la competenza ad indicare misure di riparazione, al di là di quanto esplicitamente previsto nel Patto, sulla base di un'interpretazione estensiva dell'art. 2(3) del Patto medesimo[548]. Anche altri organi di controllo quasi-giurisdizionali, nelle loro decisioni su ricorsi individuali, indicano allo Stato colpevole di una violazione quali misure di riparazione esso dovrebbe adottare nei confronti degli individui vittime; e ciò in relazione a tutte le violazioni del trattato. In sostanza, si è affermato, nella prassi, un potere implicito di tali organi in materia di *riparazione generale*[549].

Sotto un secondo aspetto, le decisioni di tali organi sulle misure di riparazione, pur non essendo in teoria vincolanti, vengono di regola rispettate dagli Stati. Pertanto è sfumata anche la differenza fra la riparazione decisa da una corte internazionale e la riparazione raccomandata da un organo di controllo quasi-giurisdizionale.

In realtà, da un esame complessivo della prassi, ci sembra si possa trarre anche un'altra conclusione; cioè che si sia ormai affermata, nel diritto internazionale contemporaneo, una norma internazionale consuetudinaria, che impone allo Stato autore di una violazione dei diritti umani di fornire una riparazione a favore degli individui vittime della violazione[550]. Si tratta adesso di precisare il contenuto di questa norma.

19.2. *Contenuto del diritto*

Come si è detto, la giurisprudenza e la prassi degli organi di controllo sui diritti umani dimostrano che le decisioni di tali organi stabiliscono una riparazione che è *direttamente a favore degli individui vittime*, anche se l'obbligo di riparare spetta poi in pratica allo Stato autore della

---

[546] Vedi, ad esempio, CCPR, artt. 9(5) e 14(6).

[547] Vedi, per tutti, Bartolini (2009), Cap. II, spec. p. 175 ss.

[548] Cfr. HRCtee, General Comment No. 31, 26 May 2004, par. 16.

[549] Bartolini (2009), p. 201.

[550] Su questo tema vedi Pisillo Mazzeschi (1999b), p. 149 ss.; Id. (2003); Id. (2004b), p. 39 ss.; Id. (2008), pp. 365-373 e 422-424; D'Argent (2005), p. 27 ss.; Bartolini (2009).

violazione[551]. Pertanto, si può concludere che l'individuo è titolare di un diritto alla riparazione per violazione dei diritti umani, che gli è attribuito *direttamente* dal diritto internazionale e non solo dall'eventuale diritto interno di applicazione del diritto internazionale[552].

Si noti che anche il Progetto di articoli della CDI sulla responsabilità degli Stati non esclude, ed anzi lascia intendere implicitamente, che gli individui possono essere titolari di diritti derivanti da illeciti di Stati[553]. Per noi, questa conclusione è scontata, poiché crediamo che gli individui siano destinatari diretti delle norme internazionali sui diritti umani, ivi comprese quelle norme secondarie in materia di responsabilità che siano strutturalmente applicabili agli individui.

Qualora si volesse accogliere una tesi più restrittiva sul contenuto del diritto individuale alla riparazione nel diritto internazionale consuetudinario, si dovrebbe quantomeno ammettere che tale diritto si è affermato per le gravi violazioni dei diritti umani fondamentali e del diritto umanitario. Su questo aspetto la prassi degli organi internazionali di controllo sui diritti umani è ormai consolidata. A tale prassi si possono aggiungere: il parere della Corte internazionale di giustizia sulla *Costruzione di un muro nel territorio palestinese occupato*[554]; la risoluzione dell'Assemblea Generale delle NU del 2005 sui diritti delle vittime di gravi violazioni dei diritti umani e del diritto umanitario[555]; il Rapporto della Commissione internazionale di inchiesta sul Darfur[556]; la risoluzione dell'*Institut de Droit International* sull'immunità degli Stati adottata nel 2009[557].

19.2.1. *Restrizioni e limiti. Conflitto fra il diritto alla riparazione e le immunità internazionali (rinvio)*

Il diritto alla riparazione per violazione dei diritti umani è soggetto a deroghe in stati di emergenza ed a restrizioni e limiti, in maniera analoga a quanto si verifica per il diritto di accesso alla giustizia. Pertanto, su questi aspetti, rinviamo a quanto abbiamo detto a proposito di quest'ultimo diritto.

19.3. *Obblighi*

Si tratta adesso di determinare la natura e la struttura degli obblighi degli Stati che corrispondono al diritto individuale alla riparazione. Su questo argomento è difficile da-

---

[551] Su questa prassi vedi Bartolini (2009), Capp. III e IV.

[552] Vedi Pisillo Mazzeschi (1999b); Id. (2003); Id. (2004b), pp. 42-50.

[553] ILC, *Draft Articles on Responsibility of States for Internationally Wrongful Acts*, 1 August 2001, artt. 33(2) e 48(2)(b). Cfr. anche UN Doc. A/56/10: *Report of the ILC on the Work of its Fifty-third Session (2001), Chapter IV, State Responsibility*, par. 4. Vedi anche Crawford (2002), p. 27, il quale ha affermato che il Progetto di articoli sulla responsabilità degli Stati non ha voluto affrontare la responsabilità dello Stato nei confronti degli individui; ma ha implicitamente ammesso che tale responsabilità è configurabile nel diritto internazionale contemporaneo.

[554] ICJ, *Legal Consequences of the Construction of a Wall*, parr. 147, 152, 153.

[555] *Basic Principles and Guidelines on the Right to a Remedy and Reparation for Victims of Gross Violations of International Human Rights Law and Serious Violations of International Humanitarian Law*.

[556] *Report of the International Commission of Inquiry on Darfur to the United Nations Secretary General, Pursuant to Security Council Resolution 1564 of 18 September 2004*, Geneva, 25 January 2005, parr. 595-599.

[557] IDI, Third Commission Resolution, *Resolution on the Immunity from Jurisdiction of the State and of Persons Who Act on Behalf of the State in Case of International Crimes*, 10 September 2009.

re una risposta unitaria, perché la riparazione, in materia di diritti umani così come nel diritto internazionale in generale, può assumere tre forme classiche: *restitutio in integrum*, risarcimento monetario del danno e soddisfazione. Oggi vi è una certa tendenza ad aggiungere, a queste tre forme, le garanzie di non ripetizione dell'illecito[558] e (in materia di diritti umani) la riabilitazione della vittima[559]. Ci occuperemo solo delle tre forme classiche.

L'obbligo dello Stato responsabile della violazione di *risarcire* il danno, sia agli individui vittime sia eventualmente ad altri Stati, è sempre un obbligo positivo di risultato, perché il suo adempimento non è soggetto ad alea.

Più complessa è invece la situazione a proposito della *restitutio in integrum*, che è evidentemente anche la forma preferibile di riparazione, quand'essa è concretamente possibile, sia in generale sia in materia di diritti umani[560]. Quando la *restitutio* si risolve nell'obbligo di emanare, modificare o abrogare legislazione, essa costituisce un obbligo di risultato. La stessa conclusione vale, in linea di principio, nel caso in cui la *restitutio* imponga allo Stato l'adozione o l'abrogazione di un provvedimento amministrativo o giurisdizionale. Più difficile è giudicare il caso in cui la *restitutio* imponga allo Stato di prendere una misura di carattere materiale (o concreto), perché allora la risposta può cambiare a seconda del tipo di misura richiesta. Infatti l'esecuzione di alcune misure materiali non è soggetta ad alea nel risultato, ad esempio il rilascio di un detenuto; mentre l'esecuzione di altre misure può essere soggetta ad alea, ad esempio il ritrovamento di una persona scomparsa. Peraltro, si può concludere che la maggior parte degli obblighi relativi alla *restitutio in integrum* si configura come obblighi di risultato.

Una conclusione simile vale per l'obbligo dello Stato di dare una *soddisfazione*. Quando la soddisfazione consiste in un riconoscimento formale della violazione, come si verifica spesso in materia di diritti umani, essa costituisce un obbligo di risultato. L'esempio classico è dato dai numerosi casi in cui gli organi internazionali di controllo hanno deciso che l'emanazione stessa di una sentenza di accertamento della violazione a carico dello Stato costituiva una soddisfazione per la vittima. La stessa conclusione vale per altri comportamenti statali, che non contengono l'elemento "diligenza", quali, ad esempio, la presentazione di scuse o l'elargizione di risarcimenti monetari simbolici o la costruzione di un monumento in memoria della vittima.

Un discorso diverso, invece, può farsi per quei casi in cui gli organi internazionali di controllo hanno richiesto allo Stato colpevole della violazione di diritti umani, a titolo di soddisfazione per le vittime, di condurre ulteriori indagini per identificare e punire i soggetti responsabili delle violazioni, o per ritrovare i corpi delle vittime, oppure di adottare certe misure per prevenire il ripetersi delle violazioni. In questi casi, l'obbligo di dare soddisfazione si configura come obbligo di *due diligence*.

---

[558] Vedi ILC, *Draft Articles on Responsibility of States for Internationally Wrongful Acts*, art. 30(b).

[559] Vedi *Basic Principles and Guidelines on the Right to a Remedy and Reparation for Victims of Gross Violations of International Human Rights Law and Serious Violations of International Humanitarian Law*, art. IX(21).

[560] Ciò non vale quando la violazione dei diritti umani deriva da condizioni sociali perduranti di iniquità. In questi casi, evidentemente, la *restitutio in integrum* sarebbe negativa e lo Stato deve invece modificare tali condizioni sociali per prevenire la ripetizione delle violazioni.

Infine, conviene precisare che le misure di riparazione concrete dovrebbero essere decise caso per caso sulla base dei bisogni effettivi delle vittime, tenendo anche conto delle loro esigenze sociali e culturali; ciò al fine di garantire un migliore livello di realizzazione dei loro diritti.

20. *Diritti basilari degli imputati. Legalità penale e irretroattività dei reati e delle pene*

Nel diritto internazionale dei diritti umani, vi sono molte norme convenzionali che si occupano, anche in maniera dettagliata, dei diritti degli imputati nei processi penali. Esse sono contenute, di solito, nelle disposizioni dedicate all'equo processo. Tuttavia, a noi interessano ora soltanto quei diritti che possono essere considerati come "fondamentali", perché trovano fondamento, oltreché nel diritto pattizio, nel diritto internazionale generale. Si potrebbe parlare di diritti umani "basilari" o "primari" degli imputati. Questi sono, a nostro parere, i diritti che le persone accusate di illeciti penali hanno in virtù del principio di legalità penale e del principio, collegato, di irretroattività dei reati e delle pene.

20.1. *Norme*

Il principio di legalità, in materia penale, si esprime nel brocardo latino "*nullum crimen sine lege, nulla poena sine lege*"; cioè nella regola che nessuno può essere condannato per un reato o punito con una pena che non erano già previsti al momento della commissione del reato. Inoltre, questo principio include anche, logicamente, l'altro principio più specifico della irretroattività della legge penale: esso significa che nessuna legge penale può essere applicata ad un reato che era stato commesso prima che la legge entrasse in vigore e che eventuali pene più gravi, che siano state stabilite dopo la commissione di un reato, non sono applicabili a tale reato. Ma l'effetto retroattivo è considerato legittimo quando la nuova legge prevede pene più leggere rispetto alla vecchia legge (regola della *lex mitior*).

Questi principi derivano da una lunga tradizione storica e sono contenuti in molte carte costituzionali. In Italia, ad esempio, essi sono sanciti in maniera sintetica dall'art. 25 della Costituzione:

> "Nessuno può essere distolto dal giudice naturale precostituito per legge.
> Nessuno può essere punito se non in forza di una legge che sia entrata in vigore prima del fatto commesso […]" [561].

Nel diritto internazionale, questi principi sono contenuti nei più importanti atti e trattati sui diritti umani. La Dichiarazione universale, all'art. 11(2), proclama che:

> "No one shall be held guilty of any penal offence on account of any act or omission which did not constitute a penal offence, under national or international law, at the time

[561] Vedi anche gli artt. 1 ("Reati e pene: disposizione espressa di legge") e 2 ("Successione di leggi penali") del codice penale italiano.

when it was committed. Nor shall a heavier penalty be imposed that the one that was applicable at the time the penal offence was committed".

La Convenzione europea, nell'art. 7, par. 1, riprende una formula quasi identica a quella della Dichiarazione universale ed aggiunge la regola della *lex mitior*. Ma poi, nel par. 2, prevede una importante, ma controversa, clausola di "precisazione" (o di "eccezione"), secondo la quale:

> "This Article shall not prejudice the trial and punishment of any person for any act or omission which, at the time when it was committed, was criminal according to the general principles of law recognised by civilised nations".

Il Patto sui diritti civili e politici, nell'art. 15, contiene una norma del tutto simile all'art. 7 della Convenzione europea; ma, nella clausola di "precisazione", parla di atti criminali secondo i principi generali di diritto riconosciuti "by the community of nations". Degno di nota è poi l'art. 49 della Carta dei diritti fondamentali dell'UE, che riprende e specifica in maggior dettaglio le regole previste dall'art. 15 del Patto sui diritti civili e politici; ed aggiunge la regola che la severità delle pene non deve essere sproporzionata rispetto al crimine.

Altri trattati regionali sui diritti umani contengono disposizioni che, pur stabilendo i due principi di base (legalità penale e irretroattività dei reati e delle pene), sono più sintetiche rispetto a quelle sopra indicate; e soprattutto si distaccano da esse perché non prevedono la clausola di "precisazione" relativa agli atti criminali secondo i principi riconosciuti dalle nazioni civili (o dalla comunità delle nazioni). In questo senso, si possono citare l'art. 9 della Convenzione americana, l'art. 7(2) della Carta africana e l'art. 15 della Carta araba.

A nostro avviso, il principio di legalità penale e l'altro principio, conseguente, di irretroattività dei reati e delle pene, si sono affermati nel diritto internazionale generale. La prassi degli organi internazionali di controllo conferma questa conclusione. Pertanto, i diritti "basilari" degli imputati che derivano da tali principi devono essere considerati come diritti umani "fondamentali". Più difficile è, invece, stabilire se analoga conclusione valga anche per la clausola di "precisazione" relativa ai crimini secondo i principi riconosciuti dalle nazioni civili, la quale, come si è visto, è contenuta solo in alcuni trattati. In realtà, molto dipende dall'interpretazione che si voglia dare a tale clausola [562].

20.2. *Contenuto dei diritti*

I principi di legalità penale e di irretroattività dei reati e delle pene conferiscono agli imputati diritti che devono essere considerati come inderogabili in stati di emergenza. Ciò risulta dai principali trattati sui diritti umani [563]. A noi sembra che si tratti anche di diritti assoluti, come vedremo meglio qui di seguito [564].

---

[562] Vedi *infra*, par. 20.2.

[563] Vedi, ad es., CCPR, art. 4(2); ECHR, art. 15(2).

[564] Una conclusione diversa dovrebbe essere raggiunta qualora si ritenesse che i suddetti principi subiscono una vera e propria eccezione, quando si tratti di reprimere atti considerati come crimini sulla base dei principi generali di diritto riconosciuti dalle nazioni civili. Sul punto vedi Pustorino (2019), pp. 153-154.

Ciò premesso, i problemi principali sul contenuto dei diritti in oggetto sono: *a*) la qualificazione del carattere "penale" degli illeciti e delle sanzioni; *b*) i requisiti richiesti agli Stati per il rispetto del principio di legalità; *c*) il significato preciso della clausola relativa ai crimini secondo i principi riconosciuti dalle nazioni civili.

Il primo problema si pone perché i due principi si applicano al settore penale ed il concetto di "illecito penale" può cambiare a seconda dei vari ordinamenti giuridici. Ma è chiaro che gli organi internazionali di controllo dei trattati sui diritti umani adottano una qualificazione "autonoma" del concetto di "illecito penale"; cioè che non si fonda (o non si fonda soltanto) su quella dei sistemi nazionali interni. In particolare, la Corte europea, nella sua giurisprudenza sull'art. 6 della Convenzione europea, ha sviluppato, fin dal noto caso *Engel*[565], tre criteri: *a*) la qualificazione adottata dall'ordinamento dello Stato in questione; *b*) la natura dell'illecito, cioè il fatto che la norma violata abbia destinatarietà generale ed uno scopo deterrente e punitivo; *c*) il grado di severità della sanzione[566]. Questa qualificazione "autonoma", operata in concreto e non sulla base di fattispecie legali astratte[567], ha consentito alla Corte di ritenere attinenti alla materia penale certi illeciti che, nei diritti interni, venivano qualificati come amministrativi o tributari[568]. Ciò ha provocato reazioni critiche da parte di alcune corti statali.

Il secondo problema concerne i requisiti richiesti affinché sia rispettato il principio di legalità. Lo Stato deve avere norme penali che siano *accessibili, chiare e prevedibili*, in modo tale da poter essere facilmente conoscibili da parte di tutti i destinatari. Questi criteri si applicano non solo alle norme scritte, ma anche alle interpretazioni giurisprudenziali di tali norme[569]. Si noti che la Corte europea, ai fini dell'applicabilità dell'art. 7 della Convenzione, ha ritenuto che, dai criteri di prevedibilità e conoscibilità della legge penale, derivi la necessità di un elemento di carattere intellettuale (quantomeno: coscienza e volontà) nella condotta dell'autore dell'infrazione[570].

Infine, il terzo problema riguarda la clausola relativa ai crimini secondo i principi generali di diritto riconosciuti dalle nazioni civili (o dalla comunità delle nazioni), che è prevista dalla Convenzione europea, dal Patto sui diritti civili e politici e dalla Carta dei diritti fondamentali dell'UE. Questa clausola pone due questioni interpretative.

La prima è se la formula dei "principi generali" debba essere intesa come un riferimento al diritto internazionale esistente (*rectius* ad una delle fonti di tale diritto)[571] oppure a principi che sono in via di formazione o consolidazione, ma che non possono ancora essere considerati come diritto internazionale[572]. Ci sembra che la prima interpretazione sia preferibile.

---

[565] ECtHR, *Engel and Others v. The Netherlands*.

[566] Vedi Focarelli (2001), pp. 125-134. Per altre sentenze della Corte europea vedi Id. (2013), pp. 166-167; Zagrebelski *et al.* (2019), pp. 256-260.

[567] Zagrebelski *et al.* (2019), p. 248.

[568] Vedi, ad esempio, in materia di *ne bis in idem* (art. 4 del Protocollo n. 7 alla Convenzione europea), ECtHR, *Grande Stevens and Others v. Italy*, parr. 94-101 e 222.

[569] Vedi Pustorino (2019), p. 153, che cita ECtHR, *Contrada v. Italy (No. 3)*.

[570] Vedi Zagrebelski *et al.* (2019), pp. 260-261 e la giurisprudenza ivi citata.

[571] Per questa tesi vedi Kälin, Künzli (2009), p. 463; Focarelli (2013), pp. 167-168; Pustorino (2019), pp. 153-154.

[572] Così Zagrebelski *et al.* (2019), p. 272.

La seconda questione è se la clausola in oggetto debba essere interpretata come un'eccezione al principio di irretroattività dei reati e delle pene[573] oppure se essa si limiti a "precisare" tale principio, specificando che esso si applica anche quando si tratta di crimini previsti da una fonte un po' particolare e di difficile reperimento e definizione, quali i principi generali riconosciuti dalle nazioni civili[574]. L'ambiguità della clausola deriva, probabilmente, dal suo scopo originario, che era quello di evitare il ripetersi delle contestazioni che erano state sollevate dalla difesa degli imputati durante il Processo di Norimberga, a proposito dell'accusa di crimini contro l'umanità, giudicati contrari al principio di irretroattività del diritto penale. Pertanto, la funzione della clausola era, ed è, quella di permettere la condanna di autori di crimini internazionali commessi durante la guerra o durante regimi totalitari, anche se tali crimini non erano previsti come reati dalle norme statali vigenti al momento della loro commissione.

Per questi motivi la clausola, a nostro avviso, non intende costituire un'eccezione al principio di irretroattività del diritto penale; ma piuttosto specificare che, fra le fonti del diritto internazionale, vanno compresi anche i principi generali di diritto riconosciuti dalle nazioni civili. Il riferimento a questa fonte consente maggiore flessibilità nell'applicazione del diritto internazionale, specie considerando che, in materia penale, l'apporto dei principi derivanti dagli ordinamenti statali può essere significativo. Questa interpretazione trova conferma nella prassi. Infatti, la Corte di Strasburgo ed il Comitato dei diritti umani, quando hanno dovuto affrontare casi nei quali veniva in luce la questione dell'applicazione retroattiva del diritto penale, hanno sempre affermato che gli Stati potevano giudicare gli autori dei crimini, poiché essi erano previsti dal diritto internazionale al momento della loro commissione; e pertanto hanno escluso che le norme penali avessero un'applicazione retroattiva, sia pure a titolo di eccezione. Si possono citare, fra gli altri, i casi *Streletz*[575], *Kononov*[576], *Maktouf*[577] e *Baumgarten*[578].

20.3. *Obblighi*

Ai diritti umani "basilari" degli imputati, che derivano dai principi di legalità penale e di irretroattività dei reati e delle pene, corrispondono, come al solito, obblighi statali di varia natura. Essi sono soprattutto a carico degli organi giurisdizionali e legislativi.

Fra tali obblighi rileva, in primo luogo, l'obbligo negativo degli organi statali (*in primis* dei giudici) di astenersi dall'applicare agli imputati eventuali norme penali esistenti che siano in contrasto con i due principi suddetti. In secondo luogo, vi possono essere obblighi positivi (immediati e di risultato) a carico degli organi legislativi, come quello di eliminare o modificare disposizioni normative che contrastino con i due principi. Inoltre, poiché il principio di legalità, come si è visto, impone che le norme penali siano accessibi-

---

[573] Sembra questa l'opinione di Pustorino (2019), pp. 153-154.

[574] In questo senso Zagrebelski *et al.* (2019), p. 272. Secondo Focarelli (2013), p. 167, quando si tratta di crimini internazionali, si deve presumere, in linea di massima, che il reato, anche se non previsto dal diritto interno al momento della commissione, fosse prevedibile o previsto dal diritto internazionale.

[575] ECtHR, *Streletz, Kessler and Krenz v. Germany*, parr. 75, 89 e 102 ss.

[576] ECtHR, *Kononov v. Latvia*, parr. 207 e 213.

[577] ECtHR, *Maktouf and Damjanović v. Bosnia and Herzegovina*, par. 72.

[578] HRCtee, *Baumgarten v. Germany*, par. 9.5.

li, chiare e prevedibili per tutti i destinatari, il legislatore statale dovrà anche assicurare che tali criteri siano rispettati [579]. Quest'obbligo grava anche sui giudici interni, nel momento in cui essi siano chiamati ad un'interpretazione ed applicazione del diritto penale.

Sezione VI
PROTEZIONE DELL'IDENTITÀ ESSENZIALE DELLA PERSONA

Un altro scopo preminente, nel quadro della tutela dei diritti umani, è quello di proteggere l'identità della persona, quando certe componenti essenziali di tale identità, quali la razza, l'origine etnica, il sesso, la lingua o la religione, sono sottoposte ad aggressione tramite un trattamento discriminatorio. Cioè quando una persona è soggetta a misure di esclusione, a forme di pregiudizio o addirittura di odio per motivi della sua appartenenza ad un certo gruppo o per motivi innati [580]. In questi casi, la persona è trattata in maniera discriminatoria non per il suo comportamento, ma per le caratteristiche che essa possiede come essere umano [581]. Pertanto, in queste situazioni, vi è uno stretto legame fra identità e dignità dell'individuo, e la discriminazione costituisce un vero e proprio assalto non solo all'identità della persona, ma anche alla dignità umana.

21. *Il divieto generale di discriminazione*

21.1. *Principi e norme*

Il divieto generale di discriminazione, a nostro avviso, deriva, più che da una norma, da un vero e proprio *principio generale* che sovrintende all'intero settore dei diritti umani, perché alla base di tale sistema vi sono sia l'idea dell'universalismo (come riconoscimento globale) dei diritti fondamentali sia quella, strettamente collegata, per cui gli Stati devono garantire tali diritti a *tutti gli esseri umani* senza discriminazioni [582].

Il principio di non discriminazione, infatti, viene espressamente riconosciuto come uno degli scopi principali delle Nazioni Unite, nell'art. 1(3) della Carta, secondo cui:

> "The purposes of the United Nations are: […] To achieve international co-operation […] in promoting and encouraging respect for human rights and for fundamental freedoms for all without distinction as to race, sex, language, or religion […]".

---

[579] Vedi, ad es., ECtHR, *Kafkaris v. Cyprus* e *Kasymakhunov and Saybatalov v. Russia*, nei quali la Corte ha accertato una violazione dell'art. 7 della Convenzione europea per mancanza di chiarezza e precisione, rispettivamente nella legislazione penale cipriota ed in quella russa.

[580] Kälin, Künzli (2009), p. 344.

[581] *Ibidem*, p. 345.

[582] Vedi *supra*, Cap. I, par. 4.

Il medesimo principio viene ribadito negli artt. 55 e 56 della Carta, laddove si collega il rispetto dei diritti umani da parte delle NU e degli Stati al mantenimento di relazioni pacifiche ed amichevoli fra le nazioni. Anche nella Dichiarazione universale il principio di non discriminazione ha un ruolo preminente; ma ad esso si accompagna anche il *principio di uguaglianza*. Infatti, l'art. 1 della Dichiarazione universale proclama che:

> "All human beings are born free and equal in dignity and rights [...]".

Subito dopo, l'art. 2 formula solennemente il principio di non discriminazione:

> "Everyone is entitled to all the rights and freedoms set forth in this Declaration, without distinction of any kind, such as race, colour, sex, language, religion, political or other opinion, national or social origin, property, birth or other status [...]".

Il successivo art. 7 della Dichiarazione universale ribadisce ambedue i principi [583]. Infine, come vedremo in seguito, il divieto generale di discriminazione viene stabilito da un gran numero di trattati, universali e regionali, sui diritti umani; ed è confermato da una copiosa giurisprudenza delle corti e degli altri organi internazionali di controllo sui diritti umani.

Tuttavia, conviene notare che sia il principio di non discriminazione che quello di uguaglianza hanno un contenuto ed un ambito di applicazione piuttosto ampi ed indeterminati. Si configurano quindi, a mio parere, come *principi-quadro*, il cui contenuto può essere precisato da norme più specifiche, di carattere convenzionale o consuetudinario. Ciò premesso, si tratta ora di comprendere meglio il rapporto fra i due principi e poi di verificare se essi si siano davvero concretizzati, nel diritto internazionale dei diritti umani, in norme più specifiche. La questione del rapporto fra il concetto di uguaglianza e quello di non discriminazione non è nuova, perché si è posta anche nella teoria generale del diritto e nei diritti costituzionali statali.

21.1.1. *Uguaglianza*

Il concetto giuridico di uguaglianza è complesso e multiforme, ed il suo contenuto è tuttora controverso. Qui siamo costretti ad una semplificazione estrema. La distinzione più nota è quella fra uguaglianza formale e sostanziale. L'uguaglianza formale richiede un trattamento uguale degli uguali, secondo la nota formula aristotelica. Invece l'uguaglianza sostanziale tende a cambiare lo *status quo*, per rimuovere gli ostacoli di fatto che impediscono un'uguaglianza concreta. Un esempio della distinzione fra uguaglianza formale e sostanziale è fornito dai due commi dell'art. 3 della Costituzione italiana. Il primo comma recita:

> "Tutti i cittadini hanno pari dignità sociale e sono eguali davanti alla legge, senza distinzione di sesso, di razza, di lingua, di religione, di opinioni politiche, di condizioni personali e sociali".

Il secondo comma stabilisce che:

---

[583] UDHR, art. 7: "All are equal before the law and are entitled without any discrimination to equal protection of the law. All are entitled to equal protection against any discrimination in violation of this Declaration and against any incitement to such discrimination".

> "È compito della Repubblica rimuovere gli ostacoli di ordine economico e sociale, che, limitando di fatto la libertà e l'eguaglianza dei cittadini, impediscono il pieno sviluppo della persona umana e l'effettiva partecipazione di tutti i lavoratori all'organizzazione politica, economica e sociale del Paese".

Si deve aggiungere che il principio di uguaglianza formale si traduce, in moltissimi ordinamenti giuridici, nelle *due norme più specifiche* della uguaglianza dinanzi alla legge e della uguale protezione della legge. La prima norma stabilisce a favore del destinatario il diritto alla medesima interpretazione ed applicazione della legge; e quindi il suo rispetto è affidato al giudice ed all'interprete. Invece, la norma sulla uguale protezione della legge prevede a favore del destinatario il diritto di essere trattato ugualmente dalla legge; e quindi il suo rispetto è affidato al legislatore.

Nel diritto internazionale dei diritti umani, queste due norme, che specificano e concretizzano il principio di uguaglianza formale, si trovano in alcuni documenti o trattati; ma essi non sono numerosi. Come si è visto, l'art. 7 della Dichiarazione universale contiene ambedue le norme:

> "All are equal before the law and are entitled without any discrimination to equal protection of the law [...]".

Una formula identica è contenuta nella prima frase dell'art. 26 del Patto sui diritti civili e politici; mentre formule simili si trovano nella Convenzione americana (art. 24), nella Carta africana (art. 3) e nella Carta araba (art. 11). Invece, altri trattati contengono soltanto la norma sulla uguaglianza dinanzi alla legge. Ad esempio, l'art. 20 della Carta dei diritti fondamentali dell'UE dispone:

> "Everyone is equal before the law".

Infine, vi sono trattati importanti che non prevedono né il principio generale di uguaglianza né le due norme che lo specificano. In questo senso è esemplare la Convenzione europea dei diritti dell'uomo, che contiene solo disposizioni sul divieto di discriminazione.

Quali conclusioni si possono trarre sul principio di uguaglianza (formale) nel diritto internazionale? A noi sembra che le disposizioni convenzionali sul principio di uguaglianza, con i suoi due corollari dell'uguaglianza dinanzi alla legge e di uguale protezione della legge, siano di numero piuttosto limitato. Per di più, le poche norme pattizie esistenti hanno un contenuto generico e indeterminato. Cosa significa, nel diritto internazionale, affermare che tutti hanno diritto alla medesima interpretazione ed applicazione della legge? Oppure che tutti hanno diritto ad essere trattati ugualmente dalla legge? Ci sembra che queste regole internazionali sull'uguaglianza siano incomplete, perché in sostanza rinviano per la loro applicazione ed interpretazione ai legislatori ed ai giudici interni degli Stati. E gli ordinamenti statali possono completare e specificare in maniera diversa fra loro tali regole.

Pertanto, a nostro avviso, il numero esiguo delle norme convenzionali sull'uguaglianza ed il loro contenuto indeterminato ed incompleto inducono ad escludere che si sia formata in materia una norma consuetudinaria, con i suoi due corollari.

21.1.2. *Non discriminazione*

Il discorso, invece, è differente per quanto riguarda il principio generale di non discriminazione. In realtà anche tale principio (o divieto generale di discriminazione) è controverso nella teoria generale del diritto e nei diritti costituzionali degli Stati. In sintesi, si può dire che esistono due modelli applicativi diversi (o, se si vuole, due interpretazioni diverse) del principio. Secondo un primo modello, il principio di non discriminazione viene visto semplicemente come l'aspetto negativo del principio di uguaglianza. Pertanto, si suole dire che è vietato un trattamento disuguale degli uguali, senza motivi oggettivi e ragionevoli. E, inversamente, che è vietato trattare in maniera uguale situazioni che siano significativamente diverse. A nostro parere, il problema di questo modello è che esso si limita a riprodurre il contenuto generico ed indeterminato del principio di uguaglianza.

Invece, in base ad un secondo modello, il principio di non discriminazione è più preciso e completo rispetto a quello di uguaglianza, poiché presuppone che si stabiliscano *i criteri di discriminazione vietati*; cioè i motivi che non possono essere invocati per giustificare un trattamento disuguale. Ad esempio, si può stabilire che è vietata la discriminazione per motivi di razza o di sesso, o per altri motivi espressamente indicati.

È questa seconda concezione quella che è stata accolta nel diritto internazionale dei diritti umani. Infatti, il divieto di discriminazione, come già detto, è contenuto in tutti i principali documenti e trattati sui diritti umani; ma esso viene *sempre* specificato, con un elenco esplicito dei criteri di discriminazione vietati. In questo senso, si sono già citati l'art. 1(3) della Carta delle NU e l'art. 2 della Dichiarazione universale. Il Patto sui diritti civili e politici, usando una formula assai simile a quella della Dichiarazione universale, stabilisce, all'art. 2(1), che:

> "Each State Party to the present Covenant undertakes to respect and to ensure to all individuals within its territory and subject to its jurisdiction the rights recognized in the present Covenant, without distinction of any kind, such as race, colour, sex, language, religion, political or other opinion, national or social origin, property, birth or other status".

Quindi l'art. 26 del Patto, dopo aver stabilito nella prima frase il principio di uguaglianza, prosegue specificando che:

> "In this respect, the law shall prohibit any discrimination and guarantee to all persons equal and effective protection against discrimination on any ground such as race, colour, sex, language, religion, political or other opinion, national or social origin, property, birth or other status".

L'art. 14 della Convenzione europea ha un contenuto quasi identico a quello dell'art. 2(1) del Patto sui diritti civili e politici. E molto simile è il contenuto delle norme sul divieto di discriminazione contenute negli altri principali trattati sui diritti umani, quali il Patto sui diritti economici, sociali e culturali (art. 2(2)), la Convenzione americana (art. 1(1)), la Carta africana (art. 2), la Carta araba (art. 3), la Carta sociale europea (riveduta) (art. E), la Carta dei diritti fondamentali dell'UE (art. 21(1)), la Convenzione sui diritti del fanciullo (art. 2(1)).

Si deve, tuttavia, notare che la maggior parte di queste norme stabilisce un divieto di discriminazione c.d. "accessorio"; cioè che opera soltanto in collegamento con gli altri diritti umani sostanziali previsti dal trattato in questione. In altri termini, vi deve essere discriminazione nel godimento di uno dei diritti garantiti dal trattato. Invece, un numero minore di disposizioni stabilisce un divieto di discriminazione c.d. "autonomo"; cioè che protegge le persone dalla discriminazione *anche* nel godimento di diritti diversi da quelli elencati nel trattato in questione. Esempi sono dati dall'art. 21(1) della Carta dei diritti fondamentali dell'UE e dall'art. 1 del Protocollo n. 12 alla Convenzione europea, che integra l'art. 14 della Convenzione (che conteneva un divieto di discriminazione solo "accessorio").

Quanto all'elenco dei criteri di discriminazione vietati, si può rilevare che esso, nei vari trattati, è talora esemplificativo e talora tassativo. La prima formulazione è preferibile, perché consente alla norma di adattarsi più facilmente all'evoluzione del contesto sociale e dei nuovi motivi di discriminazione che possono divenire via via rilevanti a livello internazionale. Inoltre, vi sono alcune differenze nei criteri previsti dai vari trattati; ma, ad un loro esame comparativo, risulta che alcuni criteri sono quasi sempre previsti: essi sono la razza, il colore, il sesso, la lingua, la religione, le opinioni politiche o di altro genere, l'origine nazionale o sociale, la proprietà, la nascita.

Da questo fatto si ricava una conclusione importante; e cioè che, nel diritto internazionale dei diritti umani, il divieto di discriminazione ha uno scopo generale ed unitario, che *non corrisponde* necessariamente ai divieti di discriminazione previsti nei diritti statali. Tale scopo, come avevamo già accennato, è quello di proibire i trattamenti diversi delle persone fatti per motivi che costituiscono anche componenti dell'identità delle persone medesime. Cioè di vietare che una persona sia sottoposta a misure discriminatorie a causa della sua appartenenza ad un certo gruppo o per motivi innati[584]. In questi casi, la discriminazione colpisce la persona non per il suo comportamento, ma per i caratteri che essa possiede come essere umano. Infatti l'identità di una persona dipende in gran parte dalla sua razza, dalla sua origine etnica, dal suo sesso, dalla sua lingua, dalla sua religione, ecc. Sono i caratteri che definiscono ciascun individuo. Pertanto, come si era detto, visto lo stretto legame fra l'identità di un individuo e la sua dignità, la discriminazione costituisce un'aggressione alla dignità umana[585]. Ciò spiega l'importanza del divieto di discriminazione nel quadro del diritto internazionale dei diritti umani.

21.1.3. *Il divieto generale di discriminazione come principio-quadro*

Dobbiamo adesso chiederci se il divieto generale di discriminazione, contenuto nelle norme convenzionali citate, sia incorporato anche in una norma di diritto internazionale generale. A nostro avviso, la risposta è affermativa; ma, come si è detto sopra, ci sembra più corretto parlare di un principio generale del diritto internazionale, e più precisamente di un principio-quadro che sovraintende e controlla il settore dei diritti umani, piuttosto che di una norma consuetudinaria. Ciò perché il suo contenuto, pur essendo più preciso rispetto a quello del principio di uguaglianza, è pur sempre ampio, comprendendo una vasta serie di criteri di discriminazione. Vedremo in seguito che, quantomeno per alcuni di tali criteri, si sono create la prassi e l'*opinio iuris* necessarie per la formazione di una norma consuetudinaria specifica[586].

Tuttavia, questo principio-quadro è utile, perché conferisce unitarietà alle norme più specifiche, convenzionali e consuetudinarie, sul divieto di discriminazione; e serve come parametro di riferimento per la loro interpretazione. Per comprendere ciò, conviene adesso

---

[584] Kälin, Künzli (2009), p. 344.

[585] *Ibidem*, p. 345.

[586] Vedi *infra*, par. 22, sul divieto di discriminazione razziale.

approfondire il discorso sul contenuto del divieto di discriminazione e sul modo con cui esso funziona.

21.2. *Contenuto del divieto*

Per precisare il contenuto del divieto di discriminazione, si devono individuare i suoi elementi costitutivi. Infatti, sarebbe sbagliato pensare che ogni distinzione fra persone costituisca una discriminazione. Occorrono invece alcune precise condizioni. In primo luogo, occorre che vi sia un *trattamento diseguale fra persone o situazioni uguali*, costituito, ad esempio, da distinzioni, limiti, restrizioni, esclusioni, punizioni o preferenze. In secondo luogo, occorre che il trattamento diseguale crei uno *svantaggio* rispetto ad altre persone che hanno le stesse caratteristiche o che si trovino in situazioni simili [587].

In terzo luogo, come si è già detto, occorre che il trattamento diseguale e svantaggioso sia fatto sulla base di uno dei *motivi di discriminazione vietati*. Ma si noti che non sempre esiste un collegamento diretto e immediato fra trattamento diseguale e motivo di discriminazione. A questo proposito, rileva la distinzione fra discriminazioni *dirette* ed *indirette*. La discriminazione diretta (o formale) si realizza quando il trattamento diseguale è direttamente collegato ad uno dei motivi di discriminazione vietati (ad esempio, il sesso). Invece, la discriminazione indiretta si verifica quando il trattamento diseguale non è esplicitamente collegato ad uno dei criteri vietati (ad esempio, il sesso), ma, di fatto, produce effetti sfavorevoli soltanto o prevalentemente per le persone che hanno quelle caratteristiche (ad esempio, le donne).

In quarto luogo, prima di poter concludere che un trattamento è discriminatorio, occorre di solito (ma non sempre) verificare se esso non sia *giustificato*. Più esattamente, si deve verificare se la differenza di trattamento abbia giustificazioni oggettive e ragionevoli, perché persegue uno *scopo legittimo* e, in caso di risposta positiva, se tale differenza sia *proporzionata*, cioè necessaria e non eccessiva per perseguire tale scopo. Le due condizioni dello scopo legittimo e della proporzionalità risultano chiaramente dalla prassi degli organi internazionali di controllo dei trattati sui diritti umani. Ad esempio, il Comitato dei diritti umani ha affermato che:

> "not every distinction constitutes discrimination, in violation of article 26, but that distinction must be justified on reasonable and objective grounds, in pursuit of an aim that is legitimate under the Covenant" [588].

La Corte di Strasburgo adotta un approccio simile. Con una formula celebre, nel *Caso linguistico belga*, la Corte ha sostenuto che:

---

[587] Conviene precisare che una discriminazione può talora consistere, anziché nel trattamento diverso di situazioni eguali, nel trattamento eguale di situazioni che siano significativamente diverse. In questo caso la discriminazione (c.d. materiale) deriva dal fatto che non vengono tenuti in considerazione certi elementi distintivi della situazione, che richiedono invece considerazione. Cfr. Zagrebelsky *et al.* (2016), p. 141.

[588] HRCtee, *Love et al. v. Australia*, par. 8.2. Vedi anche HRCtee, General Comment No. 18, 10 November 1989, par. 13: "[…] not every differentiation of treatment will constitute discrimination, if the criteria for such differentiation are reasonable and objective and if the aim is to achieve a purpose which is legitimate under the Covenant".

"[…] the principle of equality of treatment is violated if the distinction has no objective and reasonable justification. The existence of such a justification must be assessed in relation to the aim and effects of the measure under consideration, regard being had to the principles which normally prevail in democratic societies. A difference of treatment in the exercise of a right laid down in the Convention must not only pursue a legitimate aim: Article 14 […] is likewise violated when it is clearly established that there is no reasonable relationship of proportionality between the means employed and the aim sought to be realized"[589].

Anche la Corte interamericana[590] ed altri organi internazionali di controllo adottano un simile *test*.

La questione delle giustificazioni assume particolare rilevanza nel caso delle discriminazioni fondate sull'origine nazionale, ad esempio nel trattamento dei migranti. È chiaro che uno Stato può legittimamente fare differenze di trattamento fra cittadini e stranieri, e che ciò non costituisce di per sé discriminazione; ma le differenze di trattamento devono perseguire uno scopo legittimo ed essere proporzionate. Inoltre, i diritti umani "fondamentali", come il diritto alla vita, il divieto di tortura o trattamenti inumani, i diritti di sussistenza, il divieto di arresti o detenzioni arbitrari, il diritto di accesso alla giustizia, devono essere garantiti agli stranieri senza alcuna restrizione[591].

21.3. *Obblighi*

Il divieto generale di discriminazione impone agli Stati, in primo luogo, l'obbligo negativo di astenersi dal discriminare le persone per uno dei motivi vietati ed in maniera ingiustificata. In secondo luogo, esso impone anche numerosi obblighi positivi di varia natura: ad esempio, l'obbligo di prevenire e reprimere discriminazioni di persone da parte di altri individui e l'obbligo di adottare misure legislative ed amministrative in vari settori della vita sociale, volte ad eliminare le discriminazioni. Tra gli obblighi positivi, vi possono essere anche quelli di adottare trattamenti preferenziali di protezione a favore di persone o gruppi svantaggiati (ad esempio, donne, disabili, minoranze) per rimediare, sulla base del principio di *uguaglianza sostanziale*, a situazioni di svantaggio strutturale[592]. In questo senso, si può citare, ad esempio, l'art. 4(1) della Convenzione sull'eliminazione della discriminazione contro le donne:

"Adoption by States Parties of temporary special measures aimed at accelerating de facto equality between men and women shall not be considered discrimination as defined in the present Convention […] these measures shall be discontinued when the objectives of equality of opportunity and treatment have been achieved".

[589] ECtHR, *Belgian Linguistic Case*, par. 10 (The Law – B. Interpretation adopted by the Court).

[590] IACtHR, *Proposed Amendments of the Naturalization Provisions of the Constitution of Costa Rica*, parr. 56-57.

[591] Così anche Kälin, Künzli (2009), p. 490.

[592] Cfr. Focarelli (2013), p. 228.

22. *Il divieto di discriminazione razziale*

Merita un sintetico cenno a sé il tema del divieto di discriminazione razziale, intesa in senso ampio, come comprensiva delle discriminazioni fondate sulla razza, il colore o l'origine etnica, e come comprensiva delle politiche di *apartheid*. L'importanza di questo tema è confermata dal fatto che la comunità internazionale gli ha dedicato una particolare attenzione.

Si deve premettere che, come si è già detto, nel diritto internazionale sono vietate le discriminazioni che colpiscono le persone per i motivi che costituiscono componenti della loro identità come esseri umani. Pertanto, tali discriminazioni rappresentano sempre un attacco all'identità essenziale delle persone. Tuttavia, ciò non significa che tutte le discriminazioni siano poste sul medesimo piano o che esse abbiano tutte la medesima gravità. La prassi internazionale ed il consenso della comunità internazionale indicano che certe discriminazioni colpiscono in maniera particolarmente severa la dignità umana. Si tratta, in particolare, delle discriminazioni fondate sulla razza, il colore, o l'origine etnica. L'*apartheid* costituisce una pratica sistematica di discriminazione razziale.

La comunità internazionale ha condotto una lotta speciale volta alla eliminazione della discriminazione razziale. Essa si è svolta anche in conseguenza di tragiche esperienze storiche, più o meno risalenti, quali la schiavitù, il colonialismo, l'Olocausto nazista ed il regime di *apartheid* in Sudafrica. Per le azioni svolte nel quadro delle NU, si possono ricordare, fra l'altro, le prime iniziative e poi gli sviluppi a favore del principio di autodeterminazione dei popoli, la ferma condanna del Sudafrica negli anni 1960, la Convenzione del 1965 contro la discriminazione razziale[593] e la Convenzione del 1973 contro l'*apartheid*[594]. Queste due convenzioni sono molto importanti. Abbiamo già descritto, in sintesi, il loro contenuto e ci limiteremo qui a sottolineare alcuni aspetti che riguardano le nozioni di "razza" e di "*apartheid*".

La Convenzione del 1965 contro la discriminazione razziale cerca di eliminare tale discriminazione in tutte le sue forme e di combattere le dottrine razziste[595]. Essa afferma, nel suo Preambolo, che:

> "[...] any doctrine of superiority based on racial differentiation is scientifically false, morally condemnable, socially unjust and dangerous [...]"[596]

e che:

> "[...] discrimination between human beings on the ground of race, colour or ethnic origin is an obstacle to friendly and peaceful relations among nations and is capable of disturbing peace and security among peoples [...]"[597].

Come si vede, la discriminazione razziale viene considerata addirittura come un ostacolo ai rapporti pacifici fra gli Stati ed una minaccia per la pace e la sicurezza internazionale.

---

[593] Vedi *supra*, Cap. IV, par. 5.2.3.

[594] Vedi *supra*, Cap. IV, par. 5.2.4.

[595] CERD, Preamble, par. 10.

[596] *Ibidem*, par. 6.

[597] *Ibidem*, par. 7.

Peraltro, la nozione di "razza", se riferita agli esseri umani, solleva una serie di problemi [598]. Le concezioni biologiche di razza, per molto tempo dominanti, sono oggi superate dalla scienza, che ha dimostrato che esse sono infondate; poiché la biologia evolutiva ha dimostrato che non esistono gruppi razziali fissi o discontinui, e che quindi possano essere biologicamente definiti. In sostanza, si ritiene oggi comunemente che le categorie razziali siano costrutti sociali. In effetti, la Convenzione del 1965 sembra rifiutare le concezioni biologiche di razza ed essere invece influenzata dalle esperienze storiche del colonialismo e del regime di *apartheid* in Sudafrica [599]. Se si segue questa impostazione, la nozione di "razza" non dipende più da differenze di carattere biologico; ma piuttosto da un *fattore sociale* di attribuzione della "razza" e di esclusione e disprezzo del "diverso da sé". In altri termini, si tende ad associare la nozione di razza ad un gruppo di persone *percepite come inferiori* da altri gruppi, a causa di certi caratteri fisici evidenti e/o di certi caratteri culturali.

Questa concezione è più moderna e corretta, perché ammette che tutti gli esseri umani sono biologicamente uguali e non possono essere discriminati per motivi biologico-genetici. Ma essa, paradossalmente, fondandosi non più su fattori scientifici bensì su fattori sociali piuttosto ardui da definire, rende più difficile individuare le persone che hanno diritto a non esser discriminate per motivi di razza [600], salvo che nelle situazioni in cui in uno Stato esistano norme o prassi diffuse che emarginano esplicitamente certi gruppi, come è avvenuto nel caso nel regime di *apartheid* in Sudafrica. Il Comitato sulla eliminazione della discriminazione razziale ha cercato di risolvere questo problema, affermando che l'identificazione di un individuo, come membro di un particolare gruppo razziale o etnico, dovrà essere fondata, se non esistono motivi contrari, sulla *autoidentificazione* da parte dell'individuo interessato [601]. Tuttavia, questo criterio, di carattere soggettivistico, non ci sembra molto preciso.

La Convenzione del 1973 contro l'*apartheid*, che era già una pratica vietata dall'art. 3 della Convenzione del 1965, ha soprattutto lo scopo di punire penalmente tale pratica, dichiarata espressamente dalla Convenzione come un crimine contro l'umanità, che viola i principi del diritto internazionale e della Carta delle NU, e che costituisce una grave minaccia alla pace e sicurezza internazionale. La nozione di *apartheid* è evidentemente più facile a definirsi rispetto a quella di razza; e comunque la Convenzione del 1973 prevede una definizione molto dettagliata di tale crimine [602].

La prassi degli organi internazionali di controllo sui diritti umani conferma che la discriminazione razziale è considerata come la forma più grave ed odiosa di discriminazione, tale da incidere addirittura sul concetto di democrazia, che presuppone una società aperta alle diversità. La Corte europea, ad esempio, nel caso *D.H. and Others*, ha affermato che:

---

[598] Vedi Kälin, Künzli (2009), p. 368.

[599] Vedi CERD, Preamble, par. 5.

[600] Kälin, Künzli (2009), p. 369.

[601] CteeERD, General Recommendation No. VIII concerning the interpretation and application of article 1, paragraphs 1 and 4 of the Convention (Identification with a Particular Racial or Ethnic Group), 22 August 1990.

[602] CSPCA, art. II.

"Racial discrimination is a particularly invidious kind of discrimination and, in view of its perilous consequences, requires from the authorities special vigilance and a vigorous reaction. It is for this reason that the authorities must use all available means to combat racism, thereby reinforcing democracy's vision of a society in which diversity is not perceived as a threat but as a source of enrichment [...]"[603].

La medesima Corte, nel caso *Nachova*, a proposito dell'obbligo degli Stati di investigare su atti di violenza razzista, ha detto che:

"[W]here there is suspicion that racial attitudes induced a violent act is particularly important that the official investigation is pursued with vigour and impartiality, having regard to the need to reassert continuously society's condemnation of racism and ethnic hatred and to maintain the confidence of minorities in the ability of the authorities to protect them [...] [W]hen investigating violent incidents [...] State authorities have the additional duty to take all reasonable steps to unmask any racist motive [...]"[604].

Inoltre, la Corte europea, nel caso *Moldovan*, ha ritenuto che la discriminazione razziale da parte di organi statali può, in certi casi, essere considerata anche come una forma di trattamento inumano e quindi costituire una violazione dell'art. 3 della Convenzione europea[605].

Su queste basi, ci sembra si possa concludere che la prassi e l'*opinio iuris* della comunità internazionale abbiano prodotto, nel tempo, lo sviluppo ed il consolidamento di una norma consuetudinaria, che vieta la discriminazione per motivi di razza, colore o etnia; e che il divieto di pratiche discriminatorie, riflettendo valori essenziali e irrinunciabili di tale comunità, abbia la natura di *ius cogens*.

23. *Il divieto di discriminazione contro le donne ed il diritto consuetudinario*

Si è detto sopra che il divieto generale di discriminazione è contemplato da un principio-quadro, che sovraintende a norme più particolari, convenzionali o consuetudinarie, che regolano *divieti specifici di discriminazione*. Ma ci sembra che, fra tali norme particolari, soltanto quella sul divieto di discriminazione razziale, appena esaminata, sia regolata dal diritto consuetudinario e quindi conferisca quei diritti umani "fondamentali" che sono oggetto del presente capitolo.

Tuttavia, per la sua importanza, merita qualche cenno qui anche l'azione della comunità internazionale volta all'eliminazione della discriminazione contro le donne[606]. Naturalmente, l'intero sistema della tutela internazionale dei diritti umani si fonda sul presupposto che tali diritti siano applicabili, nella stessa maniera, ad uomini e donne. Ma è noto che, nella storia dell'umanità ed anche nella società contemporanea, persistono disuguaglianze

---

603 ECtHR, *D.H. and Others v. Czech Republic*, par. 179.

604 ECtHR, *Nachova and Others*, Judgment of 26 February 2004, parr. 157-158; Id., *Nachova and Others*, Judgment of 6 July 2005, par. 160.

605 ECtHR, *Moldovan and Others v. Romania (No. 2)*, par. 113.

606 Più avanti, parleremo dei divieti di discriminazione collettiva (contro minoranze e popoli indigeni). Vedi *infra*, Cap. VI, parr. 17 e 18.

a svantaggio delle donne. È quindi logico che la comunità internazionale si sia posta l'obiettivo di agire per cercare di eliminare la discriminazione contro le donne.

In un primo tempo, peraltro, gli atti ed i trattati sui diritti umani si sono limitati a contenere disposizioni sul divieto generale di discriminazione che contemplassero anche il sesso fra i motivi di discriminazione proibiti. Con questa tecnica, come è stato notato [607], si creano norme sul *divieto di discriminazione per motivi di sesso* che operano in maniera *simmetrica*, cioè nello stesso modo per uomini e donne; e che tendono ad ottenere un'uguaglianza *formale*, che sia fondata soprattutto sulla legislazione degli Stati. Un esempio paradigmatico di questo approccio è dato dal combinato disposto degli artt. 2(1) e 26 del Patto sui diritti civili e politici. Tuttavia, questo tipo di norme, operando solo a livello formale, non è efficace per combattere contro la discriminazione *di fatto* nei confronti delle donne radicata storicamente nella società; cioè contro situazioni di discriminazione strutturale o sistemica.

In un secondo tempo, un'azione più incisiva viene iniziata, nel quadro delle Nazioni Unite, con la Convenzione sull'eliminazione della discriminazione contro le donne del 1979 [608], preceduta da un'analoga dichiarazione di principi [609]. Qui l'accento si sposta dal divieto di discriminazione per motivi di sesso al *divieto di discriminazione contro le donne*. Ma non è solo una questione terminologica: si tratta invece di predisporre una protezione soltanto a favore delle donne; cioè norme che operino in maniera *asimmetrica* [610] e che tendano a rimuovere gli ostacoli che impediscono alle donne di raggiungere un'uguaglianza *sostanziale*, nel godimento dei diritti umani, che non si fondi soltanto sulla legislazione, ma anche nella società.

Questo scopo, e questo diverso approccio al problema, risultano chiari dall'intera Convenzione del 1979, il cui contenuto abbiamo già sintetizzato in precedenza [611]. Qui ci limitiamo a ricordare che la Convenzione stabilisce, a carico degli Stati parti, una serie di obblighi positivi volti ad eliminare la discriminazione contro le donne in vari settori della loro vita privata, pubblica, economica e sociale. Essa prevede anche che gli Stati possano adottare "*affirmative actions*"; cioè misure speciali temporanee favorevoli solo alle donne, tese ad accelerare una uguaglianza di fatto fra uomini e donne [612]. La prassi del Comitato sulla eliminazione della discriminazione contro le donne conferma questa impostazione più moderna e realistica del problema.

L'idea che si debba predisporre una protezione speciale per le donne, specie nei settori e nelle situazioni di loro maggiore vulnerabilità, trova realizzazione anche in una serie di strumenti internazionali di carattere settoriale e specifico, ad esempio trattati sulla protezione delle donne nel campo del lavoro, trattati contro la tratta delle donne e la prostitu-

---

[607] Kälin, Künzli (2009), pp. 357-360.

[608] Convention on the Elimination of All Forms of Discrimination against Women (CEDAW), 18 December 1979.

[609] Declaration on the Elimination of Discrimination against Women, 7 November 1967.

[610] Vedi Kälin, Künzli (2009), pp. 357 e 360-363.

[611] Vedi *supra*, Cap. IV, par. 5.2.5.

[612] CEDAW, art. 4: "Adoption by States Parties of temporary special measures aimed at accelerating de facto equality between men and women shall not be considered discrimination as defined in the present Convention [...]".

zione, norme di diritto umanitario designate alla protezione delle donne, dichiarazioni ed altri atti tesi a proteggere la violenza contro le donne.

Quest'ultimo tema è oggetto anche di un recente ed importante trattato nel quadro del Consiglio d'Europa: la Convenzione di Istanbul contro la violenza nei confronti delle donne e la violenza domestica del 2011 [613]. La Convenzione è molto ampia e stabilisce a carico degli Stati parti una serie dettagliata di obblighi, che riguardano, fra l'altro, misure di prevenzione (Cap. III), di protezione e sostegno (Cap. IV), di modifiche legislative interne relative alle indagini ed i processi civili e penali contro i responsabili degli abusi (Capp. V e VI), impegni di cooperazione internazionale (Cap. VIII). È previsto anche un meccanismo di controllo, affidato ad un gruppo di esperti indipendenti ("GREVIO"), che ha, peraltro, il compito tradizionale di esaminare i rapporti degli Stati parti e di adottare raccomandazioni. Ci sembra che la parte più innovativa della Convenzione sia costituita dalle dettagliate disposizioni relative alle indagini ed i procedimenti giurisdizionali contro i responsabili delle violenze ed ai risarcimenti spettanti alle vittime. Tuttavia, è chiaro che tali disposizioni, per essere efficaci, necessitano di attuazione interna da parte degli Stati.

In conclusione, si può sostenere che il divieto di discriminazione per motivi di sesso ed il divieto di discriminazione contro le donne siano entrati a far parte del diritto internazionale generale? Ci sembra che, purtroppo, la risposta debba essere negativa: la permanenza di tradizioni storiche di disuguaglianze fra uomini e donne in molti Paesi del mondo impedisce ancora la formazione della prassi e dell'*opinio iuris* generalizzate ed uniformi della comunità internazionale, che sono necessarie per la formazione di una norma consuetudinaria [614]. La stessa conclusione vale per la formazione di un eventuale principio generale di diritto riconosciuto dalle nazioni *in foro domestico.* Tuttavia, è anche vero che, quantomeno sul divieto di discriminazione per motivi di sesso, il consenso della comunità internazionale sta sempre più crescendo.

Sezione VII

PROTEZIONE DELLA VOLONTÀ E IDENTITÀ DEI POPOLI

Si è parlato finora di diritti umani *individuali*; ed in effetti la grande maggioranza dei diritti umani si caratterizza in questo modo, perché essi hanno tradizionalmente lo scopo di proteggere gli individui nei confronti dello Stato (o di altri enti titolari di obblighi relativi ai diritti umani). Questo carattere *individualistico* dei diritti umani, che trova le sue radici nel patrimonio culturale dell'Occidente, è stato spesso criticato, ma è tuttora dominante.

Peraltro, vi sono anche diritti umani che hanno lo scopo di proteggere un *gruppo di*

---

[613] Council of Europe Convention on prevention and combating violence against women and domestic violence, Istanbul, 11 May 2011.

[614] Anche l'adesione di un gran numero di Stati alla Convenzione del 1979 perde gran parte del suo valore se si considerano le numerose e importanti riserve formulate da molti Stati, soprattutto con riguardo a certi articoli "chiave" della Convenzione (artt. 2 e 16).

persone (popoli, minoranze, popoli indigeni) nei confronti dello Stato. Si parla, in questi casi, di diritti umani *collettivi*. Di questi diritti ci occuperemo in seguito [615]. Tuttavia, conviene qui esaminare un particolare diritto dei popoli, che possiamo includere fra i diritti umani "fondamentali", perché è protetto dal diritto internazionale generale. Si tratta del diritto dei popoli all'autodeterminazione, che ha la funzione essenziale di salvaguardare il valore della *volontà* e della *identità* di questi enti collettivi.

Si deve ribadire che, nel diritto internazionale, il popolo deve essere inteso come un'entità distinta rispetto allo Stato e che, quando si parla di norme sui diritti umani dei popoli, si fa riferimento a "norme che si occupano del popolo come contrapposto allo Stato, che si occupano dei governati come contrapposti ai governanti, che tendono [...] a tutelare il popolo rispetto all'apparato che lo governa" [616].

24. *Diritto dei popoli all'autodeterminazione*

24.1. *Il principio di autodeterminazione. Origine e sviluppo*

Il principio di autodeterminazione dei popoli, la cui importanza nel sistema complessivo del diritto internazionale va ben oltre il settore dei diritti umani, ha un'origine politica ed ideologica ed ha poi acquistato efficacia normativa. Esso fu proclamato inizialmente, a livello internazionale, da Lenin nell'Unione Sovietica e poi dal Presidente statunitense Wilson, sia pure con accezioni e contenuti parzialmente diversi [617]. L'idea politica alla base del principio era quella di dare un ruolo alla volontà ed alle aspirazioni dei popoli nelle relazioni internazionali, tradizionalmente riservate esclusivamente alla volontà degli Stati; e cioè ai governanti. L'autodeterminazione era concepita come principio democratico: i popoli avrebbero dovuto essere liberi da oppressioni esterne, specie dal dominio coloniale; ed avrebbero dovuto essere liberi di scegliere i propri governanti.

È chiaro che, così concepito, il principio di autodeterminazione dei popoli introduceva elementi dinamici e sovversivi nell'assetto tradizionale delle relazioni internazionali, erodeva il principio di sovranità territoriale degli Stati e metteva in crisi i regimi coloniali.

Nel periodo fra le due guerre mondiali, il principio fu applicato in Europa, ma non nelle colonie, dove vigeva in gran parte il sistema dei Mandati nel quadro della Società delle Nazioni. Tuttavia, la situazione cambiò con la redazione della Carta delle Nazioni Unite. La Carta sancisce il principio di autodeterminazione dei popoli negli artt. 1(2), 55 e 56. L'art. 1(2) prevede, fra i fini delle NU, quello:

> "to develop friendly relations among nations based on respect for the principle of [...]self-determination of peoples [...]".

Anche l'art. 55 parla di:

> "peaceful and friendly relations among nations based on respect for the principle of [...] self-determination of peoples".

---

[615] Vedi *infra*, Cap. VI, parr. 17-19.

[616] Conforti (2015), p. 27.

[617] Vedi, per tutti, Cassese (1984), pp. 154-155; Id. (1995), pp. 14-23.

L'art. 56 stabilisce che tutti gli Stati membri si impegnano ad agire per il raggiungimento degli obiettivi fissati dall'art. 55. Per la verità, nella Carta il principio di autodeterminazione aveva un contenuto programmatico e non ben precisato. Ma, negli anni successivi, l'intensa azione delle Nazioni Unite a favore del processo di decolonizzazione ha posto in primo piano l'importanza del principio, che era diventato una parte importante dell'agenda dell'Organizzazione. E ciò negli anni nei quali il Patto sui diritti civili e politici ed il Patto sui diritti economici, sociali e culturali venivano negoziati.

Infatti il principio di autodeterminazione è stato sancito, in maniera identica, nell'art. 1 di ambedue i Patti:

> "1. All peoples have the right of self-determination. By virtue of that right they freely determine their political status and freely pursue their economic, social and cultural development [...]
>
> 3. The States Parties to the present Covenant, including those having responsibility for the administration of Non-Self-Governing and Trust Territories, shall promote the realization of the right of self-determination, and shall respect that right, in conformity with the provisions of the Charter of the United Nations".

Nel frattempo il principio veniva ribadito in alcune solenni dichiarazioni di principi dell'Assemblea Generale delle NU, come la Dichiarazione del 1960 sull'indipendenza dei popoli coloniali[618], quella del 1962 sulla sovranità permanente sulle risorse naturali[619], e quella del 1970 sulle relazioni amichevoli fra gli Stati[620]. Pertanto, il principio si è progressivamente consolidato come giuridicamente vincolante nel diritto internazionale generale. Anche la Corte internazionale di giustizia ha riconosciuto tale carattere del principio nella sentenza del 1995 nel caso relativo al *Timor Orientale*[621] ed in alcuni importanti pareri, quale quello del 1971 sulla *Namibia*[622], quello del 1975 sul *Sahara occidentale*[623], quello del 2004 sul *Muro in Palestina*[624], quello del 2010 sul *Kosovo*[625], ed infine quello del 2019 sulla *Separazione dell'Arcipelago di Chagos*[626].

Tuttavia, come è stato notato dalla migliore dottrina[627], il principio di autodeterminazione costituisce un *principio-quadro*, che ha un contenuto generale ed indeterminato e che non indica i vari settori specifici nei quali esso deve trovare attuazione. Esso è stato poi completato da alcune *norme consuetudinarie*, che specificano, in relazione a singole aree, il contenuto normativo di tale principio. Conviene quindi esaminare queste norme,

---

[618] *Declaration on the Granting of Independence to Colonial Countries and Peoples*, GA Resolution 1514 (XV), 14 December 1960.

[619] *Permanent Sovereignty over Natural Resources*, GA Resolution 1803 (XVII), 14 December 1962.

[620] *Declaration on Principles of International Law Concerning Friendly Relations and Co-operation among States in accordance with the Charter of the United Nations*, GA Resolution 2625 (XXV), 24 October 1970.

[621] ICJ, *East Timor*, par. 29.

[622] ICJ, *Legal Consequences for States of the Continued Presence of South Africa in Namibia*, par. 52.

[623] ICJ, *Western Sahara*, par. 54.

[624] ICJ, *Legal Consequences of the Construction of a Wall in the Occupied Palestinian Territory*, par. 156.

[625] ICJ, *Accordance with International Law of the Unilateral Declaration of Independence in respect of Kosovo*, par. 79.

[626] ICJ, *Legal Consequences of the Separation of the Chagos Archipelago from Mauritius in 1965*, par. 155.

[627] Cassese (1995), pp. 126-133; Id. (2006), p. 136.

facendo anzitutto una distinzione fra autodeterminazione "esterna" ed autodeterminazione "interna".

24.2. *Diritto di autodeterminazione "esterna"*

Il diritto di autodeterminazione "esterna" significa che i popoli hanno diritto di divenire uno Stato indipendente e sovrano, o di associarsi o integrarsi con un altro Stato indipendente. Questo concetto è bene espresso nel seguente passaggio della citata Dichiarazione dell'Assemblea Generale delle NU del 1970 sulle relazioni amichevoli fra gli Stati:

> "The establishment of a sovereign and independent State, the free association with an independent State or the emergence into any other political status freely determined by a people constitute modes of implementing the right of self-determination by that people".

Ma si deve subito precisare che, nel diritto internazionale consuetudinario, l'ambito di applicazione di questo principio è molto più ristretto di quando comunemente si pensi, perché esso incontra *tre limiti* importanti.

Il primo limite deriva dal fatto che il principio si applica soltanto in *tre situazioni* o, se si vuole, a tre categorie di popoli. Infatti, se si esaminano le dichiarazioni degli Stati e la loro prassi effettiva, si deve concludere che il principio si applica solo alle seguenti ipotesi: *a*) ai popoli soggetti a dominazione coloniale; *b*) ai popoli di territori che sono stati conquistati ed occupati con la forza; *c*) ai popoli sottoposti ad un regime di *apartheid*. In altri termini, si sono formate norme consuetudinarie che hanno specificato il principio di autodeterminazione "esterna" soltanto in queste tre aree[628]. E sono norme di *ius cogens* e che stabiliscono obblighi *erga omnes*.

Un secondo limite è dato dal *carattere irretroattivo* del principio, nel caso dei popoli di territori che sono stati acquistati ed occupati con la forza. L'irretroattività significa che il principio non si applica quando la dominazione straniera risale ad un'epoca nella quale il principio non esisteva ancora, cioè prima della fine degli anni 1940. Ciò ha evidentemente lo scopo di non rimettere in discussione l'integrità di moltissimi Stati, che si sono storicamente formati prima di tale periodo, anche sulla base di eventi bellici, uso della forza e processi di conquista[629].

Infine, il terzo limite, più controverso nel suo contenuto, deriva dalla *nozione di popolo* e dal rapporto fra "popolo" e "minoranze". Una prima concezione, più tradizionale[630], ritiene che la nozione di popolo, ai fini della norma sull'autodeterminazione, coincida sostanzialmente con l'idea di *demos*, cioè di un gruppo di persone, generale ed indistinto, appartenente ad una certa entità territoriale. In altri termini, il popolo avrebbe carattere statuale-territoriale, e quindi sarebbe formato dall'unione degli abitanti di uno Stato o, qualora siano in corso processi di cambiamento che vedano emergere nuovi enti aventi diritto all'autodeterminazione, dall'intera popolazione dell'unità territoriale che era amministrata

---

[628] D'altra parte, l'ambito di applicazione attuale del principio risulta ancora più limitato, se si considera che due di queste tre ipotesi si riferiscono a fenomeni storici che appartengono al passato.

[629] Tuttavia, la tesi del carattere irretroattivo del principio, pur essendo dominante in dottrina, è messa in dubbio, in presenza di certe circostanze, da autorevoli studiosi. Vedi Crawford (2006), pp. 73 e 704-705.

[630] Vedi Tancredi (2001), p. 624.

come unità a sé durante la sottoposizione a dominio straniero. È chiaro che, secondo questa concezione, il concetto di popolo e quello di minoranza, che coincide piuttosto con l'idea di *éthnos*, sono nettamente separati.

Invece, partendo da una seconda concezione, la nozione di popolo si dovrebbe ampliare fino a comprendere anche "il popolo in senso etnico", identificato sulla base di criteri soggettivi (il senso di identificazione dei singoli membri del gruppo) ed oggettivi (lingua, cultura, religione, storia, tradizioni comuni, ecc.). Questa nozione estensiva di popolo finirebbe per ricomprendere anche le minoranze, o quantomeno alcune minoranze.

Vi è poi una tesi intermedia[631], secondo la quale la nozione di popolo avrebbe prevalentemente carattere etnico, ma dovrebbe essere integrata e completata da altri elementi, quali la dimensione del gruppo che aspira ad essere popolo, il suo riconoscimento a livello costituzionale ed il fatto che tale gruppo abbia un proprio *status* giuridico distinto.

In realtà, a nostro avviso, la prassi internazionale, in materia di autodeterminazione "esterna" dei popoli e di tentativi di secessione, conferma che la comunità internazionale riconosce ed accetta la nozione più tradizionale di "popolo" ed intende mantenere distinti i concetti di popolo e di minoranze[632]. Come vedremo[633], il discorso è in parte diverso per quanto riguarda l'autodeterminazione "interna". Pertanto, si deve concludere che il principio di autodeterminazione "esterna" non può essere invocato per legittimare pretese secessionistiche da parte di minoranze o di circoscrizioni territoriali etnicamente distinte dal resto del Paese (eccetto che nel caso di *apartheid*). Il diritto internazionale non intende favorire le secessioni da parte di minoranze; e, semmai, qualora la secessione di fatto riesca e si stabilizzi con un nuovo Stato, tale diritto può soltanto prendere atto della nuova situazione esistente, sulla base del principio di effettività.

In dottrina, alcuni autori sostengono che questa regola dovrebbe subire un'eccezione nel caso della c.d. *remedial secession*, cioè quando una minoranza all'interno di un Paese sia sottoposta a gravi violazioni dei diritti umani. Questa tesi è stata sostenuta anche dinanzi alla Corte internazionale di giustizia, nel caso del *Kosovo*[634]; ma la Corte non si è pronunciata su questo punto. Invece, la Corte Suprema del Canada, nel caso della *Secessione del Quebec*, sembra favorevole alla *remedial secession*, ma solo in casi eccezionali, quando i diritti del popolo vengano violati in modo grave e massiccio[635]. A nostro avviso, una norma consuetudinaria sulla *remedial secession* non si è ancora affermata nel diritto internazionale.

24.2.1. *Destinatari del diritto*

Lo Stato che governa illecitamente un territorio (o che pratica un regime di *apartheid*) è obbligato a consentire l'autodeterminazione del popolo. Ma si pone un problema per

---

[631] Vedi, ad es., la definizione di "popolo" che è stata data dall'UNESCO in un rapporto del 1989: *Final Report and Recommendations, International Meeting of Experts on Further Study of the Concept of the Rights of Peoples*, 27-30 November 1989, par. 22.

[632] In questo senso vedi anche Cassese (1995), pp. 348-349. Tuttavia questo autore (*ibidem*, pp. 348-363) propone, *de lege ferenda*, di estendere a certi gruppi etnici e minoranze i diritti di autodeterminazione esterna ed interna.

[633] Vedi *infra*, par. 24.3 e, per i popoli indigeni, Cap. VI, par. 18.

[634] ICJ, *Accordance with International Law of the Unilateral Declaration of Independence in respect of Kosovo*, par. 82.

[635] Supreme Court of Canada, *Re Secession of Quebec*, par. 138.

quanto riguarda i destinatari del corrispondente diritto. Si può davvero parlare di un vero e proprio diritto soggettivo internazionale dei popoli all'autodeterminazione?

Secondo alcuni autori [636], la risposta sarebbe negativa, poiché i rapporti di diritto internazionale intercorrerebbero in modo esclusivo tra gli Stati. Ciò sarebbe dimostrato dal fatto che solo gli altri Stati possono adottare misure sanzionatorie e fornire appoggio ai movimenti di liberazione nazionale che vogliono esercitare il loro diritto all'autodeterminazione.

Tuttavia, a noi sembra che questa interpretazione del principio sia riduttiva e risenta di un certo scetticismo nei confronti della soggettività internazionale dei gruppi di individui. A nostro avviso, il principio di autodeterminazione ha per destinatari formali non solo gli altri Stati, ma anche i popoli. Il fatto che i popoli non abbiano la possibilità di azionare garanzie internazionali a difesa del loro diritto non incide sull'esistenza di tale diritto. Anche gli individui non hanno, in molti casi, la possibilità di far valere sul piano internazionale certi diritti che sono loro attribuiti dal diritto internazionale; ma ciò non pregiudica l'esistenza di tali diritti. Ciò perché, come si è già avuto modo di dire [637], la titolarità di diritti sulla base di norme primarie del diritto internazionale non dipende dalla titolarità di garanzie di attuazione di tali diritti sulla base di norme secondarie.

Pertanto i popoli, cui spetta l'autodeterminazione, vantano un vero e proprio diritto soggettivo internazionale nei confronti dello Stato oppressore ed anche nei confronti degli Stati terzi, poiché questi ultimi devono astenersi dall'assistere lo Stato oppressore [638].

24.2.2. *Obblighi*

Gli Stati che opprimono i popoli, nelle tre situazioni in cui questi ultimi hanno il diritto di autodeterminazione "esterna", hanno l'obbligo negativo di consentire l'esercizio di tale diritto; ed in particolare di astenersi dal ricorrere alla minaccia o all'uso della forza contro tali popoli. D'altra parte, anche gli Stati terzi, come si è detto sopra, hanno un obbligo negativo: quello di astenersi dall'aiutare o assistere lo Stato oppressore.

Vi sono inoltre altri obblighi degli Stati, che derivano dal principio di autodeterminazione "esterna" dei popoli, ma che non attengono direttamente ai diritti umani, perché riguardano altri settori del diritto internazionale sui quali tale principio ha avuto un impatto. L'esempio principale è dato dal regime di acquisto della sovranità territoriale in violazione del principio di autodeterminazione: lo Stato responsabile della violazione ha l'obbligo di restituzione del territorio e tutti gli altri Stati hanno l'obbligo di negare effetti extraterritoriali agli atti di governo emanati in tale territorio [639].

24.3. *Diritto di autodeterminazione "interna"*

Si è parlato finora, soprattutto, del principio di autodeterminazione "esterna". Peraltro,

---

[636] Conforti (2015), p. 31.

[637] Vedi *supra*, Cap. I, par. 7.2 e Cap. III, par. 3.2.

[638] Vedi Cassese (1995), pp. 143-145; Id. (2006), p. 137.

[639] Vedi, per tutti, Conforti (2018), pp. 209-210. Secondo altri autori, tutti gli Stati avrebbero invece l'obbligo più incisivo di disconoscere l'acquisto illegittimo di sovranità. Cfr., ad es., Cassese (2006), p. 137.

anche se il principio è nato storicamente con tale connotazione, in chiave essenzialmente anticolonialista, con il tempo si è venuto affermando anche un suo aspetto "interno". Si parla quindi oggi anche di un diritto dei popoli all'autodeterminazione "interna".

In realtà, il contenuto di questo diritto è controverso. Il significato più comune è quello secondo cui il popolo di uno Stato sovrano ha diritto ad un governo che lo rappresenti ovvero ha il diritto di scegliere liberamente il proprio governo. Questo concetto, in realtà, sembra emergere anche dall'art. 1(1) dei due Patti delle Nazioni Unite del 1966. Tuttavia, si tratta di un concetto in apparenza semplice, ma che si presta a interpretazioni differenti; ed anche la nozione di "popolo" sembra essere più flessibile ed estensiva in materia di autodeterminazione "interna".

Secondo una prima interpretazione, l'autodeterminazione "interna" andrebbe intesa nel senso che i gruppi nazionali ed etnici all'interno di uno Stato avrebbero diritto a che il governo attribuisca loro importanza e tenga in debito conto le loro aspirazioni tramite strumenti quali plebisciti o referendum[640]. In un'accezione leggermente diversa, lo Stato, all'interno del quale esistono gruppi nazionali o etnici, dovrebbe concedere loro un elevato *grado di autonomia e di autogoverno nella sfera politica.* Ci sembra che sia questo il significato attribuito al diritto di autodeterminazione "interna" dalla Corte Suprema del Canada nel caso della *Secessione del Quebec*[641].

Ma esiste anche una seconda interpretazione del concetto di autodeterminazione "interna", che si è diffusa specie fra gli Stati occidentali. Questo concetto dovrebbe essere inteso come espressione del principio di legittimazione democratica dei governi. In altri termini, esso significherebbe il diritto del popolo ad una *forma di governo democratica*, cioè un vero e proprio diritto umano alla democrazia. Ma è chiaro che una simile interpretazione del principio di autodeterminazione "interna" comporta il non riconoscere valore giuridico a tale principio, quanto meno a livello universale, poiché esistono ancora numerosissimi Stati che non si conformano a forme di governo democratiche.

Infine, vi è anche un terzo significato del principio di autodeterminazione "interna", probabilmente quello che più tende a sminuirne il valore. Secondo questa tesi, il principio attribuirebbe ai destinatari soltanto singoli *diritti umani di partecipazione politica*, che possono essere fatti valere tramite gli organi internazionali di controllo sui diritti umani[642].

A nostro parere, il principio di autodeterminazione "interna" va inteso nel primo significato; cioè come diritto di "popoli" (ed anche di gruppi nazionali ed etnici) all'interno di uno Stato di ottenere un elevato grado di autonomia politica. Tuttavia, non ci sembra che questo diritto si sia affermato come norma consuetudinaria internazionale, eccetto che nel caso dell'*apartheid*[643]. Inoltre, si sta formando una norma consuetudinaria che attribuisce il diritto di autodeterminazione "interna", inteso in quest'ultimo significato, ai popoli indigeni. Ma questo tema sarà trattato in seguito[644].

---

[640] Vedi Cassese (1984), p. 158.

[641] Supreme Court of Canada, *Re Secession of Quebec*, par. 126.

[642] Vedi Focarelli (2015), p. 124. Sui diritti di partecipazione politica nel quadro dell'Unione Europea, vedi Starita (2011).

[643] In altri termini, i gruppi razziali, ai quali sia negato pieno accesso al governo del proprio paese, hanno diritto a invocare sia l'autodeterminazione "interna" che quella "esterna". Vedi Cassese (1984), pp. 157-158.

[644] Vedi *infra*, Cap. VI, par. 18.

Capitolo VI

ALTRI DIRITTI UMANI

1. *Introduzione*

Questo capitolo sarà dedicato ai diritti umani che, in linea di massima, non fanno parte della categoria dei diritti umani "fondamentali", quale da noi definita [1]. Si tratta di un gran numero di diritti; e pertanto dovremo limitarci ad un loro quadro sintetico, raggruppandoli, come si era detto [2], sulla base della natura delle attività umane che ciascun gruppo mira a proteggere.

Tuttavia, anche se questi diritti non toccano gli aspetti cruciali della vita, integrità fisica, libertà, sicurezza e identità delle persone o della volontà ed identità dei popoli, e non hanno, di solito, carattere assoluto, non si deve sottovalutare la loro rilevanza. Essi, infatti, hanno, nel loro complesso, la funzione di tutelare aspetti assai importanti della vita privata, sociale e pubblica delle persone. Più in particolare, i diritti individuali hanno lo scopo di proteggere: *a*) la vita privata e familiare; *b*) le attività intellettuali e culturali; *c*) le attività politiche; *d*) le attività economiche; *e*) le libertà di movimento. A questi diritti individuali, si devono aggiungere alcuni diritti umani collettivi, specie a favore di minoranze e di popoli indigeni.

Sezione I

PROTEZIONE DELLA SFERA PRIVATA E FAMILIARE

La protezione della sfera privata e familiare delle persone da ingerenze da parte dello Stato o di altri enti o di individui, che sono estranei rispetto a tale sfera, appartiene alla tradizione classica delle libertà civili di origine occidentale. Questa tradizione si è poi estesa al sistema del diritto internazionale dei diritti umani; ma la sua importanza non è uguale in tutti gli Stati membri della comunità internazionale. In questo ambito, rilevano soprattutto due diritti umani, che sono fra loro collegati, ma che conviene trattare separatamente: *a*) il diritto al rispetto della vita privata; *b*) il diritto alla vita familiare. Quest'ultimo diritto comprende, come vedremo, anche il diritto di sposarsi e di formare una famiglia [3].

---

[1] Vedi *supra*, Cap. V, parr. 1-6.

[2] Vedi *supra*, Cap. V, par. 1.

[3] Secondo un'altra impostazione, il diritto alla vita privata potrebbe essere considerato come un concetto

2. *Diritto al rispetto della vita privata*

2.1. *Norme*

I più importanti atti e trattati internazionali sui diritti umani prevedono norme sul diritto al rispetto della vita privata, inteso principalmente come diritto alla *privacy*. In molti casi, la norma pertinente si occupa anche, congiuntamente, del rispetto della vita familiare, sempre nell'ottica prevalente della protezione da intromissioni indebite [4]. Ma vi sono anche trattati, più recenti e con un approccio più attuale, che tengono separati i due diritti: ad esempio, la Convenzione sui diritti dei disabili contiene una disposizione (art. 22) sul rispetto della *privacy* ed un'altra (art. 23) sul rispetto per la casa e per la famiglia. Infine, vi sono trattati che *non* prevedono alcuna norma sul rispetto della vita privata: l'esempio più importante è dato dalla Convenzione africana.

Il diritto al rispetto della vita privata è contenuto nella Dichiarazione universale che, all'art. 12, proclama che:

> "No one shall be subjected to arbitrary interference with his privacy, family, home or correspondence, not to attacks upon his honour and reputation. Everyone has the right to protection of the law against such interference or attacks".

Il Patto sui diritti civili e politici stabilisce il medesimo diritto, all'art. 17, con una formula quasi identica a quella della Dichiarazione universale. L'art. 8 della Convenzione europea parla di rispetto per la vita privata (anziché di divieto di interferenza con la *privacy*) ed è più completo e dettagliato, perché prevede anche le restrizioni legittime a tale diritto. Secondo tale disposizione:

> "1. Everyone has the right to respect for his private and family life, his home and his correspondence. 2. There shall be no interference by a public authority with the exercise of this right except such as is in accordance with the law and is necessary in a democratic society in the interests of national security, public safety, or the economic well-being of the country, for the prevention of disorder or crime, for the protection of health or morals, or for the protection of the rights and freedoms of others".

Altre disposizioni sul diritto al rispetto della vita privata, ma con una formulazione piuttosto sintetica, sono contenute in altri trattati generali sui diritti umani, quali la Convenzione americana (art. 11), la Carta araba (art. 21) e la Carta dei diritti fondamentali dell'UE (art. 7); ed in trattati settoriali, quali la Convenzione sui diritti del fanciullo (art. 16) e la Convenzione sui diritti dei disabili (art. 22).

---

ampio, che comprende il diritto alla *privacy*, il diritto alla famiglia ed il diritto di sposarsi e fondare una famiglia. In questo senso vedi Kälin, Künzli (2009), p. 381 ss. Ancora diversa è l'opinione di chi ritiene che il diritto alla vita privata e familiare costituisca una sorta di "contenitore", nel quale sono confluiti ulteriori diritti nascenti da problematiche contemporanee, quali, ad es., il diritto alla protezione dei dati personali, il diritto all'oblio, i diritti delle coppie dello stesso sesso. Cfr. Pustorino (2019), p. 155 ss.

[4] Come vedremo, questi trattati contengono anche altre disposizioni che si occupano *soltanto* della protezione della famiglia e/o del diritto di sposarsi e fondare una famiglia. Vedi *infra*, par. 3.

2.2. *Contenuto del diritto*

Il diritto al rispetto della vita privata non è inderogabile in stati di emergenza, né ha carattere assoluto, poiché è soggetto ad una serie di limiti e restrizioni, che possono variare a seconda dei singoli trattati. Le restrizioni più frequenti sono quelle per motivi di sicurezza nazionale, ordine pubblico, prevenzione dei reati, protezione della salute, della morale e della reputazione altrui [5].

Lo scopo generale di questo diritto è quello di garantire all'individuo un'autonomia nelle questioni che attengono alla sua sfera privata. Pertanto, il suo contenuto è assai ampio e generale. Infatti, nel quadro di questo contenuto, si possono distinguere molti *aspetti* diversi della vita degli individui che ricadono nell'ambito della vita privata (individuale e sociale), e che sono evidenziati dalla prassi degli organi internazionali di controllo.

Un primo aspetto, classico, riguarda la libertà dell'individuo di non subire ingiustificate *interferenze e intrusioni*, da parte dello Stato o di altri soggetti. Qui vengono in rilievo questioni legate a forme di sorveglianza statale dell'individuo, tramite intercettazioni telefoniche o tecniche di video-sorveglianza o raccolta di informazioni private da parte della polizia o di servizi di *intelligence*. Rientrano in questo ambito anche il rispetto delle comunicazioni e del domicilio delle persone, anche se talora questi temi vengono considerati come oggetto di diritti collegati ed autonomi.

Un secondo aspetto riguarda il diritto alla *riservatezza*. Qui sono pertinenti molte questioni relative alla protezione e conservazione dei dati personali, con particolare importanza per i dati riguardanti la salute. In linea di principio, un uso dei dati personali effettuato da un soggetto diverso dall'interessato può costituire un pregiudizio al diritto alla riservatezza [6]. Vengono in considerazione anche tematiche legate al diritto della persona all'accesso ai propri dati, al c.d. diritto all'oblio, alla cessione della *privacy*, alla diffusione indebita di fotografie o altre immagini relative alla vita privata della persona. È chiaro che oggi, nell'era di *internet* e dei *social networks*, il diritto alla riservatezza ha assunto un'importanza centrale e presenta molti profili problematici.

Un terzo aspetto è quello del diritto all'onore e *reputazione* personale. Questo diritto viene spesso in rilievo nei casi in cui deve essere bilanciato con altri diritti umani, quali, ad esempio, le libertà di espressione e di stampa. Il diritto alla reputazione è stato anche invocato da alcune persone, sospettate di attività terroristiche, ed i cui nomi sono stati pubblicati su *internet* in certe "liste nere" (*black lists*) predisposte dal Consiglio di Sicurezza delle NU nel quadro di "sanzioni mirate" (*targeted sanctions*) contro i terroristi. Questa vicenda è stata oggetto di una nota prassi giurisprudenziale [7].

Un quarto aspetto, molto importante, concerne il diritto al *nome* ed all'*identità* personale. Il diritto al nome, come elemento essenziale dell'identità, è espressamente tutelato da alcune norme specifiche convenzionali, e viene in rilievo nella prassi specie in relazione al diritto di cambiare il proprio nome [8], al diritto dei genitori di scegliere il nome dei figli [9], al

---

[5] Vedi, ad es., l'elenco delle restrizioni stabilito dall'art. 8(2) della Convenzione europea.

[6] Zagrebelsky *et al.* (2016), p. 256.

[7] Vedi, ad es., CFI, *Kadi*; ECJ, *Kadi*; EGC, *Kadi*; EctHR, *Al-Jedda v. UK*; *Nada v. Switzerland*. Vedi anche Focarelli (2013), pp. 172-174.

[8] HRCtee, *Coeriel and Aurik v. The Netherlands*.

possibile trattamento discriminatorio nell'uso dei nomi del padre e della madre [10], al diritto di conoscere le proprie origini biologiche come elemento essenziale per la propria identificazione [11].

Il diritto all'identità personale comprende anche l'identità e l'*orientamento sessuale* delle persone. La prassi internazionale si è occupata di vari casi relativi a persone che avevano effettuato un cambiamento chirurgico del sesso e che volevano il riconoscimento del loro nuovo *status*, anche a fini meramente burocratici [12]. Il diritto all'identità sessuale a sua volta ricomprende anche il diritto di rispettare le relazioni intime fra individui, compresi i rapporti sessuali consensuali fra adulti del medesimo sesso. Nel celebre caso *Dudgeon*, la Corte europea ha condannato il Regno Unito per una legislazione che puniva con sanzioni penali i comportamenti omosessuali fra adulti maschi e consenzienti, nella loro vita privata [13]. Anche l'*identità culturale* può entrare nell'ambito di applicazione del diritto alla vita privata. La Corte europea si è occupata di questo tema in alcuni casi relativi ai Rom [14].

Un quinto aspetto, che ricade nell'ambito della vita privata, riguarda l'integrità fisica e mentale e la *salute* delle persone [15]. Qui vengono in considerazione questioni relative a trattamenti sanitari obbligatori per bambini o imposti ad adulti senza il loro consenso, a diritti di accesso ad informazioni su problemi di salute e scelte di trattamenti medici, a libertà di scelta delle persone su modalità di fine vita o di suicidio assistito. In alcune di queste questioni, possono rilevare anche altri diritti umani, quali, ad esempio, il divieto di trattamenti inumani o degradanti, o il divieto di detenzioni arbitrarie. Anche tematiche relative all'aborto possono ricadere nell'ambito di applicazione del diritto alla vita privata e di altri diritti umani, quali il diritto alla vita.

Infine, anche problemi connessi all'*ambiente* possono rientrare nel contenuto del diritto al rispetto della vita privata. In particolare, la Corte europea, pur in assenza del diritto ad un ambiente sano nella Convenzione europea, ha finito per ritenere che dall'art. 8 (diritto alla vita privata e familiare) si possa trarre una tutela indiretta in tema di danni ambientali, nel senso che immissioni di fumi, rumori, odori nella vita privata e nel domicilio di un individuo, possano violare l'art. 8. Ha inoltre sostenuto che da tale articolo si può dedurre il diritto delle persone di essere informate dei possibili pericoli derivanti da inquinamento ambientale [16].

2.3. *Obblighi*

Al contenuto, assai ampio e diversificato, del diritto alla vita privata corrispondono, a carico degli Stati, molti obblighi aventi diversa natura. Gli obblighi più tradizionali sono quelli, di carattere *negativo*, che richiedono agli Stati di astenersi dall'interferire nella sfera

[9] ECtHR, *Guillot v. France*, parr. 21-22.

[10] ECtHR, *Burghartz v. Switzerland.*

[11] ECtHR, *Gaskin v. UK.*

[12] ECtHR, *Goodwin Christine v. UK*, Judgment of 11 July 2002.

[13] ECtHR, *Dudgeon v. UK*, parr. 47 e 60-61.

[14] Vedi, ad es., ECtHR, *Connors v. UK*.

[15] Vedi Zagrebelsky *et al.* (2016), pp. 253-255, anche per la giurisprudenza ivi citata.

[16] Vedi *infra*, par. 20.2.

privata delle persone, intesa come integrità fisica e mentale, ed anche come libertà di stabilire e mantenere rapporti con familiari ed altre persone [17]. Questi obblighi si collegano, ad esempio, alle citate misure, da parte di autorità statali, di sorveglianza illegittima delle persone, o delle comunicazioni o del domicilio, o di diffusione indebita di foto, immagini o altri dati privati. Ma altri obblighi negativi riguardano divieti di certi trattamenti sanitari o di misure suscettibili di produrre danni ambientali che incidono sulla vita privata delle persone. Anche certi provvedimenti legislativi possono essere vietati (e quindi oggetto di obblighi negativi), come dimostra il sopra citato caso *Dudgeon*.

Peraltro, nella prassi più recente, la protezione effettiva del diritto al rispetto della vita privata ha finito per produrre un sempre maggior numero di obblighi positivi (sia di risultato che di *due diligence*) a carico degli Stati. Un primo gruppo di tali obblighi attiene alle misure (normative, amministrative, giudiziarie ed esecutive) che devono essere prese dallo Stato per *prevenire e reprimere* violazioni della sfera privata di una persona provenienti da individui terzi (i c.d. obblighi positivi "orizzontali" dello Stato) [18]. È chiaro che, nella società contemporanea, le intromissioni illegittime nella vita privata delle persone provengono più spesso da individui privati che non da autorità statali. Si pensi, ad esempio, alle violazioni della *privacy* o del diritto all'immagine personale da parte di giornali, televisioni, *social networks* o altri strumenti mediatici [19].

Un secondo gruppo di obblighi positivi degli Stati si collega ad altri aspetti del diritto alla vita privata, che abbiamo sopra indicato. Lo Stato deve emanare *legislazione* che garantisca una protezione effettiva di tale diritto o modificare norme che presentino lacune. Ad esempio, possono esservi obblighi normativi in materia di diritto di cambiare il nome o di scegliere il nome dei figli, o di diritto delle persone alla conoscenza delle proprie origini biologiche, o di diritto di cambiamento del sesso, o di diritto di accedere ad informazioni su questioni di salute, o di libera scelta di trattamenti sanitari. In certi casi, lo Stato deve anche adottare misure concrete o esecutive, quali, ad esempio, quelle necessarie per garantire un certo livello di *privacy* alle persone in stato di custodia o di detenzione [20].

3. *Diritto alla vita familiare*

3.1. *Norme*

Nei trattati ed altri atti internazionali sui diritti umani, le norme sul diritto alla vita familiare sono più numerose rispetto a quelle sul rispetto della vita privata. Infatti, come si

---

[17] Vedi Kälin, Künzli (2009), p. 392; Pustorino (2019), p. 157.

[18] Vedi *supra*, Cap.II, par. 10.4 e, più ampiamente, sugli obblighi di prevenzione e repressione, *supra*, Cap.V, parr. 7.3.2 e 7.3.3. Per un celebre esempio di obblighi "orizzontali" di carattere normativo vedi ECtHR, *X and Y v. The Netherlands*, par. 23.

[19] Focarelli (2013), pp. 170-173, nota che talora sono le persone stesse a "vendere" la propria *privacy* a centri di potere politico ed economico in cambio di vantaggi economici. Il problema allora non è più quello, tradizionale nella logica dei diritti umani, della tutela del singolo dal potere dello Stato, bensì quello dell'incapacità dello Stato "di orientare la condotta dei singoli in modo conforme ai diritti umani per il bene dell'intera collettività".

[20] Kälin, Künzli (2009), p. 393.

era accennato, vi sono molte norme che si occupano *congiuntamente* del rispetto della vita privata e di quella familiare (nell'ottica prevalente del divieto di interferenze indebite). Ad esse vanno aggiunte numerose altre disposizioni che sono dedicate soltanto alla vita familiare e, di solito, dal punto di vista, diverso e più ampio, della *protezione della famiglia* e del diritto di sposarsi e formare e crescere una famiglia. Per questi motivi, abbiamo ritenuto opportuno trattare separatamente il diritto al rispetto della vita privata ed il diritto alla vita familiare. Esamineremo quest'ultimo, per motivi di sintesi, solo nel quadro dei trattati generali sui diritti umani.

Il Patto sui diritti civili e politici, in aggiunta all'art. 17 già ricordato, contiene l'art. 23, secondo il quale:

> "1. The family is the natural and fundamental group unit of society and is entitled to protection by society and the State. 2. The right of men and women of marriageable age to marry and to found a family shall be recognized. 3. No marriage shall be entered into without the free and full consent of the intending spouses. 4. States Parties to the present Covenant shall take appropriate steps to ensure equality of rights and responsibilities of spouses as to marriage, during marriage and at its dissolution. In the case of dissolution, provision shall be made for the necessary protection of any children".

Anche la Convenzione americana, in aggiunta all'art. 11, prevede l'art. 17, sui diritti della famiglia, che ha un contenuto simile a quello dell'art. 23 del Patto sui diritti civili e politici. Lo stesso modello è adottato dagli artt. 21 e 33(1) e (2) della Carta araba.

Vi sono poi dei trattati, come si era già detto, che non prevedono disposizioni sul rispetto della vita privata; ma soltanto sulla protezione della famiglia e del matrimonio. Un esempio è costituito dal Patto sui diritti economici, sociali e culturali, che contiene una norma assai lunga e dettagliata (art. 10) sulla protezione della famiglia. Un altro esempio è dato dalla Carta africana. Merita citare i primi due paragrafi del suo art. 18, i quali stabiliscono che:

> "1. The family shall be the natural unit and basis of society. It shall be protected by the State which shall take care of its physical health and moral. 2. The State shall have the duty to assist the family which is the custodian of morals and traditional values recognized by the community".

3.2. *Contenuto del diritto*

Anche il diritto alla vita familiare non è inderogabile in stati di emergenza e non ha carattere assoluto. In particolare, i trattati sopra citati prevedono limiti per quanto riguarda il divieto di interferenze con la vita familiare.

Lo scopo del diritto alla vita familiare è quello, assai generale, di proteggere la famiglia. Pertanto anche il contenuto del diritto è molto ampio e, nel suo ambito di applicazione, rientra una pluralità di *aspetti* o manifestazioni della vita familiare, quali il diritto di non subire intromissioni nella vita familiare, il diritto di sposarsi e di fondare una famiglia, i rapporti personali e patrimoniali fra i coniugi, la parità fra i coniugi, la filiazione, la cura, il mantenimento e l'istruzione dei figli, l'adozione, etc. Anche in questo caso, la prassi degli organi internazionali di controllo sui diritti umani evidenzia questa molteplicità di aspetti.

Prima di dar conto sinteticamente di questi aspetti, si pone il problema preliminare circa la definizione del *concetto di famiglia* accolto dai trattati sui diritti umani. Questo concetto non è univoco in tutti i trattati. Per il Comitato dei diritti umani, poiché il Patto sui diritti civili e politici ha valenza universale, è più difficile trovare un consenso su un concetto preciso di "famiglia" ai sensi degli artt. 17 e 23 del Patto. Pertanto il Comitato tende a rinviare al concetto di famiglia esistente nell'ordinamento giuridico statale in questione. Invece, la Corte europea è riuscita a dare una definizione più autonoma di "famiglia", ritenendo che rientrino nello scopo dell'art. 8 della Convenzione europea sia la famiglia legittima sia quella naturale, per quanto riguarda i rapporti con i figli. Quanto ai rapporti fra adulti, per la Corte rilevano sia il rapporto di coniugio sia i rapporti di fatto, per questi ultimi tenendo conto della eventuale convivenza, della durata del rapporto e dell'esistenza di un impegno comune per i figli [21]. Si discute nei tempi più recenti sul fatto se il rapporto fra coppie dello stesso sesso costituisca o meno una famiglia. Anche altri organi internazionali di controllo dei trattati sui diritti umani tendono oggi ad intendere la famiglia come un'unione non solo formale, ma anche fattuale.

Ciò premesso, come si è detto, molti aspetti diversi della vita familiare vengono presi in esame dalla prassi degli organi internazionali di controllo. Ricordiamo solo i principali. Un primo aspetto riguarda questioni relative al *matrimonio*, al diritto di sposarsi, all'uguaglianza fra i coniugi, ai rapporti fra coppie di fatto. Un secondo aspetto, molto importante, riguarda questioni circa il nome e cognome dei figli, la *filiazione*, le scelte relative alla nascita dei figli, le forme di procreazione medicalmente assistite, l'*adozione* e l'affidamento dei figli minori nei casi di crisi fra i genitori. Queste ultime questioni sono molto frequenti e sono oggetto di una prassi assai estesa, nella quale si sta affermando sempre di più il principio dell'interesse superiore del minore.

Un terzo aspetto, che ricade nell'ambito di applicazione del diritto alla vita familiare, riguarda il principio dell'unità e del *ricongiungimento familiare* e le numerose questioni che si pongono in relazione a ingresso, soggiorno ed espulsione di stranieri e migranti. Come è noto, qui si pongono di solito problemi di bilanciamento fra il diritto alla vita familiare e le esigenze di ordine pubblico, pubblica sicurezza e sanità pubblica dello Stato. La prassi degli organi internazionali di controllo in questa materia è assai abbondante e piuttosto complessa. Infine, un quarto aspetto, più specifico ma anch'esso importante, riguarda le questioni legate ai rapporti familiari dei *detenuti*. Lo stato di detenzione richiede evidentemente una serie di limiti e restrizioni, ma non fa venir meno il diritto dei detenuti a mantenere legami con i propri familiari, tramite colloqui, comunicazioni e corrispondenza.

3.3. *Obblighi*

Le norme sul diritto alla vita familiare impongono agli Stati obblighi, negativi e positivi, che sono simili a quelli, sopra esaminati, che derivano dal diritto al rispetto della vita privata. Pertanto, possiamo rinviare al discorso già fatto in relazione a tali obblighi, anche per quanto riguarda la progressiva estensione della sfera di applicazione degli obblighi positivi nella prassi degli organi internazionali di controllo. Del resto ciò è logico, perché,

---

[21] ECtHR, *B. v. UK*.

come si è visto, anche lo scopo, il contenuto e l'ambito di applicazione del diritto alla vita familiare sono assai vasti e coprono una pluralità di aspetti. La protezione effettiva della famiglia, in tutte le sue manifestazioni, richiede evidentemente agli Stati di adottare misure positive di vario genere [22].

Sezione II
PROTEZIONE DELLE ATTIVITÀ INTELLETTUALI E CULTURALI

Il diritto internazionale dei diritti umani ha, fra i suoi scopi, anche quello di proteggere la sfera delle attività intellettuali e culturali delle persone. Questa tutela si realizza tramite una serie di diritti umani, che anch'essi sono nati nella civiltà occidentale come diritti e libertà civili, ma che si sono poi estesi ad altre parti del mondo [23]. Fra tali diritti, i più rilevanti sono: *a*) la libertà di pensiero, di coscienza e di religione; *b*) la libertà di espressione e di opinione; *c*) il diritto all'istruzione; *d*) il diritto alla vita culturale. La libertà di espressione viene talora considerata anche come un diritto appartenente alla sfera politica [24].

4. *Libertà di pensiero, di coscienza e di religione*

4.1. *Norme*

La libertà di pensiero, di coscienza e di religione è proclamata dall'art. 18 della Dichiarazione universale nei seguenti termini:

> "Everyone has the right to freedom of thought, conscience and religion; this right includes freedom to change his religion or belief, and freedom, either alone or in community with others and in public or private, to manifest his religion or belief in teaching, practice, worship and observance".

La Convenzione europea, all'art. 9, contiene una disposizione simile ma più complessa, che riprende, nel par. 1, il contenuto della Dichiarazione universale, ma poi aggiunge, nel par. 2, la possibilità di porre quei limiti, alla libertà di manifestare la religione o i pensieri, che siano prescritti dalla legge e che siano necessari in una società democratica per proteggere la sicurezza pubblica, l'ordine pubblico, la salute, la morale o i diritti altrui [25].

---

[22] Cfr. anche Pustorino (2019), p. 169.

[23] Tuttavia, anche questi diritti non hanno acquisito, in tutti gli Stati membri della comunità internazionale, quell'elevato grado di importanza che hanno sempre avuto negli Stati di tradizione occidentale.

[24] Per questa opinione vedi Kälin, Künzli (2009), pp. 466-474.

[25] ECHR, art. 9: "1. Everyone has the right to freedom of thought, conscience and religion; this right includes freedom to change his religion of belief and freedom, either alone or in community with others and in public or private, to manifest his religion or belief, in worship, teaching, practice and observance. 2. Freedom to

Il Patto sui diritti civili e politici, all'art. 18, riprende in gran parte la formulazione dell'art. 9 della Convenzione europea, ma aggiunge il divieto di coercizioni che possano pregiudicare le libertà stabilite dalla norma e l'impegno degli Stati di rispettare la libertà dei genitori di istruzione morale e religiosa dei propri figli. Inoltre, il Patto contiene una norma (art. 27) sui diritti culturali, religiosi e linguistici di persone appartenenti a minoranze.

Altre norme convenzionali pertinenti sono l'art. 12 della Convenzione americana, l'art. 8 della Carta africana, l'art. 30 della Carta araba e l'art. 10 della Carta dei diritti fondamentali dell'UE. Quest'ultima contiene anche una disposizione sul diritto all'obiezione di coscienza. Fra le norme contenute nei trattati settoriali sui diritti umani, si possono ricordare l'art. 5(d)(vii) della Convenzione sull'eliminazione della discriminazione razziale e l'art. 12 della Convenzione sui diritti dei lavoratori migranti.

4.2. *Contenuto delle libertà*

Lo scopo generale di queste norme è quello di consentire alle persone: *a*) di pensare liberamente, senza subire influenze da parte dello Stato o di altri soggetti; *b*) di mantenere e sviluppare liberamente le convinzioni della propria coscienza; *c*) di avere e manifestare una religione o un credo. Sembra pertanto che queste norme intendano regolare tre diverse libertà, più che tre diverse manifestazioni della medesima libertà. Ma, in realtà, le tre libertà sono strettamente collegate e spesso non è facile distinguere fra loro. Questo collegamento viene evidenziato anche dagli organi internazionali di controllo sui diritti umani, che hanno affermato che le libertà di pensiero, coscienza e religione garantiscono il pluralismo ideologico e quindi rappresentano un pilastro della società democratica[26].

Tuttavia, ciò non significa che le tre libertà siano inderogabili in stati di emergenza né che abbiano natura assoluta. Quest'ultimo aspetto è più complicato e va precisato. Infatti, si è affermata, nella prassi e nella dottrina, la distinzione fra il c.d. *forum internum*, cioè i processi strettamente interni alla persona, che producono le sue convinzioni di pensiero, coscienza e religione, ed il c.d. *forum externum,* cioè le manifestazioni esterne o esteriori di tali convinzioni. Si ritiene che l'esercizio delle tre libertà nel *forum internum* della persona non possa subire limiti o restrizioni da parte dello Stato, il quale, ad esempio, non può costringere un individuo ad adottare o abbandonare una certa fede religiosa tramite uso di coercizioni o punizioni, né imporre un giuramento di appartenenza religiosa[27]. Al contrario, le manifestazioni esterne della religione o delle convinzioni di un individuo possono essere soggette a limiti e restrizioni. Il par. 2 dell'art. 9 della Convenzione europea chiarisce bene questo aspetto.

Per comprendere meglio il contenuto delle libertà di pensiero, coscienza e religione, si devono precisare queste *nozioni*, alla luce della prassi degli organi internazionali di controllo. In primo luogo, tale prassi indica che rientrano, nell'ambito di applicazione delle norme sopra indicate, non le idee o i giudizi meramente personali, ma quelle idee che sia-

---

manifest one's religion or beliefs shall be subject only to such limitations as are prescribed by law and are necessary in a democratic society in the interests of public safety, for the protection of public order, health or morals, or for the protection of the rights and freedoms of others".

[26] Vedi, ad es., ECtHR, *Kokkinakis v. Greece*, par. 31.

[27] Vedi, ad es., ECtHR, *Buscarini and Others*, parr. 39-41.

no caratterizzate da un grado sufficiente di cogenza, serietà, coesione e importanza[28] e quelle idee che siano coerenti su certi problemi fondamentali[29]. Gli organi di Strasburgo, ad esempio, hanno ritenuto che, fra le convinzioni protette dall'art. 9 della Convenzione europea, vi siano il pacifismo[30] ed il rifiuto della forza militare[31].

In secondo luogo, vi è il problema, più delicato, di definire con precisione il significato di "religione" o di "convinzione religiosa". Questo problema non si pone per le religioni storiche, praticate e riconosciute in tutto il mondo, come il Cristianesimo, l'Islam, l'Induismo, il Buddismo o l'Ebraismo; ma per le religioni nuove o minoritarie e per le c.d. "sette religiose". La giurisprudenza della Corte europea, pur tendendo ad evitare una nozione autonoma di "religione" e quindi essendo incline a rinviare alle qualificazioni statali di tale nozione, non ha rinunciato ad esercitare un certo controllo sulla questione, al fine di garantire il rispetto della libertà religiosa[32]. È stata riconosciuta natura religiosa, ad esempio, ai Testimoni di Geova, a Scientology ed al c.d. movimento Osho. Il Comitato dei diritti umani, invece, ha accolto una nozione ampia di "religione", affermando che l'art. 18 del Patto sui diritti civili e politici "protects theistic, non-theistic and atheistic beliefs, as well as the right not to profess any religion or belief. The terms belief and religion are to be broadly construed"[33]. Inoltre, il Comitato ha aggiunto che:

> "[t]he freedom to manifest religion or belief may be exercised 'either individually or in community with others and in public or private'. The freedom to manifest religion or belief in worship, observance, practice and teaching encompasses a broad range of acts"[34].

Ciò premesso, conviene ora accennare agli aspetti principali che ricadono nell'ambito di applicazione delle libertà di pensiero, coscienza e religione e le questioni più frequenti che si sono poste nella prassi degli organi internazionali di controllo. Un primo aspetto riguarda il diritto di non adottare una certa religione e quello di cambiare la propria religione. A questo proposito, sono sorte questioni sul fatto che certi Stati proibiscono agli aderenti ad una certa religione di convertirsi ad un'altra[35], o sul fatto che altri Stati impongono alle persone di adottare una certa religione[36]. Un secondo aspetto riguarda il diritto di non rivelare le proprie convinzioni filosofiche o religiose. Può costituire una violazione della libertà religiosa, ad esempio, la circostanza che una persona sia costretta a rivelare la propria credenza religiosa dinanzi ad un tribunale[37] o in un documento di identità[38].

Un terzo aspetto rilevante attiene alle *obiezioni di coscienza* al servizio militare o a certe pratiche mediche che vengono giustificate come espressione della libertà di coscienza e

---

[28] Vedi, ad es., ECtHR, *Leela Forderkreis E.V. and Others*, par. 80; *Campbell and Cosans*, par. 36.

[29] Vedi ECmHR, *X v. Federal Republic of Germany*, Decision of 10 March 1981.

[30] ECmHR, *Arrowsmith v. UK*.

[31] ECtHR, *Bayatyan v. Armenia*, parr. 110-111.

[32] Zagrebelsky *et al.* (2016), p. 291.

[33] HRCtee, General Comment No. 22, 30 July 1993, par. 2.

[34] *Ibidem*, par. 4.

[35] HRCtee, Concluding Observations: *Yemen* (2002), par. 20.

[36] ACmHPR, *Amnesty International and Others v. Sudan*, parr. 74 e 76.

[37] ECtHR, *Alexandridis v. Greece*, par. 31 ss.

[38] ECtHR, *Sinan Işik v. Turkey*, parr.37-53, 60; *Grzelak v. Poland*, par. 93.

di religione. La Corte europea ha riconosciuto, in linea di principio, un diritto all'obiezione di coscienza[39]; ma non un diritto al rifiuto di servizi civili alternativi al servizio militare. Invece, il Comitato dei diritti umani ha mutato nel tempo la sua prassi. In un primo momento, infatti, esso affermava che l'art. 18 del Patto sui diritti civili e politici non riconosce il diritto all'obiezione di coscienza[40], salvo poi giungere a conclusioni diametralmente opposte. Nel caso *Aminov* il Comitato ha affermato che:

> "[t]he right to conscientious objection to military service inheres in the right to freedom of thought, conscience and religion. It entitles any individual to an exemption from compulsory military service if such service cannot be reconciled with that individual's religion or beliefs. The right must not be impaired by coercion"[41].

Un quarto aspetto riguarda i *segni religiosi* e gli indumenti aventi significato religioso. La questione del c.d. velo islamico, che per alcuni Stati musulmani è obbligatorio indossare e per alcuni Stati occidentali è vietato nei luoghi pubblici, è stata oggetto di numerose decisioni, non sempre uniformi, da parte degli organi internazionali di controllo. La Corte europea ha, di solito, deciso che il divieto statale di indossare il velo è legittimo, se persegue in maniera proporzionata lo scopo di proteggere l'ordine pubblico, la sicurezza pubblica o i diritti altrui[42]. Il Comitato dei diritti umani ha, invece, assunto un atteggiamento più favorevole alla libertà di indossare il velo[43], salvo che il divieto sia giustificato da motivi di sicurezza[44].

Un quinto aspetto, che rientra nell'ambito di applicazione delle norme in oggetto, riguarda l'importanza assegnata in uno Stato alla religione maggioritaria, specie in relazione al diritto dei genitori di educare i figli secondo le proprie convinzioni. Ad esempio, nel caso dell'*insegnamento religioso* nelle scuole pubbliche, la Corte di Strasburgo ha ritenuto legittimo che i programmi diano maggiore spazio alla religione maggioritaria dello Stato in questione[45]. La questione del crocefisso nelle aule scolastiche pubbliche ha interessato da vicino l'Italia nel controverso caso *Lautsi*. La ricorrente si lamentava della presenza del crocefisso in tutte le aule della scuola frequentata dai suoi due figli, ritenendola contraria al principio di laicità sul quale era improntata l'educazione loro impartita. Nella sentenza di primo grado, nel 2009, la Camera della Corte europea ha affermato che la presenza del crocefisso costituiva una violazione del diritto alla libertà religiosa[46]. Nella sentenza successiva, nel 2011, la Grande Camera ha ribaltato le conclusioni raggiunte in primo grado[47]. Altre questioni che si

---

[39] ECmHR, *X v. Germany*, Decision of 5 July 1977, par. 1; ECtHR, *Thlimmenos v. Greece*, par. 50; ECtHR, *Ebrahimian v. France*, par. 53.

[40] HRCtee, *L.T.K. v. Finland*, Decision of 9 July 1985, parr. 5.2-6.

[41] HRCtee, *Matkarim Aminov v. Turkmenistan*, par. 9.7.

[42] Vedi, ad es., ECtHR, *Şahin v. Turkey*; *Köse and 93 Other Applicants v. Turkey*. Cfr. anche altre decisioni citate da Focarelli (2013), p. 192.

[43] HRCtee, *Hudoyberganova v. Uzbekistan*, par. 6.2.

[44] Vedi, ad es., HRCtee, *Singh Bhinder v. Canada*, parr. 6-7, dove il Comitato ha ritenuto legittimo il licenziamento di un lavoratore delle ferrovie canadesi che si rifiutava di indossare il casco protettivo imposto dalla legge per motivi di sicurezza, perché la sua religione Sikh gli chiedeva di indossare sempre il turbante.

[45] ECtHR, *Hasan and Eylem Zengin* v. *Turkey*, par. 63.

[46] ECtHR, *Lautsi v. Italy*, Judgment of 3 November 2009, parr. 54-55.

[47] ECtHR, *Lautsi and Others v. Italy*, Judgment of 18 March 2011, parr. 72-76.

sono poste, nella giurisprudenza della Corte europea, relative all'insegnamento scolastico in rapporto con la religione, sono quelle dell'educazione sessuale obbligatoria in Danimarca, ritenuta dai genitori contraria alla fede cristiana [48]; e della pratica delle punizioni corporali in una scuola scozzese [49]. La prassi del Comitato dei diritti umani è più netta, poiché essa è rigorosa nel ritenere che l'istruzione scolastica debba avvenire in maniera neutrale ed oggettiva rispetto a qualsiasi religione [50].

Infine, un sesto aspetto, importante, riguarda la *blasfemia*. In molti casi, il diritto alla libertà religiosa ed al rispetto delle convinzioni religiose di una persona può trovarsi in contrasto con il diritto alla libertà di espressione di altre persone, come nel caso di un film o un articolo di stampa o una vignetta satirica [51] che manifestino un'opinione offensiva nei confronti di una religione. La Corte europea ha generalmente fatto prevalere il diritto alla libertà religiosa, ritenendo giustificate le misure restrittive prese dallo Stato che limitavano l'espressione di opinioni critiche od offensive [52]. Invece, la Corte interamericana sembra più favorevole a far prevalere la libertà di espressione [53].

4.3. *Obblighi*

Alle libertà di pensiero, coscienza e religione corrispondono obblighi degli Stati che hanno prevalentemente carattere negativo; cioè di astensione dalle interferenze in tali libertà individuali. Tuttavia, vi sono anche alcuni obblighi positivi: ad esempio, lo Stato deve operare con diligenza per impedire che il libero esercizio dei diritti in oggetto sia impedito da terze persone [54]. Inoltre, per fare un altro esempio, se lo Stato offre nelle scuole un'istruzione religiosa fondata su una particolare religione, ha l'obbligo di offrire agli alunni la possibilità di optare per alternative o di esentare gli alunni dall'istruzione di tale religione [55].

5. *Libertà di opinione e di espressione*

5.1. *Norme*

La libertà di opinione e di espressione è riconosciuta in tutti gli atti ed i trattati sui diritti umani di carattere generale ed in molti trattati di carattere settoriale. Ma le formule usate dalle pertinenti disposizioni non sono identiche: talora si parla di libertà di opinione e di espressione, ambedue comprensive della libertà di informazione; talora quest'ultima è

---

[48] ECtHR, *Kjeldsen, Busk Madsen and Pedersen v. Denmark*, par. 53.

[49] ECtHR, *Campbell and Cosans v. UK*, par. 41.

[50] Nel caso *Leirvåg*, ad esempio, il Comitato ha ritenuto che l'insegnamento obbligatorio di una corrente religiosa cristiana nelle scuole norvegesi (il CKREE) violasse l'art. 18, par. 4, del Patto sui diritti civili e politici, poiché esso non era impartito in maniera imparziale e oggettiva. Cfr. HRCtee, *Leirvåg et al. v. Norway*.

[51] È noto il caso delle vignette satiriche pubblicate in Danimarca nel 2005 contro Maometto.

[52] Vedi, ad es., ECtHR, *Otto-Preminger-Institut v. Austria*, parr. 47-48 e 52; *Wingrove v. UK*, par. 64; *Dubowska and Skup v. Poland*, par. 2.

[53] IACtHR, *Olmedo Bustos et al. v. Chile*, Judgment of 5 February 2001, parr. 71, 73 e 79.

[54] ECtHR, *Members of the Gldani Congregation of the Jehovah's Witnesses v. Georgia*, parr. 133-134.

[55] Kälin, Künzli (2009), p. 419.

considerata come una parte della sola libertà di espressione; talora invece si parla solo di libertà di espressione come comprensiva delle libertà di opinione e di informazione. In realtà, queste differenze ci sembrano più terminologiche che sostanziali. Comunque, noi adotteremo la terminologia prevalente, che parla di libertà di opinione e di espressione e che include nella seconda la libertà di informazione.

La Dichiarazione universale, all'art. 19, proclama che:

> "Everyone has the right to freedom of opinion and expression; this right includes freedom to hold opinions without interference and to seek, receive and impart information and ideas through any media and regardless of frontiers".

Come si può notare, la Dichiarazione parla di un diritto alla libertà di opinione e di espressione, che include anche la libertà di informazione. Invece, l'art. 10 della Convenzione europea, con una formula diversa, prevede il diritto alla libertà di espressione come un concetto più ampio, inclusivo della libertà di opinione e di informazione. Infatti, l'art. 10, par. 1, stabilisce:

> "Everyone has the right to freedom of expression. This right shall include freedom to hold opinions and to receive and impart information and ideas without interference by public authority and regardless of frontiers [...]".

Quindi il par. 2 dell'art. 10 specifica che l'esercizio delle suddette libertà può essere soggetto a quelle formalità, condizioni, restrizioni o pene, che siano prescritte dalla legge e siano necessarie in una società democratica per la protezione di una serie piuttosto ampia di interessi pubblici che vengono espressamente elencati.

Il Patto sui diritti civili e politici contiene una norma che, a nostro avviso, è sintetica ma completa e ben formulata. L'art. 19 del Patto distingue fra il diritto di opinione, che non è soggetto a interferenze (par. 1), e la libertà di espressione, che include il diritto di informazione (par. 2), e che è soggetta alle restrizioni prescritte dalla legge e necessarie per proteggere i diritti altrui, la sicurezza nazionale, l'ordine pubblico, la salute pubblica e la morale (par. 3). L'art. 20 aggiunge che devono essere proibiti dalla legge ogni propaganda della guerra ed ogni sostegno all'odio nazionale, razziale o religioso, che costituisca incitamento alla discriminazione, all'ostilità o alla violenza.

Altre norme convenzionali pertinenti, sulle libertà di opinione ed espressione, sono l'art. 13 della Convenzione americana[56], l'art. 9 della Carta africana, l'art. 32 della Carta araba e l'art. 11 della Carta dei diritti fondamentali dell'UE. Con riguardo ai trattati sui diritti umani di carattere settoriale, si possono citare l'art. 5(d)(viii) della Convenzione contro la discriminazione razziale, l'art. 13 della Convenzione sui diritti del fanciullo, l'art. 13 della Convenzione sui diritti dei lavoratori migranti, e l'art. 21 della Convenzione sui diritti delle persone disabili.

5.2. *Contenuto delle libertà*

Le libertà di opinione e di espressione non hanno il carattere dell'inderogabilità in stati di emergenza né quello dell'assolutezza. In particolare, esse sono soggette alle restrizioni

[56] Il quale tuttavia è intitolato "Freedom of Thought and Expression".

che vengono volta per volta specificate dai vari trattati. Sono significativi gli esempi diversi di restrizioni che sono contenuti nell'art. 10(2) della Convenzione europea e nell'art. 19(3) del Patto sui diritti civili e politici.

Gli scopi generali delle libertà di opinione ed espressione sono chiari. In primo luogo, esse sono uno dei cardini fondamentali per la protezione delle attività intellettuali e culturali degli individui e per lo sviluppo della loro stessa personalità. In secondo luogo, esse perseguono uno scopo politico, perché costituiscono uno dei fondamenti essenziali della società democratica e pluralista [57] ed una delle condizioni fondamentali del suo progresso [58]. Il legame fra queste libertà e la democrazia emerge chiaramente dalla prassi degli organi internazionali di controllo: l'idea di fondo è che esse abbiano un ruolo essenziale per mantenere e sviluppare un sistema effettivamente democratico per due motivi: *a*) perché contribuiscono al progresso ed allo sviluppo di ogni persona umana; *b*) perché permettono di controllare, giudicare e criticare l'operato dei pubblici poteri. Con riguardo a questo secondo aspetto, la Corte europea ha definito spesso la libertà di espressione, in maniera assai efficace, come il "cane da guardia" della democrazia [59]. Strettamente legato vi è il tema del pluralismo: infatti la Corte europea ha spesso affermato [60] che, senza pluralismo, tolleranza ed apertura mentale, non vi può essere una società democratica. In tal modo, si è stabilito un legame stretto, e assai importante, fra tre valori fondamentali: libertà di espressione, democrazia e pluralismo.

Venendo alle nozioni di libertà di opinione e di espressione, si deve, in primo luogo, notare che la seconda (secondo la concezione prevalente cui abbiamo sopra aderito) include anche il diritto di *informazione*. Quest'ultimo deve essere inteso non solo come diritto di comunicare informazioni di vario genere e attraverso ogni mezzo, ma anche come diritto *di cercare e di ricevere* informazioni. Si tratta di un elemento di grande importanza, che incide notevolmente sulla nozione della libertà di espressione. Infatti, al concetto tradizionale di libertà di espressione, come diritto umano di autonomia della persona, che deve essere tutelata rispetto ad ingerenze indebite da parte dello Stato (e che pertanto impone allo Stato soprattutto obblighi negativi di astensione), si è con il tempo aggiunta una concezione nuova della libertà di espressione, che viene ad essere intesa anche come diritto umano di partecipazione della persona, che deve essere tutelata nel suo diritto di cercare e ricevere informazioni ed opinioni, e di avere gli strumenti conoscitivi per formarsi una propria opinione autonoma e consapevole (e ciò pertanto impone allo Stato anche obblighi positivi).

In secondo luogo, in relazione alle forme ed ai mezzi di espressione e di informazione, le norme convenzionali suddette e la loro prassi interpretativa hanno chiarito che i diritti in oggetto includono *ogni forma* di espressione di opinioni, informazioni o idee, ed anche *ogni mezzo* con il quale esse vengano diffuse [61], ad esempio carta stampata [62], radio, televi-

[57] Vedi, ad es., ECtHR, *Zana v. Turkey*, par. 51.

[58] ECtHR, *Handyside v. UK*, par. 49; *Hadjianastassiou v. Greece*, par. 67; *Perinçek v. Switzerland*, par. 196.

[59] Vedi, ad es., ECtHR, *Thorgeir Thorgeirson v. Island*, par. 31; *Jersild v. Denmark*, par. 31; *Goodwin v. UK*, Judgment of 27 March 1996, par. 39.

[60] Vedi, ad es., ECtHR, *Handyside*, par. 49; *Lingens*, par. 41; *Oberschlick*, par. 57; *Informationsverein Lentia and Others*, par. 38; *Janowski*, par. 30.

[61] Vedi, ad es., ECtHR, *Oberschlick*; *Jersild*; *De Haes and Gijsels*.

[62] ECtHR, *Perna v. Italy*, par. 39.

sione, cinematografia e *internet*[63]. Rimane allo Stato la possibilità di disciplinare in maniera diversa le varie forme di espressione e informazione[64]. È evidente che, visti i progressi tecnologici realizzatisi negli ultimi decenni in materia di forme e mezzi di diffusione delle informazioni, questo aspetto della libertà di espressione si è venuto notevolmente a complicare e pone notevoli problemi nella società contemporanea.

Un terzo aspetto, assai importante, del contenuto della libertà di espressione, riguarda *la natura ed il contenuto* delle informazioni, opinioni ed idee che sono oggetto di protezione. La giurisprudenza degli organi internazionali di controllo ha chiarito che la tutela copre *tutte* le opinioni, informazioni o idee, a prescindere dalla loro oggettiva rilevanza, tenendo conto soprattutto dell'interesse sociale che esse rivestono; e che tali idee o informazioni possono assumere varie forme: i discorsi politici, il giornalismo, l'espressione culturale ed artistica, l'insegnamento, i dibattiti religiosi, ecc.[65]. In particolare, la Corte europea ha affermato che la protezione vale anche per le opinioni che non sono condivise, che offendono, che sono provocatorie e scioccanti, e che disturbano lo Stato o certi settori della popolazione. A questo proposito, la Corte ha fatto delle affermazioni assai notevoli, che sono divenute giustamente famose. Nel caso *Handyside*[66], essa ha detto:

> "[...] The Court's supervisory functions oblige it to pay the utmost attention to the principles characterizing a 'democratic society'. Freedom of expression constitutes one of the essential foundations of such a society, one of the basic conditions for its progress and for the development of every man. Subject to paragraph 2 of Article 10 [...], it is applicable not only to 'information' or 'ideas' that are favourably received or regarded as inoffensive or as a matter of indifference, but also to those that offend, shock or disturb the State or any sector of the population. Such are the demands of that pluralism, tolerance and broadmindedness without which there is no 'democratic society' [...]"[67].

Tuttavia, sebbene l'oggetto della tutela stabilito dalle norme sulla libertà di espressione sia assai ampio, non tutte le idee ed opinioni possono essere espresse senza conseguenze. L'incitamento all'odio, ad atti discriminatori o alla violenza, ad esempio, non è protetto dalla libertà di espressione. Lo stesso si può dire per i discorsi razzisti fondati sull'intolleranza xenofoba, antisemita, islamofobica, religiosa o di altro genere[68].

5.3. *Obblighi*

Infine, vi è la questione degli obblighi a carico degli Stati, che corrispondono alle libertà di opinione, espressione ed informazione. Si è già detto che tali libertà, nelle loro conce-

---

[63] ECtHR, *Cengiz and Others v. Turkey*, par. 52.

[64] Si è già visto, ad esempio, che l'art. 10(1) della Convenzione europea prevede che gli Stati possano sottoporre ad un regime di autorizzazione le imprese di radiodiffusione, cinematografiche e televisive.

[65] Ad esempio, nel caso *Kivenmaa* il Comitato dei diritti umani ha chiarito che il diritto di esprimere opinioni politiche (nel caso di specie attraverso la distribuzione di volantini e l'esposizione di striscioni), anche riguardanti i diritti umani, è protetto dall'art. 19 del Patto sui diritti civili e politici, e non ha rinvenuto alcun motivo per accogliere le restrizioni rivendicate dallo Stato e stabilite dal par. 3 dell'art. 19. Vedi HRCtee, *Kivenmaa v. Finland*, par. 9.3.

[66] ECtHR, *Handyside*, par. 49.

[67] Per affermazioni simili vedi ECtHR, *Lingens*, par. 41; *Oberschlick*, parr. 57-59.

[68] Su questo punto alcuni trattati sono espliciti: vedi, ad es., CCPR, art. 20(2); ACHR, art. 13(5).

zioni più tradizionali, impongono allo Stato specie obblighi negativi; ma che, attualmente, esse richiedono che lo Stato assolva anche numerosi obblighi positivi. Fra questi, vi sono sia quello di intervenire per assicurare le libertà contro lesioni derivanti da altri individui [69], sia quello di adottare norme e prassi favorevoli all'esercizio delle libertà in parola.

Sull'obbligo positivo di legiferare, ad esempio, si può ricordare la sentenza della Corte europea del 2012 nel caso *Centro Europa 7 c. Italia*, in materia di concessioni per la diffusione televisiva su frequenze terrestri, nella quale la Corte ha affermato che, nel settore dei media audiovisivi, lo Stato ha, fra l'altro, un obbligo positivo di creare un adeguato quadro normativo ed amministrativo per garantire il pluralismo effettivo [70]. Un altro esempio interessante, che riguarda il diritto di informazione, è dato dalla sentenza della Corte interamericana nel caso *Claude-Reyes* [71]. La Corte ha stabilito che il rifiuto da parte delle autorità del Cile di fornire informazioni ai tre ricorrenti circa un progetto che prevedeva la deforestazione di una regione del Cile (che avrebbe potuto mettere a repentaglio l'ecosistema del paese e il suo sviluppo economico) aveva violato la libertà di espressione *ex* art. 13 della Convenzione americana. La Corte ha sottolineato che la libertà di espressione comprende anche il diritto e la libertà di cercare, ricevere e distribuire informazioni di ogni tipo, ivi comprese quelle in possesso delle autorità statali. Di conseguenza, gli Stati hanno l'obbligo positivo di fornire tali informazioni [72].

6. *Diritto all'istruzione*

6.1. *Norme*

Anche il diritto all'istruzione è previsto da atti e trattati sui diritti umani di carattere sia generale che settoriale. L'art. 26 della Dichiarazione universale è così formulato:

> "1. Everyone has the right to education. Education shall be free, at least in the elementary and fundamental stages. Elementary education shall be compulsory. Technical and professional education shall be made generally available and higher education shall be equally accessible to all on the basis of merit.
>
> 2. Education shall be directed to the full development of the human personality and to the strengthening of respect for human rights and fundamental freedoms. It shall promote understanding, tolerance and friendship among all nations, racial or religious groups, and shall further the activities of the United Nations for the maintenance of peace.
>
> 3. Parents have a prior right to choose the kind of education that shall be given to their children".

Come si può notare, l'art. 26, con una formulazione ambiziosa, stabilisce tre componenti principali del diritto all'istruzione: *a*) il diritto di ricevere un'istruzione; *b*) gli scopi generali dell'istruzione; *c*) il diritto dei genitori di scegliere il tipo di istruzione dei figli.

Il Patto sui diritti economici, sociali e culturali regola il diritto all'istruzione nell'art.

---

[69] Vedi, ad es., ECtHR, *Young, James and Webster*, par. 55; *Dink v. Turkey*, parr. 106, 137-139.

[70] ECtHR, *Centro Europa 7 s.r.l. and Di Stefano*, par. 134.

[71] IACtHR, *Claude-Reyes et al. v. Chile.*

[72] *Ibidem*, par. 77 ss.

13, in maniera assai ampia e dettagliata; e riprende l'impostazione della Dichiarazione universale, ma con un linguaggio più prudente. Il par. 1 stabilisce, in via di principio, che gli Stati parti riconoscono il diritto di ogni individuo all'istruzione ed anche gli scopi generali dell'istruzione, simili a quelli già indicati nella Dichiarazione universale. Ma il par. 2, che è il più importante perché precisa e specifica il diritto di ricevere un'istruzione, è formulato in termini di obblighi statali "a realizzazione progressiva" [73]. Infatti, in esso gli Stati parti assumono una serie di impegni relativi alle varie fasi dell'istruzione delle persone; ma soltanto "with a view to achieving the full realization of this right". La formula è quella classica, in materia di diritti economici, sociali e culturali, che richiama la natura degli obblighi generali assunti dagli Stati parti ai sensi dell'art. 2, par. 1, del Patto [74].

In realtà, nell'art. 13, l'unico impegno netto riguarda la fase dell'istruzione primaria, poiché si prevede che: "Primary education shall be compulsory and available free to all" [75]. Con riguardo alle altre fasi dell'istruzione, gli impegni degli Stati sono meno rigorosi [76]. Per di più, anche l'obbligo relativo all'istruzione primaria, nel successivo art. 14 del Patto, assume il carattere di obbligo "a realizzazione progressiva", in un numero ragionevole di anni, per quegli Stati che non sono in grado di assicurare subito l'attuazione di tale obbligo [77]. Infine, i parr. 3 e 4 dell'art. 13 stabiliscono la libertà dei genitori di scegliere le scuole per i propri figli, ma con una serie di precisazioni e di limiti a tutela dei diritti dello Stato in materia di istruzione.

Il diritto all'istruzione è, invece, regolato in maniera più sintetica dalla Convenzione europea. L'art. 2 del Protocollo n. 1 alla Convenzione stabilisce che:

> "No person shall be denied the right to education. In the exercise of any functions which it assumes in relation to education and to teaching, the State shall respect the right of parents to ensure such education and teaching in conformity with their own religious and philosophical convictions".

Il diritto in oggetto è inoltre previsto dal Protocollo di San Salvador (art. 13), dalla Carta africana (art. 17), dalla Carta dei diritti fondamentali dell'UE (art. 14), dalla Carta araba (art. 41). Nel quadro dei trattati settoriali sui diritti umani, si possono ricordare l'art. 5(e)(v) della Convenzione contro la discriminazione razziale, l'art. 10 della Convenzione per l'eliminazione della discriminazione contro le donne, gli artt. 28, 29(2) e 32(1) della Convenzione sui diritti del fanciullo, l'art. 30 della Convenzione sui diritti dei lavoratori migranti, l'art. 24 della Convenzione sui diritti delle persone disabili, l'art. 11 della Carta africana sui diritti e il benessere del fanciullo, e gli artt. 12-14 della Convenzione quadro europea sulla protezione delle minoranze. Conviene citare anche la Convenzione UNE-

---

[73] Vedi *supra*, Cap. III, par. 5.3.

[74] Art. 2(1): "Each State Party to the present Covenant undertakes to take steps [...] to the maximum of its available resources, with a view to achieving progressively the full realization of the rights recognized in the present Covenant, by all appropriate means [...]".

[75] CESCR, art. 13(2)(a).

[76] CESCR, art. 13(2)(b) e (c).

[77] CESCR, art. 14: "Each State Party to the present Covenant which, at the time of becoming a Party, has not been able to secure [...] compulsory primary education, free of charge, undertakes, within two years, to work out and adopt a detailed plan of action for the progressive implementation, within a reasonable number of years, to be fixed in the plan, of the principle of compulsory education free of charge for all".

SCO del 1960 contro la discriminazione nell'istruzione. Infine, vi sono alcuni trattati di diritto internazionale umanitario che contengono disposizioni sul diritto all'istruzione [78].

Alcune di queste disposizioni sono ampie e dettagliate, perché riprendono, grosso modo, la formulazione dell'art. 13 del Patto sui diritti economici, sociali e culturali. Ne sono esempi l'art. 13 del Protocollo di San Salvador, l'art. 41 della Carta araba, gli artt. 28, 29 e 32 della Convenzione sui diritti del fanciullo. Altre disposizioni, invece, sono più sintetiche. Ad esempio, l'art. 17(1) della Carta africana si limita a stabilire che "Every individual shall have the right to education".

6.2. *Contenuto del diritto*

Il diritto all'istruzione non è inderogabile in stati di emergenza né ha carattere assoluto. Anche il diritto di ricevere un'istruzione primaria, come si è visto, può essere limitato nel caso in cui uno Stato non abbia le sufficienti risorse [79]. Il contenuto del diritto all'istruzione si può ricavare dal complesso delle norme convenzionali sopra citate. Tali norme perseguono gli scopi generali che erano già indicati in maniera chiara dall'art. 26 della Dichiarazione universale: *a*) quello di garantire a tutte le persone un accesso all'istruzione (diritto di ricevere un'istruzione); *b*) quello di garantire una libera scelta dell'istruzione, specie da parte dei genitori; *c*) quello di garantire che l'istruzione persegua finalità che non siano in contrasto con i diritti umani.

Da questi scopi, si deduce che il diritto all'istruzione si compone di *tre elementi principali*. Il primo elemento riguarda l'*accesso* all'istruzione. Molte norme convenzionali stabiliscono che l'istruzione primaria deve essere obbligatoria e gratuitamente accessibile a tutti. Ciò ha indotto alcuni autori a sostenere che il diritto di accesso all'educazione primaria costituisce il contenuto essenziale (*core content*) del diritto all'istruzione [80]. Per parte nostra, abbiamo già detto che non condividiamo la tesi circa un presunto contenuto essenziale (*core content*) dei diritti umani. Un discorso diverso, invece (che affronteremo in seguito) è quello di stabilire se gli Stati abbiano un obbligo minimo essenziale (*minimum core obligation*) di garantire un accesso all'educazione primaria. Un altro aspetto importante dell'accesso all'istruzione riguarda il diritto di accedere ad essa *senza discriminazioni* [81]. Questo diritto non comporta l'obbligo dello Stato di incrementare le disponibilità degli istituti di istruzione [82]; bensì deve essere inteso come il diritto di accesso non discriminatorio ad istituti di istruzione già esistenti [83].

Il secondo elemento del diritto all'istruzione riguarda la *libera scelta* dell'istruzione. Ciò significa che ogni persona (ed i genitori per i figli) è libera di scegliere l'istruzione che preferisce e lo Stato deve rispettare tale scelta e garantire il pluralismo dei percorsi e servizi scolastici [84].

---

[78] Vedi GC III, art. 38; GC IV, artt. 50 e 94; AP I, art. 52(3).

[79] CESCR, art. 14.

[80] Vedi, in questo senso, anche Kälin, Künzli (2009), p. 405.

[81] Vedi Focarelli (2013), pp. 218-219.

[82] Vedi ECtHR, *Leyla Şahin v. Turkey*, par. 137.

[83] Vedi ECtHR, *Belgian Linguistic Case*. Cfr. anche Kälin, Künzli (2009), pp. 406-407.

[84] Focarelli (2013), pp. 218-219.

Infine il terzo elemento del diritto all'istruzione riguarda l'impegno degli Stati a far sì che l'istruzione sia diretta al pieno sviluppo della persona umana ed al *rispetto dei diritti umani*. Tuttavia, si deve notare che questo elemento del diritto all'istruzione non è presente in tutti i trattati; e che esso ha carattere alquanto vago e generico.

6.3. *Obblighi*

Quanto agli obblighi degli Stati, che corrispondono ai vari aspetti del diritto all'istruzione, essi sono, come al solito, di varia natura. Alcuni sono obblighi negativi e immediati, come quello di non interferire nelle libere scelte dei genitori sui percorsi scolastici dei figli. Molti sono "a realizzazione progressiva", come avviene normalmente in materia di diritti culturali, ad esempio, gli obblighi dello Stato relativi all'accesso alle fasi superiori dell'istruzione [85]. Ma vi sono anche obblighi positivi immediati, sia di risultato che di *due diligence*.

La questione più interessante riguarda l'obbligo degli Stati di garantire a tutti un'educazione primaria. Il Comitato dei diritti economici, sociali e culturali sostiene che tale obbligo costituisce un obbligo minimo essenziale (*minimum core obligation*) e non un obbligo a realizzazione progressiva. Infatti il Comitato, nel suo Commento Generale n. 3, ha affermato che:

> "[...] a State party in which any significant number of individuals is deprived [...] of the most basic forms of education is, prima facie, failing to discharge its obligations under the Covenant. If the Covenant were to be read in such a way as not to establish such a minimum core obligation, it would be largely deprived of its raison d'être" [86].

Ci sembra che questa tesi possa essere accolta in linea di massima. Tuttavia, si deve notare che il Comitato medesimo aggiunge che ogni accertamento sul fatto se uno Stato abbia eseguito il suo *minimum core obligation* deve anche tener conto dei vincoli dati dalla disponibilità di risorse [87]. Uno Stato può escludere la propria responsabilità se dimostra che ha fatto ogni sforzo per usare tutte le risorse a sua disposizione nel tentativo di adempiere, in maniera prioritaria, il suddetto obbligo.

7. *Diritto alla vita culturale*

7.1. *Norme*

Il diritto alla vita culturale non è fra i diritti umani più ampiamente riconosciuti nella comunità internazionale, forse anche per la complessità che deriva dalle molte definizioni diverse di "cultura" [88]. Tuttavia, diversi trattati riconoscono il diritto delle persone di partecipare alla vita culturale e di godere dei vantaggi delle creazioni artistiche e scientifiche.

---

[85] Vedi CESCR, art. 13(2)(b) e (c).

[86] CteeESCR, General Comment No. 3, 14 December 1990, par. 10.

[87] *Ibidem*, par. 10.

[88] Vedi Weissbrodt, de la Vega (2007), p. 177.

Pertanto, il diritto alla vita culturale ha una sua specificità nel diritto internazionale dei diritti umani, anche se è chiaro che certi suoi aspetti sono già protetti da altri diritti umani, quali il diritto alla vita privata, le libertà di pensiero, coscienza e religione, le libertà di opinione ed espressione, il diritto all'istruzione. Pertanto, vi è un rapporto di complementarietà fra questi diversi diritti. Conviene, inoltre, premettere che il tema dei diritti umani culturali delle persone va tenuto distinto da quello, assai ampio, della protezione dei beni culturali nel diritto internazionale, che costituisce un settore diverso rispetto a quello dei diritti umani. Peraltro, anche in questo caso, esistono collegamenti ed interazioni fra i due temi.

Il diritto alla vita culturale è già previsto, nei suoi elementi essenziali, dalla Dichiarazione universale, il cui art. 27 proclama che:

> "1. Everyone has the right freely to participate in the cultural life of the community, to enjoy the arts and to share in scientific advancement and its benefits.
> 2. Everyone has the right to the protection of the moral and material interests resulting from any scientific, literary or artistic production of which he is the author".

Il Patto sui diritti economici, sociali e culturali contiene una norma più complessa ed analitica, l'art. 15, che peraltro, nel par. 1, riprende in termini quasi identici il contenuto della Dichiarazione universale:

> "1. The States Parties to the present Covenant recognize the right of everyone: a) To take part in cultural life; b) To enjoy the benefits of scientific progress and its applications; c) To benefit from the protection of the moral and material interests resulting from any scientific, literary or artistic production of which he is the author".

Nei successivi parr. 2, 3 e 4 dell'art. 15, gli Stati parti assumono alcuni obblighi piuttosto vaghi e generici. Essi si impegnano a prendere misure per conseguire la piena realizzazione del diritto alla vita culturale, incluse quelle relative alla conservazione, sviluppo e diffusione della scienza e della cultura; si impegnano a rispettare la libertà di ricerca scientifica; ed infine riconoscono i benefici della cooperazione internazionale in questi settori.

Altre norme dettagliate sul diritto alla vita culturale, in gran parte ispirate all'art. 15 del Patto sui diritti economici, sociali e culturali, sono contenute nel Protocollo di San Salvador (art. 14), nella Carta araba (art. 42) e nella Convenzione sui diritti delle persone disabili (art. 30). Gli altri trattati sui diritti umani contengono norme assai più sintetiche. Si possono ricordare l'art. 17(2) della Carta africana, l'art. 13 della Carta dei diritti fondamentali dell'UE, l'art. 13(e) della Convenzione per l'eliminazione della discriminazione contro le donne, l'art. 31 della Convenzione sui diritti del fanciullo, gli artt. 43(1)(g) e 45(1)(d) della Convenzione sui diritti dei lavoratori migranti. Ad esempio, l'art. 17(2) della Carta africana si limita a stabilire:

> "Every individual may freely take part in the cultural life of his community".

Infine, si deve ricordare che, accanto alle norme che si occupano dei diritti culturali degli individui, vi sono quelle dedicate ai diritti culturali collettivi, che appartengono alle minoranze ed ai popoli indigeni. Ma questo tema sarà trattato più avanti [89].

---

[89] Vedi *infra*, parr. 17 e 18.

7.2. *Contenuto del diritto*

Il contenuto del diritto alla vita culturale si deduce soprattutto dall'art. 15 del Patto sui diritti economici, sociali e culturali e dalle altre norme convenzionali che a tale disposizione si ispirano. Esso comprende tre elementi principali [90]: *a*) il diritto di partecipare alla vita culturale; *b*) il diritto di usufruire dei benefici della ricerca scientifica e di condurre tale ricerca; *c*) il diritto di usufruire della protezione degli interessi derivanti agli autori dai loro prodotti scientifici, letterari ed artistici.

Il primo elemento (diritto di partecipare alla vita culturale) comprende sia comportamenti "passivi" delle persone, quali la partecipazione ad eventi culturali, a mostre di pittura e scultura, a spettacoli musicali, teatrali, cinematografici e simili; sia comportamenti "attivi", quali creazioni artistiche e culturali di vario genere. Ma il diritto di creazione artistica può essere soggetto a restrizioni e limiti, per difendere altri valori, quali l'ordine pubblico, la morale, l'onore e la reputazione di altre persone. La Corte europea, ad esempio, ha affermato che i limiti stabiliti dall'art. 10(2) della Convenzione europea alla libertà di espressione operano anche in relazione alle creazioni ed espressioni artistiche, quali la pittura [91] o la letteratura.

Anche il secondo elemento (diritti relativi alla ricerca scientifica) protegge comportamenti sia "passivi" che "attivi". Infatti, da una parte, tutela la libertà delle persone di essere informate dei risultati delle ricerche scientifiche, per poterne trarre benefici. Questo aspetto risulta nitidamente dall'art. 15(1)(b) del Patto sui diritti economici, sociali e culturali. D'altra parte, viene tutelata anche la libertà di condurre ricerca scientifica, come risulta, fra l'altro, dal par. 3 del medesimo art. 15, per il quale gli Stati si impegnano a rispettare "the freedom indispensable for scientific research".

Infine, il terzo elemento (diritto degli autori alla tutela dei propri prodotti scientifici, letterari ed artistici) è stato oggetto di un apposito Commento Generale da parte del Comitato sui diritti economici, sociali e culturali [92]. Il Comitato ha approfondito anche il contenuto normativo di questo diritto [93]. Per "autori" si devono intendere individui o gruppi di individui o comunità; ma non persone giuridiche. I benefici per gli autori devono derivare da una "protezione effettiva", che tuttavia non riflette necessariamente il livello di protezione che si trova nei regimi giuridici di protezione della proprietà intellettuale. La protezione degli "interessi morali" degli autori include soprattutto il loro diritto di essere riconosciuti come i creatori delle opere e di opporsi alle loro modifiche. Infine, la protezione degli "interessi materiali" degli autori riflette il legame di questo diritto con il diritto di proprietà; ma non deve necessariamente estendersi per tutta la vita dei medesimi.

7.3. *Obblighi*

Al diritto alla vita culturale, nei suoi molteplici aspetti, corrispondono obblighi degli Stati di varia natura. Ad esempio, un obbligo negativo è quello dello Stato di non interferire nel

---

[90] Vedi Kälin, Künzli (2009), pp. 409-412.

[91] Vedi, ad es., ECtHR, *Müller and Others v. Switzerland*, parr. 33-36.

[92] CteeESCR, General Comment No. 17, 12 January 2006.

[93] *Ibidem*, parr. 6-24.

diritto delle persone di usufruire passivamente della cultura tramite libri o film o spettacoli o di usufruirne attivamente tramite la scrittura di libri o l'esecuzione di opere artistiche. Un obbligo positivo e di *due diligence* dello Stato è quello di proteggere il diritto alla cultura delle persone da interferenze da parte di altre persone. Un obbligo positivo ed "a realizzazione progressiva" dello Stato è quello di prendere misure per conseguire la piena realizzazione della conservazione, sviluppo e diffusione della scienza e della cultura, come è previsto, ad esempio, dall'art. 15(2) del Patto sui diritti economici, sociali e culturali.

Sezione III
PROTEZIONE DELLE ATTIVITÀ POLITICHE

Fra gli scopi del diritto internazionale dei diritti umani vi è anche quello di proteggere la sfera delle attività politiche (intese sia in senso lato che ristretto) delle persone. Ciò si realizza tramite alcuni diritti che, storicamente, sono considerati come appartenenti alla prima generazione dei diritti umani. Quelli più significativi, che qui di seguito tratteremo, sono: *a*) la libertà di riunione e di associazione; *b*) il diritto di partecipazione alla vita politica e pubblica, che comprende anche il diritto a libere elezioni e quello di accesso a pubblici impieghi.

8. *Libertà di riunione e di associazione*

8.1. *Norme*

Le libertà di riunione e di associazione sono sancite unitariamente dall'art. 20 della Dichiarazione universale nei seguenti termini:

> "1. Everyone has the right to freedom of peaceful assembly and association
> 2. No one may be compelled to belong to an association".

Inoltre, l'art. 23(4) della Dichiarazione stabilisce il diritto di ogni individuo di fondare ed aderire ai sindacati, per la protezione dei propri interessi.

La Convenzione europea, nell'art. 11, par.1, riprende il contenuto della Dichiarazione universale, ma menziona separatamente le due libertà:

> "Everyone has the right to freedom of peaceful assembly and to freedom of association with others, including the right to form and to join trade unions for the protection of his interests".

Quindi la Convenzione, nel par. 2 del medesimo art. 11, aggiunge una disposizione sulle restrizioni legittime alle libertà di riunione e di associazione. Le restrizioni devono essere prescritte dalla legge e necessarie in una società democratica, per la protezione della sicurezza nazionale o della sicurezza pubblica, per la prevenzione dei reati, per la protezione della salute o della morale o dei diritti altrui. Inoltre, si precisa che possono essere imposte restrizioni legittime sull'esercizio delle due libertà da parte di membri delle forze armate, della polizia o dell'amministrazione statale.

Il Patto sui diritti civili e politici dedica due norme dettagliate, separate e distinte, alla liberta di riunione (art. 21) ed alla libertà di associazione (art. 22). Ciascuna norma contiene un elenco delle restrizioni legittime, sostanzialmente simili a quelle previste dalla Convenzione europea. La Convenzione americana, negli artt. 15 e 16, adotta la medesima impostazione del Patto. Altre norme pertinenti, nei trattati sui diritti umani di carattere generale, sono gli artt. 10 e 11 della Carta africana; l'art. 24, parr. 5, 6 e 7, della Carta araba; l'art. 5 della Carta sociale europea (riveduta); e l'art. 12 della Carta dei diritti fondamentali dell'UE.

Nel quadro dei trattati settoriali sui diritti umani, si possono ricordare l'art. 5(d)(ix) della Convenzione contro la discriminazione razziale; l'art. 7(c) della Convenzione per l'eliminazione della discriminazione contro le donne; l'art. 15 della Convenzione sui diritti del fanciullo; gli artt. 26 e 40 della Convenzione sui diritti dei lavoratori migranti; e l'art. 29(b) della Convenzione sui diritti delle persone disabili.

Inoltre, conviene notare che il diritto di riunione privata nella propria abitazione è garantito dal diritto al rispetto della vita privata ed il diritto di riunione religiosa è tutelato in maniera specifica dalla libertà di religione [94]. Infine, il diritto di fondare sindacati e di aderirvi è previsto anche da alcuni trattati stipulati nel quadro dell'Organizzazione internazionale del lavoro.

8.2. *Contenuto delle libertà*

Le libertà di riunione e di associazione possono essere considerate come diritti politici in senso lato, poiché esse sono essenziali per la protezione delle attività politiche e sociali delle persone in ogni forma di regime democratico e pluralistico. Esse, peraltro, non hanno natura né di diritti inderogabili in stati di emergenza né di diritti assoluti. Infatti, ambedue le libertà sono soggette ad una serie di restrizioni, come risulta chiaramente dalle norme sopra indicate e dalla prassi [95].

Conviene distinguere fra i contenuti delle due libertà, poiché, pur essendo esse reciprocamente funzionali [96], sono differenti i comportamenti cui si riferiscono.

La libertà di riunione comprende sia le riunioni private sia quelle tenute in luogo pubblico, come, ad esempio, sit-in, marce e cortei, purché di carattere pacifico. Le riunioni possono avere natura politica, economica, sociale, sportiva o artistica. La nozione di "riunione" data dagli organi internazionali di controllo è, di solito, ampia ed autonoma rispetto alle definizioni date nei diversi sistemi nazionali. La libertà appartiene sia agli organizzatori della riunione sia a coloro che vi partecipano [97]. Nel caso di riunioni e manifestazioni violente, sono giustificati gli interventi delle autorità, ma con forme e mezzi che non superino i limiti della necessità e della proporzionalità [98].

Anche la nozione di "associazione" è ampia ed autonoma; ed essa implica una pluralità

---

[94] Vedi Focarelli (2013), p. 208.

[95] Vedi, ad es., HRCtee, *Kivenmaa v. Finland*, par. 9.2; *Zalesskaya v. Belarus*, par. 10.6.

[96] Zagrebelski *et al.* (2019), p. 365.

[97] ECtHR, *Djavit An v. Turkey*, par. 56.

[98] ECtHR, *Taranenko v. Russia*, parr. 80-97.

di soggetti, stabilmente e volontariamente associati. Nelle associazioni rientrano anche i sindacati [99], i partiti politici e le ONG. La libertà di associazione comprende anche, in termini positivi, il diritto di fondarne una, organizzarla e ottenerne il riconoscimento giuridico, per poter operare efficacemente [100]. Essa implica anche, in termini negativi, il diritto di non aderire ad alcuna associazione e quello di non essere costretto a rimanervi [101]. Ci si può chiedere se la libertà di associazione protegga solo gli individui o anche le associazioni medesime. La risposta sembra variare a seconda dei trattati. Ad esempio, i diritti protetti dalla Convenzione europea possono essere invocati dinanzi alla Corte di Strasburgo anche dalle persone giuridiche, mentre solo le persone fisiche possono indirizzare reclami individuali al Comitato dei diritti umani [102].

Nella prassi, si sono verificati alcuni casi interessanti relativi al divieto o allo scioglimento di partiti politici [103]. La Corte europea ha, di solito, ritenuto che lo scioglimento di un partito politico sia un'interferenza grave con la libertà di associazione e quindi sia giustificata solo nell'ipotesi in cui il partito costituisca una minaccia alla vita democratica dello Stato [104]. Tuttavia, nel caso *Refah Partisi* [105], ha ritenuto che fosse legittimo lo scioglimento di un partito da parte della Corte costituzionale turca, perché giustificato per proteggere la sicurezza nazionale, i diritti altrui e la prevenzione della criminalità.

8.3. *Obblighi*

Anche in questo caso, gli obblighi degli Stati, che corrispondono ai diritti di riunione e di associazione, sono di varia natura. Prima di tutto, gli Stati hanno l'obbligo negativo di non proibire le libertà di riunione ed associazione delle persone, e di non interferire nel loro esercizio. In secondo luogo, hanno l'obbligo positivo (immediato e di risultato) di emanare norme ed adottare prassi amministrative (qualora non siano già esistenti), per tutelare tali libertà.

In terzo luogo, gli Stati hanno anche una serie di obblighi positivi e immediati volti a proteggere le persone, tramite misure preventive e repressive, da interferenze nelle loro libertà da parte di terzi. Come si è già detto più volte, questi obblighi di protezione sono talora di risultato e talora di *due diligence*. Infine, si può ritenere che gli Stati abbiano anche alcuni obblighi positivi "a realizzazione progressiva", volti a promuovere nel tempo quelle associazioni che perseguono lo sviluppo e la conoscenza dei diritti umani.

---

[99] Sul diritto di costituire sindacati e di aderirvi vedi anche CESCR, art. 8, e *infra*, par. 10.

[100] Vedi HRCtee, *Korneenko and Others v. Belarus*, par. 7.2.

[101] Vedi, ad es., ECtHR, *Sørensen and Rasmussen v. Denmark*, parr. 33 e 54-77. I giudici di Strasburgo hanno condannato la Danimarca per la violazione dell'art. 11, in quanto i ricorrenti, nel periodo in cui avevano prestato servizio presso una compagnia di distribuzione, erano stati obbligati ad aderire, prima o dopo l'assunzione, ad uno specifico sindacato. Vedi anche ECtHR, *Young, James and Webster v. UK*, parr. 64-65; *Sigurjónsson v. Iceland*, par. 41; *Gustafsson v. Sweden*, parr. 51-54.

[102] Vedi Kälin, Künzli (2009), p. 477.

[103] Vedi Focarelli (2013), pp. 210-211.

[104] Vedi, ad es., ECtHR, *Case of United Communist Party of Turkey and Others v. Turkey*, par. 61; *Ouranio Toxo v. Greece*, parr. 40-41.

[105] ECtHR, *Refah Partisi (the Welfare Party) and Others v. Turkey*, parr. 67, 110-115, 119-123, 132-135.

9. *Diritto di partecipazione alla vita politica e pubblica. Libere elezioni ed accesso a pubblici impieghi*

9.1. *Norme*

L'art. 21 della Dichiarazione universale è così formulato:

> "1. Everyone has the right to take part in the government of his country, directly or through freely chosen representatives.
> 2. Everyone has the right of equal access to public service in his country.
> 3. The will of the people shall be the basis of the authority of government; this will shall be expressed in periodic and genuine elections which shall be by universal and equal suffrage and shall be held by secret vote or by equivalent free voting procedures".

Come si vede, questa disposizione prevede tre diritti diversi, ma fra loro strettamente collegati: *a*) il diritto di partecipazione alla vita politica e pubblica; *b*) il diritto di accesso agli impieghi pubblici; *c*) il diritto a libere elezioni. In realtà, come vedremo, il secondo ed il terzo diritto funzionano come specificazioni del primo.

Il Patto sui diritti civili e politici riprende, in termini molto simili, il contenuto dell'art. 21 della Dichiarazione universale, ma specificando che i tre diritti politici sono riservati ai soli cittadini e che consentono restrizioni, purché non siano "irragionevoli". Infatti, l'art. 25 del Patto recita:

> "Every citizen shall have the right and the opportunity, without any of the distinctions mentioned in article 2 and without unreasonable restrictions:
> a) To take part in the conduct of public affairs, directly or through freely chosen representatives;
> b) To vote and to be elected at genuine periodic elections which shall be by universal and equal suffrage and shall be held by secret ballot, guaranteeing the free expression of the will of the electors;
> c) To have access, on general terms of equality, to public service in his country".

Altre norme pertinenti, nei trattati sui diritti umani di carattere generale, sono: l'art. 3 del Protocollo n. 1 alla Convenzione europea, l'art. 23 della Convenzione americana, l'art. 13 della Carta africana, l'art. 24, parr. 1, 2, 3 e 4, della Carta araba, gli artt. 39 e 40 della Carta dei diritti fondamentali dell'UE. Tuttavia, queste norme non sono del tutto uniformi: ad esempio, l'art. 3 del Protocollo n. 1 alla Convenzione europea comprende solo il diritto a libere elezioni, mentre l'art. 13 della Carta africana non comprende tale ultimo diritto, e gli artt. 39-40 della Carta dei diritti fondamentali dell'UE prevedono solo il diritto di voto al Parlamento europeo ed alle elezioni municipali. Nel quadro dei trattati settoriali sui diritti umani, si possono ricordare l'art. 5(c) della Convenzione contro la discriminazione razziale, l'art. 7 della Convenzione contro la discriminazione verso le donne e l'art. 29 della Convenzione sui diritti dei disabili.

Conviene sottolineare che queste norme non intendono garantire un concetto universalmente accettato di democrazia, né promuovere uno specifico sistema di governo su tutti gli altri [106]; ma si limitano a stabilire alcuni diritti dei cittadini di partecipazione alla vita politica del proprio paese.

---

[106] Weissbrodt, de la Vega (2007), p. 113.

Ma un discorso diverso vale per la Convenzione europea, nel cui Preambolo si dichiara che i diritti umani e le libertà fondamentali "are best maintained […] by an effective political democracy" e che gli Stati europei "have a common heritage of political traditions, ideals, freedom and the rule of law". Su questa base, la Corte europea ha più volte dichiarato che una forma di governo democratica e pluralistica è una componente essenziale dell'ordine pubblico europeo [107]; e che la democrazia è il solo modello politico contemplato dalla Convenzione europea [108].

9.2. *Contenuto dei diritti*

Come si è già detto, dalla maggior parte delle norme convenzionali sopraindicate emergono tre diritti politici, i quali, pur essendo fra loro collegati, hanno contenuti ed ambiti di applicazione diversi. Un loro carattere comune è che essi non sono inderogabili in stati di emergenza, né hanno natura assoluta.

Il primo diritto viene definito, nei suddetti trattati, talora come diritto di partecipare al governo del proprio paese [109], talora come diritto di partecipare alla condotta degli affari pubblici [110], e talora in ambedue i modi [111]. A noi sembra che la definizione più precisa e completa sia quella di *diritto di partecipazione alla vita politica e pubblica* [112]. Tuttavia, si deve ammettere che questo diritto ha un contenuto assai vago e generale. Il Comitato dei diritti umani, nel suo Commento Generale n. 25 [113], ha affermato che il concetto di "direzione degli affari pubblici", contenuto nell'art. 25 del Patto sui diritti civili e politici, è un concetto ampio, che comprende l'esercizio di poteri di governo da parte di tutti gli organi statali:

> "The conduct of public affairs […] is a broad concept which relates to the exercise of political power, in particular the exercise of legislative, executive and administrative powers. It covers all aspects of public administration, and the formulation and implementation of policy at international, national, regional and local levels. The allocation of powers and the means by which individual citizens exercise the right to participate in the conduct of public affairs protected by article 25 should be established by the constitution and other laws" [114].

Il Comitato ha anche affermato che:

> "Article 25 lies at the core of democratic government based on the consent of the people […]" [115].

---

[107] Vedi, ad es., ECtHR, *Mathieu-Molin and Clerfayt v. Belgium*, par. 47; *Case of United Communist Party of Turkey and Others v. Turkey*, par. 45; *Sadak and Others v. Turkey (No. 2)*, par. 32.

[108] Vedi, ad es., ECtHR, *Zdanoka v. Latvia*, Judgment of 17 June 2004, par. 78; *Zdanoka v. Latvia*, Judgment of 16 March 2006, par. 98; *Ahmed and Others v. UK*, par. 52.

[109] UDHR, art. 21; ACHR, art. 23; ACHPR, art. 13.

[110] CCPR, art. 25; ArCHR, art. 24(2).

[111] CERD, art. 5(c); CEDAW, art. 7(b).

[112] In questo senso vedi CRPD, art. 29. In dottrina, si parla talora di "diritto di partecipazione politica": cfr. Weissbrodt, de la Vega (2007), p. 113.

[113] HRCtee, General Comment No. 25, 12 July 1996.

[114] *Ibidem*, par. 5.

[115] *Ibidem*, par. 1.

Ma il medesimo Comitato, nel caso *Marshall*, è stato più cauto, perché ha detto che:

> "[...] article 25(a) of the Covenant cannot be understood as meaning that any directly affected group, large or small, has the unconditional right to choose the modalities of participation in the conduct of public affairs. That, in fact, would be an extrapolation of the right to direct participation by the citizens, far beyond the scope of article 25(a)" [116].

Pertanto, si può concludere che il par. *a*) dell'art. 25, nonostante la sua formulazione ambiziosa, non garantisce a ogni cittadino un diritto preciso e specifico di partecipazione diretta agli affari pubblici; ma, tutt'al più, il diritto che gli Stati, nei propri ordinamenti interni, non gli pongano restrizioni o discriminazioni irragionevoli quando egli intende esercitare il suo diritto di partecipazione. Inoltre, ci sembra che il diritto di partecipazione alla vita politica e pubblica, nel par. *a*) dell'art. 25 e nelle altre norme convenzionali analoghe che lo regolano, funzioni come una sorta di "diritto-quadro", che trova poi applicazioni specifiche nel diritto di accesso ai pubblici impieghi e nel diritto a libere elezioni.

In effetti, il *diritto di accesso agli impieghi pubblici* ha un contenuto più preciso e circoscritto. Tuttavia, anche questo diritto va correttamente interpretato: esso non garantisce alle persone di ottenere un lavoro all'interno del servizio pubblico, ma soltanto l'opportunità "in condizioni generali di eguaglianza" di ottenerne uno [117]. Inoltre, il diritto di accesso agli impieghi pubblici significa che i processi di assunzione, promozione, sospensione e congedo in tali impieghi devono rispettare criteri di oggettività e ragionevolezza, e soprattutto non devono essere discriminatori [118].

Ma è il terzo diritto politico, fra quelli qui in esame, che è il più importante. Anche se la sua definizione non è identica nelle norme convenzionali sopraindicate, esso può essere definito, in sintesi, come il *diritto a libere elezioni*; cioè il diritto di veder indette libere elezioni e di parteciparvi come elettore e come candidato.

Per la verità, ci si potrebbe chiedere se le norme convenzionali sopra citate attribuiscano *direttamente* all'individuo un vero e proprio diritto elettorale. Qualche dubbio potrebbe derivare, ad esempio, dall'art. 3 del Protocollo n. 1 alla Convenzione europea, secondo cui:

> "The High Contracting Parties undertake to hold free elections at reasonable intervals by secret ballot, under conditions which will ensure the free expression of the opinion of the people in the choice of the legislature".

La formula letterale dell'art. 3 sembra prevedere soltanto un impegno ad indire elezioni preso dagli Stati tra di loro [119]. Tuttavia, la Corte europea ha affermato, fin dalle prime sentenze in materia, che la norma in questione riconosce anche un vero e proprio diritto *individuale* a vedere indette le elezioni ed a parteciparvi, sia come elettore che come candidato [120]. Inoltre, la nozione di "elezioni" dell'art. 3 del Protocollo n. 1, nonostante si riferisca solo all'elezione degli organi legislativi dello Stato, è stata interpretata in senso estensivo

---

[116] HRCtee, *Marshall et al. and the Mikmaq tribal society v. Canada*, par. 5.5. In questo caso, i ricorrenti lamentavano la violazione dell'art. 25, in quanto non erano stati invitati a partecipare alle conferenze costituzionali del Canada in qualità di rappresentanti della popolazione aborigena dei Mikmaq.

[117] HRCtee, *Kall v. Poland*, par. 13.2.

[118] Vedi, ad es., HRCtee, *Hinostroza Solís v. Peru*, par. 6.2. Cfr. anche Kälin, Künzli (2009), p. 485.

[119] Zagrebelsky *et al.* (2016), p. 337.

[120] ECtHR, *Mathieu-Molin and Clerfayt v. Belgium*, parr. 46-51.

da parte degli organi di Strasburgo [121]. D'altra parte, in altri trattati sui diritti umani, la norma pertinente è chiara nel conferire direttamente agli individui il diritto di votare e di essere eletto in libere elezioni. Esemplari, in questo senso, sono l'art. 25(b) del Patto sui diritti civili e politici, l'art. 23(b) della Convenzione americana e l'art. 24(3) della Carta araba.

Inoltre, si noti che il diritto di essere eletti è altrettanto importante che il diritto di votare. Su questo punto, il Comitato dei diritti umani ha affermato che:

> "The effective implementation of the right and the opportunity to stand for elective office ensures that persons entitled to vote have a free choice of candidates. Any restrictions on the right to stand for elections, such as minimum age, must be justifiable on objective and reasonable criteria" [122].

Altri aspetti importanti del contenuto normativo del diritto a libere elezioni riguardano la nozione stessa di "libere elezioni", i ragionevoli intervalli fra i periodi elettorali, il principio di segretezza del voto e le restrizioni legittime a tale diritto. Si ritiene, di solito, che le elezioni siano libere se esse si svolgono nel rispetto di altri diritti umani, quali la libertà di espressione, di riunione e di associazione; e se i loro risultati sono riconosciuti ed eseguiti dai governi. Il principio di segretezza del voto è fondamentale per assicurare che le elezioni siano libere. Per di più, le elezioni devono essere tenute secondo intervalli di tempo ragionevoli.

Il discorso è più complesso circa la legittimità di restrizioni al diritto di voto in libere elezioni. Le norme convenzionali sopraindicate non prevedono restrizioni o limiti a tale diritto, se non quello della sua applicabilità ai soli cittadini. Tuttavia la prassi della Corte europea, della Corte interamericana e del Comitato dei diritti umani ha riconosciuto che esistono altri limiti di carattere implicito, che gli Stati possono porre, purché nel rispetto di certi criteri. Per la Corte europea, le restrizioni al diritto di voto non devono essere arbitrarie né sproporzionate, né interferire con la libera espressione di opinione da parte del popolo. Più in particolare, secondo la Corte, per quanto riguarda l'elettorato attivo, alcune persone possono essere escluse dal diritto al voto per motivazioni legate all'età o perché si tratta di condannati con sanzione penale o di detenuti. Invece, non è stata considerata legittima l'esclusione di coloro che sono sotto tutela o curatela per infermità mentale, indipendentemente dalla gravità dell'infermità [123]. Quanto all'elettorato passivo, vi possono essere in taluni casi delle limitazioni, purché siano rispettati i criteri di proporzionalità e di non arbitrarietà.

Secondo il Comitato dei diritti umani, ogni restrizione, che sia applicata al diritto di voto ed al diritto di essere eletto, deve essere fondata su criteri oggettivi e ragionevoli [124]. Si può ricordare, ad esempio, il caso *Yevdokimov e Rezanov*, che riguardava il divieto assoluto di voto imposto dalla Russia a tutte le persone dichiarate colpevoli e condannate alla reclusione, mentre scontavano la loro pena. Il Comitato condannò la Russia per violazione

---

[121] Essa comprende non solo gli organi che esercitano funzioni legislative in senso stretto, come i parlamenti, ma anche organi che hanno una posizione di rilievo nel processo legislativo. Vedi ECtHR, *Matthews v. UK*, parr. 50-54.

[122] HRCtee, General Comment n. 25, 12 July 1996, par. 15.

[123] Vedi ECtHR, *Scoppola v. Italy (no. 3)*, parr. 81-110.

[124] Vedi HRCtee, General Comment No. 25, 12 July 1996, par. 4. Vedi anche ECtHR, *Hirst v. UK (No. 2)*, par. 60.

dell'art. 25(b) del Patto sui diritti civili e politici, ritenendo che la misura restrittiva adottata dalla Russia non fosse conforme al requisito della ragionevolezza [125].

9.3. *Obblighi*

Ai tre diritti umani in oggetto corrispondono obblighi degli Stati aventi varia natura. Per quanto riguarda il diritto di partecipazione alla vita politica e pubblica, ci sembra, come si è accennato sopra, che gli Stati non abbiano assunto, a livello internazionale, obblighi vincolanti ed immediati nei confronti dei propri cittadini, se non quello, generale, di non porre, nei propri ordinamenti interni, restrizioni o discriminazioni irragionevoli a tale diritto. Quest'obbligo comporta soprattutto misure positive di carattere normativo, poiché lo Stato deve eliminare normative interne che contengano restrizioni o discriminazioni irragionevoli.

Al diritto del cittadino di accesso agli impieghi pubblici corrispondono obblighi statali un po' più precisi, che sono diretti a tutti gli organi dello Stato e non solo a quelli legislativi. Gli Stati, come si è visto, si impegnano a rispettare criteri oggettivi, ragionevoli e non discriminatori nei processi che riguardano l'assunzione, promozione, sospensione e congedo in tali impieghi dei propri cittadini.

Infine, vi sono gli obblighi relativi al diritto dei cittadini a libere elezioni. Si è notato che tale diritto ha un contenuto piuttosto ampio e complesso, poiché comprende vari aspetti del diritto di votare e di essere votati. Anche i corrispondenti obblighi degli Stati sono molteplici ed hanno varia natura: molti di essi attengono alla garanzia dei requisiti richiesti dalla nozione di "libere elezioni" e si configurano come obblighi positivi a carico degli organi legislativi nazionali.

Sezione IV
PROTEZIONE DELLE ATTIVITÀ ECONOMICHE

Nel diritto internazionale dei diritti umani, vi sono numerose norme che hanno lo scopo di proteggere le persone nella realizzazione delle loro attività economiche. Si parla a questo proposito di diritti economici, una categoria piuttosto ampia di diritti umani, che vengono di solito inquadrati fra quelli di "seconda generazione", con riferimento principale al loro sviluppo storico nel quadro delle Nazioni Unite [126]. In realtà, questa classificazione non è sempre corretta, poiché alcuni di questi diritti, come vedremo, hanno un'origine anteriore rispet-

---

[125] HRCtee, *Yevdokimov and Rezanov v. Russia*, par. 7.5. I criteri di oggettività e ragionevolezza si applicano anche al diritto di essere eletto. Nel caso *Bwalya*, il Comitato dei diritti umani condannò lo Zambia per la violazione dell'art. 25, lett. b), non avendo potuto il ricorrente, un esponente di spicco di un partito politico di opposizione all'ex Presidente, partecipare alla campagna elettorale e candidarsi per il proprio partito, senza motivi ragionevoli. HRCtee, *Bwalya v. Zambia*, par. 6.6.

[126] Vedi *supra*, Cap. III, par. 4.1 e Cap. IV, par. 4.

to alla creazione delle Nazioni Unite. Fra i numerosi diritti economici, ci limiteremo ad esaminare quelli che riteniamo più importanti; e cioè: *a*) il diritto al lavoro [127]; *b*) il diritto di proprietà.

10. *Diritto al lavoro*

10.1. *Norme*

Il diritto al lavoro viene qui inteso in senso ampio, come comprensivo di una serie di diritti più specifici che tutelano i lavoratori [128]. È su questa base che si può sostenere che il diritto al lavoro ha un'origine storica più antica rispetto al sistema di tutela dei diritti umani delle Nazioni Unite [129]. Infatti, l'esigenza di proteggere i lavoratori ed i loro diritti a livello internazionale risale, come si ricorderà, al Trattato di pace di Versailles, al Patto della Società delle Nazioni ed alla istituzione dell'Organizzazione Internazionale del Lavoro (ILO) nel 1919.

Fin da allora, l'ILO è stata assai attiva ed ha prodotto nel tempo numerose convenzioni e raccomandazioni [130], che hanno dato vita a un vasto insieme di standard internazionali del lavoro (*international labour standards*) [131], riguardanti un'amplissima gamma di aspetti relativi alle condizioni di lavoro. Molti di questi standard sono assai specifici e dettagliati. Alcuni di essi sono comunemente ritenuti fondamentali (c.d. *core labour standards*) e sono stati ribaditi nel 1998 nella *ILO Declaration on Fundamental Principles and Rights at Work*. In realtà, sotto l'egida dell'ILO, si è venuto affermando un regime giuridico piuttosto complesso in materia di lavoro, che fa parte, a sua volta, di un ampio settore del diritto internazionale, che si suole denominare come diritto internazionale del lavoro (*international labour law*).

Tuttavia conviene, lasciando da parte il sistema dell'ILO, concentrarsi sul diritto al lavoro ed i diritti dei lavoratori soltanto *nell'ottica dei diritti umani*. In effetti, il diritto al lavoro come diritto umano è proclamato già nell'art. 23 della Dichiarazione universale, secondo cui:

> "1. Everyone has the right to work, to free choice of employment, to just and favourable conditions of work and to protection against unemployment.
> 2. Everyone, without any discrimination, has the right to equal pay for equal work.
> 3. Everyone who works has the right to just and favourable remuneration ensuring for himself and his family an existence worthy of human dignity, and supplemented, if necessary, by other means of social protection.
> 4. Everyone has the right to form and to join trade unions for the protection of his interests".

---

127 Il divieto di lavori forzati o obbligatori è stato già esaminato (*supra*, Cap. V, par. 15).

128 Vedi Pustorino (2019), p. 189, che parla di diritto al lavoro come di un "contenitore", nel quale sono confluiti con il tempo diritti più specifici.

129 Ma vedi (*supra*, Cap. I, parr. 2.8 e 2.10) i limiti del sistema di protezione dei lavoratori nel periodo fra le due guerre mondiali.

130 189 convenzioni e 205 raccomandazioni.

131 Si consulti, in generale, *www.ilo.org*.

Inoltre, la Dichiarazione, all'art. 24, enuncia che ognuno ha diritto al riposo ed al tempo libero, compresi ragionevoli limiti alle ore di lavoro e ferie periodiche retribuite. Come si può notare, già la Dichiarazione universale enuclea le principali componenti del diritto al lavoro: *a*) libera scelta del lavoro; *b*) giuste e favorevoli condizioni di lavoro; *c*) protezione dalla disoccupazione; *d*) non discriminazione nella remunerazione; *e*) diritto ad una giusta remunerazione; *f*) protezione sociale dei lavoratori; *g*) diritto di costituire sindacati e di aderirvi.

Il Patto sui diritti economici, sociali e culturali si occupa in maniera assai estesa del diritto al lavoro, nelle sue componenti sopra indicate. Le disposizioni rilevanti sono gli artt. 6, 7, 8 e 9. L'art. 6 è dedicato al *diritto al lavoro in generale* ed alla *libera scelta* del lavoro; ed è formulato in maniera piuttosto prudente, nell'ottica prevalente degli obblighi statali "a realizzazione progressiva". Nel par. 1, gli Stati contraenti riconoscono il diritto al lavoro, che implica il diritto di ogni individuo di ottenere la possibilità di guadagnarsi la vita con un lavoro liberamente scelto o accettato, e si impegnano a prendere le misure appropriate (*appropriate steps*) per garantire tale diritto. Nel par. 2, si descrivono, in maniera esemplificativa, le misure che gli Stati devono prendere per assicurare la piena realizzazione del diritto al lavoro: esse comprendono programmi di orientamento e formazione tecnica e professionale, l'elaborazione di politiche e tecniche atte ad assicurare uno sviluppo economico, sociale e culturale ed un pieno impiego produttivo.

L'art. 7 del Patto è dedicato al diritto di godere di *giuste e favorevoli condizioni di lavoro*. Gli Stati parti riconoscono questo diritto e affermano che tali condizioni di lavoro dovrebbero garantire, in particolare: *a*) una remunerazione che assicuri a tutti i lavoratori un equo salario ed un'eguale remunerazione per un eguale lavoro ed un'esistenza decorosa; *b*) la sicurezza e l'igiene nel lavoro; *c*) un'eguale possibilità di promozione nel lavoro fondata sull'anzianità di servizio e sulla competenza; *d*) il diritto al riposo, ad una ragionevole limitazione delle ore lavorative ed alle ferie periodiche retribuite. L'art. 8 si occupa del diritto di costituire *sindacati* e di aderirvi. Esso costituisce una specificazione, nell'ottica dei diritti dei lavoratori, del diritto più generale di associazione, di cui abbiamo già parlato [132]. Nell'art. 8, gli Stati parti si impegnano anche a garantire il diritto di sciopero, purché esso venga esercitato in conformità alle leggi di ciascun paese. L'art. 9 è dedicato alla sicurezza sociale. Gli Stati parti riconoscono il diritto di ogni individuo alla *sicurezza sociale*, ivi comprese le assicurazioni sociali.

Fra i trattati regionali sui diritti umani, sono particolarmente importanti la Carta sociale europea (riveduta) e la Carta dei diritti fondamentali dell'UE. La prima contiene numerose disposizioni che regolano in maniera dettagliata i diritti dei lavoratori. Essi comprendono, fra gli altri, il diritto al lavoro (art. 1), il diritto a giuste condizioni di lavoro (art. 2), il diritto a condizioni di lavoro sicure e sane (art. 3), il diritto ad un'equa remunerazione (art. 4), il diritto di organizzarsi (art. 5), il diritto di contrattazione collettiva (art. 6), il diritto alla sicurezza sociale (art. 12), il diritto di eguaglianza in materia di impiego senza discriminazione per motivi di sesso (art. 20), il diritto partecipare al miglioramento delle condizioni di lavoro (art. 22). La Carta dei diritti fondamentali dell'UE regola il diritto al lavoro negli artt. 27-32.

---

[132] Vedi *supra*, par. 8.

Nel quadro degli altri sistemi regionali, merita ricordare gli artt. 34(g) e 45(b) e (c) della Carta dell'OAS; gli artt. 6, 7 e 8 del Protocollo di San Salvador; gli artt. 15 e 29(6) della Carta africana; e l'art. 34 della Carta araba.

Inoltre, vi sono alcuni trattati settoriali sui diritti umani che contengono disposizioni sul principio di non discriminazione in materia di lavoro: l'art. 5(e)(i-ii) della Convenzione contro la discriminazione razziale; l'art. 11 della Convenzione per l'eliminazione della discriminazione contro le donne; l'art. 25 della Convenzione sui diritti dei lavoratori migranti; l'art. 27 della Convenzione sui diritti delle persone disabili. Infine, vi sono alcune norme convenzionali sul divieto di certe forme di sfruttamento del lavoro dei fanciulli. Si possono ricordare gli artt. 32-36 della Convenzione sui diritti del fanciullo; l'art. 34(3) della Carta araba; gli artt. 15 e 16 della Carta africana sui diritti ed il benessere del minore [133]; nonché alcune convenzioni dell'ILO specificamente dedicate al lavoro dei fanciulli o al divieto del loro sfruttamento [134].

10.2. *Contenuto del diritto*

Il diritto al lavoro in generale, ed i diritti specifici di tutela dei lavoratori che dal primo derivano, non hanno, in linea di massima, natura inderogabile in stati di emergenza, né carattere assoluto. Ma ciò non vale per il divieto di lavoro forzato [135] ed il divieto di sfruttamento di certe forme di lavoro minorile.

Quanto al contenuto di tali diritti, non si possono qui approfondire i contenuti dei numerosi e dettagliati diritti specifici dei lavoratori previsti nelle norme convenzionali. Pertanto ci limitiamo a qualche cenno sul diritto al lavoro in generale, specie alla luce dell'art. 6 del Patto sui diritti economici, sociali e culturali, che è la norma più importante in materia.

Il diritto al lavoro, ai sensi dell'art. 6, va inteso, in primo luogo, in stretto legame con il diritto alla libera scelta del lavoro. In altri termini, il par. 1 dell'art. 6 non intende attribuire ad ogni persona il diritto di ottenere un lavoro né il diritto di ottenere un impiego dallo Stato; ma, più semplicemente, il diritto di scegliere o accettare liberamente un lavoro, fra varie possibili offerte, senza interferenze da parte dello Stato; nonché il diritto di scegliere, per guadagnarsi da vivere, un certo tipo di lavoro [136]. Secondo il Comitato sui diritti economici, sociali e culturali, l'art. 6 stabilisce anche il diritto di non essere privati ingiustamente (*unfairly*) del lavoro [137]. Per di più, non si tratta di un diritto assoluto, perché può subire restrizioni, sulla base dell'art. 4 del Patto.

Tuttavia, il par. 2 dell'art. 6 è più ambizioso, perché, come si è visto, per assicurare la piena realizzazione del diritto al lavoro, gli Stati si impegnano a prendere una serie di mi-

---

[133] African Charter on the Rights and Welfare of the Child, 1° July 1990.

[134] Vedi, ad es., la ILO Convention No. 138 concerning Minimum Age for Admission to Employment (1973); e la ILO Convention No. 182 concerning the Prohibition and Immediate Action for the Elimination of the Worst Forms of Child Labour (1999).

[135] Vedi *supra*, Cap. V, par. 15.

[136] Vedi Kälin, Künzli (2009), p. 428.

[137] CteeESCR, General Comment No. 18, 6 February 2006, parr. 4 e 6.

sure. Ma si tratta per lo più di obblighi "a realizzazione progressiva" [138] e talora soltanto di impegni di natura politica [139]. D'altronde, il Comitato sui diritti economici, sociali e culturali riconosce:

> "the existence of structural and other obstacles arising from international factors beyond the control of States which hinder the full enjoyment of article 6 in many States parties" [140].

Il discorso è in parte diverso in relazione all'art. 7 del Patto, che si occupa del diritto a giuste e favorevoli condizioni di lavoro, e che ha, come si è visto sopra, un contenuto più preciso. Anche su tale disposizione esiste un Commento Generale del Comitato sui diritti economici, sociali e culturali [141], che serve a chiarire le varie componenti di tale diritto, quali la remunerazione, le condizioni di lavoro sicure e sane, l'eguale opportunità di promozione nel lavoro, il riposo, le ferie ed i limiti agli orari di lavoro.

Qualche cenno merita anche la Carta sociale europea. Come si è visto, essa contiene regole assai dettagliate sui diritti dei lavoratori. In proposito, si deve sottolineare il fatto che il Comitato europeo dei diritti sociali sta sviluppando recentemente una prassi interessante, che dimostra che alcuni di questi diritti hanno carattere giustiziabile ed impongono obblighi immediati a carico degli Stati [142].

10.3. *Obblighi*

Anche in questo caso, al diritto al lavoro ed ai vari diritti specifici dei lavoratori corrispondono obblighi degli Stati di natura diversa.

Molti degli obblighi sopra descritti, come si è detto, si configurano come tipici obblighi "a realizzazione progressiva". Lo stesso diritto al lavoro in generale, previsto dall'art. 6 del Patto sui diritti economici, sociali e culturali, è esplicitamente formulato in tal senso. Infatti si parla di "steps to be taken by a State party [...] to achieve the full realization of this right". Tuttavia, gli Stati hanno anche obblighi negativi: ad esempio, il divieto dello Stato o di enti pubblici di imporre alle persone un lavoro non liberamente accettato. Vi sono poi obblighi positivi immediati, sia di risultato che di *due diligence*. Un esempio dei primi è l'obbligo statale di eliminare eventuali leggi o prassi discriminatorie in materia di lavoro. Un esempio dei secondi è l'obbligo dello Stato di prevenire violazioni dei diritti dei lavoratori da parte di terzi.

Infine, vi sono, in questo settore, anche alcuni impegni di carattere politico e programmatico degli Stati, che non possono essere considerati come veri e propri obblighi giuridici. Ad esempio, l'impegno degli Stati, contenuto nell'art. 6, par. 2, del Patto sui diritti economici, sociali e culturali, di elaborare politiche atte ad assicurare uno sviluppo economico, sociale e culturale ed un pieno impiego produttivo.

---

[138] *Ibidem*, par. 19.

[139] *Ibidem*, parr. 38-47.

[140] *Ibidem*, par. 5.

[141] CteeESCR, General Comment No. 23, 27 April 2016.

[142] Vedi, ad es., ECteeSR, *Finnish Society of Social Rights v. Finland*, Decision of 8 September 2016; *Confederazione Generale Italiana del Lavoro (CGIL) v. Italy*.

11. *Diritto di proprietà*

11.1. *Norme*

Il diritto al rispetto della proprietà privata ha una posizione importante nella tradizione occidentale e nelle celebri dichiarazioni sui diritti umani del XVII e XVIII secolo [143]. Tuttavia, la sua affermazione nel diritto internazionale dei diritti umani è stata più controversa, a causa delle opinioni contrastanti circa l'importanza di tale diritto fra i Paesi occidentali, da una parte, ed i Paesi socialisti e quelli in via di sviluppo, dall'altra parte.

Questa diversità di opinioni si era già manifestata, nella prima metà del 1900, in relazione al tema della protezione dei beni degli stranieri e, in particolare, degli investimenti delle società straniere nei Paesi in via di sviluppo. Il problema si era posto specie per la prassi delle nazionalizzazioni, iniziata dopo la fine della Prima Guerra Mondiale e ripresa con vigore nel secondo dopoguerra. Per molto tempo si sono confrontate, fra tali gruppi di Stati, tesi assai diverse sulla questione della legittimità delle nazionalizzazioni di proprietà straniere e sulla misura, i tempi e le modalità dell'indennizzo. In estrema sintesi, i Paesi industrializzati erano favorevoli alla massima protezione degli investimenti stranieri, e quindi all'esistenza di alcuni limiti di legittimità internazionale per le nazionalizzazioni ed al diritto ad un indennizzo "pronto, adeguato ed effettivo" (*prompt, adequate and effective*), mentre i Paesi in via di sviluppo sostenevano l'assoluta libertà dello Stato territoriale di nazionalizzare i beni stranieri e contestavano le regole occidentali relative all'indennizzo. Queste diversità, in relazione al tema degli investimenti stranieri, si sono tuttavia attenuate in tempi più recenti [144].

Il contrasto ideologico fra gli Stati, circa l'importanza del diritto di proprietà, ha avuto un impatto anche sul diritto internazionale dei diritti umani, come si evince anche dal confronto fra la Dichiarazione universale del 1948 ed i Patti delle Nazioni Unite del 1966. Infatti, la Dichiarazione universale, prevalentemente ispirata dalle concezioni occidentali, riconosce il diritto di proprietà nell'art. 17, che è così formulato:

"1. Everyone has the right to own property alone as well as in association with others
2. No one shall be arbitrarily deprived of his property".

Invece, i due Patti del 1966, influenzati in gran parte dalle concezioni dei diritti umani dei Paesi socialisti e di un gruppo di Paesi in via di sviluppo [145], non contengono alcuna disposizione che stabilisce il diritto di proprietà. Tuttavia, i redattori dei Patti raggiunsero una sorta di compromesso fra le diverse opinioni, poiché i Patti contengono alcune disposizioni che sono indirettamente rilevanti per la protezione della proprietà [146]. Ad esempio, in ambedue i Patti si prevede che la proprietà non può essere motivo di discriminazione [147];

[143] Vedi, ad es., il Bill of Rights inglese del 13 febbraio 1689, la Dichiarazione dei diritti della Virginia del 12 giugno 1776, la Dichiarazione di indipendenza degli USA del 4 luglio 1776, la Déclaration des droits de l'homme et du citoyen francese del 26 agosto 1789.

[144] Vedi, per tutti, Conforti (2018), pp. 250-252.

[145] Vedi *supra*, Cap. III, par. 4.1 e Cap. IV, par. 5.1.

[146] Vedi Weissbrodt, de la Vega (2007), p. 91.

[147] CCPR, art. 2(1); CESCR, art. 2(2).

e che i popoli hanno diritto di disporre delle proprie ricchezze e risorse naturali [148]. Inoltre, l'art. 11 del Patto sui diritti economici, sociali e culturali stabilisce, fra l'altro, il divieto per gli Stati di distruggere, in certe circostanze, terreni o abitazioni o di sradicare le persone da certe loro proprietà. Infine, nel Patto sui diritti civili e politici, una protezione implicita della proprietà deriva dai diritti ad un ricorso interno effettivo e ad un equo processo [149], i quali impongono agli Stati di giudicare sulle legittimità di certe confische o espropriazioni di proprietà. Ed infatti il Comitato dei diritti umani ha avuto occasione di decidere su alcuni casi che incidevano sul diritto di proprietà.

Tuttavia, si deve notare che questa presa di posizione assai prudente sul diritto di proprietà, contenuta nei due Patti, non è stata seguita dalla maggioranza dei trattati sui diritti umani. Infatti, i principali trattati regionali riconoscono esplicitamente tale diritto. Assai importante è l'art. 1 del Protocollo n. 1 alla Convenzione europea (*Protection of property*), il quale stabilisce che:

> "Every natural or legal person is entitled to the peaceful enjoyment of his possessions. No one shall be deprived of his possessions except in the public interest and subject to the conditions provided for by law and by the general principles of international law.
>
> The preceding provisions shall not, however, in any way impair the right of a State to enforce such laws as it deems necessary to control the use of property in accordance with the general interest or to secure the payment of taxes or other contributions or penalties".

In maniera assai simile sono formulati l'art. 21 della Convenzione americana e l'art. 17 della Carta dei diritti fondamentali dell'UE. Anche l'art. 14 della Carta africana e l'art. 31 della Carta araba riconoscono il diritto di proprietà, sia pure con disposizioni dal contenuto più sintetico.

Vi sono, inoltre, norme sul diritto di proprietà in molti trattati settoriali sui diritti umani. Alcuni di questi trattati contengono disposizioni in materia di uguaglianza o non discriminazione nel diritto di proprietà: si possono citare l'art. 5(d)(v) della Convenzione contro la discriminazione razziale; gli artt. 15(2) e 16(1)(h) della Convenzione contro la discriminazione nei confronti delle donne; l'art. 12(5) della Convenzione sui diritti delle persone disabili. Altri trattati proteggono il diritto di proprietà di certi soggetti deboli: ad esempio, gli artt. 13 e 14 della Convenzione di Ginevra sullo status dei rifugiati; l'art. 15 della Convenzione sui diritti dei lavoratori migranti; la Convenzione relativa allo status degli apolidi [150]; la Convenzione ILO n. 169 relativa ai popoli indigeni e tribali in Paesi indipendenti [151].

Infine, il diritto di proprietà è tutelato anche dal diritto internazionale umanitario e dal diritto internazionale penale. Da una parte, le Convenzioni di Ginevra del 1949 ed i Protocolli addizionali del 1977 proteggono le somme di denaro ed altri oggetti dei prigionieri [152] e degli internati [153]; proibiscono il saccheggio e la distruzione di beni mobili e immobili in

[148] CCPR, art. 1(2); CESCR, art. 1(2).

[149] CCPR, artt. 2(3) e 14.

[150] Convention Relating to the Status of Stateless Persons, New York, 28 September 1954.

[151] Indigenous and Tribal Peoples Convention (ILO No. 169), 27 June 1989, artt. 13 e 14.

[152] GC III, art. 18.

[153] GC IV, art. 97.

territori militarmente occupati [154]; e proteggono i beni di carattere civile o essenziali per la popolazione civile [155]. D'altra parte, lo Statuto della Corte penale internazionale considera come un crimine di guerra la "extensive destruction and appropriation of property, not justified by military necessity and carried out unlawfully and wantonly" [156].

11.2. *Contenuto del diritto*

Il diritto di proprietà non è inderogabile in stati di emergenza e non ha carattere assoluto. Infatti, le norme convenzionali sopracitate prevedono, di solito, possibilità di restrizioni da parte dello Stato per motivi di interessi pubblici o generali. Per chiarire meglio il contenuto di questo diritto, conviene far riferimento soprattutto alla Convenzione europea ed alla Carta dei diritti fondamentali dell'UE.

Il Protocollo n. 1 alla Convenzione europea contiene, nell'art. 1, una norma particolarmente importante per via dell'ampia giurisprudenza sviluppata nel tempo dagli organi di Strasburgo. Tali organi hanno affermato più volte che l'art. 1, nelle sue tre frasi, contiene *tre regole diverse*, ma collegate fra loro: *a*) la prima ha carattere generale e stabilisce il principio del rispetto dei beni della persona; *b*) la seconda regola riguarda la privazione della proprietà e le condizioni a cui essa è assoggettata; *c*) la terza regola riconosce il potere dello Stato di regolamentare l'uso dei beni secondo l'interesse generale.

Secondo la Corte europea, la seconda e la terza regola attengono a situazioni particolari di interferenza con il principio generale del rispetto dei beni, e devono quindi essere interpretate alla luce di tale principio [157]. Conviene aggiungere che la Corte, quando un'interferenza nel godimento di un bene non comporta la privazione della proprietà né può essere considerata come "regolamentazione nell'uso del bene", esamina, di solito, se il caso non possa essere considerato come un'interferenza generica nel godimento del bene, ai sensi della prima regola di carattere generale, la quale funziona così da ipotesi di chiusura [158].

Quanto al concetto di "beni" (*possessions*), utilizzato dall'art. 1, gli organi di Strasburgo hanno interpretato tale nozione in maniera "autonoma" rispetto ai diritti interni degli Stati parti, ed anche in maniera assai estensiva [159], equiparandola a un "interesse sostanziale" o ad un "interesse patrimoniale" sufficientemente significativi [160]. Nel concetto di "beni" ricadono, pertanto, beni mobili e immobili, ma anche la proprietà intellettuale ed altri diritti e interessi di natura patrimoniale, come crediti [161], marchi [162], brevetti [163], concessio-

---

[154] GC IV, artt.33 e 53 e AP II, art. 4(2)(g).

[155] AP I, artt.51-54.

[156] Rome Statute, art. 8(2)(a)(iv). Vedi anche l'art. 8(2)(b)(xiii), che considera come un crimine di guerra "destroying or seizing the enemy's property unless such destruction or seizure be imperatively demanded by the necessities of war".

[157] Vedi, ad es., ECtHR, *Sporrong and Lönnroth v. Sweden*, par. 61; *Beyeler v. Italy*, par. 98; *Depalle v. France*, par. 77; *Jahn and Others v. Germany*, par. 79; *Chinnici v. Italy (no. 2)*, par. 29.

[158] Zagrebelski *et al.* (2016), p. 350.

[159] ECtHR, *Iatridis v. Greece*, par. 54; *Beyeler v. Italy*, par. 100.

[160] ECtHR, *Bozcaada Kimisis and Others v. Turkey*, parr. 41 e 50.

[161] ECtHR, *Pressos Compania Naviera S.A. and Others v. Belgium*, parr. 30-31.

[162] ECtHR, *Anheuser-Busch Inc. v. Portugal*, par. 78.

[163] ECmHR, *Smith Kline and French Laboratories Ltd v. The Netherlands*.

ni per la radio diffusione [164], permessi urbanistici [165], ecc. Sono considerati "beni", ai fini dell'art. 1, anche le "aspettative legittime", sufficientemente fondate sul diritto o sulla giurisprudenza interni, di ottenere l'effettivo godimento del bene [166]. Ma, salvo quanto appena detto, l'art. 1 copre soltanto i beni esistenti e non quelli futuri, a meno che essi non siano già stati acquisiti sulla base di un credito certo.

In relazione alla seconda regola dell'art. 1, si pone il problema di definire il concetto di "privazione" della proprietà. Con tale nozione si intende la perdita di un diritto di proprietà o di altri diritti reali non solo sul piano formale, ma anche *de facto*. Ad esempio, l'espropriazione e la nazionalizzazione sono provvedimenti che privano della proprietà chi ne era titolare, così come la distruzione di un bene. Una "privazione" può essere giustificata, se soddisfa cumulativamente tre criteri: *a*) è conforme al diritto dello Stato coinvolto; *b*) è conforme al diritto internazionale; *c*) è stata effettuata nell'interesse pubblico [167]. Il requisito della conformità al diritto statale (c.d. criterio di legalità) è simile a quello previsto da varie disposizioni della Convenzione europea, e significa che la privazione deve fondarsi su norme vigenti, che siano accessibili, precise e prevedibili [168]. Il requisito della conformità al diritto internazionale (che riguarda specie l'obbligo di equo indennizzo in caso di nazionalizzazioni) si applica, secondo gli organi di Strasburgo, solo alle privazioni di proprietà di cittadini stranieri [169]. Infine, per il requisito dell'interesse pubblico, viene di solito riconosciuto agli Stati un margine di apprezzamento, legato alla considerazione di interessi politici, sociali od economici da parte dello Stato; ma comunque l'interesse pubblico va bilanciato, secondo il principio di proporzionalità, con il diritto individuale di proprietà.

La terza regola dell'art. 1 del Protocollo riguarda, come si è detto, il potere dello Stato di regolamentare l'uso dei beni nell'interesse generale o per assicurare il pagamento di imposte, contributi o ammende. La Corte europea ritiene che debbano considerarsi interventi che incidono sull'uso dei beni, e che rientrano nell'ambito di applicazione di questa regola, quelle misure statali che non si traducono per il proprietario nella perdita della proprietà del bene [170]. Ne sono esempi [171] la mancata autorizzazione ad edificare un terreno, l'imposizione di vincoli urbanistici, la revoca di licenze o concessioni, il sequestro di pubblicazioni oscene, il sequestro temporaneo dei beni degli imputati, e certe misure di confisca. Le misure dirette a disciplinare l'uso dei beni sono legittime se rispettano tre condizioni: *a*) sono conformi ad una previsione di legge; *b*) sono dirette a proteggere un interes-

[164] ECtHR, *Centro Europa 7 s.r.l. and Di Stefano v. Italy*, parr. 171-179.

[165] ECtHR, *Pine Valley Developments Ltd and Others v. Ireland*, par. 51.

[166] ECtHR, *Fabris v. France*, parr. 49-52; *Kopecký v. Slovakia*, parr. 45-52.

[167] Nel caso *Scordino*, la Corte europea ha condannato l'Italia per la violazione dell'art. 1, a seguito dell'espropriazione di alcuni terreni appartenenti ai ricorrenti. Tale espropriazione era legittima e non arbitraria, ma l'indennizzo ricevuto dai ricorrenti era stato inferiore al valore effettivo di mercato senza apparenti ragioni legate all'interesse pubblico. La Corte ritenne, pertanto, che i ricorrenti avessero subito «a disproportionate and excessive burden which cannot be justified by a legitimate aim in the public interest pursued by the authorities». Vedi ECtHR, *Scordino and Others v. Italy (no. 1)*, Judgment of 29 March 2006, parr. 99-104.

[168] Vedi Focarelli (2013), p. 231.

[169] ECtHR, *James and Others v. UK*, parr. 58-66; *Lithgow and Others v. UK*, parr. 111-119.

[170] Vedi Zagrebelski *et al.* (2016), p. 352.

[171] Vedi la giurisprudenza della Corte europea citata da Zagrebelski *et al.* (2016), p. 352, note 25-29, e da Focarelli (2013), p. 232, note 578-588.

se generale; *c*) sono necessarie e proporzionate rispetto a tale obiettivo.

Anche nell'ordinamento dell'UE, il diritto di proprietà è stato oggetto di una giurisprudenza interessante ad opera della Corte di giustizia. Secondo la Corte, il diritto di proprietà fa parte dei principi generali dell'ordinamento comunitario (ora dell'UE). Infatti tale diritto è stato poi incorporato nel citato art. 17 della Carta dei diritti fondamentali. L'art. 17 va letto insieme all'art. 16 sulla libertà d'impresa, la quale stabilisce la libertà di esercitare un'attività economica o commerciale, ed insieme alla libertà professionale (art. 15). Le tre libertà sono state, infatti, congiuntamente annoverate dalla Corte di giustizia tra i diritti fondamentali dell'ordinamento comunitario.

Peraltro, la Corte ha ritenuto che l'esercizio del diritto di proprietà non sia assoluto, bensì limitabile da parte delle Istituzioni europee, per obiettivi di interesse generale perseguiti dalla Comunità (ora UE), e in maniera proporzionata e rispettosa del diritto medesimo. A tal riguardo, fin dal caso *Nold*[172], la Corte di giustizia ha affermato:

> "If rights of ownership are protected by the constitutional laws of all the member states and if similar guarantees are given in respect of their right freely to choose and practice their trade or profession, the rights thereby guaranteed, far from constituting unfettered prerogatives, must be viewed in the light of the social function of the property and activities protected thereunder. For this reason, rights of this nature are protected by law subject always to limitations laid down in accordance with the public interest. Within the Community legal order it likewise seems legitimate that these rights should, if necessary, be subject to certain limits justified by the overall objectives pursued by the Community, on condition that the substance of these rights is left untouched"[173].

In seguito, nella nota sentenza *Kadi* del 2008[174], la Corte di giustizia ha ritenuto che l'obiettivo di interesse generale, costituito dalla lotta contro le minacce alla pace e alla sicurezza internazionale derivanti dagli atti terroristici, giustificasse, in linea generale, le restrizioni al diritto di proprietà derivanti dal congelamento di capitali ed altre risorse economiche delle persone, individuate dal Consiglio di Sicurezza o dal Comitato per le sanzioni delle NU come affiliate ad organizzazioni terroristiche. Tuttavia, la Corte ha poi ritenuto che tali restrizioni non fossero legittime, perché erano state adottate senza consentire agli interessati di esporre le proprie ragioni alle autorità competenti[175].

Più in generale, come è stato rilevato in dottrina[176], la Corte di giustizia ha mantenuto un approccio restrittivo al diritto di proprietà quando tale diritto si è trovato contrapposto con interessi generali dell'UE attinenti alla creazione del mercato interno, mentre ha interpretato in maniera più estensiva tale diritto quando esso è venuto in rilievo come elemento complementare rispetto alla realizzazione delle libertà comunitarie, quali, ad esempio, la libertà di stabilimento.

---

[172] ECJ, *Nold, Kohlen– und Baustoffgroßhandlung*. La ricorrente Nold, una società tedesca in accomandita semplice, sosteneva che le norme di vendita della Ruhrkohle AG e la loro applicazione violassero il diritto di proprietà e che l'esclusione della società dal commercio del carbone equivalesse ad un'espropriazione.

[173] *Ibidem*, par. 14.

[174] ECJ, *Kadi*, Judgment of 3 September 2008.

[175] Vedi anche, per successivi sviluppi del caso, EGC, *Kadi*; ECJ, *European Commission and Others v. Kadi*.

[176] Zagrebelsky *et al.* (2016), p. 363.

Infine, al di fuori del sistema europeo di tutela dei diritti umani, conviene notare che ha acquistato sempre più importanza il diritto di proprietà delle terre ancestrali da parte dei popoli indigeni, del quale torneremo a parlare più avanti [177]. Infatti la Corte interamericana ha incluso tale diritto nell'ambito di applicazione dell'art. 21 della Convenzione americana; e tale approccio interpretativo è stato ripreso anche dal Comitato dei diritti umani e dagli organi di controllo del sistema africano.

11.3. *Obblighi*

Al diritto di proprietà corrispondono, prima di tutto, obblighi negativi degli Stati, i quali devono astenersi dall'interferire nel godimento dei beni delle persone, salvo che nei casi in cui l'interferenza è espressamente consentita dalle varie norme convenzionali rilevanti.

Ma la tutela effettiva del diritto di proprietà comporta anche, a carico degli Stati, una serie di obblighi positivi e immediati. Ad esempio, lo Stato deve prendere le opportune misure di prevenzione e di repressione per garantire che il diritto sia protetto anche nei rapporti fra privati. Ciò comporta, fra l'altro, l'adozione di norme (primarie, secondarie e terziarie) a tutela della proprietà; ed anche di norme che siano idonee a rendere efficaci le procedure di esecuzione delle sentenze o di procedure concorsuali [178]. Un obbligo dello Stato di intervenire, per proteggere la proprietà di un privato, può prodursi anche nel caso di omissione da parte di altre autorità pubbliche, ad esempio nel caso di occupazione abusiva di immobili [179].

Sezione V
PROTEZIONE DELLE LIBERTÀ DI MOVIMENTO

Nell'ambito di quei diritti umani che hanno la funzione di tutelare gli aspetti principali della vita privata, sociale e pubblica degli individui, un ruolo importante hanno quei diritti che sono volti a proteggere la libertà di movimento (o di circolazione) delle persone [180]. Anzi, si può affermare che la loro importanza è via via cresciuta ed è oramai divenuta assai significativa nella società contemporanea, caratterizzata da grandi movimenti, individuali e collettivi, di persone. Dal punto di vista dei diritti umani, vi sono due aspetti concettuali da prendere in considerazione [181]. Il primo, che riguarda i movimenti individuali e collettivi, è che la libertà di movimento delle persone merita protezione perché costituisce

[177] Vedi *infra*, par. 18.

[178] Vedi ECtHR, *Fuklev v. Ukraine*, parr. 89-93; *Scollo v. Italy*, par. 44.

[179] Vedi ECtHR, *Casa di Cura Valle Fiorita Srl v. Italy*, parr. 46-60.

[180] Nella prassi e nella dottrina si parla talora di "libertà di movimento" e talora di "libertà di circolazione". Noi preferiamo utilizzare il primo termine in linea generale ed il secondo termine in senso più specifico, ad es. per il diritto di circolazione all'interno di uno Stato o per il diritto dell'UE, dove si è affermata la locuzione "libertà di circolazione".

[181] Questi aspetti sono bene messi in evidenza da Kälin, Künzli (2009), pp. 488-489.

una componente importante del loro sviluppo personale. Il secondo aspetto, che concerne specie i movimenti collettivi, è che i migranti, i richiedenti asilo, i rifugiati e gli sfollati sono soggetti deboli, che hanno bisogno di sicurezza e richiedono una tutela particolare.

Pertanto, si spiega perché il diritto internazionale dei diritti umani, fin dalla sua origine, si sia occupato della libertà di movimento delle persone. In effetti, la Dichiarazione universale, nel suo articolo 13, sancisce tale libertà in termini ampi, perché fa riferimento a tutte le persone [182]. L'art. 13 infatti proclama:

> "1. Everyone has the right to freedom of movement and residence within the borders of each state.
> 2. Everyone has the right to leave any country, including his own, and to return to his country".

Tuttavia, alla luce degli sviluppi successivi del regime internazionale dei diritti umani, occorre distinguere fra le libertà di movimento dei cittadini nel proprio Stato, che sono riconosciute in maniera assai ampia, ed i diritti di movimento degli stranieri, che sono invece assai più limitati. Vi sono, poi, degli stranieri che sono soggetti ad un regime di protezione particolare: si tratta di coloro che chiedono asilo, dei rifugiati e di altri migranti internazionalmente protetti. Conviene quindi tenere separate queste diverse categorie di persone: *a*) cittadini; *b*) stranieri (in generale); *c*) richiedenti asilo; *d*) rifugiati; *e*) altri migranti internazionalmente protetti.

12. *Libertà di movimento dei cittadini*

12.1. *Norme*

Dal regime internazionale convenzionale sui diritti umani, risulta che i cittadini hanno: *a*) il diritto di circolazione e di residenza nel proprio Stato; *b*) il diritto di uscire dal territorio del proprio Stato; *c*) il diritto di rientrarvi; *d*) il diritto di non essere espulsi dal territorio del proprio Stato (che deriva implicitamente dal diritto di circolazione).

Il Patto sui diritti civili e politici, riprendendo e precisando l'art. 13 della Dichiarazione universale, riconosce tali diritti dei cittadini. Peraltro, alcuni di essi (circolazione e residenza) sono estesi anche alle persone legalmente presenti nel territorio ed altri (il diritto di uscire) ad ogni persona. Infatti, l'art. 12 del Patto stabilisce che:

> "1. Everyone lawfully within the territory of a State shall, within that territory, have the right to liberty of movement and freedom to choose his residence.
> 2. Everyone shall be free to leave any country, including his own.
> 3. The above-mentioned rights shall not be subject to any restrictions except those which are provided by law, are necessary to protect national security, public order (ordre public), public health or morals or the rights and freedoms of others, and are consistent with the other rights recognized in the present Covenant.
> 4. No one shall be arbitrarily deprived of the right to enter his own country".

[182] Si noti, peraltro, che il diritto di "ritornare" è implicitamente attribuito ai soli cittadini ("the right […] to return to his country").

Come si vede, alcuni dei diritti garantiti dal Patto possono essere soggetti a restrizioni e limiti, che siano necessari per motivi di sicurezza nazionale, ordine pubblico, pubblica sanità o morale, e rispetto di diritti altrui. Tuttavia tali restrizioni, secondo la prassi del Comitato dei diritti umani, devono essere proporzionate [183].

I trattati sui diritti umani di carattere regionale contengono norme sostanzialmente simili, anche se non identiche, all'art. 12 del Patto. Ma si noti che il Protocollo n. 4 alla Convenzione europea (artt. 2 e 3) e la Convenzione americana (art. 22(1-5)) sono più completi, perché, dopo aver riconosciuto i tre diritti di movimento che sono esplicitamente previsti dal Patto, aggiungono anche, in maniera esplicita, il diritto per i cittadini di *non essere espulsi*, né con misure individuali né con misure collettive, dal territorio del proprio Stato. Invece, la Carta africana (art. 12(1-2)) e la Carta araba (artt. 26 e 27) si conformano quasi interamente all'art. 12 del suddetto Patto delle Nazioni Unite.

Infine, la Carta dei diritti fondamentali dell'UE ha caratteri piuttosto particolari, perché riflette i principi generali dell'Unione e l'*acquis communautaire* in materia di libertà di circolazione delle persone. L'art. 45 della Carta stabilisce: *a*) la libertà di circolazione e di residenza per ogni cittadino dell'Unione nel territorio degli Stati membri; *b*) la possibilità di garantire, in accordo con i Trattati, la libertà di circolazione e di residenza a cittadini di Stati terzi legalmente residenti nel territorio di uno Stato membro.

12.2. *Contenuto delle libertà*

La libertà di movimento dei *cittadini*, come si è visto, comprende in realtà *quattro diritti specifici*, il cui contenuto conviene esaminare separatamente. Si deve premettere che tale libertà, nelle sue varie componenti, non costituisce un diritto inderogabile in stati di emergenza né assoluto. Le restrizioni ed i limiti sono quelli che si trovano tradizionalmente in altri diritti umani non aventi carattere assoluto. Ma un'eccezione deve farsi per il diritto dei cittadini di non essere espulsi dal proprio paese, che non ammette restrizioni o limiti.

Passando ora ad esaminare i vari diritti specifici, conviene notare che il *diritto di circolazione e residenza entro i confini del proprio Stato* è stato oggetto di interpretazione da parte del Comitato dei diritti umani nel suo Commento Generale n. 27. Secondo il Comitato:

> "Everyone lawfully within the territory of a State enjoys, within that territory, the right to move freely and to choose his or her place of residence [...] The right to move freely relates to the whole territory of the State [...] The enjoyment of this right must not be made dependent of any particular purpose or reason for the person wanting to move or stay in a place [...] The State party must ensure that the rights guaranteed in article 12 are protected not only from public but also from private interference" [184].

Il diritto dei cittadini di scegliere liberamente la propria residenza include anche il diritto di rimanere nella residenza scelta; e quindi garantisce una protezione contro pratiche di dislocazione e ricollocazione forzata delle persone. La dislocazione forzata di popolazione può costituire anche una violazione del diritto internazionale umanitario, se essa si verifica durante periodi di conflitto armato [185].

---

183 Vedi, ad es., HRCtee, *Peltonen v. Finland*, par. 8.4; *González del Rio v. Peru*, par. 5.3.

184 HRCtee, General Comment No. 27, 2 November 1999, par. 4.

185 Vedi GC IV, art. 49; AP II, art. 17(1).

Quanto al *diritto di lasciare il territorio del proprio Stato*, esso costituisce un diritto umano storicamente assai antico, che risale addirittura alla Magna Carta del 1215 ed è stato ripreso da molti atti normativi successivi. Il Comitato dei diritti umani, a proposito di questo diritto, ha affermato:

> "Since international travel usually requires appropriate documents, in particular a passport, the right to leave a country must include the right to obtain the necessary travel documents. The issuing of passports is normally incumbent on the State of nationality of the individual"[186].

Anche il *diritto di entrare o rientrare nel proprio Stato* è stato oggetto di precisazione da parte del Comitato dei diritti umani:

> "The right of a person to enter his or her country recognizes the special relationship of a person to that country […] It implies the right to remain in one's own country. It includes not only the right to return after having left one's own country; it may also entitle a person to come to the country for the first time if he or she was born outside the country […] The right to return is of the utmost importance for refugees seeking voluntary repatriation"[187].

Infine, i cittadini hanno anche il *diritto di non essere espulsi dal territorio del proprio Stato*. Come si è detto, questo diritto, implicito in quello di libera circolazione e di residenza, viene comunque espressamente previsto in alcuni trattati. In particolare, l'art. 3, par. 1, del Protocollo n. 4 alla Convenzione europea stabilisce che:

> "No one shall be expelled, by means either of an individual or of a collective measure, from the territory of the State of which he is a national".

Termini del tutto simili sono usati dall'art. 22(5) della Convenzione americana:

> "No one can be expelled from the territory of the state of which he is a national […]".

Il termine "espulsione" viene usato in senso ampio, tale da comprendere sia misure di espulsione amministrativa e giudiziaria che misure di deportazione e di respingimento (*refoulement*).

12.3. *Obblighi*

Gli obblighi degli Stati, corrispondenti ai diritti di cui sopra, sono, come al solito, di varia natura. La maggior parte di essi si presenta come obblighi negativi; ma vi sono anche obblighi positivi ed immediati, sia di risultato che di *due diligence*. Si pensi, ad esempio, all'obbligo dello Stato di rilasciare i necessari documenti di viaggio al proprio cittadino che vuole esercitare il diritto di lasciare il proprio Paese, oppure all'obbligo di proteggere il diritto di circolazione dei cittadini da interferenze da parte di altri individui.

---

[186] HRCtee, General Comment No. 27, 2 November 1999, par. 9.

[187] *Ibidem*, par. 19.

13. *Diritti di movimento degli stranieri*

Occupiamoci adesso dei diritti umani di movimento degli stranieri, precisando che intendiamo far riferimento a *tutti* gli stranieri (compresi i migranti), senza considerare, per ora, certe categorie di stranieri soggetti ad un regime speciale di tutela, come i richiedenti asilo, i rifugiati, ed altri migranti internazionalmente protetti, dei quali ci occuperemo in seguito [188].

È necessaria un'altra precisazione preliminare. Esamineremo qui *soltanto i diritti di movimento degli stranieri* [189]. Ma è chiaro che ciò non esaurisce il tema dei diritti umani degli stranieri, poiché *tutti* gli stranieri (e tutti i migranti), in quanto persone umane, sono destinatari, in linea di principio, di *tutte* le norme internazionali sui diritti umani [190]. Tuttavia, si deve riconoscere che quest'ultima affermazione di principio va mitigata, poiché, nella realtà, molti dei diritti umani degli stranieri sono soggetti a deroghe o restrizioni giuridiche legittime da parte degli Stati o al margine di apprezzamento dei medesimi; e che altri diritti umani, in teoria applicabili agli stranieri, trovano di fatto ostacoli e difficoltà di carattere pratico alla loro attuazione effettiva [191]. Ciò nonostante, non si può dubitare che siano applicabili a tutti gli stranieri e migranti, *senza alcuna restrizione dovuta al loro status*, i diritti umani "fondamentali" [192].

Nell'esaminare i diritti di movimento degli stranieri, conviene distinguere fra le norme che regolano: *a*) il loro ingresso in uno Stato; *b*) il loro soggiorno; *c*) il loro allontanamento da tale Stato.

13.1. *Ingresso*

In base al diritto internazionale generale, ogni Stato è libero di regolare l'ammissione o ingresso degli stranieri nel proprio territorio. Ciò in base al principio di sovranità territoriale, che comporta la libertà dello Stato di stabilire la propria politica in materia di immigrazione [193]. Pertanto gli stranieri non hanno alcun diritto ad entrare nel territorio di uno Stato, a meno che quest'ultimo non abbia assunto obblighi convenzionali in materia con altri Stati, ad esempio con i c.d. trattati di stabilimento. Questa libertà degli Stati trova conferma anche nella giurisprudenza internazionale [194]. Si noti che anche la Convenzione delle Nazioni Unite del 1990 sui diritti dei lavoratori migranti non stabilisce alcun obbligo per gli Stati contraenti circa l'ingresso dei lavoratori migranti provenienti da altri Stati contraenti. Pertanto, la disciplina normativa di questo settore è lasciata, in buona parte, a regimi inter-

---

[188] Vedi *infra*, parr. 14-16.

[189] La letteratura su questo argomento è sterminata. Fra le opere più recenti si veda Calamia, Di Filippo, Gestri (2012).

[190] See *Declaration on Human Rights of Individuals Who are not Nationals of the Country in which They Live*, GA Res. 40/144 of 13 December 1985, spec. artt. 5-9. Cfr. anche Weissbrodt (2000), p. 5.

[191] Vedi Pisillo Mazzeschi (2011), pp. 556-558 e 565-569.

[192] *Ibidem*, pp. 558-565.

[193] Vedi, per tutti, Conforti (2015), p. 249.

[194] Vedi, ad es., ECtHR, *T.I. v. UK*, secondo cui gli Stati contraenti della Convenzione europea "have the right, as a matter of well-established international law and subject to their treaty obligations [...] to control the entry, residence and expulsion of aliens".

nazionali convenzionali, fra i quali spicca quello del diritto dell'Unione Europea; ed è affidata, soprattutto, al diritto interno di ogni Stato.

Tuttavia, a nostro avviso, si possono individuare, nel diritto internazionale generale, *due eccezioni* al regime generale di libertà degli Stati; cioè due norme consuetudinarie che impongono allo Stato l'obbligo, in certe circostanze eccezionali, di non respingere gli stranieri (compresi i migranti) che vogliono entrare nel proprio territorio o negli spazi soggetti alla propria "giurisdizione", e di dare loro un'accoglienza, sia pure *temporanea.*

La prima eccezione è data dalla norma consuetudinaria sull'*obbligo di soccorso in mare.* Questa norma si è formata e consolidata durante la prima metà del 1900 [195]. Essa impone agli Stati, tramite i capitani delle proprie navi, pubbliche o private, di prestare assistenza ad ogni persona trovata in mare in pericolo di vita e di procedere con la massima rapidità al suo salvataggio. Ciò si riferisce ad ogni persona umana in pericolo, a prescindere dalla sua nazionalità e dal fatto che essa sia un migrante regolare, irregolare o clandestino. Questa norma è stata riaffermata e precisata anche nella Convenzione delle NU del 1982 sul diritto del mare (art. 98) [196]; ed in vari trattati conclusi nel quadro dell'IMO, quali, ad esempio, la Convenzione di Londra del 1974 per la salvaguardia della vita umana in mare (c.d. SOLAS) [197] e la Convenzione di Amburgo del 1979 sulla ricerca ed il salvataggio marittimo (c.d. SAR) [198]. Si noti che un emendamento alla Convenzione SAR prevede l'obbligo di sbarcare le persone salvate in un "luogo sicuro" (*place of safety*) [199].

In realtà, come si è sopra accennato, l'obbligo di soccorso in mare (che si configura come obbligo *erga omnes* a carico degli Stati) non significa che lo Stato che procede al salvataggio debba concedere allo straniero un vero e proprio ingresso legittimo nel proprio territorio o sulle proprie navi o in altri spazi soggetti al proprio controllo; ma comporta l'effetto, più limitato, di concedere allo straniero in pericolo un'accoglienza di fatto, sia pure temporanea, in tali spazi. Si tratta, comunque, di un limite alla libertà generale dello Stato di respingere gli stranieri dal proprio territorio.

La norma sull'obbligo di soccorso in mare, a nostro avviso, si è radicata come norma autonoma nel diritto internazionale consuetudinario. Peraltro, essa è strettamente e funzionalmente collegata al diritto alla vita, poiché l'obbligo di soccorso in mare deriva logicamente dall'obbligo fondamentale degli Stati di proteggere il diritto alla vita delle persone, tramite misure positive di prevenzione. È chiaro, ad esempio, che, se uno Stato non presta soccorso ad imbarcazioni con migranti a bordo che sono in pericolo di vita, commette una violazione del suo obbligo di tutelare il diritto alla vita. Purtroppo, si deve rilevare, con

---

195 Vedi, di recente, Starita (2019), pp. 5-47, spec. 7-17.

196 United Nations Convention on the Law of the Sea, Montego Bay, 10 December 1982, art. 98: "1. Every State shall require the master of a ship flying its flag, in so far as he can do so without serious danger to the ship, the crew or the passengers: (a) to render assistance to any person found at sea in danger of being lost; (b) to proceed with all possible speed to the rescue of persons in distress, if informed of their need of assistance, in so far as such action may reasonably be expected of him [...]".

197 International Convention for the Safety of Life at Sea, 1 November 1974.

198 International Convention on Maritime Search and Rescue, 27 April 1979. Vedi anche IMO, Resolution MSC.167(78), Guidelines on the Treatment of Persons Rescued At Sea.

199 Adoption of Amendments to the International Convention on Maritime Search and Rescue, 1979, as Amended, MSC Res. 155(78), 78th sess, Agenda Item 26, IMO Doc MSC78/26/Add.1 annex 5 (4 June 2004, adopted 20 May 2004).

rammarico, che di recente il Governo italiano ha, più volte, omesso di rispettare il suo obbligo di soccorso in mare, ed ha addirittura promulgato decreti in contrasto con tale obbligo [200]. Si possono ricordare i noti casi *Hirsi* [201], *Diciotti* [202] e *Sea Watch 3* [203].

La seconda eccezione, al regime generale di libertà degli Stati in materia di ammissione degli stranieri, è data dal c.d. principio del *non-refoulement*, già da noi menzionato a proposito del diritto alla vita e del divieto di tortura e trattamenti o pene inumani o degradanti [204]. Conviene adesso precisare meglio il contenuto di questo principio, che va interpretato *in maniera estensiva* in base al diritto internazionale contemporaneo. In questo senso, il principio obbliga gli Stati a non respingere gli stranieri (compresi ovviamente i migranti) verso un paese nel quale sussista un serio rischio che essi possano subire *gravi violazioni dei diritti umani fondamentali*. Anche in questo caso, il divieto di respingimento non significa che lo Stato debba concedere un ingresso legittimo negli spazi soggetti alla propria sovranità o controllo; ma comporta solo un'accoglienza di fatto e temporanea dello straniero.

Per giustificare l'interpretazione estensiva del principio di *non-refoulement*, conviene spiegare sinteticamente il suo sviluppo storico. Questo principio si è affermato gradualmente nel tempo per una sorta di accumulo o integrazione fra *tre norme diverse*. La prima norma è quella, prevista nell'art. 33 della Convenzione di Ginevra del 1951 sullo *status* dei rifugiati, che vieta agli Stati di respingere "in qualsiasi modo" un rifugiato verso le frontiere di uno Stato dove "la sua vita o libertà sarebbero minacciate a motivo della sua razza, della sua religione, della sua nazionalità, della sua appartenenza ad un gruppo sociale o delle sue opinioni politiche", salvo l'eccezione di cui al par. 2 [205]. Pertanto, qui il principio protegge soltanto i rifugiati e soltanto dai pericoli derivanti dagli specifici motivi di discriminazione elencati dalla Convenzione di Ginevra. La seconda norma è quella sul divieto di tortura e di trattamenti o pene inumani o degradanti. Questa norma, come si è visto [206], è stata interpretata, nella prassi degli organi internazionali di controllo, nel senso che uno Stato non può respingere uno straniero verso un paese nel quale sussiste un serio rischio che egli possa subire tortura o trattamenti inumani o degradanti. Pertanto, il divieto di respingimento si è esteso, dal punto di visto soggettivo, a tutti gli stranieri e, dal punto di vista oggettivo, ai pericoli di violazioni del divieto di tortura ed altri trattamenti disumani. Infine, la terza norma è quella che protegge il diritto umano alla vita. Questa norma è stata interpretata, nella prassi, nel senso che uno Stato non può respingere uno straniero verso un paese nel quale egli rischia seriamente attentati alla propria vita [207].

In sostanza, a nostro parere, vi è stata nel tempo un'integrazione fra le tre norme e la loro prassi applicativa. Per effetto di tale integrazione vi è stato, in primo luogo, un am-

---

[200] Vedi il Decreto Legge n. 113 del 4 ottobre 2018 ed il Decreto Legge n. 53 del 14 giugno 2019.

[201] ECtHR, *Hirsi Jamaa and Others v. Italy*. Per un commento, vedi Liguori (2012); Lenzerini (2012).

[202] Sul caso della nave *Diciotti*, vedi Trib. Catania, sez. Reati Ministeriali, relaz. 7 dicembre 2018.

[203] Sul caso della nave *Sea Watch 3*, vedi ECtHR, *Rackete and Others v. Italy*; Trib. Agrigento(GIP), *Rackete*, ord. 2 luglio 2019. Per un commento, vedi Gradoni, Pasquet (2019); De Sena, Starita (2019).

[204] Vedi *supra*, Cap. V, parr. 7.3.1 e 8.3.1.

[205] Cioè, quando vi sono ragionevoli motivi per ritenere che il rifugiato costituisca un pericolo per la sicurezza dello Stato di rifugio o per la sua comunità.

[206] Vedi *supra*, Cap. V, par. 8.3.1.

[207] Vedi *supra*, Cap. V, par. 7.3.1.

pliamento della sfera dei soggetti che hanno diritto al *non-refoulement*. Questo diritto, in origine previsto solo a favore dei rifugiati, riguarda adesso tutti gli stranieri. In secondo luogo, vi è stato anche un ampliamento delle cause che danno diritto al *non-refoulement*. La protezione non opera soltanto per il pericolo derivante da gravi minacce motivate da specifici motivi di discriminazione, ma si è estesa anche al pericolo di subire torture o trattamenti inumani o degradanti ed al pericolo di essere privati della vita. Si deve aggiungere che la prassi recente tende ad ampliare ulteriormente le cause che danno diritto al *non-refoulement*, ad esempio, alcuni trattati hanno esteso la protezione del principio anche a coloro che fuggono da situazioni di violenza generalizzata o da conflitti armati esistenti nel loro Paese.

In definitiva, sulla base di questi sviluppi della prassi internazionale, riteniamo che oggi il principio di *non-refoulement* abbia esteso la sua protezione a tutti i pericoli di gravi violazioni dei diritti umani fondamentali. Inoltre, vi è oramai un'opinione diffusa che il principio, con tale ampio contenuto, sia entrato a far parte del diritto internazionale consuetudinario ed abbia carattere di *ius cogens*[208].

13.2. *Soggiorno*

Il regime giuridico internazionale in materia di soggiorno degli stranieri è più semplice rispetto a quello relativo al loro ingresso. Gli stranieri legalmente presenti nel territorio di uno Stato hanno il diritto di circolare liberamente nel territorio di tale Stato ed il diritto di scegliere la propria residenza. Questi due diritti, già impliciti nell'art. 13(1) della Dichiarazione universale, sono poi espressamente stabiliti dall'art. 12(1) del Patto sui diritti civili e politici; dall'art. 2(1) del Protocollo n. 4 alla Convenzione europea; dall'art. 22(1) della Convenzione americana; dall'art. 12(1) della Carta africana; e dall'art. 26(1) della Carta araba. Si può ritenere che queste norme riflettano il diritto internazionale generale. Tuttavia, si tratta di diritti soggetti a limiti e restrizioni da parte dello Stato territoriale. Ciò risulta chiaramente da tutti i trattati sopra citati[209]. Ad esempio, lo Stato territoriale può imporre ad uno straniero, per motivi di sicurezza o ordine pubblico, l'obbligo di dimora, cioè di non allontanarsi, senza autorizzazione, dal territorio del comune di dimora abituale.

Un regime giuridico speciale è previsto dalla Convenzione sui diritti dei lavoratori migranti. La nozione di "lavoratore migrante" è assai estensiva, poiché, ai sensi dell'art. 2(1) della Convenzione:

> "The term 'migrant worker' refers to a person who is to be engaged, is engaged or has been engaged in a remunerated activity in a State of which he or she is not a national".

Ciò posto, la Convenzione stabilisce in maniera assai dettagliata i diritti dei lavoratori migranti e delle loro famiglie, e prevede alcuni diritti anche a favore dei lavoratori non legalmente residenti nello Stato territoriale. Fra l'altro, essa prevede che i diritti di movimento di queste persone siano soggetti a minori restrizioni rispetto ai diritti degli altri stranieri (art. 39). Tuttavia, la Convenzione ha avuto un numero limitato di ratifiche e riflette solo in minima parte il diritto internazionale consuetudinario.

---

[208] Vedi, per tutti, Lenzerini (2009), pp. 378-389.

[209] Vedi, ad es., CCPR, art. 12(3).

13.3. *Allontanamento*

Il concetto di "allontanamento" degli stranieri da parte di uno Stato è piuttosto generico e di solito viene utilizzato per inglobare, in una nozione omnicomprensiva, tre tipi di misure statali più specifiche, che sono denominate "espulsione", "deportazione" e "estradizione"[210]. Noi useremo il termine generico. Anche il regime giuridico relativo all'allontanamento degli stranieri è soggetto, in massima parte, al principio di sovranità degli Stati. Pertanto ogni Stato è libero, in linea di principio, di allontanare gli stranieri dal proprio territorio. Tuttavia, in questo settore incidono maggiormente i limiti posti da norme consuetudinarie del diritto internazionale dei diritti umani.

In primo luogo, vi sono dei *limiti di carattere procedurale* all'espulsione. Lo straniero, se legalmente presente nel territorio di uno Stato, può essere espulso solo a seguito di una decisione fondata sul diritto; e gli deve essere consentito di opporsi e di difendersi dinanzi ad un'autorità competente. Queste due condizioni risultano nitidamente dall'art. 13 del Patto sui diritti civili e politici, secondo cui:

> "An alien lawfully in the territory of a State Party to the present Covenant may be expelled therefrom only in pursuance of a decision reached in accordance with law and shall, except where compelling reasons of national security otherwise require, be allowed to submit the reasons against his expulsion and to have his case reviewed by, and be represented for the purpose before, the competent authority or a person or persons especially designated by the competent authority".

Norme simili, anche se talora più sintetiche, sono contenute nell'art. 1(1) del Protocollo n. 7 alla Convenzione europea, nell'art. 22(6) della Convenzione americana, nell'art. 12(4) della Carta africana, nell'art. 26(2) della Carta araba, nell'art. 22, parr. 1, 2, 3 e 4, della Convenzione sui diritti dei lavoratori migranti. Tuttavia, questi limiti di carattere procedurale non sono sempre assoluti, poiché gli Stati possono derogarvi per motivi di ordine pubblico o di sicurezza nazionale o simili.

In secondo luogo, sono *vietate le espulsioni collettive*. Questo divieto è esplicitamente previsto dall'art. 4 del Protocollo n. 4 alla Convenzione europea, dall'art. 22(9) della Convenzione americana, dall'art. 12(5) della Carta africana[211], dall'art. 26(2) della Carta araba, dall'art. 22(1) della Convenzione sui diritti dei lavoratori migranti. In realtà, anche nei trattati dove il divieto non è esplicito, esso discende logicamente dal fatto che ogni espulsione richiede, secondo quanto detto sopra, una decisione individuale fondata sul diritto e la presenza di garanzie individuali di difesa.

In terzo luogo, le modalità concrete dell'espulsione o della deportazione *non devono essere "oltraggiose"* nei confronti delle persona interessata; cioè non devono essere condotte con un uso della forza che sia inutile o sproporzionato[212].

---

[210] Di solito, per "espulsione" si intende un provvedimento giuridico (giurisdizionale o amministrativo) che impone ad una persona di lasciare il territorio di uno Stato; per "deportazione" l'esecuzione forzata di un'espulsione; per "estradizione" la consegna di una persona, accusata o condannata per un reato, da uno Stato ad un altro, su richiesta del secondo Stato.

[211] Ma tale norma qualifica come espulsioni di massa quelle che sono mirate contro gruppi nazionali, razziali, etnici o religiosi.

[212] Vedi Iran/U.S. Claims Tribunal, *Yeager v. Islamic Republic of Iran*. Cfr. anche Conforti (2015), p. 249.

In quarto luogo, vi è un limite importante di carattere sostanziale, del quale abbiamo già parlato a proposito dell'ingresso degli stranieri. Il principio del *non-refoulement* (nonostante la sua denominazione) non si applica oggi soltanto nella fase del respingimento alle frontiere degli stranieri; ma anche nella fase del loro allontanamento, tramite espulsione, deportazione o estradizione. Pertanto, sussiste il divieto di allontanare gli stranieri verso Stati nei quali essi possono subire gravi discriminazioni, o rischiano torture o trattamenti disumani, o attentati alla vita o, più generalmente, rischiano di essere vittime di gravi violazioni dei diritti umani fondamentali[213].

Infine, quantomeno nel quadro di alcuni sistemi convenzionali sui diritti umani, si sta affermando anche un ulteriore limite alla libertà degli Stati di allontanare gli stranieri. In particolare, nel sistema della Convenzione europea, gli organi di Strasburgo hanno ricavato, dal diritto al rispetto della vita privata e familiare previsto dall'art. 8 della Convenzione, l'obbligo dello Stato di non espellere uno straniero quando tale espulsione provocherebbe una ingiustificata e sproporzionata *rottura dell'unità familiare*[214]. Ma questo limite non ha carattere assoluto.

14. *Diritto di asilo*

Oggi vi è la tendenza, piuttosto diffusa, a confondere il diritto di asilo con il diritto di ottenere lo *status* di rifugiato oppure ad usare il termine "asilo" in senso ampio e generico, come un contenitore che include l'istituto del "rifugio" ed altre forme di protezione internazionale dei migranti. Come vedremo, queste confusioni sono, in parte, giustificate dall'evoluzione storica che hanno avuto questi istituti nel diritto internazionale, e specie nel diritto dell'Unione Europea. Tuttavia, a nostro avviso, rimangono alcune differenze, storiche e concettuali, che fanno tuttora preferire una trattazione separata del diritto di asilo, dei diritti dei rifugiati e delle altre forme di protezione internazionale dei migranti.

Ciò premesso, si può notare che l'asilo (a differenza del "rifugio") è un istituto giuridico assai antico, che ha assunto nel tempo varie denominazioni più specifiche (asilo territoriale, extraterritoriale, politico, religioso). In senso generale, esso significa che uno Stato ammette nel suo territorio (o in un altro spazio soggetto al suo controllo) e concede protezione ad un individuo straniero (o apolide), che cerca tale protezione nei confronti di un altro Stato. Spesso l'individuo cerca di sfuggire a persecuzioni politiche da parte del proprio Stato nazionale; ma talora egli vuole fuggire da altri pericoli, quali, ad esempio, processi penali, guerre, conflitti interni, carestie, disastri ambientali.

La definizione di "asilo", data nel 1950 dall'*Institut de Droit International*, è molto ampia. Secondo l'*Institut*, l'asilo:

> "désigne la protection qu'un Etat accorde sur son territoire ou dans un autre endroit relevant de certains de ces organes à un individu que est venu la rechercher"[215].

---

[213] Naturalmente quest'obbligo riguarda tutte le persone, cittadini e stranieri; ma di fatto esso si applica specie agli stranieri, poiché l'espulsione dei cittadini è di solito esclusa dal diritto internazionale e dai diritti statali.

[214] Vedi, ad es., ECtHR, *Moustaquim v. Belgium*.

[215] Institut de Droit International, *L'asile en droit international public*, 43 AIDI, II, 1950, p. 377.

Da questa definizione risulta che il concetto di "asilo" si fonda su due elementi costitutivi: *a*) la ricerca di protezione da parte dell'individuo; *b*) la concessione da parte di uno Stato di una protezione effettiva a favore dell'individuo. Tale protezione dello Stato presuppone non solo l'ammissione, a tempo indeterminato, dello straniero nel proprio territorio, ma anche, quantomeno in linea di principio, l'impegno a non riconsegnare l'individuo allo Stato dal quale è fuggito[216].

Tuttavia, si deve osservare subito che il termine "diritto di asilo" ha *due significati del tutto diversi*; da una parte, il *diritto di uno Stato*, nei confronti di altri Stati, di concedere l'asilo ad un individuo straniero; dall'altro il *diritto di un individuo* di ottenere asilo da parte di uno Stato. Il primo diritto (che corrisponde al concetto tradizionale di asilo che ha dominato per secoli) comporta il normale esercizio della sovranità territoriale da parte dello Stato. Pertanto è pacifico che, nel diritto internazionale consuetudinario, uno Stato ha il diritto sovrano e discrezionale di garantire asilo ad ogni individuo, salvo gli eventuali limiti verso altri Stati derivanti da trattati internazionali, specie in materia di cooperazione giudiziaria e di estradizione. Ma non ci occuperemo di questo diritto di asilo, perché esso non attiene al diritto internazionale dei diritti umani.

Ci interessa, invece, il diritto umano dell'individuo di ottenere asilo da parte di uno Stato; quindi, d'ora in poi, parleremo di "diritto di asilo" solo in questo senso. Tuttavia, anche dopo aver così delimitato l'argomento, si deve notare che il diritto umano all'asilo ha assunto con il tempo, nel diritto internazionale, nei diritti statali e nel diritto dell'Unione Europea, significati e contenuti parzialmente diversi.

14.1. *Norme e contenuto del diritto*

Il diritto dell'individuo all'asilo è stato inserito nella Dichiarazione universale, il cui art. 14 recita:

> "1. Everyone has the right to seek and to enjoy in other countries asylum from persecution.
> 2. This right may not be invoked in the case of prosecutions genuinely arising from non-political crimes or from acts contrary to the purposes and principles of the United Nations"[217].

Come si può notare, la Dichiarazione riconosce esplicitamente il diritto di asilo, quantomeno di asilo politico ("*asylum from persecution*"), come uno dei diritti umani fondamentali della persona, anche se il par. 2 dell'art. 14 pone qualche limite. Tuttavia, al tempo della Dichiarazione, tale diritto era concepito più in termini programmatici, come scopo comune da raggiungere in futuro, che come un vero e proprio diritto positivo dell'individuo nei confronti dello Stato, obbligatorio per quest'ultimo. Infatti, se si esaminano i lavori preparatori dell'art. 14, si nota che vi fu una forte opposizione da parte di vari Stati ad inserire, in tale articolo, il diritto dell'individuo "to be granted asylum"; e che invece si preferì la formula meno impegnativa del diritto "to seek and enjoy [...] asylum". Inoltre, come è noto, la Dichiarazione non costituisce un atto giuridico vincolante.

---

[216] Vedi Lenzerini (2009), pp. 83-85.

[217] Vedi anche UDHR, art. 13(2).

Pertanto, ci si deve chiedere se la prassi internazionale successiva, convenzionale e di altra natura, abbia confermato o meno l'esistenza di un diritto umano all'asilo, inteso, nel senso ampio sopra indicato, come diritto di un individuo perseguitato in uno Stato di essere ammesso a tempo indeterminato ed anche protetto nel territorio di un altro Stato.

In realtà, a livello universale, i tentativi di affermare e consolidare il diritto di asilo enunciato dalla Dichiarazione universale hanno avuto scarso successo. I due Patti internazionali del 1966 non contengono alcuna norma sul diritto di asilo: il Patto sui diritti civili e politici si limita a stabilire, come si è visto, il diritto di emigrare [218]. Successivamente, nel 1967, fu adottata dall'Assemblea Generale delle NU la Dichiarazione sull'asilo territoriale [219], che aveva lo scopo di attuare l'art. 14 della Dichiarazione universale e di precisare meglio il contenuto del diritto di asilo. Tuttavia, la Dichiarazione del 1967 è deludente, perché si limita a raccomandare agli Stati di fondare le loro politiche in tema di asilo sui principi enunciati nella Dichiarazione medesima e riafferma il diritto *discrezionale* di ogni Stato di giudicare le condizioni per concedere l'asilo. Pertanto, questa Dichiarazione non ha affatto contribuito a sviluppare il diritto di asilo come diritto umano, poiché in sostanza riafferma il concetto tradizionale per cui lo Stato ha un diritto di concedere l'asilo nei confronti degli altri Stati, ma non ha un obbligo di concedere l'asilo all'individuo. In seguito, nel quadro delle Nazioni Unite, si è cercato di pervenire all'adozione di una convenzione sull'asilo territoriale. Un progetto era stato predisposto ed il testo avrebbe dovuto essere approvato a Ginevra nel 1977; ma esso non è mai stato adottato. Negli anni successivi, l'Assemblea Generale ha adottato una serie di risoluzioni con le quali invita gli Stati a non ostacolare l'istituto dell'asilo ed a cooperare con le attività dell'Alto Commissario delle NU per i rifugiati (UNHCR). Ma si tratta di meri atti di *soft law*.

Se passiamo ad esaminare gli atti internazionali di carattere regionale sui diritti umani, si deve concludere che il diritto di asilo ha fatto qualche progresso, ma non importante. Nel quadro dell'Organizzazione degli Stati americani, si può ricordare la Convenzione di Montevideo sull'asilo politico del 1933 (art. 3) [220], che però si limita a descrivere la natura umanitaria dell'asilo. Più importante è la Dichiarazione americana dei diritti e doveri dell'uomo [221], che, all'art. XXVII, proclama che:

> "Every person has the right, in case of pursuit not resulting from ordinary crimes, to seek and receive asylum in foreign territory, in accordance with the laws of each country and with international agreements".

In seguito, si può citare la Convenzione di Caracas sull'asilo territoriale del 1954 [222], che tuttavia tratta l'asilo come una mera facoltà degli Stati. Invece, la Convenzione americana contiene una disposizione, l'art. 22(7), che riproduce sostanzialmente il contenuto dell'art. XXVII della Dichiarazione americana, ma limita espressamente il diritto di asilo alle persecuzioni per "political offenses or related common crimes". La Carta africana (art.

---

[218] CCPR, art. 12(1).

[219] *Declaration on Territorial Asylum*, GA Res. 2312(XXII) of 14 December 1967.

[220] Montevideo Convention on Political Asylum, 26 December 1933.

[221] American Declaration of the Rights and Duties of Man, Ninth International Conference of American States, Bogotá, Colombia, 2 May 1948.

[222] Caracas Convention on Territorial Asylum, 28 March 1954.

12(3))[223] contiene una norma simile all'art. XXVII della Dichiarazione americana.

Per la verità, queste norme si distinguono dall'art. 14 della Dichiarazione universale, perché non prevedono soltanto un diritto dell'individuo a "cercare" asilo, bensì un diritto a "cercare e ricevere" asilo. Quindi esse sembrano garantire all'individuo un diritto ad ottenere protezione, senza lasciare allo Stato discrezionalità nel concederla. Tuttavia, ad un esame più attento, sussistono molti dubbi circa il riconoscimento di un vero e proprio diritto individuale all'asilo a livello internazionale, poiché le norme in oggetto fanno espresso riferimento alla necessità di regolare tale diritto tramite l'adozione di norme nazionali e tenendo in considerazione i pertinenti trattati internazionali. Più in particolare, l'adozione di legislazione nazionale è necessaria, sia per stabilire il contenuto della protezione garantita che per interpretare la nozione-chiave di "persecuzione".

Anche per quanto riguarda il sistema europeo di tutela dei diritti umani, il bilancio non è positivo. La Convenzione europea non contiene alcun riferimento esplicito al diritto individuale di asilo, mentre il Protocollo n. 4 alla Convenzione stabilisce soltanto il diritto di emigrare. Solo un'interpretazione estensiva e dinamica degli artt. 2 e 3 della Convenzione europea da parte degli organi di Strasburgo ha permesso di stabilire alcune garanzie per i richiedenti asilo, come quella del divieto di *refoulement*. Il Comitato dei Ministri del Consiglio d'Europa ha adottato alcune risoluzioni sul diritto di asilo, che costituiscono tuttavia anch'esse mere raccomandazioni. Il discorso invece è diverso, come vedremo, per il diritto dell'Unione Europea.

In conclusione, per rispondere alla domanda che ci eravamo posti sopra, si deve ammettere che la prassi e l'*opinio iuris* internazionali non sono sufficienti per far ritenere esistente una norma di diritto internazionale generale sul diritto di asilo, inteso nel senso *ampio* sopra indicato: cioè come il diritto di un individuo perseguitato in uno Stato, salvo che per crimini ordinari, di cercare e ricevere accoglienza a tempo indeterminato e protezione in un altro Stato. Probabilmente, anche il contenuto così ampio e vago del diritto di asilo ha reso difficile il suo recepimento in una norma consuetudinaria. In altri termini, si deve concludere che il diritto dell'individuo "to enjoy in other countries asylum from persecution", proclamato dalla Dichiarazione universale, non ha acquistato un contenuto preciso, completo e vincolante nel diritto internazionale.

Tuttavia, questa conclusione negativa deve essere parzialmente corretta sotto tre aspetti. Il primo aspetto attiene ad una *parte limitata* del contenuto del diritto di asilo; cioè ad alcuni diritti più specifici e circoscritti rispetto al diritto di asilo nella sua interezza[224]. Questi diritti permettono ad ogni individuo straniero di ottenere una sorta di asilo *provvisorio e temporaneo* dalla persecuzione in certe circostanze. Intendiamo riferirci al principio di *non-refoulement* ed al principio che proibisce l'estradizione per reati politici. Del primo principio abbiamo già parlato. Ma anche il secondo principio si è affermato sempre di più nella prassi convenzionale; e ciò ha probabilmente contribuito a formare una norma consuetudinaria. Anch'essa obbliga gli Stati a garantire ai perseguitati per motivi politici una sorta di asilo provvisorio e temporaneo.

Il secondo aspetto riguarda gli *ordinamenti giuridici interni* degli Stati. Molti Stati hanno adottato norme costituzionali o legislative che attribuiscono un diritto di asilo agli stranieri, o

---

223 La Carta araba (art. 28) prevede soltanto il diritto di "cercare" asilo.

224 Vedi Pisillo Mazzeschi (1999a), pp. 700-701.

quantomeno agli stranieri soggetti a persecuzioni politiche. In tal modo, il contenuto del diritto di asilo è stato talora precisato, rispetto a quello assai indeterminato del diritto internazionale. La Costituzione italiana, ad esempio, nell'art. 10, 3° comma, stabilisce che:

> "Lo straniero, al quale sia impedito nel suo paese l'effettivo esercizio delle libertà democratiche garantite dalla Costituzione italiana, ha diritto d'asilo nel territorio della Repubblica, secondo le condizioni stabilite dalla legge".

Come si vede, la norma ha una formula ampia, che garantisce asilo allo straniero per il fatto che proviene da un paese che nega le libertà fondamentali, anche se costui non è personalmente perseguitato[225]. Ed in effetti, in un primo tempo la giurisprudenza italiana aveva sostenuto la tesi che la Costituzione attribuisce direttamente allo straniero, che si trovi in tali condizioni, un vero e proprio diritto soggettivo all'ottenimento dell'asilo, invocabile dinanzi al giudice ordinario[226]. Tuttavia, in seguito, questa tesi è stata abbandonata dalla giurisprudenza più recente, che interpreta l'art. 10, 3° comma, della Costituzione, come un mero riferimento alle forme di protezione dei migranti che hanno trovato attuazione in Italia nei tre istituti della tutela dei rifugiati, della protezione sussidiaria e della protezione umanitaria[227].

Per fare un altro esempio, la Costituzione francese, nel suo Preambolo, afferma che:

> "tout homme persécuté en raison de son action en faveur de la liberté a droit d'asile sur les territoires de la République".

Tuttavia, poiché il diritto di asilo, attribuito dagli ordinamenti interni, ha un contenuto diverso da Stato a Stato, non si può ritenere che tali ordinamenti abbiano molto contribuito a precisare il contenuto del diritto di asilo anche a livello del diritto internazionale.

Il terzo aspetto è il più importante. Esso riguarda il fenomeno per cui il regime giuridico internazionale dell'asilo è stato via via integrato e completato dal regime internazionale dei rifugiati. Di questo regime mi occuperò in seguito[228]. Ma fin da adesso conviene notare che il diritto dei rifugiati, a partire dalla Convenzione di Ginevra del 1951 e dal Protocollo del 1967, ha dimostrato notevole forza espansiva nel suo contenuto e nel suo ambito di applicazione personale e materiale, tanto che ha finito, in gran parte, per assorbire il regime giuridico dell'asilo[229]. Questo fenomeno non deve sorprendere. Infatti, è vero che, in origine, la disciplina del diritto di asilo e quella dei rifugiati presentavano molte differenze, di origine storica, di fondamento normativo, di natura giuridica, e di contenuto[230]. Tuttavia, le due discipline condividono il medesimo scopo generale ed i medesimi effetti pratici; cioè la protezione dello Stato di accoglienza a favore di stranieri sottoposti a persecuzione. Ciò spiega la progressiva convergenza fra i due regimi giuridici ed il fatto che la disciplina normativa dei rifugiati, fin dall'inizio più dettagliata e completa anche perché di

---

[225] Vedi Favilli (2013), p. 75.

[226] Corte di Cassazione, *Allen c. Min. Int.*, sent. n. 4674/1997.

[227] Vedi, ad es., Corte cost., sent. 20 giugno 2019, n. 194; Cass., *Min. Int. c. Yarbo Musa*. Sul tema vedi anche Lenzerini (2009a).

[228] Vedi *infra*, par. 15.

[229] Vedi Conforti (2015), p. 251; Lenzerini (2009), p. 173.

[230] Vedi Lenzerini (2009), p. 145 ss., spec. 166-174.

origine convenzionale, abbia generato un processo tendente a dare via via un contenuto più preciso (ma anche più limitato) alla disciplina dell'asilo ed abbia poi finito, in gran parte, per sostituirla.

Questa evoluzione normativa si è verificata, in maniera ancora più netta, nel diritto dell'Unione Europea. Nel quadro di tale diritto il concetto di asilo è usato con *due significati diversi*, creando una certa confusione terminologica. *In senso lato* ed a-tecnico, la nozione di asilo è usata, nella c.d. politica di asilo, intendendo quest'ultimo genericamente come protezione accordata a chi fugge dal proprio Paese e richiede accoglienza[231]. Questo significato di "asilo" si avvicina a quello del diritto internazionale. Invece, *in senso stretto* e tecnico-giuridico, il concetto di asilo si riferisce ad una componente specifica della suddetta politica, la quale ricomprende tre settori normativi: *a*) norme in materia di asilo; *b*) norme sulla protezione sussidiaria; *c*) norme sulla protezione temporanea[232]. Inoltre (e questo punto è importante), le norme dell'UE sull'asilo in senso stretto *rinviano, di fatto, a quelle sulla protezione dei rifugiati* previste dalla Convenzione di Ginevra del 1951[233].

Pertanto, nel diritto dell'UE, il fenomeno di assorbimento del richiedente asilo nella figura del rifugiato si è realizzato compiutamente. Come è stato notato[234], ciò è avvenuto anche a livello terminologico, poiché, nel linguaggio corrente, per coloro che chiedono lo *status* di rifugiato, si suole dire che essi "cercano asilo". Questo sviluppo del diritto dell'UE trova conferma anche nella Carta dei diritti fondamentali dell'UE, il cui art. 18 (*Right to asylum*) recita:

> "The right to asylum shall be guaranteed with due respect for the rules of the Geneva Convention of 28 July 1951 and the Protocol of 31 January 1967 relating to the status of refugees and in accordance with the Treaty on the European Union and the Treaty on the Functioning of the European Union [...]".

Come si vede, la Carta collega il diritto individuale di asilo nel sistema dell'UE alle ipotesi di persecuzione stabilite dalla Convenzione di Ginevra, trascurando del tutto il più ampio ambito di applicazione dell'istituto dell'asilo nel diritto internazionale.

14.2. *Obblighi*

Abbiamo sopra concluso che non esiste una norma di diritto internazionale generale sul diritto di asilo, inteso come diritto di un individuo perseguitato in uno Stato di ottenere ammissione, accoglienza e protezione a tempo indeterminato in un altro Stato. Né esistono norme convenzionali che garantiscano effettivamente tale diritto individuale[235]. Di conseguenza, non si può neppure parlare di obblighi degli Stati relativi al diritto di asilo.

---

[231] Vedi, ad es., l'art. 3(2) del TUE, che elenca, fra gli obiettivi fondamentali dell'UE, quello di offrire uno spazio di libertà, sicurezza e giustizia, nel quale vengano assicurate misure appropriate "per quanto concerne [...] l'asilo [...]".

[232] Vedi l'art. 78 TFUE.

[233] Lenzerini (2009), p. 120.

[234] Conforti (2015), p. 251.

[235] Abbiamo visto sopra (par. 14.1) i limiti dell'art. 22(7) della Convenzione americana e dell'art. 12(3) della Carta africana.

Tuttavia, abbiamo sostenuto che esistono almeno due diritti più specifici e circoscritti, che derivano dal diritto di asilo: il diritto del richiedente asilo al *non-refoulement* ed il suo diritto di non essere estradato per motivi politici. A questi diritti specifici corrispondono obblighi a carico degli Stati. Di quelli relativi al divieto di *refoulement* abbiamo già parlato [236]. Anche l'obbligo di non estradare il richiedente asilo ha carattere negativo.

15. *Diritti dei rifugiati*

15.1. *Norme*

Il regime internazionale di protezione dei rifugiati è stabilito, in via principale ed a livello universale, dalla Convenzione di Ginevra del 28 luglio 1951 sullo *status* dei rifugiati e dal successivo Protocollo del 31 gennaio 1967. Come si è già detto, questo sistema convenzionale ha sviluppato molto con il tempo il suo ambito di applicazione soggettivo ed oggettivo. A livello regionale, si devono ricordare la Convenzione che regola gli aspetti specifici dei problemi dei rifugiati in Africa del 1969 [237], la Dichiarazione di Cartagena sui rifugiati del 1984 [238] e la Convenzione araba sulla disciplina dello *status* dei rifugiati del 1994 [239].

Ma è molto importante anche il regime di protezione dei rifugiati stabilito nel quadro dell'Unione Europea, che è assai complesso, ed al quale abbiamo già dedicato qualche osservazione. Questo regime ha lo scopo di stabilire regole uniformi per gli Stati membri dell'UE, tese a completare e rafforzare il sistema della Convenzione di Ginevra [240]. Le componenti principali di questo regime sono: l'art. 3(2) del Trattato sull'Unione Europea (TEU); gli artt. 77-80 del Trattato sul funzionamento dell'Unione Europea (TFUE); gli artt. 18 e 19(2) della Carta dei diritti fondamentali; il c.d. sistema Dublino, attualmente disciplinato dal regolamento 604/2013; ed infine le direttive 2011/95, 2013/32 e 2013/33.

15.2. *Contenuto dei diritti*

La Convenzione di Ginevra, nell'art. 1, definisce come rifugiato ogni persona che:

"[…] owing to well-founded fear of being persecuted for reasons of race, religion, nationality, membership of a particular social group or political opinion, is outside the country of his nationality and is unable, or owing to such fear, is unwilling to avail himself of the protection of that country; or who, not having a nationality and being outside the country of his former habitual residence as a result of such events, is unable or, owing to such fear, is unwilling to return to it".

La Convenzione, poiché si concentrava sui rifugiati che si erano originati per eventi oc-

---

[236] Vedi *supra*, par. 13.1 e Cap. V, parr. 7.3.1 e 8.3.1.

[237] OAU Convention governing the Specific Aspects of Refugee Problems in Africa, Addis-Ababa, 10 September 1969.

[238] Cartagena Declaration on Refugees, 22 November 1984.

[239] Arab Convention on Regulating Status of Refugees in the Arab Countries, adottata dalla Lega Araba nel 1994, ma non ancora in vigore.

[240] Vedi Di Filippo (2012), pp. 242-243.

corsi durante la Seconda Guerra Mondiale in Europa, conteneva anche limiti geografici e temporali[241] nella sua definizione dei "rifugiati". Tuttavia, la maggior parte degli Stati parti della Convenzione ha poi ratificato il Protocollo del 1967, che ha rimosso tali limiti.

Pertanto, il rifugiato deve possedere quattro requisiti: *a*) deve trovarsi fuori del suo paese di origine (o di residenza abituale se è apolide); *b*) non può o non vuole valersi della protezione di tale Stato; *c*) deve avere una paura ben fondata di persecuzione; *d*) la persecuzione deve fondarsi su cinque ragioni specifiche, elencate nell'art. 1. Il primo requisito è di semplice accertamento: l'individuo deve aver superato una frontiera nazionale per essere considerato come un rifugiato. Pertanto le *Internally Displaced Persons* non possono essere qualificate come rifugiati.

Il secondo requisito è quello della "rottura" dei rapporti fra il rifugiato ed il proprio Stato e quindi della protezione del secondo nei confronti del primo. Tale "rottura" può dipendere dalla volontà dello Stato, che, ad esempio, toglie la cittadinanza all'individuo, oppure, più spesso, dalla volontà dell'individuo, che rifiuta di ritornare al suo Paese per paura di persecuzione.

Il terzo requisito è più complesso e comprende due elementi. L'elemento della "paura ben fondata" richiede uno stato mentale soggettivo, ma anche motivi oggettivi che possano giustificare tale paura. Ad esempio, la persona può portare prove circa passate persecuzioni da essa subìte nel proprio Paese o anche circa persecuzioni effettuate nel proprio Paese contro individui che hanno le sue stesse caratteristiche o appartengano ai suoi stessi gruppi. Nella giurisprudenza interna degli Stati, talora si è stabilito, come requisito di prova della "paura ben fondata", lo standard restrittivo della "clear probability of persecution", e talora lo standard più flessibile della "good reason to fear persecution"[242]. L'altro elemento del terzo requisito è quello della "persecuzione". L'*UNHCR Handbook on Procedures and Criteria for Determining Refugee Status* sostiene che:

> "[...] there is no universally accepted definition of 'persecution', and various attempts to formulate such a definition have met with little success. From Article 33 of the 1951 Convention, it may be inferred that a threat to life or freedom on account of race, religion, nationality, political opinion or membership of a particular social group is always persecution. Other serious violations of human rights – for the same reasons – would also constitute persecution".

Quindi la persecuzione comprende certamente le privazioni arbitrarie della vita, la tortura, la detenzione arbitraria. Ma, secondo una parte della dottrina e della giurisprudenza[243], anche altre gravi violazioni dei diritti umani possono costituire "persecuzione". La persecuzione deriva di solito dallo Stato e dagli individui-organi statali; ma, nella prassi di molti Stati, si riconoscono come rifugiati anche le persone perseguitate da individui privati quando lo Stato di origine non è capace di proteggerle[244].

Infine, il quarto requisito richiesto, per la qualifica di rifugiato, è che la persecuzione si fondi su uno o più dei cinque motivi specificati dalla Convenzione: razza, religione, naziona-

---

[241] Si applicava agli eventi anteriori al 1° gennaio 1951. Cfr. CSR, art. 1(A)(2).

[242] Vedi Weissbrodt, de la Vega (2007), p. 75 e le sentenze *ivi* citate.

[243] *Ibidem*, pp. 76-78 e le sentenze *ivi* citate.

[244] Cfr. Kälin, Künzli (2009), p. 509.

lità, opinioni politiche, o appartenenza ad un gruppo sociale particolare. Riguardo alla persecuzione per motivi di razza, conviene far riferimento alla definizione di discriminazione razziale contenuta nell'art. 1 della Convenzione delle NU contro la discriminazione razziale[245]. La persecuzione per motivi di religione è stata definita dal suddetto *UNHCR Handbook* nei seguenti termini:

> "Persecution for 'reasons of religion' may assume various forms, e.g. prohibition of membership of a religious community, of worship in private or in public, of religious instruction, or serious measure of discrimination imposed on persons because they practise their religion or belong to a particular religious community [...]".

Le persecuzioni fondate sulla nazionalità, sulle opinioni politiche o sull'appartenenza a particolari gruppi sociali, sono state definite in maniera piuttosto precisa dalla giurisprudenza internazionale e interna.

Secondo la Convenzione di Ginevra ed il Protocollo, i rifugiati, una volta ottenuto tale *status*, sono titolari di una serie dettagliata di diritti, tra cui quelli di non essere discriminati (art. 3), di poter praticare la propria religione (art. 4), di avere il proprio stato personale disciplinato dal paese di domicilio (art. 12), di associazione (art. 15), di accesso ai tribunali (art. 16). Inoltre, hanno il diritto di avere un trattamento favorevole (e comunque non inferiore a quello accordato agli altri stranieri) con riguardo alle loro proprietà (art. 13), alle loro attività di lavoro (artt. 17-19), all'abitazione (art. 21), e all'istruzione pubblica (art. 22).

Ma la norma più importante, e più celebre, è quella dell'art. 33 della Convenzione, che stabilisce il principio del *non-refoulement*, del quale abbiamo già parlato più volte. Conviene qui ribadire che questo principio era stabilito dall'art. 33 in maniera restrittiva, perché limitato ai pericoli derivanti dai cinque motivi di discriminazione sopra indicati; ma è stato poi interpretato in maniera evolutiva nella prassi, e quindi si applica adesso a tutti i casi nei quali il rifugiato[246] rischia di essere sottoposto nel paese di eventuale invio a gravi violazioni dei diritti umani fondamentali. Tuttavia, l'art. 33 prevede un'eccezione, quando il rifugiato può essere ragionevolmente considerato un pericolo per la sicurezza dello Stato nel quale si trova o quando, essendo stato condannato per un crimine particolarmente grave, costituisce un pericolo per la comunità di tale Stato (art. 33(2)).

Passando al contenuto delle norme convenzionali regionali sulla protezione dei rifugiati, conviene notare che esse tendono ad adottare una nozione di "rifugiato" più ampia rispetto a quella della Convenzione di Ginevra e del suo Protocollo. In particolare, la Convenzione che regola gli aspetti specifici dei problemi del rifugiato in Africa riprende la definizione di rifugiato adottata dalla Convenzione di Ginevra e dal Protocollo, ma aggiunge che il termine "rifugiato" si applicherà anche:

> "to every person who, owing to external aggression, occupation, foreign domination or events seriously disturbing public order in either part or the whole of his country of origin or nationality, is compelled to leave his place of habitual residence in order to seek refuge in another place outside his country of origin or nationality"[247].

---

[245] Vedi *supra*, Cap. IV, par. 5.2.3 e Cap. V, par. 22.

[246] E più generalmente lo straniero.

[247] OAU Convention governing the Specific Aspects of Refugee Problems in Africa, art. 1(2).

Anche nel sistema interamericano, si nota una tendenza simile. La Dichiarazione di Cartagena sui rifugiati del 1984 raccomanda di estendere la nozione di rifugiato prevista dalla Convenzione di Ginevra anche a:

> "persons who have fled their country because their lives, safety or freedom have been threatened by generalized violence, foreign aggression, internal conflicts, massive violation of human rights or other circumstances which have seriously disturbed public order" [248].

La medesima impostazione è stata adottata da altri sistemi regionali: si può citare l'art. 1(2) della già citata Convenzione araba sulla disciplina dello *status* dei rifugiati [249].

Infine, conviene descrivere, sia pure in maniera assai sintetica, il contenuto del regime giuridico dei rifugiati che si è sviluppato nel quadro dell'Unione Europea. Come si è già detto, nel diritto dell'UE, si parla di norme sul diritto di asilo, ma esse in realtà fanno riferimento, come regime-quadro, al sistema di protezione dei *rifugiati* della Convenzione di Ginevra, e poi si realizzano e specificano, in maggior dettaglio, come norme di carattere sussidiario e complementare rispetto al sistema di tale Convenzione. Ciò risulta chiaro dal già citato art. 18 della Carta dei diritti fondamentali dell'UE e dall'art. 78(1) del Trattato sul Funzionamento dell'Unione Europea (TFUE), secondo cui:

> "L'Unione sviluppa una politica comune in materia di asilo, di protezione sussidiaria e di protezione temporanea, volta a offrire uno status appropriato a qualsiasi cittadino di un paese terzo che necessita di protezione internazionale e a garantire il rispetto del principio di non respingimento. Detta politica deve essere conforme alla convenzione di Ginevra del 28 luglio 1951 ed al protocollo del 31 gennaio 1967 relativi allo status dei rifugiati, e agli altri trattati pertinenti".

Ciò premesso, conviene ricordare che la normativa dell'UE è stata creata nel tempo, passando da una fase basata prevalentemente sulla cooperazione intergovernativa fra Stati membri ad una progressiva "comunitarizzazione" della materia. Attualmente, il suo fondamento riposa sull'art. 3(2) del Trattato sull'Unione Europea (TUE) e sugli artt. 77-80 del TFUE. In particolare, è importante l'art. 78 TFUE, che, dopo aver fissato, nel par. 1, gli obiettivi della politica comune europea in materia di asilo, prevede, nel par. 2, che, per conseguire tali obiettivi, il Parlamento europeo ed il Consiglio adottino una serie di misure che includono, fra l'altro: *a*) uno *status* uniforme in materia di asilo a favore di cittadini di paesi terzi; *b*) procedure comuni per l'ottenimento e la perdita di tale *status*; *c*) criteri e meccanismi di determinazione dello Stato membro competente per l'esame della domanda di asilo; *d*) norme sulle condizioni di accoglienza dei richiedenti asilo.

In effetti, gli aspetti principali del sistema comune di asilo dell'Unione Europea sono quattro, in ordine logico. Il primo riguarda la determinazione dello *Stato competente* per l'esame della domanda di asilo. Esso è disciplinato dal c.d. sistema Dublino, originariamente regolato dalla Convenzione di Dublino del 1990 [250] e dalla Convenzione di applica-

---

[248] Cartagena Declaration on Refugees, Colloquium on the International Protection of Refugees in Central America, Mexico and Panama, 22 November 1984, par. III(3). Vedi anche la San José Declaration on Refugees and Displaced Persons, 1994.

[249] Non in vigore.

[250] Dublin Convention determining the State responsible for examining applications for asylum lodged in one of the Member States of the European Communities, 15 June 1990.

zione dell'Accordo di Schengen, poi dal regolamento 343/2003 ("Dublino II")[251] ed adesso dal regolamento 604/2013 ("Dublino III")[252], che ha sostituito il precedente. Tale sistema, come è noto, prevede che la competenza ad esaminare la domanda di asilo spetti ad un unico Stato membro, individuato sulla base di alcuni criteri che vengono applicati in ordine successivo[253]. Se la domanda viene accolta, la protezione produce effetti solo in tale Stato; se invece viene respinta, essa non può essere ripresentata in un altro Stato membro. Un aspetto critico del sistema di Dublino è che esso non risolve il problema per cui certi Paesi, come quelli mediterranei, sono soggetti ad una pressione migratoria maggiore rispetto ad altri Paesi dell'UE[254]. Per questo motivo, si parla da tempo di una revisione di tale sistema, che tuttavia non è stata finora realizzata.

Il secondo aspetto riguarda le *procedure* che vengono impiegate dagli Stati membri dell'UE per il riconoscimento e la revoca della qualifica di rifugiato: esso è adesso regolato dalla direttiva 2013/32 (c.d. "procedure")[255], che ha sostituito la direttiva 2005/85[256]. Questa direttiva è molto importante, perché riguarda una materia che non è regolata dal sistema della Convenzione di Ginevra. In sintesi, la direttiva 2013/32 disciplina, in maniera assai dettagliata, gli aspetti fondamentali delle procedure volte ad accertare i requisiti per ottenere lo *status* di rifugiato[257] e le garanzie che spettano ai richiedenti in ciascuna fase della procedura. La correttezza ed adeguatezza di tali procedure è molto importante, perché altrimenti si possono creare eccessivi ostacoli per i richiedenti il rifugio ed il pericolo di loro respingimenti illegittimi.

Il terzo aspetto, ed ai nostri fini il più importante, riguarda le norme sull'attribuzione della *qualifica di rifugiato* e sul *contenuto della protezione* accordata al medesimo. Questa materia è regolata soprattutto dalla direttiva 2011/95[258] (c.d. "qualifiche"), che ha sostituito la precedente direttiva 2004/83[259]. Lo scopo di queste norme di armonizzazione è quello di integrare ed estendere la disciplina minima di protezione dei rifugiati sta-

[251] Regolamento (CE) n. 343/2003 del Consiglio, del 18 febbraio 2003, che stabilisce i criteri e i meccanismi di determinazione dello Stato membro competente per l'esame di una domanda d'asilo presentata in uno degli Stati membri da un cittadino di un paese terzo.

[252] Regolamento (UE) n. 604/2013 del Parlamento europeo e del Consiglio, del 26 giugno 2013, che stabilisce i criteri e i meccanismi di determinazione dello Stato membro competente per l'esame di una domanda di protezione internazionale presentata in uno degli Stati membri da un cittadino di un paese terzo o da un apolide.

[253] Lo Stato dove hanno già ricevuto rifugio certi familiari, oppure lo Stato che ha già rilasciato al richiedente un titolo di soggiorno o un visto, oppure lo Stato nel quale per primo il soggetto ha fatto ingresso, regolare o irregolare.

[254] Cfr. Di Filippo (2012), p. 250.

[255] Direttiva 2013/32/UE del Parlamento europeo e del Consiglio, del 26 giugno 2013, recante procedure comuni ai fini del riconoscimento e della revoca dello status di protezione internazionale.

[256] Direttiva 2005/85/CE del Consiglio, del 1° dicembre 2005, recante norme minime per le procedure applicate negli Stati membri ai fini del riconoscimento e della revoca dello status di rifugiato.

[257] Oppure lo status di protezione sussidiaria.

[258] Direttiva 2011/95/UE del Parlamento europeo e del Consiglio, del 13 dicembre 2011, recante norme sull'attribuzione, a cittadini di paesi terzi o apolidi, della qualifica di beneficiario di protezione internazionale, su uno status uniforme per i rifugiati o le persone aventi titolo a beneficiare della protezione sussidiaria, nonché sul contenuto della protezione riconosciuta.

[259] Direttiva 2004/83/CE del Consiglio, del 29 aprile 2004, recante norme minime sull'attribuzione, a cittadini di paesi terzi o apolidi, della qualifica di rifugiato o di persona altrimenti bisognosa di protezione internazionale, nonché norme minime sul contenuto della protezione riconosciuta.

bilita dal sistema della Convenzione di Ginevra[260]. In primo luogo, la direttiva stabilisce i requisiti per essere considerato "rifugiato" e adotta un'interpretazione evolutiva della nozione prevista dal sistema di Ginevra, precisando alcune nozioni controverse relative sia al timore di essere perseguitato[261] sia agli atti ed i motivi di persecuzione[262]. Tuttavia, essa non accoglie la tendenza, presente in altri sistemi regionali, ad estendere lo *status* di rifugiato a persone che sfuggono da situazioni di violenza generalizzata, conflitti, disastri naturali o massicce violazioni di diritti umani. In secondo luogo, la direttiva apporta alcuni miglioramenti alle condizioni del rifugiato rispetto a quelle previste dalla Convenzione di Ginevra[263].

Il quarto aspetto del sistema europeo comune attiene all'*accoglienza* di coloro che richiedono lo *status* di rifugiato. Esso è regolato dalla direttiva 2013/33[264], che ha sostituito la direttiva 2003/9[265]. Lo scopo è quello di armonizzare negli Stati membri le condizioni di accoglienza dei richiedenti. La direttiva contiene, fra l'altro, una serie di garanzie per le persone che vengono trattenute e norme a favore delle persone vulnerabili.

Infine, si deve ricordare la Carta dei diritti fondamentali dell'UE che, nell'art. 18 già citato, garantisce il diritto all'asilo e, nell'art. 19(2), ribadisce a favore di tutti gli individui il principio di *non-refoulement*.

15.3. *Obblighi*

Abbiamo visto che il regime giuridico internazionale e quello europeo di protezione dei rifugiati sono molto complessi, poiché comprendono una pluralità di norme e di diritti a favore dei rifugiati. Ne deriva che anche gli obblighi a carico degli Stati sono molteplici ed hanno caratteri diversi. Non è possibile qui soffermarci su tali obblighi, che comunque si deducono facilmente dal contenuto dei suddetti diritti. Conviene solo osservare che la maggior parte degli obblighi si configurano come obblighi positivi ed immediati, spesso di risultato e talora di *due diligence*. Si noti che gli obblighi contenuti nelle citate direttive dell'Unione Europea hanno le caratteristiche particolari che contraddistinguono, in linea generale, tali atti normativi.

16. *Diritti di altri migranti internazionalmente protetti*

Si tratta adesso di esaminare, sinteticamente, i diritti umani che spettano a persone che, pur non avendo titolo a chiedere asilo o *status* di rifugiati, sono costrette a lasciare le loro abitazioni e luoghi di residenza per chiedere accoglienza e protezione altrove. Queste per-

---

[260] Vedi Di Filippo (2012), pp. 244-245.

[261] Vedi gli artt. 5-8 della direttiva.

[262] Vedi gli artt. 9 e 10 della direttiva.

[263] Vedi gli artt. 20-35 della direttiva.

[264] Direttiva 2013/33/UE del Parlamento europeo e del Consiglio, del 26 giugno 2013, recante norme relative all'accoglienza dei richiedenti protezione internazionale.

[265] Direttiva 2003/9/CE del Consiglio, del 27 gennaio 2003, recante norme minime relative all'accoglienza dei richiedenti asilo negli Stati membri.

sone possono essere definite come "migranti forzati". Tuttavia, si deve distinguere fra due situazioni diverse: *a*) quella di coloro che lasciano il proprio Paese per chiedere protezione in un altro Paese (situazione simile a quella dei rifugiati e dei richiedenti asilo); *b*) quella di coloro che cercano accoglienza in un altro luogo più sicuro all'interno del proprio Paese (c.d. *internally displaced persons*).

Nell'ambito della prima situazione, si possono individuare varie forme giuridiche di protezione a favore di questi migranti, specie nel diritto dell'Unione Europea e nel diritto statale: *a*) la protezione "sussidiaria"; *b*) quella "temporanea"; *c*) quella "umanitaria".

16.1. *Protezione "sussidiaria"*

Nel sistema comune di asilo dell'Unione Europea, vi è una disciplina normativa sulla c.d. protezione "sussidiaria". Nel linguaggio dell'UE, essa compone, insieme alla disciplina sui rifugiati, il regime della c.d. "protezione internazionale". In realtà, la protezione sussidiaria ha lo scopo di assicurare una serie di diritti a quei migranti che non possono ottenere lo *status* di rifugiato, ma che sono fuggiti dal loro Paese e chiedono la protezione di un Paese dell'Unione Europea. La protezione sussidiaria è regolata soprattutto dalla direttiva 2011/95 ("qualifiche"), che stabilisce i requisiti per tale protezione, lo *status* ed il contenuto della medesima; ma anche dalla direttiva 2013/32 ("procedure") sui procedimenti per la domanda, e dalla direttiva 2013/33 ("accoglienza")[266].

Il beneficiario della protezione sussidiaria è il cittadino di un Paese terzo, o un apolide, che non ha i requisiti per essere riconosciuto come rifugiato, ma nei cui confronti sussistono fondati motivi per ritenere che, se ritornasse nel paese di origine o di dimora abituale, correrebbe un rischio effettivo di subire un grave danno[267]. Sono ritenuti come gravi danni, in alternativa: *a*) la condanna o l'esecuzione della pena di morte; *b*) la tortura o altra forma di pena o trattamento inumano o degradante; *c*) la minaccia grave e individuale alla vita o alla persona di un civile, derivante dalla violenza indiscriminata in situazioni di conflitti armati interni o internazionali[268]. Al beneficiario di protezione sussidiaria vengono estesi i diritti spettanti al rifugiato, con qualche eccezione.

16.2. *Protezione "temporanea"*

Sempre nel quadro del diritto dell'UE, è previsto un altro regime di protezione dei migranti forzati, denominato protezione "temporanea". Esso prevede per i beneficiari un livello di tutela inferiore rispetto a quello assicurato dalla protezione sussidiaria. La protezione temporanea è disciplinata dalla direttiva 2001/55[269] e riguarda le situazioni di afflus-

---

[266] Infatti, come si è detto, queste tre direttive si occupano congiuntamente (sia con norme comuni che con norme separate) delle due forme di protezione internazionale.

[267] Vedi l'art. 2(f) della direttiva 2011/95.

[268] Vedi l'art. 15 della direttiva 2011/95.

[269] Direttiva 2001/55/CE del Consiglio, del 20 luglio 2001, sulle norme minime per la concessione della protezione temporanea in caso di afflusso massiccio di sfollati e sulla promozione dell'equilibrio degli sforzi tra gli Stati membri che ricevono gli sfollati e subiscono le conseguenze dell'accoglienza degli stessi.

so massiccio di sfollati che non possono ritornare nel Paese di origine[270]. Gli "sfollati" sono definiti come:

> "i cittadini di paesi terzi o apolidi che hanno dovuto abbandonare il loro paese o regione d'origine o che sono stati evacuati [...] ed il cui rimpatrio in condizioni sicure e stabili risulta impossibile a causa della situazione del paese stesso [...] ed in particolare: i) le persone fuggite da zone di conflitto armato o di violenza endemica; ii) le persone che siano soggette a rischio grave di violazioni sistematiche o generalizzate dei diritti umani o siano state vittime di siffatte violazioni".

In sostanza, lo scopo della protezione temporanea è quello di instaurare una procedura di carattere eccezionale, che possa fornire una tutela immediata e provvisoria alle persone sfollate[271]. Infatti, gli sfollati hanno diritto ad una forma piuttosto elementare di accoglienza da parte degli Stati membri, della durata di un anno, con possibilità di proroga per un periodo massimo di un ulteriore anno[272]. La protezione temporanea non pregiudica il riconoscimento dello *status* di rifugiato ai sensi della Convenzione di Ginevra[273]. Tuttavia, come è stato notato[274], questa forma di protezione ha il difetto di non essere un meccanismo che opera in maniera continuativa, ma la cui attivazione richiede una decisione del Consiglio presa, volta per volta, in relazione ad una specifica situazione. Pertanto, si tratta di una procedura di limitata efficacia.

16.3. *Protezione "umanitaria"*

Il regime di protezione temporanea della direttiva 2001/55, appena descritto, non va confuso con la normativa italiana che ha previsto il *permesso temporaneo di soggiorno* per motivi umanitari, e che viene spesso denominata come protezione "umanitaria". Tuttavia, va precisato che tale normativa è molto cambiata nel tempo. Il Decreto legislativo n. 286/1998 ha stabilito, all'art. 5, 6° comma, che il rifiuto o la revoca del permesso di soggiorno non possono essere adottati se ricorrono "seri motivi, in particolare di carattere umanitario o risultanti da obblighi costituzionali o internazionali dello Stato italiano". Più recentemente, il Decreto legislativo n. 25/2008, all'art. 32, ha previsto che:

> "Nei casi in cui non accolga la domanda di protezione internazionale e ritenga che possano sussistere gravi motivi di carattere umanitario, la Commissione territoriale trasmette gli atti al questore per l'eventuale rilascio del permesso di soggiorno ai sensi dell'art. 5, comma 6, del decreto legislativo 25 luglio 1998, n. 286".

Inoltre, il Decreto legislativo n. 286/1998 ha introdotto un'altra forma di protezione "umanitaria", di carattere eccezionale. L'art. 20 del Decreto, infatti, prevede che il Presidente del Consiglio dei Ministri possa adottare un decreto che introduce misure temporanee di protezione per gravi necessità umanitarie durante conflitti, disastri naturali o altri

---

[270] Vedi gli artt. 1 e 2 della direttiva.

[271] Vedi l'art. 2(a) della direttiva.

[272] Art. 4 della direttiva.

[273] Art. 3(1) della direttiva.

[274] Di Filippo (2012), p. 246.

eventi molto seri che si verifichino in Paesi terzi. In passato, in Italia un regime di protezione temporanea su tali basi è stato adottato in alcune circostanze [275].

In realtà, la protezione "umanitaria" intende costituire una forma di protezione dei migranti forzosi che ha carattere residuale, ma che è assai utile, rispetto ai tre schemi di tutela internazionale previsti dal diritto dell'Unione Europea (asilo, protezione sussidiaria e protezione temporanea). Tuttavia, come è noto, recentemente il Governo italiano, con il Decreto-Legge n. 113/2018 [276], ha quasi abolito l'istituto della protezione umanitaria, introducendo una rigida tipizzazione dei casi in cui possono essere rilasciati speciali permessi di soggiorno temporanei per esigenze di carattere umanitario, e stabilendo requisiti assai restrittivi per gli individui interessati.

16.4. Internally Displaced Persons

Come si è già detto, la situazione delle *internally displaced persons* riguarda individui che sono costretti a lasciare ed abbandonare le loro abitazioni ed i loro luoghi di residenza, ma che restano all'interno del proprio Paese. Pertanto, a differenza dei richiedenti asilo, dei rifugiati e degli altri migranti forzati sopra descritti, essi non fuggono dal loro Paese per cercare accoglienza e protezione in un altro Paese. In realtà, non esiste un regime giuridico internazionale specifico per le *internally displaced persons* [277], a parte quello previsto dalla Convenzione di Kampala del 2009 [278]. Costoro, restando nello Stato di loro nazionalità, possono invocare tutti i diritti umani che spettano agli altri cittadini, nonché, nelle situazioni di conflitti armati, le medesime norme del diritto internazionale umanitario.

Tuttavia, la loro situazione di sfollati li rende particolarmente vulnerabili; e fa sì che alcuni diritti umani siano per loro di speciale importanza da un punto di vista pratico.

Per venire incontro a questa situazione, le Nazioni Unite hanno intrapreso alcune iniziative. Nel 1992 è stato istituito un Rappresentante del Segretario Generale delle NU per le *internally displaced persons*. Quindi, nel 1998, sono stati approvati i *Guiding Principles on Internal Displacement* [279], un atto di *soft law* che tuttavia è stato in seguito approvato dal *World Summit* del 2005 [280]. Questi principi prevedono una definizione piuttosto precisa del concetto di *internally displaced persons*: si tratta di individui

> "who have been forced or obliged to flee or to leave their homes or places of habitual residence, in particular as a result of or in order to avoid the effects of armed conflict, situations of generalized violence, violations of human rights or natural or human-made disasters, and who have not crossed an internationally recognized State border".

Fra i diritti umani che assumono maggior rilievo per le *internally displaced persons* si possono indicare: *a*) il divieto di trasferimenti forzati; *b*) il divieto di discriminazione; *c*) la

---

[275] Vedi Favilli (2013), p. 83.

[276] Convertito nella Legge 1° dicembre 2018, n. 132.

[277] Vedi Kälin, Künzli (2009), pp. 502-507.

[278] African Union Convention for the Protection and Assistance of Internally Displaced Persons in Africa (Kampala Convention), 23 October 2009.

[279] UN Doc. E/CN.4/1998/53/Add.2 (Annex).

[280] 2005 *World Summit Outcome*, GA Res. A/Res/60/1 (2005), par. 132.

libertà di movimento; *d*) i diritti di sussistenza, quali il diritto al cibo, all'abitazione ed alle cure sanitarie; *e*) il diritto di ritornare alle loro abitazioni quando l'emergenza sia stata superata o, in alternativa, il diritto di integrarsi in un altro luogo.

Sezione VI

DIRITTI UMANI COLLETTIVI ED OBIETTIVI POLITICI DELLA COMUNITÀ INTERNAZIONALE

Il carattere individualistico dei diritti umani costituisce un'impronta originaria della teoria dei diritti umani, che risente della forte impostazione occidentale, e questo carattere resta ancora dominante nel regime giuridico complessivo della materia. Tuttavia, con il tempo, specie per l'impatto esercitato dalla concezione dei diritti umani dei Paesi in via di sviluppo[281], tale carattere si è un po' attenuato ed è cresciuta l'idea dell'importanza dei diritti umani collettivi; cioè l'idea che si dovesse estendere l'ambito di applicazione dei diritti umani a certe collettività, o gruppi di persone, quali i popoli, le minoranze ed i popoli indigeni.

Il primo, e più importante, successo di questa concezione è rappresentato dal rapido consolidamento, nel diritto consuetudinario, del principio di autodeterminazione dei popoli, di cui abbiamo già parlato[282]. Conviene adesso volgere l'attenzione ai diritti umani delle minoranze e dei popoli indigeni.

Ci chiederemo, poi, se altri diritti umani collettivi si siano affermati nel diritto internazionale. A questo proposito, oggi si parla spesso di certi diritti dei popoli, diversi dall'autodeterminazione, che si sarebbero affermati nell'ordinamento internazionale nel quadro dei diritti umani della terza e quarta generazione. Tuttavia, a nostro avviso, come vedremo, la maggior parte di questi diritti è ancora in una fase di progressivo sviluppo e non sembra ancora oggetto di norme internazionali vincolanti, ma soltanto di impegni o di obiettivi di carattere politico della comunità internazionale.

Infine, converrà accennare al fenomeno per cui stanno emergendo, nel diritto internazionale, alcuni diritti umani nei quali la dimensione individuale è fortemente collegata a quella pubblica o collettiva. Ci sembra che ciò si realizzi in materia di sicurezza (diritto alla sicurezza umana) ed in materia di ambiente (diritto ad un ambiente sano).

17. *Diritti delle minoranze*

La protezione internazionale delle minoranze, a partire dai secoli XVI e XVII e poi soprattutto dopo la Prima Guerra Mondiale, è stata uno degli aspetti che hanno anticipato il fenomeno della generale tutela dei diritti umani, anche se gli scopi dei trattati sulle mino-

---

[281] Vedi *supra*, Cap. III, par. 4.1 e Cap. IV, par. 4.

[282] Vedi *supra*, Cap. V, par. 24.

ranze erano motivati più da ragioni politiche di stabilità in Europa che da motivazioni umanitarie[283]. Dopo la Seconda Guerra Mondiale, la protezione delle minoranze ha trovato la sua collocazione nel quadro, più moderno, della tutela internazionale dei diritti umani; ma, per la verità, non ha avuto uno sviluppo molto significativo.

Il motivo di ciò è che gli Stati sono restii a concedere molti diritti alle minoranze nel timore che ciò possa favorire le loro aspirazioni secessionistiche, le quali ovviamente si pongono in contrasto con la sovranità statale. Si consideri anche l'alto numero di minoranze religiose, etniche, linguistiche, culturali o di altro tipo presenti negli Stati della comunità internazionale; ed il fatto che molte di esse aspirano storicamente alla secessione. Ci si potrebbe chiedere perché un simile atteggiamento ostile degli Stati non sia stato manifestato nei confronti dei popoli, a proposito del diritto di autodeterminazione. I motivi principali sono due. In primo luogo, il movimento per l'autodeterminazione dei popoli ha trovato la forte spinta, non procrastinabile, per motivi politici e storici, ad opera del processo di decolonizzazione. In secondo luogo, l'autodeterminazione dei popoli riguarda essenzialmente il diritto di questi di liberarsi da una dominazione straniera realizzatasi illegittimamente e con la forza (o di un regime illegittimo di *apartheid*). Pertanto essa non mette in crisi la sovranità della grande generalità degli Stati che agiscono legittimamente; o comunque non si pone in contrasto con la sovranità statale nella stessa misura in cui lo possono fare le aspirazioni secessionistiche da parte di minoranze.

17.1. *Norme*

Si deve anzitutto constatare che la Carta delle Nazioni Unite, pur contenendo una serie di disposizioni sui territori non autonomi e sul regime internazionale di amministrazione fiduciaria di certi territori, non aveva previsto norme esplicitamente volte alla protezione delle minoranze. Per di più, anche la Dichiarazione universale non contiene alcuna disposizione sulla tutela delle minoranze; e questa esclusione è assai significativa.

È solo con il Patto sui diritti civili e politici che emerge, nel diritto internazionale dei diritti umani, una norma sui diritti delle minoranze. Essa è contenuta nell'art. 27, che recita:

> "In those States in which ethnic, religious or linguistic minorities exist, persons belonging to such minorities shall not be denied the right, in community with the other members of their group, to enjoy their own culture, to profess and practice their own religion, or to use their own language".

Si tratta di una disposizione molto importante, perché è l'unica norma sulle minoranze contenuta in un trattato sui diritti umani di carattere generale ed universale. Tuttavia, si deve sottolineare fin d'ora che l'art. 27 parla di "persone appartenenti a tali minoranze". Su questo punto ritorneremo in seguito. Fra i trattati settoriali, e sempre di carattere universale, si può ricordare la Convenzione sui diritti del fanciullo del 1989, che contiene una norma (art. 30) assai simile a quella del Patto, con la sola aggiunta di un riferimento alle persone di origine indigena[284]. Successivamente, a livello universale, l'Assemblea Gene-

---

[283] Vedi *supra*, Cap. I, par. 2.9.

[284] CRC, art. 30: "In those States in which ethnic, religious or linguistic minorities exist, a child belonging to such a minority or who is indigenous shall not be denied the right, in community with other members of his

rale delle NU ha adottato, nel 1992, la Dichiarazione sui diritti delle persone appartenenti alle minoranze nazionali o etniche, religiose e linguistiche[285].

Nel continente europeo, lo strumento giuridico più importante è costituito dalla Convenzione quadro per la protezione delle minoranze nazionali[286], adottata dal Consiglio d'Europa nel 1995. Questa Convenzione, di cui abbiamo già parlato[287], contiene una serie di principi sui diritti delle minoranze, quali la non discriminazione; la promozione di tradizioni culturali, religiose e linguistiche; le libertà di riunione, associazione, espressione, pensiero, coscienza e religione; l'accesso ai media; i diritti linguistici; i diritti di partecipazione alla vita pubblica, ecc. Tuttavia, come si era già detto, questa Convenzione stabilisce principi più che norme di dettaglio ed è dubbio che ai diritti delle minoranze corrispondano effettivamente obblighi precisi e immediati degli Stati parti. Inoltre, il Consiglio d'Europa aveva già adottato, nel 1992, la Carta europea per le lingue regionali o minoritarie[288], che cerca di promuovere il multilinguismo. Conviene ricordare che anche l'OSCE ha approvato alcuni documenti in materia di protezione delle minoranze ed ha istituito, nel 1992, un Alto Commissario per le minoranze nazionali[289].

Nel sistema interamericano dei diritti umani, non vi sono trattati specifici sulla protezione delle minoranze; ma alcune disposizioni della Dichiarazione americana dei diritti e doveri dell'uomo[290] e della Convenzione americana[291] possono offrire una tutela indiretta alle minoranze. La giurisprudenza della Corte interamericana ha affrontato alcuni aspetti importanti in relazione alle minoranze, quali la responsabilità dello Stato per sparizioni forzate o violazioni del diritto alla vita o di diritti di proprietà di gruppi minoritari o per violazioni del diritto ad una nazionalità[292].

Anche in Africa, alcune disposizioni della Carta africana sono state utilizzate per proteggere le minoranze. Ad esempio, la Commissione africana, nel caso *Amnesty International v. Sudan*, ha applicato l'art. 8 della Carta[293], sulla libera scelta di una religione, per proteggere la minoranza cattolica in Sudan e per affermare che tale Stato aveva commesso violazioni perché i cittadini non musulmani non avevano il diritto di pregare o costruire i propri luoghi di culto, oltre ad essere sottoposti a maltrattamenti, detenzioni arbitrarie ed altri abusi.

---

or her group, to enjoy his or her own culture, to profess and practice his or her religion, or to use his or her language".

[285] Declaration on the Rights of Persons Belonging to National or Ethnic, Religious and Linguistic Minorities, GA Res. 47/135 of 18 December 1992.

[286] Framework Convention for the Protection of National Minorities of 1° February 1995 (FCPNM).

[287] Vedi *supra*, Cap. IV, par. 8.3.3.

[288] European Charter for Regional or Minority Languages of 5 November 1992 (ECML). Vedi *supra*, Cap. IV, par. 8.3.2.

[289] High Commissioner on National Minorities, *www.osce.org/hcnm*.

[290] Vedi, ad es., American Declaration of the Rights and Duties of Man, artt. II, III, IV, VIII, XII, XX, XXI, XXII.

[291] Vedi, ad es., ACHR, artt. 12, 13, 15, 16, 22, 23, 24.

[292] Vedi, ad es., IACtHR, *Aloeboetoe et al. v. Suriname (Merits)*, Judgment of 4 December 1991; *Aloeboetoe et al. v. Suriname (Reparations)*, Judgment of 10 September 1993; *Case of the Girls Yean and Bosico v. Dominican Republic*. Vedi anche, *infra*, par. 18, sui diritti dei popoli indigeni.

[293] ACmHPR, *Amnesty International and Others v. Sudan*, parr. 72-76.

17.2. *Contenuto dei diritti*

Venendo adesso al contenuto dei diritti delle minoranze, si possono individuare tre problemi principali: *a*) la definizione del concetto di "minoranza"; *b*) la questione circa la titolarità individuale o collettiva dei diritti riconosciuti; *c*) i principali diritti attribuiti alle minoranze.

Il primo problema è assai importante ed investe anche il controverso rapporto fra la nozione di "minoranza" e quella di "popolo". Come si è detto parlando dell'autodeterminazione dei popoli, mentre il concetto di "popolo", secondo la tesi prevalente, si ispira all'idea di *demos*[294], quello di minoranza esprime l'idea di *éthnos*, cioè di un gruppo di persone, che si distingue perché ha in comune razza, religione, lingua, cultura e tradizioni, ed è unito in un vincolo di reciproca solidarietà. Tuttavia, questa idea generale di "minoranza" non è sufficiente per dar luogo ad una nozione giuridica precisa. Infatti, nel diritto internazionale, specie nel quadro delle Nazioni Unite, sono stati effettuati numerosi tentativi di pervenire ad una definizione esatta della nozione di "minoranza", ma senza risultati certi.

D'altra parte, il Patto sui diritti civili e politici e la Convenzione sui diritti del fanciullo non specificano cosa intendano per minoranze. Anche la Convenzione quadro europea non è riuscita a definire il concetto di "minoranze", pur riferendosi espressamente alle minoranze nazionali. Una definizione che ha ottenuto molto consenso è quella che fu proposta da Capotorti in un suo rapporto per le NU, pubblicato nel 1979, secondo cui la minoranza è:

> "[...] a group numerically inferior to the rest of the population of a State, in a non-dominant position, whose members – being nationals of the State – possess ethnic, religious or linguistic characteristics differing from those of the rest of the population, and show, if only implicitly, a sense of solidarity directed towards preserving their culture, traditions, religion or language"[295].

Gli elementi presenti in questa definizione, ed in altre simili che sono state proposte successivamente in dottrina[296], sono i seguenti: *a*) la dimensione minoritaria del gruppo rispetto alla maggioranza della popolazione di uno Stato; *b*) la posizione non dominante del gruppo; *c*) la cittadinanza dei membri del gruppo; *d*) un'identità fissata sulla base di criteri etnici, linguistici, religiosi, culturali (requisito oggettivo); *e*) la volontà dei membri del gruppo di preservare tali caratteri e di mantenere un sentimento di solidarietà reciproca (requisito soggettivo). Come si vede, si tratta di ben cinque requisiti, che devono essere tutti presenti, e che pertanto finiscono per dare una definizione piuttosto restrittiva della nozione di "minoranza". Infatti, si deve sottolineare il fatto che il Comitato dei diritti umani tende ad ampliare questa definizione, perché ha talora esteso la protezione dell'art. 27 del Patto sui diritti civili e politici anche a membri di minoranze che sono cittadini di Stati diversi da quello in questione o che sono apolidi[297].

---

[294] Cioè di un gruppo di persone appartenente ad una certa entità territoriale. Vedi *supra*, Cap. V, par. 24.2.

[295] Capotorti (1979), par. 568.

[296] Vedi, fra gli altri, Deschênes (1985), par. 181; Thornberry (1991), p. 6 ss.; Capotorti (1992), pp. 107-109; Pocar (1998), pp. 36-37; Tancredi (2001), p. 625 ss., spec. 636; Pustorino (2006), pp. 259-263; Castellino (2014), pp. 34-36.

[297] HRCtee, General Comment No. 23, 8 April 1994, par. 5.2.

Il secondo problema, forse il più rilevante, riguarda la titolarità individuale o collettiva dei diritti riconosciuti alle minoranze. Per la verità, il diritto internazionale ha sempre mostrato la tendenza a *non* riconoscere le minoranze come entità *collettive*, ma piuttosto a concedere diritti esclusivamente ai singoli individui appartenenti alle minoranze (c.d. approccio *individualista* al problema delle minoranze)[298]. In altri termini, i membri delle minoranze godono di una serie di diritti umani *individuali*, quali, soprattutto, il diritto di non discriminazione e quello di mantenere le proprie tradizioni culturali, religiose e linguistiche. Inoltre, in coerenza con questa impostazione, il diritto internazionale non riconosce alle minoranze il più classico e importante dei diritti umani collettivi; cioè il diritto all'autodeterminazione, esterna e interna[299]. Il motivo risiede evidentemente, come si era già detto, nell'interesse degli Stati alla difesa della propria sovranità e integrità territoriale.

Questa tendenza individualista si rivela fin dall'art. 27 del Patto sui diritti civili e politici, che è la norma più importante in materia, a livello di diritto internazionale universale. Infatti, secondo l'interpretazione dominante, e che ci sembra corretta, l'art. 27 si limita a riconoscere *diritti individuali*; cioè diritti culturali, religiosi e linguistici, che spettano ai singoli membri della minoranza, e non diritti collettivi della minoranza in quanto tale[300]. Ciò significa, in sostanza, che la norma non aggiunge molto al tradizionale divieto generale di discriminazione per motivi etnici, culturali, religiosi e linguistici. Inoltre, l'art. 27 è formulato più in termini di obblighi negativi (di non interferenza) che di obblighi positivi degli Stati. Il difetto evidente di questo approccio sta nel fatto che esso manca di affrontare gli svantaggi strutturali subìti dalle minoranze e la difficoltà di rispondere a certe richieste di natura collettiva delle minoranze, come quella, ad esempio, di avere proprie scuole nella propria lingua, una rappresentanza proporzionale negli enti amministrativi e politici, il riconoscimento della propria lingua come lingua ufficiale, i propri luoghi di culto, ecc. Anche la Convenzione sui diritti del fanciullo e la citata Dichiarazione delle NU del 1992 adottano il medesimo approccio *individualistico*.

Più complessa è l'interpretazione, su questo punto, della Convenzione quadro europea per la protezione delle minoranze nazionali. Secondo alcuni autori[301], questa Convenzione proteggerebbe, quantomeno in parte, diritti umani *collettivi* delle minoranze. Secondo altri[302], invece, anche questa Convenzione attribuisce diritti ai singoli membri di una minoranza nazionale e non alla minoranza in quanto tale. A nostro avviso, questa seconda tesi è più convincente, poiché quasi tutte le norme della Convenzione sono dirette a "persone appartenenti a minoranze nazionali" (*persons belonging to national minorities*).

---

[298] Vedi, fra gli altri, Meijknecht (2001), p. 171.

[299] Vedi Tancredi (2001), pp. 229 e 628.

[300] Invece, secondo una tesi minoritaria, l'art. 27 non escluderebbe alcuni diritti collettivi, poiché stabilisce che gli individui appartenenti alle minoranze possono godere dei diritti previsti "in comune con gli altri membri del proprio gruppo". Cfr. Kälin, Künzli (2009), p. 375. Ma non ci sembra che questa specificazione dell'art. 27 intenda davvero riconoscere diritti alle minoranze in quanto tali. Anche il Comitato dei diritti umani riconosce che i diritti protetti dall'art. 27 sono diritti individuali; ma aggiunge che: "they depend in turn on the ability of the minority group to maintain its culture, language and religion. Accordingly, positive measures by States may also be necessary to protect the identity of a minority [...]" (HRCtee, General Comment No. 23, par. 6.2).

[301] Kälin, Künzli (2009), pp. 348 e 377.

[302] Focarelli (2013), p. 239.

Il terzo problema, sopra posto, riguarda i contenuti sostanziali dei diritti riconosciuti alle minoranze. In primo luogo, le persone appartenenti alle minoranze hanno il diritto di non subire discriminazioni a causa del loro *status*. Pertanto opera, per tali persone, il divieto generale di discriminazione come principio-quadro, il quale prevede sempre, fra le cause di discriminazione vietate, la lingua, la religione, l'origine nazionale o altri stati. Questo principio-quadro è ribadito e specificato, in relazione alle minoranze, nelle norme convenzionali sopra esaminate. In secondo luogo, tali norme stabiliscono una serie di diritti più specifici, volti a proteggere l'identità culturale, linguistica e religiosa delle persone appartenenti alle minoranze. Tuttavia l'attuazione di questi diritti viene, in gran parte, lasciata al diritto interno degli Stati.

17.3. *Obblighi*

Il tema degli obblighi degli Stati, corrispondenti ai diritti delle minoranze, può essere trattato in maniera molto sintetica. Per quanto riguarda il divieto di discriminazione dei membri delle minoranze, possiamo rinviare al discorso fatto in relazione al divieto generale di discriminazione [303].

Quanto agli obblighi degli Stati corrispondenti ai vari diritti specifici dei membri delle minoranze, essi includono obblighi negativi (ad esempio, quello di consentire libertà di assemblea, associazione, espressione, religione) [304] e, soprattutto, obblighi positivi. Ma, come si è detto, molti degli obblighi positivi previsti dagli strumenti internazionali esistenti non sono sufficientemente precisi e completi, e richiedono misure di attuazione nei diritti nazionali [305].

18. *Diritti dei popoli indigeni*

Fin dagli anni '80 del secolo scorso, si è venuta progressivamente affermando, nel diritto internazionale, l'esigenza di affrontare il problema della discriminazione dei popoli indigeni e di creare, a favore di tali popoli, un regime giuridico di protezione *ad hoc*. I popoli indigeni sono gli "abitanti originari" di un territorio; cioè i discendenti della popolazione di un territorio che vivevano in esso prima che la popolazione adesso dominante assumesse il controllo del territorio per effetto di immigrazione e/o conquista; e che, di solito, vivono in tribù o comunità regolate da costumi o tradizioni assai diverse, socialmente, culturalmente ed economicamente, rispetto a quelle della popolazione dominante nel territorio [306].

I popoli indigeni, di solito, non hanno per obiettivo quello della secessione dallo Stato in cui abitano; ma aspirano piuttosto a forme di auto-governo, al diritto di usufruire delle

---

[303] Vedi *supra*, Cap. V, par. 21.3.

[304] Vedi, ad es., FCPNM, art. 7.

[305] Forse può essere considerato come sufficientemente preciso, quantomeno nella prassi del Comitato dei diritti umani relativa all'art. 27 del Patto, il diritto alla proprietà delle terre ancestrali da parte dei membri dei popoli indigeni e dei membri delle comuni minoranze che a tali popoli vengono assimilate.

[306] Vedi Martinez Cobo (1983), parr. 379 e 381; Id. (1986), p. 29; Kälin, Künzli (2009), p. 378; Focarelli (2013), pp. 241-242. Vedi anche Lenzerini (ed.) (2008).

loro terre "ancestrali" e delle relative risorse naturali, ed al diritto di mantenere la loro identità culturale. Queste rivendicazioni, in un primo tempo avversate dalla grande maggioranza degli Stati, hanno più recentemente trovato maggiore accoglimento, tanto che, nel 2007, è stata addirittura approvata con ampia maggioranza dall'Assemblea Generale delle NU la Dichiarazione sui diritti dei popoli indigeni [307], che, sia pure come documento non vincolante, recepisce gran parte delle loro aspirazioni.

18.1. *Norme*

In un lontano periodo storico, che va dal XVI al XIX secolo, i popoli indigeni hanno stipulato accordi con le potenze coloniali; ma la loro natura di trattati internazionali è stata quasi sempre contestata, da tribunali interni e da arbitri e corti internazionali [308]. Venendo al diritto internazionale dei diritti umani, le norme rilevanti sono poche ed esse sono costituite, in sostanza, dalla Convenzione ILO n. 107 del 1957 sulla protezione e l'integrazione delle popolazioni indigene ed altre popolazioni tribali o semi-tribali [309], la quale tuttavia è stata sostituita quasi integralmente dalla Convenzione ILO n. 169 del 1989 sui popoli indigeni e tribali [310]; dall'art. 27 del Patto sui diritti civili e politici; e dalla già citata Dichiarazione delle NU del 2007.

La Convenzione ILO n. 169 contiene una definizione dei "popoli indigeni" ed una serie di diritti che gli Stati parti si impegnano a riconoscere ad essi. In particolare, la Convenzione stabilisce che gli Stati contraenti sono obbligati a riconoscere e tutelare i valori e gli usi di tali popoli [311]; a consultarli quando adottano misure legislative o amministrative che li possano interessare [312]; a rispettare il rapporto storico-culturale dei popoli indigeni con le loro terre [313]; a tutelare certi loro diritti in materia di lavoro, di previdenza sociale e di assistenza [314]. Ma la Convenzione dell'ILO è stata ratificata da un numero esiguo di Stati [315].

Quanto all'art. 27 del Patto sui diritti civili e politici, che, come si è visto, tutela tutte le minoranze etniche, religiose o linguistiche, esso è certamente applicabile ai popoli indigeni [316]. Tuttavia, si è già detto che questa norma presenta dei limiti importanti, perché protegge i diritti individuali dei membri delle minoranze, anziché le minoranze come entità collettive. Questo approccio individualistico dell'art. 27, già di per sé difettoso per tutte le minoranze, è ancora più inadeguato per quanto riguarda i popoli indigeni, che richiedono soprattutto una tutela collettiva per la loro identità storico-culturale e per il godimento delle proprie terre e risorse naturali.

---

307 *Declaration on the Rights of Indigenous Peoples*, GA Res. 61/295, 13 September 2007.

308 Vedi Focarelli (2013), p. 243, anche per riferimenti più specifici.

309 Indigenous and Tribal Populations Convention (ILO No. 107), 26 June 1957.

310 Indigenous and Tribal Peoples Convention (ILO No. 169), 26 June 1989.

311 *Ibidem*, art. 5.

312 *Ibidem*, art. 6.

313 *Ibidem*, artt. 7, 13-19.

314 *Ibidem*, artt. 20-25.

315 Peraltro, poiché ad essa aderiscono quasi tutti gli Stati dell'America Latina, la Convenzione ha rilevanza a livello regionale.

316 Vedi, ad es., HRCtee, General Comment No. 23, 8 April 1994, par. 3.2; *Lovelace v. Canada*, par. 14; *Kitok v. Sweden*, parr. 6.3 e 9.2.

Per questi motivi, appare particolarmente importante la Dichiarazione delle NU del 2007, la quale, nonostante il proprio carattere giuridicamente non vincolante, indica che si sta progressivamente sviluppando un consenso della comunità internazionale circa l'esigenza di riconoscere i popoli indigeni come destinatari, anche in qualità di *enti collettivi*, di alcuni diritti umani.

18.2. *Contenuto dei diritti*

Abbiamo dato sopra una definizione descrittiva del concetto di "popoli indigeni", che si fonda su elementi storici e sociologici. Tuttavia, una definizione giuridica deve essere più precisa e deve anche stabilire il rapporto fra la nozione di "popoli indigeni" e le nozioni di "minoranze" e di "popoli" ai sensi del diritto internazionale [317]. In realtà, le definizioni di "popoli indigeni" contenute nelle Convenzioni OIL n. 107 e n. 169 appaiono piuttosto lacunose. Ed anche la Dichiarazione sui diritti dei popoli indigeni del 2007 ha rinunciato a fornire una definizione giuridica precisa, poiché, ai sensi del suo art. 33(1), rinvia al c.d. criterio della autoidentificazione da parte dei popoli indigeni medesimi [318]. Occorre pertanto ricavare una definizione alla luce del complesso degli atti internazionali e della prassi relativa ai popoli indigeni.

Ad un primo sommario esame, il concetto giuridico di "popoli indigeni" si presta ad essere inquadrato nel concetto più generale di "minoranze", poiché esso coincide in massima parte con l'idea di *éthnos* ed è caratterizzato quasi sempre dagli elementi costitutivi del concetto di "minoranza" [319]. Inoltre, si potrebbe sostenere che i "popoli indigeni" costituiscono minoranze *sui generis*, poiché essi sono caratterizzati da due elementi distintivi ed aggiuntivi: *a*) l'origine storica più antica dell'insediamento territoriale dei "popoli indigeni" rispetto alle "minoranze generiche"; *b*) l'importanza particolare del fattore territoriale e del rapporto funzionale fra il controllo del territorio e delle risorse naturali da parte del popolo indigeno ed il mantenimento della propria identità culturale [320].

Tuttavia, l'inquadramento del concetto di "popolo indigeno" in quello di "minoranza", sia pure con *status* di minoranza *sui generis*, non convince; e, per di più, è stato sempre respinto dai popoli indigeni medesimi, i quali erano, e sono, consapevoli che tale inquadramento presenta svantaggi notevoli dal punto di vista giuridico e di "politica normativa". In effetti, i popoli indigeni hanno sempre evitato di restare "vincolati" al debole regime giuridico internazionale delle minoranze ed hanno invece cercato, con molta tenacia, di ottenere uno *status* giuridico diverso e più favorevole; in particolare più fondato sulla tutela di diritti umani collettivi. A questo proposito, esistono vari elementi della prassi recente

---

[317] Vedi Pisillo Mazzeschi (2016), pp. 459-465.

[318] *Declaration on the Rights of Indigenous Peoples*, art. 33(1): "Indigenous peoples have the right to determine their own identity or membership in accordance with their own customs and traditions [...]".

[319] Come si è visto sopra, tali elementi sono: a) la dimensione minoritaria del gruppo rispetto alla maggioranza della popolazione di uno Stato; b) la posizione non dominante del gruppo; c) la cittadinanza dei membri del gruppo; d) un'identità fissata sulla base di criteri etnici, linguistici, religiosi, culturali (requisito oggettivo); e) la volontà dei membri del gruppo di preservare tali caratteri e di mantenere un sentimento di solidarietà reciproca (elemento soggettivo). Nei popoli indigeni, l'unico elemento che talora manca (ma raramente) è dato dall'inferiorità numerica della popolazione indigena rispetto alla maggioranza della popolazione dello Stato.

[320] Vedi Pustorino (2006), p. 261.

che mostrano la tendenza ad assimilare il concetto di "popolo indigeno" a quello più generale di "popolo". Innanzitutto, la stessa affermazione, sul piano giuridico-diplomatico, della terminologia "popoli indigeni" non può essere priva di significato. In secondo luogo, l'art. 2 della Dichiarazione delle NU del 2007 afferma esplicitamente che i popoli indigeni sono "equal to all other peoples". In terzo luogo, anche la dottrina maggioritaria ritiene che i popoli indigeni debbano essere considerati come una categoria di "popoli", ai sensi del diritto internazionale, anche se essi godrebbero di minori diritti rispetto ai popoli soggetti a dominio coloniale, a conquista od occupazione con la forza, o ad un regime di *apartheid*; in particolare, non avrebbero il diritto di autodeterminazione "esterna"[321].

Tuttavia, anche l'assimilazione (quasi totale) dei popoli indigeni ai "popoli", ai sensi del diritto internazionale, non è del tutto convincente, sia per le caratteristiche "strutturali" dei popoli indigeni, sia perché l'autodeterminazione "esterna" sta al cuore dell'affermazione dei diritti internazionali dei popoli. Pertanto, a nostro avviso, i popoli indigeni presentano molti caratteri comuni con le minoranze, ma anche alcuni caratteri comuni con i popoli, che vanno al di là della semplice terminologia. A noi sembra che il diritto internazionale consideri i popoli indigeni come un *tertium genus*, rispetto a minoranze ed a popoli: un *tertium genus* che gode di uno *status* giuridico "speciale", per così dire intermedio rispetto a quelli degli altri due gruppi. In sostanza, i popoli indigeni usufruiscono di tutti i diritti spettanti alle comuni minoranze; ma in aggiunta, in quanto *minoranze speciali* per motivi di carattere storico-politico, usufruiscono di *ulteriori* diritti, che sono tipici ed esclusivi dei popoli indigeni (quelli legati ad una forte identità culturale ed all'uso delle risorse naturali). Infine, essi godono anche di *alcuni* diritti dei popoli, sia pure in forma minore ed attenuata rispetto ai popoli (ossia il diritto di autodeterminazione "interna" e non quello di autodeterminazione "esterna").

Questa conclusione ci sembra confermata dall'esame dei singoli diritti che vengono attribuiti ai popoli indigeni dalla Dichiarazione delle NU del 2007. Ci limitiamo qui ad una sintesi di tali diritti. In primo luogo, i membri dei popoli indigeni hanno i diritti di non discriminazione che spettano a tutte le minoranze. In secondo luogo, i popoli indigeni, *anche in quanto enti collettivi*, hanno una serie di diritti specifici legati alla loro identità culturale. In terzo luogo, essi hanno alcuni diritti che tutelano la loro proprietà o possesso sulle terre, acque ed altre risorse naturali da essi storicamente detenute o utilizzate. Anche questi diritti si distinguono rispetto a quelli che spettano alle comuni minoranze. Infine, si riconosce ai popoli indigeni anche il diritto all'autodeterminazione "interna", inteso come una forma di autogoverno locale. Tuttavia questo diritto non sembra avere un carattere autonomo e senza limiti; ma appare piuttosto come strettamente e funzionalmente collegato ai diritti di identità culturale dei popoli indigeni. In altri termini, l'obbligo dello Stato territoriale di concedere forme di autogoverno locale ai popoli indigeni può essere volta per volta proporzionato rispetto allo scopo di tutelare la loro identità culturale.

In conclusione, ci sembra che la strategia politico-diplomatica dei popoli indigeni, tesa ad ottenere un regime giuridico più favorevole rispetto a quello, piuttosto debole, delle comuni minoranze, e per certi aspetti assimilabile a quello dei popoli, sia risultata nel complesso vincente. Nella Dichiarazione del 2007 essi hanno ottenuto tre importanti obiet-

---

[321] Vedi *supra*, Cap. V, par. 24.2.

tivi: *a*) un regime giuridico speciale, fondato sui diritti umani spettanti alle comuni minoranze, ma integrato ed arricchito da ulteriori diritti concernenti la propria identità culturale e le proprie risorse naturali; *b*) il diritto di autodeterminazione "interna", sia pure con certi limiti; *c*) la titolarità, anche in quanto enti collettivi, di alcuni diritti umani.

È chiaro che la Dichiarazione non ha carattere vincolante; ma i tre aspetti sopra indicati stanno trovando conferma nella prassi degli organi internazionali di controllo sui diritti umani. Si possono citare, ad esempio, le sentenze della Corte interamericana nei casi delle comunità *Awas Tingni, Yakye Axa, Moiwana, Sawhoyamaxa, Kuna*[322]; nonché alcuni casi del Comitato dei diritti umani[323]. Pertanto, ci sembra che su tali aspetti si stia sviluppando un processo di creazione di norme di diritto internazionale consuetudinario. In particolare, ciò riguarda i diritti specifici dei popoli indigeni legati alla loro identità culturale e quelli che tutelano il loro possesso di terre, acque ed altre risorse naturali. Ma non ci sembra che tale processo si sia ancora concluso[324].

18.3. *Obblighi*

Dalle conclusioni sopra raggiunte, si ricava che, quantomeno nel diritto internazionale generale ad oggi consolidato, gli obblighi giuridicamente vincolanti degli Stati nei confronti dei popoli indigeni sono, in gran parte, quelli che esistono nei confronti delle comuni minoranze[325]. Pertanto facciamo rinvio a quanto già detto in merito a tali obblighi[326].

19. *Altri diritti umani collettivi?*

Ci si deve adesso chiedere se esistano, nell'ordinamento giuridico internazionale, diritti umani collettivi diversi ed ulteriori rispetto a quelli già esaminati. Come si era accennato, oggi si tende spesso a parlare di certi nuovi diritti, che spetterebbero ai popoli (talora anche insieme agli individui), e che vengono inquadrati nei diritti umani di terza o quarta generazione. Si citano, di solito, il diritto allo sviluppo, il diritto alle risorse naturali, il diritto alla pace, il diritto alla democrazia e il diritto ad un buon governo[327]. Questi diritti, che sono stati promossi e poi sostenuti a livello internazionale specie dai Paesi in via di sviluppo, sono contenuti soprattutto in atti internazionali non vincolanti, quali risoluzioni o

---

[322] Vedi, ad es., IACtHR, *Mayagna (Sumo) Awas Tingni Community v. Nicaragua (Merits)*, parr. 116-127, 142-155; *Yakye Axa Indigenous Community v. Paraguay (Merits)*, parr. 123-156; *Moiwana Community v. Suriname (Merits)*, parr. 125-135; *Sawhoyamaxa Indigenous Community v. Paraguay*, parr. 116-144; *Saramaka People v. Suriname*, parr. 87-96, 133-137 e 147; *Kuna and Emberá Indigenous Peoples v. Panama*, parr. 111-124.

[323] Vedi, ad es., HRCtee, *Länsman (Jouni) et al. v. Finland*, parr. 10.4 e 10.5; *Mahuika et al. v. New Zealand*, par. 9.5; *Poma Poma v. Peru*.

[324] In senso diverso vedi ILA Resolution No. 5/2012, *Rights of Indigenous Peoples*, 75th Conference of the ILA, Sofia, 26-30 August 2012.

[325] Il discorso può essere diverso, e più complesso, come si è visto, nel quadro di certi sistemi convenzionali di tutela dei diritti umani, quali il sistema interamericano e quello africano.

[326] Vedi *supra*, par. 17.3.

[327] Sull'argomento vedi, soprattutto, Tomuschat (2014), pp. 149-164.

dichiarazioni di organizzazioni o di conferenze internazionali; ma alcuni di essi sono previsti anche da trattati, quali, ad esempio, la Carta africana o la Carta araba.

Tuttavia, ci si deve chiedere se si possa davvero parlare di veri e propri diritti vincolanti, ai quali corrispondano obblighi giuridici a carico degli Stati o di altri enti, oppure se essi vadano classificati come impegni o obiettivi di carattere politico assunti dagli Stati o dalla comunità internazionale nel suo insieme [328]. Un'altra tesi sostiene che, quantomeno in alcuni casi, si tratti soltanto di fattori sociali, la cui presenza in un determinato Stato favorisce la realizzazione interna dei diritti umani da parte di tale Stato [329].

Per la verità, questi "diritti" sembrano, a prima vista, possedere alcune caratteristiche comuni, che inducono a dubitare circa la loro natura giuridica obbligatoria [330]: *a*) essi sono previsti quasi sempre da atti internazionali non vincolanti; *b*) essi non appaiono sorretti dalla *diuturnitas* e dall'*opinio iuris* internazionale, che sono richieste per la formazione di norme consuetudinarie, né dal quel riconoscimento e consenso generale da parte della comunità internazionale nel suo insieme, che è richiesto per la creazione di principi generali di diritto internazionale; *c*) vi è incertezza sul fatto se i titolari dei diritti siano i popoli o gli individui o altri enti; *d*) vi sono anche dubbi sul fatto se gli Stati siano davvero i destinatari degli obblighi corrispondenti ai diritti; *e*) infine (e soprattutto), il contenuto dei "diritti" in oggetto è spesso così vago e indefinito, da far dubitare che esso abbia carattere veramente normativo.

Ciò premesso, è vero che ciascuno di questi "diritti" ha una sua specificità e potrebbe essere studiato in maniera autonoma e approfondita rispetto agli altri. Tuttavia, ai nostri fini, si può tentare un loro esame sintetico, al solo scopo di verificare se, ed eventualmente in quale misura, ciascuno di tali diritti abbia effettivamente le suddette caratteristiche, e quali conclusioni se ne possano trarre sulla sua natura giuridica. Come vedremo, le conclusioni sono simili per tutti questi "diritti".

19.1. *Diritto allo sviluppo*

Il diritto allo sviluppo è stato affermato in alcune risoluzioni della (ex) Commissione per i diritti umani e dell'Assemblea Generale delle Nazioni Unite. In particolare, la Dichiarazione dell'AG sul diritto allo sviluppo del 1986 [331] lo definisce come un diritto umano inalienabile. Ma tale definizione ha generato molto scetticismo da parte di numerosi Stati occidentali. I tentativi successivi da parte della Commissione per i diritti umani di chiarire il contenuto di tale diritto non hanno avuto successo. Tuttavia, si deve notare che il diritto allo sviluppo è previsto anche dalla Carta africana dei diritti dell'uomo e dei popoli [332].

Quanto ai titolari del diritto, secondo la Dichiarazione dell'AG del 1986, essi sono sia i popoli che gli individui; mentre invece la Carta africana lo considera soltanto un diritto dei popoli. Ma non è chiaro se la nozione di "popolo" sia usata in senso rigoroso, per contrap-

---

[328] Vedi *supra*, Cap. III, par. 5.4.

[329] Per questa tesi v. Tomuschat (2014), pp. 155-161, in relazione a democrazia, buon governo e sicurezza umana.

[330] *Ibidem*, pp. 152-154. Vedi anche Pisillo Mazzeschi (2008), pp. 302-310.

[331] *UN Declaration on the Right to Development*, GA Res. 41/128, 4 December 1986.

[332] ACHPR, art. 22: "1. All peoples shall have the right to their economic, social and cultural development with due regard to their freedom and identity and in the equal enjoyment of the common heritage of mankind. 2. States shall have the duty, individually or collectively, to ensure the exercise of the right to development".

porre il popolo allo Stato-governo, oppure se essa sia usata in senso enfatico, per significare in realtà "Stato". In altri termini, non si comprende bene se tali atti internazionali vogliano affermare che i popoli hanno un diritto allo sviluppo nei confronti dei propri governi (e saremmo allora nel campo dei diritti umani), oppure che gli Stati più poveri hanno un diritto allo sviluppo nei confronti degli altri Stati o dell'intera comunità internazionale. Pertanto, vi è anche incertezza su quali siano i veri destinatari dell'eventuale obbligo di garantire lo sviluppo.

Venendo infine al contenuto del diritto allo sviluppo, esso è troppo vago e generico per poter produrre effetti giuridici vincolanti. La Dichiarazione dell'AG del 1986 afferma che:

> "The right to development is an inalienable human right by virtue of which every human person and all peoples are entitled to participate in, contribute to, and enjoy economic, social, cultural and political development, in which all human rights and fundamental freedoms can be fully realized" [333].

È chiaro che, in questi termini, il diritto allo sviluppo appare non come un vero e proprio diritto vincolante, ma piuttosto come un obiettivo politico di ampio respiro che gli Stati e l'intera comunità internazionale si devono dare per far progredire la causa dei diritti umani. Ma non sono indicati né i mezzi, né le risorse, né i limiti giuridici che gli Stati o la comunità internazionale devono rispettare per raggiungere tale obiettivo. Inoltre, lo sviluppo dipende da una serie estesa e complessa di fattori, molti dei quali sono al di fuori delle possibilità di controllo da parte dei singoli Stati [334]. Pertanto, non si può nemmeno parlare di obblighi statali "a realizzazione progressiva", ma solo di obiettivi politici non vincolanti.

19.2. *Diritto alle risorse naturali*

Il diritto alle ricchezze e risorse naturali si presta a considerazioni assai simili a quelle, appena fatte, per il diritto allo sviluppo. Esso è stato affermato, in un primo tempo, nella Dichiarazione dell'Assemblea Generale delle NU del 1962 sulla sovranità sulle risorse naturali [335] e poi nella Carta dei diritti e doveri economici degli Stati [336], dove tuttavia si configura come un diritto degli Stati e non dei popoli né degli individui. Invece, nella Carta africana [337], il diritto alle ricchezze e risorse naturali viene attribuito ai popoli, agli Stati ed agli individui (ma per questi ultimi limitatamente ai casi di espropriazione della loro proprietà). Pertanto, vi è incertezza sugli eventuali titolari del diritto.

Quanto al suo contenuto, esso è assai vago e indeterminato. In realtà, come è stato notato in dottrina [338], il diritto degli Stati e dei popoli a disporre liberamente delle proprie ricchezze e risorse naturali non aggiunge molto al contenuto del tradizionale diritto degli Stati alla sovranità territoriale. Ha semmai il merito, di natura squisitamente politica, di indi-

---

[333] *UN Declaration on the Right to Development*, art. 1(1).

[334] Tomuschat (2014), p. 153.

[335] *Permanent Sovereignty over Natural Resources*, GA Res. 1803 (XVII), 14 December 1962, art. 1.

[336] *Charter of Economic Rights and Duties of States*, GA Res. 3281 (XXIX), 12 December 1974. Vedi spec. gli artt. 2 e 7.

[337] ACHPR, art. 21.

[338] Vedi Conforti (2018), p. 208.

rizzare tendenzialmente a favore degli Stati più deboli la disciplina normativa sul trattamento dei beni e degli investimenti degli stranieri. Pertanto, anche in questo caso, non si può parlare di un vero e proprio diritto umano alle risorse naturali; ma piuttosto di un obiettivo politico che ha assunto la comunità internazionale, sotto la spinta del movimento promosso dai Paesi in via di sviluppo per il c.d. nuovo ordine economico internazionale.

19.3. *Diritto alla pace*

Il diritto alla pace è stato proclamato prima dalla Commissione per i diritti umani, nel 1976, e poi dall'Assemblea Generale, in una dichiarazione del 1978 [339] ed in una successiva del 1984 [340], sul cui voto tuttavia molti Stati si sono astenuti. Anche alcune risoluzioni più recenti dell'Assemblea Generale sono state adottate con molti voti contrari e diverse astensioni [341]. Peraltro, il diritto alla pace è previsto dalla Carta africana [342].

Quanto ai destinatari del diritto, la Dichiarazione dell'Assemblea Generale del 1978 menziona le nazioni e gli individui, mentre la Dichiarazione del 1984 e la Carta africana parlano soltanto dei popoli. Anche in questo caso, pertanto, sussiste notevole incertezza sui destinatari dei diritti e dei corrispondenti obblighi.

Venendo, infine, al contenuto del diritto alla pace, esso è, se possibile, ancora più vago ed indefinito di quello dei diritti allo sviluppo ed alle risorse naturali. Come è stato giustamente osservato [343], lo scopo principale del sistema delle Nazioni Unite, ed uno degli scopi fondamentali dell'intero sistema giuridico internazionale, è quello di assicurare la pace e la sicurezza internazionale; e l'efficacia di tali sistemi non viene rafforzata dal mero riconoscimento di un diritto umano alla pace a favore degli individui, dei popoli e delle nazioni.

19.4. *Diritto alla democrazia*

Il diritto umano alla democrazia non viene espressamente menzionato nei principali atti e trattati sui diritti umani di carattere generale, che preferiscono contenere norme sui diritti di partecipazione alla vita politica. Si è già visto, infatti, che l'art. 21 della Dichiarazione universale stabilisce che ciascuno ha il diritto di prendere parte al governo del suo Paese (par. 1) e che la volontà del popolo sarà la base dell'autorità del governo (par. 3).

L'art. 25 del Patto sui diritti civili e politici riprende la prima affermazione della Dichiarazione universale. Ma, come è stato notato [344], la parola "democrazia" non viene usata. Il riferimento ad una società democratica compare soltanto in alcune clausole di restrizione dei diritti garantiti, come limite a tali restrizioni. Ad esempio, nell'art. 21 del Patto, sulla libertà di assemblea, si stabilisce che le restrizioni a tale libertà possono essere imposte soltanto se sono conformi alla legge e *necessarie in una società democratica*. Clausole

[339] GA Res. 33/73, 15 December 1978.

[340] GA Res. 39/11, 12 November 1984.

[341] GA Res. 57/216, 18 December 2002; GA Res. 60/163, 16 December 2005.

[342] ACHPR, art. 23 (1): "All peoples shall have the right to national and international peace and security [...]".

[343] Tomuschat (2014), p. 153.

[344] *Ibidem*, p. 155.

simili sono contenute nella norma sulla libertà di associazione ed in quella sull'equo processo[345]. D'altra parte, i due Patti delle NU del 1966 contengono una norma sul diritto dei popoli all'autodeterminazione (anche "interna"); ma tale diritto non viene di solito interpretato come equivalente al diritto alla democrazia[346].

Un approccio diverso al tema della democrazia si è verificato, nel quadro delle Nazioni Unite, a partire dalla fine degli anni 1990[347]. Il diritto alla democrazia è stato affermato dalla Commissione per i diritti umani in due risoluzioni, nel 1999 e nel 2000[348]. La Commissione ha insistito sullo stretto rapporto che esiste fra forma di governo democratica e tutela dei diritti umani[349]. Questi concetti sono stati ripresi dall'Assemblea Generale, specie nella sua risoluzione 55/96 del 2000[350], sulla quale tuttavia molti Stati si sono astenuti. In seguito, sono state approvate altre risoluzioni dell'Assemblea Generale, che hanno definito la democrazia come un "valore universale", ma hanno anche usato un linguaggio più generico e flessibile, affermando, ad esempio, che non esiste nel mondo un singolo modello di democrazia. Un fondamento normativo meno incerto per tale diritto si riscontra nel continente europeo, nell'ambito del sistema della Convenzione europea[351], dell'Unione Europea[352] e dell'OSCE[353].

La dottrina è divisa sulla questione del diritto alla democrazia e si possono identificare, in estrema sintesi, tre posizioni. Secondo una prima tesi, più "ottimistica"[354], si starebbe affermando nel diritto internazionale "una norma generale, che attribuisce a tutti gli individui sottoposti alla giurisdizione di uno Stato il diritto ad un governo democratico"[355], che finisce per coincidere con il diritto dei popoli all'autodeterminazione interna. Peraltro, il concetto di democrazia universalmente accettato comprenderebbe solo alcuni aspetti del modello generale; e cioè "un apparato di governo rappresentativo, basato su elezioni regolari, libere ed imparziali; rispetto dei diritti umani; principio di legalità"[356]. Ma il diritto alla democrazia non si sarebbe ancora cristallizzato definitivamente come un diritto riconosciuto a tutti gli individui che vivono all'interno di uno Stato.

Al contrario, sulla base di una seconda tesi più "pessimista"[357], si esclude che l'autodeterminazione, giuridicamente intesa, possa essere interpretata come diritto alla democrazia; cioè che "il diritto internazionale richieda che tutti i Governi esistenti sulla terra godano del consenso della maggioranza dei sudditi e siano da costoro liberamente scelti"[358]. Vi

---

[345] A proposito delle esclusioni del pubblico dai processi penali per motivi di pubblica sicurezza "in una società democratica".

[346] Vedi *supra*, Cap. V, par. 24.3.

[347] Vedi Tomuschat (2014), pp. 156-157.

[348] CmHR, Res. 1999/57, 27 April 1999; Res. 2000/47, 25 April 2000.

[349] Vedi CmHR, Res. 1999/57, par. 1: "democracy fosters the full realization of all human rights, and vice versa".

[350] GA Res.55/96, 4 December 2000.

[351] Vedi *supra*, par. 9.1.

[352] Vedi TEU, Preambolo e artt. 2, 10(1), 21.

[353] Vedi Charter of Paris for a New Europe, Paris, 19-21 November 1990.

[354] Cassese (2003-2004), vol. II, pp. 110-112.

[355] *Ibidem*, p. 110.

[356] *Ibidem*, p. 111.

[357] Conforti (2018), pp. 29-30.

[358] *Ibidem*, p. 29.

è una tendenza della maggioranza degli Stati a favore della legittimazione democratica dei governi; ma vi sono ancora molti paesi che non seguono questa tendenza e non vi è "una seria e generalizzata lotta contro i paesi non democratici"[359].

Vi è, infine, una terza tesi, "intermedia" e più articolata[360], che tende a vedere la democrazia soprattutto nell'ottica dei fattori sociali e del contesto delle istituzioni che favoriscono la realizzazione dei diritti umani. Da questo punto di vista, si osserva che i diritti umani di partecipazione politica già esistevano nei vari trattati sui diritti umani; ma che l'azione svolta, nell'ultimo ventennio, dalle Nazioni Unite, dal Consiglio d'Europa, dall'OSCE, dall'Unione Europea[361] e da altri enti internazionali, ha aggiunto una dimensione politica importante: adesso la democrazia viene riconosciuta come l'unica forma legittima di governo[362], anche se il concetto di democrazia non è stato ben precisato ed è restato piuttosto generico. D'altra parte, però, alcune risoluzioni recenti dell'Assemblea Generale delle NU, adottate solo a maggioranza, richiedono "un ordine internazionale democratico ed equo" (*democratic and equitable international order*); e quindi pongono il difficile problema di una democratizzazione della stessa comunità internazionale e di una redistribuzione del potere politico a livello globale[363].

Come si può notare, il tema è complesso e non può essere qui ulteriormente approfondito. A noi sembra, restringendo la questione al diritto positivo degli individui (e di gruppi di individui) ad un governo democratico, che non vi siano difficoltà teoriche a concepire gli individui come titolari di tale diritto e lo Stato/governo come destinatario del relativo obbligo. Tuttavia, al di là dei singoli diritti di partecipazione politica espressamente previsti dai trattati sui diritti umani e delle loro garanzie giurisdizionali o quasi-giurisdizionali[364], non si vede di quali mezzi giuridici possano disporre attualmente gli individui, *nel diritto internazionale*, per far valere un loro più ampio e comprensivo diritto alla democrazia nei confronti del proprio Stato.

Pertanto a noi sembra che, nella realtà concreta della prassi internazionale, alla luce degli apparati statali effettivamente esistenti, non si possa parlare di un diritto alla democrazia come di un vero e proprio diritto umano vincolante, ma piuttosto come un obiettivo politico di carattere generale che gli Stati, e l'intera comunità internazionale, si devono dare per far progredire la causa dei diritti umani. Inoltre, si può anche convenire con l'idea che l'affermazione ed il consolidamento del principio democratico costituiscano un quadro generale che favorisce e promuove il rispetto dei diritti umani[365].

19.5. *Diritto ad un buon governo*

Simili considerazioni valgono anche per il c.d. diritto umano ad un buon governo, che appare come un ulteriore sviluppo del principio democratico. Il concetto che sta alla base

---

[359] *Ibidem*.

[360] Tomuschat (2014), pp. 155-158.

[361] Per i principi democratici nel quadro dell'Unione Europea, vedi Starita (2011).

[362] Tomuschat (2014), p. 156.

[363] *Ibidem*, p. 157.

[364] Vedi *supra*, parr. 8 e 9.

[365] In questo senso vedi Tomuschat (2014), p. 155.

del principio del buon governo è che il pieno godimento dei diritti umani dipende non solo da un apparato di governo democratico, ma anche dal comportamento concreto tenuto dagli organi che governano lo Stato: trasparenza, professionalità e responsabilità di tali organi, partecipazione della società civile e aderenza al principio di legalità.

In questi termini, il principio del buon governo è stato sviluppato soprattutto da alcune organizzazioni internazionali di carattere economico, come la Banca mondiale (*World Bank*)[366], il Fondo monetario internazionale (IMF) e la Banca africana per lo sviluppo (*African Development Bank*). Tale principio è stato poi ripreso dalla Commissione per i diritti umani e quindi incluso anche nella *United Nations Millennium Declaration* del 2000[367] e nel *World Summit Outcome* del 2005[368]. Il principio ha trovato spazio anche nel diritto dell'Unione Europea[369].

A nostro parere, questo principio deve essere inteso, anch'esso, non come un vero e proprio diritto umano, ma come un principio guida di carattere politico, tendente ad assicurare una struttura di governo che sia concretamente idonea a garantire il godimento di tutti i diritti umani.

19.6. *Conclusioni*

In conclusione, i "diritti collettivi" sopra descritti[370] presentano incertezze circa il loro fondamento giuridico, i destinatari dei diritti e dei correlativi obblighi, e soprattutto circa il loro contenuto normativo. Queste incertezze, a nostro avviso, non dipendono da difetti nella formulazione di tali diritti nei pertinenti atti internazionali, ma dalla loro natura e soprattutto dal carattere dei corrispondenti obblighi. Infatti, non si tratta di diritti che lo Stato è normalmente in grado di garantire, né di diritti che lo Stato può assicurare con attività di *due diligence* e neppure di diritti che lo Stato è comunque in grado di realizzare con un impegno progressivo e protratto nel tempo.

In realtà, secondo noi, non si tratta di veri e propri diritti umani, cui corrispondono obblighi statali giuridicamente vincolanti, ma di obiettivi generali di miglioramento e di progresso sia dello Stato-apparato, sia dello Stato-comunità, sia, soprattutto, della intera comunità internazionale. La loro realizzazione crea situazioni e condizioni generali (sviluppo, piena utilizzazione delle risorse, pace, democrazia, buon governo) che sono favorevoli, e talora addirittura necessarie, per il pieno godimento di tutti i diritti umani. Ma gli atti internazionali relativi a tali obiettivi non dettano né i vincoli giuridici, né i mezzi, né le risorse per il raggiungimento di tali obiettivi di vasto e lungo respiro, che restano affidati alla discrezionalità degli Stati e che sono anche, per certi aspetti, al di fuori delle possibilità di controllo degli Stati e dell'intera comunità internazionale.

---

[366] Vedi World Bank, *Governance: The World Bank Experience*, Washington, 1994. La World Bank ha descritto il principio del buon governo nel modo seguente: "Good governance is epitomized by predictable, open, and enlightened policy-making [...], a bureaucracy imbued with a professional ethos; an executive arm of government accountable for its actions; and a strong civil society participating in public affairs; and all behaving under the rule of law" (*ivi*, p. vii).

[367] GA Res.55/2, 8 September 2000, par. 13.

[368] GA Res. 60/1, 16 September 2005, parr. 11, 21, 39.

[369] Vedi, ad es., TFUE, art. 15; EUCh, art. 41.

[370] Vedi *supra*, parr. 19.1-19.5.

Pertanto, a nostro avviso, in relazione a tali obiettivi non si può parlare, allo stato attuale, di obblighi, ma solo di obiettivi politici non vincolanti per i singoli Stati e per l'intera comunità internazionale. Tuttavia, questa conclusione negativa va ridimensionata se ci si pone nel quadro di certi sistemi convenzionali, in particolare di quello africano, favorito dal fatto che la Carta africana prevede espressamente alcuni dei suddetti diritti collettivi. Infatti, sia la Commissione che la Corte africana hanno talora ritenuto gli Stati responsabili di violazioni di tali diritti, ad esempio del diritto alle risorse naturali e di quello allo sviluppo [371]. Inoltre, non si può escludere che, con il tempo, anche altri fra i suddetti obiettivi generali si possano concretizzare in impegni più precisi e specifici, e quindi produrre veri e propri diritti ed obblighi. Ad esempio, il principio democratico e quello del buon governo potrebbero dar vita al diritto di individui e di gruppi di individui al rispetto del principio di legalità da parte dello Stato [372].

20. *Diritti umani fra interessi individuali e collettivi*

Si parla frequentemente, oggi, di alcuni "diritti" umani, che non possono essere propriamente definiti come "collettivi", perché sono volti a proteggere soprattutto le singole persone; ma che tutelano anche interessi più ampi, di natura pubblica o collettiva, che possono (o dovrebbero) essere fatti valere anche da associazioni, comitati o altri gruppi di persone. In altri termini, in questi casi, gli interessi individualistici alla tutela dei diritti umani si intrecciano fortemente con gli interessi pubblici. Ciò si verifica, soprattutto, in materia di sicurezza e di protezione dell'ambiente.

20.1. *Diritto alla sicurezza umana*

A partire dagli anni 1990, si è progressivamente sviluppato, specie nel quadro delle Nazioni Unite, il concetto di "diritto alla sicurezza umana" [373]. Questo concetto ha acquistato notorietà internazionale per merito dello *United Nations Development Programme* (UNDP), che, in un suo rapporto del 1993 [374], ha criticato l'idea tradizionale che la sicurezza debba essere concepita solo come sicurezza militare degli Stati; ed ha affermato che "security should be reinterpreted as security for people, not security for land" [375]. In seguito, l'UNDP, in altri rapporti, ha sviluppato il nuovo concetto di "sicurezza umana", sostenendo, in sintesi, che la sicurezza riguarda non solo gli Stati, ma anche gli individui ed i gruppi di individui; e che essa si deve occupare non solo della difesa dai conflitti armati, ma anche di altri pericoli per le persone, quali la fame, le malattie, la povertà, gli attacchi alla sicurezza fisica ed alla libertà ed altre forme di oppressione delle persone. Ciò nell'ottica generale della libertà delle persone dalla paura e dal bisogno. In particola-

---

[371] Vedi, ad es., ACmHPR, *SERAC and CESR v. Nigeria*, parr. 54 e 58; ACtHPR, *African Commission on Human and Peoples' Rights v. Kenya*, parr. 201 e 211.

[372] Cfr. Cassese (2003-2004), vol. II, p. 111.

[373] Pisillo Mazzeschi (2017) e la dottrina ivi citata, pp. 353-354, note 1 e 2.

[374] UNDP, *Human Development Report 1993*, New York, 1993.

[375] *Ibidem*, p. 1.

re, l'UNDP, in un rapporto del 1994[376], parla di sicurezza economica[377], sanitaria[378], ambientale[379], personale[380], comunitaria[381] e politica[382].

Questa concezione innovativa di "sicurezza umana" ha esercitato un'influenza sia su un gruppo di Stati[383] e di organizzazioni non governative, che hanno istituito il c.d. *Human Security Network*[384], sia sulle Nazioni Unite, dove sono stati istituiti comitati e commissioni *ad hoc*[385], e sono stati presentati rapporti del Segretario Generale[386] ed adottate risoluzioni dell'Assemblea Generale[387]. In sostanza, il concetto di sicurezza umana ha finito per acquisire un ruolo rilevante nella politica estera di un gruppo di Stati[388], nei dibattiti e nelle risoluzioni nell'ambito delle Nazioni Unite, fra i *policy-makers* internazionali, e nel dibattito dottrinale; ed esso ha raggiunto lo scopo di ampliare il concetto tradizionale, attinente solo alla sicurezza militare degli Stati.

Tuttavia, passando dal campo della politica a quello del diritto, il problema del concetto di "sicurezza umana" è dato dal fatto che esso ha un contenuto molto ampio, vago e indeterminato; e pertanto è difficile darne una precisa definizione, specie ai fini della sua utilizzazione nel settore dei diritti umani. Una parte della dottrina[389] sostiene che la sicurezza umana non è una nozione giuridica autonoma che intende influire sul diritto esistente, bensì solo guidare certe scelte politiche operative degli Stati. In sostanza, sarebbe solo un concetto politico, e non anche giuridico.

Invece, un'altra parte della dottrina afferma che esiste un legame fra sicurezza umana e diritti umani; e che quindi si può parlare di un diritto di individui e gruppi di individui alla sicurezza umana. Tuttavia, nell'ambito di questo orientamento dottrinale, coesistono tesi diverse sul modo di definire il contenuto di tale diritto. Secondo un'opinione[390], ad esempio, il diritto alla sicurezza umana può servire in futuro come principio unificatore di norme in tema di diritti umani, di diritto umanitario, di diritto dei rifugiati e di diritto interna-

---

[376] UNDP, *Human Development Report 1994*, New York, 1994, spec. pp. 23-25.

[377] Libertà dalla povertà.

[378] Accesso alle cure e protezione dalle malattie.

[379] Protezione dall'inquinamento.

[380] Protezione fisica contro la tortura, la guerra ed altri crimini.

[381] Diritto a mantenere le tradizioni culturali.

[382] Libertà dall'oppressione politica.

[383] Fra i principali promotori del concetto vi sono i Governi di Canada, Norvegia, Svizzera e Giappone.

[384] Il primo incontro dell'*Human Security Network* si è tenuto a Lysoen, in Norvegia, nel 1999. In seguito vi sono stati numerosi altri incontri del gruppo.

[385] Nel 2001 è stata istituita la *Commission on Human Security*. In seguito, nel 2004, l'*High-level Panel on Threats, Challenges and Change* ha presentato il documento *A More Secure World: Our Shared Responsibility*. Cfr. anche il documento *2005 World Summit Outcome*, GA Res. 60/1, 16 September 2005.

[386] Vedi, ad es., Secretary General, *Human Security*, UN Doc. A/64/701, 8 March 2010; UN Doc. A/66/763, *Follow-up to General Assembly resolution 64/291 on human security*, 5 April 2012; UN Doc. A/68/685, *Follow-up to General Assembly resolution 66/290 on human security*, 23 December 2013.

[387] Vedi, ad es., GA Res. 66/290, 10 September 2012.

[388] Alcuni Stati (Canada e Norvegia) hanno adottato il concetto di "sicurezza umana" come linea-guida per la propria politica estera.

[389] Vedi, ad es., Ryngaert, Noortmann (2014).

[390] Sunga (2009), spec. p. 143.

zionale penale. Secondo un'altra tesi [391], il diritto in oggetto non aggiungerebbe nulla ai diritti umani già esistenti, ma avrebbe la funzione di spingere gli Stati e le istituzioni internazionali verso il comune obiettivo unitario del pieno godimento dei diritti umani. Altri autori [392] ritengono che tale concetto si ricolleghi, in sostanza, a quei diritti umani che attengono ai *basic needs* della persona.

A nostro avviso, non si può ritenere che la sicurezza umana costituisca di per sé un diritto umano separato ed autonomo, e tale da imporre agli Stati obblighi immediati (di risultato o di *due diligence*) o obblighi "a realizzazione progressiva". Il suo contenuto è troppo vago, complesso e indeterminato per essere capace di conferire a individui, o gruppi di individui, veri e propri diritti da far valere contro gli Stati. La sicurezza umana appare piuttosto come una sorta di "contenitore", che comprende al suo interno un'ampia serie di diritti umani specifici, che perseguono il comune scopo di proteggere la sicurezza di individui e gruppi di individui: in particolare, il diritto alla vita, il divieto di tortura e trattamenti inumani o degradanti, il divieto di schiavitù, il diritto alla libertà e sicurezza fisica delle persone, i diritti di sussistenza.

Pertanto, se la nozione di sicurezza umana non ha creato un nuovo diritto umano autonomo, qual è il suo valore giuridico? Allo stato attuale, ci sembra che essa, nell'ottica dei diritti umani, debba essere concepita come un *obiettivo politico* di carattere generale degli Stati e della comunità internazionale nel suo insieme, tendente ad unificare e rafforzare l'effettiva realizzazione di tutti i diritti specifici attinenti alla sicurezza delle persone.

Tuttavia, il consenso che si è finora realizzato nel quadro delle Nazioni Unite su tale concetto induce a pensare che, qualora il riconoscimento e consenso della comunità internazionale si venga in futuro a consolidare, esso possa svilupparsi e concretizzarsi in un principio generale operante nel settore dei diritti umani e del diritto umanitario [393]. Il principio-contenitore "sicurezza umana" potrebbe essere utile per: *a*) orientare l'interpretazione di alcune norme specifiche sui diritti umani e sul diritto umanitario che sono ricomprese nel principio; *b*) dare coerenza sistematica a tali norme; *c*) promuovere il loro sviluppo progressivo.

20.2. *Diritto ad un ambiente sano*

L'esistenza di un diritto umano ad un ambiente sano [394] è assai controversa, specie per la carenza di fonti normative e per la indeterminatezza del suo contenuto.

Per quanto riguarda il primo aspetto, la maggior parte degli atti e dei trattati sui diritti umani di carattere generale non prevede il diritto umano ad un ambiente sano. La Dichiarazione universale, i due Patti internazionali del 1966, la Convenzione europea, la Con-

---

[391] Tomuschat (2014), pp. 159-161.

[392] Focarelli (2013), p. 54.

[393] Intendiamo fare riferimento a quei principi generali del diritto internazionale che derivano, per un processo di astrazione o induzione, da norme consuetudinarie esistenti (quelle sui diritti umani fondamentali sopra indicati). Vedi *supra*, Cap. II, par. 5.

[394] La letteratura che si occupa del diritto umano all'ambiente è vastissima. Ci limitiamo a rinviare a: Boyle, Anderson (1996); Castellaneta (2000); Francioni (2010); Anton, Shelton (2011). Di recente, vedi Rossi (2019).

venzione americana e la Carta sociale europea non contengono riferimenti a tale diritto. La stessa conclusione si ricava dai più importanti trattati sui diritti umani di carattere settoriale. Né ci sembra che possano essere interpretate come riferimenti indiretti al diritto all'ambiente le varie disposizioni, contenute nei suddetti trattati, che sono volte a proteggere la salute o, più genericamente, un tenore di vita adeguato delle persone [395].

Questo silenzio sull'ambiente, da parte dei principali strumenti internazionali sui diritti umani, si spiega per diversi motivi [396]. Il motivo più evidente è che tali strumenti sono stati predisposti in un periodo storico nel quale non si era ancora sviluppato il settore normativo del diritto internazionale dell'ambiente e, tantomeno, si era affermata l'idea che la protezione dell'ambiente deve essere considerata come un valore attinente alla dignità della persona umana ed anche un valore collettivo per l'umanità. Un altro motivo importante è che il diritto internazionale dell'ambiente si è sviluppato, specie nei primi anni, come diritto tipicamente interstatale, cioè attraverso una serie di trattati volti a disciplinare soltanto rapporti fra Stati. Questo carattere interstatale mal si conciliava con il regime dei diritti umani, fondato sui rapporti fra Stati e individui; e ciò ha creato una sorta di "barriera" fra il settore del diritto internazionale dell'ambiente ed il settore della tutela dei diritti umani.

Infatti, il diritto ad un ambiente sano, nella sua connotazione di diritto umano internazionale, è stato affermato soprattutto in atti giuridici non vincolanti. Fra i principali, possiamo ricordare la Dichiarazione di Stoccolma del 1972 [397]; le risoluzioni 37/7 del 1982 e 45/94 del 1990 dell'Assemblea Generale delle NU [398]; la Dichiarazione di Rio su ambiente e sviluppo del 1992 [399]; la Dichiarazione finale del Vertice Mondiale per lo Sviluppo Sostenibile del 2002 e l'Agenda 2030 per lo Sviluppo Sostenibile [400]; la Dichiarazione sui Diritti Umani adottata, nel 2012, dall'Associazione delle Nazioni del Sud-est Asiatico (ASEAN) [401]. Ma alcuni di questi atti, come è stato notato [402], adottano formule prudenti, insistendo sul concetto di sviluppo sostenibile [403] e sugli impegni degli Stati a proteggere l'ambiente, anziché sui diritti degli individui.

Tuttavia, si devono sottolineare alcuni aspetti importanti. In primo luogo, vi sono alcuni trattati sui diritti umani di carattere regionale, adottati a partire dagli anni 1980, che prevedono esplicitamente il diritto ad un ambiente sano. La Carta africana del 1981, nell'art. 24, stabilisce che:

> "All peoples shall have the right to a general satisfactory environment favourable to their development".

---

[395] Su queste ultime norme vedi *supra*, Cap. V, parr. 10-13.

[396] Cfr. Rossi (2019), pp. 159-160.

[397] *Declaration of the United Nations Conference on the Human Environment*, Stockholm 1972, A/CONF. 48/14/Rev. 1 and Corr.1. Vedi il Principio 1: "Man has the fundamental right to freedom, equality and adequate conditions of life, in an environment of a quality that permits a life of dignity and well-being [...]".

[398] GA Res. 37/7, *World Charter for Nature*, 28 October 1982; GA Res. 45/94, 14 December 1990, par. 1.

[399] *Rio Declaration on Environment and Development*, 14 December 1992. Vedi spec. i Principi 1 e 10.

[400] *Johannesburg Declaration of the World Summit on Sustainable Development*, 4 September 2002, par. 1; *Transforming Our World: The 2030 Agenda for Sustainable Development*, GA Res.70/1, 25 September 2015.

[401] *ASEAN Human Rights Declaration*, 19 November 2012, Principio 28(f).

[402] Tomuschat (2014), p. 151.

[403] In questo senso vedi, specialmente, le Dichiarazioni di Rio e di Johannesburg e l'Agenda 2030.

Il Protocollo di San Salvador del 1988, all'art. 11, recita:

"1. Everyone shall have the right to live in a healthy environment [...]
2. The States parties shall promote the protection, preservation, and improvement of the environment".

Anche la Carta araba del 2004 contiene una norma (art. 38) che contempla il diritto di ogni persona ad un ambiente sano. Si possono inoltre citare, fra i trattati più specifici, la Convenzione di Aarhus sull'accesso all'informazione, la partecipazione ai processi decisionali e l'accesso alla giustizia in materia ambientale [404] (art. 1) e l'Accordo regionale di Escazú (Costa Rica) sull'accesso alle informazioni, la partecipazione pubblica e la giustizia in materia ambientale in America latina e nei Caraibi [405] (art. 4).

Un secondo aspetto da sottolineare è che, negli ultimi decenni, il riconoscimento di un diritto umano ad un ambiente sano si è verificato in numerosi ordinamenti statali, spesso a livello di norme costituzionali. Questo fatto potrebbe avere un impatto sulla formazione di un principio generalmente riconosciuto dalle nazioni civili *in foro domestico* [406].

Un terzo aspetto, ancora più importante, è dato dalla prassi degli organi internazionali di controllo sui diritti umani [407]. Come è noto, nel sistema della Convenzione europea, nonostante la mancanza di una disposizione sul diritto umano all'ambiente, gli organi di Strasburgo hanno interpretato estensivamente altri diritti espressamente previsti, e specie il diritto al rispetto della vita privata e familiare, e ne hanno ricavato una tutela per il diritto umano all'ambiente, soprattutto nella sua dimensione procedurale, che si realizza nel diritto degli individui di essere informati dallo Stato su attività gravemente inquinanti o pericolose per l'ambiente [408]. Peraltro, nel quadro della Convenzione europea il diritto ad un ambiente sano, anche in virtù di certi limiti di accesso agli organi di garanzia, ha mantenuto una dimensione prevalentemente individualistica, con scarse aperture verso la "collettivizzazione" dei casi relativi alle controversie in materia ambientale.

Ciò, invece, non si è verificato in altri sistemi regionali di tutela dei diritti umani. Nel sistema interamericano, la situazione della prassi è complessa, perché il diritto umano ad un ambiente sano si intreccia, in modi talora contraddittori, con i diritti dei popoli indigeni, specie quelli attinenti alle loro terre e risorse naturali tradizionali. Talora la protezione dell'ambiente, ad esempio mediante aree ecologiche protette, è entrata in conflitto con i diritti di proprietà dei popoli indigeni; ma, più spesso, è prevalso "l'approccio secondo cui il diritto di proprietà costituisce di per sé un potente alleato della tutela ambientale" [409]. Comunque, nel sistema interamericano, l'intreccio fra interessi individuali ed interessi pubblici ad un ambiente sano è più evidente rispetto a quello della Convenzione europea.

---

[404] Convention on access to information, public participation in decision-making and access to justice in environmental matters, Aahrus, 25 June 1998.

[405] Acuerdo Regional sobre el Acceso a la Información, la Participación Pública y el Acceso a la Justicia en Asuntos Ambientales en América Latina y el Caribe, 4 Marzo 2018.

[406] Vedi *supra*, Cap. II, par. 4.

[407] Su tale prassi vedi Pavoni (2013).

[408] Vedi, ad es., ECtHR, *López Ostra v. Spain*; *Hatton and Others v. UK*, Judgment of 8 July 2003; *Fadeyeva v. Russia*; *Hardy and Maile v. UK*. Per altri esempi vedi Pavoni (2013), pp. 32-47 e 121-132.

[409] Pavoni (2013), p. 70.

Da ultimo, si deve citare un importante parere consultivo della Corte interamericana, adottato nel 2017 su “Ambiente e diritti umani” [410]. Il parere si occupa degli obblighi degli Stati in materia di protezione dell’ambiente, in relazione al diritto alla vita ed al diritto ad un trattamento umano, previsti dagli artt. 4 e 5 della Convenzione americana sui diritti umani. La Corte ha affermato l’esistenza di un autonomo diritto umano ad un ambiente sano [411], fondato sull’art. 11 del Protocollo di San Salvador e sull’art. 26 della Convenzione americana, ed ha anche chiarito gli obblighi di tutela dell’ambiente che derivano dagli artt. 4 e 5 di tale Convenzione.

La prassi sviluppatasi nel sistema africano di tutela dei diritti umani, anche se non ampia, è ancora più favorevole alla dimensione collettiva del diritto ad un ambiente sano [412]. Naturalmente, ciò è favorito dal fatto che la Carta africana prevede numerosi diritti umani di natura collettiva e che la stessa disposizione sul diritto ad un ambiente sano (art. 24) ha come destinatari i popoli. Comunque tale prassi ha un ruolo importante nel processo di progressiva affermazione del diritto umano ad un ambiente sano. Si possono qui ricordare le note decisioni *Social and Economic Rights Action Center* della Commissione africana [413] e *SERAP* della Corte ECOWAS [414].

Infine, vorremmo notare un ultimo aspetto. È vero che il diritto internazionale dell’ambiente si è sviluppato a livello interstatale. Ma oggi esso è costituito da un numero vastissimo di trattati che stabiliscono obblighi precisi e dettagliati fra gli Stati contraenti in materia di tutela ambientale, di prevenzione dall’inquinamento e di riparazione per danni ambientali. A nostro avviso, non si può escludere che *alcuni* di questi obblighi, pur essendo in linea principale di carattere interstatale, possano essere *interpretati* come obblighi che sono indirizzati *anche* agli individui e sono suscettibili di creare diritti in loro favore. Si pensi, ad esempio, a certi obblighi di informazione o a certi obblighi di riparazione per danni ambientali transfrontalieri. In altri termini, si è realizzata con il tempo una necessaria e logica convergenza, in nome della tutela dell’ambiente come scopo dell’intera umanità, fra il settore del diritto internazionale dell’ambiente e quello dei diritti umani. Questa convergenza induce a stemperare la vecchia separazione fra i due settori. In questo modo, quei diritti individuali che sono suscettibili di essere ricavati dai trattati di diritto internazionale dell’ambiente possono servire a precisare il contenuto del diritto umano ad un ambiente sano.

In conclusione, dal punto di vista delle fonti normative, ci sembra che le antiche carenze, contenute nei più risalenti trattati sui diritti umani, siano state superate grazie agli elementi che abbiamo finora evidenziato.

Resta il problema del contenuto del diritto ad un ambiente sano [415], contenuto che viene ancora ritenuto da molti come troppo vago e indeterminato, per soddisfare i requisiti richiesti per il riconoscimento di un nuovo diritto nell’ambito del regime internazionale dei diritti umani [416]. La stessa Assemblea Generale delle NU, stabilendo linee guida per gli

---

[410] IACtHR, *The Environment and Human Rights*.

[411] *Ibidem*, parr. 59 e 62-63.

[412] Vedi Pavoni (2013), pp. 96-107.

[413] ACmHPR, *Social and Economic Rights Action Center and Other v. Nigeria*.

[414] CCJ, *The Registered Trustees of the Socio-Economic Rights and Accountability Project (SERAP) v. Nigeria & UBEC*.

[415] Rossi (2019), pp. 178-179.

[416] Vedi, ad es., Tomuschat (2014), pp. 151-154.

Stati per la creazione di nuovi strumenti normativi sui diritti umani, ha stabilito fra l'altro, come requisiti, che la nuova norma:

> "(a) Be consistent with the existing body of international human rights law [...].
> (c) Be sufficiently precise to give rise to identifiable and practicable rights and obligations"[417].

Tuttavia, a ben vedere, se si esamina l'intero sistema del diritto internazionale dei diritti umani, si nota che il requisito della "precisione del contenuto" non è sempre, in realtà, rigoroso. In questo libro, abbiamo visto che il grado di precisione del contenuto dei diritti umani non è affatto uniforme, ma che, al contrario, esso è assai variabile. Vi sono alcuni diritti che hanno un contenuto preciso e ben circoscritto, altri che hanno un contenuto più ampio, altri ancora con un contenuto così esteso e complesso da poter essere considerati come "diritti-contenitori" di diritti più specifici. Naturalmente, vi è anche un limite, oltre il quale l'eccessiva vaghezza e indeterminatezza del contenuto induce ad escludere che si tratti di un vero e proprio diritto ed a classificarlo come un mero obiettivo di carattere politico e non vincolante.

Alla luce di queste premesse, ci sembra che il diritto ad un ambiente sano, pur avendo mantenuto per un certo tempo un carattere vago ed indeterminato, abbia percorso con il tempo un processo evolutivo, specie in virtù della prassi sopra ricordata, che ha via via finito per precisare il suo contenuto normativo. Questa è anche l'opinione del Relatore Speciale, nominato dal Consiglio dei diritti umani[418] per studiare gli obblighi in materia di diritti umani relativi al godimento di un ambiente sano:

> "[T]he time has come for the United Nations to formally recognize the human right to a safe, clean, healthy and sustainable environment"[419].

Il diritto ad un ambiente sano può essere inteso, in senso lato, come il diritto di individui e gruppi di individui a che gli Stati utilizzino e conservino l'ambiente nel modo migliore[420], sulla base degli standard che si sono affermati specie nella prassi del diritto internazionale convenzionale dell'ambiente. Ci sembra che a questo diritto, di carattere generale, corrispondano obblighi statali "a realizzazione progressiva"; e che in questi obblighi il bilanciamento fra doveri degli Stati relativi all'ambiente e loro "mezzi e risorse disponibili" sia assai importante; ma anche difficile[421].

Tuttavia, si possono forse individuare anche diritti più specifici, ai quali corrispondono obblighi immediati: ad esempio, l'obbligo degli Stati di prevenire, con *due diligence*, significativi danni ambientali; l'obbligo di reprimere le relative violazioni; e l'obbligo di dare la riparazione alle vittime. Infine, vi sono alcuni diritti procedurali delle persone, che sono anch'essi piuttosto specifici, come, ad esempio, il loro diritto di essere informate su certe attività potenzialmente inquinanti e di partecipare a certe procedure di valutazione dei rischi ambientali.

---

[417] GA Res. 41/120, *Setting international standards in the field of human rights*, 4 December 1986, par. 4 (c).

[418] HRC, *Human rights and the environment*, A/HRC/RES/19/10, 19 April 2012.

[419] Vedi GA, *Human rights obligations relating to the enjoyment of a safe, clean, healthy and sustainable environment*, 19 July 2018 (A/73/188), par. 37.

[420] Cfr. Rossi (2019), pp. 179-181.

[421] Vedi *supra*, Cap. III, par. 5.3.

BIBLIOGRAFIA SELETTIVA

Abi-Saab G. (1985), "Reflexions on the Contemporary Processes of Developing International Law, Ninth Gilberto Amado Memorial Lecture", delivered at the International Law Commission on 25 June 1985.

Abi-Saab G. (1987), "Cours général de droit international public", *RC*, vol. 207, pp. 1-464.

Abi-Saab G. (1988), "Entangled Treaty and Custom", in Dinstein Y. (ed.), *International Law at a Time of Perplexity: Essays in Honour of Shabtai Rosenne*, Nijhoff, Dordrecht, p. 717 ss.

Acconci P. (2001), *Tutela della salute e diritto internazionale*, Cedam, Padova.

Ackerly B. (2008), *Universal Human Rights in a World of Difference*, CUP, Cambridge-New York.

Addo M.K. (ed.) (2006), *International Law of Human Rights*, Ashgate, Aldershot.

Ago R. (1938), "La regola del previo esaurimento dei ricorsi interni in tema di responsabilità internazionale", *Archivio di diritto pubblico*, Padova, p. 178 ss.

Ago R. (1939), "Le delit international", *RC*, vol. 68, pp. 415-554.

Ago R. (1977), "Sixième rapport sur la responsabilité des Etats", *ACDI*, 1977 (II-1).

Aja Agwu F. (2014), "The African Court of Justice and Human Rights: the future of international criminal justice in Africa", *Africa Review*, vol. 6, pp. 30-43.

Alexidze L. (1981), "Legal Nature of *Jus Cogens* in Contemporary International Law", *RC*, vol. 172, pp. 221-270.

Alston P. (1987), "Out of the abyss; the challenges confronting the new UN Committee on economic, social and cultural rights", *HRQ*, vol. 9, pp. 332-381.

Alston P., Goodman R. (2013), *International Human Rights. The Successor to International Human Rights in Context: Law, Politics and Morals. Text and Materials*, OUP, Oxford.

Anaya J. (2004), *Indigenous Peoples in International Law*, 2ª ed., OUP, Oxford.

Anton D.K., Shelton D. (2011), *Environmental Protection and Human Rights*, CUP, Cambridge.

Balboni M. (ed.) (2017), *The European Convention on Human Rights and the Principle of Non-Discrimination*, Editoriale Scientifica, Napoli.

Barret J.Q. (2010), "Raphael Lemkin and 'Genocide' at Nuremberg, 1945-1946", in Safferling C.M., Conze E.A. (eds.), *The Genocide Convention Sixty Years After Its Adoption*, Asser Press, The Hague, pp. 35-54.

Bartolini G. (2009), *Riparazione per violazione dei diritti umani e ordinamento internazionale*, Jovene, Napoli.

Bassiouni M.C. (1990), "A Functional Approach to 'General Principles of International Law'", *Mich. JIL*, vol. 11, pp. 768-818.

Baxi U. (2012), *The Future of Human Rights*, OUP, New Delhi-New York.

Baxter R. (1965-66), "Multilateral Treaties as Evidence of Customary International Law", *BYBIL*, vol. 41, pp. 275-300.

Baxter R. (1970), "Treaties and Custom", *RC*, vol. 129, pp. 27-105.

Bedjaoui M. (1979), *Towards a New International Economic Order*, Holmes & Meier Publishers, New York-London.

Benvenisti E. (2008), "The Conception of International Law as a Legal System", *GYIL*, vol. 50, pp. 393-405.

Benvenisti E. (2012), *The International Law of Occupation*, OUP, Oxford.

Benvenisti E. (2018), "The Margin of Appreciation, Subsidiarity and Global Challenges to Democracy", *Journ. Int. Disp. Settl.*, vol. 9, pp. 240-253.

Bestagno F. (2003), *Diritti umani e impunità. Obblighi positivi degli Stati in materia penale*, Vita e Pensiero, Milano.

Bestagno F. (a cura di) (2009), *I diritti economici, sociali e culturali. Promozione e tutela nella comunità internazionale*, Vita e Pensiero, Milano.

Bianchi A. (1997), "Overcoming the Hurdle of State Immunity in the Domestic Enforcement of International Human Rights", in Conforti B. and Francioni F. (eds.), *Enforcing International Human Rights in Domestic Courts*, Nijhoff, The Hague-Boston-London, pp. 405-439.

Bianchi A. (1999), "Immunity Versus Human Rights: The *Pinochet* Case", *EJIL*, vol. 10, pp. 237-277.

Bianchi A. (2004), "L'immunité des états et les violations graves des droits de l'homme: la fonction de l'interprète dans la détermination du droit international", *RGDIP*, vol. 108, pp. 63-101.

Bianchi A. (2008), "Human Rights and the Magic of *Jus Cogens*", *EJIL*, vol. 19, pp. 491-508.

Boerefijn I. (2009), "Impact on the Law of Treaty Reservations", in Kamminga M.T., Scheinin M. (eds.), *The Impact of Human Rights Law on General International Law*, OUP, Oxford-New York, pp. 63-97.

Bonetti P. (2005), "Terrorismo e stranieri nel diritto italiano. Disciplina legislativa e profili costituzionali. I parte. L'applicazione agli stranieri delle norme comuni sul terrorismo", in *Diritto, immigrazione e cittadinanza*, vol. 3, pp. 13-41.

Bourgeois H., Wouters J., "Methods of Identification of International Custom: A New Role for *Opinio Juris*?", in Pisillo Mazzeschi R., De Sena P. (eds.), *Global Justice, Human Rights and the Modernization of International Law*, Springer, Cham (Switzerland), pp. 69-111.

Boyle A.E., Anderson M.R. (eds.) (1996), *Human Rights Approaches to Environmental Protection*, Clarendon Press, Oxford.

Brownlie I. (1998), *The Rule of Law in International Affairs*, Nijhoff, The Hague.

Brownlie I. (2008), *Principles of Public International Law*, 7ª ed., OUP, Oxford-New York.

Buergenthal T., Shelton D., Stewart D.P. (2004), *International Human Rights in a Nutshell*, 3ª ed. (2° rep.), West Group, St. Paul.

Bufalini A. (2013), "La natura del divieto di detenzione arbitraria secondo il *Working Group on Arbitrary Detention* del Consiglio dei diritti umani", *DUDI*, vol. 7, pp. 525-531.

Calamia A.M., Di Filippo M., Gestri M. (a cura di) (2012), *Immigrazione, Diritto e Diritti: profili internazionalistici ed europei*, Cedam, Padova.

Caligiuri A., Cataldi G., Napoletano N. (a cura di) (2010), *La tutela dei diritti umani in Europa: tra sovranità statale e ordinamenti sovranazionali*, Cedam, Padova.

Campiglio C. (1995), *Il principio di reciprocità nel diritto dei trattati*, Cedam, Padova.

Cançado Trindade A.A. (2005), "International Law for Humankind: Towards a New *Jus Gentium*. General Course on Public International Law", *RC*, vol. 316, pp. 9-440, vol. 317, pp. 9-332.

Cançado Trindade A.A. (2012), *Le droit international pour la personne humaine*, Pédone, Paris.

Cannizzaro E. (2000), *Il principio della proporzionalità nell'ordinamento internazionale*, Giuffrè, Milano.
Cannizzaro E. (2012), *Diritto internazionale*, Giappichelli, Torino.
Cannone A. (2018), *Violazioni di carattere sistemico e Convenzione europea dei diritti dell'uomo*, Cacucci, Bari.
Capotorti F. (1979), *Study on the Rights of Persons Belonging to Ethnic, Religious and Linguistic Minorities*, UN Doc. E/CN.4/Sub.2/384/Rev.1.
Capotorti F. (1992), "Il regime delle minoranze nel sistema delle Nazioni Unite e secondo l'art. 27 del Patto sui diritti civili e politici", *Riv. int. dir. uomo*, pp. 102-112.
Carli E. (2019), *La Politica di Sicurezza e di Difesa Comune dell'Unione europea. Profili di responsabilità internazionale*, Giappichelli, Torino.
Carpanelli E. (2013), "*Extraordinary renditions* e diritti umani: alcune riflessioni sul caso *Abu Omar*", *DUDI*, vol. 7, pp. 315-330.
Carrillo Salcedo J.A. (1997), "Reflections on the Existence of a Hierarchy of Norms in International Law", *EJIL*, vol. 8, pp. 583-595.
Cassella S. (dir. publ.) (2018), *Le standard de* due diligence *et la responsabilité internationale, SFDI, Journée d'etudes du Mans*, Pédone, Paris.
Cassese A. (1984), *Il diritto internazionale nel mondo contemporaneo*, Il Mulino, Bologna.
Cassese A. (1995), *Self-Determination of Peoples. A Legal Reappraisal*, CUP, Cambridge.
Cassese A. (2000), "The Martens Clause: Half a Loaf or Simply Pie in the Sky?", *EJIL*, vol. 11, pp. 187-216.
Cassese A. (2003), *International Criminal Law*, OUP, Oxford.
Cassese A. (a cura di P. Gaeta) (2003-2004), *Diritto internazionale, Vol. I: I lineamenti* (2003), *Vol. II: Problemi della comunità internazionale* (2004), Il Mulino, Bologna.
Cassese A. (2004), *I diritti umani nel mondo contemporaneo*, Laterza, Bari.
Cassese A. (a cura di P. Gaeta) (2006), *Diritto internazionale*, Il Mulino, Bologna.
Cassese A. (2012), "A Plea for a Global Community Grounded in a Core of Human Rights", in Cassese A. (ed.), *Realizing Utopia. The Future of International Law*, OUP, Oxford, pp. 136-144.
Cassese A. (2013), *Diritto internazionale* (a cura di P. Gaeta), 2ª ed., Il Mulino, Bologna.
Cassese A., Gaeta P. (2008), *Le sfide attuali del diritto internazionale*, Il Mulino, Bologna.
Castellaneta M. (2000), "L'individuo e la protezione dell'ambiente nel diritto internazionale", *RDI*, vol. 83, pp. 913-964.
Castellino J. (2014), "International Law and Self-Determination: Peoples, Indigenous Peoples, and Minorities", in Walter C., Von Ungern-Sternberg A., Abushov K. (eds.), *Self-Determination and Secession in International Law*, OUP, Oxford, pp. 27-44.
Cataldi G. (2006), "Le deroghe ai diritti umani in stato di emergenza", in Pineschi L. (a cura di), *La tutela internazionale dei diritti umani. Norme, garanzie, prassi*, Giuffrè, Milano, pp. 752-772.
Cataldi G. (2007), "Diritti inderogabili", in Flores M., Groppi T., Pisillo Mazzeschi R. (a cura di), *Diritti Umani. Cultura dei diritti e dignità della persona nell'epoca della globalizzazione: Dizionario*, Utet, Torino, vol. I, pp. 382-385.
Cataldi G. (2012), "Articolo 15", in Bartole S., De Sena P., Zagrebelsky V. (a cura di), *Commentario breve alla Convenzione europea per la salvaguardia dei diritti dell'uomo e delle libertà fondamentali*, Cedam/Kluwer, Padova, pp. 555-564.
Cataldi G. (2019), "Sulla recente prassi in materia di comunicazioni di deroga alla Convenzione europea dei diritti dell'uomo", in Sicilianos L.A., Motoc I.A., Spano R., Chenal R. (eds.), *Regards croisés sur la protection nationale et internationale des droits de l'homme, Liber Amicorum Guido Raimondi*, Wolf Legal Publishers, Tilburg (The Netherlands).

Charney J.I. (1993), "Universal International Law", *AJIL*, vol. 87, pp. 529-551.

Chowdhury A.R., Bhuiyan J.H. (eds.) (2010), *An Introduction of International Human Rights Law*, Brill, Leiden-Boston.

Citroni G., Scovazzi T. (2013), *La tutela internazionale dei diritti umani*, Parte III del *Corso di diritto internazionale* (a cura di T. Scovazzi), Giuffrè, Milano.

Clapham A. (1993), *Human Rights in the Private Sphere*, Clarendon Press, Oxford.

Clapham A. (2006), *Human Rights Obligations of Non-State Actors*, OUP, Oxford.

Clapham A., Kamminga M. (eds.) (2004), *Extraterritorial Application of Human Rights Treaties*, Intersentia, Antwerp.

Combacau J. (1986), "Le droit international: bric-à-brac ou système?" *Archives de philosophie du droit*, vol. 31, pp. 85-105.

Combacau J., Sur S. (2006), *Droit international public*, 7ª ed., LGDJ, Paris.

Conforti B. (2006), *Diritto internazionale*, 7ª ed., Editoriale Scientifica, Napoli.

Conforti B. (2007), "Unité et fragmentation du droit international: glissez, mortels, n'appuyé pas", *RGDIP*, vol. 111, pp. 5-18.

Conforti B. (2015), *Diritto internazionale*, 10ª ed., Editoriale scientifica, Napoli.

Conforti B. (2018), *Diritto internazionale*, 11ª ed. (a cura di M. Iovane), Editoriale scientifica, Napoli.

Cornelisse G. (2010), *Immigration Detention and Human Rights. Rethinking Territorial Sovereignty*, Nijhoff, Leiden-Boston.

Craven M. (2000), "Legal Differentiation and the Concept of the Human Rights Treaty in International Law", *EJIL*, vol. 11, pp. 489-519.

Crawford J. (1993), "Democracy and International Law", *BYBIL*, vol. 63, pp. 113-133.

Crawford J. (2002), "The ILC's Articles on Responsibility of States for Internationally Wrongful Acts: A Retrospect", *AJIL*, vol. 96, pp. 874-890.

Crawford J. (2006), *The Creation of States in International Law*, 2ª ed., Clarendon Press, Oxford.

Crawford (2013), "Change, Order, Change: The Course of International Law. General Course on Public International Law", *RC*, vol. 365, pp. 9-389.

D'Amato A. (1971), *The Concept of Custom in International Law*, Cornell University Press, Ithaca-London.

D'Argent P. (2005), "Le droit de la responsabilité internationale complété? Examen des principes fondamentaux et directives concernant le droit à un recours et à la réparation des victimes de violations flagrantes du droit international des droits de l'homme et de violations graves du droit international humanitaire", *AFDI*, vol. 51, pp. 27-55.

D'Aspremont J. (2011), *Formalism and the Sources of International Law*, OUP, Oxford.

Daniele L. (2014), *Diritto dell'Unione europea. Sistema istituzionale-Ordinamento-Tutela giurisdizionale-Competenze*, 5ª ed, Giuffrè, Milano.

Davis H. (2013), *Human Rights Law Directions*, OUP, Oxford.

De Frouville O. (2004), *L'intangibilité des droits de l'homme en droit international*, Pedone, Paris.

De Martens G.F. (1975), *Nouveau Recueil Général de Traités*, Tome XX, Gottingue, 1875 (Klaus reprint 1975).

De Schutter O. (2010), *International Human Rights Law. Cases, Materials, Commentary*, CUP, Cambridge.

De Sena P. (2002), *La nozione di giurisdizione statale nei trattati sui diritti dell'uomo*, Giappichelli, Torino.

De Sena P. (2004), "Esigenze di sicurezza nazionale e tutela dei diritti dell'uomo nella recente

prassi europea", in Boschiero N. (a cura di), *Ordine internazionale e valori etici, VIII Convegno della SIDI (Verona, 2003)*, Editoriale Scientifica, Napoli, pp. 195-268.
De Sena P. (2016), "Proportionality and Human Rights in International Law: Some ... 'Utilitarian' Reflections", *RDI*, vol. 99, pp. 1009-1025.
De Sena P., De Vittor F. (2005), "State Immunity and Human Rights: The Italian Supreme Court Decision on the *Ferrini* Case", *EJIL*, vol. 16, pp. 89-116.
De Sena P., Saccucci A. (2007), "Diritti fondamentali", in Flores M., Groppi T., Pisillo Mazzeschi R. (a cura di), *Diritti Umani. Cultura dei diritti e dignità della persona nell'epoca della globalizzazione: Dizionario*, vol. I, Utet, Torino, pp. 376-382.
De Sena P., Starita M. (2019), "Navigare fra istanze 'Stato-centriche' e 'cosmopolitiche': il caso 'Sea Watch' in una prospettiva conflittuale", *SIDIBlog*, 14 luglio 2019.
De Wet E. (2004), "The Prohibition of Torture as an International Norm of jus cogens and Its Implications for National and Customary Law", *EJIL*, vol. 15, pp. 97-121.
De Wet E., Vidmar J. (eds.) (2012), *Hierarchy in International Law: The Place of Human Rights*, OUP, Oxford.
Deschênes J. (1985), *Proposal concerning a definition of the term "minority"*, UN Doc. E/CN.4/Sub.2/31.
Di Filippo M. (2012), "L'ammissione di cittadini stranieri", in Calamia A.M., Di Filippo M., Gestri M. (a cura di), *Immigrazione, Diritto e Diritti: profili internazionalistici ed europei*, Cedam, Padova, pp. 81-126.
Di Stasi A. (2010), *Diritti umani e sicurezza regionale. Il sistema europeo*, Editoriale Scientifica, Napoli.
Di Stefano A., Sapienza R. (a cura di) (2012), *La tutela dei diritti umani e il diritto internazionale*, Editoriale Scientifica, Napoli.
Dinstein Y. (2006), "The Interaction between Customary International Law and Treaties", *RC*, vol. 322, pp. 243-428.
Dipla H. (1994), *La responsabilité de l'Etat pour violation des droits de l'homme: problèmes d'imputation*, Pédone, Paris.
Dominicé C. (2013), "La societé internationale à la recherche de son équilibre. Cours général de droit international public", *RC*, vol. 370, pp. 9-392.
Doswald-Beck L. (2011), *Human Rights in Time of Conflict and Terrorism*, OUP, Oxford.
Dupuy P.M. (2002), "L'unité de l'ordre juridique international. Cours général de droit international public", *RC*, vol. 297, pp. 9-490.
Dupuy P.M. (2018), "From a Community of States Towards a Universal Community?", in Pisillo Mazzeschi R., De Sena P. (eds.), *Global Justice, Human Rights and the Modernization of International Law*, Springer, Cham (Switzerland), pp. 47-66.

Eide A. (1984), "The International Human Rights System", in Eide A. *et al.* (eds.), *Food as a Human Right*, Tokyo, pp. 152-161.
Ergec R. (1987), *Les droits de l'homme à l'épreuve des circonstances exceptionnelles. Etude sur l'article 15 de la Convention européenne des droits de l'homme*, Bruylant, Bruxelles.
Ergec R. (2006), *Protection européenne et internationale des droits de l'homme*, Bruylant, Bruxelles.

Favilli C. (a cura di) (2011), *Procedure e garanzie del diritto di asilo*, Cedam/Kluwer, Milano.
Favilli C. (2013), *Migration Law in Italy*, Kluwer, Alphen aan den Rijn.
Favuzza F. (2018), *Security Detention in Times of Armed Conflict: The Relevance of International Human Rights Law*, Kluwer/Cedam, Milano.

Ferrari Bravo L. (2002), *Lezioni di diritto internazionale*, 4ª ed., Editoriale Scientifica, Napoli.
Focarelli C. (2001), *Equo processo e Convenzione europea dei diritti dell'uomo. Contributo alla determinazione dell'ambito di applicazione dell'art.6 della Convenzione*, Cedam, Padova.
Focarelli C. (2008), *Lezioni di diritto internazionale*, voll. III, Cedam, Padova.
Focarelli C. (2012-2013), *Diritto internazionale*, 2ª ed., voll. IIII, Cedam, Padova.
Focarelli C. (2013), *La persona umana nel diritto internazionale*, Il Mulino, Bologna.
Focarelli C. (2015), *Trattato di diritto internazionale*, Utet/Kluwer, Torino-Milano.
Focarelli C. (2017), *Diritto internazionale*, 4ª ed., Kluwer/Cedam, Milano.
Focarelli C. (2019), *Diritto internazionale*, 5ª ed., Kluwer/Cedam, Milano.
Forlati S. (2005), *Diritto dei trattati e responsabilità internazionale*, Giuffrè, Milano.
Forman L. (2016a), "Can minimum core obligations survive a reasonableness standard of review under the optional protocol to the International Covenant on Economic, Social and Cultural Rights?", *Ottawa Law Review*, vol. 47, pp. 557-576.
Forman L. *et al.* (2016b), "Conceptualising minimum core obligations under the right to health: How should we define and implement the 'morality of the depths'", *The International Journal of Human Rights*, vol. 20, pp. 531-548.
Forsythe D.P. (2012), *Human Rights in International Relations*, CUP, Cambridge.
Franchi M., Viarengo I. (2016), *Tutela internazionale dei diritti umani. Casi e materiali*, Giappichelli, Torino.
Francioni F. (2007), "The Right of Access to Justice under Customary International Law", in Francioni F. (ed.), *Access to Justice as a Human Right*, OUP, Oxford, pp. 1-55.
Francioni F. (2010), "International Human Rights in an Environmental Horizon", *EJIL*, vol. 21, pp. 41-55.
Francioni F. (2018), "Global Justice, Equality and Social Inclusion: What Kind of 'Modernization' of International Law?", in Pisillo Mazzeschi R., De Sena P. (eds.), *Global Justice, Human Rights and the Modernization of International Law*, Springer, Cham (Switzerland), pp. 225-238.
Francioni F., Scheinin M. (eds.) (2008), *Cultural Human Rights*, Nijhoff, Leiden.
Franck T.M. (1990), *The Power of Legitimacy Among Nations*, OUP, New York-Oxford.
Franck T.M. (1992), "The Emerging Right to Democratic Governance", *AJIL*, vol. 86, pp. 46-91.
Freeman M., Van Ert G. (2006), *International Human Rights Law: Texts, Cases and Materials*, Irwin Law, Toronto.
Friedmann W.G. (1964), *The Changing Structure of International Law*, Stevens, London.

Gaeta P. (ed.) (2009), *The UN Genocide Convention. A Commentary*, OUP, Oxford.
Gaja G. (1981), "*Jus Cogens* beyond the Vienna Convention on the Law of Treaties", *RC*, vol. 172, pp. 271-316.
Gaja G. (1986), "Principi del diritto (diritto internazionale)", *ED*, vol. XXXV, pp. 533-546.
Gaja G. (2012), "General Principles of Law", *EPIL*, ed. online, OUP, Oxford.
Gaja G. (2014), "The Protection of General Interests in the International Community. General Course on Public International Law (2011)", *RC*, vol. 364, pp. 13-185.
Gearty C., Douzinas C. (eds.) (2012), *The Cambridge Companion to Human Rights Law*, CUP, Cambridge.
Gergen J.A. (1995-1996), "Human Rights and the Foreign Sovereign Immunities", *Virg. JIL*, vol. 36, pp. 765-800.
Gradoni L., Pasquet L. (2019), "Lisistrata a Lampedusa: una riflessione sul caso Sea Watch 3", *SIDIBlog*, 6 luglio 2019.
Guastini R. (1993), *Le fonti del diritto e l'interpretazione*, Giuffrè, Milano.

Hannikainen L. (1988), *Peremptory Norms (jus cogens) in International Law. Historical Developments, Criteria, Present Status*, Publishing Finnish Lawyers' Company, Helsinki.
Hannum H. (ed.) (2004), *Guide to International Human Rights Practice*, 4ª ed., Transnational Publishers, Ardsley-New York.
Hannum H., Shelton D.L., Anaya S.J., Celorio L. (2018), *International Human Rights: Problems of Law, Policy and Practice*, 6ª ed., Wolters Kluwer, New York.
Henckaerts J.M., Doswald-Beck L. (2005), ICRC, *Customary International Humanitarian Law*, 3 vols., CUP, Cambridge.
Henkin L. (1989), "International Law: Politics, Values and Functions", *RC*, vol. 216, pp. 9-400.
Henkin L. (1995), "Human Rights", *EPIL*, vol. 2, pp. 886-893.
Henkin L. (1995-96), "Human Rights and State Sovereignty", *Geor.JICL*, vol. 25, pp. 31-45.
Henkin L., Cleveland S.H., Helfer L.R., Neuman G.L., Orentlicher D.F. (2009), *Human Rights*, Foundation Press, New York.
Hennebel L., Tigroudja H. (2016), *Traité de droit international des droits de l'homme*, Pédone, Paris.
Higgins R. (1976-77), "Derogations under Human Rights Treaties", *BYBIL*, vol. 48, pp. 281-319.

Iovane M. (2000), *La tutela dei valori fondamentali nel diritto internazionale*, Editoriale Scientifica, Napoli.
Iovane M. (2007), "Gross violations of human rights", in Flores M., Groppi T., Pisillo Mazzeschi R. (a cura di), *Diritti Umani. Cultura dei diritti e dignità della persona nell'epoca della globalizzazione: Dizionario*, vol. 1, Utet, Torino, pp. 675-680.
Iovane M. (2008), "La participation de la société civile à l'élaboration et à l'application du droit international de l'environnement", *RGDIP*, vol. 112, pp. 465-520.

Janis M.W., Kay R.S., Bradley A.W. (2008), *European Human Rights Law: Text and Materials*, 3ª ed., OUP, Oxford-New York.
Jennings R.Y. (1979), "Treaties as Legislation", in Wilner G.M. (ed.), *Jus et Societas. Essays in Tribute to Wolfgang Friedmann*, Springer, The Hague, pp. 159-168.
Joseph S., Schultz J, Castan M. (2004), *The International Covenant on Civil and Political Rights*, 2ª ed., OUP, Oxford.

Kälin W., Künzli J. (2009), *The Law of International Human Rights Protection*, OUP, Oxford-New York.
Kälin W., Künzli J. (2019), *The Law of International Human Rights Protection*, 2ª ed., OUP, Oxford.
Kamminga M.T. (2009), "Impact on State Succession in Respect of Treaties", in Kamminga M.T., Scheinin M. (eds.), *The Impact of Human Rights Law on General International Law*, OUP, Oxford-New York, pp. 99-109.
Kamminga M.T., Scheinin M. (eds.) (2009), *The Impact of Human Rights Law on General International Law*, OUP, Oxford-New York.
Kamto M. (2002), "Une troublante 'Immunité totale' du Ministre des affaires étrangères", *RBDI*, vol. 35, pp. 518-530.
Kelsen H. (1966), *Principles of International Law*, 2ª ed., Holt, Rinehart and Winston, New York.
Kolb R. (2001a), *Théorie du* ius cogens *international. Essai de relecture d'un concept*, PUF, Paris.
Kolb R. (2001b), "La structure constitutionnelle du droit international public", *Can.YBIL*, vol. 39, pp. 69-115.

Koskenniemi M., Leino P. (2002), "Fragmentation of International Law? Post-modern Anxieties", *Leiden JIL*, vol. 15, pp. 553-579.

Krause K., Scheinin M. (eds.) (2009), *International Protection of Human Rights: A Textbook*, Åbo Akademi University Institute for Human Rights, Turku.

Lattanzi F. (1983), *Garanzie dei diritti dell'uomo nel diritto internazionale generale*, Giuffrè, Milano.

Lemkin R. (1944), *Axis Rule in Occupied Europe: Laws of Occupation, Analysis of Government, Proposals for Redress*, Carnegie Endowment for International Peace, Washington, D.C.

Lenzerini F. (ed.) (2008), *Reparations for Indigenous Peoples: International and Comparative Perspectives*, OUP, Oxford.

Lenzerini F. (2009), *Asilo e diritti umani. L'evoluzione del diritto d'asilo nel diritto internazionale*, Giuffrè, Milano.

Lenzerini F. (2009a), "The Evolution of Italian Jurisprudence concerning the Relationship between the Constitutional Right of Asylum and the Recognition of Refugee Status", *It.YIL*, vol. 19, pp. 139-156.

Lenzerini F. (2012), "Il principio del *non-refoulement* dopo la sentenza *Hirsi* della Corte europea dei diritti dell'uomo", *RDI*, vol. 95, pp. 721-761.

Lenzerini F. (2014), *The Culturalization of Human Rights Law*, OUP, Oxford.

Liguori A. (2012), "La Corte europea dei diritti dell'uomo condanna l'Italia per i respingimenti verso la Libia del 2009: il caso *Hirsi*", *RDI*, vol. 95, pp. 415-443.

Lochak D. (2009), *Les droits de l'homme*, La Découverte, Paris.

Marchesi A. (2011), *La protezione internazionale dei diritti umani. Nazioni Unite e organizzazioni regionali*, Franco Angeli, Milano.

Martinez Cobo J. (1983), *Study of the Problem of Discrimination Against Indigenous Populations, Conclusions, Proposals and Recommendations*, UN Doc. E/CN.4/Sub.2/1983/21/Add.8, 30 September 1983.

Martinez Cobo J. (1986), *Study of the Problem of Discrimination Against Indigenous Populations*, UN Doc. E/CN.4/Sub.2/1986/7 and Add. 1-4.

McCorquodale R. (ed.) (2003), *Human Rights*, Aldershot/Hants, Ashgate-Darmouth.

McDonald R.St.J. (1997), "Derogations under Article 15 of the European Convention on Human Rights", *Col. JTL*, vol. 36, pp. 225-267.

McDougal M.S. (1980), *Human Rights and World Public Order: the basic policies of an international law of human dignity*, Yale University Press, New Haven.

Meijknecht A. (2001), *Towards International Personality: The Position of Minorities and Indigenous Peoples in International Law*, Intersentia, Antwerpen-Groningen-Oxford.

Meron T. (ed.) (1984), *Human Rights in International Law: Legal and Policy Issues*, Clarendon Press, Oxford.

Meron T. (1986), "On a Hierarchy of International Human Rights", *AJIL*, vol. 80, pp. 1-23.

Meron T. (1989), *Human Rights and Humanitarian Norms as Customary Law*, Clarendon Press, Oxford.

Meron T. (2003), "International Law in the Age of Human Rights. General Course on Public International Law", *RC*, vol. 301, pp. 9-490.

Meron T. (2006), *The Humanization of International Law*, Nijhoff, Leiden-Boston.

Moeckli D., Shah S., Sivakumaran S. (eds.) (2010), *International Human Rights Law*, OUP, Oxford-New York.

Moore J.B. (1898), *History and Digest of the International Arbitrations to which the United States has been a Party*, vol. I, Washington.
Moriarty B., Massa E. (eds.) (2012), *Human Rights Law*, OUP, Oxford.
Mosler H. (1980), *The International Society as a Legal Community*, Sijthoff, Alphen aan den Rijn.
Mowbray A. (2004), *The Development of Positive Obligations under the European Convention on Human Rights by the European Court of Human Rights*, Hart, Oxford-Portland.
Mullerson R. (1993), "The Continuity and Succession of States by Reference to the Former USSR and Yugoslavia", *ICLQ*, vol. 42, pp. 473-493.

Nigro R. (2005), "Giurisdizione ed obblighi positivi degli Stati parti della Convenzione europea dei diritti dell'uomo: il caso *Ilaşcu*", *RDI*, vol. 88, pp. 413-440.
Nigro R. (2018), *Le immunità giurisdizionali dello Stato e dei suoi organi e l'evoluzione della sovranità nel diritto internazionale*, Kluwer/Cedam, Milano.
Nowak M. (2003), *Introduction to the International Human Rights Regime*, Nijhoff, Leiden-Boston.
Nowak M., McArthur E. (2008), *The United Nations Convention against Torture: A Commentary*, OUP, Oxford.

Oberdorff H. (2012), *Droits de l'homme et libertés fondamentales*, LGDJ, Paris.
Orakhelashvili A. (2006), *Peremptory Norms in International Law*, OUP, Oxford.

Padelletti M.L. (2003), *La tutela della proprietà nella Convenzione europea dei diritti dell'uomo*, Giuffrè, Milano.
Parlett K. (2011), *The Individual in the International Legal System: Continuity and Change in International Law*, CUP, Cambridge.
Pavoni R. (2013), *Interesse pubblico e diritti individuali nella giurisprudenza ambientale della Corte europea dei diritti umani*, Editoriale Scientifica, Napoli.
Pellet A. (2000), "'Droits-de-l'hommisme' et droit international, Gilberto Amado Memorial Lecture", 18 July 2000, United Nations.
Picone P. (2005), "Obblighi *erga omnes* e codificazione della responsabilità degli Stati", *RDI*, vol. 88, pp. 893-954.
Picone P. (2008), "La distinzione fra norme internazionali di *jus cogens* e norme che producono obblighi *erga omnes*", *RDI*, vol. 91, pp. 5-38.
Pineschi L. (a cura di) (2006), *La tutela internazionale dei diritti umani. Norme, garanzie, prassi*, Giuffrè, Milano.
Pisillo Mazzeschi R. (1984), *Risoluzione e sospensione dei trattati per inadempimento*, Giuffrè, Milano.
Pisillo Mazzeschi R. (1989), "*Due Diligence" e responsabilità internazionale degli Stati*, Giuffrè, Milano.
Pisillo Mazzeschi R. (1994a), "La dottrina pura del diritto di Kelsen e la realtà del diritto internazionale contemporaneo", *Diritto e Cultura*, vol. IV, pp. 43-66.
Pisillo Mazzeschi R. (1994b), "Trattati e consuetudine nella codificazione del diritto internazionale", *Com. int.*, vol. 49, pp. 196-222.
Pisillo Mazzeschi R. (1999a), "Il diritto di asilo 50 anni dopo la Dichiarazione universale dei diritti dell'uomo", *Riv. int. dir. uomo*, vol. 12, pp. 694-703.
Pisillo Mazzeschi R. (1999b), "International Obligations to Provide for Reparation Claims?", in Randelzhofer A., Tomuschat C. (eds.), *State Responsibility and the Individual: Repara-*

tion in Instances of Grave Violations of Human Rights, Nijhoff, The Hague-London-Boston, pp. 149-172.

Pisillo Mazzeschi R. (2003), "Reparation Claims by Individuals for State Breaches of Humanitarian Law and Human Rights: An Overview", *JICJ*, vol. 1, pp. 339-347.

Pisillo Mazzeschi R. (2004a), *Esaurimento dei ricorsi interni e diritti umani*, Giappichelli, Torino.

Pisillo Mazzeschi R. (2004b), "The Marginal Role of the Individual in the ILC's Articles on State Responsibility", *It.YIL*, vol. 14, pp. 39-51.

Pisillo Mazzeschi R. (2008), "Responsabilité de l'État pour violation des obligations positives relatives aux droits de l'homme", *RC*, vol. 333, pp. 175-506.

Pisillo Mazzeschi R. (2009), "Impact on the Law of Diplomatic Protection", in Kamminga M.T., Scheinin M. (eds.), *The Impact of Human Rights Law on General International Law*, OUP, Oxford-New York, pp. 211-233.

Pisillo Mazzeschi R. (2011), "The Relationship between Human Rights and the Rights of Aliens and Immigrants", in Fastenrath U. *et al.* (eds.), *From Bilateralism to Community Interest: Essays in Honour of Judge Bruno Simma*, OUP, Oxford, pp. 552-573.

Pisillo Mazzeschi R. (2012), "Il rapporto fra norme di *ius cogens* e la regola sull'immunità degli Stati: alcune osservazioni critiche sulla sentenza della Corte internazionale di giustizia del 3 febbraio 2012", *DUDI*, vol. 6, pp. 310-326.

Pisillo Mazzeschi R. (2014a), "La protezione internazionale dei diritti dell'uomo e il suo impatto sulle concezioni e metodologie della dottrina giuridica internazionalistica", *DUDI*, vol. 8, pp. 275-318.

Pisillo Mazzeschi R. (2014b), "Human Rights and the Modernization of International Law", in Lenzerini F., Vrdoljak A.F. (eds.), *International Law for Common Goods: Normative Perspectives on Human Rights, Culture and Nature*, Hart, Oxford-Portland, pp. 89-101.

Pisillo Mazzeschi R. (2014c), "Organi degli Stati stranieri (immunità giurisdizionale degli)", *ED-Annali*, vol. VII, Milano, cc. 735-794.

Pisillo Mazzeschi R. (2016), "Popoli indigeni", in *Enciclopedia di Bioetica e Scienza Giuridica, Parte giuridica*, ESI, Napoli, pp. 459-473.

Pisillo Mazzeschi R. (2017), "Sicurezza umana e diritto internazionale", in Triggiani E., Cherubini F., Ingravallo I., Nalin E., Virzo R. (a cura di), *Dialoghi con Ugo Villani*, vol. I, Cacucci, Bari, pp. 353-362.

Pisillo Mazzeschi R. (2018a), "Le chemin étrange de la due diligence: d'un concept mystérieux à un concept surévalué", in Cassella S. (dir. publ.), *Le standard de* due diligence *et la responsabilité internationale, SFDI, Journée d'etudes du Mans*, Pédone, Paris, pp. 323-337.

Pisillo Mazzeschi R. (2018b), "Coordination of Different Principles and Values in International Law", *GYIL*, vol. 61, pp. 209-250.

Pisillo Mazzeschi R., De Sena P. (eds.) (2018), *Global Justice, Human Rights and the Modernization of International Law*, Springer, Cham (Switzerland).

Pisillo Mazzeschi R., Viviani A. (2018), "General Principles of International Law: from Rules to Values?", in Pisillo Mazzeschi R., De Sena P. (eds.), *Global Justice, Human Rights and the Modernization of International Law*, Springer, Cham (Switzerland), pp. 113-161.

Pocar F. (1998), "Note sulla giurisprudenza del Comitato dei diritti dell'uomo in materia di minoranze", in Bartole S., Olivetti Rason N., Pegoraro L. (a cura di), *La tutela giuridica delle minoranze*, Cedam, Padova, pp. 31-39.

Provost R. (2002), *International Human Rights and Humanitarian Law*, CUP, Cambridge-New York.

Pustorino P. (1995), "Sull'applicabilità diretta e la prevalenza della Convenzione europea dei diritti dell'uomo nell'ordinamento italiano", *Riv. int. dir. uomo*, pp. 23-37.
Pustorino P. (1998), *L'interpretazione della Convenzione europea dei diritti dell'uomo nella prassi della Commissione e della Corte di Strasburgo*, Editoriale Scientifica, Napoli.
Pustorino P. (2006), "Questioni in materia di tutela delle minoranze nel diritto internazionale ed europeo", *Studi integr. eur.*, vol. 1, pp. 259-279.
Pustorino P. (2019), *Lezioni di tutela internazionale dei diritti umani*, Cacucci, Bari.

Ragazzi M. (1997), *The Concept of International Obligations Erga Omnes*, OUP, Oxford.
Robert J., Duffar J. (2009), *Droits de l'homme et libertés fondamentales*, LGDJ, Paris.
Robertson A.H., Merrils J.G. (1996), *Human Rights in the World. An Introduction to the Study of the International Protection of Human Rights*, 4ª ed., Manchester University Press, Manchester-New York.
Robertson G. (1999), *Crimes against Humanity: The Struggle for Global Justice*, Allen Lane/Penguin Press, London.
Rodley N.S. (1999), *The Treatment of Prisoners in International Law*, 2ª ed., OUP, Oxford.
Ronzitti N. (1978), "La disciplina dello *ius cogens* nella Convenzione di Vienna sul diritto dei trattati", *CS*, vol. XV, p. 243 ss.
Ronzitti N. (1984), "Trattati contrari a norme imperative del diritto internazionale?", in *Studi in onore di Giuseppe Sperduti*, Giuffrè, Milano, pp. 209-272.
Ronzitti N. (2007), "Ius cogens", in Flores M., Groppi T., Pisillo Mazzeschi R. (a cura di), *Diritti Umani. Cultura dei diritti e dignità della persona nell'epoca della globalizzazione: Dizionario*, vol. II, Utet, Torino, pp. 805-808.
Ronzitti N. (2016), *Introduzione al diritto internazionale*, 5ª ed., Giappichelli, Torino.
Rossi V. (2019), "Il riconoscimento del diritto universale a un ambiente sano: questioni aperte e percorsi evolutivi", in Cataldi G. (a cura di), *I diritti umani a settant'anni dalla Dichiarazione universale delle Nazioni Unite*, vol. I, Editoriale Scientifica, Napoli, pp. 157-189.
Russo D. (2012), *L'efficacia dei trattati sui diritti umani*, Giuffrè, Milano.
Ryngaert C., Noortmann M. (2014), "Human Security and International Law: The Challenge of Non-State Actors", in Ryngaert C. *et al.* (eds.), *Human Security and International Law: The Challenge of Non-State Actors*, Intersentia, Cambridge, pp. 1-11.

Saccucci A. (2005), *Profili di tutela dei diritti umani tra Nazioni Unite e Consiglio d'Europa*, Cedam, Padova.
Saccucci A. (2018), *La responsabilità internazionale dello Stato per violazioni strutturali dei diritti umani*, Editoriale Scientifica, Napoli.
Sands Ph. (2017), *La strada verso Est*, Guanda, Milano.
Scelle G. (1934), *Précis de Droit des Gens. Principes et systématique, Deuxième partie*, Recueil Sirey, Paris.
Schachter O. (1991), *International Law in Theory and Practice*, Nijhoff, Dordrecht-Boston-London.
Scheinin M. (2009), "Impact on the Law of Treaties", in Kamminga M.T., Scheinin M. (eds.), *The Impact of Human Rights Law on General International Law*, OUP, Oxford-New York, pp. 23-36.
Scheinin M. (2013), "Core Rights and Obligations", in Shelton D. (ed.), *Oxford Handbook of International Human Rights Law*, OUP, Oxford, pp. 527-540.
Scovazzi T. (a cura di) (2013), *Corso di diritto internazionale, Parte III*, Giuffrè, Milano.
Scovazzi T., Citroni G. (2007), *The Struggle against Enforced Disappearance and the 2007 United Nations Convention*, Nijhoff, Leiden-Boston.

Shabas W. (2009), *Genocide in International Law. The Crime of Crimes*, CUP, Cambridge.
Shelton D. (2010), *Regional Protection of Human Rights*, OUP, Oxford.
Shelton D. (2014), *Advanced Introduction to International Human Rights Law*, Edward Elgar, Cheltenham.
Shue H. (1980), *Basic Rights: Subsistence, Affluence, and US Foreign Policy*, Princeton University Press, Princeton.
Shue H. (1996), *Basic Rights: Subsistence, Affluence, and US Foreign Policy*, 2ª ed., Princeton University Press, Princeton.
Sicilianos L.A. (1993), "The Relationship Between Reprisals and Denunciation or Suspension of a Treaty", *EJIL*, vol. 4, pp. 341-359.
Sicilianos L.A. (2002), "The Classification of Obligations and the Multilateral Dimension of the Relations of International Responsibility", *EJIL*, vol. 13, pp. 1127-1145.
Sicilianos L.A. (2012), "L'influence des droits de l'homme sur la structure du droit international", *RGDIP*, vol. 116, pp. 5-30 e 241-274.
Sieghart P. (1983), *The International Law of Human Rights*, Clarendon Press, Oxford.
Simma B. (1970), "Reflections on Article 60 of the Vienna Convention on the Law of Treaties and Its Background in General International Law", *ÖZöR*, vol. 20, pp. 5-81.
Simma B. (1985), "Self-contained Regimes", *Neth.YIL*, vol. 16, pp. 111-136.
Simma B. (1993), "International Human Rights and General International Law: A Comparative Analysis", in *Collected Courses of the Academy of European Law*, vol. IV, Book 2, EUI, Florence, pp. 153-236.
Simma B. (1994), "From Bilateralism to Community Interest in International Law", *RC*, vol. 250, pp. 217-384.
Simma B. (2009), "Universality of International Law from the Perspective of a Practitioner", *EJIL*, vol. 20, pp. 265-297.
Simma B., Alston P. (1992), "The Sources of Human Rights Law: Custom, *Jus Cogens*, and General Principles", *Aus.YIL*, vol. 12, pp. 82-108.
Simma B., Paulus A.L. (1999), "The Responsibility of Individuals for Human Rights Abuses in Internal Conflicts: A Positivist View", *AJIL*, vol. 93, pp. 302-316.
Simma B, Pulkowski D. (2006), "Of Planets and the Universe: Self-contained Regimes in International Law", *EJIL*, vol. 17, pp. 483-529.
Sommario E. (2018), *Stati d'emergenza e trattati a tutela dei diritti umani*, Giappichelli, Torino.
Spencer J., Spencer M. (2005), *Human Rights*, Sweet & Maxwell, London.
Ssenyonio M. (2009), *Economic, Social and Cultural Rights in International Law*, Hart, Oxford.
Starita M. (2011), *I principi democratici nel diritto dell'Unione Europea*, Giappichelli, Torino.
Starita M. (2019), "Il dovere di soccorso in mare e il diritto di obbedire al diritto (internazionale) del comandante della nave privata", *DUDI*, vol. 13, pp. 5-47.
Steiner H.J., Alston P., Goodman R. (2008), *International Human Rights in Context: Law, Politics, Morals. Text and Materials*, 3ª ed., OUP, Oxford.
Sudre F. (1995), "Droits intangibles et/ou droits fondamentaux: y a-t-il des droits prééminents dans la Convention européenne des droits de l'homme?", in *Liber Amicorum Marc-André Eissen*, Bruylant, Bruxelles, pp. 381-398.
Sudre F. (2001), *Droit international et européen des droits de l'homme*, 5ª ed., PUF, Paris.
Sudre F. (2006), *Droit européen et international des droits de l'homme*, 8ª ed., PUF, Paris.
Sunga L.S. (2009), "The Concept of Human Security: Does It Add Anything of Value to International Legal Theory or Practice?", in Frick M.L., Oberprantacher A. (eds.), *Power and Justice in International Relations: Interdisciplinary Approaches to Global Challeges*, Ashgate, Farham (UK), pp. 131-146.

Suy E. (1983), "Droits des traités et droits de l'homme", in *Festschrift für Hermann Mosler*, Springer, Berlin, pp. 935-947.
Svensson-McCarthy A.L. (1998), *The International Law of Human Rights and States of Exception. With Special Reference to the* Travaux Preparatoires *and Case-Law of the International Monitoring Organs*, Nijhoff, The Hague-Boston-London.
Symonides J. (ed.) (2003), *Human Rights: International Protection, Monitoring, Enforcement*, Unesco Publishing/Ashgate, Paris.

Talmon S. (2015), "Determining Customary International Law: The ICJ's Methodology between Induction, Deduction and Assertion", *EJIL*, vol. 26, pp. 417-443.
Tams C. (2005), *Enforcing Obligations* Erga Omnes *in International Law*, CUP, Cambridge.
Tancredi A. (2001), *La secessione nel diritto internazionale*, Cedam, Padova.
Thirlway H.W.A. (1972), *International Customary Law and Codification*, Sijthoff, Leiden.
Thornberry P. (1991), *International Law and the Rights of Minorities*, Clarendon Press, Oxford.
Tladi D. (2016), *First report on peremptory norms of general international law* (jus cogens), A/CN.4/693, 8 March 2016.
Tladi D. (2017), *Second report on peremptory norms of general international law* (jus cogens), A/CN.4/706, 16 March 2017.
Tladi D. (2018), *Third report on peremptory norms of general international law* (jus cogens), A/CN.4/714, 12 February 2018.
Tladi D. (2019), *Fourth report on peremptory norms of general international law* (jus cogens), A/CN.4/727, 31 January 2019.
Tomuschat C. (1993), "Obligations Arising for States without or against Their Will", *RC*, vol. 241, pp. 195-374.
Tomuschat C. (1999), "International Law: Ensuring the Survival of Mankind on the Eve of a New Century. General Course on Public International Law", *RC*, vol. 281, pp. 9-438.
Tomuschat C. (2014), *Human Rights: Between Idealism and Realism*, 3ª ed., OUP, Oxford.
Tomuschat C. (2018), "General International Law: A New Source of International Law?", in Pisillo Mazzeschi R., De Sena P. (eds.), *Global Justice, Human Rights and the Modernization of International Law*, Springer, Cham (Switzerland), pp. 185-204.
Tomuschat C., Thouvenin J.M. (eds.) (2006), *The Fundamental Rules of the International Legal Order. Jus Cogens and Obligations Erga Omnes*, Nijhoff, Leiden.
Tomuschat C., Pisillo Mazzeschi R., Thurer D. (eds.) (2016), *Conciliation in International Law. The OSCE Court of Conciliation and Arbitration*, Brill/Nijhoff, Leiden-Boston.
Treves T. (2005), *Diritto internazionale. Problemi fondamentali*, Giuffrè, Milano.
Tunkin G.I. (1974), *Theory of International Law*, transl. by W.E. Butler, George Allen & Unwin Ltd., London.
Tuosto C. (2012), *Il sistema delle Nazioni Unite per la tutela dei diritti umani. Limiti e proposte di riforma*, Editoriale Scientifica, Napoli.

Van Alebeek R. (2000), "The *Pinochet* Case: International Human Rights Law on Trial", *BYBIL*, vol. 71, pp. 29-70.
Van Dijk P., Van Hoof J.H., Van Rijn A., Zwaak L. (eds.) (2006), *Theory and Practice of the European Convention on Human Rights*, 4ª ed., Intersentia, Antwerp-Oxford.
Verdross A. (1966), "*Jus Dispositivum* and *Jus Cogens* in International Law", *AJIL*, vol. 60, pp. 55-63.
Verdross A. (1968), "Les principes généraux de droit dans le système des sources du droit in-

ternational public" in Guggenheim P. (ed.), *Recueil d'études de droit international en hommage à P. Guggenheim*, Georg, Geneva, pp. 521-530.

Viarengo I. (2005), "Deroghe e restrizioni alla tutela dei diritti umani nei sistemi internazionali di garanzia", *RDI*, vol. 88, pp. 955-996.

Villani U. (2005), *Studi su La protezione internazionale dei diritti umani*, Luiss University Press, Roma.

Villani U. (2015), *Dalla Dichiarazione universale alla Convenzione europea dei diritti dell'uomo*, 2ª ed., Cacucci, Bari.

Villani U. (2017), *Istituzioni di Diritto dell'Unione europea*, 5ª ed. riv., Cacucci, Bari.

Viviani A. (2005), *Crimini internazionali e responsabilità dei leader politici e militari*, Giuffrè, Milano.

Voyiakis E. (2003), "Access to Court v. State Immunity", *ICLQ*, vol. 52, pp. 297-332.

Weil P. (1983), "Towards Relative Normativity in International Law?", *AJIL*, vol. 77, pp. 413-442.

Weil P. (1992), "Le droit international en quête de son identité. Cours général de droit international public", *RC*, vol. 237, pp. 1-369.

Weissbrodt D. (2000), *Prevention of Discrimination: The Rights of Non-Citizens: final Report of the Special Rapporteur*, 25 May 2000, UN Doc. E/CN.4/Sub.2/2003/23 and Add.1.

Weissbrodt D., de la Vega C. (2007), *International Human Rights Law. An Introduction*, University of Pennsylvania Press, Philadelphia.

Weissbrodt D.S., Aolain F.N., Newman F.C., Fitzpatrick J. (eds.) (2009), *International Human Rights: Law, Policy and Process*, LexisNexis, Newark.

Wood M. (2013), *First report on formation and evidence of customary international law*, UN Doc. A/CN.4/663, 17 May 2013.

Wouters J., Ryngaert C. (2009), "Impact on the Process of the Formation of Customary International Law", in Kamminga M.T., Scheinin M. (eds.), *The Impact of Human Rights Law on General International Law*, OUP, Oxford-New York, pp. 111-131.

Zagrebelsky V., Chenal R., Tomasi L. (2016), *Manuale dei diritti fondamentali in Europa*, Il Mulino, Bologna.

Zagrebelsky V., Chenal R., Tomasi L. (2019), *Manuale dei diritti fondamentali in Europa*, 2ª ed., Il Mulino, Bologna.

Zanghì C. (2013), *La protezione internazionale dei diritti dell'uomo*, 3ª ed., Giappichelli, Torino.

Zanghì C., Panella L. (2019), *La protezione internazionale dei diritti dell'uomo*, 4ª ed., Giappichelli, Torino.

Zappalà S. (2011), *La tutela internazionale dei diritti umani*, Il Mulino, Bologna.

Finito di stampare nel mese di settembre 2020
nella LegoDigit s.r.l. – Via Galileo Galilei, 15/1
38015 Lavis (TN)